Model Document Practice!

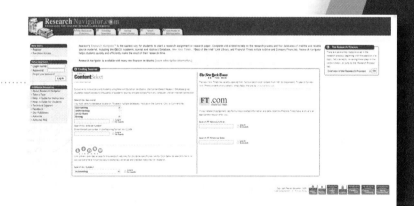

The documents below model different types of writing or writing for different purposes.

Documents that display this symbol allow you to view annotations for a variety of different elements. (Flash plug-in required)

Documents that display this symbol open as PDF files. (Adobe plug-in required)

Documents that display this symbol are quizzes.

You will need Adobe Reader and Flash to view these documents. If you do not have the

Letters
- Letter 1: Standard Letter Parts
- Letter 2: Request Action
- Letter 3: Request (Product Inquiry)
- Letter 4: Request Information
- Letter 5: Request (Product Inquiry)
- Letter 6: Making a Claim
- Letter 7: Making a Claim
- Letter 8: Positive
- Letter 9: Routine Reply
- Letter 10: Granting Claim (Your Company at Fault)
- Letter 11: Granting Claim (Client at Fault)
- Letter 12: Granting Claim (3rd part. at Fault)
- Letter 13: Granting a Claim
- Letter 14: Goodwill
- Letter 15: Goodwill
- Letter 16: Negative News
- Letter 17: Negative News - Direct Approach
- Letter 18: Negative News - Direct Approach (Collection)
- Letter 19: Negative News - Indirect Approach
- Letter 20: Bad News about Transaction

In *MyBusCommLab* you can see real-world examples of technical communication documents and immediately apply what you have learned.

Grammar Practice!

Assess and improve your grammar skills with a robust grammar component!

Research Help!

With Research Navigator and EBSCO's ContentSelect you can access newspaper archives and thousands of print journals and take advantage of online research tools!

Save Time. Improve Results.
www.pearsoned.ca/mybuscommlab

Business Communication ESSENTIALS

SECOND CANADIAN EDITION

COURTLAND L. BOVÉE

Professor of Business Communication

C. Allen Paul Distinguished Chair

Grossmont College

JOHN V. THILL

Chief Executive Officer

Communication Specialists of America

JEAN A. SCRIBNER

British Columbia Institute of Technology

Pearson Canada
Toronto

Library and Archives Canada Cataloguing in Publication

Bovée, Courtland L.
    Business communication essentials / Courtland L. Bovée, John V. Thill,
Jean A. Scribner. — 2nd Canadian ed.

Includes index.
First Canadian ed. written by Courtland L. Bovée . . . [et al.].
ISBN 978 0 13-223053-7

    1. Business communication—Textbooks. I. Thill, John V. II. Scribner, Jean
III. Title.

HF5718.B69 2010   651.7   C2008-905732-5

ISBN-13: 978-0-13-223053-7
ISBN-10: 0-13-223053-4

Vice-President, Editorial Director: Gary Bennett
Editor-in-Chief: Ky Pruesse
Acquisitions Editor: David Le Gallais
Sponsoring Editor: Carolin Sweig
Marketing Manager: Loula March
Developmental Editor: Jennifer Murray
Production Editors: Tara Tovell, Mary Ann Blair
Copy Editor: Tara Tovell
Proofreader: Melissa Hajek
Production Coordinator: Janis Raisen
Compositor: Macmillan Publishing Solutions
Art Director: Julia Hall
Cover and Interior Design: Opus House Inc./Sonya Thursby
Cover Image: Firstlight

1 2 3 4 5   13 12 11 10 09

Printed and bound in United States.

Contents in Brief

Contents

8 Writing Bad-News Messages ... 154

9 Writing Persuasive Messages ... 179

10 Understanding and Planning Business Reports and Proposals ... 208

11 Writing and Completing Business Reports and Proposals ... 237

Preface

Business Communication Essentials offers you the opportunity to practise communication skills that will help you get jobs and be promoted in today's workplace. The new, redesigned second Canadian edition is student-friendly and features the most extensive end-of-chapter activities available, including questions, exercises, assignments, and cases. Packaged with Grammar-on-the-Go, this edition gives you access to tools to build your language skills while you develop your business communication know-how.

Some of the changes in this edition include

- **Streamlined format and improved readability** so you can navigate the extensive materials easily
- Tips for building positive interpersonal relationships with co-workers in each chapter's new **On the Job** feature
- More emphasis on **analyzing audiences**, including opportunities to explore how generational and cultural differences impact workplace communication
- **Increased emphasis on email**, the preferred method of business communication
- **48 new activities and cases**. New activities explore the impact of social technologies in business communication and include exercises on the use of blogs, wikis, Facebook, and other collaborative technologies. Cases are included on podcasting, virtual meetings, instant messaging, eco-literacy, and other engaging topics from today's workplace.
- **Running cases** at the end of each chapter. Follow the career developments of Noreen and Kwong as they work through typical communication challenges you will find in business.
- **More resumé samples** and employment-related documents
- Increased focus on **document design** to allow readers to find information fast

A summary of the changes to the seventh edition of the *MLA Handbook for Writers of Research Papers*, published in 2009, is available online through MyBusCommLab. A print booklet is available for order or packaging (ISBN 978-0-13-209095-7).

Learning About Business Communication

Business Communication Essentials' integrated learning system helps you develop your communication skills so you will be prepared for the workplace. Please read through the next few pages to learn more about the features of the text and to help you learn and apply the communication skills needed for a successful career.

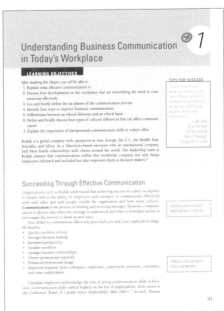

Learning Objectives are listed on the first page of each chapter. Each chapter's learning objectives provide a clear overview of the key concepts students are expected to master.

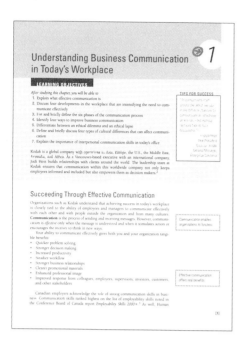

Tips for Success give you advice from Canadian business leaders or communication experts on the chapter's topic. Diverse Canadian businesses are profiled.

Marginal Notes highlight key points in the text and are good tools for reviewing concepts.

Pointers appear near many sample documents, giving you a concise list of writing tips. You will also find these pointers handy when you are on the job and need to refresh your memory about effective writing techniques.

The Three-Step Writing Process, which includes planning, writing, and completing, offers you a practical strategy for writing business messages. This process is applied throughout the text to all business communication tasks.

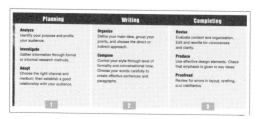

Model Documents provide a wide selection of documents that you can examine, critique, and revise. In addition, pairs of poor and improved drafts help you recognize the best writing practices.

On the Job boxes offer tips for career success and emphasize the soft skills employers value.

Reviewing Key Points summarizes main content in an easy-to-read list at the end of each chapter. These lists are no substitute for reading the chapters, but they can help you quickly get the gist of a section, review a chapter, and locate areas of greatest interest.

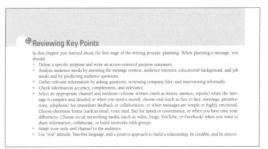

Practising Your Business Communication Skills

Applying what you learn through practising is the best way to develop your confidence and ability as a communicator. Completing the end-of-chapter activities will help you develop and improve your skills. Here are the review and practice activities you will find in each chapter.

Test Your Knowledge provides questions that review the chapter topics.

Apply Your Knowledge

1. Some writers argue that planning messages wastes time because they inevitably change their plans as they go along. How would you respond to this argument? Briefly explain.
2. As a member of the public relations department, what medium would you recommend using to inform the local community that your toxic-waste cleanup program has been successful? Why?
3. When composing business messages for your company, how can you create a professional image?
4. Considering how fast and easy it is, should email replace meetings and other face-to-face communication in your company? Why or why not?
5. **Ethical Choices** Your manager has asked you to draft a memo for her signature to the board of directors, informing them that sales in the new line of gourmet fruit jams have far exceeded anyone's expectations. As a member of the marketing department, you happen to know that sales of moderately priced jams have declined quite a bit (many customers have switched to the more expensive jams). You were not directed to add that tidbit of information. Should you write the memo and limit your information to the expensive gourmet jams? Or should you include the information about the decline in moderately priced jams? Please explain.

Apply Your Knowledge offers exercises to get you thinking about the concepts explained in the chapter.

Running Cases present realistic business situations encountered by Noreen and Kwong as they work toward their career goals. Working through these case studies will help you learn to complete on-the-job communication tasks. Watch the *Perils of Pauline* videos available on MyBusCommLab for additional interactive case studies.

Practise Your Knowledge

EXERCISES FOR PERFECTING YOUR WRITING

Choosing the Approach Indicate whether the direct or the indirect approach would be best in each of the following situations. Write *direct* or *indirect* in the space provided.
1. _____ A letter asking when next year's automobiles will be put on sale locally.
2. _____ A letter from a recent college graduate requesting a letter of recommendation from a former instructor
3. _____ A letter turning down a job applicant
4. _____ An announcement that because of high heating costs, the plant temperature will be held at 18°C during winter.
5. _____ A final request to settle a delinquent debt

Drafting Persuasive Messages If you were trying to persuade people to take the following actions, how would you organize your argument? Write *direct* or *indirect* in the space provided.
6. _____ You want your boss to approve your plan for hiring two new people.
7. _____ You want to be hired for a job.
8. _____ You want to be granted a business loan.
9. _____ You want to collect a small amount from a regular customer whose account is slightly past due.
10. _____ You want to collect a large amount from a customer whose account is seriously past due.

Selecting Specific and Precise Words In the following sentences, replace vague phrases (underlined or in italics) with concrete phrases. Make up any details you might need.
11. We will be opening our new facility _sometime this spring_.
12. You can now purchase our new Leaf-Away lawn and lawn blower _at a substantial savings_.
13. After the reception, we were surprised that _such a large number attended_.
14. The new production line has been operating _with increased efficiency_ on every run.
15. Over the holiday, we hired a crew to _expand the work area_.
16. The two reporters _____ (_ran after_) every lead enthusiastically.
17. Even large fashion houses have to match staff size to the normal _____ (_seasonal ups and downs_).
18. The _____ (_bright_) colours in that ad are keeping customers from seeing what we have to sell.
19. Health costs _____ (_suddenly rise_) when management forgets to emphasize safety issues.
20. Once we solved the zoning issue, new business construction _____ (_moved forward_), and the district has been flourishing ever since.

Avoiding Clichés Rewrite these sentences to replace the clichés with fresh, personal expressions:
21. Being a jack-of-all-trades, Dave worked well in his new selling job.
22. Moving Leslie into the accounting department, where she was literally a fish out of water, was like putting a square peg into a round hole, if you get my drift.
23. I knew she was at death's door, but I thought the doctor would pull her through.
24. Movies aren't really my cup of tea; as far as I am concerned, they can't hold a candle to a good book.
25. It's a dog-eat-dog world out there in the rat race of the asphalt jungle.

Practise Your Knowledge provides you with a wide variety of exercises and activities allowing you to explore how to decide how to handle situations and participate effectively on teams.

Expand Your Knowledge

Best of the Web

Compose a Better Business Message At Purdue University's Online Writing Lab (OWL), you'll find tools to help you improve your business messages. For advice on composing written messages, for help with grammar, and for referrals to other information sources, you'll be wise to visit this site. Purdue's OWL offers online services and an introduction to internet search tools. You can also download a variety of handouts on writing skills. Check out the resources at the OWL home page and learn how to write a professional business message.
http://owl.english.purdue.edu

EXERCISES
1. Explain why positive wording in a message is more effective than negative wording. Why should you be concerned about the position of good news or bad news in your written message?
2. What points should you include in the close of your business message? Why?

Although Purdue University's Online Writing Lab is acknowledged as one of the best online writing sites available on the internet, many Canadian universities and colleges have online writing resources. Explore a few of these sites to find help with grammar, writing, documentation, and ESL-related resources, and for links to other online writing centres.
University of New Brunswick at Saint John Writing Centre
http://www.unbsj.ca/studentservices/writingcentre/
Queen's University—The Writing Centre
http://www.queensu.ca/writingcentre/
The University of Ottawa Writing Centre. "Hypergrammar" tutorials at.
http://www.arts.uottawa.ca/writcent/hypergrammar/

Exploring the Web on Your Own

Review a chapter-related website on your own to learn more about writing business messages.
1. Write it right by paying attention to the writing tips at Bull's Eye Business Writing Tips.
www.basic-learning.com/wbwt

Expand Your Knowledge offers internet-based activities to help you further improve your business communication skills and learn about best practices

Cases at the end of specific chapters offer you a chance to apply the three-part writing process to scenarios from the real world.

Business Communication Notebook centres on one of four themes: ethics, technology, intercultural communication, and workplace skills.

MyBusCommLab is a website that offers you videos and interactive exercises to improve your communication skills.

The following icons can be found throughout the text and refer to you to further practice exercises and interactive activities on MyBusCommLab.

Work with interactive documents and practise improving incorrectly written documents. By using the Final Draft decision tool, you can create an improved version of email messages, letters, memos, reports, and resumés.

Document **Makeovers**

Model your own documents from a wide selection of sample letters, memos, emails, and instant messages from real companies.

Model Document

Access visual rhetoric and web design tutorials, an annotated list of valuable web resources and a student bookshelf offering links to communication and writing resources.

Document **Design**

 **Activities** Practise your communication skills using interactive activities that mirror real tasks in business.

 **Exercises** Practise your grammar and critical thinking skills with additional self-graded exercises.

 Interact and make decisions as you watch *The Perils of Pauline*, in which a recent graduate deals with real-world communication situations on her first job.

Student Supplements

Grammar-on-the-Go will help you to develop your language skills so that your business writing style is clear and grammatically correct. Grammar-on-the-Go opens with a diagnostic test of English skills. Brief discussions of grammar, mechanics, and usage are followed by Practice Sessions and three-level series of exercises. **See inside back cover for more details**.

MyBusCommLab is a state-of-the art, interactive and instructive solution for business communication, designed to be used as a supplement to a traditional lecture course or to be set up to administer an online course. MyBusCommLab combines multimedia, tutorials, video, audio, simulations, animations, and assessments to engage you in your learning. You can learn at your own rate, completing exercises and having them evaluated for instant feedback.

MyBusCommLab includes access to Research Navigator, Pearson's fully searchable online collection of academic and popular journals.

Get started with the personal access code packaged with your new copy of the text. Personal access codes for MyBusCommLab can also be purchased separately.

Instructor Supplements

Instructor's Resource CD-ROM (ISBN: 978-0-13-207134-5) This CD-ROM brings together many of the instructor resources for the text, including the following components:

Instructor's Manual provides chapter outlines, suggested solutions to exercises, a pop quiz for each chapter, and fully formatted documents for *every* case in the letter-writing chapters. Additional resources include diagnostic tests of English skills and supplemental grammar exercises.

Test Item File includes over 1500 multiple choice, true/false, and fill-in-the-blank questions. This test bank is offered in both Word and MyTest formats (see below).

PowerPoint Presentations cover the key points in each chapter.

MyTest from Pearson Education Canada is a powerful assessment generation program that helps instructors easily create and print quizzes, tests, and exams, as well as homework or practice handouts. Questions and tests can be authored online, allowing instructors ultimate flexibility and the ability to manage assessments at anytime, from anywhere. To access MyTest please go to www.pearsonmytest.com.

Technology Specialists from Pearson work with faculty and campus course designers to ensure that Pearson technology products, assessment tools, and online course materials are tailored to meet your specific needs. This highly qualified team is dedicated to helping schools take full advantage of a wide range of educational resources, by assisting in the integration of a variety of instructional materials and media formats. Your local Pearson Education sales representative can provide you with more details on this service program.

CourseSmart is a new way for instructors and students to access textbooks online anytime, from anywhere. With thousands of titles across hundreds of courses, CourseSmart helps instructors choose the best textbook for their class and give their students a new option for buying the assigned textbook as a lower cost eTextbook. For more information, visit www.coursesmart.com.

Most of these instructor supplements are also available for download from a password-protected section of Pearson Education Canada's online catalogue. See your local sales representative for details.

Acknowledgments

The dedicated professionals at Pearson Education Canada made working on this book a pleasure. Sponsoring editor Carolin Sweig and developmental editor Jennifer Murray provided excellent advice and support in shaping the second Canadian edition. I am also very grateful to production and copy editor Tara Tovell for her clarity and attention to detail while preparing the manuscript for production and overseeing the proofreading process. Thanks also to Simon Bailey, new media development editor, for his assistance in integrating MyBusCommLab for this text.

Thank you to my supportive colleagues in the Communication Department at British Columbia of Technology, in particular Gretchen Quiring for her valuable suggestions and to Linda Matsuba, business librarian, for her knowledge of Canadian business. Special thanks also go to Christopher Wilson at Kwantlen Polytechnic University for his advice, to Kerri Shields of Centennial College for contributing the running cases, and to Caroline Jellinck of Ray & Berndtson/Tanton Mitchell for her employment-related feedback and extensive contacts in Canadian business.

Many educators from across Canada have contributed to the development of this text. I would like to thank the following instructors who took the time to give me detailed suggestions.

Bonnie Benoit, SAIT Polytechnic
Rebecca Book, Keyano College
Sarah Bowers, Langara College
Neil Carter, Sault College
Bill Corcoran, Grande Prairie Regional College
Brent Cotton, Georgian College
Les Hanson, Red River College
Tanya Haye, Douglas College
Paul Hutchinson, Niagara College of Applied Arts and Technology
Pamela Ip, Kwantlen Polytechnic University
Keith Johnson, University of the Fraser Valley
Linda Large, Canadore College
Diana M. Lohnes-Mitchell, Nova Scotia Community College
Alexandra Richmond, Kwantlen Polytechnic University
Heather Thompson, Saint Mary's University
Bruce Watson, SAIT Polytechnic

A final thanks goes to my two daughters, Casey and Anna, for their encouragement.

Jean A. Scribner
Vancouver, B.C.

Understanding Business Communication in Today's Workplace

LEARNING OBJECTIVES

After studying this chapter, you will be able to
1. Explain what effective communication is
2. Discuss four developments in the workplace that are intensifying the need to communicate effectively
3. List and briefly define the six phases of the communication process
4. Identify four ways to improve business communication
5. Differentiate between an ethical dilemma and an ethical lapse
6. Define and briefly discuss four types of cultural differences that can affect communication
7. Explain the importance of interpersonal communication skills in today's office

Kodak is a global company with operations in Asia, Europe, the U.S., the Middle East, Australia, and Africa. As a Vancouver-based executive with an international company, Judi Hess builds relationships with clients around the world. The leadership team at Kodak ensures that communication within this worldwide company not only keeps employees informed and included but also empowers them as decision makers.[2]

Succeeding Through Effective Communication

Organizations such as Kodak understand that achieving success in today's workplace is closely tied to the ability of employees and managers to communicate effectively with each other and with people outside the organization and from many cultures. **Communication** is the process of sending and receiving messages. However, communication is *effective* only when the message is understood and when it stimulates action or encourages the receiver to think in new ways.

Your ability to communicate effectively gives both you and your organization tangible benefits:
- Quicker problem solving
- Stronger decision making
- Increased productivity
- Steadier workflow
- Stronger business relationships
- Clearer promotional materials
- Enhanced professional image
- Improved response from colleagues, employees, supervisors, investors, customers, and other stakeholders

Canadian employers acknowledge the role of strong communication skills in business. Communication skills ranked highest on the list of employability skills noted in the Conference Board of Canada report *Employability Skills 2000+*.[3] As well, Human

> Communication enables organizations to function.

> Effective communication offers real benefits.

Resources and Social Development Canada (HRSDC) has created a list of "Essential Skills" by interviewing over 4000 workers and employers across the country. These skills include

- Document use
- Writing
- Oral communication
- Working with others
- Thinking skills

You will practise these skills in many of this book's exercises and assignments. Building confidence in these skills will help you get and keep a satisfying career job. Learn more about Essential Skills by visiting the HRSDC website at **www.hrsdc.gc.ca/en/hip/hrp/ essential_skills/essential_skills_index.shtml**. To help you develop your communication skills for career success, this book includes tips from human resource managers aimed at helping you get and succeed in a first business position.

People aren't born writers or speakers. The more they write and speak, the more their skills improve. This course teaches you how to create effective messages and helps you improve your communication skills through practice in an environment that provides honest, constructive criticism. Working hard in this course will not only improve your writing skills but will also help you avoid making costly mistakes on the job.

No matter what career you pursue, this course will help you discover how to collaborate in teams, listen well, master nonverbal communication, and participate in productive meetings. You'll learn about communicating across cultures and through the internet. You'll learn a three-step process for writing business messages, and you'll get specific tips for writing emails, letters, memos, reports and making oral presentations. You'll learn how to write effective resumés and job application letters and how to handle employment interviews. Plus, this text offers a superb collection of communication examples.

Before we get to all these topics, consider some of the communication challenges you'll be facing in today's workplace as you communicate in an organizational setting.

> In this course, you will learn how to create effective business messages.

Adapting to the Changing Workplace

Good communication skills are more vital today than ever before because people need to adapt to a workplace that is constantly changing. Effective communication will help you meet challenges such as advances in technology, the need to access vast amounts of information, the growth of globalization and workforce diversity, the increasing use of teams in the workplace, and the need for good interpersonal communication skills.

> Effective communication helps us adapt to change.

- **Communicating amid advancing technology.** The internet, email, instant messaging (IM), social media, voice mail, faxes, pagers, and other wireless devices have revolutionized the way people communicate. These tools increase the speed, frequency, and reach of our communication (see Figure 1.1). People from opposite ends of the world can work together seamlessly, 24 hours a day, whether they are at the office, in a car, in an airport, in a hotel, or at home. Technology reveals your communication skill with every email, phone conversation, or videoconference.[4] Today, you have to think not only about what you're going to say and how you're going to say it but also about whether to communicate in person or use technology. Even when communicating in a global company over great distances, Judi Hess has found it important to "build relationships face to face" through visits and meetings in addition to using communication technologies to work remotely.
- **Communicating in the age of information.** In today's workplace, you must know how to find, evaluate, process, and communicate information effectively and efficiently. Plus, you must be able to use what information you receive to make strong, speedy decisions. Unfortunately, people are so inundated with information, they tend to ignore messages they see as less important. Your challenge is to get your audience's

FIGURE 1.1 Technology and Communication: Effective Email

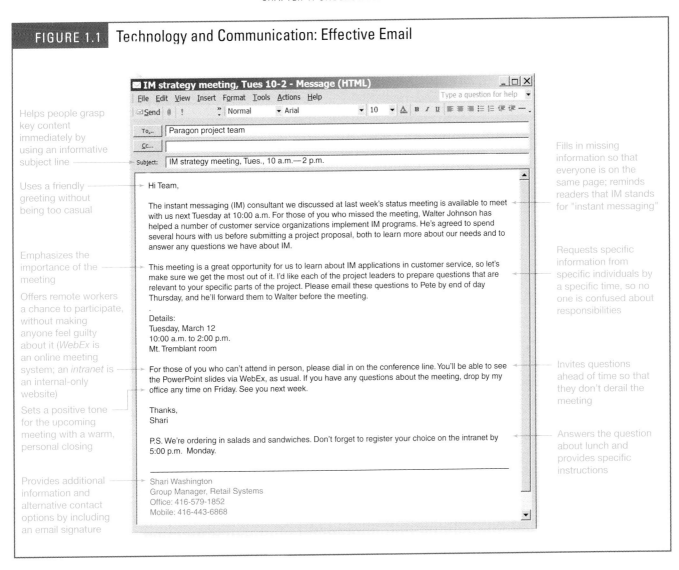

attention and to make your messages easy to skim or "scannable" so that your audience will read and act on them.

- **Communicating in the age of connectivity.** Web 2.0 technologies, such as social or "peer" media including blogs, wikis, YouTube, and networking sites (for example, Facebook or MySpace), increase people's ability to connect, collaborate, and interact. These technologies are having a powerful effect on the way companies can communicate with employees, customers, and the public, with over 25 percent of online consumers visiting social networking sites by 2007.[5] A **wiki**, for example, is a site that allows multiple authors to construct content and participate in its editing. **Blogs** are online personal journals of entries (or **"posts"**) that offer readers an ongoing conversation and opportunity to participate in it. While the technologies change rapidly, the focus on relationship and connectivity is timeless, making your ability to write concise, focused messages an essential skill. Your challenge is to hone your communication skills so that you can respond to interactive communications in an appropriate and considered way. Having a positive presence online will be influenced by the effectiveness of your communication skills.

- **Communicating globally and within a culturally diverse workforce.** More and more businesses are crossing national boundaries to compete on a global scale. More than two million North Americans now work for multi-national employers, and the number of foreign companies with plants in Canada is increasing.[6] Plus, the Canadian

> Scannable messages help readers cope with information overload.

workforce includes growing numbers of people with diverse ethnic backgrounds. To communicate effectively, you must understand other backgrounds, personalities, and perceptions. "Understanding the culture of the people you are going to do business with is key for achieving success and can change the style of the communication," says Hess. Kodak keeps in touch with staff in many different countries by using video calls and teleconferences, live webcasts, and globally linked internal voice mail and email systems. Cultural and language barriers among staff from many different language groups are overcome through careful planning and management of communication.

- **Communicating in team-based organizations.** Traditional management style is changing in today's fast-paced, e-commerce environment.[7] Successful companies no longer limit decisions to a few managers at the top of a formal hierarchy. Instead, organizations use teams and work groups to collaborate and make fast decisions. As Chapter 2 discusses in detail, before you can function in a team-based organization, you must understand how groups interact. You must be a good listener and correctly interpret all the nonverbal cues you receive from others. Such interaction requires a basic understanding of the communication process in organizational settings.

Understanding the Communication Process

The communication process has six steps.

Effective communication doesn't occur haphazardly in organizations. Nor does it happen all at once. Communication is a dynamic, two-way process that can be broken down into six phases (see Figure 1.2):

1. **The sender has an idea.** You conceive an idea and want to share it.
2. **The sender encodes the idea.** You decide on the message's form (word, facial expression, gesture), length, organization, tone, and style—all of which depend on your idea, your audience, and your personal style or mood.
3. **The sender transmits the message.** You select a **communication channel** (verbal or nonverbal, spoken or written) and a **medium** (telephone, letter, memo, email, report, face-to-face exchange). This choice depends on your message, your audience's location, your need for speed, and the formality required.
4. **The receiver gets the message.** Your audience must receive the message. If you send a letter, your receiver has to read it before understanding it. If you're giving a speech, your audience has to be able to hear you, and they have to be paying attention.

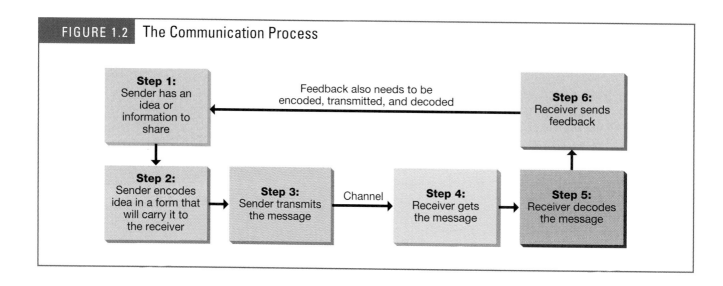

FIGURE 1.2 The Communication Process

5. **The receiver decodes the message.** Your receiver must absorb, understand, and mentally store your message. If all goes well, the receiver interprets your message correctly, assigning the same meaning to your words as you intended.
6. **The receiver sends feedback.** After decoding your message, the receiver responds in some way and signals that response to you. This feedback enables you to evaluate the effectiveness of your message: If your audience doesn't understand what you mean, you can tell by the response and refine your message.

As Figure 1.2 illustrates, the communication process is repeated until both parties have finished expressing themselves.[8] To communicate effectively, don't cram too much information into one message. Instead, limit the content of your message to a specific subject, and use this repeated back-and-forth exchange to provide additional information or details in subsequent messages.

Improving Business Communication

In the coming chapters, you'll find real-life examples of both good and bad communication, with explanations of what's good or bad about them. After a while you'll begin to see a pattern. You'll notice that four themes keep surfacing: (1) committing to ethical communication, (2) adopting an audience-centred approach, (3) improving your intercultural sensitivity, and (4) improving your workplace sensitivity. Close attention to these themes will help you improve your business communication.

Committing to Ethical Communication

Ethics refers to the principles of conduct that govern a person or a group. Unethical people say or do whatever it takes to achieve an end. Ethical people are generally trustworthy, fair, impartial, respectful of the rights of others, and concerned about the impact of their actions on society. Ethics is "knowing the difference between what you have a right to do and what is the right thing to do."[9]

Ethical communication includes all relevant information, is true in every sense, and is not deceptive in any way. By contrast, unethical communication can include falsehoods and misleading information (or exclude important information). Some examples of unethical communication include[10]

- **Plagiarism.** Stealing someone else's words or work and claiming it as your own
- **Selective misquoting.** Deliberately omitting damaging or unflattering comments to paint a better (but untruthful) picture of you or your company
- **Misrepresenting numbers.** Increasing or decreasing numbers, exaggerating, altering statistics, or omitting numerical data
- **Distorting visuals.** Making a product look bigger or changing the scale of graphs and charts to exaggerate or conceal differences

An ethical message is accurate and sincere. It avoids language that manipulates, discriminates, or exaggerates. To communicate ethically, do not hide negative information behind an optimistic attitude, don't state opinions as facts, and be sure to portray graphic data fairly. Be honest with employers, co-workers, and clients, and never seek personal gain by making others look better or worse than they are. Don't allow personal preferences to influence your perception or the perception of others. In short, act in good faith.

On the surface, such ethical practices appear fairly easy to recognize. But deciding what is ethical can be quite complex.

RECOGNIZING ETHICAL CHOICES Every company has responsibilities to various groups: customers, employees, shareholders, suppliers, neighbours, the community, and the country. Unfortunately, what's right for one group may be wrong for another.[11] Moreover,

You can improve your business communication by
- Committing to ethical communication
- Adopting an audience-centred approach
- Improving your intercultural sensitivity
- Improving your workplace sensitivity

 Activities

For business communication to be effective, it must be ethical.

Avoid unethical practices when preparing your business messages.

as you attempt to satisfy the needs of one group, you may be presented with an option that seems right on the surface but that somehow feels wrong. When people must choose between conflicting loyalties and weigh difficult trade-offs, they are facing a dilemma.

> When choosing between two ethical alternatives, you are facing an ethical dilemma.

An **ethical dilemma** involves choosing between alternatives that aren't clear-cut (perhaps two conflicting alternatives are both ethical and valid, or perhaps the alternatives lie somewhere in the vast grey area between right and wrong). Suppose you are president of a company that's losing money. You have a duty to your shareholders to try to cut your losses and a duty to your employees to be fair and honest. After looking at various options, you conclude that you'll have to lay off 500 people immediately. You suspect you may have to lay off another 100 people later on, but right now you need those 100 workers to finish a project. What do you tell them? If you confess that their jobs are shaky, many of them may quit just when you need them most. However, if you tell them that the future is rosy, you'll be stretching the truth.

> When choosing an alternative that is unethical or illegal, you are experiencing an ethical lapse.

Unlike a dilemma, an **ethical lapse** is making a clearly unethical or illegal choice. Suppose you have decided to change jobs and have discreetly landed an interview with your company's largest competitor. You get along well with the interviewer, who is impressed enough with you to offer you a position on the spot. Not only is the new position a step up from your current job, but the pay is also double what you're getting now. You accept the job and agree to start next month. Then as you're shaking hands with the interviewer, she asks you to bring along profiles of your current company's 10 largest customers when you report for work. Do you comply with her request? How do you decide between what's ethical and what is not?

> For ethical guidance, first look to the law.

MAKING ETHICAL CHOICES One place to look for guidance is the law. If saying or writing something is clearly illegal, you have no dilemma: You obey the law. However, even though legal considerations will resolve some ethical questions, you'll often have to rely on your own judgment and principles. One guideline: If your intent is honest, your message is ethical, even though it may be factually incorrect. However, if your intent is to mislead or manipulate your audience, the message is unethical, regardless of whether it is true. You might look at the consequences of your message and opt for the solution that provides the greatest good to the greatest number of people—a solution that you can live with.[12] You might ask yourself[13]

> To help make an ethical decision, you can ask yourself four questions.

- **Is this message legal?** Does it violate civil law or company policy?
- **Is this message balanced?** Does it do the most good and the least harm? Is it fair to all concerned in the short term as well as the long term? Does it promote positive, win-win relationships? Did you weigh all sides before drawing a conclusion?
- **Is it a message you can live with?** Does it make you feel good about yourself? Does it make you proud? Would you feel good about your message if a newspaper published it? If your family knew about it?
- **Is this message feasible?** Can it work in the real world? Have you considered your position in the company? Your company's competition? Its financial and political strength? The likely costs or risks of your message? The time available?

One way to help you make your messages ethical is to consider your audience: What does your audience need? What will help your audience the most?

Adopting an Audience-Centred Approach

> An effective business message focuses on its audience.

Adopting an audience-centred approach means focusing on and caring about the members of your audience, making every effort to get your message across in a way that is meaningful to them. To create an effective message, you need to learn as much as possible about the biases, education, age, status, and background of your audience. When you address strangers, try to find out more about them; if that's impossible, try to project yourself into their position by using your common sense and imagination. By writing and speaking from your audience's point of view, you can help them understand and accept your message—an approach that is discussed in more detail in Chapter 3, "Planning Business Messages." Audience focus takes on special importance when you're communicating with someone from another culture. You will improve your business communication tremendously by becoming more sensitive to the differences that exist among people from various cultures.

Improving Your Intercultural Sensitivity

To communicate more effectively, be aware of and sensitive to cultural differences. **Culture** is a shared system of symbols, beliefs, attitudes, values, expectations, and norms for behaviour. Members of a culture have similar assumptions about how people should think, behave, and communicate, and they all tend to act on those assumptions in much the same way.

Yet, from group to group, cultures differ widely. When you write to or speak with someone from another culture, you encode your message using the assumptions of your own culture. However, the members of your audience decode your message using the assumptions of their culture, so your intended meaning may be misunderstood.[14]

For example, when Japanese auto manufacturer Mazda opened a plant in North America, officials passed out company baseball caps and told employees that they could wear the caps at work, along with their mandatory company uniform (blue pants and khaki shirts). The employees assumed that the caps were a *voluntary* accessory, and many decided not to wear them. This decision upset Japanese managers, who regarded this behaviour as a sign of disrespect. Managers believed that employees who really cared about the company would *want* to wear the caps. However, the North American employees resented being told what they should *want* to do.[15]

You can improve your ability to communicate effectively across cultures by recognizing such cultural differences, by overcoming your tendency to judge others based on your own standards, by polishing your written intercultural skills, and by polishing your oral intercultural skills.

RECOGNIZING CULTURAL DIFFERENCES Problems arise when we assume, wrongly, that other people's attitudes and lives are like ours. A graduate of one intercultural training program said, "I used to think it was enough to treat people the way I wanted to be treated. But [after taking the course] . . . I realized you have to treat people the way *they* want to be treated."[16] You can improve intercultural sensitivity by recognizing and accommodating cultural differences in such areas as context, ethics, social customs, and nonverbal communication.

Context **Cultural context** is the pattern of physical cues, environmental stimuli, and implicit understanding that conveys meaning between two members of the same culture (see Table 1.1 on page 8). In a **high-context culture** such as South Korea or Taiwan, people rely less on verbal communication and more on the context of nonverbal actions and environmental setting to convey meaning. A Chinese speaker expects the audience to *discover* the essence of a message and uses indirectness and metaphor to provide a web of meaning.[17] In high-context cultures, the rules of everyday life are rarely explicit; instead, as individuals grow up, they learn how to recognize situational cues (such as gestures and tone of voice) and how to respond as expected.[18]

On the other hand, in a **low-context culture** such as Canada, Germany, or the United States, people rely more on verbal communication and less on circumstances and cues to convey meaning. An English speaker feels responsible for transmitting the meaning of the message and often places sentences in chronological sequence to establish a cause-and-effect

Activities

Effective business communicators take cultural differences into account.

Improve your cultural sensitivity by
- Recognizing cultural differences
- Overcoming the tendency to stereotype
- Polishing your written intercultural communication skills
- Polishing your oral intercultural communication skills

Cultural differences exist in areas such as context, ethics, social custom, and nonverbal communication.

Activities

To communicate with one another, members of different cultures rely on the context of physical cues, environmental stimuli, and implicit understanding to different degrees.

| TABLE 1.1 | How Cultural Context Affects Business Communication |

IN LOW-CONTEXT COMPANIES	IN HIGH-CONTEXT COMPANIES
Executive offices are separate with controlled access.	Executive offices are shared and open to all.
Workers rely on detailed background information.	Workers do not expect or want detailed information.
Information is highly centralized and controlled.	Information is shared with everyone.
Objective data are valued over subjective relationships.	Subjective relationships are valued over objective data.
Business and social relationships are discrete.	Business and social relationships overlap.
Competence is valued as much as position and status.	Position and status are valued much more than competence.
Meetings have fixed agendas and plenty of advance notice.	Meetings are often called on short notice, and key people always accept.

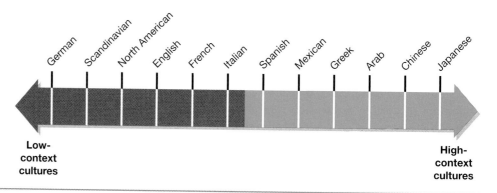

Low-context cultures — German, Scandinavian, North American, English, French, Italian, Spanish, Mexican, Greek, Arab, Chinese, Japanese — High-context cultures

To communicate in high-context cultures, members rely less on words and more on context.

To communicate in low-context cultures, members rely more on words and less on context.

Members of different cultures have different views of what is ethical and even legal.

pattern.[19] In low-context cultures, rules and expectations are usually spelled out through explicit statements such as "Please wait until I'm finished" or "You're welcome to browse."[20]

Contextual differences are apparent in the way cultures approach problem solving, negotiations, and decision making. For example, in lower-context cultures such as Germany, business people want to make decisions as quickly and efficiently as possible. However, in higher-context cultures such as Greece, business people consider it a mark of good faith to spend time on each little point before reaching a decision. Even in Canada, contextual differences between French and English Canada influence styles of negotiation and decision making. The French, the British, and the North Americans are ranked as having low-context cultures, with British falling in the middle of the three.[21]

Ethics Legal and ethical behaviours are also affected by cultural context. For example, because members of low-context cultures value the written word, they consider written agreements binding. They also tend to view laws with flexibility. However, members of high-context cultures put less emphasis on the written word and consider personal pledges more important than contracts. Plus, they tend to adhere more strictly to the law.[22]

Legal systems differ from culture to culture. In the United Kingdom and Canada, an individual is presumed innocent until proved guilty, a principle rooted in British common law. However, in Mexico and Turkey, an individual is presumed guilty until proved innocent, a principle rooted in the Napoleonic code.[23] These distinctions are particularly important if your firm must communicate about a legal dispute in another country.

Social Customs In any culture, the rules of social etiquette may be formal or informal. Formal social rules are specifically taught "rights" and "wrongs" of how to behave in common social situations (such as table manners at meals). When formal rules are violated, people can explain why they feel upset. However, informal social rules are usually learned by watching how people behave and then imitating that behaviour, so these rules are more difficult to identify (such as how males and females are supposed to behave, or when it's appropriate to use a person's first name). When informal rules are violated, people often feel uncomfortable without knowing exactly why.[24]

Differences in social values are apparent in the way various cultures define manners, think about time, recognize status, and value wealth. For example, the predominant U.S. view is that money solves many problems, that material comfort is a sign of superiority and is earned by individual effort, and that people who work hard are better than those who don't. But other cultures condemn materialism, some prize communal effort above that of the individual, and some value a more carefree lifestyle. Canadians, for example, place a high value on collective goals such as a national health-care program, trust government more than Americans do, and believe in a social safety net.[25] However, even within Canada values can differ by region.

> Whether formal or informal, the rules governing social custom differ from culture to culture.

Nonverbal Communication The simplest hand gestures change meaning from culture to culture, so interpreting nonverbal elements according to your own culture can be dangerous. Differences in nonverbal communication are apparent in body language and in the varying attitudes toward personal space. For example, Canadian business people usually stand about 1.6 m apart during a conversation. However, this distance is uncomfortably close for people from Germany or Japan and uncomfortably far for Arabs and Latin Americans. (See more on nonverbal communication in Chapter 2.)

OVERCOMING ETHNOCENTRISM Being aware of cultural differences is only the first step in improving your intercultural communication. To communicate across cultures successfully, you must be able to overcome our human tendency to judge others by our own standards. When communicating across cultures, your effectiveness depends on maintaining an open mind. Unfortunately, many people lapse into **ethnocentrism**, the belief that their own cultural background is superior to all others. They lose sight of the possibility that their words and actions can be misunderstood, and they forget that they are likely to misinterpret the actions of others.

> Ethnocentrism blocks effective communication because it closes the mind to new information.

When you first begin to investigate the culture of another group, you may attempt to understand the common tendencies of that group's members by **stereotyping**—predicting individuals' behaviour or character on the basis of their membership in a particular group or class. For example, Japanese visitors often stereotype Americans as people who walk fast, are wasteful in using space, speak directly, ask too many questions in the classroom, don't respect professors, are disrespectful of age and status, lack discipline, and are extravagant.[26]

> Stereotyping can be useful, but only as a first step in learning about another culture.

Stereotyping may be useful in the beginning, but your next step is to move beyond it to relationships with real people. Unfortunately, when ethnocentric people stereotype, they tend to do so on the basis of limited, general, or inaccurate evidence. They frequently develop biased attitudes toward a group, and they fail to move beyond that initial step.[27] So instead of talking with Abdul Karhum, a unique human being, ethnocentric people are talking to "an Arab." They may believe that all Arabs are, say, hagglers, so Abdul Karhum's personal qualities cannot alter such preconceptions. His every action is forced to fit the preconceived image, even if that image is wrong.

To overcome ethnocentrism, follow a few simple suggestions:

- **Acknowledge distinctions.** Don't ignore the differences between another person's culture and your own.
- **Avoid assumptions.** Don't assume that others will act the same way you do, that they will operate from the same assumptions, or that they will use language and symbols the same way you do.

> Seven tips will help you improve your written intercultural skills.

- **Avoid judgments.** When people act differently, don't conclude that they are in error, that their way is invalid, or that their customs are inferior to your own.

Too often, both parties in an intercultural exchange are guilty of ethnocentrism and prejudice. Little wonder, then, that misunderstandings arise when communicating across cultures.

Activities

POLISHING YOUR WRITTEN INTERCULTURAL SKILLS The letter in Figure 1.3 illustrates an effective intercultural communication. To help you prepare effective written communications for multicultural audiences, remember these tips:[28]

- **Use plain English.** Use short, precise words that say exactly what you mean and rely on specific terms and concrete examples to explain your points.
- **Address international correspondence properly.** The order and layout of address information vary from country to country, so follow the conventions that appear in the company's letterhead.

FIGURE 1.3 **Effective Intercultural Letter**

- **Cite numbers carefully.** Use figures (27) instead of spelling them out (twenty-seven).
- **Avoid slang, idioms, jargon, and abbreviations.** Acronyms (such as CAD/CAM) and unfamiliar product names may also lead to confusion.
- **Be brief.** Construct sentences that are short and simple.
- **Use short paragraphs.** Each paragraph should stick to one topic and use transitions.
- **Hire a translator when language is a barrier.**

POLISHING YOUR ORAL INTERCULTURAL SKILLS When speaking in English to people who speak English as a second language, you may find these tips helpful:

Activities

- **Speak slowly** and pronounce words clearly. Pause at the end of your sentences to make one point at a time. Rephrase your sentences if the listener appears confused. Choose simpler words and avoid repeating the same words in a louder voice. Use concrete words to convey objective messages. Avoid overuse of adjectives such as "fantastic" or "fabulous," which people from other cultures might consider overly dramatic.
- **Avoid talking down** to the other person. Say "Am I going too fast?" rather than "Is this too difficult for you?"
- **Pay attention to feedback.** Be alert to signs of confusion in your listener. Realize that nods and smiles do not necessarily mean understanding. If the other person's body language seems at odds with the message, take time to clarify the meaning. Clarify your intent through examples and repetition.
- **Listen carefully and patiently.** Let others finish what they have to say. If you interrupt, you may miss something important and show lack of respect. When you do not understand a comment, ask the person to repeat it. You can do this politely by saying "I'm sorry but I did not quite hear your comment."

> Four tips will help you improve your oral intercultural skills.

In short, take advantage of the other person's presence to make sure that your message is getting across and that you understand his or her message too.

Improving Your Workplace Sensitivity

ADAPTING TO CULTURAL DIVERSITY The Canadian workforce includes immigrants and people from a variety of ethnic backgrounds (such as Canadians from Chinese, Indian, and Filipino cultures) who often bring their own languages and cultural customs to the workplace. Today's workforce is made up of people who differ in race, gender, age, culture, family structure, religion, and educational background. Nineteen percent of Canadian wage earners in 2001 were born outside the country.[29] Such **cultural diversity** affects how business messages are conceived, planned, sent, received, and interpreted in the workplace. To communicate more effectively with people at work, learn all you can about the cultures of the people around you. Read books and articles about these cultures, and talk to people who have intercultural business experience.

> Today's culturally diverse workforce is made up of men and women from various nations, ethnic backgrounds, age groups, and races.

BEING SENSITIVE TO GENERATIONAL DIFFERENCES Workplace sensitivity also requires awareness of differences in communication preferences for workers of varying ages. For the first time in Canadian history, many workplaces employ up to four generations of workers.[30] The three generations most represented in the workplace are the "Baby Boomers" (born 1941–1960), "Generation X" (born 1961–1976), and "Generation Y" or the "Millennials" (born 1977–1992). The members of each generation have been shaped by defining events in their developmental years, which have affected their outlooks on life and work. For example, the Millennials are the first group born into a digital society and are completely comfortable with using communication technology. Their preference for social media channels of communication such as Facebook is

> Be sensitive to generational differences when selecting the way you communicate in the office.

different from communication channels favoured among employees or managers from earlier generations, who may prefer face-to-face conversation, telephone messages, or email.[31] Diverse generations working side by side can result in friction due to differing attitudes, ethics, values, and behaviours, so increased sensitivity to these differences is important for communicators.

BEING SELF-AWARE AND CONSIDERATE OF OTHERS Increased use of technology and time spent "plugged in" can result in lack of experience in "soft skills" or interpersonal communication skills. Yet these skills, including politeness, ability to converse socially, awareness of others' feelings, diplomacy, and responsiveness, are more important than ever. In a recent survey, human resource managers ranked job applicants' soft skills higher than analytical and technical skills.[32] Strong interpersonal communication skills depend on being self-aware and aware of others. Those who are not self-aware may not realize that their habits, hygiene, or communication styles are annoying to those around them. For example, in an open plan office, the employee who speaks loudly or leaves a cellphone to ring unattended on her desk will disturb those working nearby. Understanding business etiquette or standards of behaviour expected in the office can help you fit into the workplace. Business etiquette differs from social etiquette but shares the basic tenant that individuals should act in ways that make others around them comfortable. Though many offices are less formal than in the past, still certain behaviours will be viewed as more courteous than others and effective business communicators strive to be courteous.

In Medieval times, politeness was a form of class distinction because only wealthy people were educated in a code of conduct, called "chivalry." Today, however, codes of conduct are not restricted to wealthy classes. Most office environments function according to a generally understood agreement about what constitutes polite behaviour.

In today's workplace, where people from many different backgrounds work closely together, the concept of civility is highly valued. Employees with bad manners distract others and lower productivity. Resolving interpersonal conflicts among staff members costs Canadian business in management time and company money. One study showed that "over 65% of performance problems result from strained relationships between employees, not from deficits in individual skill or motivation,"[33] and another study estimated up to "30% of a typical manager's time is spent dealing with conflict"[34] Many firms have increased emphasis on business etiquette by providing training programs and coaching to improve civility in the workplace.[35]

Throughout this book you will find other tips on how to create and maintain positive, polite work relationships, be aware of business etiquette, and refine your interpersonal communication skills.

POLISHING YOUR WORKPLACE SENSITIVITY SKILLS You can communicate more effectively in a culturally diverse workplace by following these best practices from successful intercultural business people.[36]

Educate Yourself
- **Recognize your own cultural biases.** Learn to identify when your assumptions are different from another person's. Assume differences until similarity is proved. Look beyond superficial differences and don't be distracted by dress or appearance.
- **Investigate the receivers' values.** Before you send a message, put yourself in the receivers' shoes to imagine their feelings or interests on the topic and the way the message will reach them. Learn how respect is communicated in various cultures and age groups (through eye contact, gestures, dress, and so on). Learn when to be direct or indirect, and which channels of communication would be preferred by the receiver.

- **Focus on the individual.** Communicate with each person as an individual, not as a stereotypical representative. Emphasize common ground. Look for similarities from which to work.

Adjust Your Attitude

- **Take responsibility for communication.** Don't assume it is the other person's job to communicate with you. Be patient and persistent. If you want to communicate with someone from another culture, don't give up easily.
- **Empathize.** Before you send a message, imagine the receiver's feelings and point of view.
- **Withhold judgment.** Listen to the whole story and accept differences in others without judging them. Learn to control frustration and tolerate ambiguity when placed in an unfamiliar and confusing situation.
- **Be flexible.** Be prepared to change your habits and attitudes when communicating with someone from another culture or age group.

This advice will help you communicate with anybody, regardless of culture.

> Courteous behaviour helps your career and office productivity.

ON THE JOB

Create a Professional Persona

Being courteous can help get others to cooperate with you and help you advance in your career. You can improve how others perceive you by

- Being punctual
- Greeting associates politely
- Expressing appreciation
- Dressing for your professional role
- Being sensitive to the needs of others
- Keeping emails and voice mails short
- Ensuring your cellphone is turned off in meetings or in a shared space with co-workers
- Keeping personal and professional boundaries separate

Self-Assess Your Office Courtesy

Using *MyBusCommLab's* Research Navigator, research "business etiquette" to iden-tify ways you can make a positive impression in the workplace. Getting along with oth-ers in an office can be challenging. How do you rate your office courtesy?

Element of Courtesy	Always	Frequently	Occasionally	Never
I use polite language and avoid swearing.	_____	_____	_____	_____
I say plea se" and "thank you" when others do things for me.	_____	_____	_____	_____
I match the formality of my communication style to my audience's preferences.	_____	_____	_____	_____
I respect others' space and clean up my work area or lunch space.	_____	_____	_____	_____
I respect personal/professional boundaries by not asking questions about workmates' finances/personal lives.	_____	_____	_____	_____
I avoid raising my voice when working near others.	_____	_____	_____	_____
I avoid gossiping.	_____	_____	_____	_____

Reviewing Key Points

Activities

In this chapter you learned that communication is important to the way organizations function. Changes in technology have increased the speed, frequency, and reach of business communication. As a communicator, you must focus messages on action and make them easy to scan to help readers manage information overload. To be a successful communicator, especially in team-based organizations, you need to be aware of audience needs and cultural differences.

You also learned about the six phases of communication—sending, encoding, transmitting, receiving, decoding, and giving feedback—and that effective business communication is ethical, audience centred, and sensitive to cultural differences. High-context cultures such as China and Japan rely on nonverbal actions and environment to convey meaning whereas low-context cultures such as Canada, the United States, and Germany rely more on words and less on circumstances and cues.

You can be sensitive to diversity in the workplace and overcome cultural barriers by
* Withholding judgment and recognizing differences
* Understanding varying social customs regarding gestures, sense of time, and use of space
* Being flexible
* Keeping messages simple and limited in scope
* Using repetition
* Using plain English
* Being courteous

mybuscommlab Go to MyBusCommLab at www.pearson.ca/mybuscommlab for online exercises and problems.

Practise Your Grammar

Exercises

Effective business communication starts with strong grammar skills. To improve your grammar skills, go to MyBusCommLab or Grammar-on-the-Go, where you'll find exercises and diagnostic tests to help you produce clear, effective communication.

Test Your Knowledge

Exercises

1. What benefits does effective communication give you and your organization?
2. How are social technologies changing communication in the workplace?
3. How can information overload affect communication?
4. What effects do globalization and workforce diversity have on communication?
5. How are teams changing business communication?
6. In which phases of the communication process are messages encoded and decoded?
7. Define ethics, and explain what ethical communication encompasses.
8. What is an audience-centred approach to communication?
9. In what four general areas can you expect to observe cultural differences?
10. What are tips for communicating effectively in a diverse workplace?

Apply Your Knowledge

1. How does your understanding of the communication process help you conduct business more effectively?
2. Do you think that written or spoken messages would be more susceptible to cultural misunderstanding? Why?
3. Your company has relocated to Vancouver, where a Vietnamese subculture is strongly established. Many employees will be from this subculture. As a member of the human resources department, what suggestions can you make to improve communication between management and the Vietnamese Canadians your company is hiring?

4. What kinds of workplace problems can be created in communications among employees of different generations (for example, between the "Boomers" and "Generation X")? How could generational differences influence the choice of method for communicating between two people from different generations?

5. **Ethical Choices** Because of your excellent communication skills, your boss always asks you to write his reports for him. But when the CEO compliments him on his logical organization and clear writing style, your boss responds as if he'd written all those reports himself. What kind of ethical choice does this represent? What can you do in this situation? Briefly explain your solution and your reasoning.

Running Cases

Video

CASE 1: Noreen

Noreen is working toward a Bachelor of Business Administration (BBA) and takes her studies via distance education through a Canadian university. She works full time at Petro-Go, an international fuel company, in one of their call centres as a customer service representative (CSR). She is the team leader for a group of CSRs located in the Go Points program department. Her future career goal is to complete her BBA and obtain a senior management position within a large international firm. Noreen is on the social committee and her manager asks her to organize a potluck lunch for 40 employees in her call centre department.

QUESTIONS

a. Suggest an appropriate type of communication (e.g., casual conversation, formal letter, meeting, memo, email, bulletin board notice) and briefly explain your choice.

b. Is this a horizontal flow or a downward flow of communication? Formal or informal?

c. What must Noreen consider when planning this event?

d. What must Noreen consider when communicating the plans?

e. What communication barriers might she encounter and how should she overcome those barriers?

YOUR TASK

Assume all the plans are arranged and now Noreen just needs to notify the guests. Write an email that she will send to the 40 employees in her department. Ensure the necessary details are in the invitation. Exchange emails with another student and ask for constructive criticism on how to improve your communication.

CASE 2: Kwong

Kwong, a new Canadian, is enrolled in a three-year co-op diploma program in accounting at a local college. He is currently in his third semester and will be placed in a co-op position next term. There he will apply what he has learned in his studies and, at the same time, gain valuable work experience. His future career goal is to complete the Chartered General Accountant (CGA) requirements and then open his own accounting firm. Kwong will be interviewed by a prospective co-op employer. He needs to be successful in the interview to obtain the placement.

QUESTIONS

a. What research should Kwong do before the interview?

b. Which employability skills do you think Kwong may currently possess and which skills may he still need to develop? (Refer to Figure 1.2 on page 4)

c. How will he emphasize his strong skills and de-emphasize his weaker skills during the interview?

d. What ethical choices may Kwong have to make?

e. What communication barriers may Kwong be faced with (both oral and written)? Give a specific example.

YOUR TASK

Make a list of the employability skills you believe you possess. Make a list of the employability skills you believe you need to improve. Visit the Human Resources and Social Development Canada website for more information about employability skills: www.hrsdc.gc.ca/en/hip/hrp/essential_skills/essential_skills_index.shtml.

⊘ Practise Your Knowledge

ACTIVITIES

1. **Analyze This Document** Your boss wants to send a brief email message welcoming employees recently transferred to your department from your Hong Kong branch. The boss asked a new hire to draft the message and has asked you to follow up on it and make any necessary revisions before the message is sent. The recipients all speak English. What changes would you suggest—and why? Would you consider this message to be audience centred? Why or why not?

   Hey, I wanted to welcome you ASAP to our little family here in B.C. It's high time we shook hands in person and not just across the sea. I'm stoked about getting to know you, and I for one will do my level best to sell you on Canada.

2. **Ethical Choices** In less than a page, explain why you think each of the following is or is not ethical.
   a. De-emphasizing negative test results in a report on your product idea
   b. Taking a computer home to finish a work-related assignment
   c. Telling an associate and close friend that she'd better pay more attention to her work responsibilities or management will fire her
   d. Recommending the purchase of excess equipment to use up your allocated funds before the end of the fiscal year so that your budget won't be cut next year

3. **The Changing Workplace: Always in Touch** Technological devices such as faxes, cellular phones, electronic mail, instant messaging, and voice mail are making business people easily accessible at any time of day or night, at work and at home. What kind of impact might frequent intrusions have on their professional and personal lives? Please explain your answer in less than a page.

4. **Internet** As a manufacturer of aerospace, energy, and environmental equipment, Lockheed Martin has developed a code of ethics that it expects employees to abide by. Visit Lockheed Martin's website at **www. lockheedmartin.com**. Click on "Ethics" (in the pull-down menu under "About Us"), then follow the link to "Partners in Setting the Standards" and review the company's code of ethics. In a brief paragraph, describe three specific examples of things you could do that would violate these provisions. Now scroll down and study the list of "Warning Signs" of ethics violations and take the "Quick Quiz." In another brief paragraph, describe how you could use this advice to avoid ethical problems as you write business letters, memos, and reports. Submit both paragraphs to your instructor.

5. **Ethical Choices** Your boss often uses you as a sounding board for her ideas. Now she seems to want you to act as an unofficial messenger. You are to pass her ideas along to the staff, without mentioning her involvement. Then she wants you to inform her of what staff members say, without telling them you're going to repeat their responses. What questions should you ask yourself as you consider the ethical implications of this situation? Write a short paragraph explaining the ethical choice you will make in this situation.[37]

6. **Self-Introduction** Write a paragraph or prepare a two-minute oral presentation introducing yourself to your instructor and your class. Include such things as your background, interests, achievements, and goals.

7. **Teamwork** Your boss has asked your work group to research and report on corporate child-care facilities. Of course, you'll want to know who (besides your boss) will be reading your report. Working with two team members, list four or five other things you'll want to know about the situation and about your audience before starting your research. Briefly explain why each of the items on your list is important.

8. **Communication Process: Analyzing Miscommunication** Use the six phases of the communication process to analyze a miscommunication you've recently had with a co-worker, supervisor, classmate, teacher, friend, or family member. What idea were you trying to share? How did you encode and transmit it? Did the receiver get the message? Did the receiver correctly decode the message? How do you know? Based on your analysis, what do you think prevented your successful communication in this instance?

9. **Ethical Choices** Your department has been given the critical assignment of selecting the site for your company's new plant. After months of negotiations with landowners, numerous cost calculations, and investments in ecological, social, and community impact studies, your boss is about to recommend building the new plant on the Georgian Bay site. Now, just 15 minutes before your team's big presentation to top management, you discover a possible mistake in your calculations: Site-purchase costs appear to be $50 000 more than you calculated, nearly 10 percent over budget. You don't have time to recheck all your figures, so you're tempted to just go

ahead without mentioning it and ignore any discrepancies. You're worried that management won't approve this purchase if your department can't present a clean, unqualified solution. You also know that many projects run over their original estimates, so you can probably work the extra cost into the budget later. What will you decide to do?

Your task: In a few paragraphs, explain the decision you made.

10. **Intercultural Sensitivity: Recognizing Differences** Your boss represents a Canadian toy company that's negotiating to buy miniature truck wheels from a manufacturer in Osaka, Japan. In the first meeting, your boss explains that your company expects to control the design of the wheels as well as the materials that are used to make them. The manufacturer's representative looks down and says softly, "Perhaps that will be difficult." Your boss presses for agreement, and to emphasize your company's willingness to buy, he shows the prepared contract he's brought with him. However, the manufacturer seems increasingly vague and uninterested.

Your task: What cultural differences may be interfering with effective communication in this situation? Explain briefly in an email message to your instructor.

11. **Teamwork** Working with two other students, prepare a list of 10 examples of slang or idioms (in your own language) that would probably be misinterpreted or misunderstood during a business conversation with someone from another culture. Next to each example, suggest other words you might use to convey the same message. Do the alternatives mean exactly the same as the original slang or idiom?

12. **Intercultural Communication: Studying Cultures** Choose a specific country, such as India, China, Korea, Thailand, or Nigeria, with which you are not familiar. Research the culture and write a brief summary of what a Canadian business person would need to know about concepts of personal space and rules of social behaviour in order to conduct business successfully in that country.

13. **Multicultural Workforce: Bridging Differences** Differences in gender, age, and physical abilities contribute to the diversity of today's workforce. Working with a classmate, role-play a conversation in which
    a. A woman is being interviewed for a job by a male personnel manager
    b. An older person is being interviewed for a job by a younger personnel manager
    c. A person using a wheelchair is being interviewed for a job by a person who can walk

How did differences between the applicant and the interviewer shape the communication? What can you do to improve communication in such situations?

14. **Intercultural Sensitivity: Understanding Attitudes** You are assistant to the director of marketing for a telecommunications firm based in Germany. You're accompanying your boss to negotiate with an official in Guangzhou, China, who's in charge of selecting a new telephone system for the city. Your boss insists that the specifications be spelled out in detail in the contract. However, the Chinese negotiator argues that in developing a long-term business relationship, such minor details are unimportant.

Your task: What can you suggest that your boss do or say to break this intercultural deadlock and obtain the contract so that both parties are comfortable? Outline your ideas in a brief email message to your instructor.

15. **Teamwork: Adapting to Differences**

Part One: In a group of three, research one of the following generations each: Generation Y/Millennials; Generation X; Baby Boomers.

Design a five-part table (one for each group member) and use it to summarize facts about the generation. Cover the following main topics:
    a. Birth years range
    b. Age range now, and include two famous people of this generation
    c. Big events that occurred when this generation was between the ages of 5 and 20
    d. Common values attributed to the generation
    e. Preferences this generation has in receiving information and communicating

Include a list of your sources and bring them, along with your completed table, to the next class.

Part Two: Deliver a 1–2 minute informal presentation to your group about the generation.

Part Three: Summarize what you learned about other generations from your group's presentations.

16. **Communicating Using Social Technologies: Assessing a Blog** Find a company on the internet that has a blog. Read a few of the journal entries and 5 to 10 comments posted about the entries. Write three short pieces and submit them to your instructor:
    1. A paragraph describing the purpose of the blog and the type of content being discussed. What is the background of the blogger? Why would people "follow" this blog (or not)? How would you characterize the relationship between the commentators and the blogger? Explain why.

2. A paragraph assessing the effectiveness of the blog based on what you have read. Why do you believe the blog is effective or ineffective?

3. A 45-character summary of your opinion about this blog, as if you were posting this comment online on Twitter, a social networking site where people post comments and follow the comments of others.

Note: You can use a blog search engine such as Google Blog Search or Technorati to help you find a blog that has a huge influence.

Expand Your Knowledge

Best of the Web

Check Out These Resources at the Business Writer's Free Library The Business Writer's Free Library is a terrific resource for business communication material. Categories of information include basic composition skills, basic writing skills, correspondence, reference material, and general resources and advice. Log on and read about the common errors in English, become a word detective, ask Miss Grammar, review samples of common forms of correspondence, fine-tune your interpersonal skills, learn about blogs, newsgroups, and more. Follow the links and improve your effectiveness as a business communicator.
www.managementhelp.org/commskls/cmm_writ.htm

EXERCISES

1. How do the objectives of professional writing differ from the objectives of composition and literature?
2. What is the purpose of feedback?
3. What are some basic guidelines for giving feedback?

Exploring the Web on Your Own

Review these chapter-related websites on your own to learn more about achieving communication success in the workplace.

1. Netiquette Home Page, www.albion.com/netiquette. Learn the dos and don'ts of online communication at this site, then take the Netiquette Quiz.
2. You Can Work from Anywhere, www.youcanworkfromanywhere.com. Click on this site's Info and Tech Center and follow the links. Review the tips, tools, articles, ideas, and other helpful resources to improve your productivity as a telecommuter, mobile, or home-based worker.
3. Email Help, www.net-market.com/email.htm. Learn the ins and outs of email at this site so that your email will stand out from the crowd. Do you agree with all the suggestions? Explain your answer in a brief email to your instructor.

Test Your Intercultural Knowledge

Never take anything for granted when you're doing business in a foreign country. All sorts of assumptions that are valid in one place can cause you problems elsewhere if you fail to consider that customs may vary. Here are several true stories about business people who blundered by overlooking some simple but important cultural differences. Can you spot the wrong assumptions that led these people astray?

1. You're tired of the discussion and you want to move on to a new topic. You ask your Australian business associate, "Can we table this for a while?" To your dismay, your colleague keeps right on discussing just what you want to put aside. Are Australians that inconsiderate?

2. You finally made the long trip overseas to meet the new German director of your division. Despite slow traffic, you arrive only four minutes late. His door is shut, so you knock on it and walk in. The chair is too far away from the desk, so you pick it up and move it closer. Then you lean over the desk, stick out your hand, and say, "Good morning, Hans, it's nice to meet you." Of course, you're baffled by his chilly reaction. Why?

3. Your meeting went better than you'd ever expected. In fact, you found the Japanese representative for your new advertising agency to be very agreeable; she said yes to just about everything. When you share your enthusiasm with your boss, he doesn't appear very excited. Why?

4. You've finally closed the deal, after exhausting both your patience and your company's travel budget. Now, two weeks later, your Chinese customers are asking for special considerations that change the terms of the agreement. How could they do this? Why are they doing it? And, most important, what should you do?

In each case the problems have resulted from inaccurate assumptions. Here are the explanations of what went wrong:

1. To "table" something in Australia means to bring it forward for discussion. This is the opposite of what North Americans usually mean. The English that's spoken in Australia is closer to British than to North American English. If you are doing business in Australia, become familiar with the local vocabulary. Note the tendency to shorten just about any word whenever possible, and adding "ie" to it is a form of familiar slang: for example, *brolly* (umbrella) and *lollie* (candy). And yes, it's true: "G'day" is the standard greeting. Use it.

2. You've just broken four rules of German polite behaviour: punctuality, privacy, personal space, and proper greetings. In time-conscious Germany, you should never arrive even a few minutes late. Also, Germans like their privacy and space, and they adhere to formal greetings of "Frau" and "Herr," even if the business association has lasted for years.

3. The word *yes* may not always mean "yes" in the Western sense. Japanese people may say *yes* to confirm they have heard or understood something but not necessarily to indicate that they agree with it. You'll seldom get a direct no. Some of the ways that Japanese people say no indirectly include "It will be difficult," "I will ask my supervisor," "I'm not sure," "We will think about it," and "I see."

4. For most North American business people, the contract represents the end of the negotiation. For Chinese business people, however, it's just the beginning. Once a deal is made, Chinese negotiators view their counterparts as trustworthy partners who can be relied on for special favours—such as new terms in the contract.

Applications for Success

Learn how to improve your cultural savvy and gain an international competitive advantage. Visit Cultural Savvy (www.culturalsavvy.com) by Joyce Millet & Associates and read the country reports and cultural tips. Follow the site's links to tips, articles, books, and more.

Answer the following questions:
1. Why should you avoid humour when communicating with people of a different culture?
2. Every culture has its own business protocol. What should you know about a culture's business protocol before you transact business within that culture?
3. What are some examples of cultural gift-giving taboos?

Communicating in Teams: Listening, Nonverbal, and Meeting Skills

After studying this chapter, you will be able to

1. Explain how teams contribute to an organization's decision-making process
2. Outline four elements that are necessary to plan a productive meeting
3. Explain four ways to increase productivity during meetings
4. List and briefly explain the five phases of the listening process
5. Discuss three barriers to effective listening and some strategies for overcoming them
6. List several of the techniques for improving the way you answer phone calls, make phone calls, and use voice mail
7. Identify six categories of nonverbal communication

As vice-president responsible for human resources, communication, and corporate affairs for Xerox Canada, Tony Martino relies on effective communication among team members and between teams and upper management. He uses meetings to bring people together to solve business problems and help ensure that participants will be committed to the implementation. "To succeed," says Martino, "you need to gather as much input as possible to develop a good business solution. Listening, clarifying, testing understanding, and truly hearing what people are saying makes the difference in teamwork and success."

Working in Teams

A **team** is a unit of two or more people who work together to achieve a goal. Team members share a mission and the responsibility for working to achieve it.[1] Teams are important in today's workplace. At their best, teams offer an extremely useful forum for making key decisions. Teams help organizations succeed by[2]

- **Increasing information and knowledge.** By aggregating the resources of several individuals, teams bring more information and expertise to the decision-making process.
- **Increasing the diversity of views.** Team members bring a variety of perspectives to decision-making tasks.
- **Increasing the acceptance of a solution.** Because team members share in making a decision, they are more likely to support that decision enthusiastically and encourage others to accept it.
- **Increasing performance levels.** Working in teams can unleash vast amounts of creativity and energy in workers who share a sense of purpose and mutual accountability. Teams also contribute to performance levels by filling the individual worker's need to belong to a group, reducing employee boredom, increasing feelings of dignity and self-worth, and reducing tension among workers.

 **Activities**

Team members have a shared mission and are collectively responsible for their work.

Teams contribute to an organization's performance.

At their worst, teams are unproductive and frustrating, and they waste everyone's time. Team members must be careful to avoid the following:

- **Groupthink.** When belonging to a team is more important to members than making the right decision, that team may develop groupthink, the willingness of individuals to set aside their personal opinions and go along with everyone else, even if everyone else is wrong. Groupthink not only leads to poor decisions and ill-advised actions but can even induce people to act unethically.
- **Hidden agendas.** Some team members can have private motives that affect the group's interaction. Sam might want to prove that he's more powerful than Laura, Laura might be trying to share the risks of making a decision, and Don might be looking for a chance to postpone doing "real" work. Each person's hidden agenda can detract from a team's effectiveness.
- **Free riders.** Some team members don't contribute their fair share to the group's activities because they aren't being held individually accountable for their work. The free-ride attitude can cause certain tasks to go unfulfilled.
- **High coordination costs.** Aligning schedules, arranging meetings, and coordinating individual parts of a project can eat up a lot of time and money.

Effective teams have a clear sense of purpose, communicate openly and honestly, reach decisions by consensus, think creatively, remain focused, review progress regularly, and resolve conflict effectively.[3] The purpose of developing an effective team is to get members to collaborate on necessary tasks, and much of that collaboration takes place in meetings.

Preparing, Conducting, and Attending Meetings

A great deal of the oral communication that takes place in the workplace happens in small-group meetings. Unfortunately, too many meetings are unproductive. Some managers have recently reported that little more than half their meetings were actually productive and that a quarter of them could have been handled by a phone call or an email.[4] To ensure productivity, take great care when planning, conducting, and attending meetings, and make sure you follow up.

Preparing for Team Meetings

Before you call a meeting, be sure that one is truly needed. Perhaps you could accomplish your purpose more effectively in an email or through individual conversations or through written conversations using a social technology such as a wiki. If you do require the interaction of a group, be sure to bring the right people together in the right place for just enough time to accomplish your goals. To avoid the high cost of travel, companies also use videoconferencing to bring participants together. IBM uses Second Life 3D virtual world technology to hold meetings.[5] Participants are represented by their avatars and present their ideas either by speaking through headsets or by sending written messages in real time. The key to all kinds of productive meetings is careful planning of purpose, participants, location, and agenda:

- **Decide on your purpose.** Most meetings are one of two types: In *informational meetings,* participants share information and sometimes coordinate action. Briefings may come from each participant or from the leader. In *decision-making meetings,* participants persuade, analyze, and solve problems. They are often involved in brainstorming sessions and debates.
- **Select participants.** Invite only those people whose presence is essential. If the session is purely informational and one person will be doing most of the talking, you can include a relatively large group. However, if you're trying to solve a problem,

develop a plan, or reach a decision, try to limit participation to between 6 and 12 people.[6]

- **Choose an appropriate location.** Decide where you'll hold the meeting, and reserve the location. For work sessions, morning meetings are usually more productive than afternoon sessions. Also, consider the seating arrangements. Are rows of chairs suitable, or do you need a conference table? Plus, pay attention to room temperature, lighting, ventilation, acoustics, and refreshments.
- **Set and follow an agenda.** Meeting agendas help prepare the participants. Although small, informal meetings may not require a formal agenda, even they benefit if you prepare at least a list of matters to be discussed. Distribute the agenda to participants several days before the meeting so that they know what to expect and can come prepared to respond to the issues at hand.

<aside>Productive meetings have the right purpose, include the right people, take place at the right location and time, and have a clear agenda.</aside>

A typical agenda format (shown in Figure 2.1) may seem stiff and formal, but it helps you start and end your meetings on time and stay on track. Doing so sends a signal of good organization and allows attendees to meet other commitments.

An effective agenda focuses on action, answering three key questions: (1) What do we need to do in this meeting to accomplish our goals? (2) What issues are of greatest importance? (3) What information must be available in order to discuss these issues?[7] Agendas also include the names of the participants, the time, the place, and the order of business. Make sure agenda items are specific, in order to help all attendees prepare in advance with facts and figures.

Conducting and Attending Meetings

The success of any meeting depends largely on the effectiveness of its leader. If the leader is prepared and has selected participants carefully, the meeting will generally be productive.

KEEP THE MEETING ON TRACK A good meeting is a cross-flow of discussion and debate, not a series of dialogues between individual members and the leader. Good leaders occasionally guide, mediate, probe, stimulate, and summarize, but mostly they let others thrash out their ideas. That's why it's important for leaders to avoid being so domineering that they close off suggestions. Of course, they must also avoid being so passive that they lose control of the group. A meeting leader is responsible for

- **Developing and circulating an agenda in advance so that participants come prepared.**
- **Keeping the meeting moving along.** If the discussion lags, call on those who haven't been heard.
- **Pacing the presentation and discussion.** Limit the time spent on each agenda item so that you'll be able to cover them all.
- **Summarizing meeting achievements.** As time begins to run out, interrupt the discussion and summarize what has been accomplished; however, don't be too rigid. Allow enough time for all the main ideas to be heard, and give people a chance to raise related issues.

<aside>Don't be so rigid that you cut off discussion too quickly.</aside>

<aside>Don't let one or two members dominate the meeting.</aside>

ENCOURAGE PARTICIPATION The best meetings are those in which everyone participates, so don't let one or two people dominate your meeting while others doodle on their notepads. To draw out the shy types, ask for their input on issues that particularly pertain to them. You might say something like, "Roberta, you've done a lot of work in this area. What do you think?" For the overly talkative, simply say that time is limited and others need to be heard from. As you move through your agenda, stop at the end of each

| FIGURE 2.1 | Meeting Agenda |

AGENDA

PLANNING COMMITTEE MEETING

Monday, October 21, 2009
10:00 A.M. to 11:00 A.M.

Executive Conference Room

		Person	Proposed Time
1.	Call to Order		
2.	Approval of Agenda		
3.	Approval of Minutes from Previous Meeting		
4.	Chairperson's Report on Site Selection Progress		
5.	Subcommittee Reports		
	a. New Markets	Alan	5 minutes
	b. New Products	Jennifer	5 minutes
	c. Finance	Craig	5 minutes
6.	Old Business—Decide Pricing Policy for New Products	Terry	10 minutes
7.	New Business		
	a. Review Carson and Canfield Data on New Product Sales	Sarah	10 minutes
	b. Decide Restructuring of Product Territories due to New Product Introductions	Edith	10 minutes
8.	Announcements		
9.	Adjournment		

Activities

An effective agenda tells participants
- What must be done
- What issues are important
- What information is necessary for discussion
- Who is attending
- When and where the meeting is being held
- The order in which business will be handled

item, summarize what you understand to be the feelings of the group, and state the important points made during the discussion. Use whiteboards, flipcharts, or laptops to record key content for the group and to stimulate group participation.

If you're a meeting participant, try to contribute to both the subject of the meeting and the smooth interaction of the participants. Use your listening skills and powers of observation to size up the interpersonal dynamics of the people; then adapt your behaviour to help the group achieve its goals. Speak up if you have something useful to say, but don't monopolize the discussion.

CLOSE EFFECTIVELY At the conclusion of the meeting, tie up the loose ends. Either summarize the general conclusion of the discussion or list the actions to be taken. Wrapping things up ensures that all participants agree on the outcome, and it gives people a chance

Productive meetings end with a review of what's been accomplished and who's responsible for doing what.

to clear up any misunderstandings. Before the meeting breaks up, briefly review who has agreed to do what by what date.

Activities

Document **Makeovers**

Minutes of the meeting remind everyone of what happened and who needs to take action.

Following Up

As soon as possible after the meeting, make sure all participants receive a copy of the minutes or notes, showing recommended actions, schedules, and responsibilities. Generally, a person appointed to record prepares a set of minutes for distribution to all attendees and other interested parties. An informal meeting may not require minutes. Instead, attendees simply make their own notes on their copies of the agenda. Follow-up is then their responsibility, although the meeting leader may need to remind them to do so through an email or a phone call. Briefly summarize the meeting outcomes even if you have met only with one person. Record any decisions made and actions planned, including who will do what, by when. Then, send it to those involved to ensure that understanding is achieved. Figure 2.2 contains sample minutes.

FIGURE 2.2 Typical Meeting Minutes

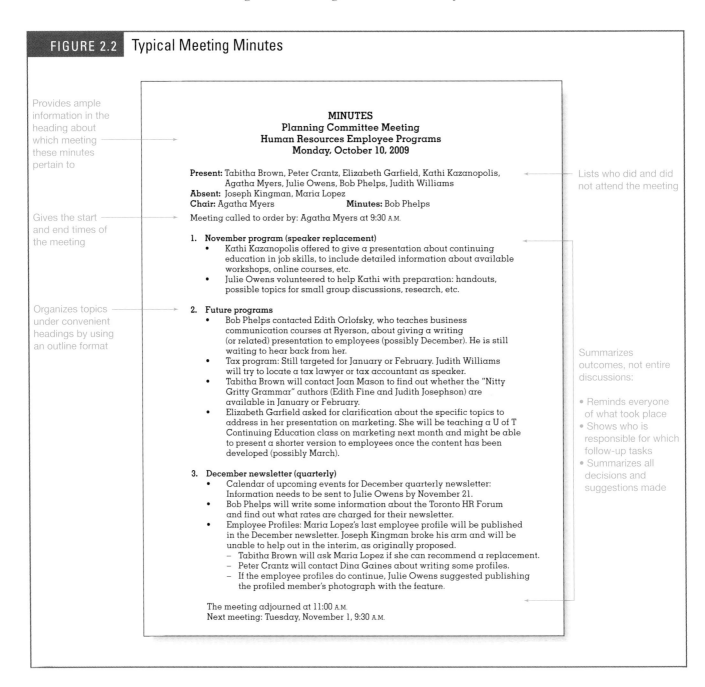

Provides ample information in the heading about which meeting these minutes pertain to

Gives the start and end times of the meeting

Organizes topics under convenient headings by using an outline format

MINUTES
Planning Committee Meeting
Human Resources Employee Programs
Monday, October 10, 2009

Present: Tabitha Brown, Peter Crantz, Elizabeth Garfield, Kathi Kazanopolis, Agatha Myers, Julie Owens, Bob Phelps, Judith Williams
Absent: Joseph Kingman, Maria Lopez
Chair: Agatha Myers   **Minutes:** Bob Phelps

Meeting called to order by: Agatha Myers at 9:30 A.M.

1. **November program (speaker replacement)**
   • Kathi Kazanopolis offered to give a presentation about continuing education in job skills, to include detailed information about available workshops, online courses, etc.
   • Julie Owens volunteered to help Kathi with preparation: handouts, possible topics for small group discussions, research, etc.

2. **Future programs**
   • Bob Phelps contacted Edith Orlofsky, who teaches business communication courses at Ryerson, about giving a writing (or related) presentation to employees (possibly December). He is still waiting to hear back from her.
   • Tax program: Still targeted for January or February. Judith Williams will try to locate a tax lawyer or tax accountant as speaker.
   • Tabitha Brown will contact Joan Mason to find out whether the "Nitty Gritty Grammar" authors (Edith Fine and Judith Josephson) are available in January or February.
   • Elizabeth Garfield asked for clarification about the specific topics to address in her presentation on marketing. She will be teaching a U of T Continuing Education class on marketing next month and might be able to present a shorter version to employees once the content has been developed (possibly March).

3. **December newsletter (quarterly)**
   • Calendar of upcoming events for December quarterly newsletter: Information needs to be sent to Julie Owens by November 21.
   • Bob Phelps will write some information about the Toronto HR Forum and find out what rates are charged for their newsletter.
   • Employee Profiles: Maria Lopez's last employee profile will be published in the December newsletter. Joseph Kingman broke his arm and will be unable to help out in the interim, as originally proposed.
     – Tabitha Brown will ask Maria Lopez if she can recommend a replacement.
     – Peter Crantz will contact Dina Gaines about writing some profiles.
     – If the employee profiles do continue, Julie Owens suggested publishing the profiled member's photograph with the feature.

The meeting adjourned at 11:00 A.M.
Next meeting: Tuesday, November 1, 9:30 A.M.

Lists who did and did not attend the meeting

Summarizes outcomes, not entire discussions:

• Reminds everyone of what took place
• Shows who is responsible for which follow-up tasks
• Summarizes all decisions and suggestions made

Listening to Others

Just as follow-up is the responsibility of team members, so is each person's ability to listen. Without effective listening skills on the part of every team member, meetings could not take place. Your ability to listen effectively is directly related to your success in meetings, conversations, phone calls, and other group relationships. Unfortunately, most of us listen at or below a 25 percent efficiency rate: We remember only about half of what's said in a 10-minute conversation, and we forget half of that within 48 hours.[8] In addition, when questioned about material we've just heard, we are likely to get the facts mixed up. That's because although we listen to words, we don't necessarily hear their meaning.[9]

> Most people need to improve their listening skills.

The Listening Process

By understanding the process of listening, you begin to understand why oral messages are so often lost. Listening involves five related activities, which usually occur in sequence:[10]

> Listening involves five steps.

1. **Receiving:** Physically hearing the message and taking note of it. Physical reception can be blocked by noise, impaired hearing, or inattention.
2. **Interpreting:** Assigning meaning to sounds according to your own values, beliefs, ideas, expectations, roles, needs, and personal history. The speaker's frame of reference may be quite different from yours, so you may need to determine what the speaker really means.
3. **Remembering:** Storing a message for future reference. As you listen, you retain what you hear by taking notes or by making a mental outline of the speaker's key points.
4. **Evaluating:** Applying critical thinking skills to weigh the speaker's remarks. You separate fact from opinion and evaluate the quality of the evidence.
5. **Responding:** Reacting once you've evaluated the speaker's message. If you're communicating one on one or in a small group, the initial response generally takes the form of verbal feedback. If you're one of many in an audience, your initial response may take the form of applause, laughter, or silence. Later on, you may act on what you have heard.

Obstacles to Effective Listening

A large part of becoming a good listener is the ability to recognize and overcome a variety of physical and mental barriers, including

- **Prejudgment.** To function in life, people must operate on some basic assumptions. However, these assumptions can be incorrect or inappropriate in new situations. Moreover, some people listen defensively, viewing every comment as a personal attack, so they distort messages by tuning out anything that doesn't confirm their assumptions.
- **Self-centredness.** Some people tend to take control of conversations, rather than listen. If a speaker mentions a problem, self-centred listeners eagerly relate their own problems, trivializing the speaker's concerns by pointing out that their own difficulties are much worse. No matter what the subject, these people know more than the speaker does, and they're determined to prove it.
- **Selective listening.** When you listen selectively (also called *out-listening*), you let your mind wander to things such as whether you brought your dry-cleaning ticket to work. You tune out until you hear something that gets your attention. Thus, you don't remember what the speaker *actually* said; you remember what you *think* the speaker *probably* said.[11]

> Effective listening is blocked when
> - You jump to conclusions and close your mind to additional information
> - Self-centred listeners shift their attention from the speaker to themselves
> - Selective listeners tune out the speaker

One reason people's minds tend to wander is that they think faster than they speak. Most people speak at about 120 to 150 words per minute. However, studies indicate that, depending on the subject and the individual, people can process information at 500 to 800 words per minute.[12] The disparity between rate of speech and rate of thought can be used to pull one's thoughts together, but some listeners let their minds wander and just tune out.

> Your mind can process information more than four times faster than the rate of speech.

Strategies for Effective Listening

> Ten tips will help you improve your listening.

Document **Makeovers**

Effective listening strengthens organizational relationships, enhances product delivery, alerts the organization to innovation from both internal and external sources, and allows the organization to manage growing diversity both in the workforce and in the customers it serves.[13] Good listening gives you an edge and increases your impact when you speak (see Table 2.1). However, effective listening requires a conscious effort and a willing mind. To improve your listening skills, heed the following tips:

- **Find areas of interest.** Look beyond the speaker's style by asking yourself what the speaker knows that you don't.
- **Judge content, not delivery.** Evaluate and criticize the content, not the speaker. Review the key points. Do they make sense? Are the concepts supported by facts?
- **Keep quiet.** Don't interrupt. Depersonalize your listening so that you decrease the emotional impact of what's being said and are better able to hold your rebuttal until you've heard the total message.
- **Listen for ideas.** Listen for concepts and key ideas as well as for facts, and know the difference between fact and principle, idea and example, and evidence and argument.
- **Take careful notes.** Take meaningful notes that are brief and to the point.
- **Work at listening.** Look for unspoken messages. Often the speaker's tone of voice or expressions will reveal more than the words themselves. Provide feedback. Let the

TABLE 2.1	Distinguishing Effective Listeners from Ineffective Listeners
EFFECTIVE LISTENERS	INEFFECTIVE LISTENERS
Listen actively	Listen passively
Take careful and complete notes	Take no notes or ineffective notes
Make frequent eye contact with the speaker (depends on culture to some extent)	Make little or no eye contact
Stay focused on the speaker and the content	Allow their minds to wander; are easily distracted
Mentally paraphrase key points to maintain attention level and ensure comprehension	Fail to paraphrase
Give the speaker nonverbal cues (such as nodding to show agreement or raising eyebrows to show surprise or skepticism)	Fail to give the speaker nonverbal feedback
Save questions or points of disagreement until an appropriate time	Interrupt whenever they disagree or don't understand
Overlook stylistic differences and focus on the speaker's message	Are distracted by or unduly influenced by stylistic differences; are judgmental
Make distinctions between main points and supporting details	Unable to distinguish main points from details

speaker know you're with him or her. Maintain eye contact. Provide appropriate facial expressions.

- **Block out competing thoughts.** Fight distractions by closing doors, turning off radios or televisions, and moving closer to the speaker.
- **Paraphrase the speaker's ideas.** Paraphrase or summarize when the speaker reaches a stopping point.
- **Stay open-minded.** Keep an open mind by asking questions that clarify understanding; reserve judgment until the speaker has finished.
- **Capitalize on the fact that thought is faster than speech.** Stay ahead of the speaker by anticipating what will be said next and by thinking about what's already been said.

Listening to what someone is saying is crucial to business success, whether you're conversing with someone face to face, listening to a speaker during a meeting, or having a conversation over the phone. But telephone conversations and voice mail involve more than simply listening.

Using Telephones and Voice Mail

Just as important as how you plan, conduct, and participate in meetings is how you communicate using the telephone and voice mail. In fact, some experts estimate that 95 percent of most companies' daily contacts come via the telephone.[14]

When using the telephone and voice mail, your communication loses a great deal of the nonverbal richness that accompanies face-to-face conversations. Even so, your attitude and tone of voice can convey your confidence and professionalism effectively. Your voice and attitude can impress others with your eagerness to help, your willingness to listen, and your ability to communicate clearly.

> Telephones and voice mail are essential for organizations to conduct business effectively.

Receiving Telephone Calls Effectively

When people call your place of business, they want to know, first, that they will reach someone who can help them and, second, that doing so will be quick and easy. They don't want to be passed from department to department. They don't want to hold while their party finishes up with someone else. And they don't want to get stuck talking with someone who lacks the knowledge or the ability to get them the information or the action they need.

If you answer the phone for someone who is unable to take the call right away, note the caller's name, telephone number, and a brief but accurate message—assuring the caller that the appropriate person will get the message and return the call. Likewise, if you will be away from your telephone for any length of time, forward your calls so that anyone calling you won't have to be transferred again and again.[15]

To be as effective as possible when receiving calls, observe the following helpful tips:[16]

- **Answer promptly and with a smile.** Answer within two or three rings. Also, answering with a smile makes you sound friendly and positive. Speak clearly, and don't rush your greeting. Speak slowly enough for people to understand what you're saying.
- **Identify yourself.** Announce the company name, the department, and your own name. Keep your manner friendly and professional so that the conversation begins pleasantly and positively, building an instant relationship with your caller.
- **Establish the needs of your caller.** Immediately ask, "How may I help you?" If you know the caller's name, use it to affirm a sense of warmth and personal interest. Also, use continuity expressions to show that you're listening (e.g., "Oh yes," "I see," or

> Six tips will help you answer telephone calls effectively.

"That's right"). Keep focused on the subject at hand, and don't interrupt with pointless questions.

Handle calls in a confident, positive, helpful manner.

- **Be positive.** If you can, answer callers' questions promptly and efficiently. If you can't help, tell them what you can do for them. Explain that you will find the necessary information. Avoid conveying a lack of confidence; that is, don't use vague phrases, such as "I'm really not sure whether . . . " or "It may be that . . . "
- **Take complete, accurate messages.** Obtain as much information as you can so that you know how to process the call. Repeat names, telephone and fax numbers, email addresses, and dates to make sure you have them right. Always take a return number, even if the caller assures you it is known. And don't forget to write neatly so that whoever gets your message can read it.
- **Give reasons for your actions.** If you absolutely must put a caller on hold briefly or transfer the call, explain to the caller what you are doing and why. Don't leave callers on hold for long periods of time. If it's necessary to hunt for information or to take another call, offer to call back.

Making Effective Telephone Calls

The key to making effective telephone calls is planning. Know precisely why you're calling and exactly what you need from the person you're calling. Before you make the call, gather all the materials you may need to refer to, and briefly outline or jot down notes about what you're going to say. To be as effective as possible when making phone calls, keep in mind the following tips:[17]

Plan your calls so that you can be efficient.

Seven tips will help you make telephone calls more effectively.

- **Be ready before you call.** Anticipate the conversation and plan ahead how you will handle any possible outcomes. Make an outline or notes and have them in front of you, along with a pad for taking notes. Also make sure you have at your fingertips any other necessary materials: account numbers, catalogues, electronic files, cost figures, and so on.
- **Schedule the call.** Decide ahead of time when you will call. Consider your own readiness, the time of day, and whether your contact is located in a different time zone. Don't call people first thing in the morning when they are answering mail and starting their day. Likewise, don't call anyone last thing at night when they're heading out of the office.
- **Eliminate distractions.** Don't call from a noisy pay phone or from an area where background noise will interfere with your concentration and your ability to hear and be heard. Similarly, don't tap a pencil or make other noises that might be picked up and amplified over the phone wires.
- **Make a clear, comprehensive introduction.** Immediately identify the person you're calling, give your own name and organization, briefly describe the reason for your call, and greet the person. This opening starts the call on a positive note. Keep your tone friendly, and always ask, "Is this a good time to talk briefly, or should I call you back?"
- **Don't take up too much time.** Avoid talking too slowly, spending too much time in small talk, or complaining about how difficult it is to get in touch with this person. Speak quickly and clearly, and get right to the point of the call.
- **Maintain audience focus throughout the call.** Ask questions and give clear answers so that both of you understand the call and can decide together what action is needed.
- **Close in a friendly, positive manner.** Double-check all vital information by summarizing what you've discussed. Check to see that you both agree on any action that either party will take. Thank the other person for his or her time, and if you promise to phone back, make sure you do so.

FIGURE 2.3 Using Voice Mail

Voice mail lets you send, store, and retrieve verbal messages. Voice mail is part of what is now called *voice processing,* which can include an automatic attendant, automatic call distribution, email and paging integration, call forwarding, call screening, and many other features.[18]

Voice mail can be used to replace short memos and phone calls that need no response. It is most effective for short, unambiguous messages. Like email, it solves time-zone difficulties and reduces a substantial amount of interoffice paperwork.[19] Use voice mail to avoid interruptions caused by taking calls during meetings or other work sessions.

RECORDING A GREETING
Before recording your outgoing greeting for your own voice mail system, organize your thoughts.[20] You want your message to be accurate and concise. The following tips may also help you make your voice mail greeting more effective:[21]

- **Be brief.** Your message should not take longer than 30 seconds.
- **Be accurate.** Specifically state what callers should do.
- **Sound professional.** Make sure your voice is businesslike but cheerful. Never eat, drink, chew gum, or suck candy while recording a message. Speak slowly. Don't say names or phone numbers so fast that they can't be understood.
- **Keep your callers in mind.** Encourage callers to leave detailed messages. Also remind them to leave a phone number (especially frequent callers who may assume you have it handy).
- **Make options logical and helpful.** Limit options to three or four. Make one of the options an easy way to reach a live operator without bouncing from one menu option to another. When describing options, state the action first and then the key to press.
- **Keep your personal greeting current.** Update your greetings to reflect your schedule and leave special announcements. Don't forget to change your message when you go on vacation or plan to be away from your desk for an extended period of time.

RESPONDING
- **Respond promptly.** Check your voice mail messages regularly and return all necessary calls within 24 hours.

LEAVING A MESSAGE
When you leave a message on someone else's voice mail system, think about your message in advance, and plan it carefully. Remember the following tips:[22]

- **Keep the message simple.** Save the complicated details to give in person. Leave your name, number, and purpose for calling. Designate a specific time when you can be reached (or say you'll call the person back at a specific time). Give just enough detail to get your message across so that the receiver can evaluate whether to call you back. Don't forget to repeat your name and phone number at the end of the message.
- **Sound professional.** Give your message a headline so that the listener can quickly judge its priority. Speak clearly, slowly, and loudly. Remember to smile while recording, so that your tone will be pleasant. Avoid background noise as much as possible, and before using a cellphone, consider the effect of a bad connection or interruption.
- **Avoid personal messages.** Remember, someone else may be in the room when your message is played back.
- **Replay your message before leaving the system.** Use this option whenever it is available, in order to listen to your message objectively and make sure it is clear.
- **Don't leave multiple, repetitious messages.** Rather than a series of messages with the same information, simply leave one detailed message and follow that up with a fax or an email.
- **Never hide behind voice mail.** Don't use it to escape unpleasant encounters, and make sure to give praise in person.[23]

Use voice mail for short, straightforward messages.

Seven tips will help you record a more effective voice mail greeting.

Plan messages in advance to focus on the main ideas and be concise.

Six tips will help you leave more effective voice mail messages.

Understanding Nonverbal Communication

When using telephones and voice mail, the way you sound is important—your tone and your attitude shape the way other people perceive you and your message. Tone goes beyond the words you use. Although sound, tone, and attitude are nonverbal, they communicate an important message to your receivers. Your ability to use and interpret nonverbal communication is just as important as all the other skills discussed so far.

The most basic form of communication is **nonverbal communication**: all the cues, gestures, facial expressions, spatial relationships, and attitudes toward time that enable people to communicate without words. Nonverbal communication differs from verbal methods in terms of intent and spontaneity. You generally think about verbal messages, if only for a moment. However, when you communicate nonverbally, you sometimes do so unconsciously—you don't mean to raise an eyebrow or to blush. Nonverbal communication is always ongoing and when you are aware and control it, nonverbal communication can help you form a positive impression.

The Importance of Nonverbal Communication

> Nonverbal communication is more reliable and more efficient than verbal communication.

Actions do speak louder than words. In fact, most people can deceive others much more easily with words than they can with their bodies. Words are relatively easy to control; body language, facial expressions, and vocal characteristics are not. By paying attention to a person's nonverbal cues, you can detect deception or affirm a speaker's honesty.

Also, nonverbal communication is efficient. When you have a conscious purpose, you can often achieve it more economically with a gesture than with words. A wave of the hand, a pat on the back, a wink—all are streamlined expressions of thought. Even so, nonverbal communication usually blends with speech, carrying part of the message to augment, reinforce, and clarify the spoken word.

Improving Your Nonverbal Communication

The thousands of forms of nonverbal communication can be grouped into some general categories. Just remember, the interpretation of these nonverbal signals varies from culture to culture (see Figure 2.4). When communicating orally, pay attention to your nonverbal cues, and avoid giving others conflicting signals.[24] Keep in mind that few gestures convey meaning in and of themselves; they must be interpreted in clusters, and they should reinforce your words, not replace them. You can improve your nonverbal communication by following the tips listed below.

> The face and eyes command particular attention as sources of nonverbal messages.

FACIAL EXPRESSION Your face is the primary site for expressing your emotions; it reveals both the type and the intensity of your feelings.[25] Your eyes are especially effective for indicating attention and interest, influencing others, regulating interaction, and establishing dominance. In fact, eye contact is so important in North America that even when your words send a positive message, averting your gaze can lead your audience to perceive a negative one. Maintain the eye contact an audience expects.[26] Some people try to manipulate their facial expressions to simulate an emotion they do not feel or to mask their true feelings. It is more effective, however, to be as honest as possible in communicating your emotions. Smile genuinely. Faking a smile is obvious to observers.

> Body language reveals a lot about a person's emotions and attitudes.

GESTURE AND POSTURE By moving your body, you can express both specific and general messages, some voluntary and some involuntary. Many gestures—a wave of the hand, for example—have a specific and intentional meaning, such as "hello" or "goodbye." Other types of body movement are unintentional and express a more general message. Slouching, leaning forward, fidgeting, and walking briskly are all unconscious signals that reveal whether you feel confident or nervous, friendly or hostile, assertive or passive, powerful or powerless. Be aware of your posture and gestures.

VOCAL CHARACTERISTICS Like body language, your voice carries both intentional and unintentional messages. Consider the sentence "What have you been up to?" If you repeat that question four or five times, changing your tone of voice and stressing various words, you can intentionally convey quite different messages. However, your vocal characteristics also reveal many things you're unaware of. Your tone and volume, your accent and speaking pace, and all the little *um*'s and *ah*'s that creep into your speech say a lot about who you are, your relationship with the audience, and the emotions underlying your words.

> Your tone of voice carries meaning, whether intentional or not.

PERSONAL APPEARANCE People respond to others on the basis of their physical appearance. When people think you're capable and attractive, you feel good about yourself, and that feeling affects your behaviour, which in turn affects other people's perceptions of you. Although body type and facial features impose limitations, most people are able to control their attractiveness to some degree. Grooming, clothing, accessories, "style"—all modify a person's appearance. If your goal is to make a good impression, adopt the style of the people you want to impress.

> Physical appearance and personal style contribute to one's identity.

TOUCHING BEHAVIOUR Touch is an important vehicle for conveying warmth, comfort, and reassurance. Perhaps because it implies intimacy, touching behaviour is governed in various circumstances by relatively strict customs that establish who may touch whom and how. The accepted norms vary, depending on the gender, age, relative status, and cultural background of the persons involved. In business situations, touching suggests dominance, so a higher-status person is more likely to touch a lower-status person than the other way around. Touching has become controversial, however, because it can sometimes be interpreted as sexual harassment. Leave people a comfort zone. Adapt a handshake that matches your personality and intention.

> Touching behaviour is governed by customs.

USE OF TIME AND SPACE Like touch, time and space can be used to assert authority. Some people demonstrate their importance by making other people wait; others show respect by being on time. People can also assert their status by occupying the best space. In

> Punctuality and comfort zones vary by culture and authority.

FIGURE 2.4   Avoiding Nonverbal Mishaps

	In Canada	In Other Cultures
Handshake	A firm grip should last for several seconds.	Japanese traditionally prefer a slight bow of the head; some Southeast Asians prefer to press their palms together in a slight praying motion; when people do shake hands in the Middle East and Far East, gentle pressure is preferred (a firm handshake is considered aggressive).
Eye contact	Direct, sustained eye contact is considered a sign of friendliness, strength, and trustworthiness.	In countries such as Japan and South Korea, eye contact can be considered aggressive.
Thumbs up	This gesture expresses a variety of positive meanings, from "yes" to "nice job."	This gesture means "one" in Germany and "five" in Japan; it's an obscene gesture in Australia and some other countries.
"OK" sign	The "OK" sign indicates approval or assurance.	The "OK" sign means "zero" or "worthless" in France; indicates money in Japan; is an obscene gesture in Germany, Brazil, and some other countries.
Smile	A genuine smile indicates happiness, agreement, or friendliness.	Good news: A simple smile works everywhere in the world!

Canadian and U.S. companies, the chief executive often has the corner office and the best view. Apart from serving as a symbol of status, space can determine how comfortable people feel talking with each other. When others stand too close or too far away, we are likely to feel ill at ease. Again, attitudes toward punctuality and comfort zones vary from culture to culture, so be aware of varying attitudes toward time.

ON THE JOB

Checklist for Attending a Meeting

Do You ...

☐ review the agenda/prepare for your role at the meeting?

☐ arrive early?

☐ turn your cellphone and other electronic devices off?

☐ wait to be seated until the leader and others have taken their places?

☐ listen carefully and avoid interrupting others?

☐ control your nonverbal messages to present a positive, attentive persona?

☐ make your points concisely?

☐ make notes of key decisions for follow-up?

☐ ask questions to clarify but only if the answers cannot be found out another way?

☐ avoid asking questions that pertain just to your role that you could clarify after the meeting?

☐ avoid taking or sending text messages?

Reviewing Key Points

In this chapter you learned how effective teams contribute to an organization's success by involving employees in decision making, by increasing the diversity of perspectives and amount of information brought to tasks, and by increasing a sense of belonging among employees. In meetings, staff members get together to share ideas and solve problems. When you are the meeting leader, you

- Organize the agenda
- Keep people on track
- Clarify and summarize results

When you are a meeting participant, listen actively, present ideas concisely, and help facilitate the group's work. Good listeners

- Stay focused on the topic being discussed
- Avoid interrupting
- Block out competing thoughts
- Keep open minds

When you work with others, interpret and send nonverbal messages by being aware of what is conveyed in tone of voice, attitude, gestures, facial expressions, and sounds.

When using the telephone,

- Plan ahead so that calls and voice mail can be focused and concise
- Handle calls in an organized and polite manner to create positive impressions with clients and co-workers

Participating in teams and meetings, listening, and managing nonverbal communication and telephone communication are all important for career success.

mybuscommlab   Go to MyBusCommLab at www.pearson.ca/mybuscommlab for online exercises and problems.

Practise Your Grammar

 Exercises

Visit MyBusCommLab or Grammar-on-the-Go to work on your language skills.

Test Your Knowledge

 Exercises

1. In what four ways do organizations benefit from team decision making?
2. What seven things must effective teams do?
3. How should a meeting leader prepare?
4. What questions should an agenda answer?
5. What activities make up the listening process?
6. Name the three main barriers to effective listening.
7. Of the 10 strategies listed to help you listen effectively, list and explain five.
8. Explain why your attitude and tone of voice are so important when using the telephone and voice mail.
9. In what six ways can an individual communicate nonverbally?
10. Of the dozen tips listed to improve nonverbal communication, list and explain five.

Apply Your Knowledge

1. Whenever your boss asks for feedback, she blasts anyone offering criticism, which causes people to agree with everything she says. You want to talk to her about it, but what should you say? List some of the points you want to make when you discuss this issue with your boss.
2. At your last department meeting, three people monopolized the entire discussion. What might you do at the next meeting to encourage other department members to participate voluntarily?
3. Jason never seems to be paying attention during weekly team meetings. He has never contributed to the discussion, and you've never even seen him take notes. He says he wants to support the team but that he finds it difficult to focus during routine meetings. List some ideas you could give him that might improve his listening skills.
4. How can nonverbal communication help you run a meeting? For example, how can it help you call a meeting to order, emphasize important topics, show approval, express reservations, regulate the flow of conversation, and invite a colleague to continue with a comment?
5. **Ethical Choices** As team leader, you've just received a voice mail message from Tanya Moore, asking to lead next week's meeting. She's been with the company for six weeks and with your team for three. From what you've already observed, she's opinionated (a bit of a know-it-all), and she tends to discourage the more reserved team members from speaking up.

    You can't allow her to run next week's meeting, and without improvement in her attitude toward others, she may never be ready to lead. You consider three options for explaining your view of her position: (1) leaving her a friendly voice mail message, (2) meeting with her, or (3) sending her a friendly email message. What should you do? Explain your choice.
6. **Ethical Choices** Strange instant messages occasionally pop up on your computer screen during your team's virtual meetings, followed quickly by embarrassed apologies from one of your colleagues in another city. You eventually figure out that this person is working from home, even though he says he is in the office. You recognize his name and know he reports to your counterpart in the other city. As well as being disruptive to your meetings, the messages suggest that he's running a sideline business from his home. Instant messaging is crucial to your team's communication and you are concerned about the frequent disruptions, not to mention your colleague's potential ethical violations. What should you do? Explain your choice.

Running Cases

Video

CASE 1: Noreen

Noreen is planning to attend a WebEx online meeting today at 11:00 A.M. Her boss at Petro-Go has asked her to participate in the meeting with other Go Points team leaders from around the world. The group is to compile statistics regarding the Go Points program as well as discuss strategies for expanding the program and improving customer retention. They are to submit a report in one week detailing their findings and suggestions.

Noreen begins the set-up and login process on her computer at 10:45 A.M. She finds that because she has never participated in a WebEx conference, she is unable to prepare her computer. She calls the technical department, and a technician comes to set it up for her. She finally connects with the group at 12:30 P.M. By this time they are ending the meeting and planning to meet tomorrow at the same time. Noreen apologizes and explains what happened, but feels rather embarrassed.

The next day Noreen connects on time, but is somewhat behind on the discussion because she does not know what was discussed the day before. She tries her best to share information, but is scrambling to find the data she needs to share with the group. The group divides the workload between them and asks everyone to meet online again at 11:00 A.M. in three days to share and review their work. Noreen types her team's statistics and suggestions for expanding and finishes early. When she meets the group again she discovers that not only did everyone type their team's statistics and suggestions for expanding the program, they also compared their team's performance with two other office teams and gave suggestions for improving customer retention. Noreen was not aware they were supposed to include all of this information. One team leader volunteered to compile everything and said he would contact the others tomorrow if he had questions. Noreen knew she would be out of the office for the next three days on training.

The report was finished on time, but Noreen's team's section was incomplete. Her boss was not happy.

QUESTIONS

a. Why did Noreen not know what was expected?
b. What could Noreen have done differently to ensure communication would not break down?
c. Should Noreen have alerted the others to the fact that her section was incomplete?
d. Should the group have gone ahead with the report without Noreen's completed section?
e. What could Noreen have done to ensure that she had done the task correctly?

YOUR TASK

Write an email from Noreen to her boss explaining what happened and apologizing for the errors. She should admit fault and offer suggestions for correcting the situation.

CASE 2: Kwong

Kwong is working on a group project for his business communication class. His group members are Mohamed, Gopan, and Marie. The project is to choose a company and research its channels and methods of communication. The group will submit a formal report and deliver a presentation.

The group divides the tasks for the project: Kwong will create the PowerPoint slides, Marie and Mohamed will gather the information, and Gopan will create the formal report.

Mohamed does not attend the next class. The group sends several emails to Mohamed over the course of the next four days, but they get no response. The group emails the professor to make her aware of the situation and to ask for guidance on how to proceed.

The day the project is due, Mohamed meets Gopan outside the classroom door. They have a loud argument that the class overhears. The teacher asks Kwong's group to stay after class to discuss any problems their group may have. The class begins, and Kwong's group does not allow Mohamed to present with them, nor do they accept his work.

After class Gopan complains that Mohamed did his part incorrectly and did not participate. Marie says she came with Mohamed's part done and added it to their project, so they would not lose marks. Mohamed tells the group that he had family problems and apologizes for his absence. Mohamed is willing to accept a zero grade. The professor discusses appropriate behaviour with the team. Gopan apologizes for yelling at Mohamed, and they shake hands.

The next day, when each member emails the professor their peer evaluation forms, both Mohamed and Kwong say they do not wish to work in a group with Gopan again. The group members each give Mohamed a low grade because of his lack of participation.

QUESTIONS

a. Do you think having a group contract from the beginning of the group assignment would have helped the situation? Could a contract have helped ensure that communication would not break down?

b. Was the group being mean by making the professor aware of Mohamed's non-participation? Why did they inform her?

c. Why do you think Mohamed did not wish to work with Gopan again? Why do you think Kwong did not wish to work with Gopan again?

d. What could Gopan have done differently? What could Mohamed have done differently?

e. Should the group have let Mohamed present with them?

YOUR TASK

Create an email to your professor evaluating Gopan's, Mohamed's, Marie's, and Kwong's individual performance on this group assignment. Rate them on
1. cooperation
2. participation
3. contribution
4. demonstrated interest
5. communication

Give a brief explanation as to why you rated each member the way you did.

⊙ Practise Your Knowledge

ACTIVITIES

1. **Agenda Preparation** A project leader has made notes about covering the following items at the quarterly budget meeting. Prepare a formal agenda by putting these items into a logical order and rewriting them, where necessary, to phrase items in parallel form and to focus clearly on needed action.

   Budget Committee Meeting to be held on December 12, 2009, at 9:30 A.M.

   - I will call the meeting to order.
   - Site director's report: A closer look at cost overruns on Greentree site.
   - The group will review and approve the minutes from last quarter's meeting.
   - I will ask the finance director to report on actual vs. projected quarterly revenues and expenses.
   - I will distribute copies of the overall divisional budget and announce the date of the next budget meeting.
   - Discussion: How can we do a better job of anticipating and preventing cost overruns?
   - Meeting will take place in Conference Room 3 with WebEx active for remote employees.
   - What additional budget issues must be considered during this quarter?

2. **Teamwork** With a classmate, attend a local community or campus meeting where you can observe group discussion. Take notes individually during the meeting and then work together to answer the following questions:
   a. What is your evaluation of this meeting? In your answer, consider (1) the leader's ability to clearly state the meeting's goals, (2) the leader's ability to engage members in a meaningful discussion, and (3) the group's listening skills.
   b. How well did the individual participants listen? How could you tell?
   c. What nonverbal communication did you observe during the meeting? Was it positive or negative? Did the sender appear to be aware of the messages?
   d. Compare the notes you took during the meeting with those of your classmate. What differences do you notice? How do you account for these differences?

3. **Meeting Productivity: Analyzing Agendas** Obtain a copy of the agenda from a recent campus or work meeting. Does this agenda show a start time or end time? Is it specific enough that you, as an outsider, would be able to understand what was to be discussed? If not, how would you improve the agenda?

4. **Listening Skills** Find a short videoblog or YouTube post about listening. It could be a comedy routine about listening or advice from a consultant that you have found online. Summarize the key points made in the clip, document the source, and be prepared to present your summary to classmates in a 2-minute oral presentation. Bring the source/link to class.

5. **Listening Skills: Overcoming Barriers** Identify some of your bad listening habits and make a list of some ways you could correct them. For the next 30 days, review your list and jot down any improvements you've noticed as a result of your effort.

6. **Listening Skills: Self-Assessment** How good are your listening skills? Rate yourself on each of the following elements of good listening; then examine your ratings to identify where you are strongest and where you can improve, using the tips in this chapter.

Element of Listening	Always	Frequently	Occasionally	Never
1. I look for areas of interest when people speak.	——	——	——	——
2. I focus on content rather than delivery.	——	——	——	——
3. I wait to respond until I understand the content.	——	——	——	——
4. I listen for ideas and themes, not isolated facts.	——	——	——	——
5. I take notes only when needed.	——	——	——	——
6. I really concentrate on what speakers are saying.	——	——	——	——
7. I stay focused even when the ideas are complex.	——	——	——	——
8. I keep an open mind despite emotionally charged language.	——	——	——	——

7. **Telephones and Voice Mail** You are interested in the hiring policies of companies in your area. You want information about how often entry positions need to be filled, what sort of qualifications are required for these positions, and what range of pay is offered. Plan out your phone call. Think about what you will say (1) to reach the person who can help you, (2) to gain the information you need, (3) in a voice mail message. Once you've planned out your approach, call three companies in your area, and briefly summarize the results of these calls.

8. **Virtual Meetings** Virtual world culture is an aspect of social networking technology that has applications in business not just for meetings, but also for training and collaboration. To prepare yourself for participating in a 3D virtual meeting, explore what it is like to move around in virtual worlds by creating an avatar in Second Life. You can get training to assist you in making your first visit to a virtual world by using your browser to find www.secondlife.astd.com.
Write a short summary of your experience in an email to your professor. Include three paragraphs summarizing what happened, the advantages and disadvantages of virtual representation of yourself, and how nonverbal communication is used or affected in the virtual environment.

9. **Nonverbal Communication: Analyzing Written Messages** Select a business letter and envelope that you have received at work or at home. Analyze their appearance. What nonverbal messages do they send? Are these messages consistent with the content of the letter? If not, what could the sender have done to make the nonverbal communication consistent with the verbal communication?

10. **Nonverbal Communication: Analyzing Body Language** Describe what the following body movements suggest when they are exhibited by someone during a conversation. How do such movements influence your interpretation of spoken words?
    a. Shifting one's body continuously while seated
    b. Twirling and playing with one's hair
    c. Sitting in a sprawled position
    d. Rolling one's eyes
    e. Extending a weak handshake

11. **Nonverbal Communication: Self-Assessment** What type of "persona" do you want to have in the workplace? What nonverbal signals can you send to create this persona? In meetings, others form an impression about your work abilities. How can you ensure that you come across as confident, competent, and easy to get along with?

Element of Nonverbal Communication	Always	Frequently	Occasionally	Never
I stand tall to appear confident.	_____	_____	_____	_____
I walk with purpose.	_____	_____	_____	_____
I greet others when I pass.	_____	_____	_____	_____
I maintain eye contact when speaking with others.	_____	_____	_____	_____
I dress appropriately for the type of workplace.	_____	_____	_____	_____
I avoid provocative clothing.	_____	_____	_____	_____
I avoid controversial slogans on clothing.	_____	_____	_____	_____
I wear appropriate shoes for my workplace.	_____	_____	_____	_____
I maintain personal hygiene.	_____	_____	_____	_____
I take off hats when working inside.	_____	_____	_____	_____
I open doors for others if I get to them first.	_____	_____	_____	_____
I unplug my iPod/electronic devices when in meetings and presentations.	_____	_____	_____	_____

➲ Expand Your Knowledge

Best of the Web

Building Teams in the Cyber Age If you want to learn about building effective teams, you can read many excellent books on the subject. But you might be surprised by just how much information on team building you can find on the internet. One good starting point is the Free Management Library site affiliated with the Management Assistance Program (MAP) for non-profits. Consult the library site at www.mapfornonprofits.org and follow links to team building through the "Group Skills" and "Group Dynamics" choices. Explore some of the links to learn more about teams and teamwork.

EXERCISES

1. Under "Related Library Topics" select "Team Building." Click on "Being an Effective Team Member" to find "Being a Valuable Team Member." Of the meeting roles discussed here, which roles come naturally to you? Which of the negative roles mentioned affect groups in which you participate?

2. Under "Basics of Team Building" find "How to Build Your Team" and take the team assessment test. What should you concentrate on to improve your teamwork?

Exploring the Web on Your Own

Review these chapter-related websites on your own to learn more about achieving communication success in the workplace.

1. About.com: Human Resources has many links, articles, and research reports on the subject matter of teams.
   http://humanresources.about.com/od/involvementteams/a/twelve_tip_team.htm

2. Effective Meetings.com has dozens of tips on how to run effective meetings—from the basics to advanced facilitation skills.
   www.effectivemeetings.com/meetingplanning/index.asp

What You Should Know About Videoconferencing Versus Face-to-Face Meetings

Ever since AT&T unveiled a videophone at the 1964 World's Fair, two-way TV has been touted as the next revolution in communication. Videoconferencing has always been a good idea, but its high costs and technical complexity had put off widespread acceptance—until now.

Today videoconferencing is better, faster, and more user friendly. System quality makes participants feel as if they are in the same room. Furthermore, the costs of installing videoconferencing systems have dropped dramatically in the last few years. Installations range in price from $10 000 for a portable TV monitor unit to $250 000 for a fully outfitted conference room with a giant screen and remote-control video camera. Software such as WebEx can enable videoconferencing at desktops. In some cases, the time and cost savings from reduced corporate travel could pay for these systems in less than one year.

Spurred by such cost savings and a heightened fear of flying, cancelled flights, and long airport delays following the terrorist attacks of September 11, 2001, sales of videoconferencing equipment are soon expected to top $40 billion. Companies that have considered videoconferencing for years are now being pressured by customers and suppliers to install such services. In fact, the hottest first-class seat is no longer on an airplane—instead, it's in front of a videoconferencing camera.

Will videoconferencing make face-to-face meetings obsolete? Probably not. You still need to seal important deals with personal handshakes—especially when conflicts or emotions are involved or when a relationship requires personal interaction to flourish. But videoconferencing will likely change the way people meet. For instance, lower-priority meetings and even details of merger talks could take place without participants leaving their hometown offices. "There's been far too much travelling around the country for 30 minute meetings," says one corporate executive. "It's foolish to have 15 people from different places fly thousands of miles to sit opposite each other at a conference table. . . . It doesn't make any sense. It never made any sense." As one frequent business traveller put it, with videoconferencing, "there is no reason to get on a plane unless you absolutely need to."

Applications for Success

Learn more about videoconferencing skills by reading Penny Tremblay's article on presentation skills using videoconferencing at **www.baytoday.ca/content/business/editorials/recent.asp?w=55**. Gather some tips on presenting using the technology at the University of Guelph's site at **www.tss.uoguelph.ca/cts/vidcontip.html**. As well, read about WebEx by visiting **www.webex.com**. Follow links for tips on presenting.

Assume you are an assistant to the director of communications at Morris & McWhinney, a law firm with branches in Vancouver, Calgary, and Toronto. The partners have asked your boss to investigate whether the firm should use videoconferencing and purchase any equipment needed. To begin, your boss asks you to examine the general pros and cons. Do the following:

1. Summarize your own opinion about whether videoconferencing is appropriate for meetings that your firm conducts. Are there any meetings that would not be right for videoconferencing?
2. Make a list of videoconferencing's advantages and disadvantages and uses for Morris & McWhinney.
3. Based on the results of your examination (and assuming that money is no object), make your own recommendation to your boss to either purchase or not purchase the equipment.

Planning Business Messages

LEARNING OBJECTIVES

After studying this chapter, you will be able to

1. Describe the three-step writing process
2. List four questions that can help you test the purpose of your message
3. Discuss six ways to satisfy your audience's information needs
4. Identify six elements to consider when choosing a channel and medium
5. Specify six ways to establish a good relationship with your audience
6. Explain how to use the "you" attitude when writing messages
7. Give examples of bias-free language and explain its importance

From its beginning as a small regional bank in Halifax in 1875 to its international presence in global financial services, RBC Financial Group has built its success by creating strategies to accommodate changes in markets, customers, and employee needs. Today, RBC has 60 000 employees serving customers in branches, online, and through automated services.[1] Its network has grown to nearly 2000 branches in Canada and the United States, more than 4000 automated banking machines, and more than 2.5 million online clients. Communicating face to face with their various audiences is not always an option for RBC staff. Instead, they must make use of a wide range of available channels and media, as well as new technologies, to make their messages effective.

Creating Audience-Centred Messages

Like RBC Royal Bank's managers, you'll face a variety of communication assignments in your career, both oral and written. Some of your tasks will be routine, needing little more than jotting down a few sentences; others will be more complex, requiring reflection, research, and careful document preparation. Whatever the situation, you can make your messages more effective by making them

- **Action-oriented.** Business messages provide information, solve a problem, or request the resources necessary to accomplish a goal. Every message has a specific purpose.
- **Audience-centred.** Business messages help audiences understand issues, collaborate on tasks, or take action. Each message considers the audience's needs, background, and viewpoint.
- **Concise.** Business messages respect everyone's time by presenting information clearly and efficiently. Every message should be as short as it can be without detracting from the subject.

One of the best ways to create effective business messages is to follow a systematic writing process.

What Is the Three-Step Process?

The three-step writing process covers planning, writing, and completing business messages.

The writing process outlined in Figure 3.1 can help you write more effective messages. As the figure shows, this process may be viewed as three simple steps: planning, writing, and completing.

PLANNING First, think about the fundamentals of your message. Clarify your purpose in communicating and analyze audience members so that you can tailor your message to their needs and expectations. Gather the information that will inform, persuade, or motivate your audience. Then adapt your message by selecting the channel and medium that will suit both your needs and those of your audience. Finally, establish a good relationship with your audience. Planning is the focus of this chapter.

WRITING Once you've planned your message, the next step is to organize your ideas and compose your first draft. In this stage, you commit your thoughts to words, create sentences and paragraphs, and select illustrations and details to support your main idea. Writing business messages is discussed in Chapter 4.

COMPLETING After writing your first draft, it's time to step back to review the content and organization for overall style, structure, and readability. You'll want to revise and rewrite until your message comes across clearly and effectively; then edit your message for grammar, punctuation, and format. In this stage produce your message, putting it into the form that your audience will receive. The last step is to proof the final document for typos, spelling errors, and other mechanical problems. Completing business messages is discussed in Chapter 5.

How Does the Three-Step Process Work?

Try to budget your time for each step.

Because so many of today's business messages are composed under pressure, allocating your time among these three steps can be a challenge. But whether you have 30 minutes or two days, try using roughly half of your time for planning—for deciding on your purpose, getting to know your audience, and immersing yourself in your subject matter. Devote less than a quarter of your time to writing your document. Then use more than

---

FIGURE 3.1 | The Three-Step Writing Process

Planning	Writing	Completing
Analyze Identify your purpose and profile your audience. **Investigate** Gather information through formal or informal research methods. **Adapt** Choose the right channel and medium; then establish a good relationship with your audience.	**Organize** Define your main idea, group your points, and choose the direct or indirect approach. **Compose** Control your style through level of formality and conversational tone. Choose your words carefully to create effective sentences and paragraphs.	**Revise** Evaluate content and organization. Edit and rewrite for conciseness and clarity. **Produce** Use effective design elements. Check that emphasis is given to key ideas. **Proofread** Review for errors in layout, spelling, and mechanics.
1	2	3

a quarter of your time for completing the project (so that you don't shortchange important final steps such as revising and proofing).[2]

There is no right or best way to write all business messages. As you work through the writing process presented in Chapters 3, 4, and 5, try not to view it as a list of how-to directives but as a way to understand the various tasks involved in effective business writing.[3] Effective communicators complete all three steps, although they may not necessarily complete them in 1-2-3 order. Some jump back and forth from one step to another; some compose quickly and then revise; others revise as they go along. But for the sake of organization, we'll start with planning, the first step of the writing process.

The order of the three steps is flexible.

Analyzing the Situation and Identifying Your Audience

When planning a business message, the first thing you need to think about is your purpose. For a business message to be effective, its purpose and its audience must complement each other.

Define Your Purpose

All business messages have a **general purpose**: to inform, to persuade, or to collaborate with your audience. Business messages also have a **specific purpose**. To help you define the specific purpose of your message, ask yourself what you hope to accomplish with your message and what your audience should **DO** or think after receiving your message.

Business messages have an "action" purpose.

Write a purpose statement to help you focus your message. Focus on the **ACTION** you want. Often when people write in business, it is because something needs to happen or has happened. What action do you want? One technique to develop an **action-based purpose statement** is to complete this sentence: *"I want my reader to . . .* Use a verb to express your action purpose. Also consider the context or circumstances in which you are communicating when developing your purpose statement. Ask yourself these questions:

- **Is my purpose realistic?** If your purpose involves a radical shift in action or attitude, go slowly. Consider proposing the first step and using your message as the beginning of a learning process.
- **In which context will the message be received?** What are the circumstances surrounding the message? For example, is it the right time to be asking or telling? If an organization is undergoing changes of some sort, you may want to defer your message until things stabilize and people can concentrate on your ideas.
- **Is the right person delivering this message?** Although you may have done all the work, having your boss deliver your message could get better results because of his or her higher status. What is your relationship to the reader? Are you writing to a peer or to a supervisor or client?
- **Is my purpose acceptable to the organization?** Even though you want to fire off an angry reply to an abusive letter attacking your company, your supervisors might prefer that you regain the customer's goodwill. Your response must reflect the organization's priorities.

Once you have identified a clear purpose in communicating, take a good look at your intended audience.

Develop an Audience Profile

Who are your audience members? What are their attitudes? What do they need to know? And why should they care about your message? The answers to such questions will indicate which material you'll need to cover and how to cover it (see Figure 3.2 on page 42).

Ask yourself some key questions about your audience.

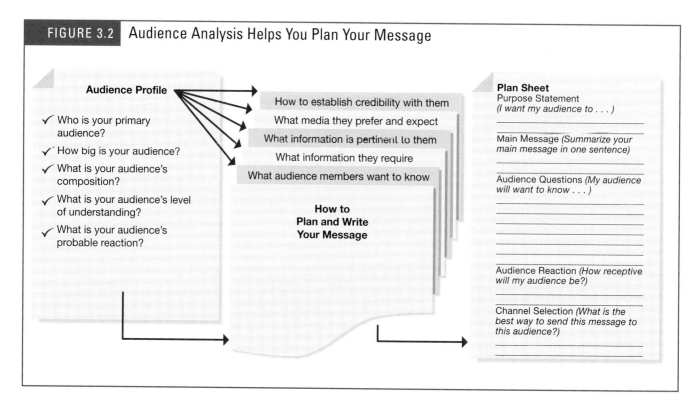

FIGURE 3.2 Audience Analysis Helps You Plan Your Message

Profile your audience by
- Identifying key decision makers
- Determining audience size
- Looking for common interests
- Estimating audience understanding
- Predicting audience reactions and questions about your topic

Identify your primary audience. Will anyone else be affected by the message? You may need to analyze the needs of both a primary and secondary audience.

- **Determine the size of your audience.** A report for a large audience requires a more formal style, organization, and format than one directed to three or four people in your department. Also, respond to the particular concerns of key individuals. The head of marketing would need different facts than the head of production or finance would need.

- **Define your audience's composition.** Look for common interests that tie audience members together across differences in culture, education, age, status, or attitude. Include evidence that touches on everyone's area of interest. To be understood across cultural and age barriers, consider how audience members think and learn, what they value, as well as what style they expect.[4]

- **Assess the way in which the audience prefers to get information.** While Boomers (those born between 1941 and 1961) prefer print, Millennials (those born between 1977 and 1992) often prefer visual and online channels of communication, finding things out by looking on the internet or consulting peers. Consider the dilemma faced by WorkSafeBC, the Workers' Compensation Board in British Columbia. Young workers between the ages of 18 and 26 experience a high rate of injury and fatalities. To reach these Millennials, WorkSafeBC produced a series of 60 videos on working safely and posted them to YouTube. In addition, they created a website called Raise Your Hand.com in which young people tell their injury stories, peer-to-peer. These choices show excellent audience analysis because the channels of communication (1) matched the age group's style and method of getting information, and (2) suited the intention of conveying emotional content through powerful storytelling—both effective tools in persuasion. The technology also gave the sender a way to track the numbers of people who view the material and ensure the messages were effective in reaching the audience.

Audience questions often include
- What
- Who
- When
- Where
- Why
- How

- **Gauge your audience's level of understanding.** If audience members share your general background, they'll understand your material without difficulty. If not, you must educate them. Include only enough information to accomplish your objective, gearing your coverage to your primary audience (the key decision makers).

- **Estimate your audience's probable reaction.** If you expect a favourable response, you can state conclusions and recommendations up front and offer minimal supporting evidence. If you expect resistance, you can introduce conclusions gradually, with more proof. Assess audience expectations. How much work time should you devote to this message? Is the audience expecting 1 page or 50? Chapter 4 discusses how audience reaction affects message organization.

Use a Plan Sheet

To develop ideas for the content of your messages, use the plan sheet in Figure 3.2. Once you focus yourself by stating an action purpose, write your main message in one sentence. This summary statement can be part of the introduction to your communication and it will help focus the receiver.

The plan sheet can also help you generate content to include in your communication. Pretend the audience has read the main message, then predict what questions would follow. List the audience questions on the plan sheet. Later, you can use these questions to select the content, organize it, and create headings—thus creating a reader-oriented document design.

Investigating the Topic

Before you compose your message, you'll most likely need to gather some information to communicate to your audience. When writing long, formal reports, you'll conduct formal research to locate and analyze all the information relevant to your purpose and your audience. Formal techniques for finding, evaluating, and processing information are discussed in Chapter 11.

Other kinds of business messages require less formal information gathering. For example, you may simply try to consider others' viewpoints. Put yourself in someone else's position to consider what that person or group might be thinking, feeling, or planning. Or your company's files may be a good source of the information you need for a particular memo or email message. Consider company annual reports, financial statements, news releases, memos, marketing reports, and customer surveys for helpful information.

> For many messages, collect information informally through networking.

Chatting with supervisors, colleagues, or customers can help you gather information. Conducting telephone or personal interviews is a convenient way to investigate. And don't forget to ask your audience for input. If you're unsure of what audience members need from your message, ask them through casual conversation (face to face or over the phone), informal surveys, or unofficial interviews.

> Ask the audience for feedback.

Be careful when deciding what information to include in your messages. Make sure your information is

> Double-check your information.

- **Complete.** One good way to test the thoroughness of your message is to use the journalistic approach: Check to see whether your message answers *who, what, when, where, why,* and *how.*
- **Accurate.** Your organization is legally bound by any promises you make, so be sure your company can follow through. Check with the appropriate people before you make the commitment. Also, review all mathematical or financial calculations, check all dates and schedules, and examine your own assumptions and conclusions.
- **Ethical.** Messages can be unethical simply because information is omitted. You need to include enough detail to avoid misleading your audience. Include as much information as you believe best fits your definition of complete.
- **Pertinent.** Choose and emphasize the points that affect your audience the most. Whereas engineers may be interested in customer reaction to product design, shipping managers might want to know when customers receive the product. For an unknown audience, use your common sense to identify points of particular interest. Factors such as job, location, income, or education can give you a clue.

Adapting Your Message to Your Audience and Purpose

By now you know why you're writing, you know the audience you're writing to, and you have most of the information you need. But before beginning to write your message, think of how to make it serve both your audience and your purpose. To adapt your message, select a channel and a medium that fit your purpose and satisfy your audience's expectations. In addition, you need to establish a good relationship with your audience.

Select the Best Channel and Medium

Selecting the best channel and medium for your message can make the difference between effective and ineffective communication.[5] You must choose between the oral and written channels, and you must consider all the media within each one.

The *oral channel* includes media such as face-to-face conversation, telephone calls, speeches, presentations, and meetings. The chief advantage of oral communication is the opportunity it provides for immediate feedback. Your choice between a face-to-face conversation and a telephone call would depend on audience location, message importance, and your need for the sort of nonverbal feedback that only body language can reveal.

The *written channel* includes media that range from the scribbled notes people use to jog their own memories to formal reports that rival magazines in graphic quality. The most common written media is email, but other common business written media include reports, letters, and memos (see Appendix A for business document formats). Written messages have one big advantage: They let you plan and control the message.

In addition to the traditional forms of oral and written media, both channels have electronic forms. Oral media also include voice mail, podcasts, vodcasts, webcasts, teleconferencing, videoconferencing, and many more. Written media also include email, faxing, computer conferencing (with groupware), websites, blogs, wikis, instant messaging, and more. With the growing use of online social networking technologies such as Facebook and YouTube, oral, written, and visual communication can be used together to connect with customers, co-workers, and the public and can provide instantaneous feedback for businesses.

The trick to choosing the best channel and medium is to select the tool that does the best overall job in each situation (see Table 3.1). To choose the channel and medium that will best match your purpose and audience, consider the following elements:

- **Message style and tone.** You wouldn't write a report with the same level of informality that you might use in an email message. To emphasize the formality of your message, use a more formal medium, such as a memo or a letter.
- **Possibility for feedback.** Different media offer varying levels of feedback. The more feedback possible, the richer the medium. Traditionally, face-to-face conversation is richest because it provides immediate verbal and nonverbal feedback. However, social networking technologies (such as blogs and networking sites) now offer instantaneous feedback and participation with multiple audiences across the world.[6] On the other hand, unaddressed documents such as fliers are leanest because they offer no feedback at all. Use leaner media (notes, memos, letters) for simple, routine messages; use richer media (meetings, videos) for complex, non-routine messages; and use phone calls, email, and voice mail for messages in between. Consider social networking media when you want to engage in conversations with your audience for collaboration, relationship building, and feedback.
- **Audience perception.** To emphasize the confidentiality of a message, use voice mail rather than a fax, send a letter rather than a memo, or plan on a private conversation rather than a meeting. To instil an emotional commitment, consider video or a videoconference. If you can get together, face-to-face conversation, however, can be more complete.[7]

Different types of messages require different communication channels and media.

In general, use an oral channel if your purpose is to collaborate with the audience.

A written channel increases the sender's control but eliminates the possibility of immediate feedback.

When choosing a channel and medium, consider six elements:
- Message style
- Opportunity for feedback
- Audience perception
- Timing
- Cost
- Audience expectation

TABLE 3.1	Choosing the Best Channel and Medium

USE WRITTEN CHANNELS WHEN

- You need no immediate feedback
- Your message is detailed, complex, or requires careful planning
- You need a permanent, verifiable record
- Your audience is large and geographically dispersed
- You want to minimize the distortion that can occur when messages pass orally from person to person
- Immediate interaction with the audience is either unimportant or undesirable
- Your message has no emotional component

USE ORAL CHANNELS WHEN

- You want immediate feedback from the audience
- Your message is relatively simple and easy to accept
- You need no permanent record
- You can assemble your audience conveniently and economically
- You want to encourage interaction to solve a problem or reach a group decision
- You want to read the audience's body language or hear the tone of their response
- Your message has an emotional component

USE ELECTRONIC FORMS WHEN

- You need speed or simultaneous collaboration
- You're physically separated from your audience
- Time zones differ
- You must reach a dispersed audience personally
- You seek to build relationships with two-way communication
- Your audience prefers interactive media

- **Time.** If your message is urgent, you'll probably use the phone, send a fax, or send your message by next-day mail.
- **Cost.** You wouldn't think twice about telephoning an important customer overseas if you just discovered your company had erroneously sent the wrong shipment. But you'd probably choose to fax or email a routine order acknowledgement to your customer in Australia.
- **Audience expectation.** Consider which media your audience expects or prefers.[8] You expect your university or college to deliver your degree/diploma by hand at graduation or in the mail, not by fax. Moreover, culture influences channel preference. People in Canada and Germany prefer written messages, whereas people in Japan prefer oral ones.[9] North American workers prefer email and voice mail because it helps with the continent's multiple time zones; whereas German and French workers prefer traditional paper-based media and find long, detailed voice mails irritating.[10]

Establish a Good Relationship with Your Audience

Once you've chosen an appropriate channel and medium, you're still not ready to start writing. Effective communicators do more than simply convey information. They make sure that they establish a good relationship with their audience.

To give the right impression in your message, think carefully about who you are and who your audience is. Since a good relationship is based on sincerity, respect, and courtesy, show yours by using the "you" attitude, emphasizing the positive, establishing your credibility, being polite, using bias-free language, and projecting the company's image (see Figure 3.3 on page 46).

FIGURE 3.3 Establishing a Good Relationship in Business Messages

Provides enough information to identify the warranty, the customer, etc.

Includes specific date the warranty expires

Avoids bias by not mentioning the repair person as either male or female

Uses the "you" attitude to explain the warranty without blaming the reader

Emphasizes the positive, with helpful information, and ends on a friendly note

Uses the pronoun "you" correctly, emphasizing the positive by implying the refusal to pay for a new motor and any spoiled food

Includes relevant information in language that is easy for the reader to understand

Provides detailed information about what the reader might do to avoid such costs in the future

EPPLER APPLIANCES
7142 Agricola Street, Halifax, NS B3K YG2
Voice: (902) 768-1927   Fax: (902) 768-1928

September 9, 2009

Mr. Joseph Carpaccio
Carpaccio's Ristoranti
16 Basin Drive
Wolfville, NS B4P 1X3

Dear Mr. Carpaccio:

Subject: Burned-out Freezer Motor, Invoice # 3770 46 010122

Thank you for your letter about freezer repairs. Your Crown Freezer is under limited warranty until November 15, and to help you defray a portion of your unforeseen costs, we would like to pay the standard $45 for the service call. The cheque is enclosed.

You received a copy of the warranty with your freezer, and I've enclosed another copy for your convenience. As you can see, Crown Freezers are designed to endure everyday use in a typical commercial kitchen. Their top-quality materials and performance rating guarantee that they will perform effectively and efficiently under normal operating conditions, which must exclude running for extended periods of time with the door open.

With only two months left on your limited warranty, you might consider purchasing an extended manufacturer's warranty. The basic warranty covers parts and labour for five years for only $75. Plus, you can purchase additional business insurance for just $135 more per year, which covers parts, labour, and damages—regardless of the cause. The enclosed brochure gives all the details, or you can visit our website at www.eppler.com.

Sincerely,

Kjiersten Lejunhud

Kjiersten Lejunhud
Customer Relations

Enclosures (3)

Express your message in terms of the audience's interests and needs.

USE THE "YOU" ATTITUDE To project your audience-centred approach, adopt a "you" attitude—that is, speak and write in terms of your audience's wishes, interests, hopes, and preferences. On the simplest level, you replace terms that refer to you and your company with terms that refer to your audience. Use *you* and *yours* instead of *I, me, mine, we, us,* and *ours:*

Instead of

To help us process this order, we must ask for another copy of the requisition.

We are pleased to announce our new flight schedule from Montreal to Toronto, which is every hour on the hour.

Use

So that your order can be filled promptly, please send another copy of the requisition.

Now you can take a plane from Montreal to Toronto every hour on the hour.

However, using *you* and *yours* requires finesse. If you overdo it, you're likely to create some rather awkward sentences, and you run the risk of sounding like a high-pressure carnival barker.[11] The "you" attitude is not intended to be manipulative or insincere. You can use *you* 25 times in a single page and still ignore your audience's true concerns. It's the thought and sincerity that count, not the pronoun. If you're talking to a retailer, try to think like a retailer; if you're writing to a dissatisfied customer, imagine how you would feel at the other end of the transaction. The important thing is your attitude toward audience members and your appreciation of their position.

In fact, on some occasions you'll do better to avoid using *you*. For instance, using *you* in a way that sounds dictatorial is impolite. Or, when someone makes a mistake, you may want to minimize ill will by pointing out the error impersonally. You might say, "We have a problem," instead of "You caused a problem."

Be sure to consider the attitudes and policies of your organization and those of other cultures. In some cultures, it is improper to single out one person's achievements because the whole team is responsible for the outcome; using the pronoun *we* or *our* is more appropriate. Similarly, some companies have a tradition of avoiding references to *you* and *I* in their memos and formal reports. If you work for a company that expects a formal, impersonal style, confine your use of personal pronouns to informal emails, letters, and memos.

EMPHASIZE THE POSITIVE Another way of establishing a good relationship with your audience is to emphasize the positive side of your message.[12] Stress what is or will be instead of what isn't or won't be. Most information, even bad news, has some redeeming feature. If you can make your audience aware of that feature, your message will be more acceptable.

Avoid Being Negative	**Say What You *Can* Do**
It is impossible to repair your vacuum cleaner today.	Your vacuum cleaner will be ready by Tuesday.
We apologize for inconveniencing you during our remodelling.	The renovations now underway will help us serve you better.

If you're trying to persuade the audience to buy a product, pay a bill, or perform a service for you, emphasize audience benefits by pointing out what's in it for them. Don't focus on why *you* want them to do something. An individual who sees the possibility for personal benefit is more likely to respond positively to your appeal.

Avoid Focusing on Your Needs	**Focus on Reader Benefits**
Please buy this book so that I can make my sales quota.	The plot of this novel will keep you in suspense to the last page.
We need your contribution to the Variety Club.	You can help a child make friends and build self-confidence through your donation to the Variety Club.

In general, try to state your message without using words that might hurt or offend your audience. Substitute mild terms (euphemisms) for those that have unpleasant connotations. You can be honest without being harsh:

Avoid Harsh Language	**Use Subtle Language**
cheap merchandise	bargain prices
toilet paper	bathroom tissue

Sidenotes:

Don't overdo the "you" attitude.

Avoid using *you* and *yours* when doing so
- Makes you sound dictatorial
- Makes someone else feel guilty
- Goes against your organization's style

Explain what you have done, what you can do, and what you will do—not what you haven't done, can't do, or won't do.

Show audience members how they will benefit from complying with your message.

On the other hand, don't carry euphemisms to extremes. If you're too subtle, people won't know what you're talking about. You won't be helping your audience by "derecruiting" workers to the "mobility pool" instead of telling them that they have six weeks to find another job.

> People are more likely to react positively to your message when they have confidence in you.

ESTABLISH YOUR CREDIBILITY If you're unknown to your audience members, you'll have to earn their confidence before you can win them to your point of view. You want people to trust that your word is dependable and that you know what you're doing. Your **credibility** (or believability) is based on how reliable you are and how much trust you evoke in others.

If you're communicating with a familiar group, your credibility has probably already been established, so you can get right down to business. But if audience members are complete strangers or, worse, if they start off with doubts about you, you'll need to devote the initial portion of your message to gaining credibility.

Try to show an understanding of your audience's situation. Sometimes you can call attention to the things you have in common. If your audience shares your professional background, you might say, "As a fellow engineer [or lawyer, doctor, teacher, or whatever], I'm sure you can appreciate this situation." Also, use technical or professional terms that identify you as a peer.

> To enhance your credibility
> - Show that you understand the other person's situation
> - Explain your own credentials or ally yourself with a credible source
> - Back up your claims with evidence, not exaggerations
> - Use words that express confidence
> - Believe in yourself and your message

You can explain your credentials. Your title or the name of your organization might be enough to impress your audience with your abilities. You might mention the name of someone who carries some weight with your audience ("Professor Goldberg suggested that I contact you") or quote a recognized authority on your subject. Just be careful not to sound pompous.

Avoid exaggerating your claims. A mail-order catalogue promised: "You'll be absolutely amazed at the incredible blooms on this healthy plant." Terms such as *amazing, incredible, extraordinary, sensational,* and *revolutionary* exceed the limits of believability, unless they're supported with some sort of proof. Similarly, support compliments with specific points. Don't appear to be currying favour with compliments that are overblown and insincere.

Avoid Exaggerating
My deepest heartfelt thanks for the excellent job you did. It's hard these days to find workers like you. You are just fantastic! I can't stress enough how happy you have made us with your outstanding performance.

Be Specific
Thanks for the fantastic job you did filling in for Sandi at the convention with just an hour's notice. Despite the difficult circumstances, you managed to attract several new orders with your demonstration of the new line of coffee makers. Your dedication and sales ability are truly appreciated.

Finally, avoid revealing any lack of confidence. Try not to undermine your credibility with vague sentiments or by using words such as *if, hope,* and *trust.* Avoid communicating an uncertain attitude that undermines your credibility. State your case with authority so that your audience has no doubts.

Avoid Creating Doubt
We hope this recommendation will be helpful.

If you'd like to order, mail us the reply card.

Be Definite
We're glad to make this recommendation.

To order, mail the reply card.

BE POLITE Being polite is another good way to earn your audience's respect. By being courteous to members of your audience, you show consideration for their needs and feelings. Express yourself with kindness and tact. Venting your emotions rarely improves the situation and can jeopardize your audience's goodwill. Instead, be gentle when expressing yourself:

> Try to express the facts in a kind and thoughtful manner.

Avoid Accusation	Be Tactful
You really fouled things up with that last computer run.	Let's go over what went wrong with the last computer run so that the next run goes smoothly.
You've been sitting on my order for two weeks, and we need it now!	We are eager to receive our order. When can we expect delivery?

In general, written communication requires more tact than oral communication. When you're speaking, your words are softened by your tone of voice and facial expression. Plus, you can adjust your approach according to the feedback you get. But written communication is stark and self-contained. If you hurt a person's feelings in writing, you can't soothe them right away. What you say in writing in email, on Facebook, or on the internet has permanence and can be spread around at rapid speed. The connectivity allowed by the internet has made the old expression "spread by word of mouth" take on a much more powerful role in our society. Be careful to guard your credibility and image and act responsibly with material sent to you in the "wired" world.

USE BIAS-FREE LANGUAGE Bias-free language avoids unethical, embarrassing blunders in language related to gender, race, ethnicity, age, and disability. Good communicators make every effort to correct biased language (see Table 3.2 on page 50). To keep your messages bias-free, avoid the following:

> Avoid biased language that might offend your audience.

- **Gender bias.** Avoid sexist language by using the same label for everyone (don't use *chairperson* for a woman and then use *chairman* for a man). Reword sentences to use *they* or to use no pronoun at all. Remember, the preferred title for women in business is *Ms.*, unless the individual asks to be addressed as *Miss* or *Mrs.* or has some other title, such as *Dr.*
- **Racial and ethnic bias.** The central principle is to avoid language suggesting that members of a racial or an ethnic group have stereotypical characteristics. The best solution is to avoid identifying people by race or ethnic origin unless such a label is relevant.
- **Age bias.** As with gender, race, and ethnic background, mention the age of a person only when it is relevant. When referring to older people, avoid such stereotyped adjectives as *spry* and *frail*.
- **Disability bias.** No painless label exists for people with a physical, mental, sensory, or emotional impairment. Avoid mentioning a disability unless it is pertinent. However, if you must refer to someone's disability, avoid terms such as *handicapped, crippled,* or *retarded*. Put the person first and the disability second.[13]

PROJECT THE COMPANY'S IMAGE Even though establishing a good relationship with the audience is your main goal, give some thought to projecting a professional image for your company. When you communicate with outsiders, on even the most routine matter, you serve as the spokesperson for your organization. The impression you make can enhance or

> Subordinate your own style to that of the company.

TABLE 3.2	Tips for Overcoming Bias in Language	
EXAMPLES	UNACCEPTABLE	PREFERABLE
Gender Bias		
Using words containing "man"	Man-made	Artificial, synthetic, manufactured, constructed
	Businessman	Executive, business manager, business person
	Salesman	Sales representative, salesperson, clerk, sales agent
	Foreman	Supervisor
Using female-gender words	Authoress, actress, stewardess	Author, actor, flight attendant
Using special designations	Woman doctor, male nurse	Doctor, nurse
Using "he" to refer to "everyone"	The average worker . . . he	The average worker . . . he or she
Identifying roles with gender	The typical executive spends four hours of his day in meetings.	Most executives spend four hours a day in meetings.
	the nurse/teacher . . . she	nurses/teachers . . . they
Identifying women by marital status	Ian Hanomansing and Sandi Ian Hanomansing and Ms. Renaldo	Ian Hanomansing and Sandi Renaldo Mr. Hanomansing and Ms. Renaldo
Racial and Ethnic Bias		
Assigning stereotypes	My Indian assistant speaks more articulately than I do.	My assistant speaks more articulately than I do.
	Jim Wong is an unusually tall Asian.	Jim Wong is tall.
Identifying people by race or ethnicity	Adrienne Clarkson, Chinese-Canadian journalist and governor general of Canada	Adrienne Clarkson, journalist and governor general of Canada
Age Bias		
Including age when irrelevant	Mary Kirazy, 58, has just joined our trust department.	Mary Kirazy has just joined our trust department.
Disability Bias		
Putting the disability before the person	Crippled workers face many barriers on the job.	Workers with physical disabilities face many barriers on the job.
	An epileptic, Tracy has no trouble doing her job.	Tracy's epilepsy has no effect on her job performance.

damage the reputation of the entire company. Thus, your own views and personality must be subordinated, at least to some extent, to the interests and style of your company. Your role as an ambassador for your company has never been more important than in the wired world. What employees say about the company on the internet can have a profound effect on business. A Comcast installer caught on video sleeping on a client's sofa during a maintenance call provided entertainment on YouTube but an image problem for the company.[14]

ON THE JOB

Using the "Grapevine" in Person and Online

Having positive relationships with co-workers and managers also extends to informal communication in the office. The "grapevine" or informal communication network often provides a useful source of information about company values and a way to connect with co-workers. However, office gossip, when harmful and personal, can get people fired. Knowing how to participate in informal communication in your office can help your career. Calgary-based communication expert Merge Gupta-Sunderji offers these tips:[15]

- Could you repeat the information to the person it is about? If no, do not discuss it.
- Is the information harmful or about personal matters? If yes, don't participate in a conversation about it.
- Watch what you say on email, blogs, and sites such as Facebook or Twitter. There is no such thing as a private electronic conversation.
- Do not spread malicious rumours.
- Remember that work-related social functions are extensions of the workplace.

Reviewing Key Points

In this chapter you learned about the first stage of the writing process: planning. When planning a message, you should

- Define a specific purpose and write an action-oriented purpose statement.
- Analyze audience needs by assessing the message context, audience interests, educational background, and job needs and by predicting audience questions.
- Gather relevant information by asking questions, reviewing company files, and interviewing informally.
- Check information accuracy, completeness, and relevance.
- Select an appropriate channel and medium—choose written (such as letters, memos, reports) when the message is complex and detailed or when you need a record; choose oral (such as face to face, meetings, presentations, telephone) for immediate feedback or collaboration, or when messages are simple or highly emotional. Choose electronic forms (such as email, voice mail, fax) for speed or convenience, or when you have time zone differences. Choose social networking media (such as wikis, blogs, YouTube, or Facebook) when you want to share information, collaborate, or build networks with groups.
- Adapt your style and channel to the audience.
- Use "you" attitude, bias-free language, and a positive approach to build a relationship, be credible, and be sincere.

mybuscommlab   Go to MyBusCommLab at www.pearson.ca/mybuscommlab for online writing exercises.

Practise Your Grammar

Exercises

Effective business communication starts with strong grammar skills. To improve your grammar skills, go to MyBusCommLab or Grammar-on-the-Go, where you'll find interactive exercises and diagnostic tests to help you produce clear, effective communication.

Test Your Knowledge

 Exercises

1. What are the three steps in the writing process?
2. What two types of purposes do all business messages have?
3. What do you need to know in order to develop an audience profile?
4. What are four methods of informal information gathering?
5. When including information in your message, what four conditions must you satisfy?
6. What are the main advantages of oral communication? Of written media?
7. What six elements must you consider when choosing a channel and medium?
8. What is the "you" attitude, and how does it differ from an "I" attitude?
9. How can you establish your credibility when communicating with an audience of strangers?
10. How can you establish a good relationship with your audience?

Apply Your Knowledge

1. Some writers argue that planning messages wastes time because they inevitably change their plans as they go along. How would you respond to this argument? Briefly explain.
2. As a member of the public relations department, what medium would you recommend using to inform the local community that your toxic-waste cleanup program has been successful? Why?
3. When composing business messages for your company, how can you create a professional image?
4. Considering how fast and easy it is, should email replace meetings and other face-to-face communication in your company? Why or why not?
5. **Ethical Choices** Your manager has asked you to draft a memo for her signature to the board of directors, informing them that sales in the new line of gourmet fruit jams have far exceeded anyone's expectations. As a member of the marketing department, you happen to know that sales of moderately priced jams have declined quite a bit (many customers have switched to the more expensive jams). You were not directed to add that tidbit of information. Should you write the memo and limit your information to the expensive gourmet jams? Or should you include the information about the decline in moderately priced jams? Please explain.

Running Cases

 Video

CASE 1: Noreen

Noreen's manager informs her of a new Petro-Go company promotion for Canadian customers owning a Go Points card. The first step is to prepare the service stations.

The promotion details are: (1) Cardholders will now receive double points when they purchase more than $30 of gasoline in one visit (regular points up to $30 and then double points over $30). (2) Cardholders will earn a new reward redemption—Petro-Go gift certificates ($20 certificate for a 250-point redemption). (3) Cardholders will win a free 6-litre container of windshield washer fluid when their accumulated points reach each 1000-point interval (1000, 2000, 3000).

Noreen is asked to create a letter to inform the service station owners/operators of when the promotion begins, how it will be advertised, what the promotion offers, and how they will use their equipment to offer and track this promotion. An instruction booklet on where and how to place signs, how to update equipment, and how to manage card points will be attached to the letter. Noreen needs to prepare this booklet by gathering information from past promotional materials and then choosing only what she needs for this task. This letter needs to be distributed as soon as possible. There is much to be done.

QUESTIONS

a. What information must Noreen gather?

b. Why is it so important that Noreen's letter be concise and accurate?

c. What would be the best way to distribute this information to the service stations?

d. What will the audience's general attitude be toward the message?

e. How many key ideas are in this letter? How will Noreen emphasize them?

YOUR TASK

The station owners/operators need to know how and where to put up promotional signs, and how to update point-of-sale machines and registers using key codes and sequences. Write two sets of instructions for the service stations—the first set will be for a reader who has never used that type of machine or provided a promotion before, and the second set will be for a reader who is familiar with that type of machine and has provided promotions in the past. Use your imagination. Briefly explain how your two audiences affect your instructions.

CASE 2: Kwong

Kwong has done some research into Canadian business culture. He has also attended several college workshops to improve his English and speaking skills. Thanks to his efforts and improved understanding he has now obtained a co-op placement with Accountants For All accounting firm. With the tax season quickly approaching, Kwong's manager knows that their previous customers will once again look for an accounting firm to help them file their tax returns. Kwong's manager asks him to produce a promotional letter that will help bring back previous customers.

QUESTIONS

a. What does Kwong need to plan?

b. How should he get started?

c. What information should Kwong put in this promotional letter?

d. How should Kwong organize his letter?

e. How much detail does he need to provide?

YOUR TASK

List five messages you have received lately, such as direct-mail promotions, letters, email messages, phone solicitations, and lectures. For each, determine the general and the specific purpose; then, answer the following questions:

1. Was the message well timed?

2. Did the sender choose an appropriate medium for the message?

3. Did the appropriate person deliver the message?

4. Was the sender's purpose realistic?

⊙ Practise Your Knowledge

EXERCISES

Purpose Statements For each of the following communication tasks, state a specific purpose (if you have trouble, try beginning with "I want to tell you that . . .").

1. A report to your boss, the store manager, about the outdated items in the warehouse

2. A memo to clients about your booth at the upcoming trade show

3. A letter to a customer who hasn't made a payment for three months

4. A memo to employees about the office's expensive water service bills

5. A phone call to a supplier checking on an overdue parts shipment

6. A report to future users of the computer program you have chosen to handle the company's mailing list

Audience Profiles For each communication task below, write brief answers to three questions: (1) Who is my audience? (2) What is my audience's general attitude toward my subject? (3) What does my audience need to know? Predict a list of audience questions.

7. A final-notice collection letter from an appliance manufacturer to an appliance dealer, sent 10 days before initiating legal collection procedures

8. An unsolicited sales letter asking readers to purchase DVDs at near-wholesale prices

9. Fliers to be attached to doorknobs in the neighbourhood, announcing reduced rates for chimney lining or repairs

10. A cover letter sent along with your resumé to a potential employer

11. A request (to the seller) for a price adjustment on a piano that incurred $150 in damage during delivery to a banquet room in the hotel you manage

Media and Purpose Describe a message you have received lately (such as a direct-mail promotion, letter, email message, phone solicitation, or a lecture). Determine its purpose; then answer the questions listed.

12. What was the general purpose of the message?

13. What was its specific purpose? What action did the writer want to happen? Where was the action stated?

14. Was the message well timed?

15. Did the sender choose an appropriate medium for the message?

16. Did the appropriate person deliver the message?

17. Was the sender's purpose realistic?

Audience and Purpose Read the scenario below. Identify a specific (action) purpose, describe a few characteristics of the audience, sum up your main message, then predict and list audience questions that need to be answered in the communication. Select an appropriate channel for communicating your message.

You work as a supervisor at Sport Right, a sports clothing retailer, in the local mall. It bothers you that the merchandise is frequently lying over racks or on the floor by the end of a shift and that the items are often misplaced around the store. The manager, Sandi Johal, has been out of the store for the last few weeks in training courses. Even when she is around, though, things get pretty messy out on the floor. Each shift has enough people but they don't seem to worry about the appearance of the store. You decide to approach Sandi to solve this problem.

18. Use the plan sheet in Figure 3.2 (on page 42) to develop a plan. Make up the details you need to complete your plan.

The "You" Attitude Rewrite the following sentences to reflect your audience's viewpoint.

19. We request that you use the order form supplied in the back of our catalogue.

20. We insist that you always bring your credit card to the store.

21. We want to get rid of all our 15-inch monitors to make room in our warehouse for the 19-inch screens. Thus we are offering a 25 percent discount on all sales this week.

22. I am applying for the position of bookkeeper in your office. I feel that my grades prove that I am bright and capable, and I think I can do a good job for you.

23. As requested, we are sending the refund for $25.

Emphasizing the Positive Revise these sentences to be positive rather than negative.

24. To avoid the loss of your credit rating, please remit payment within 10 days.

25. We don't make refunds on returned merchandise that is soiled.

26. Because we are temporarily out of Baby Cry dolls, we won't be able to ship your order for 10 days.

27. You failed to specify the colour of the blouse that you ordered.

28. You should have realized that waterbeds will freeze in unheated houses during winter. Therefore, our guarantee does not cover the valve damage and you must pay the $9.50 valve-replacement fee (plus postage).

Emphasizing the Positive Revise the following sentences to replace unflattering terms (in italic):

29. The new boss is _____ (*stubborn*) when it comes to doing things by the book.

30. When you say we've doubled our profit level, you are _____ (*wrong*).

31. Just be careful not to make any _____ (*stupid*) choices this week.

32. Jim Riley is _____ (*incompetent*) for that kind of promotion.

33. Glen monopolizes every meeting by being _____ (*a loudmouth*).

Courteous Communication Revise these sentences to make them more courteous:

34. You claim that you mailed your cheque last Thursday, but we have not received it.
35. It is not our policy to exchange sale items, especially after they have been worn.
36. You neglected to sign the enclosed contract.
37. I received your email, in which you assert that our shipment was three days late.
38. We are sorry you are dissatisfied.
39. You failed to enclose your instructions for your new will.
40. We request that you send us the bond by registered mail.

Using Bias-Free Language Rewrite each of the following sentences to eliminate bias:

41. For an Indian, Maggie certainly is outgoing.
42. He needs a wheelchair, but he doesn't let his handicap affect his job performance.
43. A pilot must have the ability to stay calm under pressure, and then he must be trained to cope with any problem that arises.
44. Councillor Renata Parsons, married and the mother of a teenager, will attend the debate.

Message-Planning Skills: Self-Assessment How good are you at planning business messages? Use the following chart to rate yourself on each of the following elements of planning an audience-centred business message. Then examine your ratings to identify where you are strongest and where you can improve.

Element of Planning	Always	Frequently	Occasionally	Never
1. I start by defining my purpose.	____	____	____	____
2. I analyze my audience before writing a message.	____	____	____	____
3. I investigate what my audience wants to know.	____	____	____	____
4. I check that my information is accurate, ethical, and pertinent.	____	____	____	____
5. I consider my audience and purpose when selecting media.	____	____	____	____
6. I adopt the "you" attitude in my messages.	____	____	____	____
7. I emphasize the positive aspects of my message.	____	____	____	____
8. I establish my credibility with audiences of strangers.	____	____	____	____
9. I express myself politely and tactfully.	____	____	____	____
10. I use bias-free language.	____	____	____	____
11. I am careful to project my company's image.	____	____	____	____

Expand Your Knowledge

Best of the Web

Instant Messaging at Work Many companies are adopting chat technologies to provide online customer support and connect workers in different departments or worksites. If you are new to instant messaging, log on to Marshall Brain's How Stuff Works website and learn all about instant messaging and see why this form of communication is so popular. Use it to collaborate on a project with teammates. Instant messaging is becoming a valuable tool in the workplace. www.howstuffworks.com/instant-messaging.htm

EXERCISES

1. What are the key advantages and disadvantages of instant messaging?
2. What is the difference between a chat room and instant messaging?
3. Is instant messaging a secure way to communicate?

Exploring the Web on Your Own

Review these chapter-related websites on your own to learn more about achieving communication success in the workplace:

1. Learn more about the writing process, English grammar, style and usage, words, and active writing at Garbl's Writing Resources Online, **www.garbl.com**.
2. Discover how email works and how to improve your email communications by following the steps at Learn the Net—Harness Email, **www.learnthenet.com/english/section/email.html**.

Caution! Email Can Bite

Gone are the days when memos were dictated, typed, revised, retyped, photocopied, and circulated by inter-office "snail" mail. Today, email messages are created, sent, received, and forwarded in the blink of an eye, and at the stroke of a key. But this quick and efficient method of communication can cause a great deal of trouble for companies.

One of the greatest features—and dangers—of email is that people tend to treat it far more informally than other forms of business communication. They think of email as casual conversation and routinely make unguarded comments. Moreover, they are led to believe that "deleting" email destroys it permanently. But that's a dangerous misunderstanding of technology.

Even after you delete an email message, it can still exist on the system's hard drive and backup storage devices at both the sender's and the recipient's location. Deleting files only signals the computer that the space required to store the message is no longer needed. The space is so marked, but the data that occupy that space continue to exist until the computer overwrites it with new data. Thus, deleted messages are recoverable—even though doing so is an involved and expensive process—and they can be used as court evidence against you and your company. Embarrassing email has played a big role in corporate battles. In the high-profile Microsoft court battle, for instance, email emerged as the star witness.

So how can companies guard against potential email embarrassment and resulting litigation? Besides restricting the use of email by employees, monitoring employees' email, developing company email policies, and reprimanding or terminating offenders, companies can train their employees to treat email as any other form of written communication. Perhaps one of the best ways to ensure that employee messages won't come back to haunt the company is to teach employees that email messages are at least as permanent as letters and memos—if not more so.

To make sure that you use email effectively, efficiently, and safely, follow these guidelines:
- Don't send large files (including large attachments) without prior notice.
- Proofread every message.
- Respect other people's electronic space by sending messages only when necessary.
- Respond to messages quickly.
- Avoid overusing the label "urgent."
- Be careful about using the "reply all" button.
- Remember that email isn't always private.

Applications for Success

Improve your email skills by visiting The Art of Writing Email (**www.net-market.com/email.htm**). Whether you're working for a company or for yourself, be sure to give your email messages as much consideration as you give more formal types of communication.

Answer the following questions:
1. Why do you think that most people treat email so casually?
2. What kinds of things do you think a company should address in an email policy?
3. Do you think that companies have the right to monitor employees' email? Please explain.

Writing Business Messages

LEARNING OBJECTIVES

After studying this chapter, you will be able to

1. Explain why good organization is important to both you and your audience
2. List the four activities required to organize business messages effectively
3. Summarize five features of an effective outline
4. Identify three factors you must consider before choosing a direct or an indirect approach
5. Explain four things you should avoid to achieve a conversational tone in business messages
6. Describe five techniques for selecting the best words when writing business messages
7. Discuss three measures you can take to help you create more effective sentences
8. List four methods of establishing transitions to make paragraphs coherent

Julie Galle is writer/producer for the official website of The Weather Channel, weather.com. Whether writing a short news item about a snowstorm in the Prairies or a lengthy report on the effects of global warming, Galle must organize and compose her messages so that members of her audience can easily understand the information, believe it, and quickly apply it to their own lives. Galle limits the scope of her articles and carefully organizes them. Although short news stories may require only the briefest notes of a few facts, Galle prepares outlines for long pieces. For non-news items and long reports, she usually writes three drafts: for style, for covering meteorological points, and for proofing grammar and punctuation.[1]

> ## TIPS FOR SUCCESS
>
> "My college professor said to take what you know, close your eyes, and pretend you're running home and opening the door and saying, 'Hey, Mom, guess what?' The next words will be your first line."
>
> —Julie Galle
> Writer/Producer
> weather.com

Organizing Your Message

Today, more than ever, writers need the ability to be clear about their intentions, focus on the key points, and form concise messages. The immediate and shorter forms of messaging used for email on BlackBerries, posts on the web, or online conversations make good writing skills critical. Misinterpreted messages waste time, lead to poor decision making, and shatter business relationships. So you can see how valuable clear writing and good organization can be.[2] Successful communicators like Julie Galle rely on good organization to make their messages meaningful.[3]

> Poor organization costs time, efficiency, and relationships.

What exactly makes a particular organization "good"? Although the definition of good organization varies from country to country, in Canada and the United States it generally means creating a linear message that proceeds point by point and delivers the main message near the beginning. Putting the main message in the opening is direct, and the direct approach is the most commonly used organizing strategy in business because of the routine nature of most messages. When the message is not straightforward or may be negative, an indirect pattern of organization can be used. However, in most routine business messages, getting to the point will be appreciated by your readers. Consider Figure 4.1.

FIGURE 4.1 Letter with Improved Organization

Model Document

Poor

General Nutrition Corporation has been doing business with ComputerTime since I was hired six years ago. Your building was smaller then, and it was located on the corner of Macdonald Avenue and 2nd N.W. Jared Mallory, our controller, was one of your first customers. I still remember the day. It was the biggest cheque I'd ever written. Of course, over the years, I've gotten used to larger purchases.

— Takes too long to get to the point

Our department now has 15 employees. As accountants, we need to have our computers working so that we can do our jobs. The CD-RW drive we bought for my assistant, Suzanne, has been a problem. We've taken it in for repairs three times in three months to the authorized service centre, and Suzanne is very careful with the machine and hasn't abused it. She does like playing interactive adventure games on lunch breaks. Anyway, it still doesn't work right, and she's tired of hauling it back and forth. We're all putting in longer hours because it is our busy season, and none of us has a lot of spare time.

— Includes irrelevant material

— Gets ideas mixed up

— Leaves out necessary information

This is the first time we've returned anything to your store, and I hope you'll agree that we deserve a better deal.

Sincerely,

Jill Saunders

Improved

GNC LiveWell.

Pointers for Good Organization
- Get to the point right away, and make the subject and purpose clear—unless your message is negative.
- Include only information that is related to the subject and purpose.
- Group ideas and present them in a logical way.
- Include all necessary information.

September 13, 2009

ComputerTime
556 Seventh Avenue
Peterborough, ON K9J M8I

Dear Customer Service Representative:

EXCHANGING A CD-RW DRIVE

States purpose clearly →

GNC bought an Olympic Systems, Model PRS-2, CD-RW drive from your store on November 15, 2008, during your pre-Christmas sale, when it was marked down to $199.95. We didn't use the unit until January because it was bought for my assistant, who unexpectedly took six weeks' leave from mid-November through December. You can imagine her frustration when she first tried using it and it didn't work, so we'd like to exchange the faulty CD-RW drive.

— Focuses on action needed

In January, we took the drive to the authorized service centre and were assured that the problem was merely a loose connection. The service representative fixed the drive, but in April we had to have it fixed again—another loose connection. For the next three months, the drive worked reasonably well, although the response time was occasionally slow. Two months ago, the drive stopped working again. Once more, the service representative blamed a loose connection and made the repair. Although the drive is working now, it isn't working very well. The response time is still slow, and the motor seems to drag sometimes.

— Explains the situation so that reader will understand the problem

— Presents ideas logically

States precisely what adjustment is being requested →

Although all the repairs have been relatively minor and have been covered by the one-year warranty, we are not satisfied with the drive. We would like to exchange it for a similar model from another manufacturer. If the new drive costs more than the old one, we will pay the difference, even though we generally look for equipment with substantial business discounts.

Includes all necessary information and no irrelevant facts →

GNC has done business with your store for six years and until now has always been satisfied with your merchandise. Please call us at (705) 327-1892 before September 25 to let us know whether we can exchange the drive.

— Motivates action from the reader in the close

Sincerely,

Jill Saunders

Jill Saunders

General Nutrition Corporation, 300 Sixth Avenue, Timmins, ON P8N 8R6
Tel: (705) 288-4600

The poorly written draft displays weak organization, but the organization is much improved in the revised version. Before you begin to write, think about what you're going to say to this particular reader, and how that reader may prefer to get the message.

What does good organization do for you? First and foremost, it saves you time. Your draft goes more quickly because you're not putting ideas in the wrong places or composing material you don't need. In addition, you can use your organizational plan to get some advance input from your audience, making sure you're on the right track before spending hours working on your draft. And, if your project is large and complex, you can even use your organizational plan to divide the writing job among co-workers.

In addition to helping you, good organization:

- **Helps your audience understand your message.** By making your main point clear at the outset, and by focusing on audience interests, your well-organized message will satisfy your audience's need for information.
- **Helps your audience accept your message.** Even when your message is logical, you need to select and organize your points in a diplomatic way. Softening refusals and leaving a good impression enhance credibility and add authority to your messages.
- **Saves your audience time.** Audience members receive only the information they need, and because that information is relevant, brief, and logically placed, your audience can follow your thought pattern without a struggle.

When writing messages at weather.com, Julie Galle achieves good organization by defining the main idea, limiting the scope, grouping supporting points, and establishing their sequence by selecting either a direct or an indirect approach.

Define the Main Idea

In addition to having a general purpose and a specific purpose, all business messages gain focus when they begin with a **main idea** or general interest statement that sums up the message. The rest of your document supports, explains, or demonstrates this point. Your main idea is not the same as your topic. The broad subject of your message is the topic, and your main idea makes a statement about that topic. The topic is "*what*" you are writing about. The main idea is the "*so what*" about the topic.

In longer documents and presentations, you'll need to unify a mass of material, so you'll need to define a main idea that encompasses or summarizes all the individual points you want to make. For tough assignments like these, you may want to take special measures to define your main idea.

Limit the Scope

Determine the scope of your message (its length and detail) by analyzing your audience's needs. Decide how much to write by predicting what questions the audience would have about your main idea.

Regardless of how long the message will be, focus on three or four major points—five at the very most. According to communication researchers, that's all your audience will remember.[4] Instead of introducing additional points, you can more fully develop complex issues by supporting your points with a variety of evidence.

Group Your Points in an Outline

Once you have narrowed the scope of your message, you must provide supporting details in the most logical and effective way. Constructing an outline of your message is a great way to visualize how your major points and supporting details will fit together. Whether you use the outlining features provided with word-processing software or simply jot

Most disorganized communication suffers from problems with clarity, relevance, grouping, and completeness.

Good organization saves time, strengthens relationships, and improves efficiency.

To organize a message
- Define your main idea
- Limit the scope
- Group your points
- Choose the direct or indirect approach

The topic is the broad subject; the main idea makes a statement about the topic.

Focus on three or four major points (not more than five), regardless of message length.

FIGURE 4.2 Common Outline Forms

ALPHANUMERIC OUTLINE

I. First Major Point
  A. First subpoint
  B. Second subpoint
    1. Evidence
    2. Evidence
II. Second Major Point
  A. First subpoint
    1. Evidence
    2. Evidence
  B. Second subpoint

DECIMAL OUTLINE

I.0 First Major Point
  1.1 First subpoint
  1.2 Second subpoint
    1.2.1 Evidence
    1.2.2 Evidence
2.0 Second Major Point
  2.1 First subpoint
    2.1.1 Evidence
    2.1.2 Evidence
  2.2 Second subpoint

An outline or a schematic diagram will help you visualize the relationship among parts of a message.

down three or four points on the back of an envelope, your outline will keep you on track and help you cover the important information. You're no doubt familiar with the basic outline format (see Figure 4.2).

Remember that outlines
- Use numbers (or letters and numbers) to identify each point
- Indent points to show which ideas are of equal status
- Divide a topic into at least two parts
- Ensure that each group of ideas is separate and distinct

The main idea states the action you want your audience to take and why.

Figure 12.3 (in Chapter 12) shows an outline of a 30-minute presentation. When outlining your message, begin with a purpose statement and your main idea. To help you establish the goals and general strategy of your message, the main idea summarizes two things: (1) what you want audience members to do or think and (2) why they should do so. Everything in your message must either support the main idea or explain its implications.

Major supporting points clarify your main idea.

Next, you state the major supporting points. Try to identify between three and five major points that support and clarify your message in more concrete terms. If you come up with more, go back and look for opportunities to combine some of your ideas.

Finally, illustrate your major supporting points with evidence—facts and examples that help your audience understand and remember your message. In a long, complex message, you may need to carry the outline down several levels; in short, informal business documents, numbers are rarely used. Just remember that every level is a step along the chain from the abstract to the concrete, from the general to the specific. The lowest level contains the individual facts and figures that make up your evidence.

Choose Between the Direct and the Indirect Approach

Once you've defined your ideas and outlined your message, choose the basic approach you'll use to present your points. When addressing a Canadian or U.S. audience with few cultural differences, you have two options:
- **Direct approach (deductive).** The main idea comes first (a recommendation, conclusion, or request), followed by the evidence. Use this approach when your audience will be neutral about your message or pleased to hear from you.

 **Model** Document

- **Indirect approach (inductive).** The evidence comes first, and the main idea comes later. Use this approach when your audience may be displeased about or may resist what you have to say.

Before you can choose one of these approaches, you must have a good idea of how your audience is likely to react to your purpose and message. Consider whether the culture of the audience has a preference for an indirect approach. The direct approach is generally fine when audience members will be receptive—if they are eager, interested, pleased, or even neutral. But you may have better results with the indirect approach if audience members are likely to resist your message—if they are displeased, uninterested, or unwilling (see Figure 4.3).

Bear in mind, however, that each message is unique. No simple formula will solve all your communication problems. Sometimes you'll want to get directly to the point, even if your message is unpleasant. Also, the direct approach may be better for long messages, regardless of your audience's attitude, because delaying the main idea could cause confusion and frustration. So before choosing a direct or an indirect approach, consider all three of the following factors:

- **Audience reaction:** Positive, neutral, or negative
- **Message length:** Short memos and letters (discussed in Chapter 6) or long reports, proposals, and presentations (discussed in Chapters 10, 11, and 12)
- **Message type:** (1) routine, good-news, and goodwill messages (Chapter 7); (2) bad-news messages (Chapter 8); or (3) persuasive messages (Chapter 9)

Just remember, your first priority is to make your message clear. Your other main priority is to consider how your reader will want to hear it. In the following brief discussions, note how the opening, body, and close all play an important role in getting your message across, regardless of message type.

> Use direct order if the audience's reaction is likely to be positive and indirect order if it is likely to be negative.

> Audience reaction can range from eager to unwilling.

> Choice of approach depends on audience reaction, message length, and message type.

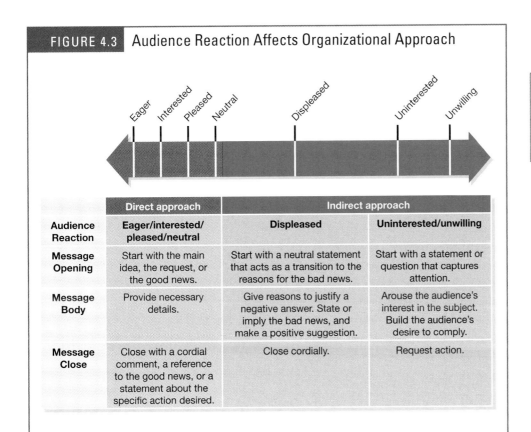

FIGURE 4.3 Audience Reaction Affects Organizational Approach

	Direct approach	Indirect approach	
Audience Reaction	Eager/interested/ pleased/neutral	Displeased	Uninterested/unwilling
Message Opening	Start with the main idea, the request, or the good news.	Start with a neutral statement that acts as a transition to the reasons for the bad news.	Start with a statement or question that captures attention.
Message Body	Provide necessary details.	Give reasons to justify a negative answer. State or imply the bad news, and make a positive suggestion.	Arouse the audience's interest in the subject. Build the audience's desire to comply.
Message Close	Close with a cordial comment, a reference to the good news, or a statement about the specific action desired.	Close cordially.	Request action.

Composing Your Message

Once you've completed the planning process and organized your message, you're ready to begin composing your first draft. If your schedule permits, put aside your outline for a day or two. Then review it with a fresh eye, looking for opportunities to improve the flow of ideas. Once you begin writing, you may discover as you go along that you can improve on your outline. Feel free to rearrange, delete, and add ideas, as long as you don't lose sight of your purpose.

As you compose your first draft, try to let your creativity flow. Don't try to draft and edit at the same time or worry about getting everything perfect. Just put down your ideas as quickly as you can. You'll have time to revise and refine the material later. Once you have all your thoughts and ideas jotted down, begin shaping your message. Start by paying attention to your style and tone. Try to select words that match the tone you want to achieve. Next, create effective sentences and develop coherent paragraphs. The following sections discuss each of these elements.

> Composition is the process of drafting your message; polishing it is a later step.

Control Your Style and Tone

Style is the way you use words to achieve a certain tone, or overall impression. You can vary your style—your sentence structure and vocabulary—to sound forceful or objective, personal or formal, colourful or dry. The right choice depends on the nature of your message and your relationship with your audience.

> When composing your message, you can vary the style to create a tone that suits the occasion.

USE A CONVERSATIONAL TONE Most business messages aim for a conversational tone, using plain language that sounds businesslike without being stuffy, stiff, wordy, or full of jargon. To achieve a conversational tone in your messages, try to avoid obsolete and pompous language, intimacy, humour, and preaching or bragging. Table 4.1 illustrates that conversational tone ranges along a continuum from formal to informal.

Avoid Obsolete Language Business language used to be much more formal than it is today, and some out-of-date phrases still remain. You can avoid using such language if you ask yourself, "Would I say this if I were talking with someone face to face?"

> To achieve a warm but businesslike tone
> - Don't use obsolete language
> - Don't be too familiar
> - Use humour only with great care
> - Don't preach or brag

Obsolete	Up to Date
in due course	today, tomorrow (or a specific time)
permit me to say that	(omit—permission is not necessary)
we are in receipt of	we have received
pursuant to	(omit)
In closing, I'd like to say	(omit)
we wish to inform you	(omit—just say it)
attached please find	enclosed is
please be advised that	(omit)

Avoid False Familiarity Don't mention anything about anyone's personal life unless you know the individual very well. Avoid phrases such as "just between you and me" and "as you and I are well aware." Be careful about sounding too folksy or chatty; such a familiar tone may be seen as an attempt to seem like an old friend when, in fact, you're not.

Avoid Humour Using humour can backfire, especially if you don't know your audience very well. What seems humorous to you may be deadly serious to others. Plus, what's funny today may not be in a week or a month. Moreover, when you're communicating

TABLE 4.1	Formal, Conversational, and Informal Tones

FORMAL TONE	CONVERSATIONAL TONE	INFORMAL TONE
Reserved for the Most Formal Occasions	Preferred for Most Business Communication	Reserved for Communication with Friends and Close Associates
Dear Ms. Navarro:	Dear Ms. Navarro:	Hi Gabriella:
We are enclosing the information that was requested during our telephone communication of May 14. As was mentioned at that time, Metro Clinic has significantly more doctors of exceptional quality than any other health facility in the province.	Here's the information you requested during our telephone conversation on Friday. As I mentioned, Metro Clinic has the best doctors and more of them than any other facility in the province.	Just sending along the information you asked for. As I said on Friday, Metro Clinic has more and better doctors than any other facility in the province.
As you were also informed, our organization has quite an impressive network of doctors and other health-care professionals with offices located throughout the province. In the event that you should need a specialist, our professionals will be able to make an appropriate recommendation.	In addition, we have a vast network of doctors and other health professionals with offices throughout the province. If you need a specialist, they can refer you to the right one.	We also have a large group of doctors and other health professionals with offices close to you at work or at home. Need a specialist? They'll refer you to the right one.
You would be entitled to use the numerous programs that we provide to assist you and your family in achieving the highest level of health possible. We are especially proud of our health hotline, which allows you to speak with a registered nurse 24 hours a day, seven days a week.	You and your family can also participate in numerous health programs, such as smoking-cessation classes, health fairs, nutritional guidance, and a 24-hour hotline whose registered nurse can answer your questions seven days a week.	You and your family can get and stay healthy, thanks to our health fairs and numerous classes to improve your overall fitness. We even have a health hotline where you can get answers to your health questions all day, every day.
If you have questions or would like additional information, you may certainly contact me during regular business hours.	If you would like more information, please call anytime between 9:00 and 5:00, Monday through Friday.	Just give me a ring if you want to know more (any time from 9:00 to 5:00).
Most sincerely yours,	Sincerely,	Take care,
Samuel G. Berenz	Samuel G. Berenz	Sam

across cultures, chances are slim that your audience will appreciate your humour or even realize that you're trying to be funny.[5]

Use Plain English

Plain English is a way of writing and arranging technical materials so that your audience can understand your meaning. Because it's close to the way people normally speak, plain English is easily understood by people with only a grade eight or nine education. If you've ever tried to make sense of an overwritten or murky passage in a legal document or credit agreement, you can understand why governments and corporations endorse the plain-English movement.[6]

> Plain English is close to spoken English and can be easily understood.

Avoid Overwriting

The applicability of the general information and administrative procedures set forth below accordingly will vary depending on the investor and the record-keeping system established for a shareholder's investment in the Fund. Participants in RRSPs and other plans should first consult with the appropriate persons at their employer or refer to the plan materials before following any of the procedures below.

Use Simple, Clear Language

If you are investing through a large retirement plan or other special program, follow the instructions in your program material.

> Plain English is also helpful for intercultural communication.

Plain English lacks the precision necessary for scientific research, intense feeling, and personal insight, but it is invaluable in general business messages. Even though it's intended for audiences who speak English as their primary language, plain English can also help you simplify the messages you prepare for audiences who speak English only as a second or even third language. For example, by choosing words that have only one interpretation, you will surely communicate more clearly with your intercultural audience.[7]

Select the Best Words

To compose effective messages, you must choose your words carefully.[8] Good business writing is learned by imitation and practice. As you read business journals, newspapers, and even novels, make a note of the words you think are effective and keep them in a file. Then look through them before you draft your next letter or report. Try using some of these words in your document. You may be surprised at how they can strengthen your writing.

> Correctness is the first consideration when choosing words.

First, pay close attention to correctness. Using words correctly is important. If you make grammatical or usage errors, you lose credibility with your audience, and grammatical errors are distracting. If you have doubts about what is correct, look up the answer. You can also consult any number of special reference books and resources available in libraries, in bookstores, and on the internet. Most authorities agree on the basic conventions.

> Effectiveness is the second consideration when choosing words.

Just as important as selecting the correct word is selecting the most suitable word for the job at hand. Word effectiveness is generally more difficult to achieve than correctness, particularly in written communication. Good writers work at their craft to produce messages that are clear, concise, and accurate.

BLEND ABSTRACT AND CONCRETE WORDS An **abstract word** expresses a concept, quality, or characteristic. Abstractions are usually broad, encompassing a category of ideas. They are often intellectual, academic, or philosophical. *Love, honour, progress, tradition,* and *beauty* are abstractions.

A **concrete word** stands for something you can touch or see. Concrete terms are anchored in the tangible, material world. *Chair, table, horse, rose, kick, kiss, red, green,* and *two* are concrete words; they are direct, clear, and exact.

> In business communication, use concrete, specific terms whenever possible; use abstractions only when necessary.

Abstractions permit us to rise above the common and tangible. They allow us to refer to concepts such as *morale, productivity, profits, quality, motivation,* and *guarantees.* Even though they're indispensable, abstractions can be troublesome. They tend to be fuzzy and subject to many interpretations. They also tend to be boring. It isn't always easy to get

TABLE 4.2	Selecting the Most Effective Words

AVOID WEAK PHRASES	USE STRONG TERMS
Wealthy business person	Tycoon
Business prosperity	Boom
Hard times	Slump

AVOID UNFAMILIAR WORDS	USE FAMILIAR WORDS
Ascertain	Find out, learn
Consummate	Close, bring about
Peruse	Read, study
Circumvent	Avoid
Increment	Growth, increase
Unequivocal	Certain

AVOID CLICHÉS	USE PLAIN LANGUAGE OR OMIT
Scrape the bottom of the barrel	Strain shrinking resources
An uphill battle	A challenge
Writing on the wall	Prediction
Call the shots	Be in charge
Feel free to	(omit)
Cost an arm and a leg	Expensive
A new ballgame	Fresh start
Worst nightmare	Strong competitor; disaster
Fall through the cracks	Be overlooked
Do not hesitate to call	Please call
Thank you in advance for your cooperation	We would appreciate your cooperation

> For effective messages, choose familiar words.

> To make a good impression, avoid clichés.

excited about ideas, especially if they're unrelated to concrete experience. The best way to minimize such problems is to blend abstract terms with concrete ones, the general with the specific. State the concept, then pin it down with details expressed in more concrete terms. Instead of referring to a *sizable loss*, talk about a *loss of $32 million*. Save the abstractions for ideas that cannot be expressed any other way.

CHOOSE STRONG WORDS Choose words that express your thoughts most clearly, specifically, and dynamically. Nouns and verbs are the most concrete, so use them as much as you can. Adjectives and adverbs have obvious roles, but use them sparingly—they often evoke subjective judgments. Verbs are especially powerful because they tell what's happening in the sentence, so make them dynamic and specific; for example, replace *rise* or *fall* with *soar* or *plummet*. However, always consider your audience when deciding word choice. For example, if you are reporting negative financial information to a client, you would not choose words such as *plummet*.

> Good business communicators choose strong words.

AVOID JARGON Handle technical or professional terms with care. As Julie Galle puts it, meteorological terminology and jargon can add precision and authority to a weather message, but many people don't understand the jargon. When deciding whether to use technical jargon, let your audience's knowledge guide you. For example, when addressing a group of engineers or scientists, it's probably fine to refer to *meteorological effects on microwave propagation*; otherwise, refer to the *effects of weather on radio waves*.

> Use jargon only if your readers know the term.

Create Effective Sentences

In English, words don't make much sense until they're combined in a sentence to express a complete thought. Thus the words *Jill*, *receptionist*, *the*, *smiles*, and *at* can be organized

In English, word order is important when constructing sentences.

into "Jill smiles at the receptionist." Now that you've constructed the sentence, you can begin exploring the possibilities for improvement, looking at how well each word performs its particular function. Nouns and noun equivalents are the topics (or subjects) that you're communicating about. Verbs and related words (or predicates) make statements about those subjects. In a complicated sentence, adjectives and adverbs modify the nouns and verbs, and various connectors hold the words together. You can make your sentences more effective by using all four types of sentences, emphasizing key thoughts through sentence style, and selecting active or passive voice.

USE ALL FOUR TYPES OF SENTENCES Sentences come in four basic varieties: simple, compound, complex, and compound-complex. A **simple sentence** has one main clause (a single subject and a single predicate), although it may be expanded by nouns and pronouns serving as objects of the action and by modifying phrases. Here's a typical example (with the subject underlined once and the predicate verb underlined twice):

You can choose from four types of sentences:
• Simple
• Compound
• Complex
• Compound-complex

Profits have increased in the past year.

A compound sentence has two main clauses that express two or more independent but related thoughts of equal importance, usually joined by *and, but,* or *or.* In effect, a compound sentence is a merger of two or more simple sentences (independent clauses) that are related. For example:

Wage rates have declined by 5 percent, and employee turnover has been high.

The independent clauses in a compound sentence are always separated by a comma or by a semicolon (in which case the conjunction—*and, but, or*—is dropped).

A **complex sentence** expresses one main thought (the independent clause) and one or more subordinate thoughts (dependent clauses) related to it, often separated by a comma. The subordinate thought, which comes first in the following sentence, could not stand alone:

Although you may question Gerald's conclusions, you must admit that his research is thorough.

A compound-complex sentence has two main clauses, at least one of which contains a subordinate clause:

Profits have increased in the past year, and although you may question Gerald's conclusions, you must admit that his research is thorough.

Vary your style by balancing the four types of sentences.

To make your writing as effective as possible, balance all four sentence types. If you use too many simple sentences, you won't be able to properly express the relationships among your ideas. If you use too many long, compound sentences, your writing will sound monotonous. On the other hand, an uninterrupted series of complex or compound-complex sentences is hard to follow.

EMPHASIZE KEY THOUGHTS WITH SENTENCE STYLE Sentence style varies from culture to culture. In English, try to make your sentences grammatically correct, efficient, readable, interesting, and appropriate for your audience. For most business audiences, clarity and efficiency take precedence over literary style, so strive for straightforward simplicity. In every message, some ideas are more important than others. You can emphasize these key ideas through your sentence style.

Reflect Relationships with Sentence Type One obvious technique for emphasizing key ideas is to choose the type of sentence to match the relationship of the ideas you want to express. If you have two ideas of equal importance, express them as two simple sentences or as one compound sentence. However, if one of the ideas is less important than the other, place it in a dependent clause to form a complex sentence. By making the first thought subordinate to the second, you establish a cause-and-effect relationship:

> Because the chemical products division is the strongest in the company, its management techniques should be adopted by the other divisions.

Allocate More Space to the Important Ideas Another way to emphasize key ideas is to give important points the most space. When you want to call attention to a thought, use extra words to describe it. Consider this sentence:

> The chairperson of the board called for a vote of the shareholders.

To emphasize the importance of the chairperson, you might describe her more fully:

> Having considerable experience in corporate takeover battles, the chairperson of the board called for a vote of the shareholders.

You can increase the emphasis even more by adding a separate, short sentence to augment the first:

> The chairperson of the board called for a vote of the shareholders. She has considerable experience in corporate takeover battles.

Make Important Ideas the Subject You can also call attention to a thought by making it the subject of the sentence. In the following example, the emphasis is on the person:

> *I* can write letters much more quickly using a computer.

However, by changing the subject, the computer takes centre stage:

> The *computer* enables me to write letters much more quickly.

Place Important Ideas First or Last Another way to emphasize an idea is to place it at either the beginning or the end of a sentence:

> **Less Emphatic:** We are cutting the *price* to stimulate demand.

> **More Emphatic:** To stimulate demand, we are cutting the *price*.

If you want to downplay the idea, put it in the middle of the sentence.

> **Less Emphatic:** Mexico, *which has lower wage rates,* was selected as the production point for the electronic parts.

> **More Emphatic:** *Wage rates are lower in Mexico,* so the electronic parts are manufactured there.

> **Most Emphatic:** The electronic parts are manufactured in Mexico, *which has lower wage rates than Canada.*

Techniques like these give you a great deal of control over the way your audience interprets what you have to say.

CHOOSE ACTIVE OR PASSIVE VOICE Your choice of active or passive voice also affects the tone of your message. You're using active voice when the grammatical subject performs the action and the object (the "acted upon") follows the verb, as in: "John rented the office." You're using passive voice when the grammatical subject receives the action: "The office was rented by John." Here, the passive voice combines the helping verb *to be* with the past tense of the verb *rent*.

Emphasize important ideas by
- Using sentence type to reflect the relationship between ideas
- Giving important ideas more space
- Making the important idea the subject of the sentence
- Putting important ideas at the beginning or at the end of the sentence

---

Emphasize key ideas.

Beginnings and endings are emphatic positions in sentences.

USE ACTIVE VOICE IN GENERAL Active sentences generally sound less formal and usually make it easier for the reader to figure out who performed the action. Passive voice de-emphasizes the actor and implies action done by something or someone.

Passive	**Active**
The new procedure is thought by the president to be superior.	The president thinks the new procedure is superior.
Taxes were raised by Council.	The Council raised the taxes.
It is necessary that the report be finished by Friday.	Finish the report by Friday.

> Active sentences are stronger than passive ones.

Using the active voice produces shorter, stronger sentences and makes your writing more vigorous, concise, and generally easier to understand.[9] Using the passive voice, while not wrong grammatically, is cumbersome, wordy, and often unnecessarily vague, and it can make sentences longer.

> Use passive sentences to soften bad news, to put yourself in the background, or to create an impersonal tone.

USE PASSIVE VOICE FOR DIPLOMACY OR OBJECTIVITY Using the passive voice makes sense in some situations because it can help you focus on your audience and demonstrate the "you" attitude. Use the passive when you want to
- Be diplomatic about pointing out a problem or error of some kind (the passive version seems less like an accusation)
- Point out what's being done without taking or attributing either the credit or the blame (the passive version leaves the actor completely out of the sentence)
- Avoid personal pronouns in order to create an objective tone (the passive version may be used in a formal report, for example)

Active Voice Focuses on the Actor	**Passive Voice Can Leave out the Actor**
You lost the shipment.	The shipment was lost.
I am analyzing the production line to determine the problem.	The production line is being analyzed to determine the problem.
We have established criteria to evaluate capital expenditures.	Criteria have been established to evaluate capital expenditures.

Develop Coherent Paragraphs

A *paragraph* is a cluster of sentences all related to the same general topic. It is a unit of thought, separated from other units by skipping a line or indenting the first line. A series of paragraphs makes up an entire composition. Each paragraph is an important part of the whole, a key link in the train of thought. As you compose your message, think about the paragraphs and their relationship to one another.

> A paragraph contains sentences that pertain to a single thought.

ADAPT PARAGRAPH LENGTH Paragraphs vary widely in length and form. You can communicate effectively in one short paragraph or in pages of lengthy paragraphs, depending on your purpose, your audience, and your message. The typical paragraph contains three basic elements: a topic sentence, related sentences that develop the topic, and transitional words and phrases.

USE DEVELOPMENT TECHNIQUES Paragraphs can be developed in many ways. Six of the most common techniques are illustration, comparison or contrast, cause and effect, classification, problem and solution, and chronology. Your choice of technique depends on your subject, your intended audience, and your purpose:

> Six ways to develop paragraphs:
> - Illustration
> - Comparison or contrast
> - Cause and effect
> - Classification
> - Problem and solution
> - Chronology

- **Illustration:** Giving examples that demonstrate the general idea
- **Comparison or contrast:** Using similarities or differences to develop the topic

- **Cause and effect:** Focusing on the reasons for something
- **Classification:** Showing how a general idea is broken into specific categories
- **Problem and solution:** Presenting a problem and then discussing the solution
- **Chronology:** Following the sequence of occurrence.

Table 4.3 presents samples of each method; however, in practice, you'll often combine two or more methods of development in a single paragraph. To add interest, you might begin by using illustration, shift to comparison or contrast, and then shift to problem and solution. However, before settling for the first approach that comes to mind, consider the alternatives. Think through various methods before committing yourself. If you fall into the easy habit of repeating the same old paragraph pattern time after time, your writing will be boring.

ACHIEVE UNITY AND COHERENCE Every properly constructed paragraph is *unified*—it deals with a single topic. The sentence that introduces this topic is called the **topic sentence**. In business, the topic sentence is generally explicit, rather than implied, and is often the first sentence in the paragraph. The topic sentence gives readers a summary of the general idea that will be covered in the rest of the paragraph.

The sentences that explain the topic sentence round out the paragraph. These related sentences must all have a bearing on the general subject and must provide enough specific details to make the topic clear. These developmental sentences are all more specific than the topic sentence. Each one provides another piece of evidence to demonstrate the general truth of the main thought. Also, each sentence is clearly related to the general idea being developed; the relation between the sentences and the idea is what gives the

> The topic sentence
> - Reveals the subject of the paragraph
> - Indicates how the subject will be developed

TABLE 4.3	Methods of Paragraph Development

TECHNIQUE	EXAMPLE
Illustration	Some of our most popular products are available through local distributors. For example, Sysco Foods; Westons carries our frozen soups and entrees. The Dandipak carries our complete line of seasonings, as well as the frozen soups. Island Farms, also a major distributor, now carries our new line of frozen desserts.
Comparison or Contrast	In previous years, when the company was small, the recruiting function could be handled informally. The need for new employees was limited, and each manager could comfortably screen and hire her or his own staff. Today, however, Norco Cycles must undertake a major recruiting effort. Our successful bid on the Costco contract means that we will be doubling our labour force over the next six months. To hire that many people without disrupting our ongoing activities, we will create a separate recruiting group within the human resources department.
Cause and Effect	The heavy-duty fabric of your Wanderer tent probably broke down for one of two reasons: (1) a sharp object punctured the fabric, and without reinforcement, the hole was enlarged by the stress of erecting the tent daily for a week, or (2) the fibres gradually rotted because the tent was folded and stored while still wet.
Classification	Successful candidates for our supervisor trainee program generally come from one of several groups. The largest group, by far, consists of recent graduates of accredited data-processing programs. The next largest group comes from within our own company, as we try to promote promising clerical workers to positions of greater responsibility. Finally, we do occasionally accept candidates with outstanding supervisory experience in related industries.
Problem and Solution	Selling handmade toys by mail is a challenge because consumers are accustomed to buying heavily advertised toys from major chains. However, if we develop an appealing online catalogue, we can compete on the basis of product novelty and quality. In addition, we can provide craftsmanship at a competitive price: a rocking horse of birch, with a hand-knit tail and mane; a music box with the child's name painted on the top; a real First Nations teepee, made by Blackfoot artisans.

Paragraphs are developed through a series of related sentences that provide details about the topic sentence.

Because each paragraph covers a single idea, use transitional words and phrases to show readers how paragraphs relate to each other.

paragraph its unity. A paragraph is well developed when it contains enough information to make the topic sentence convincing and interesting.

In addition to being unified and well developed, effective paragraphs are *coherent;* that is, they are arranged in a logical order so that the audience can understand the train of thought. When you complete a paragraph, your readers automatically assume that you've finished with a particular idea. You achieve coherence by using transitions to show the relationship between paragraphs and among sentences within paragraphs. **Transitions** are words or phrases that tie ideas together and show how one thought is related to another. They help readers understand the connections you're trying to make. You can establish transitions in various ways:

* **Use connecting words:** *and, but, or, nevertheless, however, in addition,* and so on.
* **Use key term repeats.** Echo a word or phrase from a previous paragraph or sentence: "A system should be established for monitoring inventory levels. *This system* will provide . . ."
* **Use a pronoun that refers to a noun used previously:** "Ms. Arthur is the leading candidate for the president's position. *She* has excellent qualifications."
* **Use words that are frequently paired:** "The machine has a *minimum* output of . . . Its *maximum* output is . . ."

Here is a list of transitions frequently used to move readers smoothly between sentences and paragraphs:

Additional detail:	moreover, furthermore, in addition, besides, first, second, third, finally
Causal relationship:	therefore, because, accordingly, thus, consequently, hence, as a result, so
Comparison:	similarly, here again, likewise, in comparison, still
Contrast:	yet, conversely, whereas, nevertheless, on the other hand, however, but, nonetheless
Condition:	although, if
Illustration:	for example, in particular, in this case, for instance
Time sequence:	formerly, after, when, meanwhile, sometimes
Intensification:	indeed, in fact, in any event
Summary:	in brief, in short, to sum up
Repetition:	that is, in other words, as I mentioned earlier

Although transitional words and phrases are useful, they're not sufficient in themselves to overcome poor organization. Your goal is first to put your ideas in a strong framework and then to use transitions to link them even more strongly.

You can use transitions inside paragraphs, between paragraphs, and between major sections.

Consider using a transitional device whenever it might help the reader understand your ideas and follow you from point to point. You can use transitions inside paragraphs to tie related points together and between paragraphs to ease the shift from one distinct thought to another. In longer reports, transitions that link major sections or chapters are often complete paragraphs that summarize the ideas presented in the section just ending and serve as mini-introductions to the information that will be covered in the next section. Here's an example:

> Given the nature of this product, the alternatives are limited. As the previous section indicates, we can stop making it altogether, improve it, or continue with the current model. Each of these alternatives has advantages and disadvantages, which are discussed in the following section.

ON THE JOB

If you use direct, concise style, you will be saving other people's time.

Form your message in as few words as possible but then check the tone—if you are too direct you will sound abrupt and bossy. You may need to add a few words to show consideration for the reader's feelings. Using concise, clear, and courteous style helps you build relationships at work.

Reviewing Key Points

In this chapter you learned how to
- Organize your message according to your audience's needs.
- Assess whether reaction to your idea will be positive, neutral, or negative so that you could choose an appropriate approach. If reaction is neutral, positive, or only mildly negative, choose a direct approach so that you can put the main idea near the beginning of the document. Use an indirect approach if resistance to your idea is strong.
- Compose by writing down your ideas and then revising to vary sentences and to choose effective words for a concise, clear, and friendly style and tone.
- Use plain English, familiar words, and active voice.
- Think about what ideas need emphasis and make those ideas prominent by leaving space around them or by making them the subjects of sentences.
- Ensure that your paragraphs are developed with a main idea and supporting details and examples.
- Build unity and coherence through use of transitional phrases and connecting words.

mybuscommlab   Go to MyBusCommLab at www.pearson.ca/mybuscommlab for online exercises.

Practise Your Grammar

 Exercises

Effective business communication starts with strong grammar skills. To improve your grammar skills, go to MyBusCommLab or Grammar-on-the-Go, where you'll find exercises and diagnostic tests to help you produce clear, effective communication.

Test Your Knowledge

Exercises

1. How does planning help you organize more effective messages?
2. How does good organization help your audience?
3. What four steps help you organize messages more effectively?
4. What three elements do you consider when choosing between a direct and an indirect approach?
5. How do you achieve a conversational tone?
6. How does an abstract word differ from a concrete word?
7. In what three situations should you use passive voice?
8. How can you use sentence style to emphasize key thoughts?
9. What is the purpose of the topic sentence in a paragraph?
10. What functions do transitions serve?

Apply Your Knowledge

1. Does good organization help you or your audience more? Please explain.
2. Some people feel that preparing an outline for a business message is a waste of time. Do you agree or disagree? Please explain.
3. Would you use a direct or an indirect approach to ask employees to work overtime to meet an important deadline? Please explain.
4. Which approach would you use to let your boss know that you'll be out half a day this week to attend a relative's funeral—direct or indirect? Why?
5. **Ethical Choices** Do you think that using an indirect approach to overcome audience resistance is manipulative? Discuss the ethical issues in your answer.

Running Cases

Video

CASE 1: Noreen

Now that the letter has gone to the service station owners/operators, informing them of the upcoming promotion (see the case in Chapter 3), Noreen's manager at Petro-Go has asked her to send an informative, promotional letter to all existing Canadian Go Points customers.

The promotion details are:

1. Canadian cardholders will now receive double points when they purchase more than $30 of gasoline in one visit (regular points up to $30 then double points over $30).
2. There is a new reward redemption available— Petro-Go gift certificates ($20 certificate for a 250-point redemption).
3. A free gift of a 6-litre container of windshield washer fluid is available when accumulated points reach each 1000-point interval (1000, 2000, 3000).

Of course, the letter must be approved by the manager before it will be distributed.

QUESTIONS

a. Is the direct or indirect approach best for this message? Why?
b. How will Noreen use the "you" attitude in the letter?
c. Why is it so important that Noreen's letter use bias-free language?
d. How will this letter differ in tone from the one sent to the employees?
e. What considerations will Noreen think of when developing the paragraphs for the letter?

YOUR TASK

Create the letter. Apply the skills you have learned in Chapters 3 and 4. (Remember to create a company logo.) Use Appendix A to select a letter format.

Now, consider how Noreen would put this information into a webpage. Write a list of some factors she would have to consider when adding this information to the existing company website.

CASE 2: Kwong

Kwong is working on producing a promotional letter for Accountants For All that will entice past customers to return this upcoming tax season. He has checked the database and discovered addresses and email accounts for past customers.

He informs his manager of his plan to email all past customers with the promotional news as well as deliver

the letter through postal mail. The main promotional points Kwong wishes to convey are:

1. 20 percent discount for repeat customers
2. 10 percent discount for families of four or more, students, or seniors; and only one promotional discount may be applied

QUESTIONS

a. How should Kwong begin the letter?

b. How will Kwong emphasize the promotional discounts?

c. How will he make the message easier to read?

d. What should the subject line read in the email message?

e. Why send both email and postal mail?

YOUR TASK

Create the letter. Apply the skills you have learned in Chapters 3 and 4. (Remember to create a company logo.) Once the letter is complete, create the email message. Apply the skills you have learned in Chapters 3 and 4 and use Appendix A to select an appropriate letter format.

Practise Your Knowledge

EXERCISES FOR PERFECTING YOUR WRITING

Choosing the Approach Indicate whether the direct or the indirect approach would be best in each of the following situations. Write *direct* or *indirect* in the space provided.

1. _____ A letter asking when next year's automobiles will be put on sale locally
2. _____ A letter from a recent college graduate requesting a letter of recommendation from a former instructor
3. _____ A letter turning down a job applicant
4. _____ An announcement that because of high heating costs, the plant temperature will be held at 18°C during winter.
5. _____ A final request to settle a delinquent debt

Drafting Persuasive Messages If you were trying to persuade people to take the following actions, how would you organize your argument? Write *direct* or *indirect* in the space provided.

6. _____ You want your boss to approve your plan for hiring two new people.
7. _____ You want to be hired for a job.
8. _____ You want to be granted a business loan.
9. _____ You want to collect a small amount from a regular customer whose account is slightly past due.
10. _____ You want to collect a large amount from a customer whose account is seriously past due.

Selecting Specific and Precise Words In the following sentences, replace vague phrases (underlined or in italics) with concrete phrases. Make up any details you might need.

11. We will be opening our new facility sometime this spring.
12. You can now purchase our new Leaf-Away yard and lawn blower at a substantial savings.
13. After the reception, we were surprised that such a large number attended.
14. The new production line has been operating with increased efficiency on every run.
15. Over the holiday, we hired a crew to expand the work area.
16. The two reporters _____ (*ran after*) every lead enthusiastically.
17. Even large fashion houses have to match staff size to the normal _____ (*seasonal ups and downs*).
18. The _____ (*bright*) colours in that ad are keeping customers from seeing what we have to sell.
19. Health costs _____ (*suddenly rise*) when management forgets to emphasize safety issues.
20. Once we solved the zoning issue, new business construction _____ (*moved forward*), and the district has been flourishing ever since.

Avoiding Clichés Rewrite these sentences to replace the clichés with fresh, personal expressions:

21. Being a jack-of-all-trades, Dave worked well in his new selling job.
22. Moving Leslie into the accounting department, where she was literally a fish out of water, was like putting a square peg into a round hole, if you get my drift.
23. I knew she was at death's door, but I thought the doctor would pull her through.
24. Movies aren't really my cup of tea; as far as I am concerned, they can't hold a candle to a good book.
25. It's a dog-eat-dog world out there in the rat race of the asphalt jungle.

Choosing Simple and Familiar Words In the following sentences, replace long words (in italics) with short, simple ones:

26. Management _____ (*inaugurated*) the recycling policy six months ago.
27. I'll miss working with you when my internship _____ (*terminates*).
28. You can convey the same meaning without _____ (*utilizing*) the same words.
29. No one _____ (*anticipated*) that Mr. Hughes would retire so soon.
30. When Julian asked for my _____ (*assistance*), I grabbed the chance to learn more about accounting.
31. You'll never be promoted unless you _____ (*endeavour*) to be more patient.
32. I have to wait until payday to _____ (*ascertain*) whether or not I got the raise.
33. On your way back from lunch, don't forget to _____ (*procure*) more photocopy paper.
34. We'll send you an invoice when we _____ (*consummate*) the job.
35. Please _____ (*advise*) me when you're ready to begin the test.
36. John will send you a copy, once he's inserted all the _____ (*alterations*) you've requested.
37. The contract was _____ (*forwarded*) to you for your signature on July 19.
38. Grand Tree _____ (*fabricates*) office furniture that is both durable and attractive.
39. I understand from your letter that you expect a full refund, _____ (*nevertheless*) your warranty expired more than a year ago.
40. I have received _____ (*substantial*) support on this project from Claire Devon and Randy Smith.

Removing Outdated Words Rewrite the following sentences, replacing obsolete phrases with up-to-date versions. Write *none* if you think there is no appropriate substitute.

41. I have completed the form and returned it to my insurance company, as per your instructions.
42. Attached herewith is a copy of our new contract for your records.
43. Even though it will increase the price of the fence, we have decided to use the cedar in lieu of the chain link.
44. Saunders & Saunders has received your request for the Greenwood file, and in reply I wish to state that we will send you copies of Mr. Greenwood's documents only after Judge Taylor makes her ruling and orders us to do so.
45. Please be advised that your account with Credit Union Atlantic has been compromised, and we advise you to close it as soon as possible.

Using Active Voice Rewrite each sentence in active voice.

46. The raw data are submitted to the data processing division by the sales representative each Friday.
47. High profits are publicized by management.
48. The policies announced in the directive were implemented by the staff.
49. Our computers are serviced by the company.
50. The employees were represented by Janet Hogan.

Using Transitions Add transitional elements to the following sentences to improve the flow of ideas. (*Note:* You may need to eliminate or add some words to smooth out your sentences.)

51. Tim Hortons first opened in 1964 in Hamilton, Ontario. The first Tim Hortons sold only coffee and doughnuts. The chain has more than 2200 restaurants in Canada and more than 160 in the United States. Tim Hortons is growing. The chain plans to add 170 to 180 restaurants each year for the next few years. Tim Hortons plans to open restaurants in western Canada and Ontario. The chain enjoys wide popularity with Canadians. Canadians eat three times as many doughnuts per capita as Americans. Canadians consume more doughnuts per capita than any other country in the world.[10]

52. Facing some of the toughest competitors in the world, Harley-Davidson had to make some changes. The company introduced new products. Harley's management team set out to rebuild the company's production process. New products were coming to market and the company was turning a profit. Harley's quality standards were not on par with those of its foreign competitors. Harley's costs were still among the highest in the industry. Harley made a U-turn and restructured the company's organizational structure. Harley's efforts have paid off.

53. Whether you're indulging in a doughnut in Mississauga or California, Krispy Kreme wants you to enjoy the same delicious taste with every bite. The company maintains consistent product quality by carefully controlling every step of the production process. Krispy Kreme tests all raw ingredients against established quality standards. Every delivery of wheat flour is sampled and measured for its moisture content and protein levels. Krispy Kreme blends the ingredients. Krispy Kreme tests the doughnut mix for quality. Krispy Kreme delivers

the mix to its stores. Krispy Kreme knows that it takes more than a quality mix to produce perfect doughnuts all the time. The company supplies its stores with everything they need to produce premium doughnuts—mix, icings, fillings, equipment—you name it.

ACTIVITIES

1. **Revising an Outline** A writer is working on an insurance information brochure and is having trouble grouping the ideas logically into an outline. Prepare the outline, paying attention to appropriate subordination of ideas. If necessary, rewrite phrases to give them a more consistent sound.

Accident Protection Insurance Plan

- Coverage is only pennies a day
- Benefit is $100 000 for accidental death on common carrier
- Benefit is $100 a day for hospitalization as result of motor vehicle or common carrier accident
- Benefit is $20 000 for accidental death in motor vehicle accident
- Individual coverage is only $17.85 per quarter; family coverage is just $26.85 per quarter
- No physical exam or health questions
- Convenient payment—billed quarterly
- Guaranteed acceptance for all applicants
- No individual rate increases
- Free, no-obligation examination period
- Cash paid in addition to any other insurance carried
- Covers accidental death when riding as fare-paying passenger on public transportation, including buses, trains, jets, ships, trolleys, subways, or any other common carrier
- Covers accidental death in motor vehicle accidents occurring while driving or riding in or on automobile, truck, camper, motor home, or nonmotorized bicycle

2. **Developing Paragraphs** Working with six other students, divide the following six topics and write one paragraph on your selected topic. Be sure one student writes a paragraph using the illustration technique, one using the comparison-or-contrast technique, one using a discussion of cause and effect, one using the classification technique, one using a discussion of problem and solution, and one using the chronology technique. As a group, discuss what type of organization best suits each topic. Then exchange paragraphs within the team and pick out the main idea and general purpose of the paragraph one of your teammates wrote. Was everyone able to correctly identify the main idea and purpose? If not, suggest how the paragraph might be rewritten for clarity.
   a. Types of cameras (or dogs or automobiles) available for sale
   b. Advantages and disadvantages of eating at fast-food restaurants
   c. Finding that first full-time job
   d. Good qualities of my car (or house, or apartment, or neighbourhood)
   e. How to make a favourite dessert (or barbecue a steak or make coffee)
   f. How to get a driver's licence

3. **Controlling Style and Tone** In a group of three, analyze the style and tone of the following memo. How does the writer come across? What action does the writer want from the reader? Rewrite the memo using active voice and second person to create conversational style and tone.

To:	Zoe Watts, Personnel Manager
From:	William Butterworth, Health and Safety Manager
Date:	November 12, 2009
Subject:	Application of Ergonomic Principles to Computer Workstations

It is recommended that a copy of the attached booklet entitled *Guide for Computer Workstation Ergonomics* be sent to all senior managers and purchasing agents who may influence the purchase and installation of computer equipment in Bigco over the ensuing years, together with a covering letter from some appropriate upper level authority in Bigco urging them to pay attention to the selection, purchase and installation of this type of equipment in the future. Your suggestions as to the most appropriate procedure and list of recipients would be appreciated.

In the course of implementing the Health Services program for monitoring the visual and other health-related complaints of personnel working at computer stations in Bigco, numerous examples of gross violation of ergonomic principles have become evident. Obviously, there cannot be an overnight remedy to these problems as was openly acknowledged by speakers at the National Safety Society conference in Toronto last month. Improvement and conversion of this equipment will cost tens of thousands of dollars at Bigco. And it should be noted that Bigco is by no means unique. Workstation ergonomic problems exist industry wide. But, by the same token, the need for future change is becoming widely recognized and it is important that Bigco keep pace with equipment changes. Much could be done in the interim to improve the currently established workstations and lessen the legitimate health-related complaints of employees, which show a common-sense causal relationship to poor posture, poor lighting arrangements and so on. It is important that awareness be developed on the part of all those managers, supervisors, and agents who ultimately influence the selection, purchasing, and installation of computer equipment. Any suggestions as to how such awareness could be best cultivated would be appreciated.

Expand Your Knowledge

Best of the Web

Compose a Better Business Message At Purdue University's Online Writing Lab (OWL), you'll find tools to help you improve your business messages. For advice on composing written messages, for help with grammar, and for referrals to other information sources, you'll be wise to visit this site. Purdue's OWL offers online services and an introduction to internet search tools. You can also download a variety of handouts on writing skills. Check out the resources on the OWL home page and learn how to write a professional business message.
http://owl.english.purdue.edu

EXERCISES

1. Explain why positive wording in a message is more effective than negative wording. Why should you be concerned about the position of good news or bad news in your written message?
2. What points should you include in the close of your business message? Why?

Although Purdue University's Online Writing Lab is acknowledged as one of the best online writing sites available on the internet, many Canadian universities and colleges also have online writing resources. Explore a few of these sites to find help with grammar, writing, documentation, and ESL-related resources, and for links to other online writing centres.

University of New Brunswick at Saint John Writing Centre
http://www.unbsj.ca/studentservices/writingcentre/
Queen's University—The Writing Centre
http://www.queensu.ca/writingcentre/
The University of Ottawa Writing Centre. "Hypergrammar" tutorials at:
http://www.arts.uottawa.ca/writcent/hypergrammar/

Exploring the Web on Your Own

Review a chapter-related website on your own to learn more about writing business messages.
1. Write it right by paying attention to the writing tips at Bull's Eye Business Writing Tips,
www.basic-learning.com/wbwt

Workplace Skills

Beating Writer's Block: Ten Workable Ideas to Get Words Flowing

Putting words on a page or on a screen can be a real struggle. Some people get stuck so often that they develop a mental block. If you get writer's block, here are some ways to get those words flowing again:

- **Use positive self-talk.** Stop worrying about how well or easily you write, and stop thinking of writing as difficult, time-consuming, or complicated. Tell yourself that you're capable and that you can do the job. Also, recall past examples of your writing that were successful.
- **Know your purpose.** Be specific about what you want to accomplish. What action do you want to happen as a result of this piece of writing? Without a clear purpose, writing can indeed be impossible.
- **Visualize your audience.** Picture audience backgrounds, interests, subject knowledge, and vocabulary (including the technical jargon they use). Such visualization can help you choose an appropriate style and tone for your writing.
- **Create a productive environment.** Write in a place that's for writing only, and make that place pleasant. Set up "writing appointments." Scheduling a session from nine-thirty to noon is less intimidating than an indefinite session. Also, keep your mind fresh with scheduled breaks.
- **Make an outline or a list.** Even if you don't create a formal outline, at least jot down a few notes about how your ideas fit together. As you go along, you can revise your notes, so long as you end up with a plan that gives direction and coherence.
- **Just start.** Put aside all worries, fears, distractions—anything that gives you an excuse to postpone writing. Then start putting down any thoughts you have about your topic. Don't worry about whether these ideas can actually be used; just let your mind range freely.
- **Write the middle first.** Start wherever your interest is greatest and your ideas are most developed. You can follow new directions, but note ideas to revisit later. When you finish one section, choose another without worrying about sequence. Just get your thoughts down.
- **Push obstacles aside.** If you get stuck at some point, don't worry. Move past the thought, sentence, or paragraph, and come back to it later. Prime the pump simply by writing or talking about why you're stuck: "I'm stuck because . . ." Also try brainstorming. Before you know it, you'll be writing about your topic.
- **Read a newspaper or magazine.** Try to find an article that uses a style similar to yours. Choose one you'll enjoy so that you'll read it more closely.
- **Work on nontext segments.** Work on a different part of the project, such as formatting or creating graphics or verifying facts and references.

Remember, when deadlines loom, don't freeze in panic. Concentrate on the major ideas first, and save the details for later, after you have something on the page. If you keep things in perspective, you'll succeed.

Applications for Success

Learn more about beating writer's block. Visit Writer's Block at http://owl.english.purdue.edu/owl/resource/567/01. Another way to overcome writer's block is to limit the scope of your message. Suppose you are preparing to recommend that top management install a new heating system (using the cogeneration process). The following information is in your files.

- History of the development of the cogeneration heating process
- Scientific credentials of the developers of the process
- Risks assumed in using this process
- Your plan for installing the equipment in your building
- Stories about its successful use in comparable facilities
- Specifications of the equipment that would be installed
- Plans for disposing of the old heating equipment
- Costs of installing and running the new equipment
- Advantages and disadvantages of using the new process
- Detailed 10-year cost projections
- Estimates of the time needed to phase in the new system
- Alternative systems that management might wish to consider

Do the following:

1. Limit the scope of this message by eliminating any topics that aren't essential.
2. Arrange the remaining topics so that your report will give top managers a clear understanding of the heating system and a balanced, concise justification for installing it.
3. List the ways you procrastinate, and discuss what you can do to break these habits.
4. Analyze your own writing experiences. What negative self-talk do you use? What might you do to overcome this tendency?

[77]

Completing Business Messages

After studying this chapter, you will be able to

1. List the main tasks involved in completing a business message
2. Identify nine techniques for improving the clarity of your writing
3. Discuss four methods for making your writing more concise
4. Explain how four design elements affect your document's appearance
5. Clarify the types of errors you look for when proofreading
6. Describe seven ways to improve your proofreading process

As senior adviser to the premier, Jamie Baillie ran the Office of the Premier, ensuring that the government's agenda was communicated to the public as clearly and concisely as possible. He wrote memoranda, strategic plans, and briefing notes for the premier and reviewed communication plans, major speeches, and paid media campaigns. "I have been known to revise an important document eight or nine times in order to ensure that the message fits with the overall communications goals of government. The tolerance for error or even mixed messages is low, so it is essential to revise and edit to get details right."[1]

Revising Your Message

Successful business people care about saying precisely the right thing in precisely the right way. Look back at the diagram of the three-step writing process (Figure 3.1 on page 40). You can see that completing your message consists of three tasks: revising, producing, and proofreading your message.

Although the tendency is to separate revision from composition, revision occurs throughout the writing process. You revise as you go along; then you revise again after you've completed the first draft. Ideally, you should let your draft age a day or two before you begin the revision process, so that you can approach the material with a fresh eye. Then read through the document quickly to evaluate its overall effectiveness (its content, organization, style, and tone) before you begin revising for finer points such as clarity and conciseness.

> Revision takes place during and after preparing the first draft.

In your first pass, spend a few extra moments on the beginning and ending of the message. These are the sections that have the greatest impact on the audience. Be sure that the opening of a letter or memo has the main message summarized and is geared to the reader's probable reaction. Ask, "What should be emphasized?" Is "reader action" located in an emphatic spot? In longer messages, check to see that the first few paragraphs establish the subject, purpose, and organization of the material. Review the conclusion to be sure that it summarizes the main idea and leaves the audience with a positive impression.

> The beginning and end of a message have the greatest impact on readers.

As you revise your messages, you'll find yourself rewriting sentences, passages, and even whole sections to improve their effectiveness. Look closely at the revised message in

FIGURE 5.1 Sample Edited Letter (Excerpt)

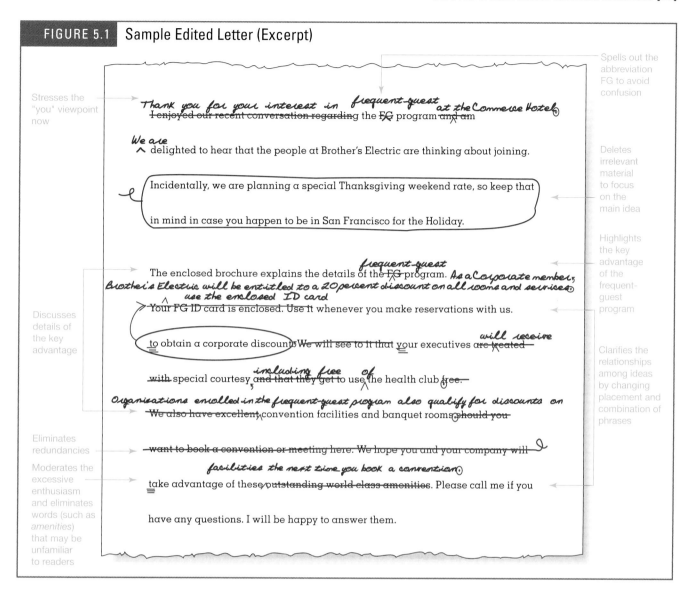

Figure 5.1. It has been edited using the proofreading marks shown in Appendix C. As you can see, the revisions provide the requested information in a more organized fashion, in a friendlier style, and with clearer mechanics.

Sometimes you'll find that you can solve the most difficult problem in a sentence simply by removing it. When you come upon a troublesome element, ask yourself, "Do I need it at all?" You may find that the element was causing a problem because it was trying to do an unnecessary job.[2]

| Solve some problems by deleting them. |

Rewrite and Edit for Clarity

Once you've reviewed your message for overall effectiveness, you'll want to make sure that your message is clear. Perhaps a sentence is so cluttered that the reader can't unravel it, or it's constructed in such a way that the reader can interpret it in several ways.[3] The goal is to enable the audience to read the document once and understand one precise meaning.

| Clarity avoids confusion. |

BREAK UP OVERLY LONG SENTENCES Don't connect too many clauses with *and*. If you find yourself stuck in a long sentence, you're probably trying to make the sentence do more than it can reasonably do, such as express two dissimilar thoughts. You can often clarify your writing style by separating a string into individual sentences. Try not to take compound sentences too far, as shown in the following table.

| In many cases, the parts of a compound sentence should be separated into two sentences. |

Too Long
The magazine will be published January 1, and I'd better meet the deadline if I want my article included.

Improved
The magazine will be published January 1. I'd better meet the deadline if I want my article included.

> Don't be afraid to present your opinions without qualification.

REWRITE HEDGING SENTENCES Sometimes you have to write *may* or *seems* to avoid stating a judgment as a fact. Nevertheless, when you have too many such hedges, you aren't really saying anything. Avoid overqualifying your sentences:

Hedging
I believe that Mr. Johnson's employment record seems to show that he may be capable of handling the position.

Definite
Mr. Johnson's employment record shows that he is capable of handling the position.

> When you use the same grammatical pattern to express two or more ideas, you show that they are comparable thoughts.

IMPOSE PARALLELISM When you have two or more similar (parallel) ideas to express, use the same grammatical pattern for each related idea—parallel construction. Repeating the pattern makes your message more readable: It tells readers that the ideas are comparable, and it adds rhythm. Parallelism can be achieved by repeating the pattern in words, phrases, clauses, or entire sentences.

Not Parallel
Miss Simms had been drenched with rain, bombarded with telephone calls, and her boss shouted at her.

Ms. Reynolds dictated the letter, and next she signed it and left the office.

To waste time and missing deadlines are bad habits.

Interviews are a matter of acting confident and to stay relaxed.

Parallel
Miss Simms had been drenched with rain, bombarded with telephone calls, and shouted at by her boss.

Ms. Reynolds dictated the letter, signed it, and left the office.

Wasting time and missing deadlines are bad habits.

Interviews are a matter of acting confident and staying relaxed.

> Make sure that modifier phrases are really related to the subject of the sentence.

CORRECT DANGLING MODIFIERS Sometimes a modifier is not just an adjective or an adverb but an entire phrase modifying a noun or a verb. Be careful not to leave this type of modifier dangling with no connection to the subject of the sentence. The first unacceptable example in the following group implies that the red sports car has both an office and the legs to walk there. The second example shows one frequent cause of dangling modifiers: passive construction. Avoid placing modifiers close to the wrong nouns and verbs:

Dangling Modifiers
Walking to the office, a red sports car passed her.

Working as fast as possible, the budget was soon ready.

After a three-week slump, we increased sales.

Corrected
A red sports car passed her while she was walking to the office.

Working as fast as possible, the committee soon had the budget ready.

After a three-week slump, sales increased.

> Stringing together a series of nouns may save a little space, but it causes confusion.

REWORD LONG NOUN SEQUENCES Avoid stringing too many nouns together. When nouns are strung together as modifiers, the resulting sentence is hard to read. You can clarify such a sentence by putting some of the nouns in a modifying phrase. Although you add a few more words, your audience won't have to work as hard to understand the sentence.

Too Many Nouns
The aluminum window sash installation company will give us an estimate on Friday.

Clear
The company that installs aluminum window sashes will give us an estimate on Friday.

REPLACE CAMOUFLAGED VERBS Watch for word endings such as *ion, tion, ing, ment, ant, ent, ence, ance,* and *ency.* Most of them change verbs into nouns and adjectives. Liberate the verbs to create a more powerful style.

> Turning verbs into nouns or adjectives weakens your writing style.

Noun Forms	"Liberated" Verbs
The manager undertook implementation of the rules.	The manager implemented the rules.
Verification of the shipments occurs weekly.	Shipments are verified weekly.

Also try not to transform verbs into nouns (writing "we performed an analysis of" rather than "we analyzed"). To prune and enliven your messages, use verbs instead of noun phrases:

Wordy Noun Forms	Concise, Powerful Verbs
reach a conclusion about	conclude
make a discovery of	discover
give consideration to	consider

CLARIFY SENTENCE STRUCTURE Keep the subject and predicate of a sentence as close together as possible. When subject and predicate are far apart, readers have to read the sentence twice to figure out who did what. Try not to separate subject and predicate:

> Subject and predicate (the verb and all the words that belong to it) should be placed as close together as possible, as should modifiers and the words they modify.

Scattered	Focused
A 10 percent decline in market share, which resulted from quality problems and an aggressive sales campaign by Armitage, the market leader in the Maritimes, was the major problem in 2004.	The major problem in 2004 was a 10 percent loss of market share, which resulted from both quality problems and an aggressive sales campaign by Armitage, the market leader in the Maritimes.

Similarly, adjectives, adverbs, and prepositional phrases usually make the most sense when they're placed as close as possible to the words they modify:

Misplaced Modifier	Clear
Our antique desk is suitable for busy executives with thick legs and large drawers.	With its thick legs and large drawers, our antique desk is suitable for busy executives.

CLARIFY AWKWARD REFERENCES To save words, business writers sometimes use expressions such as *the above-mentioned, as mentioned above, the aforementioned, the former, the latter,* and *respectively.* These words cause readers to jump from point to point, which hinders effective communication. Use specific references, even if you must add a few more words:

> Be specific in your references.

Awkward	Clear
The Law Office and the Accounting Office distribute computer supplies for legal secretaries and beginning accountants, respectively.	The Law Office distributes computer supplies for legal secretaries; the Accounting Office distributes those for beginning accountants.

MODERATE YOUR ENTHUSIASM An occasional adjective or adverb intensifies and emphasizes your meaning, but too many can ruin your writing. Try not to display too much enthusiasm:

> Business writing shouldn't be gushy.

Over the Top

We are extremely pleased to offer you a position on our staff of exceptionally skilled and highly educated employees. The work offers extraordinary challenges and a very large salary.

Businesslike

We are pleased to offer you a position on our staff of skilled and well-educated employees. The work offers challenges and an attractive salary.

Rewrite and Edit for Conciseness

> Conciseness means efficiency.

Many business documents today are swollen with words and phrases that do no new work. In fact, a majority of executives responding to one survey complained that most written messages are too long.[4] Because executives are more likely to read documents that efficiently say what needs to be said, it's especially important to weed out unnecessary material. As you rewrite and edit your messages, concentrate on how each word contributes to an effective sentence and how that sentence develops a coherent paragraph.

Most first drafts can be cut by 50 percent.[5] Eliminate every word that serves no function, replace every long word that could be a short word, and remove every adverb that adds nothing to the meaning already carried in the verb.

To test whether every word counts, try removing phrases or words that don't appear to be essential. If the meaning is unchanged, leave those elements out. For instance, *very* can be a useful word to achieve emphasis, but more often it's clutter. There's no need to call someone "very methodical." The person is either methodical or not. As you begin your editing task, simplify, prune, and strive for order.

> Be on the lookout for inefficient phrases and excessive or confusing relative pronouns and articles.

DELETE UNNECESSARY WORDS AND PHRASES Some combinations of words have one-word equivalents that are more efficient. Avoid using wordy phrases:

Wordy	**Concise**
for the sum of	for
in the event that	if
on the occasion of	on
prior to the start of	before
in the near future	soon
have the capability of	can
at this point in time	now
due to the fact that	because
in view of the fact that	because
until such time as	when
with reference to	about

In addition, avoid the clutter of too many or poorly placed relative pronouns (*who, that, which*). Even articles can be excessive (mostly too many *the*'s):

Awkward	**Clear**
Cars that are sold after January will not have a six-month warranty.	Cars sold after January will not have a six-month warranty.
Employees who are driving to work should park in the underground garage.	Employees driving to work should park in the underground garage.

However, well-placed relative pronouns and articles prevent confusion. Make sure to use enough relative pronouns to be clear:

Confusing	Clear
The project manager told the engineers last week the specifications were changed.	The project manager told the engineers last week *that* the specifications were changed.
	The project manager told the engineers *that* last week the specifications were changed.

SHORTEN LONG WORDS AND PHRASES Short words are generally more vivid and easier to read than long ones are. The idea is to use short, simple words, *not* simple concepts.[6] Try to get rid of overly long words:

Inflated	Plain English
During the preceding year, the company accelerated productive operations.	Last year the company sped up operations.
The action was predicated on the assumption that the company was operating at a financial deficit.	The action was based on the belief that the company was losing money.

By using infinitives in place of some phrases, you not only shorten your sentences but also make them clearer. Be careful to use infinitives rather than wordy phrases:

> Short words and infinitives are generally more vivid than long words and phrases, and they improve the readability of a document.

Wordy	Concise
He went to the library for the purpose of studying.	He went to the library to study.
The employer increased salaries so that she could improve morale.	The employer increased salaries to improve morale.

ELIMINATE REDUNDANCIES In some word combinations, the words tend to say the same thing. For instance, "visible to the eye" is redundant because *visible* is enough; nothing can be visible to the ear. Try not to repeat meanings:

> Remove unneeded repetition.

Redundant	Concise
absolutely complete	complete
basic fundamentals	fundamentals
follows after	follows
reduce down	reduce
free and clear	free
refer back	refer
repeat again	repeat
collect together	collect
future plans	plans
return back	return
important essentials	essentials
midway between	between
end result	result
actual truth	truth
final outcome	outcome
uniquely unusual	unique
surrounded on all sides	surrounded

In addition, avoid using double modifiers with the same meaning.

Redundant	Concise
modern, up-to-date equipment	modern equipment

Avoid starting sentences with *it* and *there*.

RECAST "IT IS/THERE ARE" STARTERS If you start a sentence with an indefinite pronoun (an expletive) such as *it* or *there*, odds are that the sentence could be shorter. Make sure that your sentences start with a strong subject.

Wordy	**Focused**
It would be appreciated if you would sign the lease today.	Please sign the lease today.
There are five employees in this division who were late to work today.	Five employees in this division were late to work today.

Producing Your Message

Once you have revised and refined your message from start to finish, you are ready to produce it. You want to give your message an attractive, contemporary appearance by designing your document carefully. Also, make sure that your design uses graphics and visual elements to reinforce key ideas.

Before you can proofread your final version, you must produce it in some readable form.

Select the Right Design Elements

REFLECT A MODERN APPEARANCE The way you package your ideas has a lot to do with how successful your communication will be. The first thing your readers notice about your message is its appearance. If your document looks tired and out of date, it will give that impression to your readers—even if your ideas are innovative. Good looks can help you get your message across, especially to busy readers.

Effective page design is simple, unified, and balanced.

EMPHASIZE MAIN PARTS When designing your message, balancing graphics and text is important. The visual elements should be carefully selected to highlight key points. Consider the memo in Figure 5.2. The bar chart in this memo is centred to give a formal impression, and the colour used in the graphic is balanced by the letterhead logo. The headings emphasize the organizational divisions and important content.

You can use a variety of design elements, such as white space, margin and line justification, typefaces, and type styles to make your message look professional, interesting, and up to date. You can use text boxes to emphasize important information. But be careful—too many design elements will confuse your audience. If you will be designing a lot of documents that contain a variety of elements, you would be wise to take a course in page layout or at least to read further about effective design techniques.

White space provides contrast and prevents crowding.

USE WHITE SPACE TO SHOW ORGANIZATION **White space** is the part of a document that is free of text or artwork. It provides visual contrast for your readers, and perhaps even more important, it gives their eyes a resting point. White space includes the open area surrounding headings and margin areas, the vertical space between columns, the space created by ragged line endings, the paragraph indents or extra space between unindented paragraphs, and the horizontal space between lines of text. White space is used to show organizational divisions such as with the double spacing between paragraphs. White space opens up the page and prevents crowding. In today's busy workplace, readers want to scan quickly for information. Crowded text cannot be scanned.

Headings emphasize important content.

USE HEADINGS TO EMPHASIZE KEY CONTENT Just as white space is used to show organizational divisions, so are headings and subheadings. Headings are short phrases that label and summarize sections of the document. Use headings to direct the reader's eye to key content and signal organizational divisions. Documents with headings are easy for readers to scan, enhancing readability. Guidelines for headings are discussed in the next chapter on page 104.

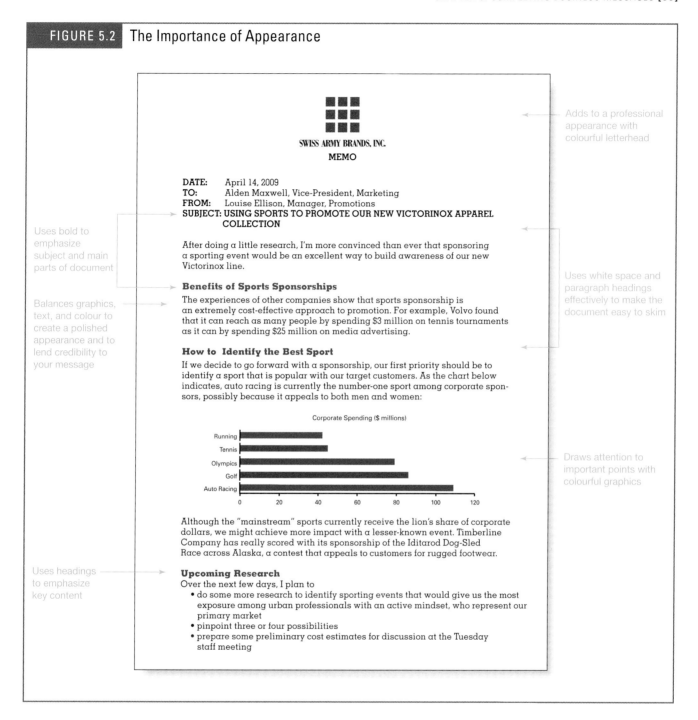

FIGURE 5.2 The Importance of Appearance

Adds to a professional appearance with colourful letterhead

Uses bold to emphasize subject and main parts of document

Balances graphics, text, and colour to create a polished appearance and to lend credibility to your message

Uses white space and paragraph headings effectively to make the document easy to skim

Draws attention to important points with colourful graphics

Uses headings to emphasize key content

SWISS ARMY BRANDS, INC.
MEMO

DATE: April 14, 2009
TO: Alden Maxwell, Vice-President, Marketing
FROM: Louise Ellison, Manager, Promotions
SUBJECT: USING SPORTS TO PROMOTE OUR NEW VICTORINOX APPAREL COLLECTION

After doing a little research, I'm more convinced than ever that sponsoring a sporting event would be an excellent way to build awareness of our new Victorinox line.

Benefits of Sports Sponsorships

The experiences of other companies show that sports sponsorship is an extremely cost-effective approach to promotion. For example, Volvo found that it can reach as many people by spending $3 million on tennis tournaments as it can by spending $25 million on media advertising.

How to Identify the Best Sport

If we decide to go forward with a sponsorship, our first priority should be to identify a sport that is popular with our target customers. As the chart below indicates, auto racing is currently the number-one sport among corporate sponsors, possibly because it appeals to both men and women:

Corporate Spending ($ millions)

Although the "mainstream" sports currently receive the lion's share of corporate dollars, we might achieve more impact with a lesser-known event. Timberline Company has really scored with its sponsorship of the Iditarod Dog-Sled Race across Alaska, a contest that appeals to customers for rugged footwear.

Upcoming Research
Over the next few days, I plan to
- do some more research to identify sporting events that would give us the most exposure among urban professionals with an active mindset, who represent our primary market
- pinpoint three or four possibilities
- prepare some preliminary cost estimates for discussion at the Tuesday staff meeting

IMPROVE READABILITY THROUGH MARGINS AND LAYOUT **Margins** define the space around your text and between text columns. They're influenced by the way you place lines of type, which can be set (1) justified (flush on the left and flush on the right), (2) flush left with a ragged right margin, (3) flush right with a ragged left margin, or (4) centred. Ample margins improve the reader's ability to move through text quickly. The column of space left in the margin of this text allows the summary notes to be highlighted for speed-reading and review.

Justified type "darkens" your message's appearance, because the uniform line lengths lack the white space created by ragged margins. It also tends to make your message look more like a form letter and less like a customized message. Justified type is often considered more difficult to read.

Flush-left, ragged-right type "lightens" your message's appearance. It gives a document an informal, contemporary feeling of openness. Spacing between words is the same, and only long words that fall at the ends of lines are hyphenated.

Margins frame your text.

Flush-left, ragged-right type gives your message an open feeling.

TABLE 5.1	Common Typefaces
SAMPLE SERIF TYPEFACE Times Roman is often used for text. TIMES ROMAN IS HARDER TO READ IN ALL CAPS.	**SAMPLE SANS SERIF TYPEFACE** Helvetica is often used for headings. HELVETICA IS A CLEANER FACE, EVEN IN ALL CAPS.

CHOOSE EASY-TO-READ TYPEFACES **Typeface** refers to the physical design of letters, numbers, and other text characters. Most computers offer many choices of fonts or typefaces. Each typeface influences the tone of your message, making it look authoritative, friendly, expensive, classy, casual, and so on. Choose fonts that are appropriate for your message.

> Serif typefaces are commonly used for text.

Serif typefaces have small crosslines (called serifs) at the ends of each letter stroke (see Table 5.1). Serif faces such as Times Roman (packaged with most laser printers) are commonly used for text; they can look busy and cluttered when set in large sizes for headings or other display treatments. Typefaces with rounded serifs can look friendly; those with squared serifs can look official.

> Sans serif typefaces are commonly used for headings.

Sans serif typefaces have no serifs. Faces such as Helvetica (packaged with most laser printers) are ideal for display treatments that use larger type. Sans serif faces can be difficult to read in long blocks of text. They look best when surrounded by plenty of white space—as in headings or in widely spaced lines of text.

Limit the number of typefaces in a single document.[7] In general, use no more than two typefaces on a page. Many great-looking documents are based on a single sans serif typeface for heads and subheads, with a second serif typeface for text and captions. Using too many typefaces clutters the document and reduces your audience's comprehension.

> Use boldface for emphasis.

USE TYPE STYLES TO DRAMATIZE IMPORTANT INFORMATION **Type style** refers to any modification that lends contrast or emphasis to type. Most computers offer <u>underlining</u>, **boldface**, *italic*, and other highlighting and decorative styles. Using boldface type for subheads breaks up long expanses of text. Too much boldfacing will darken the appearance of your message and make it look heavy. You can set isolated words in boldface type in the middle of a text block to draw more attention to them. However, if you boldface too many words, you might create a "checkerboard" appearance in a paragraph.

Use italic type to set off text but notice that italic is a weak typeface. Boldface will create a more dramatic effect. Italic can also be used to identify a quote or to indicate the title of a publication and is often used in captions. Boldface type and italic are most effective when reserved for key words—those words that help readers understand the main point of the text.

> Avoid using type styles that slow your readers down such as all capitals or underlining.

As a general rule, don't use any style that slows your audience's progress through your message. For instance, using underlining or all-uppercase letters can interfere with your reader's ability to recognize the shapes of words and thus slow the reader's progress.

Make sure the size of your type is proportionate to the importance of your message and the space allotted. Small type in a sea of white space appears lost. Large type squeezed into a small area is hard to read and visually cramped. For most business messages, use a type size of 10 to 12 points.

Make Design Elements Effective

> For effective design, pay attention to
> • Consistency
> • Balance
> • Restraint
> • Detail

Make all design elements work together. Effective document design guides your readers through your message, so be sure to focus on being consistent, maintaining balance, showing restraint, being detail-oriented, and using whatever technological tools you can (see Table 5.2).

TABLE 5.2	Five Pointers for Making Design Elements Effective
POINTER	**WHAT TO DO**
Be consistent throughout a message	Keep margins, typeface, type size, and spacing consistent from document to document (and sometimes even from message to message). Also be consistent when using recurring design elements, such as vertical lines, columns, and borders.
Balance all visual elements	Create a pleasing design by balancing the space devoted to text, artwork, and white space.
Use the best technology available	Word-processing and desktop publishing programs help you combine text and graphics for a professional, inviting appearance. They add a first-class finish with attractive typefaces and color graphics. They also let you manage document style with formatting commands that you can save and apply as needed—to ensure consistency from section to section and from document to document. Technology can turn a plain piece of text into a dazzling, persuasive document.
Strive for simplicity in design	Don't clutter your message with too many design elements, too much highlighting, or too many decorative touches.
Pay attention to design details	When headings and subheadings appear at the bottom of a column or a page, readers can be offended because the promised information doesn't appear until the next column or page. Plus, narrow columns with too much space between words can be distracting.

Avoid last-minute compromises. Don't reduce type size or white space to squeeze in text. If you've planned your message so that your purpose, your audience, and your message are clear, you can design your document to be effective.[8] Start by thinking about your medium (press release, magazine or newsletter article, brochure, direct-mail package, slide presentation, formal report, business letter, or internal memo). Once you've decided on a medium for your message, make it look interesting and easy to read and understand.

Use Computers to Improve Your Documents

Whether you're composing your message, adding graphics, or revising your first draft, technology helps you do so more efficiently, and it helps you produce more professional-looking results. Word processors give you the ability to delete and move text easily, with features such as automatic list numbering, page numbering, and dating.

> Spell checkers, grammar checkers, and computerized thesauruses can all help with the revision process, but they can't take the place of good writing and editing skills.

USE SOFTWARE

For Editing When it's time to revise and polish your message, your word processor helps you add, delete, and move text with functions such as *cut and paste* (taking a block of text out of one section of a document and pasting it in somewhere else) and *search and replace* (tracking down words or phrases and changing them if you need to). In addition, the AutoCorrect feature allows you to store words you commonly misspell or mistype, along with their correct spelling. So if you frequently type *teh* instead of *the*, AutoCorrect will automatically correct your typo for you. Finally, software tools such as revision marks keep track of proposed editing changes electronically and provide a history of a document's revisions. The revisions appear in a different font colour from the original text, giving you a chance to review changes before accepting or rejecting them.

For Checking Spelling and Grammar Three advanced software functions can help bring out the best in your documents: a *spell checker*, a *thesaurus*, and a *grammar checker*. Just don't rely on grammar or spell checkers to do all your revision work. For example, spell checkers cannot tell the difference between *their* and *there*. Moreover, some of the "errors" they do detect may actually be proper names, technical words, words that you misspelled on purpose, or simply words that weren't included in the spell checker's dictionary.

> Spelling and grammar checkers have their limitations.

Grammar checkers are even more limited, so it's up to you to decide whether each flagged item should be corrected or left alone, and it's up to you to find the errors that your spell and grammar checkers have overlooked.[9]

For Making Graphics *Graphics software* can help you create simple diagrams and flow charts (see Chapter 11) or you can create your pictures from scratch, use *clip art* (collections of uncopyrighted images), or scan in drawings or photographs.

Proofreading Your Message

Most readers view attention to detail as a sign of your professionalism. Whether you're writing a one-paragraph memo or a 500-page report, if you let mechanical errors slip through, your readers wonder whether you're unreliable. For example, a resumé with a typo in it may be rejected.

What to Look for When Proofreading

To ensure that your message is letter perfect, proofread it. Give some attention to your overall format. Have you followed accepted conventions and company guidelines for laying out the document on the page (margin width, number of columns, page numbering)? Have you included all the traditional elements that belong in documents of the type you're creating? Have you been consistent in handling heading styles, exhibit titles, source notes, and other details? (To resolve questions about format and layout, see Appendix A.)

Check your document for correct grammar, usage, and punctuation. Also look for common spelling errors and typos. Check for missing material: a missing source note, exhibit, or paragraph. Look for design errors; for example, make sure that all headings and text appear in the right typeface and that columns within tables and exhibits are aligned. Graphic characters such as ampersands and percent signs may appear when they should be spelled out, and numerical symbols might be incorrect. Look closely at the type to spot problems such as extra spacing between lines or between words, a short line of type ending a paragraph at the top of a new page, a heading that's been left hanging at the bottom of a page, or incorrect hyphenation. For a quick reminder of what to look for when proofreading, see Table 5.3.

How to Adapt the Proofreading Process

How many and what sorts of errors you catch when proofreading depend on how much time you have and what type of document you are preparing. The more routine your document, the less time you'll need to spend proofreading it. Proofreading may require patience, but it adds credibility to your document. To help make your proofreading more effective and ensure that your document is error-free, remember the following pointers:

- **Multiple passes.** Go through the document several times, focusing on a different aspect each time. The first pass might be to look for omissions and errors in content. The second pass could be for layout, spacing, and other aesthetic features. A final pass might be to check for typographical, grammatical, and spelling errors.
- **Perceptual tricks.** Your brain has been trained to ignore typos. Try (1) reading each page from the bottom to the top (starting at the last word in each line), (2) placing your finger under each word and reading it silently, (3) making a slit in a sheet of paper that reveals only one line at a time, and (4) reading the document aloud and pronouncing each word carefully.
- **Impartial reviews.** Have a friend or colleague proofread the document for you. Others are likely to catch mistakes that you continually fail to notice. (All of us have blind spots when it comes to reviewing our own work.)

You can use graphics software to add visual elements to your message.

Your credibility is affected by your attention to the details of mechanics and form.

The types of details to look for when proofreading include language errors, missing material, design errors, and typographical errors.

Allow time for thorough proofreading.

Focus on one aspect at a time.

TABLE 5.3	Proofreading Tips

LOOK FOR WRITING ERRORS

☑ Typographical mistakes

☑ Misspelled words

☑ Grammatical errors

☑ Punctuation mistakes

LOOK FOR MISSING ELEMENTS

☑ Missing text sections

☑ Missing exhibits (drawings, tables, photographs, charts, graphs, and so on)

☑ Missing source notes, copyright notices, or other reference items

LOOK FOR DESIGN AND FORMATTING MISTAKES

☑ Incorrect or inconsistent font selections

☑ Column sizing, spacing, and alignment

☑ Margins

☑ Special characters

☑ Clumsy line and page breaks

☑ Page numbers

☑ Page headers and footers

☑ Adherence to company standards

- **Distance.** If you have time, set the document aside and proofread it the next day.
- **Vigilance.** Avoid reading large amounts of material in one sitting, and try not to proofread when you're tired.
- **Focus.** Concentrate on what you're doing. Try to block out distractions, and focus as completely as possible on your proofreading task.
- **Caution.** Take your time. Quick proofreading is not careful proofreading.

ON THE JOB

Creating Impressions Through Your Email

In a large company many people will only get to know others in the company by receiving their emails. By ensuring your documents are free of errors and have positive, concise style, you will be creating a persona for yourself that helps others see you as someone who can be trusted to do a good job.

Reviewing Key Points

This chapter describes what to do in the third step of the three-step writing process. To complete a business document be sure to

- Allow time for thorough revision.
- Start with checking the content. Pay attention to the opening—does it say what the document is about? Is the body of the document complete? Are all predicted reader questions answered in the document? Where is the action you want readers to take—is it noticeable and emphasized because it is in the beginning and end, the most emphatic parts of the document?

- Use bulleted and numbered lists.
- Use boldface, colour, and other typographical elements conservatively.
- Write informative headings that stand on their own and are consistent in their wording.
- Write concise summaries and descriptions that are informative and crystal clear.

5. **Write effective links and place them strategically:**
   - Use a combination of textual and graphical hyperlinks, but don't overdo graphics, since they slow down document loading time.
   - Avoid self-referential terms such as "click here" or "follow this link."
   - Use absolute directions.
   - Write informative hyperlinks so that the content of subsequent pages is obvious.
   - Place your links strategically and carefully.

6. **Establish your credibility (important because anyone can post material on a website):**
   - Include your name and the name of your sponsor (if applicable) on every webpage.
   - Provide contact information (at least an email address) so that readers can get in touch with you or your sponsor easily.
   - Include posting and revision dates for your information.
   - Make sure your content is error-free.

Applications for Success

 Document **Design**

Writing for the web (**www.useit.com/papers/webwriting**) offers you a huge amount of information on web writing. Visit this site and access research on how users read on the web and get tips on how to adapt your writing for online readers. Find links to many resources including computer industry style guides for web writing.

Do the following:

1. Select any webpage and critique the headings. Do they make sense on their own? Do they include hyperlinks? Does the author use colour or boldface effectively? What changes, if any, would you recommend?

2. Select any webpage and critique the effectiveness of the written hyperlinks. Does the author use self-referential terms or absolute directions? Is the writing concise? Are linked words embedded in a sentence or paragraph to provide the reader with context? Are the hyperlinks placed effectively?

3. Select a short article from any print magazine or newspaper. Now rewrite the article in a format suitable for the web, using the techniques discussed in this workshop. Focus on writing only one webpage. Include some hyperlinks on that page and in your article (but don't take the time to develop material for the linked page).

Working with Memos, Email, Letters, and Instant Messages

After studying this chapter, you will be able to

1. Explain the difference between internal and external communication
2. Discuss how memos, email, letters, and instant messages differ in format
3. Summarize four techniques you can use to improve message readability
4. Distinguish between descriptive and informative headings
5. Describe four methods you can use to improve the readability of email messages
6. Define email etiquette and give examples
7. Name three business message categories that determine your writing strategy

Based in Winnipeg, Ferguson Walker Marketing Communications has handled communication for many prominent businesses such as Canada Safeway, McDonald's Restaurants of Canada, James Richardson & Sons Limited, GM, and the Pan American Games. "All messages need to be carefully planned. For instance, understanding your audience and subject matter are critical in deciding the tone and formality of the message," says Colin Ferguson. You need to know when to use a casual tone and when to be formal. You also need to know when to send an email, memo, letter, or instant message.[1]

Using Memos, Email, Letters, and Instant Messages

Although a lot of business communication is oral (taking place in face-to-face conversations, in meetings, during phone conversations, and in voice mail), a significant amount of your time will be spent writing emails, memos, and letters. Business messages are also conveyed using social technologies developed especially for collaboration and relationship building. These social technologies (Facebook, blogs, wikis, and other networking sites) offer interactivity and feedback. But no matter what the form of delivery, the principles of putting your ideas into print are constant. Since the dominant method of sending business messages is via email, this chapter devotes the most space to tips for writing email. But many of the strategies for writing effective emails also apply to writing memos, letters, instant messages, and other online written messages for business. This chapter will help you discern differences among memos, emails, letters, and instant messages. Best practices for writing and commenting on blogs, wikis, and other online media are evolving.

> Understanding the differences among memos, emails, letters, and instant messages is important.

Internal and External Communication

Internal communication refers to the exchange of information and ideas within an organization. You use email and sometimes memos for the routine, day-to-day communication within the organization. Internal communication helps employees develop a clear sense of the organization's mission, identify potential problems, and react quickly to changes.

> Internal communication is the way employees exchange information within an organization.

Just as internal communication carries information throughout the organization, **external communication** carries it into and out of the organization. Companies constantly exchange messages in emails and letters with customers, vendors, distributors, competitors, investors, journalists, and community representatives.

These external messages also perform an important public relations function. External communication helps employees create a favourable impression of their company, plan for and respond to crises, and gather useful information. Email is often used for external communication (1) in response to email messages that you receive, (2) when the purpose of your message is informal, and (3) when your audience accepts email as appropriate.

Many companies are also using online or peer media such as blogs and social networking sites for external communication. New technologies are used when the purpose of the message includes forming an interactive relationship with the receiver, when the audience expects and is comfortable with the technology, and when the company has the technological resources to support its immediate and interactive nature. Yet in all these forms of communication—whether text message, blog post, Facemail (an email sent using Facebook), or regular email—the essential skill is the ability to write a clear, concise, and focused message. Since many of the new technologies are also used in social settings, the business person has to make the shift into a style and tone acceptable for representing a company. When Facebook is used to send messages among friends it can be very informal, but when a company creates a group and uses the technology, the tone and style must match the nature of the business.

Format Differences

Most memos, emails, letters, and instant messages are relatively brief—generally less than two pages long (often less than a page for email). Letters are the most formal of the four. Memos are less formal, and instant messages are the least formal of all. For in-depth format information, see Appendix A: Format and Layout of Business Documents. When trying to distinguish among these four types of documents, keep the following format differences in mind.

MEMOS Being less formal than letters, most memos begin with a title, such as *Memo, Memorandum,* or *Interoffice Correspondence.* They use *To, From, Date,* and *Subject* headings to emphasize the needs of the readers (who usually have time only to skim messages). Figure 6.1 is a typical memo at Carnival Corporation (responding to a request for data on passenger capacity). The comments in the left margin point out typical memo format elements.

The Carnival writer might have chosen to respond using email. However, the data being provided are clearest in table form, and tabular material comes out more reliably in print.

Memos do not have salutations. Good memos discuss only one topic and use a conversational tone. Memos generally have no complimentary close or signature. Because of their open construction and informal method of delivery (either interoffice mail or email), memos are less private than letters.

Use memos and email for internal communication.

External communication is the way employees exchange information outside the organization.

Use letters and email for external communication.

Different media have varying levels of formality:
- Formal = letters
- Less formal = memos/email
- Least formal = instant messages

 **Activities**

 Document **Makeovers**

Memos have elements such as
- To
- From
- Date
- Subject

| FIGURE 6.1 | A Typical Memo |

Includes a
title—in
this case,
also adds
the company
name and
a graphic

Carnival

INTERNAL MEMORANDUM

Uses typical
memo heading

TO: Lauren Eastman, Assistant Director, Sales
FROM: Brad Lymans, Operations Manager
DATE: June 11, 2009
SUBJECT: CAPACITY FOR CARNIVAL CORPORATION CRUISE SHIPS

Uses prominent
subject line

Includes no
inside address
or salutation

Here is the capacity information you requested along with a brief
explanation of the figures:

Opens with
the specific
information
requested
and sticks
to a single
subject
throughout
the memo

Current Capacity

Cruise Brand	Number of Ships	Passenger Capacity	Primary Market
Carnival	15	30 020	North America
Holland America	10	13 348	North America
Costa	7	9 200	Europe
Cunard	2	2 458	Worldwide
Seabourn	6	1 614	North America
Windstar	4	756	North America
Airtours-Sun	4	4 352	Europe
Total	48	61 748	

Presents data
in an easy-to-
read table in
the body, helps
clarify that data
with factual
information,
and anticipates
reader's needs
by including
additional
information
to help
the reader
interpret the
data

All passenger capacities are calculated based on two passengers per cabin,
even though some cabins can accommodate three or four passengers.

Uses headings
to show
organization

Future Trends
Cruising capacity has grown in recent years, and management expects it to
continue because all the major cruise companies are planning to introduce
new ships into service. Carnival Corporation will build 16 additional cruise
ships over the next 5 years, increasing the company's passenger capacity by
36 830, which will bring the total to 98 578.

To use this new capacity, we must increase our share of the overall vacation
market. Keep in mind that demand for cruises may be affected by (1) the
strength of the countries where the ships operate; (2) political instability in
areas where the ships travel; and (3) adverse incidents involving cruise
ships in general.

More Information
Please call me at local 829 if you have any further questions or need any
additional data.

Closes on a
positive,
friendly note

Includes no
complimentary
close or
signature

FIGURE 6.2   A Typical Email Message

Uses a typical email heading that lets the reader know the purpose of the message with an informative subject line

Always provides information on To, From, and Subject

Uses an informal salutation for email to peers

Opens by stating the specific request for information

Communicates one clear and concise objective, in the body, and clearly states what is expected of the reader

Includes a brief complimentary close and a typed name

Includes contact information in case email is forwarded to someone else

Closes cordially, making a statement about the specific action requested

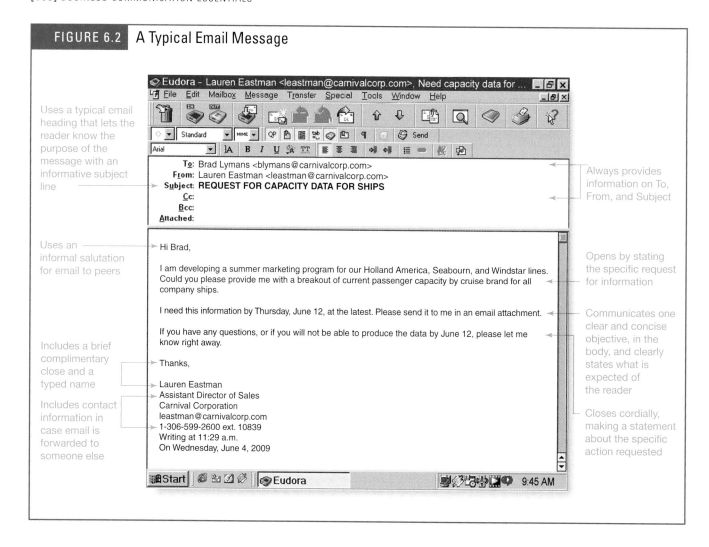

EMAIL MESSAGES Email has become the most commonly used form of business communication. Like memos, email messages begin with *To, From, Date,* and *Subject* information. The heading section also may include information about copies and attachments. The date is automatically inserted into the document by the program. Figure 6.2, is a typical email message (here, a request for capacity data at Carnival Corporation). The comments in the left-hand margin point out typical email format elements.

For email messages a salutation is optional; however, a greeting can add a friendly tone. Because the information in the header is often very brief, you may want to include contact information with your name at the end of the email, especially if the email is going outside the company.

Email has a reputation for speed and informality. Nevertheless, you'll want to write your email messages carefully. Appearance, organization, and style are just as important for electronic messages as for any other type of business message.

Email messages have elements such as
- Heading (often brief, including information about copies and attachments)
- Salutation (optional but highly recommended)
- Complimentary closing (optional but highly recommended)
- Typed name of sender
- Contact information (optional but recommended)

FIGURE 6.3	A Typical Letter

Uses letterhead stationery

Includes the date after the heading

Uses a typical inside address

Greets the recipient with a salutation

Includes a subject line to highlight the main idea

States the message clearly

Includes a complimentary close

Follows close with a signature block

Also includes typist's initials

Save the Wolves Foundation
4542 Western Highway • Red Deer, AB T4N 5H5
(403) 266-6223 • (403) 723-3229
www.wolves.org

March 13, 2009

Mr. Sam Davis, Managing Editor
The Times Magazine
468 Foothills Drive
Calgary, AB T5Y 2P5

Dear Mr. Davis:

SUPPORTING THE WOLF RELOCATION PROGRAM

Thank you for your recent editorial supporting the Alberta wolf relocation program. We are as dedicated to preserving domestic livestock herds as are the ranchers who own them. However, killing the wolf predators is both a short-term and a short-sighted solution. We'd like your readers to have some additional information, besides the excellent points you made.

Every one of the 45 wolves we've captured and relocated this year has been examined by a veterinarian. The wolves receive inoculations to prevent rabies, among other diseases. Therefore, the relocated wolves pose little threat of disease to wildlife, their pack, or the occasional domestic animal or human who might encounter them.

In the wilderness areas where they will be relocated, wolves help keep the population of caribou, moose, and deer under control, and they cull injured or sick animals from the herd. However, wolves fear human beings and will avoid people whenever possible. Our North American wolves do not attack humans.

In addition, your readers will be interested to know a little more about wolves in general. Wolves have strong family ties and often mate for life. Female wolves give birth to about four to six pups, and both parents supply food and help train the pups. In fact, the wolf pack is usually a family group. And just as families call to their children, wolves sometimes howl to keep their pack together.

We invite those of your readers who would like to join our efforts to call 1-800-544-8333 to receive more information.

Sincerely,

Carroll Paulding

Carroll Paulding
President

sg

Opens by telling what prompted the letter, clearly stating the purpose, and identifying two audiences for this information: the magazine editor and his readers

Provides specific relocation-program details in the body, reassures readers about their personal safety, and anticipates the needs of the second audience by providing information that was not requested

Closes cordially, clearly stating the invitation where the reader will notice it

LETTERS Although the format for a letter depends on the traditions of the organization, it does have some generally accepted characteristics. For example, consider the letter in Figure 6.3. Alberta's Save the Wolves Foundation seeks to raise funds for relocating wolves from other Canadian provinces into selected wilderness areas in North America. The foundation tries to educate the public and garner support, so it communicates externally. Figure 6.3 is a letter from the foundation to representatives of the mass media. Comments in the left margin point out format elements.

Most business letters appear on letterhead stationery, which includes the company's name and address and other contact information. The first thing to appear after the letterhead is the date. Next comes the inside address, which identifies the person receiving the letter. And after that comes the salutation, usually in the form of *Dear Mr.* or *Ms. Last Name*. A subject line summarizes the topic and acts as a title and filing reference. The message comes next, often running several paragraphs and sometimes running over to a second page. After the message is the complimentary close, usually *Sincerely* or *Yours truly*. And last comes the signature block: space for the signature, followed by the sender's printed name and title.

Letters have elements such as
- Letterhead
- Date
- Inside address
- Salutation
- Subject line
- Complimentary close
- Signature block

FIGURE 6.4 A Typical Instant Message

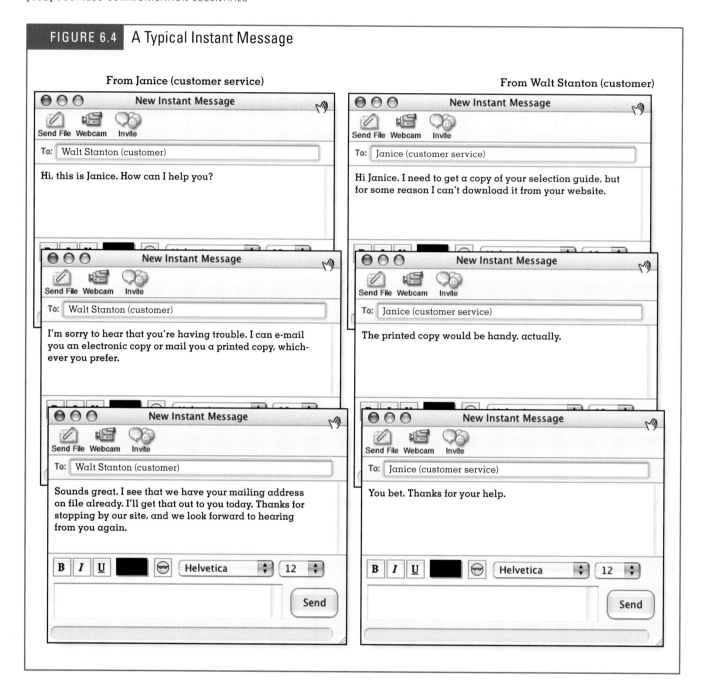

INSTANT MESSAGES AND ONLINE MESSAGES As speedy as email can be, it sometimes isn't fast enough. Instant messaging (IM) lets you know who on your list of contacts is online at the very moment you are. Then you can send multiple messages back and forth in real time, without having to click through all the reply and send steps that email requires. The format is informal, just a small window on your computer screen, which displays your entire conversation—your messages and your contact's responses (see Figure 6.4).

Instant messaging is used by many companies for communicating with business associates and customers. Businesses use IM to replace in-person meetings and phone calls, to supplement online meetings, and to interact with customers. The benefits of IM in the workplace are numerous. It allows rapid response to urgent messages, costs less than both phone calls and email, can mimic conversation more closely than email, and is available on a wide range of devices from PCs to phones to personal digital assistants. To learn more about how IM works, check out http://computer.howstuffworks.com/instant-messaging.htm. For the latest on the business applications of IM, log on to www.instantmessagingplanet.com.

In some companies, such as Telus and Starbucks, Facebook is used to form networks with customers and informal social networks among employees. Facebook offers the ability to build relationships, get feedback, and send messages among whole groups of linked customers and/or employees. These messages can easily and rapidly be shared throughout the wider networks of participants. Though informal, what you say and how you say it can have a lasting effect among those you work with or depend on for promotion, cooperation, or sales.

Electronic messages have a reputation for speed and informality, but you'll want to exercise care in writing your instant messages and other forms of online messages, such as comments you post on business networking sites (e.g., LinkedIn). Blogs, wikis, and comments you post online in your business role represent your company, and once posted, they have permanence on the internet. Appearance, organization, and style are just as important for electronic messages as for any other type of business message. People receiving your text messages on a BlackBerry will appreciate your concise and direct style. In fact, you can take several steps to improve readability and help your audience accept your short business messages.

Improving Readability in Short Business Messages

Make your message easier to skim by varying sentence length, using shorter paragraphs, using lists and bullets, and adding effective headings and subheadings. Most business writers know that busy readers seldom read every word of a message on their first pass. Instead, they typically skim a message, reading only certain sections carefully to assess the value of the document. If they determine that the document contains valuable information or requires a response, they will read it more carefully when time permits.

> Make your messages easy to skim.

Vary Sentence Length

To increase interest, use a variety of both short and long sentences. Although good business writers use short sentences most of the time, too many short sentences in a row can make your writing choppy.

- Long sentences are well suited for grouping or combining ideas, listing points, and summarizing or previewing information.
- Medium-length sentences (those with about 20 words) are useful for showing the relationships among ideas.
- Short sentences emphasize important information.

> Using a variety of short, medium-length, and long sentences makes your message more interesting.

Most good business writing has an average sentence length of 20 words or fewer. (Varying sentence length can create translation problems for international readers, so stick to short sentences for audiences abroad.)[2]

Keep Paragraphs Short

Short paragraphs (of seven lines or fewer) are easier to read than long ones, and they make your writing look inviting. Most business readers are put off by large blocks of text. Unless you break up your thoughts somehow, you'll end up with a three-page paragraph that's guaranteed to intimidate even the most dedicated reader.

> Short paragraphs are easier to read than long ones.

As you write your message, try to use a variety of paragraph lengths. But be careful to use one-sentence paragraphs only occasionally and only for emphasis. When you want to package a big idea in short paragraphs, break the idea into subtopics and treat each subtopic in a separate paragraph—being careful to provide plenty of transitional elements.

Use Lists and Bullets

Set off important ideas in a list—a series of words, names, or items. Lists can show the sequence of your ideas, heighten visual impact, and help readers find your key points. In addition, lists simplify complex subjects, ease the skimming process for busy readers, and give the reader a breather.

> Lists help you focus your reader's attention on important points.

You can separate list items with numbers, letters, or bullets (a general term for any kind of graphical element that precedes each item). Bullets are generally preferred over numbers or letters, unless the sequence of events is critical (if the steps in a process must be completed in a specific order, for example).

When using lists, introduce them clearly so that people know what they're about to read. One way to introduce a list is to use an introductory or lead-in sentence:

> The board of directors met to discuss the revised annual budget. To keep expenses in line with declining sales, the directors voted to
> * Cut everyone's salary by 10 percent
> * Close the employee cafeteria
> * Reduce travel expenses

Another way to introduce a list is to use a complete introductory sentence, followed by a colon:

> To accomplish our mission, our team will follow three steps:
> 1. Find out how many employees would use on-site daycare facilities.
> 2. Determine how much space the daycare centre would require.
> 3. Estimate the cost of converting conference rooms for the on-site facility.

If necessary, add further discussion after the lists to complete your thought.

The items in a list should be in parallel form. If one list item begins with a verb, all list items should begin with a verb. If one is a noun phrase, all should be noun phrases:

Avoid Nonparallel List Items	**Use Parallel List Items**
• Improve our bottom line	• Improving our bottom line
• Identification of new foreign markets for our products	• Identifying new foreign markets for our products
• Global market strategies	• Developing our global market strategies
• Issues regarding pricing and packaging size	• Resolving pricing and packaging issues

For additional discussion of parallelism, see "Rewrite and Edit for Clarity" in Chapter 5.

Use Headings and Subheadings

A heading is a brief title that cues readers to the content of the section that follows. Headings and subheadings serve several important functions. They

* **Show Organization.** Headings show your reader at a glance how the document is organized. They are labels that group related paragraphs together, organizing your material into short sections.
* **Grab Attention.** Informative, inviting, and in some cases intriguing headings grab the reader's attention, make the copy easier to read, and help readers find the parts they need to read—or skip.
* **Make Connections.** Using headings and subheadings visually indicates shifts from one idea to the next, helping readers see the relationship between subordinate and main ideas.

Headings fall into two categories. **Descriptive headings** ("Cost Considerations") identify a topic but do little more. **Informative headings** ("Reducing Costs by Changing Suppliers") sum up the content of the text below them. A well-written informative heading is self-contained; readers can understand it without reading the rest of the document. Use informative headings whenever possible. Keep your headings brief, and use parallel construction as you would for an outline, a list, or a series of words.

Document **Makeovers**

Improving Readability in Email Messages

Email can be as informal and casual as a conversation between old friends. But it can also emulate "snail mail" by using conventional business language, a respectful style, and a more formal format—by using a traditional greeting, formalized headings, and a formal closing and signature.[3] As with any business communication, how formal you make your message depends on your audience and your purpose.

Be sure to use correct spelling and proper grammar for your electronic messages. Spelling, grammar, capitalization, and punctuation still count in cyberspace.[4] To improve email readability even more, be sure to make your subject lines informative, make your message easy to follow, personalize your messages, and observe basic email etiquette.

Make Subject Lines Informative

Always use subject lines in memos, emails, and letters. To capture your audience's attention, make your subject line informative. Do more than just describe or classify message content. Build interest with key words, actions, or benefits. Make subject lines short, specific, and action-oriented. Using verbs, especially participle forms ("ing"), will make the style active. Keep subject lines positive or neutral in tone. If the message is negative, use a topic subject line that does not disclose the message. Otherwise, tell the whole story in this one short phrase.[5]

Ineffective Subject Line	Effective Subject Line
July sales figures	Sending figures for July sales
Tomorrow's meeting	Bringing consultant's report to Friday's meeting
Marketing report	Supplying budget for marketing report
Employee parking	Revised resurfacing schedule for parking lot
Status report	Warehouse remodelling on schedule

Change Subject Lines When Replying

In emails, if you are exchanging multiple emails on the same topic, periodically modify the subject line of your message to reflect the revised message content. Most email programs will copy the subject line when you click the Reply button. It can be confusing to have multiple emails with the same subject line in your electronic files. Moreover, they may have absolutely nothing to do with the original topic. Modifying the subject line with each new response will prevent reader confusion and can make it easier to locate a message at a later date.

Make Your Email Messages Easy to Follow

Avoid lines that run off screen or wrap oddly by using the Enter key to limit lines to 80 characters (60 if email will be forwarded). Avoid styled text (boldface, italic), unless your receiver's system can read it.[6] Write short, focused, logically organized paragraphs. And try to limit email to one screen; otherwise, write like a reporter—starting with the "headline" and adding detail in descending order of importance.[7] That way you'll be sure to get your point across as early as possible, in case your reader doesn't have the time or interest to finish reading your message.

Personalize Email Messages

Adding a salutation to your email message makes it more personal. Naturally, whether you use a formal greeting (*Dear Professor Ingersol*) or a more casual one (*Hi, Marty*) depends on your audience and your purpose. Your complimentary closing and signature also personalize your email message. In most cases, use simple closings, such as *Thanks* or *Regards*, rather than more traditional business closings, such as *Sincerely yours*. However, you may want to use a more formal closing for international email.

For your signature, you can simply type your name on a separate line. Or you may want to use a *signature file,* a short identifier that can include your name, company, postal address, fax number, other email addresses, and so on. You can also use a digital copy of your handwritten signature, which is becoming acceptable as legal proof in business transactions, especially when accompanied by the date stamp that is automatically inserted by your email program.

You can improve email readability by
- Writing informative subject lines
- Making messages visually easy to follow
- Personalizing your messages
- Observing basic email etiquette

Subject lines in email messages and memos should identify message content and build interest.

Subject lines should be
- A phrase (short)
- Specific (informative)
- Focused on action

You can make email messages easier to follow by
- Wording the subject line precisely
- Limiting message length
- Covering the most important points first

Personalize email by adding a salutation, a complimentary closing, and a signature.

Observe Basic Email Etiquette

The best business communicators know how to communicate quickly and courteously. They know how to refrain from putting into writing anything that could come back to haunt them. And they know how important it is to proofread email messages before sending them. Following basic email etiquette means being courteous, brief, and careful.

BE COURTEOUS Common courtesy is an important consideration when sending any communication. Since email creates a false sense of intimacy, it is tempting to write less carefully than you would when composing a memo or letter. However, you should always think about how your messages affect your various audiences; that includes thinking about more than just message content.

- **Send only necessary messages.** Do your best not to add to your audience's information overload.
- **Know who your audience is.** Before clicking on the Send button, double-check your addressees to make sure you've included everyone necessary and no one else.
- **Know your audience's culture.** Don't assume that your audience reads and understands your language. Make sure you know the culture and language of your readers before you begin to write.
- **Be clear about time.** In international email, be sure to use a 24-hour military time format (say 18:00 instead of 6:00 P.M.). Also, indicate the appropriate time zone— Eastern Standard Time (EST), Pacific Daylight Time (PDT), and so on.

> Never write email when you are angry.

- **Respect your audience's schedule.** Identify messages that require no response by including words such as "for your information only" in your subject line or opening comments. And don't waste time sending jokes or chain letters.
- **Don't flame.** A negative email message containing insensitive, insulting, or critical comments is called a *flame.* If you're upset about something or angry with someone, compose yourself before composing your email.

- **Use the priority feature with care.** Many email programs allow you to assign a priority to your message, such as *high, normal,* or *low.* Make sure the priority assigned to your message matches its urgency. Do not overuse "urgent."

BE BRIEF Make sure that you craft tight, meaningful messages. Cover only what is necessary. Identify the issue, add the relevant facts, suggest a resolution, offer possible obstacles, present a timetable for response, and ask for agreement.

- **Narrow your scope.** Stick to one purpose. If you find yourself with two or three purposes, write separate emails. This narrow scope not only helps your readers focus on your message but also facilitates filing and forwarding.

> Avoid wasting readers' time.

- **Write short messages.** Short, direct messages have a much better chance of being understood and acted on than long, roundabout ones. However, don't edit your email messages so much that your readers cannot understand them.
- **Rely on short sentences.** Long sentences are particularly hard to read on screen. Whenever possible, break up long sentences into short, concise ones. If you need to write longer sentences now and then, make sure they are logically and clearly written.

CONTROL TONE The tone of your email should reflect your relationship to the reader and the formality of the situation. Tone is the "sound" of your writing and often shows your attitude to the reader. Tone problems are caused when writers misjudge their relationships to readers; they may talk down to them, sound bossy, negative, or self-centred. Writers who use inflated language can create a pompous tone. Writing an email when you are angry can result in your anger coming across in the tone; for example, saying "Once again you submitted the incorrect form . . ." conveys impatience and lacks regard for the dignity of the receiver—it sends the message, "You did it again, dummy!"

> Create a friendly or neutral tone depending on your relationship to the reader and the nature of the topic.

Tone can range from very informal to formal, depending on the nature of the topic, the relationship of the writer to the reader, and the intention of the message. For example,

TABLE 6.1	Examples of Controlling Tone	
TECHNIQUES FOR CONTROLLING TONE	INFORMAL	FORMAL
Choice of Person/Voice	You can pick up your paycheque at 3 P.M. (second person)	Paycheques may be picked up at 3 P.M. (no person/passive voice)
Word Choice		
Choose words with an appropriate level of formality for the audience and situation	Blue shirts are well known for their customer service. (use of nick name)	Best Buy employees are well known for their customer service. (use of full, official name)
Use plain English and simple words.	The end of the contract means we have to move out of the offices.	The termination of the contract stipulates we must vacate the offices.
Be careful of "charged" words such as "required" and other words that come across as bossy or judgmental.	Please send your travel receipts to finance for reimbursement.	Employees are required to submit receipts to the finance department to be reimbursed for legitimate travel expenses.

if you are writing an email outlining company policies to people who work for you, aim for a neutral tone that avoids preaching or being "bossy" yet conveys the seriousness of the content. If the subject of your message is routine and your relationship to the receivers is informal, your writing can be informal and friendly. Be careful, however, to avoid being too informal. Writers who are used to the informality of Facebook or other social networking sites may come across as too familiar or casual in a business context. For example, the greeting "Hey" and abbreviated language such as "u" (for "you") or "LOL" (for "laughing out loud") are too informal for most business environments. In a social network, everyone is on the same level, but in business, individuals of differing levels of authority may be involved. Knowing how you relate to the readers of your emails will help you choose a tone that is respectful and appropriate to the situation.

Formality and tone are controlled by word choice and by the writer's choice of point of view (first, second, or third person) and voice. If you want writing to sound less formal, use the second person point of view and talk to readers directly in a conversational style. Always put yourself in the reader's shoes to be aware of how the reader might feel about your message. Table 6.1 gives some examples of how tone can be shifted by changing the point of view and word choice.

 Activities

BE CAREFUL Email's speed is its greatest benefit and can also be its greatest drawback. When we sit down at the keyboard, our mindset is typically to empty our email box and move on to other business. Email prompts such quick responses that we forget to organize our thoughts. Successful email is written carefully.

Take time to avoid mistakes.

- **Be sure you hit the right reply button.** When you receive an email message, it may be addressed to you alone or to dozens of others. It may be "copied" to others or "blind copied" to recipients you don't know about. Make sure you hit the correct reply button so that only intended recipients receive your message.
- **When you choose to "reply to all," do so wisely.** Even though the original email sender may think it's a good idea to update everyone on the team, not all team members may need to see every recipient's reply.
- **Understand the use of the cc and bcc fields.** When you add addresses to the cc (courtesy copy) field, make sure that you want all recipients to see who is receiving a copy of your message. Otherwise, use the bcc (blind courtesy copy) field.
- **Slow down.** Every word matters. Even though the fast pace of technology encourages us to respond to others instantaneously, take your time and proceed at your own comfortable pace. The other party will wait.

- **Reread your message.** Avoid sending important email messages immediately after you write them. Ideally, reread them the next morning and make changes.
- **Edit email carefully.** Double-check your email message before sending it. Proofread every email message for completeness, content, fluency, punctuation, and grammar. Finally, make sure that promised documents are indeed attached.
- **Be aware of the permanence of email.** Even after you delete an email message, it can still exist on hard drives and storage devices—both yours and the receiver's. Deleted messages can not only be recovered but also be used as court evidence against you.

Proofread before you send an email.

Understanding the Categories of Brief Messages

Whether you send letters, memos, or email messages, all your messages have three parts: the opening, the body, and the close. How you handle these three parts depends on the type of message you're sending: (1) routine, good-news, and goodwill; (2) bad-news; or (3) persuasive.

Message categories dictate how you approach the opening, body, and close of your short business message.

Routine, Good-News, and Goodwill Messages

The most straightforward business messages are routine, good-news, and goodwill messages. Your readers will most likely be pleased to hear from you, or at the very least, they will be neutral. In the opening, state your main idea directly. The body of your message provides all necessary details. The close is cordial, emphasizing your good news or making a statement about the specific action desired. (Look again at Figures 6.1 on page 99, 6.2 on page 100, and 6.3 on page 101. The comments in the right-hand margins point out how the opening, body, and close are handled in these routine messages.) Routine, good-news, and goodwill messages are discussed in greater detail in Chapter 7.

Bad-News Messages

Successful communicators take a little extra care with their bad-news messages. If your audience will be disappointed, it may be best to use the indirect approach—putting the evidence first and the main idea later. Open with a neutral statement that acts as a transition to the reasons for the bad news. In the body, give the reasons that justify a negative answer before stating or implying the bad news. Your close must always be cordial. Bad-news messages are discussed further in Chapter 8.

Persuasive Messages

An indirect approach is also useful when you know that your audience will resist your message (will be uninterested in your request or unwilling to comply without extra coaxing). Before you can persuade people to do something, you must capture their attention. In the opening, mention a possible benefit, referring to a problem that the recipient might have, posing a question, or mentioning an interesting statistic. In the body, build interest in the subject and arouse your readers' desire to comply. Once you have them thinking, you can introduce your main idea. The close is cordial and requests the desired action. Persuasive messages are discussed at greater length in Chapter 9.

ON THE JOB

Making a Professional Impression in Email

Remember to make the switch from casual use of email and instant messaging to a style and tone that will convey a professional impression of you in the workplace.

- Avoid abbreviated language in email and while serving customers via instant messaging.
- Check spelling and grammar before you hit the send button.
- Use "hello" or "hi" greetings instead of "hey" or other casual greetings.

Reviewing Key Points

This chapter introduces the forms and uses of memos, emails, instant messages, and letters. The chapter explains how to choose a format, based on whether the message is intended for internal or external communication and whether the message form suits the formality of the situation.

Memos and email are used inside companies, while letters are used for more formal external communication. Email and instant messaging are used informally in both internal and external communication.

You learned how to improve overall readability in short business messages by
- Using short paragraphs of no more than seven lines
- Varying sentence patterns and length but limiting sentence length to no more than 16–20 words
- Using lists and bullets to highlight key information and items in a sequence or process
- Making list items parallel and giving them an introductory or lead-in sentence
- Giving every message a short, specific, informative, and action-oriented subject line
- Using informative headings and subheadings phrased in parallel construction to highlight sections of your documents to allow readers to find information quickly or to speed-read the material

You also learned basic email etiquette such as
- Changing the subject line of reply emails
- Being brief, courteous, and mindful of the recipient's time
- Keeping messages short, on one topic, and easy to follow
- Avoiding overfamiliarity, chain emails, and humour

mybuscommlab   Go to MyBusCommLab at www.pearson.ca/mybuscommlab for online exercises.

Practise Your Grammar

 Exercises

Effective business communication starts with strong grammar skills. To improve your grammar skills, go to MyBusCommLab or Grammar-on-the-Go, where you'll find exercises and diagnostic tests to help you produce clear, effective communication.

Test Your Knowledge

Exercises

1. Which message forms are used for internal communication? Why?
2. Which message forms are used for external communication? Why?
3. What format elements make letters more formal than memos and email?
4. How can you increase the readability of your short business messages?
5. What functions do headings serve?
6. How can you increase the readability of your email messages?
7. What are the characteristics of an effective subject line for a memo, an email, or a letter?
8. In what ways can you be courteous when preparing your email messages?
9. What are the similarities between instant messages, text messages, and online posts?
10. What are the characteristics of a well-written heading?

Apply Your Knowledge

1. Why do you think good internal communication improves employee attitudes and performance? Explain briefly.
2. What do you think is important about matching the formality of your message to the formality of the situation and audience expectations?
3. For what purposes could a company use social networking technologies? What are the advantages and disadvantages of using this technology from the company's point of view? Explain.

4. Is it ever okay to use an indirect approach when writing email? How can you put off the bad news when you have to state your purpose in the subject line? Explain.

5. **Ethical Choices** Your boss wants you to send a message to the production staff, thanking all six members for their hard work and overtime to get the new manufacturing line set up and running on schedule. Your boss has been working a lot of overtime herself; she's been under a lot of pressure, and it's beginning to show. She wants to send the thank-you message by email and asks you to work on the wording. You think each member of the production staff should receive a formal letter to keep for future promotions or other jobs. You know your boss won't like being interrupted about an issue that she thinks is off her desk, and you know how valuable her time is.

   a. Should you draft the letter and produce six copies so that you don't have to bother your boss?

   b. Should you simply draft the email message as requested to save everyone time?

   c. Should you discuss the issue with your boss, regardless of taking her away from the tasks she so desperately needs to get done?

Running Cases

Video

CASE 1: Noreen

During the month following the merger of Petro-Go and Best Gas, many staff changes were made on the Go Points and Collections teams. Noreen has continued as acting manager of the two teams and has been approached by Sandra, a team leader from Collections about some staff problems. Sandra is having problems with three employees who have recently transferred onto her team. Sandra explains that the three employees frequently return from breaks late, and though she has tried to use humour to get them to return on time, they continue to come back late several times per week. Now some of the other employees are starting to take longer breaks too.

QUESTIONS

1. What should Noreen do?

2. What may be contributing to the employees' behaviours?

3. What message should be communicated to the three employees? Should the same message be sent to the whole team?

4. What is the best way to communicate these messages? Why?

5. Who should send the message?

6. What style and tone elements should be considered when communicating with the employees?

YOUR TASK

Create an email that could be sent to all employees on the Collections team. Use a style and tone that is appropriate for the situation.

CASE 2: Kwong

As a result of Kwong's promotional flyer, Accountants For All has many new clients. Kwong has been put in charge of working with 10 new small business clients. He has to communicate two important deadlines (date by which all material must be given to him and date for the meeting to sign forms in his office) and he has to brief the clients on two different forms they must complete before the upcoming tax season. Each form has two or three points that need explanation—for example, the Claim for GST Exemption Form must have all receipts attached and include the company's GST number. Also, the Statement of Income and Expenses Form must list income monthly and include invoice numbers for each entry. The expenses have to also be listed monthly and have corresponding receipts attached.

QUESTIONS

1. Should Kwong use a form letter or an email to communicate with his new clients? Why?

2. What design elements would be useful in explaining the forms?

3. How could Kwong emphasize the two deadlines?

4. What other messages should Kwong include in the communication?

5. How can Kwong create an appropriate tone for his communication?

YOUR TASK

Write the message to the clients. Make up needed details and use document design features to emphasize important aspects of the message.

⊖ Practise Your Knowledge

Form and Audience Barbara Marquardt is in charge of public relations for a cruise line that operates out of Vancouver, B.C. She is shocked to read a letter in a local newspaper from a disgruntled passenger, complaining about the service and entertainment on a recent cruise. Marquardt will have to respond to these publicized criticisms in some way.

1. What audiences will she need to consider in her response?
2. For each of these audiences, should Marquardt send her message via letter, memo, email, or another channel of communication? Why?

Teamwork Your team has been studying a new method for testing the durability of your company's electric hand tools. Now your team needs to summarize the findings in three separate reports: (a) one for company administrators who will decide whether to purchase the new testing equipment needed for this new method, (b) one for company engineers who design and develop the hand tools, and (c) one for the trainers from the test equipment company, who would be showing your workers how to use the new testing equipment. Your team leader emphasizes that all three reports need to reach receivers quickly so that your team can receive their responses in less than a month. Working with at least two other students, answer the following questions for each of the three reports:

3. Should your team send the report by letter, memo, or email?
    a. Administrators
    b. Engineers
    c. Trainers
4. Should the language be formal or conversational?
    a. Administrators
    b. Engineers
    c. Trainers

Using Bullets Rewrite the following paragraph using a bulleted list:

5. With our alarm system, you'll have a 24-hour security guard who signals the police when there is any indication of an intruder. You'll also appreciate the computerized scanning device that determines exactly where and when the intrusion occurred. No need to worry about electrical failure, either, thanks to our backup response unit.[8]

Keeping Paragraphs Short Mark on the page where to break the following paragraph into shorter paragraphs:

6. Donner Corporation faced a major transformation, growing from a small, single-product company to a large, broadly based corporation in just three years. This changeover involved much more than simply adding on to the plant and hiring more people, because the quality of the existing staff and products was not good enough for a first-rate operation. The task therefore required both physical expansion and quality improvement. The physical expansion alone represented a major undertaking. The investment in facilities required $18 million. Over a three-year period, the organization spent more on the new plant and equipment than it had spent in the past 17 years of its operation. To raise its competitive capability, the company had to develop new programs and organizational units and, at the same time, expand and upgrade its existing operations. It also needed to double the size of its staff by recruiting high-calibre people from many fields. This staffing had to be accomplished in an increasingly competitive labour market and without benefit of an experienced human resources department.

Varying Sentence Length Revise the following paragraph to vary the length of the sentences and to shorten the paragraph so that readers find it more readable:

7. Although major league hockey remains popular, more people are attending minor league hockey games because they can spend less on admission, snacks, and parking and still enjoy the excitement of Canada's favourite game.

For example, in the 2001–02 season more than seven million fans attended regular games and one million attended the playoffs. Saskatchewan has three teams—the Moose Jaw Warriors, Saskatoon Blades, and the Regina Pats—and Manitoba has the Brandon Wheat Kings. These teams play in relatively small rinks, so fans are close enough to see and hear everything, including the sounds of the players hitting the boards or the goalie catching the puck. Best of all, the cost of a family outing to see rising stars play in a local minor league game is just a fraction of what the family would spend to attend a major league game in a much larger, more crowded arena.

Controlling Tone

8. The email below contains a number of tone problems. Discuss the email with two classmates and identify what causes the tone problems. What type of tone should this email have? Rewrite the email to achieve appropriate tone.

From: Cal Wilson <cpwilson@orgus.net>
To: All Employees
Sent: Friday, September 04, 2009 7:04 PM
Subject: Smoking at Building Entrances

It has come to my attention once again that employees continue to smoke at the entrances to our building.
Not only is this behaviour in contravention of the firm's regulations and the City bylaw, but it is also preventing customers from proper egress into our establishment.

Effective immediately no employees will smoke within five meters of the building entrances.

---

9. Write the following message in three ways to create (1) a friendly, informal tone; (2) a neutral tone; and (3) a firm, formal tone. You are an employee in the shipping department of a company of 150 employees. You are setting up a Facebook group for company employees to use for socializing and you want employees to participate in the group. You also want them to use their judgment about the types of things they say and do on the site.

Informal tone:

Neutral tone:

Formal tone:

Making Subject Lines Informative Add specific words to make the following subject lines more informative:
10. New budget figures

11. Your opinion on our current marketing brochure

12. Production schedule

ACTIVITIES

1. **Analyze This Document** Read the following document; then (1) analyze the strengths and weaknesses of each sentence and (2) revise the document so that it follows the guidelines in Chapters 3 through 6.

Dear Ms. Giraud:

Enclosed herewith please find the manuscript for your book, *Interpreting Body Art*. After perusing the first two chapters of your 1500-page manuscript, I was forced to conclude that the subject matter, tattoo art forms and piercings, is not coincident with the publishing program of Framingham Press, which to this date has issued only works on business endeavours, avoiding all other topics completely.

Although our firm is unable to consider your impressive work at the present time, I have taken the liberty of recording some comments on some of the pages. I am of the opinion that any feedback that a writer can obtain from those well versed in the publishing realm can only serve to improve the writer's authorial skills.

In view of the fact that your residence is in the Toronto area, might I suggest that you secure an appointment with someone of high editorial stature at Pearson Press, which I believe might have something of an interest in works of the nature you have produced.

Wishing you the best of luck in your literary endeavours, I remain

Arthur J. Cogswell

Editor

---

2. **Planning an Email: Learn While You Earn—Email Announcing Burger King's Educational Benefits**

Herb Lipsey, owner of the Burger King store in Moncton, is worried about employee turnover. He needs to keep 50 people on the payroll to operate the outlet, but recruiting and retaining those people is tough. The average employee leaves after about seven months, so Lipsey has to hire and train 90 people a year just to maintain a 50-person crew. At a cost of $1500 per hire, the price tag for all that turnover is approximately $60 000 a year.

Lipsey knows that a lot of his best employees quit because they think that flipping burgers is a dead-end job. But what if it weren't a dead-end job? What if a person could really get some place flipping burgers? What if Lipsey offered to pay his employees' way through college if they remained with the store? Would that keep them behind the counter?

He's decided to give educational incentives a try. Employees who choose to participate will continue to earn their usual salary, but they will also get free books and college tuition, keyed to the number of hours they work each week. Those who work from 10 to 15 hours a week can take one free course at nearby New Brunswick Community College; those who work 16 to 25 hours can take two courses; and those who work 26 to 40 hours can take three courses. The program is open to all employees, regardless of how long they have worked for Burger King, but no one is obligated to participate.

Your task Assume you are Herb's assistant. He has asked you to respond. How would you plan and write an email announcing the new educational incentives? The purpose is clear (to inform employees about the new offer), the audience has already been defined (all Moncton Burger King employees), and the medium has been chosen (an email). Now use the following questions to continue your planning, choosing the best answer for each one. Then, creating sentences of your own, draft the email based on what you've learned from this planning exercise.
1. Which sentence best expresses the email's main idea?
    a. Turnover at the Moncton Burger King costs approximately $60 000 a year.
    b. Flipping burgers doesn't have to be a dead-end job.
    c. The Moncton Burger King is offering its employees an exciting new educational program.
    d. The new educational incentive program is open to all employees, no matter how long they've worked for Burger King.
2. Which of these sentences will help you establish a good relationship with your audience?
    a. We are hoping that many of you will take advantage of the new program because it will reduce our turnover.

      b. Employees need not attend college to continue working for us.

      c. We hope that you will find the program useful.

      d. Now you can earn free college tuition while you work at Burger King.

3. What must the body of your message accomplish? (Choose all that apply.)

      a. Tell employees how to take advantage of the educational offer.

      b. Explain how working hours relate to tuition payments.

      c. Describe how Mr. Lipsey came up with his idea.

      d. Influence employees to attend college.

4. Which of the following methods will be best for conveying the relationship between hours worked and tuition paid?

      a. A two-column table with the headings: "Those Who Work" (listing hours per week) and "May Take" (listing number of courses paid for).

      b. A paragraph explaining the connection between hours worked and courses paid for.

      c. A bulleted list with parallel entries such as, "If you work 10 to 15 hours, you'll get one free course; If you work 16 to 25 hours, you'll get two free courses;" etc.

      d. A paragraph suggesting that details can be obtained from Mr. Lipsey's office for those interested in taking advantage of the program.

5. To close the email, which of the following sentences is the best choice?

      a. We hope you'll take advantage of this offer, since doing so will help us reduce our turnover problem.

      b. You don't have to take college courses to continue working for us.

      c. I'll be happy to answer any questions you might have about how working for Burger King can help you earn free college tuition; just ask me.

      d. If you're thinking of quitting, this may give you second thoughts.

Now draft an email in your own words for Herb to sign.

3. **Revising an Email: Break-Time Blues—Email Requesting a New Employee Procedure** The following message contains numerous errors related to what you've learned about planning and writing business messages. First, list the flaws you find in this version. Then follow the steps below to plan and write a better email:

To: Billing Department
From: Felicia August, Sr. Supervisor
Date: December 28, 2009
Subject: Compliance with new break procedure

Hello people,

Some of you may not like the rules about break times; however, we determined that keeping track of employees while they took breaks at times they determined rather than regular breaks at prescribed times was not working as well as we would have liked it to work. The new rules are not going to be an option. If you do not follow the new rules, you could be docked from your pay for hours when you turned up missing, since your direct supervisor will not be able to tell whether you were on a "break" or not and will assume that you have walked away from your job. We cannot be responsible for any errors that result from your inattentiveness to the new rules. I have already heard complaints from some of you and I hope this memo will end this issue once and for all. The decision has already been made.

Starting Monday, January 1, you will all be required to take a regular 15-minute break in the morning and again in the afternoon, and a regular thirty-minute lunch at the times specified by your supervisor, NOT when you think you need a break or when you "get around to it."

There will be no exceptions to this new rule!

---

1. Describe the flaws you discovered in this email.
2. Develop a plan for rewriting the email. Use the following steps to organize your efforts before you begin writing:
   a. Determine the purpose
   b. Identify and analyze your audience
   c. Define the main idea
   d. Outline the major supporting points
   e. Choose between a direct and an indirect approach
3. Now rewrite the email. Don't forget to leave ample time for revision of your own work before you turn it in.

4. **Revising an Email: Moving Day—Email Informing Employees About an Office Relocation** From what you've learned about planning and writing business messages, you should be able to identify numerous errors made by the writer of the following email. List them below, then plan and write a better email, following the guidelines given.

> To: All Office Personnel
> From: David Burke, Manager
> Date: September 27, 2009
> Subject: Get Ready
>
> Hi,
>
> We are hoping to be back at work soon, with everything running smoothly, same production schedule and no late projects or missed deadlines. So you need to clean out your desk, put your stuff in boxes, and clean off the walls. You can put the items you had up on your walls in boxes, also.
>
> We have provided boxes. The move will happen this weekend. We'll be in our new offices when you arrive on Monday.
>
> We will not be responsible for personal belongings during the move.
>
> Regards,
>
> Dave

1. Describe the flaws you discovered in this email.
2. Develop a plan for rewriting it. Use the following steps to organize your efforts before you begin writing:
   a. Determine the purpose
   b. Analyze and identify your audience
   c. Define the main idea
   d. Outline the major supporting points
   e. Choose between the direct and the indirect approach
3. Now rewrite the email. Don't forget to leave ample time for revision of your own work before you turn it in.

Expand Your Knowledge

Best of the Web

Improve Your Use of Email You've probably used email for personal communication, but writing business email can be both risky and daunting. Before you begin, learn some email etiquette by reviewing a list of dos and don'ts at www.dynamoo.com/technical/etiquette.htm. You can also get tips on email use and how companies can enforce email policies at www.emailreplies.com/Email_policy.html.

EXERCISES

1. What should a company include in an email policy for staff? How can companies follow up to ensure staff will follow the policy?
2. What's wrong with using common email jargon and abbreviations in business email, such as BTW ("by the way") or IMHO ("in my humble opinion")?
3. What is an *autoresponder*? If you're operating a website, how might it improve the effectiveness of your email communication? Can you think of situations in which it might work against your business interests?

Exploring the Web on Your Own

Review these chapter-related websites on your own to learn more about writing business messages.

1. Become fluent in your email usage, from basic set-up to advanced techniques, by taking the tutorial at **www.webteacher.org/home**. On the home page, click "Communicating," then select "Email."
2. Master email's unique challenges by studying suggestions for developing clear content, using special cues, and creating context at A Beginner's Guide to Effective Email, **www.webfoot.com**.
3. Gain more insight into the parts of a memo and their effective use by reading the handbook notes at **www.ecf.toronto.edu/~writing/handbook-memo.html**.

Cases

Apply each step in Figure 3.1 (on page 40) to the following cases, as assigned by your instructor.

EMAIL SKILLS 1. NO EXAGGERATION: SHORT EMAIL DESCRIBING INTERNSHIP DUTIES

You've been labouring all summer at an internship, learning how business is conducted. You've done work nobody else wanted to do, but that's okay. Even the smallest tasks can make a good impression on your future resumé.

This morning, your supervisor asks you to write a description of the job you've been doing. "Include everything, even the filing," she suggests, "and address it to me in an email message."

She says a future boss might assign such a task prior to a performance review. "You can practise describing your work without exaggeration—or too much modesty," she says, smiling.

YOUR TASK Using good techniques for short messages and relying on your real-life work experience, write an email that will impress your supervisor.

EMAIL SKILLS 2. SATISFACTION GUARANTEED: EMAIL FROM MOUNTAIN EQUIPMENT CO-OP

One of the nicest things about working in customer service for recreational goods and clothing retailer MEC is that company policy guarantees satisfaction, "no questions asked." This means you always get to say yes to angry customers who want a refund.

In your hand is a package from Arvin Bummel (212 Borealis Drive, Iqaluit, Nunavut X0A 0H0). You open it to find (a) one pair of wool trousers, stiff and shrunken, (b) an outfitter's guide shirt (regular), also two sizes smaller than it should be, and (c) an angry letter from Mr. Bummel saying the clothes were ruined the first time he washed them.

You're not surprised, since their labels all clearly say, "Dry Clean Only."

YOUR TASK Write a letter to Mr. Bummel granting him a refund, to be credited to his MasterCard. He sent you his receipts and by cross-checking on your inventory list, you can see that the prices are correct (pants: $69, shirt: $45). Refund him his costs, including taxes. You look into the catalogue and see a couple of washable alternatives in the same price range—the mountaineer shirt, product #12-y789 ($42) and camp pants, product #35-A224 ($74). But remember not to blame him in your letter; an MEC customer is always right.

EMAIL SKILLS TEAM SKILLS 3. MEASURING SUPPLIERS: EMAIL REQUESTING REVIEWS AT BELL CANADA

Bell Canada evaluates employees regularly to determine their performance—so why not do the same with the independent contractors the company hires to perform key functions? Nearly every department uses outside providers these days—a practice called *outsourcing*. So if there's a gap between what Bell expects from contractors and what the contractors actually deliver, shouldn't Bell tell them how they can improve their performance?

You've been discussing these questions all morning in a meeting with other members of the Employee Services Group. Your boss is convinced that regular reviews of independent contractors are essential.

"It's all about improving clarity in terms of goals and expectations," he says, adding that if contractors receive constructive feedback, Bell can develop good relationships with them instead of having to look for new service suppliers all the time.

Your boss assigns your team the task of informing all departments in your region that they'll be required to evaluate subcontractors every six months, beginning immediately. The goal of the review is to determine the performance of independent contractors so that Bell can (1) give them constructive feedback and continue a strong relationship or (2) end the relationship if service is substandard. Departments will need to rate each contractor on a scale of 1 (poor) to 5 (excellent) for each of several factors that your group is going to determine. Departments will be sending their reports to Roxanna Frost, group program manager for Bell's Executive Management and Development Group.

YOUR TASK Working as a team of three with your classmates, develop a list of factors that will help you rate the overall service of independent contractors. You'll need to consider cost, quality of work, innovation, delivery, and other factors similar to those you'd encounter in a job performance review. Then compose an email to all Bell department managers in your region. Explain the new review requirements and include your list of factors to be rated on the 1-to-5 scale.[9]

EMAIL SKILLS 4. PIZZA PROMISES

You work at John Henry's, a large mountain bike retailer in North Vancouver. You are an administrative assistant (and all round big help) to the store owner and manager. The 30 members of the staff are about to head into the peak season for mountain bike sales. Things will be hopping for the next two months. The boss has decided you should organize a pizza lunch for every Friday—free for all staff. Write an email to let employees know.

5. WAKEBOARD MANIA: LETTER FROM PERFORMANCE SKI & SURF INQUIRING ABOUT AVAILABILITY

Your boss, Bill Porter, owner of Performance Ski & Surf in Peterborough, Ontario, hasn't seen a sport this popular since in-line skating took off.

"I hope these kids don't get hurt trying to imitate the pros," Porter says. You're both admiring a picture of a professional wakeboarder catching air as he trails behind a boat on nearby Rice Lake. He's 5 metres in the air, with the short, stubby fibreglass board strapped to his feet—only he's upside down. His grimace shows the flip isn't as easy as it looks.

"Don't worry," you say. "Extreme sports are hot. Think of snowboarding. I guarantee, you'll see wakeboarding at the Olympics soon."

"Well, meanwhile, we've got to get these Wake Techs, Neptunes, and Full Tilts in stock," Porter replies. "They're outselling traditional water skis 20 to 1."

"It would be cool to see what other models the manufacturers are going to come out with for next season," you say.

"Go ahead and ask for new catalogues when you write to them about availability. And ask what kind of lead time is needed for shipping. I don't want to get caught short," Porter replies.

YOUR TASK Draft a letter Porter can send to manufacturers to inquire about availability throughout Ontario's busy summer season. It's winter now and you're well stocked, but when summer returns, your sales will rocket.

EMAIL SKILLS 6. NAP TIME: EMAIL ANNOUNCING NEW SLEEPING ROOM AT PHIDIAS & ASSOCIATES

"We're going to do what?" you ask in astonishment. But your boss is standing over your desk and he isn't smiling. Jonas T. Phidias is senior partner of Phidias & Associates, a Vancouver architectural firm, and he's completely serious.

"A nap room," he says somewhat impatiently. "We've hired a subcontractor to convert those two back offices that we haven't been using. You know what pressures our people are under to handle the stress of long hours and still be creative. Well, we'll soon be offering them the opportunity to rejuvenate with a quick, creative nap."

From his snappish tone, you realize that your response wasn't what he had expected. Quickly you compose

yourself. As you think about it, his idea makes a lot of sense. You've felt the need yourself—after working late on a rush job, you've wondered how you're supposed to be creatively inspired when you can barely get your eyes to focus. "Why, naps could be great!" you finally manage.

"Yes," he interrupts before you can go on. "It's not just about productivity—I read an article in the *Globe* recently that said many Canadians are operating on way too little sleep. Fatigue causes car accidents, illness, and long-term health problems," says Phidias. "I've just read *The Art of Napping* by William A. Anthony, and the benefits of a nap room are too great to ignore.

"Other companies are proving that naps can improve employees' mental function sufficiently to affect the bottom line. I've decided that no matter what they think of it, Phidias & Associates employees are going to take naps during working hours," he instructs as he strides away.

YOUR TASK As Phidias's assistant, write a straightforward email informing employees that the new "nap room" will be ready for their convenience in approximately three weeks, and that they will be encouraged to make good use of it. Try to keep humour out of your email. Decide how the room can be booked and if any rules should be included. Add any realistic details as needed.[10]

EMAIL SKILLS 7. ENVIRONMENTAL PLANNING: EMAIL ANNOUNCING A COMMITTEE MEETING

You've probably worked as a volunteer on a committee or with team members for class assignments. You know how hard it is to get a diverse group of individuals together for a productive meeting. Maybe you've tried different locations—one member's home, or a table at the library. This time you're going to suggest a local coffee shop.

The committee you're leading is a volunteer group planning a garbage pickup project at an area park. Your meeting goal is to brainstorm ways to encourage public participation in this environmental event, to be held next Earth Day.

YOUR TASK Develop a short email message telling committee members about the meeting. Include time, date, duration, and location (choose a place you know). Mention the meeting goal to encourage attendance.

EMAIL SKILLS 8. COMMUNITY GROUP PLANNING: PROMOTING LOCAL AND ORGANIC PRODUCERS.

You belong to a community group that promotes local and organic producers. One of your big success stories is the summer farmers' markets that started in your neighbourhood but now happen throughout the city. The last few months your group has been waiting for a response to an application you put in for federal funding for the idea of staging a community fair that would promote local organic farmers and businesses that have sustainable business practices. The target is to get 50 businesses to participate in a one-day event, so the call you just received from your president, Johanna Prozski, was just what you were waiting to hear. "Good news," she said. "We got our federal grant for the fair!"

This is good news—you now have the rest of the funds needed to get the fair going. "This is exciting! It's going to happen! We need Kira, Puru, and Meghan to begin calling companies to sell them a booth—it'll cost 125 bucks for a booth—which is a good deal," exclaimed Johanna.

"I agree," you replied. "Showcasing your company for that small amount is a good deal."

"Yeah, we'll get somewhere around 800 to 1000 people out, no problem, especially if the surrounding communities get into this event too," offered Johanna.

"What's the timeline for our people to be calling the companies they have been assigned?" you asked.

"It'd be good to know who is committed within one month," replied Johanna. "Will you email the group and let them all know the news and who needs to do what?"

"Sure, I can do that," you replied. "Remind me of the fair venue details."

"Well—we're in for the Heritage Hall on Main Street on March 30 and I believe we have from 10 to 4. Make sure everyone knows Dan offered to order the poster printing and Maurice is on for getting the city licence and permit for the event," she instructed. "And Shari agreed to price table rentals. What a great group, hey? Way better than last year when Mark and Matt paid for a bar bill with petty cash and Connor mixed up the table order—way better. Maybe we better meet in two weeks—Tuesday night, let's say 7 to 9 P.M., to iron out all the details," Johanna remarked.

"OK," you agreed. "I'll book the room at Trout Lake Community Centre for that and let everyone know what's going on."

YOUR TASK Select the appropriate information (and add any specific details you think are necessary) and write the email to the community group (make up your own group name) to update them on the grant and confirm event details and responsibilities. Remember to use document design features to make your email easy to read. You may want to use a combination of an email and an MS Word attachment for the event details.

EMAIL SKILLS 9. CELEBRATING DIFFERENCES—A REQUEST FROM HUMAN RESOURCES

You work as an assistant in human resources at Art in Motion, a production company that makes framed artwork for the retail market. The company has 340 employees in a plant just outside Vancouver. The multicultural staff have an active social club and its president, Charlotte Knutson, approached human resources about the company holding celebrations to mark special occasions for the four predominant cultures of the staff. The idea is to have the social club set up displays four times per year (at Chinese New Year, Diwali, Hanukkah, Christmas, and maybe for even more celebrations depending on staff suggestions. They requested that the staff cafeteria serve traditional foods in keeping with each celebration and play some music related to the culture.

After you got the go-ahead from the senior management team, you looked into the cost of providing a budget for displays, decorations, and music (even though the president did not ask for it) and you talked to the food services contractor, who has agreed to coordinate with the social club representatives to prepare menus for the four celebrations. The cafeteria requires only that the selection of entrees be limited to six dishes (the usual number of varied dishes) and that the menus be set well in advance to allow for purchasing deadlines. Advertising for the events would have to be created by Charlotte or a designate, but she would have to send it to you so you could use your all-staff email (and you could also edit messages to ensure they meet company standards before they are sent out). So, she would have to send you the messages a few days before they need to go out for each celebration period.

YOUR TASK Write an email to Charlotte telling her the good news and outlining requirements. Add any details you think would be useful.

EMAIL SKILLS 10. BOLGA BOO-BOO: EMAIL TO GETRADE (GHANA) LTD. FROM PIER 1 IMPORTS

When you were hired as an assistant buyer for Pier 1 Imports, you thought it would be an exciting introduction to the import-export business—the job you've always dreamed about. What a romantic way to earn a living—travelling overseas, buying products, and then shipping them back to Canada for sale. But now you've learned some of the realities of the job, and your romantic ideas are fading.

For example, Pier 1 sent a buyer to Accra, Ghana, to find local handicrafts to satisfy your customers' interests in African art. So far the local entrepreneurs are having trouble meeting the demand from large-quantity buyers like Pier 1 (and your rival, Cost Plus). A good example of what's been going wrong is the shipment that just arrived from Getrade (Ghana) Ltd., one of your best Ghanaian suppliers. You sympathize with Ladi Nylander, chairman and managing director of Getrade, who is trying hard to adapt to the specific tastes of Canadian buyers. He's hiring local artisans to carve, shape, and weave all sorts of artifacts—often from designs provided by Pier 1.

Your Pier 1 customers love bowl-shaped Bolga baskets, traditionally woven by the people of northern Ghana. You can't keep the baskets in stock, so this was to be a huge shipment—3000 Bolga baskets. Your order requested 1000 green, 1000 yellow, and 1000 magenta baskets in the traditional shape.

However, when the order came in, you found 3000 mixed-colour, flat Bolga baskets. Your overseas buyer reported that the Body Shop had ordered baskets similar to yours but with mixed-colour patterns and a flatter shape. Pier 1 may have received the Body Shop's order by mistake.

YOUR TASK As assistant buyer, you need to send an email message to Nylander at Nylander@Getrade.co.za, informing him of the error in your order. You can mention that your order and the Body Shop's may have been mixed up, a mistake that should be relatively easy to correct.

▌INSTANT
▌MESSAGES 11. "YES, WE DO PURPLE": INSTANT MESSAGE FROM LANDS' END

When clothing retailer Lands' End offered its 2500 telephone service representatives the chance to train on its new instant messaging system, "Lands' End Live," you jumped at the opportunity. As it turned out, so many volunteered for the new training that the company had to give preference to a few hundred who'd been on the job longest. You were one of the lucky ones.

Now you've had months of practice answering messages like the one you just received from a customer named Alicia. She wants to know if she can have a red Polartec Aircore-200 scarf custom monogrammed—not in the standard, contrasting wheat-coloured thread, but in radiant purple as a gift for her husband, whose favourite colours are red and purple. According to Alicia, her husband says, "Red & purple are feng shui symbols of wealth & prosperity."

On its website, Lands' End promises to fulfill nonstandard monogram requests "if technical limitations allow." You've done a quick check and yes, her husband can have his initials in bright purple on the red background.

YOUR TASK Write the instant message reply to Alicia, telling her the good news.[11]

Spin Cycle: Deciphering Corporate Doublespeak

If there's one product North American businesses can manufacture in large amounts, it's doublespeak. Doublespeak is language that only pretends to say something but that in reality hides, evades, or misleads. Like most products, doublespeak comes in many forms, from the popular buzzwords that everyone uses but no one really understands—such as *competitive dynamics* and *empowerment*—to words that try to hide meaning, such as *re-engineering, synergy,* and *restructuring.*

With doublespeak, bribes and kickbacks are called *rebates* or *fees for product testing* and used-car-parts dealers have become *auto dismantlers and recyclers.* Plus, just about everyone's job title has the word *chief* in it: chief nuclear officer, chief learning officer, chief cultural officer, chief ethics officer, chief turnaround officer, and chief creative officer. After all the "operations improvement" that corporations have undergone, you have to wonder who all those "chiefs" are leading. Never before have so many led so few.

With doublespeak, banks don't have *bad loans* or *bad debts;* they have *nonperforming credits* that are *rolled over* or *rescheduled.* And corporations never lose money; they just experience *negative cash flow, deficit enhancement,* or *negative contributions to profits.*

Of course, no one gets fired these days. People high enough in the corporate pecking order *resign for personal reasons.* Those below the lofty heights of corporate power are *involuntarily terminated* as the result of *downsizing, workforce adjustments,* and *headcount reductions.* Some companies even *implement a skills mix adjustment* or *eliminate redundancies in the human resources area.* One automobile company (that closed an entire assembly plant and eliminated more than 8000 jobs) called the action *a volume-related production schedule adjustment.*

But don't worry, if you're *dehired, deselected, surplused,* or *uninstalled,* corporations will offer you a *career change opportunity* or *vocational relocation.* In fact, hardly anyone is laid off these days. "We don't characterize it as a layoff," said one corporate doublespeaker (sometimes called a spin doctor). "We're managing our staff resources. Sometimes you manage them up, and sometimes you manage them down."

The goal of good writing is to communicate, not to confuse; to be understood, not to hide behind words. Look at this confusing excerpt from an investment document:

The applicability of the general information and administrative procedures set forth below accordingly will vary depending on the investor and the record-keeping system established for a shareholder's investment in the Fund. Participants in RRSPs and other plans should first consult with the appropriate persons at their employer or refer to the plan materials before following any of the procedures below.

As discussed in Chapter 4, *plain English* is a way of writing and arranging technical materials so that your audience can understand your meaning. Restating our excerpt in plain English reveals one simple thought: "If you are investing through a large retirement plan or other special program, follow the instructions in your program material."

Some companies are concerned that writing documents in plain English will increase their liability, but many companies are finding just the opposite. "In many ways," notes one Bell Atlantic employee, "we reduced our liability because we have created a document that is much clearer and less ambiguous." Similarly, when Citibank introduced promissory notes written in plain English, the number of collection lawsuits fell dramatically. The clearer writing simply made it easier for borrowers to understand their obligations.

Some lawyers may purposely choose obscure language to control vital information, to take advantage of those who don't know what they're signing, or profit from people who hire them to interpret the difficult language. But many legal professionals strongly endorse the plain-English movement. The plain-English movement has generated great momentum; perhaps confusing language will become obsolete.

APPLICATIONS FOR SUCCESS

For more on the subject of doublespeak, visit David Tompkins' website at www.dt.org and select "For Your Reading Pleasure" to find and read the article "Life Under the Chief Doublespeak Officer."

Answer the following questions:

1. What do you think? Isn't corporate doublespeak just another way to emphasize the positive in business situations? Or is it unethical to use business buzzwords and corporate doublespeak to ease negative impressions? Explain your position in a one-page memo or an email message to your instructor.

2. If it's unethical to use doublespeak, would you classify it as an ethical dilemma or an ethical lapse? Explain your position in a one-page memo or email message to your instructor.

3. Do the people in your field appear to value the jargon and buzzwords of their industry? If you use plain English, do you risk your reputation as a professional in your field? Please explain in a one-page memo or email message to your instructor.

4. The president of one company just learned that some of his employees have been playing a popular game called "buzzword bingo," in which participants ridicule doublespeak by tracking the jargon their bosses use during staff meetings on bingo-like cards. Some managers are complaining that it's getting out of control. In fact, as one meeting dragged on, employees tried to steer the conversation to use all the buzzwords on their cards. What can managers do to avoid these silly games?

5. Visit the following buzzword bingo website and print out a card or two: isd.usc.edu/~karl/Bingo.

6. Read the current business section of your favourite newspaper. How many buzzwords did you find?

Writing Routine Messages

LEARNING OBJECTIVES

After studying this chapter, you will be able to

1. Apply the three-step writing process to routine positive messages
2. Illustrate the strategy for writing routine requests
3. Discuss the differences among three types of routine requests
4. Illustrate the strategy for writing routine replies and positive messages
5. Explain the main differences among messages granting a claim when the company, the customer, or a third party is at fault
6. Clarify the importance of goodwill messages, and describe how to make them effective

Ernst & Young is one of the world's largest providers of professional services, with offices in 670 locations in 140 countries. Ernst & Young Canada operates in 14 Canadian cities, offering accounting, business, and financial consulting services to a variety of industries. The company also has a strong sense of corporate responsibility and has a reputation of creating goodwill through actively supporting the arts. As a managing partner, Fred Withers communicates widely with professional staff and clients. "Some people think that accountants only work with numbers," says Withers, "but the key is being able to explain them to people in a clear, professional manner." Whether requesting information from clients, or responding to routine inquires, Withers believes concise, accurate, open communication can create a positive impression for the business.[1]

Using the Three-Step Writing Process for Routine Messages

Like Fred Withers, you'll probably compose a lot of routine, good-news, and goodwill messages: orders, company policies, claims, credit, information about employees, products, operations, and so on. To produce the best messages possible, apply the three-step writing process (see Figure 7.1 on page 124):

- **Step 1: Planning routine messages.** For routine messages, you may need only a few moments to analyze your purpose and audience, investigate audience needs, and adapt your message to your readers.
- **Step 2: Writing routine messages.** Organizing and composing routine messages can be direct and quick; however, be sure to verify the customs of your intercultural audiences before deciding to use the direct approach.
- **Step 3: Completing routine messages.** No matter how short or straightforward your message, make it professional by allowing plenty of time to revise, produce, and proofread it.

Even for routine situations, you need to plan, write, and complete your messages.

FIGURE 7.1	Applying the Three-Step Writing Process to Routine Messages

Planning	Writing	Completing
Analyze • Make your purpose specific. • Know whether readers will react positively. • Learn more about them if necessary. **Investigate** • Find out what readers need to know. • Gather relevant information. **Adapt** • Verify the effectiveness of the written channel. • If written, choose the best medium. • Use the "you" attitude. • Keep your language positive and polite.	**Organize** • Define the main idea before beginning. • Group relevant points logically. • Adopt the direct approach. - Open by clearly stating the main idea. - Put all necessary details in the body. - Close cordially. **Compose** • Adapt the style and tone. • Use a conversational tone. • Use plain English.	**Revise** • Evaluate the overall effect of the message. • Be sure you've said what you want to. • Put content in the order you want. • Make the message easy to read, concise, and clear. **Produce** • Design the document to suit your readers. • Use effective design elements. • Use appropriate delivery methods. **Proofread** • Check for typos. • Check for spelling and mechanical errors. • Look for alignment problems. • Make sure print quality is acceptable.
1	2	3

Making Routine Requests

Whenever you ask for something—information, action, products, adjustments, references—you are making a request. A request is routine if it's part of the normal course of business and you anticipate that your audience will want to comply. Don't make unnecessary requests. If you can find information yourself, don't risk your credibility and burden others by asking them to find it for you.

Strategy for Routine Requests

Use the direct approach. Open with your main idea (a clear statement of your request). In the body give details and justify your request. Then close by requesting specific action and concluding cordially.

BEGIN WITH THE REQUEST To begin, ask yourself what you want readers to do or to understand as a result of reading your message. Place your request first; however, be careful not to be abrupt or tactless. Follow these guidelines:

* **Pay attention to tone.** Even though you expect a favourable response, instead of demanding action ("Send me your catalogue no. 33A"), soften your request with words such as *please.*
* **Assume your audience will comply.** Assume that once the reason is clearly understood, your audience will comply with your request. An impatient demand is unnecessary.
* **Avoid beginning with personal introductions.** Don't start with, "I am the senior corporate writer at UnumProvident, and I'm looking for information on . . . " Such a beginning buries the main idea so that the actual request may be lost.

Activities

Organize your routine messages according to the direct approach.

Keep your direct approach from being harsh or discourteous.

 Document **Makeovers**

- **Punctuate questions and polite requests differently.** A polite request in question form requires no question mark ("Would you please help us determine whether Kate Kingsley is a suitable applicant for this position"). A direct question does require a question mark ("Did Kate Kingsley demonstrate an ability to work smoothly with clients?").
- **Be specific.** State precisely what you want. For example, if you request the latest census figures from a government agency, be sure to say whether you want a page or two of summary figures or a detailed report running several thousand pages.

EXPLAIN AND JUSTIFY YOUR REQUEST Use the body of your message to explain your request. Try to make the explanation grow smoothly and logically from your opening remarks. When you request information, tell readers why you need the information and explain how they might benefit from granting the request.

You can use the body of your routine request to list a series of questions. You might ask about the technical specifications, exact dimensions, and precise use of a complex piece of machinery. When listing a series of questions, just keep a few basics in mind:

- **Ask the most important questions first.** Number your questions, and list them logically in descending order of importance. If cost is your main concern, begin by asking, "What does the C-704 cost?" Then you can ask related but more specific questions, perhaps about the availability of a product ("How many C-704s do you usually have in stock?") or its warranty ("What warranty do you provide with the C-704?").
- **Ask only relevant questions.** Don't waste your reader's time; ask only those questions central to your request. If your questions need simple yes-or-no answers, provide boxes to check; otherwise, use open-ended questions to elicit the information you want: Ask "How fast can you ship the unit?" or "When will you ship the unit?" rather than "Can you ship the unit?"
- **Deal with only one topic per question.** Break down multiple requests. If you have an unusual or complex request, list the request and then provide supporting details in a separate, short paragraph. Use paragraph headings to make your reader's job easier.

> Numbered lists help readers sort through multiple related items or multiple requests.

REQUEST SPECIFIC ACTION IN A COURTEOUS CLOSE Close your message with three important elements:

- **A specific request for action.** Restate your request and ask that readers respond by a specific time ("Please send the figures by April 5 so that I can return first-quarter results to you before the May 20 conference").
- **Contact information.** Help your reader respond easily by including your phone number, office hours, and other contact information.
- **An expression of appreciation or goodwill.** Sincerely express your goodwill and appreciation; however, don't thank readers "in advance" for cooperating. If a reader's response warrants a thank you, send it after you've received the reply.

> In the closing, "make the action easy."

Types of Routine Requests

The types of routine requests are numerous, from asking favours to requesting credit. Many of the routine messages that you'll be writing will likely fall into major categories. The following sections discuss three of these categories: placing orders, requesting information and action, and making claims and requesting adjustments.

PLACING ORDERS Today, many companies make paperless orders by using computer-generated order forms. These forms provide a list of products with a description of each item and information such as the catalogue number, name or trade name, colour, size, and unit price. Your job is to fill in the quantity, compute the total amount due, and provide the shipping address.

If you do need to draft an order letter, follow the same format as you would on an order form.

- **Opening.** Start with the general request.
- **Body.** Include specific information about the items you want. Put this information in columns, double-space between the items, and total the price at the end.
- **Close.** Specify the delivery address, which may differ from the billing address. Also indicate how the merchandise is to be shipped. Finally, in any letter including a payment, mention the amount enclosed and explain how the amount was calculated.

Here's an example of an effective order:

Please send the following items to the above address. I am ordering from your current spring–summer catalogue:

COUNT	STOCK I.D.	DESCRIPTION	ITEM PRICE	TOTAL PRICE
3	139-24	Daily appointment books (black)	$ 8.95	$ 26.85
50	289-90	Mechanical pencils (0.5 mm/black)	1.69	84.50
5	905-18	Wrist pads (grey)	6.99	34.95
10	472-67	CD-R disks (50/box)	17.99	179.90
		TOTAL SALES		$326.20
		SHIPPING		FREE
		AMOUNT DUE		$326.20

My cheque #1738 for $326.20 is enclosed. Please ship these supplies via Purolator to the address on the letterhead.

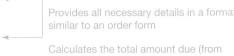 States general request first

Provides all necessary details in a format similar to an order form

Calculates the total amount due (from information on tax and shipping that was provided in the catalogue)

Includes additional important information in the close

 **Model** Document

REQUESTING INFORMATION AND ACTION Basically, a simple request says, "This is what I want to know or what I want you to do, why I'm making the request, and why it may be in your interest to help me." In more complex situations, readers might be unwilling to respond unless they understand how the request benefits them, so be sure to include this information in your explanation. Follow the direct approach:

- **Opening.** Start with a clear statement of your reason for writing.
- **Body.** Provide whatever explanation is needed to justify your request.
- **Close.** Provide a specific account of what you expect, and include a deadline if appropriate.

 Document **Makeovers**

Internal requests to fellow employees are often oral and rather casual, but sending a clear, thoughtful written memo or email message can save time and questions by helping readers understand precisely what you want (see Figure 7.2). Requests to outsiders are often made by letter, although some are sent via email. These messages are usually short and simple (see Figure 7.3 on page 128).

MAKING CLAIMS AND REQUESTING ADJUSTMENTS When you're dissatisfied with a company's product or service, you make a claim (a formal complaint) or request an **adjustment** (a claim settlement). Although a phone call or visit may solve the problem, a written claim letter documents your dissatisfaction. You may be angry or frustrated with the company, but wait until you have cooled off before you write the letter so you can adopt a more objective tone. After all, a courteous, clear, concise explanation will make a far more favourable impression than an abusive, angry letter.

 **Model** Document

In most cases, and especially in your first letter, assume that a fair adjustment will be made, and follow the plan for direct requests:

- **Opening.** Begin with a straightforward statement of the problem.
- **Body.** Give a complete, specific explanation of the details, providing any information an adjuster would need to verify your claim. Include receipts or other evidence to back up your claim.

FIGURE 7.2 Memo Requesting Action from Company Insiders

Planning

Analyze
Purpose is to request feedback from fellow employees.

Investigate
Gather accurate, complete information on program benefits and local gym.

Adapt
Office memo or email is appropriate medium. Use "you" attitude, and make responding easy.

1

Writing

Organize
Main idea is saving money while staying healthy. Save time and meet audience expectations using the direct approach.

Compose
Keep style informal but business-like. Using a "we" attitude includes readers in the decision-making process.

2

Completing

Revise
Keep it brief. Weed out overly long words and phrases. Avoid unnecessary details.

Produce
No need for fancy design elements in this memo. Include a response form.

Proofread
Review carefully for both content and typographical errors.

3

ACE
Ace Hardware Corporation

INTERNAL MEMORANDUM

TO: All Employees
FROM: Tony Ramirez, Human Resources
DATE: October 15, 2009
SUBJECT: NEW WELLNESS PROGRAM OPPORTUNITY

Routes message efficiently, with all needed information

The benefits package committee has asked me to contact everyone about an opportunity to save money and stay healthier in the bargain. As you know, we've been meeting to decide on changes in our benefits package. Last week, we sent you a memo detailing the Synergy Wellness program. Now we would like to know whether you are interested in participating in the program.

States purpose and request in opening to avoid wasting busy readers' time

Presents the situation that makes the inquiry necessary

Discount Offer
In addition to the package as described in the memo (life, major medical, dental, hospitalization), Synergy has also offered ACE Hardware a 10 percent discount. To meet the requirements for the discount, we have to show proof that at least 25 percent of our employees participate in aerobic exercise at least 3 times a week for at least 20 minutes. (Their actuarial tables show a resulting 10 percent reduction in claims.)

Facilities Access
After looking around, we discovered a gymnasium just a few blocks south on Haley Boulevard. Sports Action will give our employees unlimited daytime access to their indoor track, gym, and pool for a group fee that comes to approximately $4.50 per month per employee if at least half of us sign up.

In addition to using the track and pool, we can play volleyball, jazzercise, form our own intramural basketball teams, and much more. Our spouses and children can also participate at a deeply discounted monthly fee. If you have questions, please email or call me (or any member of the committee). Let us know your wishes on the following form.

Lists reader benefits and requests action

Your Response
Sign and return the following no later than Friday, **October 29.**

===

Provides an easy-to-use response form

_____ Yes, I will participate in the Synergy Wellness program and pay $4.50 a month.
_____ Yes, I am interested in a discounted family membership.
_____ No, I prefer not to participate.

Signature _____ _____

Employee ID Number _____

FIGURE 7.3 Letter Requesting Information from a Company Outsider

Pralle Realty

823 Viewpoint Avenue
Kingston, ON N5Y 5R6
(519) 633-3018 fax: (519) 663-3020

September 24, 2009

Mr. Harold Westerman
Agri-Lawn Services
1796 West Commercial Ave.
Kingston, ON N6T 8V2

Dear Mr. Westerman:

INFORMATION ON LAWN SERVICES

Would you please send us information about the lawn services you provide.

Pralle Realty owns approximately 27 pieces of rental property in Kingston and we're looking for a lawn service to handle all of them. We are making a commitment to provide quality housing in this university town, and we are looking for an outstanding firm to work with us.

We would appreciate your responses to these questions.

1. **Lawn care.** What is your annual charge for each location for lawn maintenance, including mowing, fertilizing, and weed control?

2. **Shrubbery.** What is your annual charge for each location for the care of deciduous and evergreen bushes, including pruning, fertilizing, and replacing as necessary?

3. **Contract.** How does Agri-Lawn Services structure such large contracts? We have enclosed a list of addresses for which we need service. What additional information do you need from us?

Please let us know your pricing by February 15. We must have a lawn-care firm in place by March 15.

Sincerely,

Kathleen Moriarity

Kathleen Moriarity
Senior Partner

Enclosure

Annotations (left):
Makes overall request in polite question form (no question mark)

Avoids making an overly broad request by using a series of specific questions

Avoids useless yes-or-no answers by including open-ended questions

Annotations (right):
Keeps reader's interest by hinting at possibility of future business

Itemizes questions in a logical sequence

Specifies a time limit in the courteous close

Pointers for Making a Routine Request

Direct Statement of the Request

- Be direct since your readers will respond favourably.
- Open by stating the main idea clearly and simply.
- Write in a polite, undemanding, personal tone.
- Before complex requests, include a brief explanation.

Justification, Explanation, and Details

- Justify the request, or explain its importance.
- Explain the benefit of responding.
- State desired actions in a positive, supportive manner.
- Itemize a complex request in a logical, numbered list.
- Limit any question to one topic.

Courteous Close with Request for Specific Action

- Courteously request a specific action.
- Make it easy to comply by including contact information.
- Indicate your gratitude.
- Clearly state any important deadline or time frame.

- **Close.** Politely request specific action or convey a sincere desire to find a solution. And don't forget to suggest that the business relationship will continue if the problem is solved satisfactorily.

Companies usually accept the customer's explanation of what's wrong, and ethically it's important to be honest when filing claims. Also, be prepared to back up your claim with invoices, sales receipts, cancelled cheques, dated correspondence, catalogue descriptions, and any other relevant documents. Send copies and keep the originals for your files. Be sure to supply your contact information and the best time to call so that the company can discuss the situation with you if necessary. For more insights into writing these kinds of messages, compare the poor and improved versions of the claim letter in Figure 7.4 (on page 130).

> Be prepared to document your claim. Send copies and keep the original documents.

Sending Routine Replies and Positive Messages

When responding positively to a request, giving good news, or sending a goodwill message, you have several goals: (1) to communicate the information or good news, (2) to answer all questions, (3) to provide all required details, and (4) to leave your reader with a good impression of you and your firm. Routine positive messages can be quite brief and to the point, but remember to be courteous, stay upbeat, and maintain a you-oriented tone.

> Routine replies and positive messages have four specific goals.

Strategy for Routine Replies and Positive Messages

 Document Makeovers

Like requests, routine replies and positive messages will generally be of interest to your readers, so you'll usually use the direct approach. Open with your main idea (the positive reply or the good news). Use the body to explain all the relevant details. Then close cordially, perhaps highlighting a benefit to your reader.

START WITH THE MAIN IDEA Begin your positive message with the main idea or good news and prepare your audience for the detail that follows. Try to make your opening clear and concise. Look at the following introductory statements. They make the same point, but one is so cluttered with unnecessary information that it buries the purpose; the other is brief, to the point, and clear:

> Before you begin, have a clear idea of what you want to say.

Instead of	Write
I am pleased to inform you that after deliberating the matter carefully, our human resources committee has recommended you for appointment as a staff accountant.	Congratulations. You've been selected to join our firm as a staff accountant, beginning March 20.

PROVIDE NECESSARY DETAIL AND EXPLANATION In the body, explain your point completely so that the audience will experience no confusion or lingering doubt. In addition to providing details in the body, maintain the supportive tone you already established in the opening. This tone is easy to continue when your message is purely good news, as in this example:

> Embed any slightly negative information in a positive context

> Your educational background and internship have impressed us, and we believe you would be a valuable addition to Green Valley Properties. As discussed during your interview, your salary will be $4500 per month, plus benefits. In that regard, please meet with our benefits manager, Paula Vellani, on Monday, March 20, at 8:00 a.m. She will assist you with all the paperwork necessary to tailor our benefit package to your family needs. She will also arrange various orientation activities to help you adapt to our company.

 Document Makeovers

FIGURE 7.4   Letter Making a Claim

Poor

We have been at our present location only three months, and we don't understand why our December utility bill is $815.00 and our January bill is $817.50. Businesses on both sides of us, in offices just like ours, are paying only $543.50 and $545.67 for the same months. We all have similar computer and office equipment, so something must be wrong.

Opens with emotion and details

Small businesses are helpless against big utility companies. How can we prove that you read the meter wrong or that the November bill from before we even moved in here got added to our December bill? We want someone to check this meter right away. We can't afford to pay these big bills.

Uses a defensive tone and blames the meter reader

This is the first time we've complained to you about anything, and I hope you'll agree that we deserve a better deal.

Closes with irrelevant information and a weak defence

Sincerely,

Laura Covington

Laura Covington
Proprietor

Improved

The European Connection
Specialist Purveyors of European Antiques
for over 30 years

P.O. Box 804 • Saint John, NB E2L 3V1
Telephone: (506) 979-7727 Fax: (506) 979-2828
EuroConnect@bellca.net

February 23, 2009

Customer Service Representative
City of Saint John Utilities
955 Cabot Street
Saint John, NB E4Y 1Z1

Dear Customer Service Representative:

REQUEST FOR METER CHECK

The utility meter in our store may not be accurate. Please send someone to check it.

Opens by clearly and calmly stating the problem

We have been at our current location since December 1, almost three months. Our monthly bill is nearly double those of neighbouring businesses in this building, yet we all have similar storefronts and equipment. In December we paid $815.00, and our January bill was $817.50—the highest bills that neighbouring businesses have paid were $543.50 and $545.67. Copies of our bills and comparable bills from the two closest stores are enclosed.

Explains details in the body so that reader can understand why Covington thinks a problem exists

Presents details clearly, concisely, and completely

Includes evidence to support the claim

If your representative could visit our store, he or she could do an analysis of how much energy we are using. We understand that you regularly provide this helpful service to customers.

We would appreciate hearing from you this week. You can reach me by calling 979-7727 during business hours.

Requests specific action in the closing and provides contact information to make responding easy

Sincerely,

Laura Covington

Laura Covington
Proprietor

Enclosure

Pointers for Making a Claim

- Gain reader understanding by praising some aspect of the product—at least explain why the product was purchased.
- Maintain a confident, factual, fair, unemotional tone.
- Present facts clearly, politely, and honestly.
- Show confidence in the reader's fairness—eliminate threats, sarcasm, hostility, and exaggeration, and use a nonargumentative tone.
- Make no accusation against any person or company—unless you can back it up with facts.
- Include evidence to substantiate any claim you make. For example, attach receipts.

However, if your routine message is mixed and must convey mildly disappointing information, put the negative portion of your message into as favourable a context as possible:

Instead of	**Write**
No, we no longer carry the Avalon line of sweaters.	The new Olympic line has replaced the Avalon sweaters that you asked about. Olympic features a wider range of colours and sizes and more contemporary styling.

The more complete description is less negative and emphasizes how the audience can benefit from the change. However, be careful using even only slightly negative information in this type of message: Use it *only* if you're reasonably sure the audience will respond positively. Otherwise, use the indirect approach (discussed in Chapter 8).

END WITH A COURTEOUS CLOSE Your message is most likely to succeed if your readers are left feeling that you have their personal welfare in mind. Accomplish this task either by highlighting a benefit to the audience or by expressing appreciation or goodwill. If follow-up action is required, clearly state who will do what next.

Types of Routine Replies and Positive Messages

Innumerable types of routine replies and positive messages are used in business every day. Many of these messages fall into three main categories: granting requests for information and action, granting claims and requests for adjustments, and sending goodwill messages.

GRANTING REQUESTS FOR INFORMATION AND ACTION If your answer to a request is yes or is straightforward information, use the direct plan: Open with the main idea (or good news), use the body for explanation and detail, and close courteously. Your prompt, gracious, and thorough response will positively influence how people think about your company, its products, your department, and you. For a good example of this type of message, see Herman Miller, Inc.'s response to Julian Zamakis's request for information about employment opportunities (see Figure 7.5 on page 132).

Many of the requests you receive will be routine and can get a standardized response. For example, a human resources department gets numerous routine inquiries about job openings. To handle repetitive queries like these, companies usually develop form responses. Although such messages are often criticized as being cold and impersonal, you can put a great deal of thought into wording them, and you can use computers to personalize and mix paragraphs. Thus, a computerized form letter prepared with care may be personal and sincere.

GRANTING CLAIMS AND REQUESTS FOR ADJUSTMENT Satisfied customers bring additional business to a firm; angry, dissatisfied customers do not. Plus, they complain to anyone who'll listen, creating poor public relations. So even though claims and adjustments may seem unpleasant, progressive business people treat them as golden opportunities for building customer loyalty.[2]

Few people go to the trouble of requesting an adjustment unless they actually have a problem. So the most sensible reaction to a routine claim is to assume that the claimant's account of the transaction is an honest statement of what happened—unless the same customer repeatedly submits dubious claims or the dollar amount is very large. When you receive a complaint, investigate the problem first to determine what went wrong and why. In addition, determine whether your company, your customer, or a third party is at fault.

When Your Company Is at Fault Refer to company errors carefully. Explain your company's efforts to do a good job, and imply that the error was an unusual incident. Here are some tips on what *not* to do:

Make sure the audience understands what to do next and how that action will benefit them.

Document **Makeovers**

Many companies use form responses to reply to similar requests.

The claims you receive are your chance to build strong relationships with customers and clients.

Finding out who is at fault helps you know how to respond to a claim.

Model Document

| FIGURE 7.5 | Email Replying to a Request for Information |

Model Document

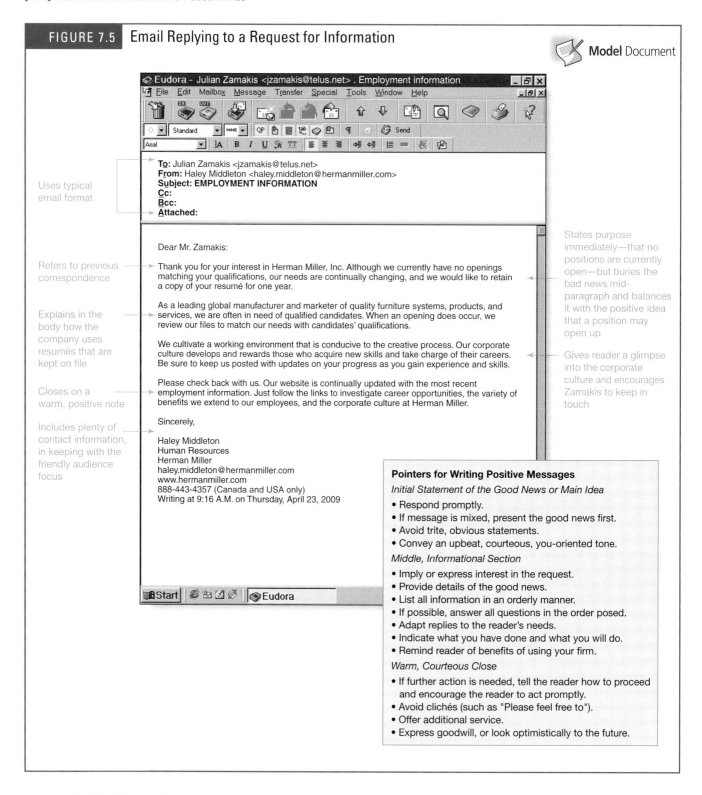

Uses typical email format

Refers to previous correspondence

Explains in the body how the company uses resumés that are kept on file

Closes on a warm, positive note

Includes plenty of contact information, in keeping with the friendly audience focus

States purpose immediately—that no positions are currently open—but buries the bad news mid-paragraph and balances it with the positive idea that a position may open up

Gives reader a glimpse into the corporate culture and encourages Zamakis to keep in touch

To: Julian Zamakis <jzamakis@telus.net>
From: Haley Middleton <haley.middleton@hermanmiller.com>
Subject: EMPLOYMENT INFORMATION
Cc:
Bcc:
Attached:

Dear Mr. Zamakis:

Thank you for your interest in Herman Miller, Inc. Although we currently have no openings matching your qualifications, our needs are continually changing, and we would like to retain a copy of your resumé for one year.

As a leading global manufacturer and marketer of quality furniture systems, products, and services, we are often in need of qualified candidates. When an opening does occur, we review our files to match our needs with candidates' qualifications.

We cultivate a working environment that is conducive to the creative process. Our corporate culture develops and rewards those who acquire new skills and take charge of their careers. Be sure to keep us posted with updates on your progress as you gain experience and skills.

Please check back with us. Our website is continually updated with the most recent employment information. Just follow the links to investigate career opportunities, the variety of benefits we extend to our employees, and the corporate culture at Herman Miller.

Sincerely,

Haley Middleton
Human Resources
Herman Miller
haley.middleton@hermanmiller.com
www.hermanmiller.com
888-443-4357 (Canada and USA only)
Writing at 9:16 A.M. on Thursday, April 23, 2009

Pointers for Writing Positive Messages

Initial Statement of the Good News or Main Idea
- Respond promptly.
- If message is mixed, present the good news first.
- Avoid trite, obvious statements.
- Convey an upbeat, courteous, you-oriented tone.

Middle, Informational Section
- Imply or express interest in the request.
- Provide details of the good news.
- List all information in an orderly manner.
- If possible, answer all questions in the order posed.
- Adapt replies to the reader's needs.
- Indicate what you have done and what you will do.
- Remind reader of benefits of using your firm.

Warm, Courteous Close
- If further action is needed, tell the reader how to proceed and encourage the reader to act promptly.
- Avoid clichés (such as "Please feel free to").
- Offer additional service.
- Express goodwill, or look optimistically to the future.

When a complaint is the result of company error, word your response carefully.

- Don't blame an individual or a specific department.
- Don't use lame excuses such as "Nobody's perfect" or "Mistakes will happen."
- Don't promise that problems will never happen again (such guarantees are unrealistic and often beyond your control).

Many response letters are written as a personal answer to a unique claim. Such letters start with a clear statement of the good news: the settling of the claim according to the customer's request. For example, when a customer complained about a defective product, Klondike Gear (a large mail-order company) responded with the personal answer shown in Figure 7.6.

FIGURE 7.6   Personalized and Form Letters Responding to Complaints

Personalized Letter

Klondike Gear
71 Blackfoot Road
Calgary, AB T5N 6G4
(403) 977-3297 fax: (403) 977-3301
www.klondikegear.com

February 7, 2009

Ms. Ellen Seargento
784 W. Douglas Ave.
Fort Smith, NT X0E 0P0

Dear Ms. Seargento:

REPLACING YOUR SWEATER

Here is your heather-blue wool-and-mohair sweater (size large) to replace the one returned to us with a defect in the knitting on the left sleeve.

Thanks for giving us the opportunity to replace your sweater. Customers' needs have come first at Klondike Gear for 27 years. Our sweaters are handmade by the finest knitters in this area.

Our newest catalogue is enclosed. Browse through it, and you'll see what wonderful new colours and patterns we have for you. Whether you are skiing or driving a snowmobile, Klondike Gear offers you the best protection from wind, snow, and cold. Let us know how we may continue to serve you and your sporting needs.

Sincerely,

John Steele

John Steele
Customer Representative

Annotations (left):
- Puts customer at ease with "you" attitude
- Includes resale and sales promotion

Annotations (right):
- Starts with a "good-news" statement: that the correct merchandise has arrived
- Thanks customer for writing about the defect
- Closes with statement of company's concern for the customer

---

Form Letter

[Date]

[Name]
[Address]
[City, Province, Postal Code]

Dear [Name]:

FILLING YOUR ORDER

Your letter concerning your recent Klondike order has been forwarded to our director of operations.

Your complete satisfaction is our goal; when you are satisfied, we are satisfied. Our customer service representative will contact you soon to assist with the issues raised in your letter.

Whether you're skiing or driving a snowmobile, Klondike Gear offers you the best protection from wind, snow, and cold—and Klondike has been taking care of customers' outdoor needs for more than 27 years! Because you're a loyal customer, enclosed is a $10 gift certificate. You may wish to consider our new line of quality snow goggles.

Thank you for taking the time to write to us. Your input helps us better serve you and all our customers.

Annotations (left):
- Puts customer at ease with "you" attitude
- Includes resale and sales promotion

Annotations (right):
- Starts with a "good-attitude" statement (not the usual good-news statement since it's going to people with various complaints)
- Never suggests that customer was wrong to write to Klondike
- Closes with statement of company's concern for all its customers

Companies also receive many claims that are quite similar. Klondike Gear has numerous customers who claim they haven't received exactly what was ordered. So the company created a form letter (see Figure 7.6), which can be customized through word processing and then individually signed.

Model Document

When complying with an unjustified claim, let the customer know that the merchandise was mistreated, but maintain a respectful and positive tone.

When the Customer Is at Fault When your customer is at fault (perhaps washing a dry-clean-only sweater in hot water), either you refuse the claim and attempt to justify your refusal or you simply do what the customer asks. Remember, if you refuse the claim, you may lose your customer—as well as many of the customer's friends, who will hear only one side of the dispute. You must weigh the cost of making the adjustment against the cost of losing future business from one or more customers.

If you choose to grant the claim, open with the good news: You're replacing the merchandise or refunding the purchase price. However, the message body needs special attention. After all, if the customer fails to realize what went wrong, you'll be committing your firm to an endless procession of returned merchandise. Your job is to help the customer understand that the merchandise was mistreated, but you must do so without being condescending ("Perhaps you failed to read the instructions carefully") or preachy ("You should know that wool shrinks in hot water"). If you insult the customer, your cash refund will be wasted because you'll lose that customer anyway. Without being offensive, the letter in Figure 7.7 educates a customer about how to treat his in-line skates.

Model Document

You have three options when a third party is at fault.

When a Third Party Is at Fault Sometimes neither you nor the claimant is at fault. Perhaps the carrier damaged merchandise in transit. Or perhaps the original manufacturer is responsible for some product defect. When a third party is at fault, you have three options:

- **Simply honour the claim.** This option is the most attractive. You satisfy your customer with a standard good-news letter and no extra explanation. You maintain your reputation for fair dealing but bear no cost (since the carrier, manufacturer, or other third party reimburses you).
- **Honour the claim but explain you're not at fault.** This option corrects any impression that the damage was caused by your negligence. You can still write the standard good-news letter, but stress the explanation.
- **Refer the reader to the third party.** This option is usually a bad choice because you fail to satisfy the customer's needs. However, use this option when you're trying to dissociate yourself from any legal responsibility for the damaged merchandise, especially if it has caused a personal injury, in which case you would send a bad-news message (see Chapter 8).

FIGURE 7.7 Letter Responding to a Claim When the Buyer Is at Fault

Planning

Analyze
Purpose is to grant a customer's claim, gently educate, and encourage further business.

Investigate
Gather information on product care, warranties, and resale information.

Adapt
Use letter format to reinforce businesslike tone. Give customer relationship utmost attention.

1

Writing

Organize
Main idea is that you're replacing the wheel assembly—even though you are not required to do so.

Compose
Use an upbeat, conversational style, but remain businesslike. Choose words carefully, especially when educating the customer. Include resale information to reinforce future business.

2

Completing

Revise
Revise for tone, focusing on conciseness, clarity, and the "you" attitude.

Produce
Avoid confusing your positive message with fussy design elements. Keep it simple.

Proofread
Review for the usual errors, and include all promised enclosures.

3

Skates
Alive!

209 Fraser Way
London, ON N5Y 3R6
(519) 332-7474 • Fax: (519) 336-5297
skates@rogers.net

August 7, 2009

Mr. Steven Cox
1172 Amber Court
Summerside, PE C1A 4Z1

Dear Mr. Cox:

REPLACING YOUR SKATE WHEELS

Thank you for contacting us about your in-line skates. Even though your six-month warranty has expired, Skates Alive! is mailing you a complete wheel assembly replacement free of charge. The enclosed instructions make removing the damaged wheel line and installing the new one relatively easy.

The "Fastrax" (model NL 562) you purchased is our best-selling and most reliable skate. However, wheel jams may occur when fine particles of sand block the smooth rotating action of the wheels. These skates perform best when used on roadways and tracks that are relatively free of sand. We suggest that you remove and clean the wheel assemblies (see enclosed directions) once a month and have them checked by your dealer about every six months.

Because of your location, you may want to consider our more advanced "Glisto" (model NL 988) when you decide to purchase new skates. Although more expensive than the Fastrax, the Glisto design helps shed sand and dirt quite efficiently and should provide years of carefree skating.

Enjoy the enclosed copy of "Rock & Roll," with our compliments. Inside, you'll read about new products, hear from other skaters, and have an opportunity to respond to our customer questionnaire.

All of us at Skates Alive! wish you healthy skating.

Sincerely,

Candace Parker

Candace Parker
Customer Service Representative

Enclosure

Acknowledges reader communication, keeps opening positive by avoiding words such as "problem," and conveys the good news right away

Explains the problem without blaming the customer by avoiding the pronoun "you" and by suggesting ways to avoid future problems

Adds value by enclosing a newsletter that invites future response from customer

Includes sales promotion in the body, encouraging the customer to "trade up"

Closes positively, ending on a "feel good" note that conveys an attitude of excellent customer service

Pointers for Granting a Claim
- In the opening, state the good news: you're honouring the claim.
- Thank the reader for writing.
- In the body, explain how you'll grant the claim.
- Don't argue with reader's version of events.
- Keep your explanation objective, nonvindictive, and impersonal.
- Apologize only when appropriate; then do so crisply, with no overly dramatic tone.
- Keep your tone supportive.
- In the closing, remind the reader how you are honouring the claim.
- Encourage the reader to look favourably on your company or product.
- Clarify any actions the reader must take.

Model Document

SENDING GOODWILL MESSAGES You can enhance your relationships with customers, colleagues, and other business people by sending friendly, unexpected notes for special occasions. Effective goodwill messages must be sincere, honest, and avoid exaggeration. Back up any compliments with specific points. Remember, readers often regard restrained praise as being more sincere:

Instead of	Write
Words cannot express my appreciation for the great job you did. Thanks. No one could have done it better. You're terrific! You've made the whole firm sit up and take notice, and we are ecstatic to have you working here.	Thanks again for taking charge of the meeting in my absence. You did an excellent job. With just an hour's notice, you managed to coordinate the legal and public relations departments so that we could present a united front in the negotiations. Your communication abilities are truly appreciated.

Activities

Taking note of significant events in someone's personal life helps cement the business relationship.

Congratulations Reasons for sending congratulations include the highlights in people's personal lives—weddings, births, graduations, and successes. A prime opportunity for sending goodwill messages is to congratulate someone for a significant business achievement—perhaps for being promoted or for attaining an important civic position. The improved congratulatory note in Figure 7.8 moves swiftly to the good news.

You may congratulate business acquaintances on their own achievements or on the accomplishments of a spouse or child. You may also take note of personal events, even if you don't know the reader well. Of course, if you're already friendly with the reader, you can get away with a more personal tone.

Activities

A message of appreciation documents a person's contributions.

Appreciation An important business quality is the ability to recognize the contributions of employees, colleagues, suppliers, and other associates. Your praise does more than just make the person feel good; it encourages further excellence. Moreover, a message that expresses appreciation may become an important part of someone's personnel file. So when you write, specifically mention the person or people you want to praise. The brief email message that follows expresses gratitude and reveals the happy result:

> Thank you for sending the air-conditioning components via overnight delivery. You allowed us to satisfy the needs of two customers who were getting very impatient with the heat.
>
> Special thanks to Susan Brown, who took our initial call and never said, "It can't be done." Her initiative on our behalf is greatly appreciated.

A condolence message shows you care.

Condolences In times of serious trouble and deep sadness, written expressions of sympathy leave their mark. Granted, this type of message is difficult to write, but don't let such difficulty keep you from responding promptly. Those who have experienced a health problem, the death of a loved one, or a business misfortune appreciate knowing that they're not alone.

Condolences are seldom written on letterhead. Use a plain note card with matching envelope. Open with a brief statement of sympathy, such as "I was deeply sorry to hear of your loss." In the body, mention the good qualities or the positive contributions made by the deceased. State what the person or business meant to you. In the close, you can offer your condolences and your best wishes. One considerate way to end this type of message is to say something that will give the reader a little lift, such as a reference to a brighter future.

FIGURE 7.8 Letter Congratulating a Business Acquaintance

Planning	Writing	Completing
Analyze Purpose is to create goodwill with industry business associates. **Investigate** Gather information on specific accomplishments of the reader's firm. **Adapt** Letter format lets reader use your message (perhaps even reproduce it) as an industry testimonial. **1**	**Organize** Main idea is to congratulate the reader. The direct approach is perfect for this welcome news. **Compose** A conversational tone complements the slightly formal style, since this is your first contact with the reader. Avoid generalized praise by mentioning specific, concrete accomplishments. **2**	**Revise** Review for consistency in tone, word choice, and sentence structure. **Produce** A simple design avoids distracting your reader from the message. **Proofread** Create a positive first impression by being especially careful to send an error-free message. **3**

Poor

We are so pleased when companies that we admire do well. When we attended our convention in Halifax last month, we heard about your firm's recent selection to design and print media advertisements for the National Association of Business Suppliers (NABS).

→ Sounds condescending and self-centred—expressing the reason but failing to actually congratulate the reader

We have long believed that the success of individual franchises is directly linked to the healthy growth of the industry at large. Lambert, Cutchen & Browt is the only firm for the job.

→ Seems insincere because of the lack of supporting reasons and the exaggeration ("only you can do the job")

We wish you the best of luck with your new ad campaign. Congratulations on a job well done!

→ Congratulating the reader in the close seems like an afterthought

Sincerely,

Janice McCarthy

Janice McCarthy
Director, Media Relations

Improved

Office DEPOT, Canada

200 Fort Garry Road, Winnipeg, MB R3K 6J5   (204) 278-4800

March 3, 2009

Mr. Ralph Lambert, President
Lambert, Cutchen & Browt, Inc.
1435 Leeds Avenue
Hamilton, ON L8N 3T2

Dear Mr. Lambert:

CONGRATULATIONS ON YOUR SUCCESS

Congratulations on your firm's recent selection to design print media advertisements for the National Association of Business Suppliers (NABS). We learned of your success at our convention in Halifax last week.

Uses body to make compliment more effective by showing knowledge of the reader's work, while avoiding exaggeration →

We admire your success in promoting associations of other industries such as soft drinks, snack food, and recycling. "Your Dream Vision 2008" ads for the bottling industry were both inspirational and effective in raising consumer awareness. The campaign you design for NABS is sure to yield similar positive responses.

Closes by expressing interest in following the future success of the firm →

You can be sure we will follow your media campaign with great interest.

Sincerely,

Janice McCarthy

Janice McCarthy
Director, Media Relations

tw

FIGURE 7.9 Note of Condolence

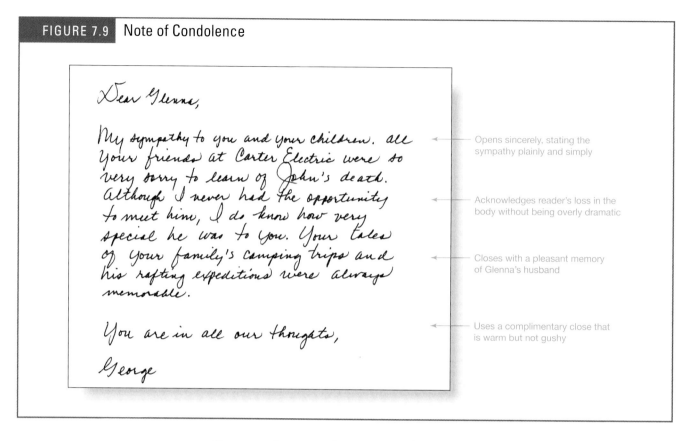

Dear Glenna,

My sympathy to you and your children. All your friends at Carter Electric were so very sorry to learn of John's death. Although I never had the opportunity to meet him, I do know how very special he was to you. Your tales of your family's camping trips and his rafting expeditions were always memorable.

You are in all our thoughts,

George

Opens sincerely, stating the sympathy plainly and simply

Acknowledges reader's loss in the body without being overly dramatic

Closes with a pleasant memory of Glenna's husband

Uses a complimentary close that is warm but not gushy

Here are a few general suggestions for writing condolence messages:

- **Keep reminiscences brief.** Recount a memory or an anecdote (even a humorous one), but don't dwell on the details of the loss, lest you add to the reader's anguish.
- **Write in your own words.** Write as if you were speaking privately to the person. Don't quote "poetic" passages or use stilted or formal phrases. If the loss is a death, refer to it as such rather than as "passing away" or "departing."
- **Be tactful.** Mention your shock and dismay, but remember that bereaved and distressed loved ones take little comfort in lines such as "Richard was too young to die" or "Starting all over again will be so difficult." Try to strike a balance between superficial expressions of sympathy and heartrending references to a happier past or the likelihood of a bleak future.
- **Take special care.** Be sure to spell names correctly and to be accurate in your review of facts. Try to be prompt.
- **Write about special qualities of the deceased.** You may have to rely on reputation to do this, but let the grieving person know you valued his or her loved one.
- **Write about special qualities of the bereaved person.** A pat on the back helps a bereaved family member feel more confident about handling things during such a traumatic time.[3]

For an example of an effective condolence note, see Figure 7.9. George Bigalow sent the message to his administrative assistant, Glenna Case, after learning of the death of Glenna's husband.

Writing Procedures

Giving instructions in the workplace is a frequent routine task. Often you have to let clients or co-workers know how to perform an operation. Workplace instructions or procedures lay out the steps to perform the operation or task in an easy-to-follow sequence. Informal, written procedures often are sent in emails, memos, and letters. Longer, more detailed procedures that may be used by many people will be written in a separate document, put online or into a manual, or posted near where the procedures must be followed. Documenting procedures gives employees guidance in performing tasks and helps companies set performance standards.

Examples of procedures include instructions on how to log on to equipment, fill out forms, operate machines, follow guidelines for recycling, or carry out office tasks. Just like other communications you prepare, you can apply the three-step process to write an effective procedure.

Planning

In the planning stage, identify an action purpose—your purpose is to instruct the reader in how to DO something. The reader will be using the document to perform the steps. Analyze the reader's knowledge about the topic—how much or how little does the reader know and need to know? You may need to include definitions for beginners or you may be able to skip basic information for readers with advanced knowledge. For example, if your procedures are for chartered accountants, you will not have to define basic terms, but if you are writing procedures for new hires with only one year of accounting experience, more background information may be required.

What questions would the reader have about this task? Use your list of reader questions to organize the procedures. Often procedures begin with a general overview that includes

- What the procedures are about (in general)
- Any definition, background information, or specialized language used
- A preview of the main stages if the procedure is lengthy

The introductory information orients the reader to the document and provides a context for the details to follow. After the overview, list the steps. The procedure may conclude with the last step in the sequence, or it may conclude with troubleshooting suggestions. Figure 7.10 provides a WorkSafeBC sample procedure on how to lock out a piece of industrial equipment to ensure no one will energize the equipment during maintenance.

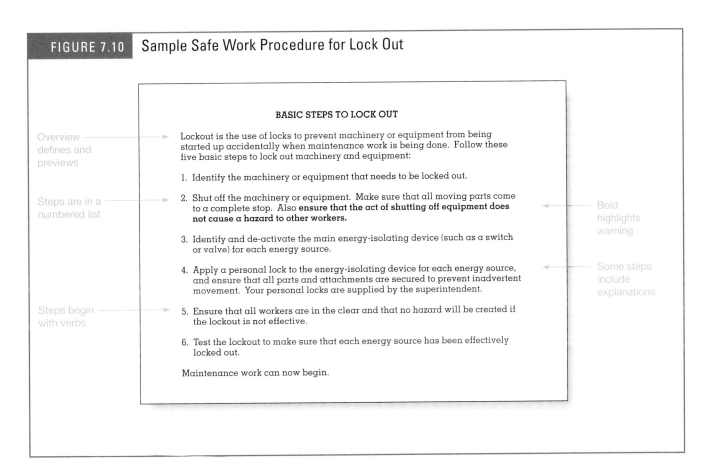

FIGURE 7.10 Sample Safe Work Procedure for Lock Out

BASIC STEPS TO LOCK OUT

Overview defines and previews

Lockout is the use of locks to prevent machinery or equipment from being started up accidentally when maintenance work is being done. Follow these five basic steps to lock out machinery and equipment:

1. Identify the machinery or equipment that needs to be locked out.

Steps are in a numbered list

2. Shut off the machinery or equipment. Make sure that all moving parts come to a complete stop. Also **ensure that the act of shutting off equipment does not cause a hazard to other workers.**

Bold highlights warning

3. Identify and de-activate the main energy-isolating device (such as a switch or valve) for each energy source.

4. Apply a personal lock to the energy-isolating device for each energy source, and ensure that all parts and attachments are secured to prevent inadvertent movement. Your personal locks are supplied by the superintendent.

Some steps include explanations

Steps begin with verbs

5. Ensure that all workers are in the clear and that no hazard will be created if the lockout is not effective.

6. Test the lockout to make sure that each energy source has been effectively locked out.

Maintenance work can now begin.

Writing

Frequently readers will not read the whole procedure before beginning. They may wait to consult the written procedures while performing the operation, so you want your procedures to be easy to scan and follow. Here are some tips on how to write effective instructions:

- Use short paragraphs for the overview.
- Put the steps into a list.
- Divide the tasks into a series of action statements.
- Begin each step with a command form verb. By beginning each step with a verb, you emphasize action.
- Number the steps when a sequence must be followed. For instructions which do not have a set order, use bullets for the list instead of numbers.
- Separate explanations from steps so they are easily distinguished.
    One way to separate them is to indent the explanations, thus distinguishing them in alignment from action statements.
- **Highlight warnings and precautions.**
- Use active voice and second person—talk directly to the reader.

Ineffective

Names and ID numbers are to be filled in on the form in the spaces provided, and the boxes below must be checked to verify your age and policy limit.

More Effective

1. Fill in your name and ID number in the spaces provided.
2. Check the boxes to verify your age and policy limit.

Completing

Keep the procedures brief by taking out unnecessary detail. Ask someone who is typical of the intended audience to use the procedures to complete the task, testing the procedures to discover where information may be missing or unclear.

Decide what needs emphasis. For example, if a warning is included, is it highlighted with boldface or set apart in space? Use document design features such as textboxes, boldface, indentation, and white space to draw attention to key parts, especially for long procedures.

USE HEADINGS AND SUBHEADINGS TO PROVIDE ACCESS Use headings to show the main organizational divisions of the procedure. Break up long lists of steps by grouping related steps and providing subheadings. Many readers do not read the document from beginning to end before attempting to perform the procedure. Instead, people will often begin the procedure, become confused about what to do part way through, then consult the written procedure to find instructions about that step. If you have provided headings, readers can more easily find the part of the procedure that interests them.

ON THE JOB

Building relationships is the key to getting things done in an organization. Four things you can do to build relationships with people at work include
- Always doing what you say you will do
- Listening to others' ideas without interrupting or judging
- Remaining positive under pressure—avoid blaming others or being defensive
- Asking people politely to do things—even if your authority would allow you to tell them to do it

Reviewing Key Points

This chapter introduced you to strategies for routine, good-news, and goodwill messages. When you write messages such as routine requests, "yes" replies, claims, and adjustments, follow the direct pattern by

- Stating the request or response at the beginning
- Explaining the details
- Closing politely, facilitating the specific action

When you respond to claims, you aim to restore and maintain customer relations, so try to accommodate the claim where possible. In order letters, precise specification is important, and in goodwill messages, sincere, specific examples are most effective. In routine correspondence, remember to

- Begin by stating the main action
- Explain *why*, *what*, or *how* in a clear, concise, courteous style and tone
- End by pointing the way to the next step—*who* will do *what*, by *when*

Written procedures tell how to carry out a workplace task. When you write procedures

- Include an overview to define the purpose of the task
- List the steps in sequence

mybuscommlab   Go to MyBusCommLab at www.pearson.ca/mybuscommlab for online exercises.

Practise Your Grammar

Exercises

Effective business communication starts with strong grammar skills. To improve your grammar skills, go to MyBusCommLab or Grammar-on-the-Go, where you'll find exercises and diagnostic tests to help you produce clear, effective communication.

Test Your Knowledge

Exercises

1. When is a request routine?
2. What are three guidelines for asking a series of questions in a routine request?
3. What information should be included in an order request?
4. Should you use the direct or indirect approach for most routine messages? Why?
5. Where in a routine message should you state your actual request?
6. How does a claim differ from an adjustment?
7. How does the question of fault affect what you say in a message granting a claim?
8. Why do firms sometimes grant claims even when they know the customer was at fault?
9. How can you avoid sounding insincere when writing a goodwill message?
10. What are six tips for writing procedures?

Apply Your Knowledge

1. When organizing request messages, why is it important to know whether any cultural differences exist between you and your audience? Explain.
2. Your company's error cost an important business customer a new client; you know it and your customer knows it. Do you apologize, or do you refer to the incident in a positive light without admitting any responsibility? Briefly explain.
3. You've been asked to write a letter of recommendation for an employee who has a disability and uses a wheelchair. The disability has no effect on the employee's ability to do the job, and you feel confident about writing the best recommendation possible. Nevertheless, you know the prospective company and its facilities aren't well suited to wheelchair access. Do you mention the employee's disability in your letter? Explain.

4. Every time you send a direct-request memo to Ted Jackson, he delays or refuses to comply. You're beginning to get impatient. Should you send Jackson an email to ask what's wrong? Complain to your supervisor about Jackson's uncooperative attitude? Arrange a face-to-face meeting with Jackson? Bring up the problem at the next staff meeting? Explain.

5. **Ethical Choices** You have a complaint against one of your suppliers, but you have no documentation to back it up. Should you request an adjustment anyway? Why or why not?

Running Cases

Video

CASE 1: Noreen

Now that Petro-Go is a larger company (see Chapter 5 for the merger with Best Gas), upper management has established a new procedure: regular semi-annual bonuses will be distributed to all employees who meet performance targets. The letter announcing this development will include a list of performance expectations and bonus goals.

Noreen is asked to write the letter on her manager's behalf informing the Go Points and Collections teams of this new bonus opportunity. Petro-Go will mail the letter, once approved, to each of the team members, letting them know that, because of their hard work over the past six months, they will each receive a bonus cheque. The cheques are enclosed with the letters. Each member will receive a bonus amount based on their individual performance and achievements captured in the Petro-Go semi-annual statistics and progress reports.

QUESTIONS

a. Is this a routine or good-news letter or both?
b. What information should Noreen begin the letter with? Why?
c. How should Noreen end the letter? Why?
d. Does Noreen need to include an announcement about the merger in this letter?
e. What tone will Noreen use in this letter?

YOUR TASK

Write the letter. Remember to use company letterhead (create it yourself) and include an enclosure notation for the two enclosures. Also thank the team for their hard work and dedication to the company over the past six months. Let the employees know they can contact Noreen if they have questions or comments.

This is confidential information, a fact that should be stated on the envelope and the letter itself. Prepare the envelope. (See Appendix A for letter and envelope formats.)

CASE 2: Kwong

Kwong's boss at Accountants For All asks him to write a letter replying to a corporate customer's request for information. Kwong needs to write to Albridge and Scranton Ltd. to give them the details of the last five years' tax summaries. John Albridge would like to know the total expenses claimed, primarily the vehicle expense deduction, and the total amount of refund/amount owed each year. Kwong needs to attach copies of each year's summary statement as well.

This is a good opportunity for Kwong to thank Albridge and Scranton Ltd. for their past business and let them know that Accountants For All looks forward to their future business.

QUESTIONS

a. Should Kwong list the information requested in the letter or simply attach the summary statements and refer the reader to those statements?
b. Is this a routine or goodwill letter or both?
c. Is the direct or indirect approach better for this letter? Why?
d. Is it best to thank the customer for their past business in the introductory part of the letter? Why or why not?
e. Where in the letter should Kwong include the information about looking forward to doing future business with Albridge and Scranton Ltd.?

YOUR TASK

Write the letter. Remember to use company letterhead (create it yourself) and include an enclosure notation. Also thank the customer for their past and anticipated future business. Leave the customer with a contact name at Accountants For All for further inquiries.

This is confidential information; the envelope and the letter itself should state this warning. Prepare the envelope. (See Appendix A for letter and envelope formats.)

Practise Your Knowledge

EXERCISES FOR PERFECTING YOUR WRITING

Revising Messages: Direct Approach Revise the following short email messages so that they are more direct and concise; develop a subject line for each revised message.

1. | **Subject line:** _____
   | I'm contacting you about your recent order for a High Country backpack. You didn't tell us which backpack you wanted, and you know we make a lot of different ones. We have the canvas models with the plastic frames and vinyl trim and we have the canvas models with leather trim, and we have the ones that have more pockets than the other ones. Plus they come in lots of different colours. Also they make the ones that are large for a big-boned person and the smaller versions for little women or kids.

2. | **Subject line:** _____
   | Thank you for contacting us about the difficulty you had collecting your luggage at the Toronto airport. We are very sorry for the inconvenience this has caused you. As you know, travelling can create problems of this sort regardless of how careful the airline personnel might be. To receive compensation, please send us a detailed list of the items that you lost and complete the following questionnaire. You can email it back to us.

Revising Messages: Direct Approach Rewrite the following sentences so that they are direct and concise.

3. We wanted to invite you to our special 40 percent off by-invitation-only sale. The sale is taking place on November 9.
4. We wanted to let you know that we are giving a tote bag and a free Phish CD with every $50 donation you make to our radio station.
5. The director planned to go to the meeting that will be held on Monday at a little before 11:00 A.M.
6. In today's meeting, we were happy to have the opportunity to welcome Paul Eccelson. He reviewed some of the newest types of order forms. If you have any questions about these new forms, feel free to call him at his office.

Audience Analysis (Teamwork) With another student, conduct an audience analysis of the following message topic: A notice to all employees about the addition of recycling bins by the elevator doors

7. What is the purpose of this message?
8. What is the most appropriate format for communicating this written message?
9. How is the audience likely to respond to this message?
10. Based on this audience analysis, would you use the direct or the indirect approach for this message? Explain your reasoning.

Revising Messages: Closing Paragraphs How would you rewrite each of the following closing paragraphs to be concise, courteous, and specific?

11. I need your response sometime soon so I can order the parts in time for your service appointment. Otherwise your air-conditioning system may not be in tip-top condition for the start of the summer season.
12. Thank you in advance for sending me as much information as you can about your products. I look forward to receiving your package in the very near future.

How Direct Is Too Direct?

Is it possible to be too direct, even if you're simply requesting information? At an event in Mexico, the president of the United States spoke bluntly of political realities, but the president of France spoke more abstractly—his style more grand, his words more beautiful. One man addressed the issues directly; the other was less direct. Which one had greater impact?

Neither speech changed global relationships, but the U.S. president was seen as a product of his outspoken culture, whereas the French president was seen as at least making his listeners feel better for a while. Countries such as France, Mexico, Japan, Saudi Arabia, Italy, and the Philippines all tend toward high-context cultures (see discussion in Chapter 1). That is, people in those countries depend on shared knowledge and inferred messages to communicate; they gather meaning more from context and less from direct statement. On a continuum of high-to-low context cultures, Canada falls between France, Britain, and the United States, having been influenced by our English and French heritage and by our proximity to the United States. So, although people in the United States believe that being direct is civil, considerate, and honest, people in high-context cultures and mid-context cultures, such as Canada, sometimes view that same directness as abrupt, rude, and intrusive—even dishonest and offensive. You might think you're doing a good thing by offering a little honest and constructive criticism to your Italian assistant, but doing so may actually hurt your assistant's dignity and could even be devastating. In fact, in high-context cultures, don't say outright, "You are wrong." People know when they've made a mistake, but if you put it into words in high-context cultures, you cause them to lose face.

To determine whether your international audience will appreciate a direct or an implied message, consider your audience's attitudes toward four factors: destiny, time, authority, and logic.

- **Destiny.** Do people in this culture believe they can control events themselves? Or are events seen as predetermined and uncontrollable? If you're supervising employees who believe that a construction deadline is controlled by fate, they may not understand your crisp email message requesting them to stay on schedule; they may even find it insulting.

- **Time.** Do people in this culture believe that time is exact, precise, and not to be wasted? Or do they view time as relative, relaxed, and necessary for developing interpersonal relationships? If you believe that time is money and you try to get straight to business in your memo to your Japanese manager, your message may be overlooked in the confusion over your lack of relationship skills and your disregard for social propriety.

- **Authority.** Do the people in this culture conduct business more autocratically or more democratically? In Mexico, rank and status are highly valued, so when communicating with people who have less authority than you do, you may need to be even more direct than you're used to being in Canada. And when communicating with people who have more authority than you do, you may need to be much less direct in Mexico than you're used to being in Canada.

- **Logic.** Do the people in this culture pursue logic in a straight line from point A to point B? Or do they communicate in circular or spiral patterns of logic? If you organize a message in a straightforward and direct manner, your message may be considered illogical, unclear, and disorganized.

You may need to ask not only how direct to be in written messages but also whether to write at all; perhaps a phone call or a visit would be more appropriate. By finding out how much or how little a culture tends toward high-context communication, you can decide whether to be direct or to rely on nuance when communicating with people in that culture.

APPLICATIONS FOR SUCCESS

For more information on the subject of intercultural communication, go to **www.executiveplanet.com**.
Answer the following questions:

1. Research a high-context culture such as Japan, Korea, or China, and write a one- or two-paragraph summary of how someone in that culture would go about requesting information.

2. When you are writing to someone in a high-context culture, would it be better to (a) make the request directly in the interest of clarity or (b) try to match your audience's unfamiliar logic and make your request indirectly? Explain your answer.

3. Germany is a low-context culture; by comparison, France and England are more high-context. These three translations of the same message were posted on a lawn in Switzerland:

a. German: "Walking on the grass is forbidden."

b. English: "Please do not walk on the grass."

c. French: "Those who respect their environment will avoid walking on the grass."

How does the language of each sign reflect the way information is conveyed in the cultural context of each nation? Write a brief (two- to three-paragraph) explanation.

Writing Bad-News Messages

After studying this chapter, you will be able to

1. Apply the three-step writing process to bad-news messages
2. Show how to achieve an audience-centred tone and explain why it helps readers
3. Describe the differences between the direct and indirect approaches to bad-news messages, and indicate when it's appropriate to use each one
4. Discuss the three techniques for saying no as clearly and kindly as possible

Bad news in the business world comes in all shapes and sizes. But even though bad news may be commonplace, most business people don't know how to communicate this type of news effectively. Working in public relations for more than 20 years, Kevin Gass has helped dozens of companies communicate bad news on such topics as health-care service cuts, Vancouver's loss of an NBA team, plant closings, and other unfavourable situations. Many companies make the mistake of pulling back from communicating, but as Gass explains, "the key is to deal effectively, fully, and quickly with the bad news. Ideally companies should turn the situation into an opportunity or, at the very least, get back to business as quickly as possible." Of course, communicating bad news isn't always easy, but the proper tone and approach can help people accept and understand your message. Public relations experts tell us that "most people will forgive just about anything if you admit to it, take responsibility for it, explain how it happened, and tell what you are doing to ensure it won't occur again."[1]

> ## TIPS FOR SUCCESS
>
> "Often audiences seem to have a premonition that bad news is coming and just as often move to a worst-case scenario. Similarly, bad news is difficult to contain; rumour often precedes fact. Credibility, for you and your organization, can hinge on the speed with which you get the difficult information out to communities, audiences, or individuals."
>
> —Kevin Gass
> Vice-President, Marketing and Communication
> B.C. Lotteries Corporation

Using the Three-Step Writing Process for Bad-News Messages

Nobody likes bad news—as Kevin Gass can attest. People don't like to get it, and they don't like to give it. Saying no can put knots in your stomach and cost you hours of sleep. The word *no* is terse and abrupt, so negative that a lot of people have trouble saying it. And for most, it's the toughest word to hear or understand. But the most damaging "no" is usually the one you don't explain.[2] The three-step writing process can help you write bad-news messages that are more effective and less damaging (see Figure 8.1).

> Saying no is difficult.

Step 1: Planning Your Bad-News Messages

To be effective, bad-news messages require extremely careful analysis. Analysis helps you know how your readers will receive your message and whether they prefer receiving it directly or indirectly, in person or in writing. Investigation provides you with all the facts your audience will need to accept the negative message. Finally, maintaining a good relationship with your audience is particularly important, in order to avoid alienating readers, so be sure to adapt your medium and tone to your audience.

> Analysis, investigation, and adaptation help you avoid alienating your readers.

FIGURE 8.1	Applying the Three-Step Writing Process to Bad-News Messages

Planning	Writing	Completing
Analyze • Verify specific purpose is worth pursuing. • Know how readers react to bad news. • Know what readers want: bad news or reasons first. **Investigate** • Ensure information is reliable and accurate. • Ensure facts support negative news. • Gather all relevant facts readers need. **Adapt** • Verify effectiveness of written channel. • Adapt medium and tone to audience. • Pay particular attention to readers' feelings.	**Organize** • Carefully define negative main idea. • Cover relevant points thoroughly. • Group relevant points logically. • Choose the direct or indirect approach with special care. **Compose** • Adapt style and tone to readers' culture. • Pay special attention to word choice. • Create sentences and paragraphs carefully.	**Revise** • Verify message is organized properly. • Be sure it says what you want it to. • Ensure message gives bad news concisely and clearly. **Produce** • Ensure design doesn't detract from bad news. • Ensure design doesn't detract from your efforts to be sensitive. **Proofread** • Correct spelling and mechanical errors. • Correct any alignment problems. • Ensure that the print quality is acceptable. • Make sure there are no misunderstandings.
1	2	3

Step 2: Writing Your Bad-News Messages

Because your main idea is negative, be careful to define it and cover relevant points thoroughly and logically. Choosing between the direct and the indirect approach takes on added importance in bad-news messages. You need to decide whether to open with the bad news or to prepare your readers with a cogent explanation before giving them the negative bits. Also, pay special attention to word choice so that you can create sentences and paragraphs that are tactful and diplomatic.

> Appropriate organization helps readers accept your negative news.

Step 3: Completing Your Bad-News Messages

Careful revision ensures that your bad-news message is organized properly, says what you want it to say, and does so concisely and clearly. It gives you a chance to make sure that your design is appropriate for the bad news and contributes to your efforts to be sensitive. As always, proofreading your message helps ensure that misunderstandings won't arise from typos, errors in spelling, or problems with mechanics.

Strategies for Bad-News Messages

Whatever the details of your particular message, when you have bad news, you want your readers to feel that they have been taken seriously, and you want them to agree that your news is fair and reasonable. When delivering bad news, you have five main goals:
- To convey the bad news
- To gain acceptance for it

Five goals of bad-news messages
- Give the bad news
- Ensure its acceptance
- Maintain the reader's goodwill
- Maintain the organization's good image
- Reduce future correspondence on the matter

- To maintain as much goodwill as possible with your audience
- To maintain a good image for your organization
- To reduce or eliminate the need for future correspondence on the matter

Accomplishing so many goals in a single message is not easy. But you can convey negative news more effectively by following these guidelines: First, adopt an audience-centred tone. Second, organize your message to meet your audience's needs and expectations by using either the direct approach, which presents the main idea before the supporting data (fully described in Chapter 7), or the indirect approach, which presents the supporting data before the main idea.

Creating an Audience-Centred Tone

Your tone helps your readers accept that your bad news represents a firm decision. Your audience-centred focus helps readers understand that, under the circumstances, your decision was fair and reasonable. Your tone helps your audience remain well disposed toward your business. And not least, your audience-centred tone helps readers preserve their pride.

When establishing tone, strive for
- Firmness
- Fairness
- Goodwill
- Respect

Experts suggest that conveying bad news in person requires listening to your audience before talking—building trust by letting people say what they feel. Bad news involves emotions, and you must acknowledge these emotions in your communication.[3] However, if you're delivering bad news in writing, you're unable to "listen" to your audience first. Nevertheless, you can certainly do your research up front and learn as much as you can about your audience. Only then are you able to demonstrate in writing that you're aware of your reader's needs, concerns, and feelings.

To adopt an audience-centred tone, pay close attention to several techniques:
- **Use the "you" attitude.** The "you" attitude is crucial to every message you write, but it's especially important in bad-news messages. Point out how your decision might actually further your audience's goals. Convey concern by looking for the best in your audience. And assume that your audience is interested in being fair, even when they are at fault.
- **Choose positive words.** The words you choose can make a letter either offensive or acceptable. You can ease disappointment by using positive words rather than negative, counterproductive ones (see Table 8.1). Just be sure not to hide the bad news.[4] Remember, you want to convey the bad news, not cover it up, even when you use the indirect approach.
- **Use respectful language.** Protect your audience's pride by using language that conveys respect and avoids an accusing tone. For instance, when your audience is at fault, observe the "you" attitude by avoiding the word *you*. Use impersonal language to explain audience mistakes in an inoffensive way. Say, "The appliance won't work after being immersed in water" instead of "The appliance doesn't work because you immersed it in water."

Several techniques will help you establish an audience-centred tone.

Using the Direct Approach

If you know that your audience prefers the bad news first, or if the situation is minor and the news will cause your audience little disappointment, use the direct approach:
- **Opening.** Start with a clear statement of the bad news.
- **Body.** Proceed to the reasons for the decision (perhaps offering alternatives).
- **Close.** End with a positive statement aimed at maintaining a good relationship with the audience.

Use the direct approach when your negative answer or information will have little personal impact.

Stating the bad news first has two advantages: (1) It makes a shorter message possible, and (2) the audience needs less time to reach the main idea of the message, the bad news

TABLE 8.1	Choosing Positive Words
AVOID A NEGATIVE TONE	**USE A POSITIVE TONE**
I *cannot understand* what you mean.	Please clarify your request.
There will be a *delay* in your order.	We will ship your order as soon as possible.
Your account is in error.	Corrections have been made to your account.
The breakage was not our *fault*.	The merchandise was broken during shipping.
Sorry for your inconvenience.	The enclosed coupon will save you $5 next time.
I was *shocked* to learn that you're unhappy.	Your letter reached me yesterday.
The enclosed statement is *wrong*.	Please recheck the enclosed statement.

itself. Some bad-news situations are more appropriate for directness than others. Use a direct approach when

- You know from experience that your audience prefers reading bad news first in any message.
- Your company prefers internal correspondence to be brief and direct regardless of whether the message is negative.
- The message, although negative, is routine and likely to have little impact.
- The intended readers see bad news frequently and expect it (such as job seekers).[5]
- You want to present an image of firmness.

Document **Makeovers**

Using the Indirect Approach

Beginning a bad news message with a blunt "no" could prevent some people from reading or listening to your reasons. Some people prefer an explanation first, and for them you would use the indirect approach, easing them into your message by explaining your reasons before delivering the bad news:

- **Opening.** Start with a buffer.
- **Body.** Continue with a logical, neutral explanation of the reasons for the bad news; then follow with a diplomatic statement of the bad news (emphasizing any good news and de-emphasizing the bad).
- **Close.** End with a positive, forward-looking statement that is helpful and friendly.

Model **Document**

Activities

> Use the indirect approach when some preparation will help your audience accept the bad news.

Presenting your reasons first increases your chances of gaining audience acceptance by gradually preparing readers for the negative news to come. The indirect approach follows a four-part sequence: buffer, reasons, bad news, positive close.

BEGIN WITH A BUFFER A **buffer** is a neutral, noncontroversial statement that is closely related to the point of the message. Some critics believe that using a buffer is manipulative and dishonest, and thus unethical. But buffers are unethical only if they're insincere. Breaking bad news with kindness and courtesy is the humane way. Considering the feelings of others is never dishonest, and that consideration helps your audience accept your message. An effective buffer is tricky to write. A good buffer expresses your appreciation for being thought of, assures the reader of your attention to the request, compliments the reader, or indicates your understanding of the reader's needs. To write effective buffers, try to make them

> A buffer is a neutral lead-in to bad news.

- **Sincere.** Never insult your audience with insincere flattery or self-promoting blather. An effective buffer never makes readers feel they are being set up or "snowed."
- **Relevant.** Don't use an unrelated buffer. You will seem to be avoiding the issue. You'll appear manipulative and unethical, and you'll lose your audience's respect. In fact, try

to base your buffer on statements made by the reader. Doing so shows that you have listened well.

- **Not misleading.** Avoid implying that good news will follow. Building up your audience's expectations at the beginning only makes the actual bad news even more surprising. Imagine your reaction to the following openings:

> Your resumé indicates that you would be well suited for a management trainee position with our company.

> Your resumé shows very clearly why you are interested in becoming a management trainee with our company.

The second opening emphasizes the applicant's interpretation of her qualifications rather than the company's evaluation, so it's less misleading but still positive.

- **Neutral.** Avoid saying "no." An audience encountering the blunt refusal right at the beginning usually reacts negatively to the rest of the message, no matter how reasonable and well phrased it is.
- **Respectful.** Avoid using a know-it-all tone. When you use phrases such as "you should be aware that," readers expect your lecture to lead to a negative response, so they resist the rest of your message.
- **Succinct.** Avoid wordy and irrelevant phrases and sentences. Sentences such as "We have received your letter," "This letter is in reply to your request," and "We are writing in response to your request" are irrelevant. Make better use of the space by referring directly to the subject of the letter.
- **Assertive.** Avoid apologizing. Unless warranted by extreme circumstances, an apology only weakens the following explanation of your unfavourable news.
- **Brief.** Avoid writing a buffer that is too long. Identify something that both you and your audience are interested in and agree on before proceeding in a businesslike way.

> To write an effective buffer, make it sincere, relevant, neutral, respectful, succinct, assertive, and brief.

Table 8.2 shows several types of buffers you could use to open a bad-news message tactfully. After you've composed a buffer, evaluate it by asking yourself four questions: Is it pleasant? Is it relevant? Is it neutral, saying neither yes nor no? Does it provide for a smooth transition to the reasons that follow? If you can answer yes to every question, you can proceed confidently to the next section of your message.

FOLLOW WITH REASONS Cover the more positive points first; then move to the less positive ones. Provide enough detail for the audience to understand your reasons, but be concise; a long, roundabout explanation may make your audience impatient. Your goal is to explain *why* you have reached your decision before you explain *what* that decision is. If you present your reasons effectively, they should convince your audience that your decision is justified, fair, and logical.

> Giving reasons shows that your decision is fair.

Highlight readers' benefits rather than focusing on why the decision is good for you or your company. For example, when denying a request for credit, you can show how your decision will keep the person from becoming overextended financially. Facts and figures are often helpful when convincing readers that you're acting in their best interests.

Avoid hiding behind company policy to cushion the bad news. If you say, "Company policy forbids our hiring anyone who does not have two years' management experience," you seem to imply that you haven't considered the person on her or his own merits. Skilled and sympathetic communicators explain company policy (without referring to it as "policy") so that the audience can try to meet the requirements at a later time.

> Be tactful by focusing on reader benefits, not hiding behind company policy, and not apologizing.

Similarly, avoid apologizing when giving your reasons. Apologies are appropriate only when someone in your company has made a severe mistake or has done something terribly wrong. If no one in the company is at fault, an apology gives the wrong impression. For example, suppose that you're refusing the application of a

TABLE 8.2	Types of Buffers		
BUFFER	STRATEGY		EXAMPLE
Agreement	Find a point on which you and the reader share similar views.		We both know how hard it is to make a profit in this industry.
Appreciation	Express sincere thanks for receiving something.		Your cheque for $127.17 arrived yesterday. Thank you.
Cooperation	Convey your willingness to help in any way you realistically can.		At Employee Services our job is to assist you.
Fairness	Assure the reader that you've closely examined and carefully considered the problem, or mention an appropriate action that has already been taken.		For the past week, we have carefully monitored those using the photocopying machine to see whether we can detect any pattern of use that might explain its frequent breakdowns.
Good news	Start with the part of your message that is favourable.		A replacement knob for your range is on its way, shipped February 10 via UPS.
Praise	Find an attribute or an achievement to compliment.		Your resumé shows a breadth of experience, which should serve you well as you progress in your career.
Resale	Favourably discuss the product or company related to the subject of the letter.		With their heavy-duty, full-suspension hardware and fine veneers, the desks and file cabinets in our Montclair line have become a hit with value-conscious professionals.
Understanding	Demonstrate that you understand the reader's goals and needs.		So that you can more easily find the printer with the features you need, we are enclosing a brochure that describes all the Panasonic printers currently available.

management trainee. A tactfully worded letter might give these reasons for the decision not to hire:

> Because these management trainee positions are quite challenging, our human relations department has researched the qualifications needed to succeed in them. The findings show that the two most important qualifications are a bachelor's degree in business administration and two years' supervisory experience.

The paragraph does a good job of stating the reasons for the refusal because it

- Provides enough detail to make the reason for the refusal logically acceptable
- Implies that the applicant is better off avoiding a program in which he or she would probably fail, given the background of potential co-workers
- Explains the company's policy as logical rather than rigid
- Offers no apology for the decision
- Avoids negative personal expressions ("You do not meet our requirements")

Even though specific reasons help audiences accept bad news, reasons cannot always be given. Don't include reasons when they involve confidential, excessively complicated, or purely negative information or when they benefit only you or your firm (by enhancing the company's profits, for example). Instead, move directly to the next section.

STATE THE BAD NEWS When the bad news is a logical outcome of the reasons that come before it, the audience is psychologically prepared to receive it. However, the audience may still reject your message if the bad news is handled carelessly. Four techniques are useful for saying no clearly and kindly.

> Well-written reasons are
> - Detailed
> - Tactful
> - Individualized
> - Unapologetic
> - Positive

> Sometimes detailed reasons should not be provided.

De-emphasize Bad News

- Minimize the space or time devoted to the bad news.
- Subordinate bad news in a complex or compound sentence ("My department is already shorthanded, so I'll need all my staff for at least the next two months"). This construction pushes the bad news into the middle of the sentence, the point of least emphasis.
- Embed bad news in the middle of a paragraph or use parenthetical expressions ("Our profits, which are down, are only part of the picture").

To handle bad news carefully, use four techniques:
- De-emphasize the bad news visually and grammatically.
- Use a conditional statement.
- Tell what you did do, not what you didn't do.
- Be clear.

Use a Conditional Statement Use a conditional (*if* or *when*) statement to imply that the audience could have received, or might someday receive, a favourable answer ("When you have more managerial experience, you are welcome to reapply"). Such a statement could motivate applicants to improve their qualifications.

Say What You *Can* Do Tell the audience what you did do, can do, or will do rather than what you did not do, cannot do, or will not do. Say "We sell exclusively through retailers, and the one nearest you that carries our merchandise is . . ." rather than "We are unable to serve you, so please call your nearest dealer." By implying the bad news, you may not need to actually state it ("The five positions currently open have been staffed with people whose qualifications match our needs"). By focusing on the positive and implying the bad news, you soften the blow.

Be Clear When implying bad news, be sure your audience understands the entire message—including the bad news. It would be unethical to overemphasize the positive. So if an implied message might leave doubt, state your decision in direct terms. Avoid overly blunt statements that are likely to cause pain and anger:

Don't let the bad news get lost by overemphasizing the positive.

Instead of	**Use**
I *must refuse* your request.	I will be out of town on the day you need me.
We *must deny* your application.	The position has been filled.
I *am unable* to grant your request.	Contact us again when you have established . . .
We *cannot afford* to continue the program.	The program will conclude on May 1.
Much as I would like to attend . . .	Our budget meeting ends too late for me to attend.
We *must reject* your proposal.	We've accepted the proposal from AAA Builders.
We *must turn down* your extension request.	Please send in your payment by June 14.

END WITH A POSITIVE CLOSE After giving your audience the bad news, end your message on an upbeat note. You might propose an attainable solution to the audience's problem ("The human resources department has offered to bring in temporary workers when I need them, and they would probably consider doing the same for you"). In a message to a customer or potential customer, an ending can include **resale information** (favourable comments about a product or service that the customer has already purchased) or **sales promotion** (favourable comments that encourage interest in goods or services the reader has not yet committed to purchase). If you've asked readers to decide between alternatives or to take some action, make sure that they know what to do, when to do it, and how to do it with ease. Whatever type of close you choose, follow these guidelines:

- **Keep it positive.** Don't refer to, repeat, or apologize for the bad news, and refrain from expressing any doubt that your reasons will be accepted (avoid statements such as "I trust our decision is satisfactory").

- **Limit future correspondence.** Encourage additional communication *only* if you're willing to discuss your decision further (avoid wording such as "If you have further questions, please write").
- **Be optimistic about the future.** Don't anticipate problems (avoid statements such as "Should you have further problems, please let us know").
- **Be sincere.** Steer clear of clichés that are insincere in view of the bad news (avoid saying, "If we can be of any help, please contact us").
- **Be confident.** Don't show any doubt about keeping the person as a customer (avoid phrases such as "We hope you will continue to do business with us").

> Make your close positive, final, optimistic, sincere, and confident.

Types of Bad-News Messages

In the course of your business career, you will write various types of bad-news messages, from refusing credit to refusing requests and giving bad news about orders. Many of the messages that you'll be writing will fall into two major categories: negative answers to routine requests and negative organizational news.

Sending Negative Answers to Routine Requests

As a business person, you can't say yes to everyone. Occasionally, your response to routine requests must simply be "no." It's a mark of your skill as a communicator to be able to say no clearly and yet not cut yourself off from future dealings with the people you refuse.

REFUSING REQUESTS FOR INFORMATION When people ask you for information and you can't honour the request, you may answer with either the direct approach or the indirect approach. However, using the direct approach may offend readers who are outside the company and may be emotionally involved in the response. Compare the poorly written draft with the improved, revised letter in Figure 8.2 (on page 162). The improved letter conveys the same negative message but without sounding offensive. As you think about the different effects of these two letters, you can see why good business writers take the time and the trouble to give negative messages the attention they deserve, even when they are only requesting information.

> Use either the direct or the indirect approach to tell someone you cannot provide what has been requested.

REFUSING INVITATIONS AND REQUESTS FOR FAVOURS When you must say no to an invitation or a requested favour, your use of the direct or the indirect approach depends on your relationship with the reader. For example, suppose the president of the local community college asks your company to host graduation on your corporate grounds, but your sales meetings will be taking place at the same time. If you don't know the president well, you'll probably use the indirect approach. See Figure 8.3 (on page 163), in which May Yee Kwan delivers this bad news in a helpful and supportive way. If you are friends with the president and work frequently on projects for the college, you might use the direct approach.

> When turning down an invitation or a request for a favour, base your choice of approach on your relationship with the reader.

Sandra, thanks for asking us to host your graduation. You know we've always supported the college and would love to do this for you. However, our company sales meetings will be going on during the same time. We'll have so many of our staff tied up with logistics, we won't have the personnel to adequately take care of the graduation.

Have you called Jerry Kane over at the Botanical Gardens? I can't think of a prettier site for graduation. Roberta in my office volunteers over there and knows Jerry. She can fill you in on the details, if you'd like to talk to her first.

Thanks again for considering us. Let's have lunch in mid-June to plan our involvement with the college for the next school year. I'll look forward to seeing you and catching up on family news.

FIGURE 8.2 Letter Refusing a Request for Information

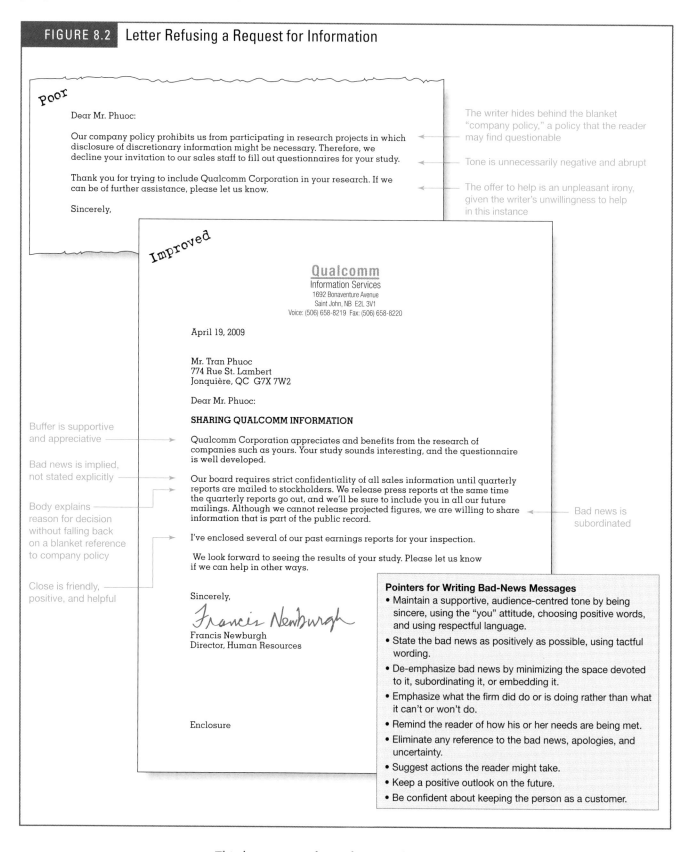

Poor

Dear Mr. Phuoc:

Our company policy prohibits us from participating in research projects in which disclosure of discretionary information might be necessary. Therefore, we decline your invitation to our sales staff to fill out questionnaires for your study.

Thank you for trying to include Qualcomm Corporation in your research. If we can be of further assistance, please let us know.

Sincerely,

The writer hides behind the blanket "company policy," a policy that the reader may find questionable

Tone is unnecessarily negative and abrupt

The offer to help is an unpleasant irony, given the writer's unwillingness to help in this instance

Improved

Qualcomm
Information Services
1692 Bonaventure Avenue
Saint John, NB E2L 3V1
Voice: (506) 658-8219 Fax: (506) 658-8220

April 19, 2009

Mr. Tran Phuoc
774 Rue St. Lambert
Jonquière, QC G7X 7W2

Dear Mr. Phuoc:

SHARING QUALCOMM INFORMATION

Qualcomm Corporation appreciates and benefits from the research of companies such as yours. Your study sounds interesting, and the questionnaire is well developed.

Our board requires strict confidentiality of all sales information until quarterly reports are mailed to stockholders. We release press reports at the same time the quarterly reports go out, and we'll be sure to include you in all our future mailings. Although we cannot release projected figures, we are willing to share information that is part of the public record.

I've enclosed several of our past earnings reports for your inspection.

We look forward to seeing the results of your study. Please let us know if we can help in other ways.

Sincerely,

Francis Newburgh

Francis Newburgh
Director, Human Resources

Enclosure

Buffer is supportive and appreciative

Bad news is implied, not stated explicitly

Body explains reason for decision without falling back on a blanket reference to company policy

Close is friendly, positive, and helpful

Bad news is subordinated

Pointers for Writing Bad-News Messages
- Maintain a supportive, audience-centred tone by being sincere, using the "you" attitude, choosing positive words, and using respectful language.
- State the bad news as positively as possible, using tactful wording.
- De-emphasize bad news by minimizing the space devoted to it, subordinating it, or embedding it.
- Emphasize what the firm did do or is doing rather than what it can't or won't do.
- Remind the reader of how his or her needs are being met.
- Eliminate any reference to the bad news, apologies, and uncertainty.
- Suggest actions the reader might take.
- Keep a positive outlook on the future.
- Be confident about keeping the person as a customer.

This letter gets right to the point but still uses some blow-softening techniques: It compliments the person and organization making the request, suggests an alternative, and looks toward future opportunities for cooperation.

HANDLING BAD NEWS ABOUT ORDERS For several reasons, businesses must sometimes convey bad news concerning orders. Also, when delivering bad news to existing or would-be customers, you have an additional challenge—resale. To make readers feel

The basic goal of a bad-news letter about orders is to protect or make a sale.

FIGURE 8.3 Letter Declining a Favour

Planning	Writing	Completing
Analyze Gauge the audience's reaction to refusal; gear level of formality to reader familiarity. **Investigate** Collect information on possible alternatives. **Adapt** For a more formal response, letterhead is best. Maintain the relationship with the "you" attitude, and focus on the reader's problem.	**Organize** Main idea is to refuse a request. Respect your reader by showing that the request received serious consideration. Use an indirect approach. **Compose** Make your style conversational but keep it businesslike. Keep the letter brief, clear, and helpful.	**Revise** Maintain a friendly tone by eliminating overly formal words and phrases. Ensure your tone is positive. **Produce** Use letterhead with a straight-forward format. **Proofread** Be careful to review for accuracy, spelling, and mechanics.
1	**2**	**3**

InfoTech

418 Glendale Drvie, Don Mills, ON M3B 2X2
Voice (416) 447-4428   Fax: (416) 447-4429
www.infotech.com

March 5, 2009

Dr. Sandra Wofford, President
Haliburton College
333 Fairley Avenue
Don Mills, ON M5T 4J6

Dear Dr. Wofford:

YOUR REQUEST FOR A GRADUATION SITE

Info Tech has been happy to support Haliburton College in many ways over the years, and we appreciate the opportunities you and your organization provide to students. Thank you for considering our grounds for your graduation ceremony.   *← Buffers bad news by demonstrating respect and recapping request*

Our company-wide sales meetings will be held during the weeks of May 29 and June 5. We will host more than 200 sales representatives and their families, and activities will take place at both our corporate campus and the Ramada Renaissance. As a result, our support staff will be devoting all their time and effort to these events.   *← States reason for the bad news explicitl and in detail*

My assistant, Roberta Seagers, suggests you contact the Municipal Botanical Gardens as a possible graduation site. She recommends calling Jerry Kane, director of public relations.   *← Suggests an alternative—showing that Kwan cares abou the college and has given the matter some thought*

We remain firm in our commitment to the college and will continue to be a corporate partner. If we can help in any other way with graduation, please let us know.   *← Closes by renewing the corporation's future support*

Sincerely,

May Yee Kwan

May Yee Kwan
Public Relations Director

Pointers for Writing Buffers and Giving Reasons

Buffer

• Express appreciation, cooperation, fairness, good news, praise, resale, or understanding.
• Introduce a relevant topic.
• Avoid apologies and negative-sounding words *(won't, can't, unable to)*.
• Be brief and to the point.

Reasons

• Smooth the transition from the favourable buffer to the reasons.
• Show how the decision benefits your audience.
• Avoid apologies and expressions of sorrow or regret.
• Offer enough detail to show the logic of your position.
• Include only factual information and only business reasons, not personal ones.
• Carefully word the reasons so that readers can anticipate the bad news.

good about continuing to do business with your firm, you want to reinforce the customer's confidence in your service or product.

When you must back-order for a customer, you have one of two types of bad news to convey: (1) You're able to send only part of the order, or (2) you're able to send none of the order. When sending only part of the order, you actually have both good news and bad news, so use the indirect approach. The buffer contains the good news (that part of the order is en route) along with a resale reminder of the product's attractiveness. After the buffer come the reasons for the delay of the remainder of the shipment. A strong close encourages a favourable attitude toward the entire transaction. For a customer whose order for a recliner and ottoman will be only partially filled, your email message might read like the one in Figure 8.4.

REFUSING CLAIMS AND REQUESTS FOR ADJUSTMENT   Almost every customer who makes a claim is emotionally involved; therefore, the indirect approach is usually the best approach for a refusal. Your job as a writer is to avoid accepting responsibility for the unfortunate situation and yet avoid blaming or accusing the customer. To steer clear of these pitfalls, pay special attention to the tone of your letter. Keep in mind that a tactful and courteous letter can build goodwill even while denying the claim. For example, Village Electronics recently received a letter from Daniel Lindmeier, who believes that his warranty covers one year, when it actually covers only three months. For the reply to his letter, see Figure 8.5 (on page 166).

When refusing a claim, avoid language that might have a negative effect on the reader. Instead, demonstrate that you understand and have considered the complaint. Then, even if the claim is unreasonable, rationally explain why you are refusing the request. Remember, don't apologize and don't rely on company policy. End the letter on a respectful note, and try to suggest some alternative action.

Sending Negative Organizational News

Refusing a request isn't the only type of bad news. At times, you may have bad news about your company's products or about its operations. Whether you're reporting to a supervisor or announcing your news to the media, the particular situation dictates whether you will use the direct or the indirect approach.

BAD NEWS ABOUT PRODUCTS   Say that you must provide bad news about a product. If you were writing to tell your company's bookkeeping department about increasing product prices, you'd use the direct approach. Although your audience would have to make some arithmetical adjustments, readers would probably be unemotional about the matter. On the other hand, if you were writing to convey the same information to customers or even to your own sales department, you would probably use the indirect approach. Customers never like to pay more, and your sales reps would see the change as weakening your product's competitive edge, threatening their incomes, and possibly threatening their jobs.

COMPANY DECISIONS AFFECTING CUSTOMERS   At least three situations require bad-news letters about company operations or performance: (1) a change in company policy or future plans that will have a negative effect on the reader, (2) problems with company performance, and (3) controversial or unpopular company operations. In trying situations, apologies may be in order. If an apology is appropriate, good writers usually make it brief and bury it somewhere in the middle of the letter. Moreover, they try to leave readers with a favourable impression by closing on a positive note.

When a change in company policy will have a negative effect on your audience state the reasons for the change clearly and carefully. The explanation section of the message convinces readers that the change was necessary and, if possible, explains

---

Use the indirect approach for both types of bad news about orders.

Model Document

Activities

Use the indirect approach in most cases of refusing a claim.

When refusing a claim
- Demonstrate your understanding of the complaint
- Explain your refusal
- Suggest alternative action

When conveying bad news about your company, focus on the reasons and on possible benefits.

FIGURE 8.4 Email Message Advising of a Back Order

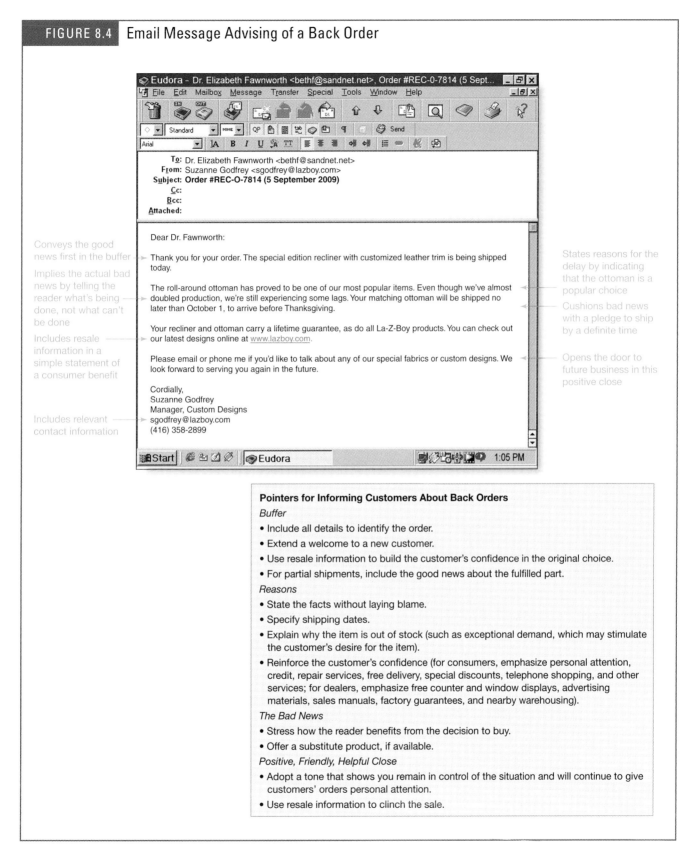

Conveys the good news first in the buffer

Implies the actual bad news by telling the reader what's being done, not what can't be done

Includes resale information in a simple statement of a consumer benefit

Includes relevant contact information

States reasons for the delay by indicating that the ottoman is a popular choice

Cushions bad news with a pledge to ship by a definite time

Opens the door to future business in this positive close

Pointers for Informing Customers About Back Orders

Buffer
- Include all details to identify the order.
- Extend a welcome to a new customer.
- Use resale information to build the customer's confidence in the original choice.
- For partial shipments, include the good news about the fulfilled part.

Reasons
- State the facts without laying blame.
- Specify shipping dates.
- Explain why the item is out of stock (such as exceptional demand, which may stimulate the customer's desire for the item).
- Reinforce the customer's confidence (for consumers, emphasize personal attention, credit, repair services, free delivery, special discounts, telephone shopping, and other services; for dealers, emphasize free counter and window displays, advertising materials, sales manuals, factory guarantees, and nearby warehousing).

The Bad News
- Stress how the reader benefits from the decision to buy.
- Offer a substitute product, if available.

Positive, Friendly, Helpful Close
- Adopt a tone that shows you remain in control of the situation and will continue to give customers' orders personal attention.
- Use resale information to clinch the sale.

how the change will benefit them. For example, if your company decided to drop orthodontic coverage from its employee dental plan, you could explain the decision this way:

> By eliminating this infrequently used benefit, we will not have to increase the monthly amount withheld from your paycheque for insurance coverage.

FIGURE 8.5 Letter Refusing a Claim

Planning	Writing	Completing
Analyze Purpose is to explain that the warranty has expired and to offer repairs that the reader can pay for. **Investigate** Briefly gather information on product warranties, terms for repair, and resale information. **Adapt** Use letter format and focus on customer relationship. **1**	**Organize** Main idea is that you're offering repairs, even though the warranty has expired. Use the indirect approach to help reader accept your message. **Compose** Make the style conversational. Choose your words carefully, and enclose a catalogue to encourage future business. **2**	**Revise** Review for logical order and tone. Be clear but friendly. **Produce** Use a clean letter format on letterhead. **Proofread** Review for accuracy and correctness. Be sure to include promised enclosures. **3**

NUMBER ONE IN ENTERTAINMENT

Village Electronics

48 College Street, Toronto, ON M5B 1H8
Voice: (416) 591-1312 • (416) 591-1316

May 3, 2009

Mr. Daniel Lindmeier
12 Wellington Square
Brantford, ON N3T 4H7

Dear Mr. Lindmeier:

REPAIRING YOUR CAMERA

[Buffers the bad news by emphasizing a point that reader and writer both agree on]

Thank you for your letter about the battery release switch on your JVC digital camera. We believe, as you do, that electronic equipment should be built to last. That's why we stand behind our products with a 90-day warranty.

[States bad news indirectly, tactfully leaving the repair decision to the customer]

[Puts company's policy in a favourable light]

Even though your JVC camera is a year old and therefore out of warranty, we can still help. Please package your camera carefully and ship it to our store in St. Catharines. Include your complete name, address, phone number, and a brief description of the malfunction, along with a cheque for $35. After examining the unit, we will give you a written estimate of the needed parts and labour. Then just let us know whether you want us to make the repairs—either by phone or by filling out the prepaid card we'll send you with the estimate.

[Helps soothe the reader with a positive alternative action]

If you choose to repair the unit, the $35 will be applied toward your bill, the balance of which is payable by cheque or credit card. If you decide not to repair the unit, the $35 will pay for the technician's time examining the unit. JVC also has service centres available in your area. If you would prefer to take the unit to one of them, please see the enclosed list.

[Closes by blending sales promotion with an acknowledgement of customer's interests]

Thanks again for inquiring about our service. I've enclosed a catalogue of our latest cameras and accessories. In June JVC is offering a "Trade-Up Special," at which time you can receive trade-in credit for your digital camera when you purchase a newer model. Come to visit Village Electronics soon.

Sincerely,

Walter Brodie

Walter Brodie
President

mk

Enclosures: List of service centres
            Catalogue

Pointers for Refusing Claims

- In the buffer, indicate your full understanding of the complaint.
- Avoid all areas of disagreement and any hint of your final decision.
- In the body, provide an accurate, factual account of the transaction.
- Avoid using a know-it-all tone, and use impersonal, passive language.
- Make the refusal clear, using tactful language (avoid words such as "reject" and "claim").
- Avoid any hint that your decision is less than final.
- Offer a counterproposal, a compromise, or a partial adjustment.
- Include resale information for the company or product.
- Emphasize your desire for a good relationship in the future.
- Offer to replace the product or to provide a replacement part at the regular price.
- In the close, make no reference to your refusal.
- Refer to enclosed sales material.
- Make any suggested action easy for readers to comply with.

FIGURE 8.6 Email Message Providing Bad News About Company Operations

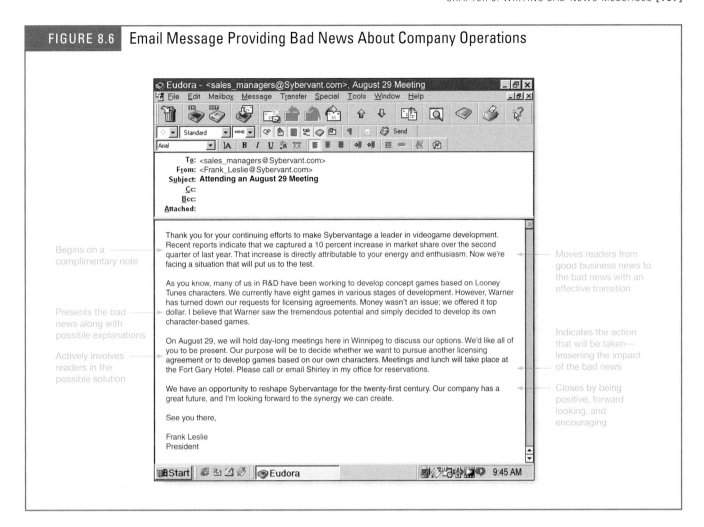

If your company is having serious performance problems, your customers and shareholders want to learn of the difficulty from you, not from complaints posted online or on YouTube. Even if the news leaks out before you announce it, counter with your own explanation as soon as possible. Social technologies make spreading rumours very easy, and it pays for a company to monitor what is being said about it so that the company can respond in a timely manner. Business is based on mutual trust; if your customers and shareholders can't trust you to inform them of your problems, they may choose to work with someone they can trust. When you do inform stakeholders, use your common sense and present the bad news in as favourable a light as possible.

If your company loses a major business customer or if an important deal falls through, you could present the bad news as an opportunity to focus on smaller, growing businesses or on new products, as the email in Figure 8.6 does. In this example, rather than dwell on the bad news, the company focuses on possible options for the future. The upbeat close and focus on action diminish the effect of the bad news.

ON THE JOB

Negative messages about people in the workplace have the potential to cause trouble in staff relationships, which then costs companies in lost productivity. To build strong, positive relationships with co-workers, avoid commenting negatively about others in office gossip sessions. Two good rules of thumb are:

1. If you don't have something good to say, keep it to yourself.
2. Could you say the comment to the person's face? If not, don't say it to others.

Reviewing Key Points

This chapter shares strategies for bad-news messages. Since no one likes to receive bad news, you'll want to pay attention to readers' feelings when you have to convey negative messages. In this chapter, you learned how to

- Send effective bad-news messages by creating an audience-centred tone.
- Choose the direct approach when you know the reader prefers bad news first, when the situation is minor, or when writing inside your organization and the company practice is to be very direct.
- Choose the indirect approach when you expect the news to be hard to accept, and to avoid having the reader reject your message before getting to the reasons. The indirect pattern for bad news includes
  - A buffer (a point of agreement, appreciation, good news, or fairness)
  - Reasons for the refusal (carefully and objectively explained with relevant facts)
  - The refusal (to de-emphasize the negativity, the refusal could be placed at the bottom of the reasons paragraph, subordinated, or implied)
  - A positive close (in which you may offer alternatives or resale information)
- Handle negative responses to requests, orders, and claims without laying blame and by restoring a goodwill relationship.
- Advise people inside and outside the company about problems with products or company operations by being straightforward, telling what you can do, and being optimistic about the future.

mybuscommlab   Go to MyBusCommLab at www.pearson.ca/mybuscommlab for online exercises.

Practise Your Grammar

 Exercises

Effective business communication starts with strong grammar skills. To improve your grammar skills, go to MyBusCommLab or Grammar-on-the-Go, where you'll find exercises and diagnostic tests to help you produce clear, effective communication.

Test Your Knowledge

Exercises

1. What are the five main goals in delivering bad news?
2. Why is it particularly important to adapt your medium and tone to your audience's needs and preferences when writing a bad-news message?
3. What are the advantages of using the direct approach to deliver the bad news at the beginning of a message?
4. What is the sequence of elements in a bad-news message that is organized using the indirect approach?
5. What is a buffer, and why do some critics consider it unethical?
6. When using an indirect approach to announce a negative decision, what is the purpose of presenting your reasons before explaining the decision itself?
7. What are four techniques for de-emphasizing bad news?
8. When and why should a company acknowledge a performance problem and communicate about it openly in today's "connected" world?

Apply Your Knowledge

1. Why is it important to end your bad-news message on a positive note? Explain.
2. If company policy changes, should you explain those changes to employees and customers at about the same time, or should you explain them to employees first? Why?
3. If the purpose of your letter is to convey bad news, should you take the time to suggest alternatives to your reader? Why or why not?
4. When a company suffers a setback, should you soften the impact by letting out the bad news a little at a time? Why or why not?
5. **Ethical Choices** Is intentionally de-emphasizing bad news the same as distorting graphs and charts to de-emphasize unfavourable data? Why or why not?

Running Cases

Video

CASE 1: Noreen

In her role as collections manager, Noreen has to write a letter informing customers with overdue accounts that the interest rate has risen by 1 percent, effective 30 days from the date on the letter. This policy means Petro-Go's current interest rate is 14 percent and in 30 days will increase to 15 percent. Overdue accounts are charged with compounding interest (i.e., interest on both the previous month's balance and the interest already charged on that month's balance).

QUESTIONS

a. What does it mean to use the "you" attitude in this type of message?
b. Is the direct or indirect approach best for this bad-news message? Why?
c. What must be considered to avoid defamation of the customer's character or reputation?
d. How will Noreen end this message on a positive note?
e. Should Noreen suggest ways for the customer to avoid paying late payment charges in this letter?

YOUR TASK

Write the letter. Remember to use company letterhead (create it yourself) and include an enclosure notation. Include a 1-800 number customers can call for further information. Both the letter and the envelope should indicate that the information is confidential. Prepare the envelope. (See Appendix A for letter and envelope formats.)

CASE 2: Kwong

Kwong has returned to Accountants For All to complete his third co-op work term required by his college program. The owner, being very impressed with Kwong's past work performance and knowing that he has completed the required courses, promotes Kwong to corporate accountant status. He asks Kwong to write a letter to an important corporate client, Trisix, informing Marion Beattie, chief financial officer, that the quote Accountants For All gave them for this year's tax services was incorrect. The actual charge will be $500 more than discussed previously in an office meeting with Accountants For All's owner. The increased fee was set because Trisix's ledger was not accurate and Accountants For All's staff had to review receipts and adjust ledger entries manually. The initial price quote did not include manual handling of receipts. The letter should attempt to maintain a good customer relationship.

QUESTIONS

a. What facts must Kwong gather before writing the letter?
b. How will he choose positive words for this bad news?
c. Kwong has chosen the indirect approach for this letter. Suggest a reasonable buffer.
d. Should Kwong apologize?
e. How will Kwong end this message on a positive note? Why is this important?

YOUR TASK

Write the letter. Apply the guidelines for writing bad-news messages that Chapter 8 discusses.

Practise Your Knowledge

EXERCISES FOR PERFECTING YOUR WRITING

Teamwork Working alone, revise the following statements to de-emphasize the bad news. (*Hint:* Minimize the space devoted to the bad news, subordinate it, embed it, or use the passive voice.) Then team up with a classmate and read each other's revisions. Did you both use the same approach in every case? Which approach seems to be most effective for each of the revised statements?

1. The airline can't refund your money. The "Conditions" segment on the back of your ticket states that there are no refunds for missed flights. Sometimes the airline makes exceptions, but only when life and death are involved. Of course, your ticket is still valid and can be used on a flight to the same destination.

2. I'm sorry to tell you, we can't supply the custom decorations you requested. We called every supplier and none of them can do what you want on such short notice. You can, however, get a standard decorative package on the same theme in time. I found a supplier that stocks these. Of course, it won't have quite the flair you originally requested.

3. We can't refund your money for the malfunctioning lamp. You shouldn't have placed a 250-watt bulb in the fixture socket; it's guaranteed for a maximum of 75 watts.

Using Buffers Answer the following questions pertaining to buffers:

4. You have to tell a local restaurant owner that your plans have changed and you have to cancel the 90-person banquet scheduled for next month. Do you need to use a buffer? Why or why not?

5. Write a buffer for a letter declining an invitation to speak at an association's annual fundraising event. Show your appreciation for being asked.

6. Write a buffer for a letter rejecting a job applicant who speaks three foreign languages fluently. Include praise for the applicant's accomplishments.

Selecting Indirect or Direct Approach Select which approach you would use (direct or indirect) for the following bad-news messages:

7. A memo to your boss informing her that one of your key clients is taking its business to a different accounting firm

8. An email message to a customer informing her that one of the books she ordered over the internet is temporarily out of stock

9. A letter to a customer explaining that the tape backup unit he ordered for his new custom computer is on back order and that, as a consequence, the shipping of the entire order will be delayed

ACTIVITIES

1. **Analyze This Document** Read the following document; then (1) analyze the strengths and weaknesses of each sentence and (2) revise the document so that it follows this chapter's guidelines.

> Your spring party sounds like fun. We're glad you've again chosen us as your caterer. Unfortunately, we have changed a few of our policies, and I wanted you to know about these changes in advance so that we won't have any misunderstandings on the day of the party.
>
> We will arrange the delivery of tables and chairs as usual the evening before the party. However, if you want us to set up, there is now a $100 charge for that service. Of course, you might want to get some friends to do it, which would save you money. We've also added a small charge for cleanup. This is only $3 per person (you can estimate because I know a lot of people come and go later in the evening).
>
> Other than that, all the arrangements will be the same. We'll provide the skirt for the band stage, tablecloths, bar setup, and of course, the barbecue. Will you have the tubs of ice with soft drinks again? We can do that for you as well, but there will be a fee.
>
> Please let me know if you have any problems with these changes and we'll try to work them out. I know it's going to be a great party.

2. **Analyze This Document** Read the following document; then (1) analyze the strengths and weaknesses of each sentence and (2) revise the document so that it follows this chapter's guidelines.

> I am responding to your letter of about six weeks ago asking for an adjustment on your fax/modem, model FM39Z. We test all our products before they leave the factory; therefore, it could not have been our fault that your fax/modem didn't work.
>
> If you or someone in your office dropped the unit, it might have caused the damage. Or the damage could have been caused by the shipper if he dropped it. If so, you should file a claim with the shipper. At any rate, it wasn't our fault. The parts are already covered by warranty. However, we will provide labour for the repairs for $50, which is less than our cost, since you are a valued customer.
>
> We will have a booth at the upcoming trade fair there and hope to see you or someone from your office. We have many new models of office machines that we're sure you'll want to see. I've enclosed our latest catalogue. Hope to see you there.

3. **Ethical Choices** The insurance company where you work is planning to raise all premiums for health-care coverage. Your company offers basic medical coverage for families and individuals as well as other insurance policies for extended health (for vision, dental, and long-term disability). The rise in rates will apply to all of the policies that your firm sells. All the policies will be expanded to include additional benefits. Your boss has asked you to read a draft of her letter to customers announcing the new, higher rates. The first two paragraphs discuss some exciting medical advances and the expanded coverage offered by your company. Only in the final paragraph do customers learn that they will have to pay more for coverage starting next year. What are the ethical implications of this draft? What changes would you suggest?

4. **Revising an Email Message: Budgetary Cutbacks at Black & Decker** The following bad-news email about travel budget cutbacks contains numerous blunders. Using what you've learned in the chapter, read the message carefully and analyze its faults. Then use the questions below to outline and write an improved message.

Date: Fri, 28 May 2009 4:20
From: M. Juhasz, Travel & Meeting Services
To: [mailing list]
CC:
BCC:
Attached:
Subject: Travel Budget Cuts Effective Immediately

Dear Travelling Executives:

We need you to start using some of the budget suggestions we are going to issue as a separate memorandum. These include using videoconference equipment instead of travelling to meetings, staying in cheaper hotels, arranging flights for cheaper times, and flying from less-convenient but also less-expensive suburban airports.

The company needs to cut travel expenses by 50 percent, just as we've cut costs in all departments of Black & Decker. This means you'll no longer be able to stay in fancy hotels and make last-minute, costly changes to your travel plans.

You'll also be expected to avoid hotel phone surcharges. And never return a rental car with an empty tank! That causes the rental agency to charge us a premium price for the gas they sell when they fill it up upon your return.

You'll be expected to make these changes in your travel habits immediately.

Sincerely,

M. Juhasz

Travel & Meeting Services

---

1. Describe the flaws you discovered in this bad-news email about company operations.
2. Develop a plan for rewriting the email, using the direct approach for company insiders. The following steps will help you organize your efforts before you begin writing:
   a. Create an opening statement of the bad news, using the "you" attitude.
   b. Decide what explanation is needed to justify the news.
   c. Determine whether you can use lists effectively.
   d. Choose some positive suggestions you can include to soften the news.
   e. Develop an upbeat closing.
3. Now rewrite the email. Don't forget to leave ample time for revision of your own work before you turn it in.

5. **Teamwork: Revising a Letter—Refusal from Home Depot to New Faucet Manufacturer** The following letter rejecting a faucet manufacturer's product presentation contains many errors in judgment. Working with your classmates in a team effort, you should be able to improve its effectiveness as a bad-news message. First, analyze and discuss the letter's flaws. How can it be improved? Use the questions below to help guide your discussion and development of an improved version.

July 15, 2009
Pamela Wilson, Operations Manager
Sterling Manufacturing
133 Industrial Avenue
Red Deer, AB T5D 2D6

Dear Ms. Wilson:

We regret to inform you that your presentation at Home Depot's recent product review sessions in Edmonton did not meet our expert panellists' expectations. We require new products that will satisfy our customers' high standards. Yours did not match this goal.

Our primary concern is to continue our commitment to product excellence, customer knowledge, and price competitiveness, which has helped make Home Depot a top-performing company with more than a thousand stores Canada-wide. The panel found flaws in your design and materials. Also, your cost per unit was too high.

The product review sessions occur annually. You are allowed to try again; just apply as you did this year. Again, I'm sorry things didn't work out for you this time.

Sincerely,

1. Describe the problems you found with this letter rejecting a product presentation.
2. Develop a plan for rewriting the letter, using the indirect approach. First, organize your thinking before you begin writing:
   a. Select a buffer for the opening, using the "you" attitude.
   b. Choose the reasons you'll use to explain the rejection.
   c. Develop a way to soften or embed the bad news.
   d. Create a conditional (if/then) statement to encourage the recipient to try again.
   e. Find a way to close on a positive, encouraging note.
3. Now rewrite the letter. Don't forget to leave ample time for revision of your own work before you turn it in.

⊘ Expand Your Knowledge

Best of the Web

Learn from Professionals. Find out more about ethical considerations of delivering bad news by visiting the Canadian Public Relations Society website and clicking on "Code of Professional Standards." Learn how important truthful communication is to a practising professional in this field.
www.cprs.ca

Use Google Scholar (http://scholar.google.com) to search for reviews of a book by Don Middleberg titled *Winning PR in the Wired World: Powerful Communication Strategies for the Noisy Digital Space* (New York: McGraw Hill, 2001). By reading a review, you can learn how the internet has changed the public's expectation of information sharing during times of crisis.

EXERCISES

1. How has the internet influenced the practice of public relations?
2. What difference do these changes in society make to companies that have bad news to deliver?
3. How has the internet changed the way companies should communicate in a crisis?

Exploring the Web on Your Own

Review these chapter-related websites on your own to learn more about the bad-news issues human resources departments are facing today.

1. Bob Rosner and Sherrie Campbell's "Workplace911" column on the Workplace911 website, **www.workplace911.com**, offers some advice for delivering bad news to your boss. Read some of the other articles to find out what kinds of issues managers have to resolve in the workplace. What are the top "headaches" reported by employees?

2. Human Resources and Social Development Canada offers extensive human resources management advice and information on its website. Visit **www.hrmanagement.ca** to read about workplace trends, labour law affecting employers, recruiting, benefits, staffing, and more.

Apply each step in Figure 8.1 on page 155 to the following cases, as assigned by your instructor.

1. TOO ANOMALOUS: LETTER DECLINING AN INVITATION FROM THE DISCLOSURE PROJECT

You work part-time for the president of the Alberta Flying Club, an organization that offers discounts on flying lessons and small plane rentals. In exchange, you get free flying lessons from the president, John Zuniga.

Like most pilots-to-be, you're interested in anomalous aerial phenomena (UFOs), so you paid close attention when Zuniga was asked if the club would sponsor a free public event in Calgary, a "Campaign for Disclosure." The request came from two club members, both retired airforce pilots who are well respected around the airport, Bill West and Chuck Macdonald. You've overheard some of their stories about their UFO encounters during airborne military manoeuvres. You also heard them say that they were threatened by superiors to "forget what they'd seen."

These two members met with Zuniga in his office, presenting him with a book and videotape from a non-profit research organization in the United States called the Disclosure Project. It was founded by Dr. Steven Greer, an emergency-room physician who gave up his doctor's salary to document the testimony of more than 400 witnesses to UFO and extraterrestrial events. These witnesses are from the United States, Canada, Britain, Russia, Australia, and other countries, and from the armed services, the CIA, NASA, CSIS, and other agencies.

When Zuniga emerges from the meeting, his face is grim, determined. "These fellas are really into it, but we can't do it," he tells you when you ask about the sponsorship.

"It's my job to encourage pilots to join this flying club," he explains. "No matter what I believe personally, this isn't an event we should sponsor. I can't have folks referring to us as 'those kooks over in Hangar 5,' much as I'd love to hear Dr. Greer speak. He's got a powerful agenda and I'd love to support him—but officially, I just can't do it."

YOUR TASK Zuniga wants you to write a letter to Bill West (12468 16 St NW, Calgary, AB T1V 4Y2), declining the sponsorship invitation: "First take a look at the Disclosure website, **www.disclosureproject.org**, and you'll know why we can't sponsor this. Then write a polite refusal. Use what you've learned to let the doctor know

we've given this event our serious consideration. Be encouraging, if you can, and let me sign the letter."[6]

2. THE BOX HALF FULL—A COMMUNICATION WITH CUSTOMERS EXPLAINING A PROBLEM WITH HOME DELIVERY

You are the office administrator for Organics to You, a small, but growing organic produce home-delivery business. The company's accounts have grown from 50 in 2007 to over 1200 today. Generally people are very happy with the quality of the fruits and vegetables.

You have good local suppliers for some of the items, but much of the produce is imported in the winter and being in the fresh food business can sometimes be a headache—like earlier this week when your warehouse received shipments from distributors that were supposed to have eight different fruit varieties and only two came in and not a single avocado (a popular fruit with all the customers) was delivered.

"Hey—the area of Mexico where the avocados are grown has been hit by a storm—the supplier can't promise to deliver any for three weeks," you tell the owner, Rina Svetic. "What's the problem with the fruit order?" Rina asks. "Well, I think it was just a screw up with the order form. For some reason Kira in the warehouse could not get the second page of the order to transmit through the fax machine on Thursday, so the whole order did not reach the distributor."

"Which distributor are we talking about?" Rina asks, hoping it is nearby. You reply, "It was the order to Sunripe in Kelowna, B.C. So now it will take a few days for the second-page items to arrive here—which means we will have extra items for the boxes filled three days from now and not as many items for those that have been filled for today."

"Bummer," says Rina. "Find alternative suppliers for the avocados and communicate with the affected customers—let them know the bad news. At least the fruit is only going to be a problem for the next three days and not the whole week. Be sure you copy the delivery drivers when you communicate with the customers so they will know the situation."

No deluxe exotics or berries this week even though most customers ordered a variety of fruits; a drag, but what can you do? And besides, some of these people are too picky. Maybe you will think of something to offer, but in the meantime, the bad news is each customer's box will have less variety for three days of deliveries and no avocados for at least one week. No guacamole for those folks this week!

YOUR TASK Prepare a communication for the approximately 720 customers who will receive deliveries over the next three days, as well as for the two delivery drivers. Consider whether you should send an email or write a letter to be included in the delivery box. Which channel of communication would be best in this situation?

3. CYBER-SURVEILLANCE: LETTER REFUSING CLAIM FROM SILENT WATCH VICTIM

You work in human resources for a company called Advertising Inflatables, which designs and builds the huge balloon replicas used for advertising atop retail stores, tire outlets, used-car lots, fast-food outlets, fitness clubs, and so on. Since you started, you've seen balloon re-creations of everything from a 17-m King Kong to a "small" 3-m pizza.

Not long ago, company management installed the "cyber-surveillance" software, Silent Watch, to track and record employees' computer usage. At the time, you sent out a memo informing all employees that they should limit their computer use and email to work projects only. You also informed them that their work would be monitored. At your boss's request, you did not mention that Silent Watch would record every keystroke of their work or that they could be monitored from a screen in their manager's office.

As it turned out, Silent Watch caught two of the sales staff spending between 50 percent and 70 percent of their time surfing internet sites unrelated to their jobs. The company docked (withheld) their pay accordingly, without warning. Management sent them a memo notifying them that they were not fired but were on probation. You considered this wise, because when they work, both employees are very good at what they do, and talent is hard to find.

But now salesman Jarod Harkington has sent you a letter demanding reinstatement of his pay and claiming he was "spied on illegally." On the contrary, company lawyers have assured management that the courts almost always side with employers on this issue, particularly after employees receive a warning such as the one you wrote. The computer equipment belongs to Advertising Inflatables, and employees are paid a fair price for their time.

YOUR TASK Write a letter refusing Mr. Harkington's claim.[7] His address is 267 Hale Avenue, Peterborough, ON, K9J 7B1.

4. NOT THIS TIME: LETTER TO VANCITY CUSTOMER DENYING ATM DEBIT ADJUSTMENTS

You work in operations in the ATM Error Resolution Department at VanCity Credit Union. Your department often adjusts customer accounts for multiple ATM debit errors. Mistakes are usually honest ones—such as a merchant swiping a customer's debit card two or three times, thinking the first times didn't "take" when they actually did.

Whenever customers call the bank about problems on their statements, they're instructed to write a claim letter to your department describing the situation and to enclose copies of receipts. Customers are notified of the outcome within 10 to 20 business days.

You usually credit their account. But this time, your supervisor is suspicious about a letter you've received from Margaret Caldwell, who maintains several hefty joint accounts with her husband at VanCity.

Three debits to her chequing account were processed on the same day, credited to the same market, Wilson's Gourmet. The debits carry the same transaction reference number, 1440022-22839837109, which is what caught Mrs. Caldwell's attention. But you know that number changes daily, not hourly, so multiple purchases made on the same day often carry the same number. Also, the debits are for different amounts ($23.02, $110.95, and $47.50), so these transactions weren't a result of repeated card swipes. No receipts are enclosed.

Mrs. Caldwell writes that the store was trying to steal from her, but your supervisor doubts that and asks you to contact Wilson's Gourmet. Manager Simon Lau tells you that he's had no problems with his equipment and mentions that food shoppers commonly return at different times during the day to make additional purchases, particularly for beverages or to pick up merchandise they forgot the first time.

Your supervisor decides this was neither a bank error nor an error on the part of Wilson's Gourmet. It doesn't matter whether Mrs. Caldwell is merely confused or trying to commit an intentional fraud. Bank rules are clear for this situation: You must politely deny her request.

YOUR TASK Write to Margaret Caldwell, 2789 Cedar Parkway, Richmond, BC, V7R 2E5, explaining your refusal of her claim number 7899. Remember, you don't want to lose this wealthy customer's business.[8]

5. PRODUCT RECALL: LETTER FROM PERRIGO COMPANY TO RETAILERS ABOUT CHILDREN'S PAINKILLER

You work at Perrigo Company in customer service, where the atmosphere has been tense lately. Your company discovered that one batch of its cherry-flavoured children's painkiller contains too much acetaminophen, and it must immediately inform retailers and the public of this dangerous error. Full and prompt disclosure is especially crucial when consumer health is involved.

Perrigo manufactures more than 900 store-brand, over-the-counter (OTC) pharmaceuticals and nutritional products. Store brands are packaged under store names, such as Save-On or London Drugs. They're priced lower than brand-name products such as Tylenol, Motrin, and NyQuil, but they offer "comparable quality and effectiveness."

Your marketing department calculates that 6500 118-mL bottles of the "children's nonaspirin elixir" (a Tylenol look-alike) are already in the hands of consumers. That leaves 1288 bottles on store shelves. The lab says the acetaminophen contained in the painkilling liquid is up to 29 percent more than labels state, enough to cause an overdose in young children, which can cause liver failure. Fortunately, only lot number 1AD0228 is affected.

The painkiller is sold under the Save-On, London Drugs, and Good Sense labels at stores throughout Canada. Consumers must be told not to give the product to children. They must check the lot number, and if the bottle is from the affected batch, they must return it to the store they bought it from for a refund.

YOUR TASK Company news releases have already notified the media about the product recall, but for legal purposes, you've been asked to write a formal letter to retailers. Explain the recall, and instruct stores to remove the product from their shelves for return to your company. Perrigo will reimburse them for refunds to customers. Include a phone number they can call with questions and pass on to customers: 1-800-321-0105.[9]

EMAIL SKILLS | TEAM SKILLS 6. SAFE SELLING: EMAIL FROM THE SPORTS AUTHORITY HEADQUARTERS ABOUT DANGEROUS SCOOTERS

You are a merchandising assistant at the Pacific regional office of The Sports Authority and you recently noted that the Consumer Product Safety Commission (CPSC) in the United States has issued a consumer advisory on the dangers of motorized scooters. You're not surprised— these trends are common in Canada, too. You have even tried the scooters yourself and lived to regret forgetting to wear elbow pads.

The popular electric or gas-powered scooters, which feature two wheels similar to in-line skates, travel 14 km to 23 km per hour. As sales have grown, so have the reports of broken arms and legs, scraped faces, and bumped heads. The problem is that, unlike a motorcycle or bicycle, a scooter can be mastered by first-timers almost immediately. Both children and adults are hopping on and riding off—without helmets or other safety gear.

Over a six-month period, the CPSC says 2250 motorized scooter injuries and 3 deaths were reported by emergency rooms around the United States. The riders who were killed, ages 6, 11, and 46, might all have lived if they'd been wearing helmets. Some provinces and states have already enacted laws restricting scooter operations.

Your stores sell a wide selection of both the foot-powered ($25 to $150) and motorized scooters ($350 to $1000). The merchandising experts you work for are as concerned about the rise in injuries as they are about the CPSC advisory's potential negative effect on sales and liability. Many consumers in Canada pay attention to these advisories. You've been assigned to a team that will brainstorm ideas for improving the situation.

For example, one team member has suggested developing a safety brochure to give to customers; another wants to train salespeople to discuss safety issues with customers before they buy. "We'd like to see increased sales of reflective gear ($6 to $15), helmets ($24), and elbow and knee pads ($19)," a store executive tells your team, "not to improve on The Sports Authority's annual revenue, but to save lives."

YOUR TASK Working in a team of three, discuss how the Sports Authority can use positive actions, including those mentioned in the case, to react to the CPSC advisory. Choose the best ideas and decide how to use them in a bad-news email notifying the chain's 15 store managers in the Pacific region about the consumer advisory. Then write the email your team has outlined.[10]

7. THE CHEQUE'S IN THE MAIL—ALMOST: LETTER FROM SUN MICROSYSTEMS EXPLAINING LATE PAYMENTS

Like everyone else working for Sun Microsystems, you were amazed that the installation of the computer company's new management information system did not go smoothly. When the new computer program was installed, errors were made that caused information to be lost. This embarrassment wasn't discovered until Sun's suppliers started clamouring for payments they hadn't received.

Terence Lenaghan (the corporate controller and your boss) has to tell 300 vendors why Sun Microsystems has failed to pay its bills on time—and why it might be late with payments again.

"Until we get these errors corrected," Lenaghan confesses to you, "we're going to have to finish some of the accounting work by hand. That means that some of our payments to vendors will probably be late next month too. I need you to write to our suppliers and let them know that there's nothing wrong with the company's financial status. The last thing we want is for our vendors to think our business is going under."

YOUR TASK Write a form letter for your boss to send to Sun Microsystem's vendors explaining that problems with your new management information system are responsible for the delays in payment.[11]

EMAIL SKILLS 8. CELLPHONE VIOLATIONS: EMAIL MESSAGE TO ASSOCIATES AT WILKES ARTIS LAW FIRM

"Company policy states that personnel are not to conduct business using cellphones while driving," David Finch reminds you. He's a partner at the law firm of Wilkes Artis in Toronto, where you work as his administrative assistant.

You nod, waiting for him to explain. He already issued a memo about this rule last year, after that 15-year-old girl was hit and killed by a lawyer from another firm. Driving back from a client meeting, the lawyer was distracted while talking on her cellphone. The girl's family sued the firm and won $30 million, but that's not the point. The point is that cellphones can cause people to be hurt, even killed.

Finch explains, "Yesterday one of our associates called his secretary while driving his car. We can't allow this. Heck, one province, some of the states, and a few countries have banned the use of hand-held cellphones while driving. From now on, any violation of our cellphone policy will result in suspension without pay, unless the call is a genuine health or traffic emergency."

YOUR TASK Finch asks you to write an email message to all employees, announcing the new penalty for violating company policy.[12]

INSTANT MESSAGES 9. SNOW DAY CLOSURE: INSTANT MESSAGE ABOUT CAMPUS SHUT-DOWN DUE TO WEATHER

You work as an administrator in the security department at Simon Fraser University on top of Burnaby Mountain, just outside Vancouver. You got to work very early this morning because you knew the drive through the winter storm would be challenging and though you made it up the mountain, you saw city buses stuck at the side of the road and quite a few vehicles having difficulty making it up the steep hill. Sure enough, as soon as you arrive in the office, your manager, Jesse Sloan, received word from the university's president that classes are to be cancelled. The winter storm has dropped significant snow and now the weather forecast is calling for more snow and freezing

rain. These conditions would make the drive up the mountain treacherous—something you just experienced first-hand! The Security Department uses the 3N System (National Notification Network) in emergencies to deliver text messages, instant messages, and emails to all staff and students. These messages can get to students whether they are on campus, at home, or on the way to campus.

YOUR TASK Jesse asks you to draft a cancellation alert, staying within the 65-word limit of many instant-messaging programs. The president also authorized the use of the gym for a temporary shelter/sleeping facility if people who are already on campus do not want to head down the hill.[13]

INSTANT MESSAGES 10. QUICK ANSWER: INSTANT MESSAGE TURNING DOWN AN EMPLOYEE REQUEST

You are stuck in a meeting, and during one of your only breaks, you get an instant message from marketing rep Arash Param, containing his request to attend a conference on the use of blogging for business, which is being held in Montreal next month. You are quite interested in exploring the use of blogs, but Arash wants your answer within the hour. If he had asked a week ago and included more information, you could have said yes. But no, he has to leave it to the last minute and catch you in this meeting. He'll just have to take no for an answer.

For one thing, you'd need to get budget approval from your group's vice-president because the conference would involve out-of-province travel; to get a green light on travel to attend any conference longer than a day or farther than Calgary (a two-hour drive from your Edmonton office) you've got to get the VP to sign off on it. As well, the high cost of the air travel and hotel for four days would also need a justification, so that should have been part of the request. You'd need a written document explaining how business blogs relate to Arash's marketing position. Not that hard to do, but the fact is, he hasn't done it. Since he waited until one hour before the deadline, none of these issues can be addressed, so you can't possibly say yes! Which is a drag because Arash is a very nice guy and you wish you could send him to the conference. Worse yet, it will have to be an instant message reply that lets him know.

YOUR TASK Write a 60–75-word instant message to Arash Param declining his request. Decide whether the direct or indirect approach is appropriate.[14]

Should Employers Use Email to Deliver Negative Messages?

Most people are more comfortable delivering bad news via email than in person or on the phone. But is it appropriate to avoid the dreaded task of explaining lay-offs and spending cuts in person by using email to break such bad news? Some think it is.

Few executives advise using email in extremely personal situations such as firing an employee, but some think it's perfectly fine to use email for other uncomfortable scenarios such as job cuts, travel restrictions, hiring freezes, and other significant spending changes. Consider these examples:

- Amazon.com called an in-person meeting to announce job cuts, but telecommuters who couldn't attend the meeting were informed via email. "I want you to know that this was a very difficult decision for the company to make . . . we know this must be very painful to hear," the email read.
- Discovery Communications used email to alert Discover.com workers that staffing changes would take place before announcing layoffs of some of its dot-com full-time employees.
- Motorola sent email to employees in its semiconductor sector explaining layoffs and other cost-cutting steps. Workers being let go were told in person, but word of what was happening went out electronically.
- Ameritrade online brokerage notified more than 2000 call-centre workers of layoffs via email.

Employers who use email to deliver bad news claim that it's a quick and effective way to get information to all employees—especially those in remote locations or home offices. With face-to-face or even voice-to-voice communication, people have a tendency to tune out the worst and sugarcoat the bad news. But delivering bad news via email lets people be more honest. Email facilitates straight talk because senders don't see the discomfort of their recipients.

However, critics cry foul when companies break job-related bad news via email. As they see it, email is too impersonal. "The only advantage is that it gives management an opportunity to duck and dodge angry employees," says one communication expert. If you want to maintain good relationships with your employees, "these kinds of things should be done in person."

Applications for Success

For more advice about email and employer/employee communication, go into MyBusCommLab and use Research Navigator to look up the key words "bad news and email" and "email etiquette."

a. Do you think employers should deliver negative messages via email? Explain your answer.
b. Why does email facilitate straight talk?
c. If you are sending bad news in an email message, how can you use an indirect approach and still include an informative subject line? Won't the subject line give away your message before you have the chance to explain your reasons? Briefly explain in a one- to two-paragraph memo or email to your instructor.

Writing Persuasive Messages

LEARNING OBJECTIVES

After studying this chapter, you will be able to

1. Discuss the planning tasks that need extra attention when preparing persuasive messages
2. Distinguish between emotional and logical appeals, and discuss how to balance them
3. Describe the AIDA plan for persuasive messages
4. List six strategies for sending sales messages
5. Explain how to adapt the AIDA plan to sales messages
6. Compare sales messages with fundraising messages

As vice-president, marketing at CTV, Mary Kreuk persuades advertisers and agencies across the country. Mary sums up her department's approach as "meeting an advertiser's need and eliminating any potential roadblock—before it is raised. Relationship building is the key." In addition to persuading external clients, CTV's marketing group also persuades internal audiences, working with programming, sales, communications, promotions, research, and television producers. In internal communication, the marketing group provides the "reason why" and always relates that reason to a particular audience's interests. For instance, when selling an idea to a producer, the "reason why" may be potential revenue, but that persuasive message by itself might fail if the proposal does not also accommodate the producer's need to maintain editorial control. Kreuk knows that recognizing the interests of the audience is an essential part of persuasive communication.

In persuasive messages, Kreuk targets the needs of audience members—not to manipulate them but to use information, logic, and reason to help them make intelligent, informed decisions.[1] She also augments these individual messages with ongoing relationship building to better work with clients on a long-term basis and to develop a level of trust that helps smooth out the rough spots. Either way, success depends on being able to identify client needs and develop strategies to meet those needs.

Using the Three-Step Writing Process for Persuasive Messages

Model Document

Savvy business people often accomplish communication goals by using techniques of persuasion—the attempt to change an audience's attitudes, beliefs, or actions.[2] Effective persuasion is "the ability to present a message in a way that will lead others to support it," says Jay Conger, author of *Winning 'Em Over.* "It makes audiences feel they have a choice, and they choose to agree."[3] In today's competitive marketplace, successful business people must be able to put together a persuasive argument. Applying the three-step writing process to your persuasive messages will help you make them as effective as possible (see Figure 9.1 on page 180).

Persuasion is the attempt to change someone's attitudes, beliefs, or actions.

| FIGURE 9.1 | Applying the Three-Step Writing Process to Persuasive Messages |

Planning	**Writing**	**Completing**

Analyze
 • Identify an "action" purpose.
 • Gauge audience needs.
 • Adapt the persuasive argument to cultural differences.
 	
 Investigate
 • Ensure information is reliable and accurate.
 • Ensure facts support your argument.
 • Gather all relevant facts readers need.
 • Identify reader benefits.
 	
 Adapt
 • Verify effectiveness of written channel.
 • Establish your credibility.
	Organize
	 • Define your main idea, limit the scope, and group related points.
	 • Use the direct approach when:
	   ○ Readers prefer the "bottom line" first.
	   ○ Your firm encourages directness.
	   ○ Your message is long or complex.
	   ○ Your authority warrants doing so.
	 • Choose the indirect approach when emotions are high.
	
	 Compose
	 • Adapt the style and tone to readers.
	 • Choose positive words.
		Revise
		 • Judge your argument objectively.
		 • Carefully match the purpose and organization to audience needs.
		
		 Produce
		 • Ensure design emphasizes benefits.
		 • Ensure the delivery method fits your purpose and audience expectations.
		
		 Proofread
		 • Strengthen your persuasive message by correcting spelling and mechanical errors.
		 • Correct any alignment problems.
		 • Make sure the print quality is acceptable.

1	2	3

Step 1: Planning Persuasive Messages

For a persuasive message, some planning tasks require more effort.

Unlike routine positive messages (discussed in Chapter 7), persuasive messages aim to influence audiences who are inclined to resist. Therefore, persuasive messages are generally longer, are usually more detailed, and often depend heavily on careful planning. Persuasive messages require that you pay particular attention to analyzing your purpose, analyzing your audience, establishing your credibility, and striving for high ethical standards.

Persuasive requests encounter two problems:
• Audiences are busy.
• Audiences receive many competing requests.

ANALYZE YOUR PURPOSE When writing a persuasive message, your purpose is to persuade people to do something different or to try something new. But people are busy, so they're reluctant to act, especially if the action takes time and offers no guarantee of any reward in return. Moreover, people receive competing requests from everywhere. When writing persuasive requests, you must be absolutely sure that your purpose is clear, necessary, and appropriate for written media. Focus on the action you want from the reader.

The questions you ask before writing a persuasive message go beyond those you would ask for other types of messages.

ANALYZE YOUR AUDIENCE Chapter 3 discusses the basics of audience analysis, but the process can become much more involved for persuasive messages. Learning about your audience's needs or concerns can take weeks—even months. Everyone's needs differ, so everyone responds differently to any given message.

Using Questions to Gauge Audience Needs The best persuasive messages are closely connected to your audience's existing desires and interests.[4] Ask yourself these important questions:
• Who is my audience?
• What are their needs?

- What do I want them to do?
- How might they resist?
- Are there alternative positions I need to examine?
- What does the decision maker consider the most important issue?
- How might the organization's culture influence my strategy?

To assess various individual needs, you can refer to specific information. **Demographics** is information about the age, gender, occupation, income, education, and other quantifiable characteristics of your audience. **Psychographics** is information about the personality, attitudes, lifestyle, and other psychological characteristics of an individual. Both types of information are strongly influenced by culture.

Considering Cultural Differences Persuasion is different in different cultures. To satisfy the needs of audience members and gain their respect, you must understand and respect their cultural differences. For example, in France, using an aggressive, hard-sell technique would probably antagonize your audience. In Germany, where people tend to focus on technical matters, plan on verifying any figures you use for support, and make sure they are exact. In North America, audiences are usually concerned with more practical matters.[5] By researching and taking into account the cultural expectations and practices of the people in your audience, you will be able to use the appropriate appeal and organize your message in a way that seems familiar and comfortable to them.

> Cultural differences influence your persuasion attempts.

ESTABLISH YOUR CREDIBILITY To persuade a skeptical or hostile audience, you must convince people that you know what you're talking about and that you're not trying to mislead them. Your *credibility* is your capability of being believed because you're reliable and worthy of confidence. Without such credibility, your efforts to persuade will seem manipulative. Some of the best ways to gain credibility are to

> Your credibility is defined by how reliable, believable, and trustworthy you are.

- Support your message with facts. Testimonials, documents, guarantees, statistics, and research results all provide seemingly objective evidence for what you have to say, which adds to your credibility. The more specific and relevant your proof, the better.
- Name your sources. Telling your audience where your information comes from and who agrees with you always improves your credibility, especially if your sources are already respected by your audience.
- Establish your expertise. Your knowledge of the subject area builds credibility.
- Establish common ground. Those beliefs, attitudes, and background experiences that you have in common with members of your audience will help them identify with you.
- Be enthusiastic and positive. Your excitement about your subject can infect your audience.
- Be objective. Your ability to understand and acknowledge all sides of an issue helps you present fair and logical arguments in your persuasive message.
- Be sincere. Your concern, genuineness, good faith, and truthfulness help you focus on your audience's needs.

> You can do a lot to establish your credibility.

STRIVE FOR HIGH ETHICAL STANDARDS Some people view the word *persuasion* as negative. They associate persuasion with dishonest and unethical practices, such as coaxing, urging, and even tricking people into accepting an idea, buying a product, or taking an unwanted or unneeded action. However, successful business people make persuasion positive. They influence audience members by providing information and aiding understanding, which allows audiences the freedom to choose.[6]

> Positive persuasion leaves your audience free to choose.

To maintain the highest standards of business ethics, make every attempt to persuade without manipulating. Choose words that won't be misinterpreted, and be sure you don't distort the truth. Focus on the members of your audience by showing honest concern for their needs and interests. Ethical business people show audiences that the benefits of an idea, a group, a product, or an action will satisfy a need they truly have.

> To maintain the highest ethics, try to persuade without manipulating.

Step 2: Writing Persuasive Messages

When writing persuasive messages, you will define your main idea, limit the scope of your message, and group your points in a meaningful way. But you must focus even more effort on choosing the direct or indirect approach. Some persuasive messages use the indirect approach, explaining reasons and building interest before revealing their purpose. However, many situations call for the direct approach.

If audience members are objective, or if you know they prefer the "bottom line" first (perhaps because it saves them time), the direct approach might be the better choice. You'll also want to use the direct approach when your corporate culture encourages directness. In addition, when a message is long or complex, your readers may become impatient if the main idea is buried seven pages in, so you may want to choose the direct approach for these messages as well.

Sandi Sidhu is administrative assistant to the athletic director at UBC. Each year, after hockey season tickets have been mailed, the cost of the athletic department's toll-free phone number skyrockets as fans call with questions about their seats, complaints about receiving the wrong number of tickets, or orders for last-minute tickets. Sidhu came up with an idea that could solve the problem, so she composed an email message that uses the direct approach (see Figure 9.2). Sidhu supports her idea with benefits, not only for the athletic department but also for the fans who buy season tickets. Plus, her reasons are so logical that the message sounds both confident and convincing.

If you use the direct approach, keep in mind that even though your audience prefers the main point up front, you'll still want to include a justification or explanation, just as Sandi Sidhu did. Don't expect your reader to accept your idea on blind faith. For example, consider the following two openers:

Poor	**Improved**
I recommend building our new retail outlet on the West Main Street site.	After comparing the four possible sites for our new retail outlet, I recommend West Main Street as the only site that fulfils our criteria for visibility, proximity to mass transportation, and square footage.

Your choice between a direct and an indirect approach is also influenced by the extent of your authority, expertise, or power in an organization. As a first-line manager writing a persuasive message to top management, you may try to be diplomatic and use an indirect approach. However, your choice could backfire if some managers perceive your indirectness as manipulative and time wasting. On the other hand, you may try to save your supervisors time by using a direct approach, which might be perceived as brash and presumptuous. Similarly, when writing a persuasive message to employees, you may use the indirect approach to ease into a major change, but your audience might see your message as weak, even wishy-washy. You need to think carefully about your corporate culture and what your audience expects before selecting your approach.

Step 3: Completing Persuasive Messages

The length and complexity of persuasive messages make applying Step 3 even more crucial to your success. When you evaluate your content, try to judge your argument objectively and appraise your credibility. When revising for clarity and conciseness, carefully match the purpose and organization to audience needs.

Use design elements to complement (not detract from) your argument. For example, use headings and lists to highlight benefits as Sandi does in Figure 9.2. Finally, meticulous proofreading will identify any mechanical or spelling errors that would detract from the credibility of your persuasive message.

Use the indirect approach when your audience will react unfavourably to your message. Use the direct approach when your message is long or complex, or when your reader prefers directness.

Choice of approach is also influenced by your position (or authority within the organization) relative to your audience's.

As with other business messages, Step 3 of the writing process helps guarantee the success of your persuasive messages.

FIGURE 9.2	Email Message Selling an Idea to a Boss

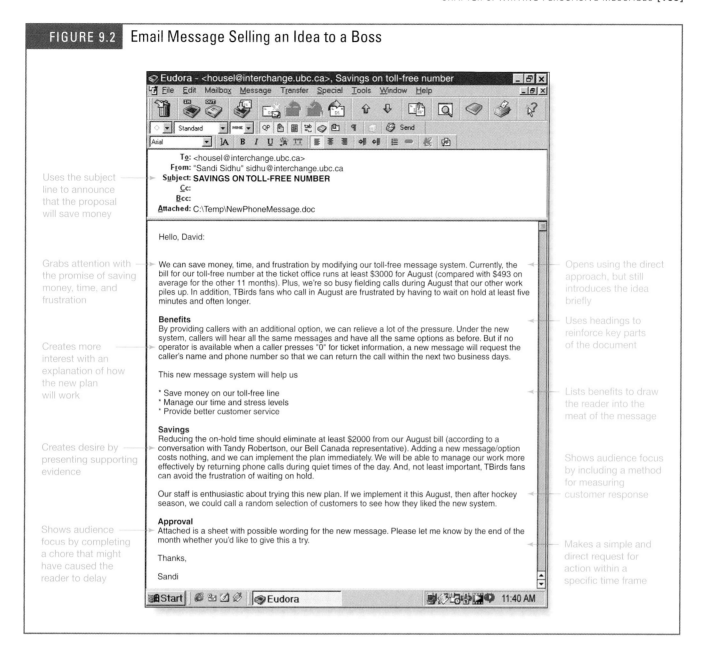

Uses the subject line to announce that the proposal will save money

Grabs attention with the promise of saving money, time, and frustration

Creates more interest with an explanation of how the new plan will work

Creates desire by presenting supporting evidence

Shows audience focus by completing a chore that might have caused the reader to delay

Opens using the direct approach, but still introduces the idea briefly

Uses headings to reinforce key parts of the document

Lists benefits to draw the reader into the meat of the message

Shows audience focus by including a method for measuring customer response

Makes a simple and direct request for action within a specific time frame

Text inside the email message figure:

To: <housel@interchange.ubc.ca>
From: "Sandi Sidhu" sidhu@interchange.ubc.ca
Subject: SAVINGS ON TOLL-FREE NUMBER
Cc:
Bcc:
Attached: C:\Temp\NewPhoneMessage.doc

Hello, David:

We can save money, time, and frustration by modifying our toll-free message system. Currently, the bill for our toll-free number at the ticket office runs at least $3000 for August (compared with $493 on average for the other 11 months). Plus, we're so busy fielding calls during August that our other work piles up. In addition, TBirds fans who call in August are frustrated by having to wait on hold at least five minutes and often longer.

Benefits
By providing callers with an additional option, we can relieve a lot of the pressure. Under the new system, callers will hear all the same messages and have all the same options as before. But if no operator is available when a caller presses "0" for ticket information, a new message will request the caller's name and phone number so that we can return the call within the next two business days.

This new message system will help us

* Save money on our toll-free line
* Manage our time and stress levels
* Provide better customer service

Savings
Reducing the on-hold time should eliminate at least $2000 from our August bill (according to a conversation with Tandy Robertson, our Bell Canada representative). Adding a new message/option costs nothing, and we can implement the plan immediately. We will be able to manage our work more effectively by returning phone calls during quiet times of the day. And, not least important, TBirds fans can avoid the frustration of waiting on hold.

Our staff is enthusiastic about trying this new plan. If we implement it this August, then after hockey season, we could call a random selection of customers to see how they liked the new system.

Approval
Attached is a sheet with possible wording for the new message. Please let me know by the end of the month whether you'd like to give this a try.

Thanks,

Sandi

Strategies for Persuasive Messages

Whether you use a direct or an indirect approach, you must convince your reader that your request or idea is reasonable by identifying benefits that appeal to reader needs. Strike a balance between emotional and logical appeals, and master the AIDA (Attention, Interest, Desire, Action) organizational approach.

Balancing Emotional and Logical Appeals

One way to persuade people is to appeal to their hearts and minds. Most persuasive messages include both emotional and logical appeals. However, finding the right balance between these two types of appeals depends on four factors: (1) the actions you wish to motivate, (2) your reader's expectations, (3) the degree of resistance you must overcome, and (4) how far you feel empowered to go in selling your point of view.[7]

When you're persuading someone to accept a complex idea, take a serious step, or make a large and important decision, lean toward logic and make your emotional appeal subtle. However, when you're persuading someone to purchase a product, join a cause, or make a donation, rely a bit more on emotion.

> Both emotional and logical appeals are needed to write successful persuasive messages.

Emotional appeals are best if subtle.

EMOTIONAL APPEALS An **emotional appeal** is based on audience feelings or sympathies; however, such an appeal must be subtle.[8] For instance, you can make use of the emotion surrounding certain words. The word *freedom* evokes strong feelings, as do words such as *success, prestige, credit record, savings, free, value,* and *comfort.* Such words put your audience in a certain frame of mind and help them accept your message. However, emotional appeals aren't necessarily effective by themselves. Emotion works with logic in a unique way: People need to find rational support for an attitude they've already embraced emotionally.

Logical appeals can use
- Analogy
- Induction
- Deduction

LOGICAL APPEALS A **logical appeal** calls on human reason. In any argument you might use to persuade an audience, you make a claim and then support your claim with reasons or evidence. When appealing to your audience's logic, you might use three types of reasoning:
- **Analogy.** With analogy, you compare your idea to something familiar to your audience. For instance, to persuade employees to attend a planning session, you might use a town meeting analogy, comparing your company to a small community and your employees to valued members of that community.
- **Induction.** With induction, you reason from specific evidence to a general conclusion. To convince potential customers that your product is best, you might report the results of test marketing in which individuals preferred your product over others. After all, if some individuals prefer it, so will others.
- **Deduction.** With deduction, you might reason from a generalization to a specific conclusion. To persuade your boss to hire additional employees, you might point to industry-wide projections and explain that industry activity (and thus your company's business) will be increasing rapidly over the next three months, so you'll need more employees to handle increased business.

 **Model** Document

Organize persuasive messages using the AIDA plan:
- Attention
- Interest
- Desire
- Action

Using AIDA for Indirect Plans

Most persuasive messages follow an organizational plan that goes beyond the indirect approach used for negative messages. The opening does more than serve as a buffer; it grabs your audience's attention. The explanation section is expanded to two sections. The first incites your audience's interest, and the second changes your audience's attitude. Finally, your close ends on a positive note with a statement of what action is needed and emphasizes reader benefits, motivating readers to take specific action. More intense than the indirect approach of bad-news messages, this persuasive approach is called the **AIDA plan**. In his letter in Figure 9.3, Randy Thumwolt uses the AIDA plan in a persuasive memo about his program to reduce Fairmont West's annual plastics costs while curtailing consumer complaints about the company's recycling record. In persuasive messages, use the AIDA plan to intensify audience reactions in each of four phases:
- **Attention.** Make your audience want to hear about your problem or idea. Write a brief and engaging opening sentence, with no extravagant claims or irrelevant points. And find some common ground on which to build your case. Thumwolt's letter gains attention by explaining the specifics of the problem he's trying to solve (see Figure 9.3).
- **Interest.** Explain the relevance of your message to your audience. Continuing the theme you started with, paint a more detailed picture with words. Get your audience thinking. Thumwolt's interest section introduces an additional, unforeseen problem with plastic product containers (see Figure 9.3). Moreover, Thumwolt emphasizes his suggestions with an easy-to-read list.
- **Desire.** Make readers want to change by explaining how the change will benefit them. Reduce resistance by predicting and answering in advance any questions readers might have. Think of why the reader will *not* want to accept your idea—then plan how to counter this resistance. What are the reader's interests? How can you satisfy these interests?

FIGURE 9.3 Persuasive Memo Using the AIDA Plan

FAIRMONT WEST SERVICES

INTERNAL MEMORANDUM

TO: Eleanor Tran, Comptroller
FROM: Randy Thumwolt, Purchasing Director
DATE: May 7, 2009
SUBJECT: COST CUTTING IN PLASTICS

In spite of our recent switch to purchasing plastic product containers in bulk, our costs for these containers are exorbitant. In my January 5 memo, I included all the figures showing that

- We purchase five tonnes of plastic product containers each year
- The price of the polyethylene terephthalate (PET) tends to rise and fall as petroleum costs fluctuate

The High Cost of Plastic
In January you approved that we purchase plastic containers in bulk during winter months, when petroleum prices tend to be lower. As a result, we should realize a 10 percent saving this year. However, our costs are still out of line, around $2 million a year.

A Recycling Plan
In addition to the cost in dollars of these plastic containers is the cost in image. We have recently been receiving an increasing number of consumer letters complaining about our lack of a recycling program for PET plastic containers, both on the airplanes and in the airport restaurants.

After conducting some preliminary research, I have come up with the following ideas:

- Provide recycling containers at all Fairmont West airport restaurants
- Offer financial incentives for the airlines to collect and separate PET containers
- Set up a specially designated dumpster at each airport for recycling plastics
- Contract with A-Batt Waste Management for collection

Savings
I've attached a detailed report of the costs involved. As you can see, our net savings the first year should run about $500 000. I've spoken to Ted Macy in marketing. If we adopt the recycling plan, he wants to build a PR campaign around it.

Action
The PET recycling plan will help build our public image while improving our bottom line. If you agree, let's meet with Ted next week to get things started.

Grabs attention by clearly stating an ongoing problem and briefly providing background information that includes specific numbers

Reminds reader of important facts that have already been established by breaking them out into a list

Builds interest by introducing an additional problem with the plastic product containers

Makes suggestions in an easy-to-read list, providing detailed support in an attachment

Creates desire by providing another reader benefit

Urges action within a specific time frame

Pointers for Writing Persuasive Messages

- Balance emotional and logical appeals to help the audience accept your message.
- Open with a reader benefit, a stimulating question, a problem, or an unexpected statement.
- Discuss something your readers can agree with, and show you understand their concerns.
- Elaborate on the main benefit, and explain the relevance of your message to your audience.
- Make audience members want to act by explaining how the action will benefit them.
- Predict reader resistance and provide reasons that overcome it.
- Back up your claims with relevant evidence.
- Confidently ask for the audience's cooperation, and stress the positive results of the action.
- Include the due date (if any) for a response, and tie it in with audience benefits.
- Include one last reminder of the audience benefit, and make the desired action easy.

Explain how you would implement complex ideas. Back up your claims to increase reader willingness to take the suggested action. Ensure that all evidence is relevant to your audience. Thumwolt emphasizes a monetary benefit and a possible public relations benefit. Most managers want to save time and money.

run high—you calculate the cost per vehicle at today's gas prices based on each vehicle getting 20 km per litre. You think a hybrid fleet would make much more sense. For one thing, the Toyota Prius gets 44 km to the litre, which would bring a big savings in fuel costs. The cost of the gas is one issue, but you also have some other concerns because your boss isn't really very eco-sensitive. In fact, your boss drives a "honking big SUV" around town and doesn't even use it for skiing or off-road activities.

You saw a program on CBC about the "green economy" and did a little research via some links on the CBC website to find CleanTech (**www.cleantech.com**) and Sustainable Development Technology Canada (**www.sdtc.ca**). You believe it makes business sense for companies to reduce greenhouse gas. You could not only accomplish this goal but also realize further economies by converting the fleet to a hybrid option. The B.C. government, like California, created a carbon tax, so over the next few years it will become even more costly to run gasoline-based engines in the province. As a result of the tax, the price of gas will go up at least 10 cents per litre within a couple of years. You also read that Sustainable Development Technology Canada has funding available for technology innovations that deliver clean water, clean soil, clean air, and reduced greenhouse emissions. You know other companies are making money by going green—even leading multinationals such as Johnson & Johnson were able to grow business by 300 percent over an eight-year period while reducing greenhouse gas by 7 percent, so you know making this change can be profitable.

YOUR TASK In MyBusCommLab, use Research Navigator to research the benefits of reducing greenhouse gas emissions for a business. You want your boss to authorize you to do a feasibility study on the possible savings of switching the company fleet to hybrid technology. As well, you could put together an application for a contribution to the change by the federal government if your boss gives you the okay to look into it. Write a persuasive email to your boss to get approval of your idea. Who knows? Maybe your idea will result in not just saving your company money but making the air cleaner for a lot of people.[23]

13. INSTANT PROMOTION: TEXT MESSAGE FROM HILTON HOTELS TO FREQUENT GUESTS

Hilton Hotels now uses an SMS (short messaging service) to send instant text message promotions to customers who've signed up as President's Club members. You work in the Toronto office in marketing, and that means you're often struggling to condense descriptions of elaborate travel packages into 65 enticing words (the system's maximum).

For example, today's promotion offers "A Golfer's Dream Come True: 'I just played a round of golf by the pyramids!'" For $575 per person per day (double room), valid through January 15, 2010, travellers can stay in the Hilton Pyramids Golf Resort near Cairo, Egypt, for seven nights/eight days, including breakfast, service charge, and tax. They'll be met at the airport, given transportation to the resort, plus two rounds of golf per person at the Dreamland Golf Course and two rounds of golf per person at the Pyramids Golf & Country Club in Soleimania Golf City, near Cairo. That's 93 words already!

But you also need to convey that the Dreamland course wraps like a serpent around the Hilton resort. Its lush greens and lakes, designed by Karl Litten, contrast sharply with the golden desert, culminating in a stunning view of the Great Pyramid of Giza, one of the seven wonders of the ancient world. The Dreamland course features the "biggest floodlit driving course in Egypt." The travel package provides transportation to this nearby course.

Rates, of course, are subject to availability and other restrictions may apply. But interested travellers should mention the code—Golf & Pyramid Golf Special—when they call Hilton Reservations Worldwide. They can also email rm_pyramids_golf@hilton.com or call the Cairo hotel directly at 20-1-8402402. That is, if you can entice them in 65 words.

YOUR TASK Write the persuasive instant message.[24]

∎EMAIL SKILLS 14. BUILDING RELATIONSHIPS USING SOCIAL TECHNOLOGIES AT PURDY'S CHOCOLATES

You work in the marketing department of Purdy's Chocolates, a family-owned business with 900 employees worldwide. Your company's website is well designed and offers news and updates to customers via a "My Purdy's" feature. However, the marketing manager thinks the company could benefit from building more of an online community and has asked you whether a blog would be a good idea. The main objective the marketing department would like to accomplish is getting more online customer engagement and feedback.

You think a blog might be useful—it would be helpful for the marketing department staff to read the comments posted by customers. Listening to customer conversation about the product could lead to more ideas for product development, and if the customers know the company is listening, it may lead to increased brand loyalty as well. You think having the CEO write a blog could be one strategy to engage people online. You also think it would be appealing because she is an inspiring business woman—her company is the largest woman-run business in B.C. By sharing some of her experiences in a blog, she could increase trust with customers and even employees. These were your initial thoughts, but you'd like to find some facts that support your idea about the business benefits of blogging. You are not sure if the best strategy is to have the CEO blog or someone else in the company. You plan to research best practices in blogging to find out. You also think that engaging customers with some kind of online opportunity for rating the products might be a good idea.

YOUR TASK Visit MyBusCommLab and use Research Navigator to learn the advantages and disadvantages of blog communication; then decide whether a blog would be a good choice for Purdy's.

Write an email to your boss, the marketing department manager, recommending whether or not a CEO blog or another online strategy would be a good choice to help achieve the marketing department's goals.

EMAIL SKILLS 15. BUILDING RELATIONSHIPS WITH EMPLOYEES THROUGH VODCASTING

You work in the human resources department of an accounting firm that has expanded from 80 employees to over 200 within the last three years. Your offices used to be all on one floor and the atmosphere was friendly and familial. However, two years ago the firm had to expand its office space and moved onto three floors. In the past, conversations around the water cooler used to keep people in touch. Now, the atmosphere has changed and most employees only know a few of their colleagues. Many of the new employees are in the age range of 23 to 30.

Your boss, the human resources department manager, recognizes there is a morale problem. You think the morale could be improved by creating a way for people to share positive company experiences. You read that Ernst & Young, an international consulting firm, created an employee contest using video. Each department in a branch of the company was given a video camera and the task of making a short video about what is good about working at Ernst & Young. Creative and entertaining videos were produced and shared on the company's website. Later some of these videos were used for recruitment, and Ernst & Young still uses employee testimonial videos on its Facebook site.[25]

Maybe a video contest for your company's departments would be a good way to get people interacting and would raise morale. You decide to persuade your boss to take this idea to the senior management team, and even though she is not that oriented toward technology, she is open to your ideas. You estimate the cost to be $4000 for cameras for ten departments plus a budget for catering for the grand finale show, and some prizes. You'd hold the finale after work as a social event. Bringing everyone together to see the finished videos would be part of the morale builder. Later, the videos would be posted on the company website.

YOUR TASK Write an email to your boss persuading her to propose a departmental video contest to senior management.

16. HELPING CHILDREN: INSTANT MESSAGE HOLIDAY FUND DRIVE AT WESTJET

At WestJet, you are one of the coordinators for the annual Employee Charitable Contributions Campaign. All year, WestJet supports a number of health and human service agencies. These groups include the CNIB, Missing Children, Hope Air, The Ontario Hospital for Sick Children, and many other deserving causes. WestJet engages employees in corporate citizenship.

During the winter holidays, WestJet also donates to agencies that cater to the needs of disadvantaged families, women, and children. The prospect of helping children enjoy the holidays, children who otherwise might have nothing, usually awakens the spirit of most employees. But some of them wait until the last minute and then forget.

They have until Friday, December 18, to come forth with cash contributions. To make it in time for holiday deliveries, they can also bring in toys, food, and blankets through Tuesday, December 22. They shouldn't have any trouble finding the collection bins; they're everywhere in the corporate office and in all airport staff lounges, and they are marked with big, bright, red banners. But some will want to call you with questions or to make (you hope) credit card donations: 1-800-532-6754, ext. 3342.

YOUR TASK It is December 14. Write a 75–100 word instant message encouraging last-minute gifts.[26]

Ethics

What You May Legally Say in a Sales Letter

As you prepare to write your sales letter, think carefully about your choice of words. False or misleading statements could land you in court, so make sure your language complies with legal and ethical standards. To keep your sales letters within the limits of the law, review the legal considerations of these typical sales phrases:

- **"Our product is the best on the market**." This statement is acceptable for a sales letter because the law permits you to express an opinion about your product. In the process of merchandising a product, statements of opinion are known as "puffery," which is perfectly legal as long as you make no deceptive or fraudulent claims.

- **"Our product will serve you well for many years to come."** This statement from a sales brochure triggered a lawsuit by a disgruntled customer who claimed the manufacturer's product lasted only a few years. The courts ruled that the statement was an acceptable form of puffery because the manufacturer did not promise that the product would last for a specific number of years.

- **"We're so confident you'll enjoy our products that we've enclosed a sample of our most popular line. This sample can be yours for only $5! Please send your payment in the enclosed, prepaid envelope."** If you include a product sample with your sales letter, your readers may keep the merchandise without paying for it. Under the law, consumers may consider unordered goods as gifts. They are not obligated to return the items to you or submit payments for unsolicited merchandise.

- **"Thousands of high school students—just like you—are already enjoying this fantastic CD collection! Order before March 1 and save!"** If your sales letter appeals to minors, you are legally obligated to honour their contracts. At the same time, however, the law permits minors to cancel their contracts and return the merchandise to you. Sellers are legally obligated to accept contracts voided by minors and any goods returned by them. Legal adult status is defined differently from province to province, ranging from age 18 to age 21.

- **"You'll find hundreds of bargains at our annual 'scratch and dent' sale! All sales are final on merchandise marked 'as is.'"** When you use the term as is in your sales letter, you are not misleading customers about the quality of your products. By warning consumers that the condition of sale items is less than perfect, you are not legally obligated to issue refunds to customers who complain about defects later on.

Applications for Success

1. You probably receive sales letters through the mail or via email all the time. Review two of these sales letters for content. List the "puffery" statements in each letter.

2. Note any statements in these sales letters that appear questionable to you. Rewrite one of the statements, carefully choosing words that won't be misleading to consumers.

3. What do you think? Are these sales letters convincing? How have they persuaded you? If you don't believe they are convincing, explain how they have failed to persuade you.

Understanding and Planning Business Reports and Proposals

> **TIPS FOR SUCCESS**
>
> "Written reports are essential for evaluating business opportunities. Without the facts, boards can't act."
> —Gerry Roy
> Chief Corporate Officer and Legal Counsel
> Inualiut Regional Corporation

The Inualiut Regional Corporation (IRC) was established in 1984 to manage the affairs of the first aboriginal Canadians from the Northwest Territories to negotiate a comprehensive land claim settlement with the Government of Canada. Today, IRC's principal business subsidiaries and interests include the land, the investment or "heritage fund," and diverse industries such as environmental services, property management, hospitality, construction, transportation, manufacturing, and oil and gas. Reports are designed to speak to many audiences; Gerry Roy writes reports that facilitate decision making among the boards of directors in this unique business setting. "Conveying an understanding of what we do and where we do it with such a diverse audience," says Roy, "requires careful message planning." Decision makers depend on well-planned reports to summarize carefully researched data, define problems, discuss pertinent issues, and analyze information.

Working with Business Reports and Proposals

Like Gerry Roy, most managers make decisions and solve problems based on the information and analyses they receive in reports, written factual accounts that objectively communicate information about some aspect of business. Reports come in all shapes and sizes, from fleeting images on a computer screen and preprinted forms to memos, letters, and formal three-volume bound manuscripts. Regardless of length or formality, most reports are used for one of six general purposes:
1. To oversee and manage company operations
2. To carry out company rules and ways of doing things
3. To obey government and legal requirements
4. To inform others of what's been done on a project
5. To guide decisions on particular issues
6. To get products, plans, or projects accepted by others

> Business reports help companies make decisions and solve business problems.

> Reports may be classified in several ways:
> - Informal or formal
> - Routine or special
> - Internal or external
> - Short or long
> - Informational or analytical

Informational Reports

Informational reports present data and facts without analyses or recommendations. Common types of informational reports include monitor/control reports, policy/procedure reports, compliance reports, and progress reports.

The purpose of informational reports is to explain.

 **Model** Document

REPORTS FOR MONITORING AND CONTROLLING OPERATIONS Managers rely on reports to learn what's happening to the operations under their control. Monitor/control reports focus on data, so they require special attention to accuracy, thoroughness, and honesty. These reports uncover problems to get them out in the open before it is too late, so they avoid covering up bad news and emphasizing only accomplishments.

Some monitor/control reports, such as strategic plans and annual budgets, establish guidelines for future action. Others, such as monthly sales reports, corporate annual reports, and scouting reports, provide detailed information about operations (see Figure 10.1) and

Monitor/control reports expose any problems that exist.

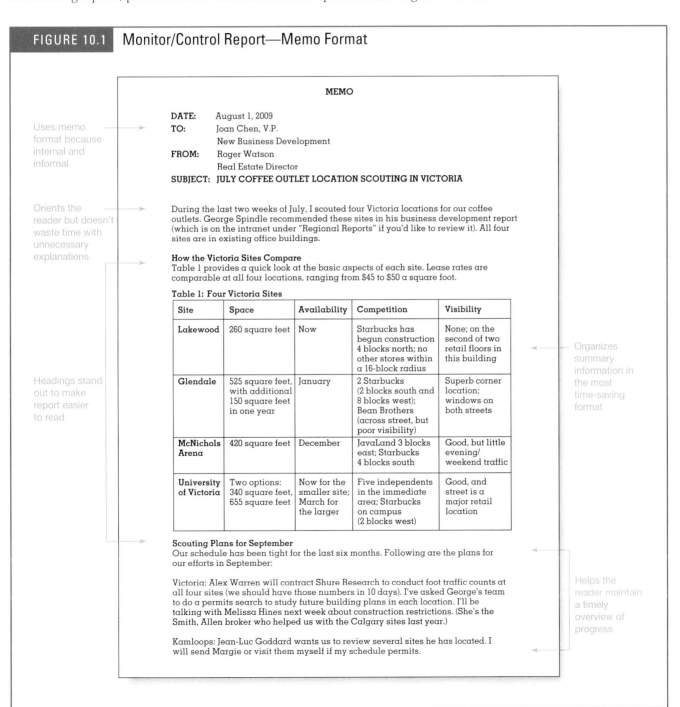

FIGURE 10.1   Monitor/Control Report—Memo Format

some reports document incidents or problems in operations so that the company has a record and can analyze problems and trends. Finally, some monitor/control reports describe what occurred during some personal activity, such as a conference, convention, or trip.

 Document Makeovers

REPORTS FOR IMPLEMENTING POLICIES AND PROCEDURES Managers provide policy and procedure reports to be read by anyone who wants a question answered. These reports present information in a straightforward manner. The rules of an organization make up lasting guidelines (such as the process for standardizing quality-control procedures or directions for how to reserve the conference room for special meetings). Less permanent issues are treated as they arise in nonrecurring reports (such as a position paper on the need for extra security precautions after a rash of burglaries in the area). Sue North's report in Figure 10.2 answers a question from her company's board of directors. The report is internal, so it is attached to an email sent to the person who asked Sue to write it. The email transmits the report and provides the key recommendation. The semiformal attachment format allows the report to be circulated to a number of different readers without having the email heading at the top of the document.

> Policy/procedure reports help managers communicate the company's standards.

FIGURE 10.2   Sample Policy Report in Semiformal Format

HIGHLAND TENNIS CLUB EMAIL

TO: Cal Smith, General Manager <csmith@highland.ca>
FROM: Sue North, Accounting Supervisor <snorth@highland.ca>
DATE: November 19, 2008 9:52 AM
SUBJECT: Effect of New Recommendations from the CICA on our Pension Accounting Policy

Here is the analysis you requested regarding whether accounting practice changes are needed as a result of the newly released recommendations from the Canadian Institute of Chartered Accountants. We will have to adjust our pension accounting methods but may wait until next fiscal year.

EFFECT OF NEW RECOMMENDATIONS FROM THE CANADIAN INSTITUTE OF CHARTERED ACCOUNTANTS

Submitted by the Accounting Department
November 19, 2009

Summary
The Board of Directors asked the Accounting Department to comment on how the Canadian Institute of Chartered Accountants' (CICA's) new recommendations on current accounting practices and new reporting requirements for employee pension plans will affect the Club. We secured a copy of the September 2008 CICA recommendations, studied the new requirements, and have summarized the details in this report.

A few procedural changes in how we report our pension plan savings will be required to comply. Overall, we suggest that we adopt the CICA recommendations but wait to implement the changes until our next actuarial report time.

New CICA Pension Recommendations
The new CICA Pension recommendations present a complex technical restructuring of how pension costs and obligations are accounted and reported. The main purposes behind these changes are to
- avoid management manipulating the company's profit and thereby losing results by over- or underfunding the pension plan.
- provide more accurate, comparative income statements within the company (from year to year), and outside the company (from one firm to another).

(Continued)

FIGURE 10.2	(Continued)

2

Impact on Highland Tennis Club
Public companies must comply with these recommendations by the fiscal year
beginning December 1, 2009. For a private organization such as ours, the
changes in accounting method would not be mandatory until the fiscal year
beginning December 1, 2010. The detailed changes are included in Attachment 1.

Cost of Implementation
To commission a new actuarial valuation to implement the recommendations will
cost the Club approximately $4500. Since we paid for an updated valuation earlier
this year, the next report is not due until January 2009. For a private organization,
the changes in accounting method are minor and do not justify the cost of
implementing the new practices immediately.

Timing
Although earlier adoption of the recommendations has been suggested, the
immediate changes in accounting method would not be significant enough to
warrant the extra expense. The best time for us to implement the new
recommendations would be the new fiscal year commencing 2010. This means that
a valuation would take place in January 2009. Since we would require a valuation
at that time under our old system, we could implement the changes at no extra cost.

Our Interim Position
We have up to three years to implement the new CICA ruling. I have reviewed an
interim position with respect to the Club's pension investments and valuation
method. We also checked with Sterling Investments, our pension consulting firm.
They have verified a conservative approach was taken in preparing our last
actuarial report. Our pension fund is currently vested with Mutual Life Assurance
and has generated an average 9 percent return during the last three years.
Therefore, the risk of being underfunded is minimal.

Conclusion and Recommendation
In conclusion, while the new rules do require us to change some procedures, there
is no compelling reason to implement the CICA recommendations immediately.

We recommend deferring implementation of the new rules until the fiscal year
beginning 2010.

Attachment 1: Pension Accounting Changes Required by CICA September 2008 Recommendations

You'll notice Sue's report is written in the first-person plural to represent her department, and that the tone is semi-formal to suit the nature of the subject matter. The opening segment provides an introduction as well as a summary of the main outcome. The headings make it easy to navigate the report's contents and read selected parts.

REPORTS FOR COMPLYING WITH GOVERNMENT REGULATIONS All compliance reports are written in response to regulations of one sort or another, most of them imposed by government agencies. The regulatory agency issues instructions on how to write the necessary reports. The important thing in such reports is to be honest, thorough, and accurate. Annual compliance reports include income tax returns and annual shareholder reports. Interim compliance reports include reports from licensed institutions such as nursing homes and child-care facilities.

REPORTS FOR DOCUMENTING PROGRESS Whether you're writing a progress report for a client or for your boss, you need to anticipate your reader's needs and provide the required information clearly and tactfully. Interim progress reports give an idea of the work that has been accomplished to date (see Figure 10.3 on page 212). In many cases these interim reports are followed by a final report at the conclusion of the contract or project. Final reports are generally more elaborate than interim reports and serve as a permanent record of what was accomplished. They focus on final results rather than on progress along the way.

> Compliance reports document and explain what a company is doing to conform to government regulations.

 **Model** Document

> Reports documenting progress on a client's contract or an internal project provide all the information readers need.

| FIGURE 10.3 | Progress Report—Letter Format |

Uses letter format, common for many external interim progress reports (final reports would usually be longer and would often be in manuscript form)

Emphasizes what has been accomplished during the reporting period (if it were a final report, it would focus on results rather than on progress)

Eases reader's understanding by making headings correspond to the tasks performed

Johnson Landscaping

820 Grandview Avenue, Saint John, NB E2L 3V9 · (506) 658-8636 johnsonlandscaping@sympatico.ca

May 31, 2009

Mr. Steve Gamvrellis, Facilities Manager
The Fairwinds Hotel
240 Kings Street
Saint John, NB E4P 2Y1

Dear Mr. Gamvrellis:

PROGRESS ON MAY LANDSCAPING

This report will bring you up to date on the landscaping done for The Fairwinds by Johnson Landscaping during the month of May 2009. Currently we are on schedule and on budget. We resolved the flooding near the receiving dock and in the next week will investigate the high soil acidity in the perennial borders.

Initial ground preparation and sprinkler system installation is complete. A total of 25 000 square feet of lawn and flower beds were tilled, raked, and levelled. Installation of the sprinkler system for 15 000 square feet of lawn and beds was completed on May 20.

WORK COMPLETED
From May 21 to May 30, shrubs and ornamental perennials were planted in 7000 square feet of beds. Beds were prepared for 3000 square feet of annuals.

PROBLEM AREAS
Lighting Options
As promised, we completed inquiries to six local lighting vendors and have found three options that meet your criteria for lighting the entrance and new arbour areas of the grounds. The estimated costs and a selection of recommended fixtures will be included in our report next month. These figures will help your committee to select the lighting before the annual budget submission in September.

Flooding
We've resolved the flooding problem discovered last month near the south end of the shipping and receiving dock. It appears that an old plumbing repair had begun to come apart under the employee cafeteria, causing water to flow under the building and occasionally flood a small portion of the new lawn area.

Perennial Beds
Unfortunately, we have uncovered a potential problem in several of the perennial borders we've created along the east side of the main building. A series of soil samples indicates an extremely high level of acidity, much higher than would occur under natural conditions. We suspect that the problem may have been caused by a small chemical spill at some point in the past. We'll try to resolve the problem next month, and I'll contact you if the solution to this problem is likely to affect your budget planning.

FUTURE WORK

1. Distribute bark mulch and plant remaining annuals.
2. Resolve the soil quality issue in the perennial bed and make soil amendments as needed.
3. Monitor and adjust the automated sprinkling system to ensure adequate watering.

Please let me know if I can answer questions about this month's work or other landscaping work. You can reach me at 778-888-9226. We appreciate your business.

Sincerely,

Shanley Johnson
Owner

Doesn't hesitate to bring up problems that need to be solved, but offers a possible solution for further investigation

Outlines plans for the coming period

Analytical Reports

To make informed decisions, managers rely on the supporting information, analyses, and recommendations presented in analytical reports. Typically, an analytical report presents a decision (or solution to a problem), often with recommendations for a number of actions. The body of the report presents all the facts (both good and bad) and persuades readers to accept the decision, solution, or recommendations that are detailed throughout the report. To persuade the reader, the writer carefully analyzes the facts and presents a compelling argument. Two of the more common examples of analytical reports are problem-solving reports and proposals.

> The purpose of analytical reports is to convince the audience that the conclusions and recommendations developed in the text are valid.

FIGURE 10.4 **Problem-Solving Report in Semiformal Format**

EMAIL FROM THE BUSINESS DEVELOPMENT DEPARTMENT

TO: Board of Directors Executive Committee
FROM: Jane Hurst <jhurst@bell.net>
SENT: Tuesday, September 10, 2009 7:04 PM
SUBJECT: Report on Establishing an Internet Retailing Site

In response to your request, we have investigated the potential for establishing an online retailing site.

The attached report gives you our findings and recommends going ahead with an online site as soon as possible.

ESTABLISHING AN INTERNET RETAILING SITE

Introduction tells who did what, when, why

On June 15, 2009, the board of directors requested the business development department to assess whether our company should add a retailing section to our website. Our staff analyzed the behaviour of our customers and major competitors and studied the overall development of electronic retailing.

Together the introduction and recommendations make a summary of the key parts of this report: "Who did what and what resulted?"

Recommendations are in an accessible list near beginning, for emphasis

Recommendations
We recommend
  1. Adding retail purchasing capabilities to our website as soon as possible.
  2. Hiring a firm that specializes in online retailing to expand our website.
  3. Integrating online retailing with our store-based and mail-order operations.

Logical and clear reasons are given to support the recommendations

Adding to the Website
First, does a retail branch of our website make financial sense? Studies suggest that our competitors are generating significant revenue from online retailing. Mosini's is the leader so far, with sales approaching $1.5 million—up from a loss only two years ago. Moreover, at least half of our competitor's online sales are from new customers from out of the area who would not have purchased in-store.

Headings identify key pass of the report

Cost
The cost of setting up a retailing function on our website is around $150 000, using an expert team and aiming for state-of-the-art features.

Potential Market
While the online market is too fluid and unpredictable to give an exact, quantitative answer to the question of how profitable an online site would be, a qualitative view of strategy indicates that we should add to our site.
• As younger consumers more comfortable with online shopping reach their peak earning years (ages 35–54), they'll be more likely to buy online than today's peak spenders.
• The web is erasing geographical shopping limits, presenting both a threat and an opportunity. Even though our customers can now shop websites anywhere in the world (so that we have thousands of competitors instead of a dozen), we can now attract customers from anywhere in the world.
• The growth in e-marketing will continue, so the sooner we get a site operational, the sooner we can work out any problems and prepare for high-volume business in the years ahead.

(Continued)

| FIGURE 10.4 | (Continued) |

Conclusions follow from the report's facts—no new information

Hiring a Consultant to Implement the Site
Implementing competitive retailing features can take anywhere from 1000 to 1500 hours of design and programming time. We have some of the expertise needed in-house, but the marketing and information systems departments have only 300 person-hours in the next six months. A web design consultant could help us get the design going sooner and could also do all the programming.

Integrating the Web into Existing Operations
The studies we reviewed showed that the most successful web retailers are careful to integrate their online retailing with their store and mail-based retailing. Companies that don't integrate carefully find themselves with higher costs, confused customers, and websites that don't generate much business. Before we begin adding to our website, we should develop a plan for integrating it with our existing marketing, accounting, and production systems. The online site could affect every department in the company, so it is vital that everyone has a chance to review the plans before we proceed.

Conclusion
- Online retailing is profitable and will grow further when younger consumers peak in earnings and spending. Web retailing capability is required to avoid losing this future business.
- Our internal IT department does not have enough person-hours to undertake the project.
- Online retailing should be integrated with all of our current operations through consultations with marketing, accounting, and production.

REPORTS FOR SOLVING PROBLEMS When solving problems, managers need both basic information and detailed analysis. Problem-solving reports typically require secondary or primary research. They are used when a problem exists and someone must investigate and propose a solution. These troubleshooting reports usually start with some background information on the problem, then analyze alternative solutions, and finally recommend the best approach.

From time to time, employees and managers write problem-solving reports to evaluate the practicality and advisability of pursuing a course of action (such as buying equipment, changing a procedure, or hiring a consultant). These feasibility reports study proposed options to assess whether any or all of them are sound. In Figure 10.4, for example, an organization's business development manager answers a question from the board of directors about whether the organization should implement an online retailing site. The semiformal report is attached to an email, which makes it easy to circulate the findings to multiple readers. Justification reports are written after a course of action has been taken to justify what was done. Audits are written to assess company compliance with regulatory requirements.

> Feasibility and justification reports study and qualify courses of action—feasibility reports are prepared before the action is taken, and justification reports are prepared after.

PROPOSALS A **proposal** is a special type of analytical report designed to get products, plans, or projects accepted by others. Proposals can be one or two pages, or they can be hundreds of pages if they involve large, complex jobs. Regardless of the size and scope, these special types of reports analyze an audience's problem, present a solution, and convince the audience that the solution presented is the best approach. Proposals are usually read by people in positions of authority.

Solicited proposals are generally prepared at the request of external parties who need something done; however, they may also be requested by such internal sources as

> Proposals present ideas and convince audiences to accept them.

management or the board of directors. Some external parties prepare an invitation to bid on their contract. Called a **request for proposal (RFP)**, such an invitation includes instructions that specify the exact type of work to be performed, along with guidelines on how and when the company wants the work completed.

> Effective solicited proposals address each item listed in the RFP.

Unsolicited proposals are usually written to obtain business or funding without a specific invitation from management or a potential client. In other words, with an unsolicited proposal, the writer makes the first move. Since readers may not know about the problem, the writer must convince them that a problem exists and that he or she can solve it. Thus, unsolicited proposals generally spend considerable time explaining why readers should take action and convincing them of the benefits of buying (or funding) something.

> An unsolicited proposal must first establish that a problem exists.

Internal Proposals **Internal proposals** are submitted to decision makers in one's own organization. They have two primary purposes: (1) to seek approval for a course of action

 **Model** Document

---

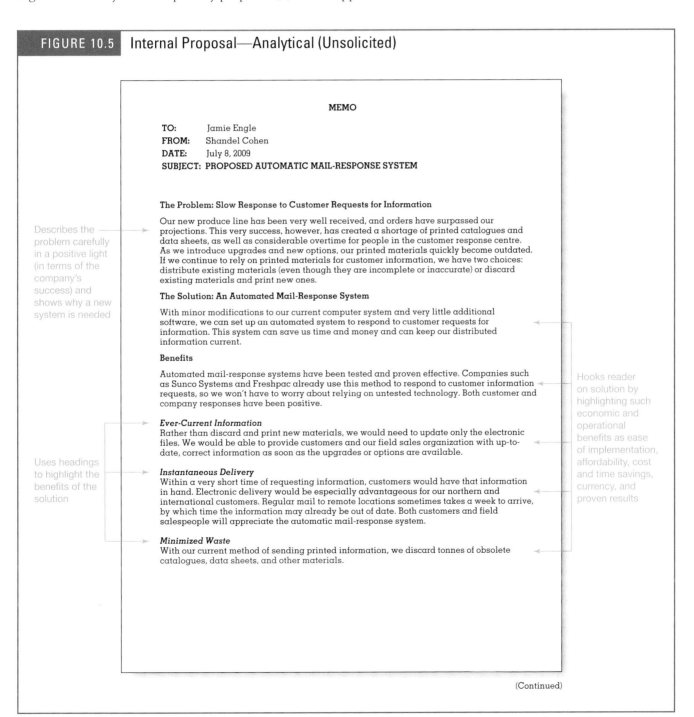

FIGURE 10.5   Internal Proposal—Analytical (Unsolicited)

Describes the problem carefully in a positive light (in terms of the company's success) and shows why a new system is needed

Uses headings to highlight the benefits of the solution

Hooks reader on solution by highlighting such economic and operational benefits as ease of implementation, affordability, cost and time savings, currency, and proven results

MEMO

TO: Jamie Engle
FROM: Shandel Cohen
DATE: July 8, 2009
SUBJECT: PROPOSED AUTOMATIC MAIL-RESPONSE SYSTEM

The Problem: Slow Response to Customer Requests for Information

Our new produce line has been very well received, and orders have surpassed our projections. This very success, however, has created a shortage of printed catalogues and data sheets, as well as considerable overtime for people in the customer response centre. As we introduce upgrades and new options, our printed materials quickly become outdated. If we continue to rely on printed materials for customer information, we have two choices: distribute existing materials (even though they are incomplete or inaccurate) or discard existing materials and print new ones.

The Solution: An Automated Mail-Response System

With minor modifications to our current computer system and very little additional software, we can set up an automated system to respond to customer requests for information. This system can save us time and money and can keep our distributed information current.

Benefits

Automated mail-response systems have been tested and proven effective. Companies such as Sunco Systems and Freshpac already use this method to respond to customer information requests, so we won't have to worry about relying on untested technology. Both customer and company responses have been positive.

Ever-Current Information
Rather than discard and print new materials, we would need to update only the electronic files. We would be able to provide customers and our field sales organization with up-to-date, correct information as soon as the upgrades or options are available.

Instantaneous Delivery
Within a very short time of requesting information, customers would have that information in hand. Electronic delivery would be especially advantageous for our northern and international customers. Regular mail to remote locations sometimes takes a week to arrive, by which time the information may already be out of date. Both customers and field salespeople will appreciate the automatic mail-response system.

Minimized Waste
With our current method of sending printed information, we discard tonnes of obsolete catalogues, data sheets, and other materials.

(Continued)

| FIGURE 10.5 | (Continued) |

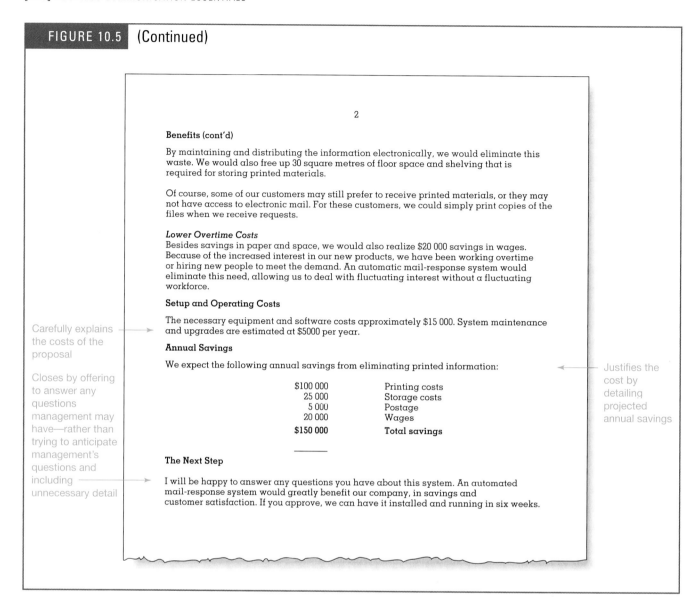

Carefully explains the costs of the proposal

Closes by offering to answer any questions management may have—rather than trying to anticipate management's questions and including unnecessary detail

2

Benefits (cont'd)

By maintaining and distributing the information electronically, we would eliminate this waste. We would also free up 30 square metres of floor space and shelving that is required for storing printed materials.

Of course, some of our customers may still prefer to receive printed materials, or they may not have access to electronic mail. For these customers, we could simply print copies of the files when we receive requests.

Lower Overtime Costs
Besides savings in paper and space, we would also realize $20 000 savings in wages. Because of the increased interest in our new products, we have been working overtime or hiring new people to meet the demand. An automatic mail-response system would eliminate this need, allowing us to deal with fluctuating interest without a fluctuating workforce.

Setup and Operating Costs

The necessary equipment and software costs approximately $15 000. System maintenance and upgrades are estimated at $5000 per year.

Annual Savings

We expect the following annual savings from eliminating printed information:

$100 000	Printing costs
25 000	Storage costs
5 000	Postage
20 000	Wages
$150 000	**Total savings**

Justifies the cost by detailing projected annual savings

The Next Step

I will be happy to answer any questions you have about this system. An automated mail-response system would greatly benefit our company, in savings and customer satisfaction. If you approve, we can have it installed and running in six weeks.

Effective internal proposals are unbiased and thoroughly explain the need, application, cost, and benefits of the proposed action.

(such as changing recruiting procedures, revising the company's training programs, or reorganizing a department) or (2) to request additional resources (such as new equipment, more employees, or extra operating funds).

Because most internal proposals advocate change, you must take extra care to understand whether your audience will feel threatened by your plan. A good internal proposal is completely unbiased and explains why a project or course of action is needed, what it will involve, how much it will cost, and how the company will benefit (see Figure 10.5).

If accepted, external proposals become legally binding documents.

External Proposals **External proposals** are submitted outside an organization to current or potential clients and government agencies. Like internal proposals, they solicit approval for projects or funds, but they differ in several ways. First, because they're directed to outsiders, external proposals are more formal. Second, external proposals are legally binding. Once approved, they form the basis of a contract, so they are prepared with extreme care, spelling out precisely what your company will provide under specific terms and conditions.

Third, audience members may not know your company, so your proposal must convince them that your organization is the best source of a product or service. You can do so by explaining your experience, qualifications, facilities, and equipment. Also, show that you clearly understand your audience's problem or need (see Figure 10.6).[1]

FIGURE 10.6 External Proposal—Analytical (Solicited)

Pointers for Preparing External Proposals

- Review the requirements stated in RFP.
- Define the scope of work.
- Determine the methods and procedures to be used.
- Estimate the requirements for time, personnel, and costs.
- Write the proposal exactly as RFP specifies—following the exact format required and responding meticulously to every point raised.
- Begin by stating the purpose of the proposal, defining the scope of work, presenting background information, and explaining any restrictions that might apply to the contract.
- In the body, give details and specify anticipated results—including methods, schedule, facilities, equipment, personnel, and costs.
- Close by summarizing key points and asking for audience decision.

JWR Remodelling Solutions

3240 Richard Road SW • Calgary, AB T3E 6R2
(403) 240-8845 • Fax: (403) 240-8846 • Email: jwr@telus.net

October 28, 2009

Mr. Daniel Yurgren
Data Dimensions
15 Foothills Lane
Calgary, AB T4M 1X2

Dear Mr.Yurgren:

PROPOSAL FOR HOME OFFICE CONSTRUCTION

Timing
JWR Remodelling Solutions would be happy to convert your existing living room area into a home office according to the specifications discussed during our October 14 meeting. We can schedule the project for the week beginning November 11, 2009 (two weeks from today). The project will take roughly three weeks to complete.

Acknowledges scope of project

Uses introduction to grab the reader's attention with expedited completion date—a key selling point

Benefits
Our construction approach is unique. We provide a full staff of licensed trades people and schedule our projects so that when one trade finishes, the next trade is ready to begin. To expedite this project, as you requested, we have agreed to overlap several trades whose work can be done concurrently.

Services Provided
JWR Remodelling Solutions will provide the following work:

- Remove baseboard, door casing, fluted casing, and sheetrock to prepare for construction of new partition wall at north end of living room.
- Partition and finish walls to create two separate storage closets at north end of living room with access through two 3'0" six-panel door units. Replace all disturbed sheetrock.
- Hang and trim new door units and replace all disturbed baseboards and door casings.
- Install 5'0" double French door unit in location of current cased opening at the SW entrance to living room adjacent to foyer. Trim appropriately.
- Provide all rough and finished electrical using recessed lighting in the ceiling and appropriate single pole switches and duplex outlets.
- Move cold air return from west wall to east wall of living room.
- Paint or finish all surfaces/trim to match specs used throughout house.

Uses body to explain how company will expedite schedule, outline approach, provide work plan, and (on the next page) list qualifications and state costs

Specifies exactly what contractor will and won't do

Exceptions
The work does *not* include custom office cabinetry, carpeting, or phone or cable wiring. We would be happy to bid on these projects in the future.

(Continued)

FIGURE 10.6 (Continued)

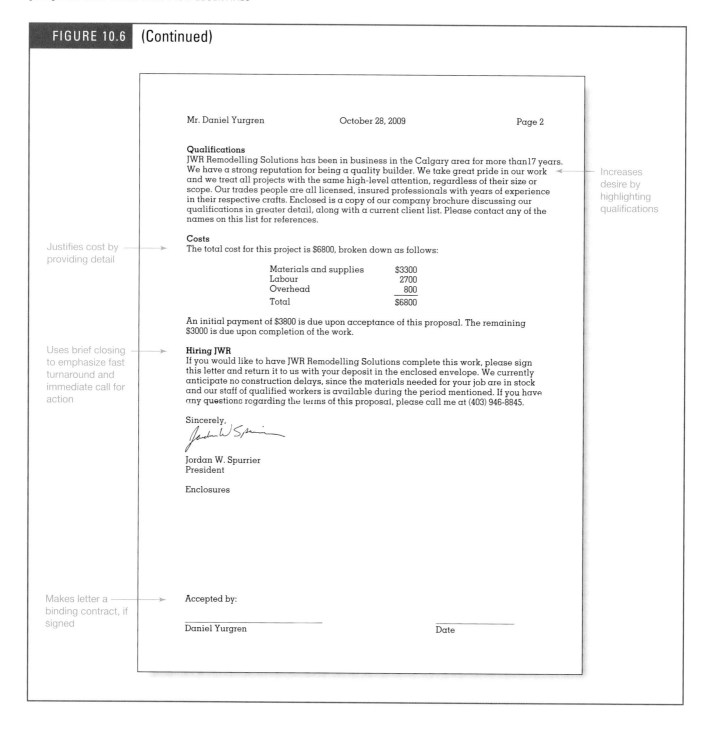

Mr. Daniel Yurgren   October 28, 2009   Page 2

Qualifications
JWR Remodelling Solutions has been in business in the Calgary area for more than 17 years. We have a strong reputation for being a quality builder. We take great pride in our work and we treat all projects with the same high-level attention, regardless of their size or scope. Our trades people are all licensed, insured professionals with years of experience in their respective crafts. Enclosed is a copy of our company brochure discussing our qualifications in greater detail, along with a current client list. Please contact any of the names on this list for references.

Increases desire by highlighting qualifications

Costs
The total cost for this project is $6800, broken down as follows:

Materials and supplies	$3300
Labour	2700
Overhead	800
Total	$6800

Justifies cost by providing detail

An initial payment of $3800 is due upon acceptance of this proposal. The remaining $3000 is due upon completion of the work.

Hiring JWR
If you would like to have JWR Remodelling Solutions complete this work, please sign this letter and return it to us with your deposit in the enclosed envelope. We currently anticipate no construction delays, since the materials needed for your job are in stock and our staff of qualified workers is available during the period mentioned. If you have any questions regarding the terms of this proposal, please call me at (403) 946-8845.

Uses brief closing to emphasize fast turnaround and immediate call for action

Sincerely,

Jordan W. Spurrier
President

Enclosures

Accepted by:

Makes letter a binding contract, if signed

_____   _____
Daniel Yurgren   Date

Applying the Three-Step Writing Process to Business Reports and Proposals

The three-step writing process applies to reports as well as to other business messages.

As with other business messages, your reports and proposals benefit when you follow the three-step writing process: (1) planning, (2) writing, and (3) completing business messages. Since much of the three-step process is covered in Chapters 3, 4, and 5, the following sections discuss only those tasks that differ for reports and proposals. The rest of this chapter focuses on Step 1, planning business reports and proposals. Chapter 11 focuses on Steps 2 and 3, writing and completing formal business reports and proposals.

Step 1: Planning Business Reports and Proposals

When planning reports and proposals, you focus on the same three tasks as for other business documents: analysis, investigation, and adaptation. Adapting your report to your audience and purpose is no different from adapting other business documents. You choose the best channel and medium, and you establish a good relationship with your audience. However, you have a few special considerations when analyzing and investigating business reports and proposals.

Analysis for Reports and Proposals

When planning reports and proposals, you will of course need to analyze your audience and purpose. Define the problem, define your specific purpose, compose a preliminary outline, and develop a work plan.

DEFINE THE PROBLEM Sometimes the person authorizing your report will define the problem you address. Other times, you will have to define the problem to be resolved. Be careful not to confuse a topic (campus parking) with a problem (the lack of enough campus parking). To help define the problem that your analytical report will address, ask yourself

- What needs to be determined?
- Why is this issue important?
- Who is involved or affected?
- Where is the trouble located?
- How did the problem originate?
- When did it start?

> When writing reports, pay special attention to analysis tasks such as defining the problem, writing the statement of purpose, developing a preliminary outline, and preparing the work plan.

> The problem you need to resolve may be defined by your superior.

Not all these questions apply in every situation, but asking them helps you define the problem and limit the scope of your discussion.

WRITE THE PURPOSE STATEMENT Writing a purpose statement will help you keep your report writing on task. Whereas defining the problem helps you know *what* you are going to investigate, the purpose statement clarifies *why* you are preparing the report. The most useful way to word your purpose statement is to begin with an infinitive phrase (*to* plus a verb). Doing so encourages you to take control and decide where you're going before you begin. For instance, in an informational report, your purpose statement can be as simple as these:

> The purpose statement defines the objective of your report.

To update clients on the progress of the research project (progress report)

To develop goals and objectives for the coming year (monitor/control report)

To explain the building access procedures (policy/procedure report)

To submit required information to the Department of Transport (compliance report)

For analytical reports, the statement of purpose is often more comprehensive. Linda Moreno is the cost accounting manager for Electrovision, a high-tech company based in Montreal, Quebec. She was recently asked to find ways of reducing employee travel-and-entertainment costs (her complete report appears in Chapter 11). Because Moreno was supposed to suggest specific ways of reducing travel and entertainment costs, she phrased her statement of purpose accordingly:

> Statements of purpose for analytical reports are often more complex than are those for informational reports.

. . . to analyze the T&E [travel and entertainment] budget, evaluate the impact of recent changes in airfares and hotel costs, and suggest ways to tighten management's control over T&E expenses.

If Moreno had been assigned an informational report instead, she might have stated her purpose differently:

> To summarize Electrovision's spending on travel and entertainment.

You can see from these two examples how much influence the purpose statement has on the scope of your report. Remember, the more specific your purpose statement, the more useful it will be as a guide to planning your report. Also, remember to double-check your purpose statement with the person who authorized the report. The authorizer may decide that the report needs to go in a different direction. Once your statement is confirmed, you can use it as the basis for your preliminary outline.

DEVELOP A PRELIMINARY OUTLINE A preliminary outline gives you a visual diagram of your report—its important points, the order in which they will be discussed, and the detail to be included (see Figure 10.7). Your preliminary outline will guide your research efforts and help you organize and compose your report. Think of your preliminary outline as a working draft that you'll revise and modify as you go along. It will look quite different from the final outline you develop to write your report. Write informative (talking) headings. Although outlines with informative headings take a little longer to write, they're generally more useful in guiding your work and easier for others to review.

PREPARE THE WORK PLAN Writing a report can be a lengthy task with several phases. In addition to organizing and writing, you'll often need to conduct primary and secondary research and prepare visuals. Developing a work plan is one way to coordinate and monitor your efforts so that you will produce quality reports quickly and efficiently.

> Once you prepare a written statement of your purpose, review it with the person who authorized the study.

> Your preliminary outline establishes the framework for your report and differs from the final outline.

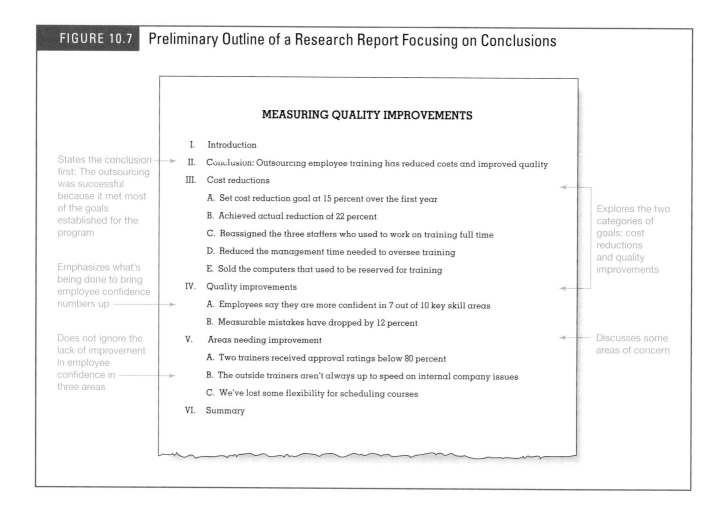

FIGURE 10.7   Preliminary Outline of a Research Report Focusing on Conclusions

MEASURING QUALITY IMPROVEMENTS

I. Introduction

II. Conclusion: Outsourcing employee training has reduced costs and improved quality

III. Cost reductions

    A. Set cost reduction goal at 15 percent over the first year

    B. Achieved actual reduction of 22 percent

    C. Reassigned the three staffers who used to work on training full time

    D. Reduced the management time needed to oversee training

    E. Sold the computers that used to be reserved for training

IV. Quality improvements

    A. Employees say they are more confident in 7 out of 10 key skill areas

    B. Measurable mistakes have dropped by 12 percent

V. Areas needing improvement

    A. Two trainers received approval ratings below 80 percent

    B. The outside trainers aren't always up to speed on internal company issues

    C. We've lost some flexibility for scheduling courses

VI. Summary

States the conclusion first: The outsourcing was successful because it met most of the goals established for the program

Emphasizes what's being done to bring employee confidence numbers up

Does not ignore the lack of improvement in employee confidence in three areas

Explores the two categories of goals: cost reductions and quality improvements

Discusses some areas of concern

If you are preparing the work plan for yourself, it can be relatively informal: a simple list of the steps you plan to take and an estimate of their sequence and timing. If you're conducting a lengthy, formal study, however, you'll want to develop a detailed work plan that can guide the performance of many tasks over a span of time. A formal plan might include the following elements (especially the first two):

- **Problem statement.** The problem statement clearly describes the issue and helps you stay focused.
- **Statement of the purpose and scope of your investigation.** The purpose statement describes what you plan to accomplish and the boundaries of your work. Stating which issues you will and will not cover is especially important with complex, lengthy investigations.
- **List of tasks to be accomplished.** For simple reports, the list of things to do will be short and probably obvious. However, longer, complex investigations require an exhaustive list so that you can plan the time needed for each task. Be sure to indicate your sources of information, the research necessary, and any constraints (on time, money, personnel, or data).
- **Description of any products that will result from your investigation.** Often, the only product of your efforts will be the report itself. In other cases, you'll need to produce something beyond a report, perhaps a new marketing plan or even a new product to sell. Make these expectations clear at the outset, and be sure to schedule enough time and resources to get the job done.
- **Review of project assignments, schedules, and resource requirements.** Indicate who will be responsible for what, when tasks will be completed, and how much the investigation will cost. If more than one person will be involved, include a brief section on coordinating report writing and production.
- **Plans for following up after delivering the report.** Follow-up can be as simple as making sure people received the information they need or as complex as conducting additional research to evaluate the results of report recommendations. Even informal follow-up can help you improve future reports and show that you care about your work's effectiveness and its impact on the organization.
- **Working outline.** Some work plans, such as the plan in Figure 10.8 (on page 222), include a tentative outline of the report. This plan was developed for a report on whether to launch a company newsletter.

> Whether you prepare an informal work plan for yourself or a detailed work plan for your team, be sure it identifies all the tasks that must be performed.

Investigation for Reports and Proposals

Model Document

In most cases you'll begin your research by looking for sources of secondary information—information on your subject that already exists and has already been collected, usually in the form of books, periodicals, newspapers, and websites. If secondary information doesn't exist or isn't helpful, then you'll need to collect first-hand, primary information for your specific needs.

> Begin your research by gathering secondary information.

GATHER SECONDARY INFORMATION Many sources of secondary information are easily accessible in print and online.[2]

Finding Information in the Library Libraries are where you'll find business books, electronic databases, newspapers, periodicals, directories, almanacs, and government publications. In addition, you'll find your most important resource: librarians. Reference librarians are trained in research techniques and can show you how to use the library's many resources:

> Reference librarians are there to assist you with your research efforts.

- **Business books.** Although less timely than journal articles, business books provide in-depth coverage of a variety of business topics. You may have better luck finding specialized information at company libraries or at a college or university library.
- **Electronic databases.** These computer-searchable collections of information are

| FIGURE 10.8 | Work Plan for a Formal Study |

Clear enough for anyone to understand without background research

Lays out the tasks to be accomplished and does so in clear, simple terms

A preliminary outline is presented for guidance, even though no description of the end product is included

States the assignments and the schedules for completing them

Delineates exactly what will be covered in the report

Includes no plans for following up

STATEMENT OF THE PROBLEM
The rapid growth of our company over the past five years has reduced the sense of community among our staff. People no longer feel like part of an intimate organization where they matter as individuals.

PURPOSE AND SCOPE OF WORK
The purpose of this study is to determine whether a company newsletter would help rebuild employee identification with the organization. The study will evaluate the impact of newsletters in other companies and will attempt to identify features that might be desirable in our own newsletter. Such variables as length, frequency of distribution, types of articles, and graphic design will be considered. Costs will be estimated for several approaches. In addition, the study will analyze the personnel and the procedures required to produce a newsletter.

SOURCES AND METHODS OF DATA COLLECTION
Survey literature in human resources journals about the impact of corporate newsletters on employee morale. Sample newsletters will be collected from 50 companies similar to ours in size, growth rate, and types of employees. The editors will be asked to comment on the impact of their publications on employee morale. Our own employees will be surveyed to determine their interest in a newsletter and their preferences for specific features. Production procedures and costs will be analyzed through conversations with newsletter editors and printers.

PRELIMINARY OUTLINE
The preliminary outline for this study is as follows:
  I. Do newsletters affect morale?
      A. Do people read them?
      B. How do employees benefit?
      C. How does the company benefit?
 II. What are the features of good newsletters?
      A. How long are they?
      B. What do they contain?
      C. How often are they published?
      D. How are they designed?
III. How should a newsletter be produced?
      A. Should it be written, edited, and printed internally?
      B. Should it be written internally and printed outside?
      C. Should it be totally produced outside?
 IV. What would a newsletter cost?
      A. What would the personnel cost be?
      B. What would the materials cost be?
      C. What would outside services costs?
  V. Should we publish a company newsletter?
 VI. If so, what approach should we take?

WORK PLAN
Each phase of this study will be completed by the following dates:

Survey literature	September 3–14, 2009
Collect/analyze newsletters	September 3–14, 2009
Interview editors by phone	September 16–20, 2009
Survey employees	September 23–27, 2009
Develop sample	September 30–October 11, 2009
Develop cost estimates	October 8–11, 2009
Prepare report	October 14–25, 2009
Submit final report	October 28, 2009

often categorized by subject areas (business, law, science, technology, and education). When using an electronic database, try to get a list of the periodicals or publications it includes, as well as the time period it covers so that you can plan to fill in any gaps for items not in the database.

- **Newspapers.** Libraries subscribe to only a select number of newspapers and store a limited number of back issues in print. However, they frequently subscribe to databases containing newspaper articles in full text (available online, on CD-ROM, or on microfilm). Also, most newspapers today offer full-text or limited editions of their papers on the internet.
- **Periodicals.** Most periodicals fall into four categories: (1) popular magazines (not intended for business, professional, or academic use), (2) trade journals (providing

news and other facts about particular professions, industries, and occupations), (3) business magazines (covering all major industries and professions), and (4) academic journals (publishing data from professional researchers and educators).

- **Directories.** Covering everything from accountants to zoos, business directories provide entries for companies, products, and individuals, and they include the names of key contacts.
- **Almanacs.** Almanacs are handy guides to factual and statistical information about countries, politics, the labour force, and so on.
- **Government publications.** For information on a law, a court decision, or current population patterns and business trends, consult government documents. A librarian can direct you to the information you want.

Finding Business Information on the Internet Today's most popular source of company and industry information is the internet, offering current news, industry trends, and company-related data on financial performance, products, goals, and employment. Remember that anyone (including you) can post anything on a website. Thus, information on the web may be biased, inaccurate, or exaggerated. Before searching the web for business information, wait until you've had a chance to learn a bit about your topic from journals, books, and commercial databases. Then you'll be able to detect unreliable information and be more selective about which websites and documents you use.

> When doing research on the internet, you need to be selective because anyone can publish anything.

A good place to start on the web is the Internet Public Library at **www.ipl.org**. Modelled after a real library, this site will provide you with carefully selected links to high-quality business resources. You can find company profiles, trade data, business news, small-business information, prepared forms and documents, biographies of executives, financial reports, job postings, online publications, and so on. Canadians frequently consult U.S.-based internet sites for business information, but be aware that U.S. political, legal, and corporate tax information will differ from what is valid in English and French Canada.

To find specific company information, consult *The Globe and Mail*'s Annual Report Service. Go to **www.wilink.com** and choose "Investor Services" to find the link to order free copies of companies' annual reports. Information about Canadian companies, markets, and economic trends can be found on Site-By-Site! The International Investment Portal & Research Center (**www.site-by-site.com**). Also, check the company's website (if it maintains one). Company sites generally include detailed information about the firm's products, services, history, mission, strategy, financial performance, and employment needs. Many sites provide links to related company information, such as news releases, and more.

> You can find all kinds of information about a company on its website.

You can obtain news releases and general company news from news release sites such as Canada NewsWire (**www.newswire.ca**). This site offers free databases of news releases from companies subscribing to their services. News release sites are also good places to look for webcasts, podcasts, announcements of new products, management changes, earnings, dividends, mergers, acquisitions, and other company information.

The web doesn't have everything. You may find nothing about small organizations, or perhaps just their address and phone number. And even if the information exists on the web, you may not be able to find it. The internet holds hundreds of millions of webpages, with hundreds of pages being added every day, and even the best internet search engines manage to index only about one-third of the pages on the web.[3]

Understanding Search Engines Search engines identify and screen web resources. They will often turn up what you're looking for, most likely along with a mountain of stuff you don't need. Not all search engines operate the same way. For instance, some engines index all the pages they find; others index only the most popular pages. Sites such as Yahoo!, Lycos, and Google offer well-known, commercially backed search engines. Google offers the option of searching for "Canada only" sites.

Using Business Databases Many college and university libraries subscribe to important business databases. Check to see whether your library has

- **Canadian Business & Current Affairs**—indexes more than 600 Canadian periodicals and newspapers, making 150 of these available to subscribers in full-text form. The most comprehensive source of business current events information in Canada.
- **SEDAR (System for Electronic Document Analysis and Retrieval)**—lists all companies on stock exchanges in Canada.
- **Cancorp Financials**—financial and management information from 13 000 Canadian companies
- **EBSCOhost Web**—includes a number of databases and full-text products including Business Source Premier and Business Wire news
- **Mergent Online**—general and financial information, annual reports, and links to newswire articles, with data on more than 10 000 public U.S. and 17 000 non-public U.S. companies
- **Statistics Canada** huge repository of accurate data about Canada[4]

Using Research Navigator You can get a head start on your research by going into MyBusCommLab and using Research Navigator. Besides giving you help with the research process, Research Navigator allows you to search electronically in the following databases: EBSCO Academic Journal and Abstract Database, the New York Times Search by Subject Archive, and the Financial Times Article Archive and Company Financials.

Conducting Effective Database Searches Whether you are using a library database or an internet search engine, follow these tips to improve your search results:[5]

- **Use multiple search engines.** Don't limit yourself to a single search engine, especially if you are looking for less popular topics. Try your search on several engines by using metacrawlers, special engines that search several search engines at once.
- **Translate concepts into key words and phrases.** If you're researching the "effect of TQM on company profits," select the keywords *TQM, total quality management, profits, sales, companies,* and *corporations.* Use synonyms or word equivalents whenever possible.
- **Use capitals and lower case characters correctly.** When a search engine is case sensitive, it will return different documents for the keywords *Chair* and *chair.* If the search engine is not case sensitive, then it will return all documents containing the word *chair,* whether capitalized or not.
- **Use variations of your terms.** Use abbreviations (*CEO, CPA*), synonyms (*man, male*), related terms (*child, adolescent, youth*), different spellings (*dialog, dialogue*), singular and plural forms (*woman, women*), nouns and adjectives (*manager, management, managerial*), and open and compound forms (*online, on line, on-line*).
- **Specify phrases or individual keywords with quotation marks.** To look for an entire phrase (*"total quality management"*), most search engines allow you to use quotation marks around the phrase. Otherwise, the search engine will look for instances where the separate words (*total, quality,* and *management*) appear somewhere on the webpage.
- **Evaluate the precision and quality of your results to refine your search if necessary.** You'll need to refine your search if you end up with more than 60 to 100 links to sort through or if your first page of results doesn't offer something of interest. Also pay attention to whether you are searching in the title, subject, or document field of the database. Each will return different results.

> By following a few guidelines, you can improve your database search results.

COLLECT PRIMARY INFORMATION Sometimes what you need is not available from sources of secondary information, or you need something beyond what is covered in secondary information. In that case, you go out into the real world to gather data yourself. The main

> Conduct primary research by collecting basic information yourself.

methods of collecting primary information are examining documents, making observations, conducting experiments, surveying people, and conducting interviews.

Documents, Observation, and Experiments Often the most useful method of collecting primary information is examining internal documents, such as company sales reports, memos, balance sheets, and income statements. You can find a great deal of information in company databases and files. A single document may be a source of both secondary and primary information. For example, when citing summaries of financial and operations data from an annual report, you're using the report as secondary information. However, the same annual report would be considered a primary source if you were analyzing its design features, comparing it with annual reports from other years, or comparing it with reports from other companies.

Another common method of collecting primary business information is making formal observations. For instance, you can observe people performing their jobs or customers interacting with a product. Conducting experiments is another method of collecting primary information, but this method is far more common in technical fields than in general business.

Surveys One of the best methods of collecting primary information is to ask people with relevant experience and opinions. Surveys include everything from a one-time, one-on-one interview to the distribution of thousands of questionnaires. When prepared and conducted properly, surveys can tell you what a cross-section of people think about a given topic. Surveys are useful only when they're reliable and valid. A survey is *reliable* if it produces identical results when repeated. A survey is *valid* if it measures what it's intended to measure. For effective surveys, follow these tips:

- **Provide clear instructions.** Respondents need to know exactly how to fill out your questionnaire.
- **Keep the questionnaire short and easy to answer.** Ask only questions that are relevant to your research. Remember that people are most likely to respond if they can complete your questionnaire within 10 to 15 minutes.
- **Develop questions that provide easy-to-analyze answers.** Numbers and facts are easier to summarize than opinions.
- **Avoid leading questions.** Questions that lead to a particular answer bias your survey. If you ask, "Do you prefer that we stay open in the evenings for customer convenience?" you'll get a yes answer. Instead, ask, "What time of day do you normally do your shopping?"
- **Ask only one thing at a time.** A compound question such as "Do you read books and magazines regularly?" doesn't allow for the respondent who reads one but not the other.
- **Pre-test the questionnaire.** Have a sample group identify questions that are subject to misinterpretation.

If you're mailing your questionnaire rather than administering it in person, include a return postage-paid envelope along with a persuasive cover letter that explains why you're conducting the research. Your letter must convince your readers that responding is important. Remember that even under the best of circumstances, you may get no more than a 10 to 20 percent response.

Interviews Getting information straight from an expert can be another effective method for collecting primary information. Interviews are planned conversations with a predetermined purpose that involve asking and answering questions. Before you decide to do one, ask yourself whether an interview is really the best way to get the information you need. Although they are relatively easy to conduct, interviews require careful planning and a lot of time.

Documentary evidence and historical records are sources of primary data.

Observation applies your five senses and your judgment to the investigation.

Developing an effective survey questionnaire requires care and skill.

Effective interviewers develop a communication plan.

- **Plan the interview.** Decide in advance what kind of information you want and how you will use it. Analyze your purpose, learn about the other person, and formulate your main idea. Then decide on the length, style, and organization of the interview.
- **Prepare interview questions.** The answers you receive are influenced by the types of questions you ask, the way you ask them, and your subject's cultural and language background.
- **Assign priorities to interview questions.** Rate your questions and highlight the most important ones. If you start to run out of time during the interview, you may have to be selective.
- **Limit the number of questions.** Don't try to cover more questions than you have time for. You can probably handle about 20 questions in a half-hour.
- **Edit your questions.** Try to make your questions as neutral and as easy to understand as possible. Then practise them several times to make sure you're ready for the interview.
- **Process interview information.** After the interview, take a few moments to write down your thoughts, go over your notes, and organize your material. Fill in any blanks while the interview is fresh in your mind.

Always give proper credit when you use someone else's material or ideas.

DOCUMENT SOURCES AND GIVE CREDIT Whenever you quote or paraphrase, you are using someone else's words or ideas. Doing so without proper credit is plagiarism. You can avoid **plagiarism** by documenting the original source (using one of the systems explained in Appendix B, "Documentation of Report Sources"). Documenting your sources is necessary for books, articles, tables, charts, diagrams, song lyrics, scripted dialogue, letters, speeches—anything that you take from someone else. Even if you paraphrase the material, you should to give credit to the person you obtained the original information from.

However, you do not have to cite a source for general knowledge or for specialized knowledge that's generally known among your readers. For example, everyone knows that Pierre Trudeau was elected prime minister. You can say so on your own authority, even if you've read an article in which the author says the same thing.

Avoiding plagiarism involves six different skills including knowing when to cite a source, how to attribute the source, and how to paraphrase, use quotation marks, integrate the citation, and make a proper reference entry. You can test yourself on your knowledge of how to avoid plagiarism by visiting MyBusCommLab. Click on "Research Process" and "Avoiding Plagiarism" to complete the tutorials and self-tests. Citing sources shows you have consulted experts and have gathered evidence from credible sources.

Analyze your results by drawing reasonable and logical conclusions and, if appropriate, developing a set of recommendations.

INTERPRET YOUR FINDINGS By themselves, the data you collect won't offer much meaning or insight. You'll need to search for relationships among the facts and the bits of evidence you've compiled. This analysis allows you to interpret your findings and thus answer the questions or solve the problem that required the report in the first place. Once you have thoroughly analyzed your information, your next step is to draw conclusions and, if requested, develop recommendations.

Summarizing Your Research

Summaries must be impartial statements of facts.

If your boss has asked you to summarize the competitive strengths and weaknesses of another company or the recent trends in a particular market, your goal is to provide an unbiased summary that is free of your own opinions, conclusions, or recommendations. If you do uncover something that sparks an idea or raises a concern, by all means communicate this revelation but do so separately; don't include such information in your summary report.

TABLE 10.1	Summarizing Effectively	
ORIGINAL MATERIAL (116 WORDS)	**45-WORD SUMMARY**	**22-WORD SUMMARY**
Our facilities costs spiralled out of control last year. The 23 percent jump was far ahead of every other cost category in the company and many times higher than the 4 percent average rise for commercial real estate in the Portland metropolitan area. The rise can be attributed to many factors, but the major factors include repairs (mostly electrical and structural problems at the downtown office), energy (most of our offices are heated by electricity, the price of which has been increasing much faster than for oil or gas), and last but not least, the loss of two sublease tenants whose rent payments made a substantial dent in our cost profile for the past five years.	Our facilities costs jumped 23 percent last year, far ahead of every other cost category in the company and many times higher than the 4 percent local average. The major factors contributing to the increase are repairs, energy, and the loss of two sublease tenants.	Our facilities costs jumped 23 percent last year, due mainly to rising repair and energy costs and the loss of sublease income.

Summarizing is not always a simple task. Identify the main idea and the key support points, and separate these from details, examples, and other supporting evidence (see Table 10.1). Focus your efforts on your audience, highlighting the information that is most important to the person who assigned the project or to those who will be reading the report.

However, don't mistake audience focus to mean that you're supposed to convey only the information your audience wants to hear. A good summary might contain nothing but bad news or information that runs counter to majority assumptions in the organization. Even if the summary isn't pleasant, effective managers always appreciate and respect honest, complete, and perceptive information from their employees.

DRAW CONCLUSIONS A conclusion is a logical interpretation of the facts in your report. Reaching good conclusions based on the evidence at hand is one of the most important skills you can develop in your business career. Make sure your conclusions are sound:

> Conclusions are interpretations of the facts.

- First, your conclusion should fulfil the original statement of purpose. After all, drawing a conclusion is why you took on the project in the first place. Reread your purpose statement. Your conclusion should answer the question posed by your purpose. A conclusion in an analytical report is often a decision that you make based on the facts of the report. In a descriptive report, where no decision is required, the conclusion may be used to sum up the key facts you have described in the report.
- Second, base your conclusion strictly on the information included in the rest of the report—all the information. Don't ignore anything, even if it doesn't support your conclusion.
- Third, don't introduce any new information in your conclusion.
- And, fourth, make sure your conclusion is logical. A logical conclusion is one that follows accepted patterns of reasoning. Your conclusions are influenced by your personal values and your organization's values; so be aware of how these biases affect your judgment.

> Check the logic that underlies your conclusions.

> Recommendations are suggestions for action.

DEVELOP RECOMMENDATIONS Whereas a conclusion interprets the facts, a recommendation suggests what to do about the conclusion. The difference between a conclusion and a recommendation can be seen in the following example:

Conclusion
On the basis of its track record and current price, I conclude that this company is an attractive buy.

Recommendation
I recommend that we offer to buy the company at a 10 percent premium over the market value of its stock.

> Good recommendations are
> • Practical
> • Acceptable to readers
> • Explained in enough detail for readers to take action

Clarify the relationship between your conclusions and your recommendations. Remember, recommendations are inappropriate in a report when you're not expected to supply them. But when you do provide recommendations in a report, try to develop them without bias. Don't let your assumptions and personal values influence them. To be credible, recommendations must be based on logical analysis and sound conclusions. They must also be practical and acceptable to your readers, the people who have to make the recommendations work. Finally, when making a recommendation, adequately describe the steps that come next. Don't leave your readers scratching their heads and saying, "This all sounds good, but what do I do on Monday morning?"

Since recommendations are often the most important information in a report, decide how you can design the document to make the recommendations easily accessible to the reader. Consider using a heading and putting recommendations in a list to emphasize them. Depending on your authority, you may emphasize action and strengthen the tone of your recommendations if you write them in second person, active command form. If you also put them in a numbered list you will assign priority and make them very accessible. On the other hand, if you have not been authorized to be so direct, you can still emphasize action but soften the tone by changing the verb form as shown in the following example.

Recommendations
To increase business, WestJet can
1. Offer a special business traveller's pass
2. Increase the number of flights that leave in the evening

Recommendations
WestJet can increase business by
1. Offering a special business traveller's pass
2. Increasing the number of flights leaving in the evening

ON THE JOB

You can build positive relationships even while you are doing research for the company. Always giving credit for the sources of information you use, or to the people who helped you, will maintain your reputation for integrity and honesty.

Reviewing Key Points

In this chapter, you looked at informational reports for monitoring operations, implementing policies, complying with regulation, and documenting progress on projects. You also learned about analytical reports for solving problems and proposing changes. You viewed internal and external proposals to get products, plans, or projects accepted by authorities. Companies may solicit or invite you to write a proposal that describes how to solve a known problem. Or, you may initiate a proposal and send it unsolicited. When you submit unsolicited proposals, you have to convince the receiver about the problem as well as the solution.

This chapter concentrates on the planning stage of the proposal writing process. In the planning stage of the writing process, you should

- Analyze the audience and write a clear purpose statement
- Define the problem and scope of the document
- Prepare a preliminary outline and a work plan for longer projects
- Research using primary and/or secondary sources to investigate the topic
- Design efficient surveys and interviews with focused, unbiased questions
- Consult important business directories, databases, and indexes such as Canadian Business and Current Affairs, SEDAR, and Industry Canada to gather facts
- Interpret evidence, summarize key facts, and develop conclusions

In Chapter 11 you will study the next stages: writing and producing the report or proposal.

mybuscommlab   Go to MyBusCommLab at www.pearson.ca/mybuscommlab for online exercises.

Practise Your Grammar

Exercises

Effective business communication starts with strong grammar skills. To improve your grammar skills, go to MyBusCommLab or Grammar-on-the-Go, where you'll find exercises and diagnostic tests to help you produce clear, effective communication.

Test Your Knowledge

Exercises

1. How are reports for monitoring and controlling operations used?
2. What functions do progress reports serve?
3. What are the two primary purposes of internal proposals?
4. How do proposal writers use an RFP?
5. How does primary information differ from secondary information?
6. How can you improve your search when using a search engine or a library database?
7. What makes a survey reliable and valid?
8. What must you do to be ethical when using material you have found in secondary sources?
9. What are the characteristics of a sound conclusion?
10. How does a conclusion differ from a recommendation?

Apply Your Knowledge

1. Why are unsolicited proposals more challenging to write than solicited proposals?
2. If secondary sources do not exist for your report's topic, where can you get information?
3. If your report includes only factual information, is it objective? Please explain.
4. After an exhaustive study of an important problem, you have reached a conclusion that you believe your company's management will reject. What will you do? Explain your answer.
5. **Ethical Choices** If you want to make a specific recommendation following your research, should you include information that might support a different recommendation? Explain your answer.

Running Cases

CASE 1: Noreen

Noreen would like to propose a new project to upper-level management: reorganizing two departments into one.

Currently, the Go Points department is on the fourth floor and staffed by 20 sales/service reps. They (1) make sales calls to existing Petro-Go credit card holders to offer the points program, (2) receive calls from existing points program customers who have enquiries, and (3) call existing points customers to announce, for example, promotions and offers.

The Petro-Go credit card department is on the third floor and staffed by 30 sales/service reps. They (1) make sales calls to recruit new credit card customers, (2) receive calls from existing credit card holders who have enquiries, and (3) call existing credit card customers to announce, for example, promotions and offers.

Noreen thinks that by joining the credit card sales/service department with the Go Points department, customers will be better served by one-stop shopping. She also feels that the credit card sales/service staff could easily modify their call routines to include information about the Go Points program, and the Go Points staff could easily be trained on the credit card policies and procedures.

QUESTIONS

a. Is this a solicited proposal?
b. How will Noreen use the "you" attitude in this proposal?
c. What costs might be involved?
d. What supporting facts or evidence do you think might help Noreen justify this proposal?
e. What are some concerns or problems that may arise during this project?

YOUR TASK

Create a work plan for Noreen to use as a guide in writing her proposal. Include the following elements:

- statement of the problem
- statement of the purpose and scope
- discussion of the tasks to be accomplished
- review of timelines and resources required

CASE 2: Kwong

Kwong applies to and gets hired by a large national telephone service provider, ET Canada, in the accounting department. He plans to complete his CGA studies part-time because he finds his expenses increasing and he needs to have more income. His goal of opening his own accounting firm is still in place but will take a little longer to achieve.

One of his first tasks is to work on the company's annual report with a team of people. The annual report will be posted on the internet and distributed to all shareholders.

QUESTIONS

a. Which type of report best describes an annual report—an analytical report, an operating report, or a progress report?
b. What information is included in a company's annual report?
c. Where will Kwong find the information he needs for the annual report?
d. What teamwork skills will Kwong need to make an effective team member?
e. How will Kwong format the headings in the report, so the reader knows where each new section begins and which sub-topics relate to which heading?

YOUR TASK

Research a public Canadian utility company. Public companies usually have more information available than private companies. Use the SEDAR (System for Electronic Document Analysis and Retrieval) website to find a list of Canadian public companies and their annual reports. Review several company annual reports for utility service providers. Make a list of the common headings and sections within the annual reports. Create a table of contents that Kwong might use in ET Canada's annual report.

⊖Practise Your Knowledge

ACTIVITIES

1. **Analyze This Document** All public companies file comprehensive annual reports. Many companies post links to these reports on their websites along with links to other company reports. Use www.sedar.com to find a company of your choice. View the company's most recent annual report and financial report. Compare the style and format of the two reports. For which audience(s) is the annual report targeted? Who is interested in the financial report? Which report do you find easier to read? More interesting? More detailed?

2. **Understanding Business Reports and Proposals: How Companies Use Reports** Interview several people working in a career you might like to enter, and ask them about the types of written reports they receive and prepare. How do these reports tie in to the decision-making process? Who reads the reports they prepare? Summarize your findings in writing, give them to your instructor, and be prepared to discuss them with the class.

3. **Internet** Read the step-by-step hints and examples for writing a funding proposal at www.learnerassociates.net. Review the entire sample proposal online. What details did the author decide to include in the appendices? Why was this material placed in the appendices and not the main body of the report? According to the author's tips, when is the best time to prepare a project overview?

4. **Analyzing the Situation: Statement of Purpose** Sales at the Style Shop, a men's clothing store where you work as the store manager, have declined for the third month in a row. Your boss is not sure whether this decline is due to a weak economy or if it's due to another, unknown reason. She has asked you to investigate the situation and to submit a report to her highlighting some possible reasons for the decline. Develop a statement of purpose for your report.

5. **Teamwork: Planning an Unsolicited Proposal** Break into small groups and identify an operational problem occurring at your campus—perhaps involving registration, university housing, food services, parking, or library services. Then develop a workable solution to that problem. Finally, develop a list of pertinent facts that your team will need to gather to convince the reader that the problem exists and that your solution will work.

6. **Preparing the Work Plan** The lawn surrounding the Town Centre shopping mall looks as if it could use better care. You're the assistant to the centre's general manager, who must approve any new contracts for lawn service. You want to prepare a formal study of the current state of your lawn's health. Your report will include conclusions and recommendations for your boss's consideration. Draft a work plan, including the problem statement, the statement of purpose and scope, a description of what will result from your investigation, the sources and methods of data collection, and a preliminary outline.

7. **Finding Secondary Information** Business people have to know where to look for secondary information when they conduct research. Prepare a list of the most important magazines and professional journals in the following fields of study:
   a. Marketing/advertising
   b. Insurance
   c. Communications
   d. Accounting

8. **Finding Information: Primary Information** Deciding how to collect primary data is an important part of the research process. Which one or more of the five methods of data collection (examining documents, making observations, surveying people, performing experiments, or conducting interviews) would you use if you were researching these questions?
   a. Has the litter problem on campus been reduced since the cafeteria began offering fewer takeout choices this year?
   b. Has the school attracted more transfer students since it waived the formal application process and allowed students at other colleges simply to send their transcripts and a one-page letter of application?
   c. Have the number of traffic accidents at the school's main entrance been reduced since a traffic light was installed?
   d. Has student satisfaction with the campus bookstore improved now that students can order their books over the internet and pick them up at several campus locations?

9. **Finding Information: Interviews** You're conducting an information interview with a manager in another division of your company. Partway through the interview, the manager shows clear signs of impatience. How should

you respond? What might you do differently to prevent this from happening in the future? Explain your answers.

10. **Avoiding Plagiarism: Practising Paraphrasing**

  a. Extracting key details and putting them into your own words takes practice. Visit MyBusCommLab and click on, in sequence, "Research Process," "APA," and "Avoiding Plagiarism" to find "Paraphrasing." Read over the samples; then complete the first two practice exercises on paraphrasing sources. Print out your results and bring them to class to exchange with another student. How closely does your paraphrasing match with your classmate's? Have you both cited the source properly?

  b. Using Research Navigator, find a two-page article and bring it to class to share with another student. Read each others' articles and summarize five key points the articles make. Exchange your summaries and identify which parts of the summary should be cited. Insert proper citations and write out your entry to be included in the reference list.

11. **Processing Information: Documenting Sources** Select five business articles from sources such as journals, books, newspapers, or websites. Develop a reference list. Using Appendix B, practise forming references in APA format. Or, practise making references using an interactive website developed by Dr. Michele Jacobsen at the University of Calgary, **www.ucalgary.ca/~dmjacobs/prosem/citing_resources.html**. Or, learn more about writing citations in APA by completing citation tutorials and exercises in MyBusCommLab in the "Research Process" section.

Expand Your Knowledge

Best of the Web

Pointers for Business Plans What's involved in a business plan? BizPlanIt.com offers tips and advice, consulting services, a free email newsletter, and a sample virtual business plan. You'll find suggestions on what details and how much information to include in each section of a business plan. You can explore the site's numerous links to business plan books and software, online magazines, educational programs, government resources, women's and minority resources, and even answers to your business plan questions.
www.bizplanit.com

EXERCISES

1. Why is the executive summary such an important section of a business plan? What kind of information is contained in the executive summary?
2. What is the product/services section? What information should it contain? List some of the common errors to avoid when planning this part.
3. What type of business planning should you describe in the exit strategy section? Why?

Exploring the Web on Your Own

Review these chapter-related websites on your own to learn more about planning and using reports in the workplace.

1. If your report writing involves researching other companies, check out Wall Street Research Network, **www.wsrn.com**, one of the most comprehensive company information sites on the internet.
2. Looking for a specific company? Try SuperPages at **www.bigbook.com** where you'll find more than 16 million listings. Select "Global Directories" to locate Canadian companies.
3. Searching for information on a company or industry? Corporate Information, **www.corporateinformation.com**, is a good place to begin your online research. It has a link to Wright Investors Source for Canadian profiles.

 # Cases

Informal Informational Reports

1. PROGRESS REPORT ON A PROJECT

YOUR TASK Plan and write a progress report on a project you are working on. Assume the instructor or supervisor of the project has asked you to document what you have completed so far, what problems you have encountered and solved, and what work is remaining on the project. If you do not have a current project, assume you are halfway through one you have completed in the past.

If your course work does not require any projects, assume you have a scholarship to attend school. As part of your scholarship requirements, you must submit a report each term that summarizes the work you have completed and what you will be taking next.

2. REPORT ON MEETING OR CONFERENCE ATTENDANCE

YOUR TASK Plan and write a personal activity report on a meeting or conference you have recently attended. If you have not attended a meeting recently, look at the student government calendar at your school for an upcoming campus meeting and attend it. Or, attend a local government meeting in your community. Write a summary of the meeting for those who were not able to attend and submit it to your professor.

3. REPORT ON TRENDS IN TUITION COSTS

Assume you work for the Canadian Students' Advisory Coalition, a non-profit group that works on behalf of post-secondary students across the country. The Advisory Coalition is monitoring tuition costs. Your supervisor has asked you to research tuition increases for the last four years in your school and one other in the nearby area. Are tuition costs going up, down, or remaining the same? For each school, once you have determined the costs for each year, calculate the percentage change in tuition costs from year to year and between first and fourth year.

YOUR TASK Using memo format, plan an informal report presenting your findings and conclusions to your supervisor. Plan to include graphics that explain your findings and support your conclusions.

Informal Analytical Reports

4. REPORT ON TIME MANAGEMENT

No doubt you have learned the importance of time management in trying to complete your studies and perhaps work part time. It is not easy to juggle classes, work obligations, and family or personal commitments and still have time for health and exercise. You have found it so challenging, in fact, that you signed up for some free counselling sessions on time management. The counsellor has asked you to keep a record of how you use your time over the course of one week. "Design a table that you can use to record your time," she said. "Record what you do in 15-minute increments for 7 days (24-hour periods); then at the end of the week, you can analyze your use of time."

At first you thought it would be tedious, but you get into it and record everything you do in a week.

YOUR TASK Design the table and record your time use for one week. At the end of the week, analyze your use of time. What categories can you use to describe the different ways you use time? How effective is your use of time? Can you see any ways to improve your use of time? What graphics could you use to show your use of time?

Write a short report to the counsellor that describes what you did and what you found out, and provides conclusions and some recommendations. Include at least two graphics. Assume the counsellor has asked you to submit your report before your next session with her. Decide what type of format would best suit this audience and subject.

5. CAREER MOVES: ASSESSING EMPLOYMENT PROSPECTS

YOUR TASK Assess the job prospects in your desired occupation and research a company that employs people in this field. Look up the trends and predictions about the occupational category and find out the hiring qualifications. To find information on occupational categories such as accountants, human resource managers, and others, consult the Canadian National Occupational Classification site at **www5.hrsdc.gc.ca/NOC-CNP/app/index.aspx?/c=e**. Look on Work Futures sites by province, such as **www.workfutures.bc.ca**. Provincial Work Futures sites contain links to those of the other provinces and territories.

Use SEDAR at www.sedar.com or Industry Canada at www.ic.gc.ca to locate a company that employs people in the occupational group you have researched. Visit the company's website. Find out whether this company would be a good hiring prospect for fellow classmates in your field. If time permits, interview a manager in the company to gather specific information for your report. Write a report that provides information on the company and assesses its employment and future prospects. Develop a conclusion based on the facts you collect and include at least one recommendation.

6. RECOMMENDATION REPORT ON SOFTWARE FOR THE OFFICE

Assume you work for a small manufacturing firm which has an office staff of three. Your supervisor has asked you to recommend some new accounting software for the company to purchase. "It has to be easy to use," she said. "None of us is really what you would call a techie," she warned. Choose two types of office software that do the same kind of job—for example, ACPAC and Simply Accounting. Read reviews of the software and identify which one you would recommend to your boss.

YOUR TASK Write a short report describing the options and recommending one product to your boss. Decide what type of format would best suit your audience and subject.

7. QUESTIONNAIRE DESIGN FOR CUSTOMER FEEDBACK

Assume you have a job with the catering firm that runs your campus food services. The regional manager of the company is interested in getting feedback from students about the service. He is interested in the customer perceptions about the quality of the food, the hours of operation, the variety in the menu, the customer service skills of the staff, and the pricing of the items.

YOUR TASK Design a questionnaire that can be used to gather customer opinions. Print a copy of it to submit to your instructor.

8. REPORT ON CUSTOMER OPINIONS

Use the questionnaire that you designed in #7 above and work with four other students to gather opinions of at least 25 people who use the campus cafeteria. Meet as a team to summarize the opinions of the surveyed customers. What can you conclude about the customer opinions?

YOUR TASK Write a short report in memo format to the firm's regional manager describing the source of the information, the main findings, and your team's conclusions.

Include a couple of recommendations based on your survey findings. Include at least one graphic in your report. Your professor will tell you whether to write one report from the team or whether you should submit individual reports based on your team's findings.

9. REPORT ON AREA RECYCLING PRACTICES AND OPPORTUNITIES

Assume you have landed an administrative job at your college. You are thrilled that some of the many ideas you had to improve the place can actually be part of your job now. One of your passions is recycling. You can't believe that some people still are not very sensitive to the need to recycle. You have noticed a number of areas on campus where recycling needs to be improved. Your supervisor was mildly interested when you brought the subject up, but she told you to describe the problem and the solution in a report. Pick an area of the campus where you have observed a lack of recycling and base your report on that area. Come up with your own ideas about how to improve recycling in this area. Consult sources on ways to motivate people to recycle or for examples on company successes in recycling.

YOUR TASK Write a short, informal report for your supervisor. Decide which format would be best suited to this situation and audience. Include a graphic to illustrate your solution.

10. UNSOLICITED PROPOSAL ON A TELEPHONE INTERVIEWING SYSTEM

How can a firm be thorough yet efficient when considering dozens of applicants for each position? One tool that may help is IntelliView, a 10-minute question-and-answer session conducted by touch-tone telephone. The company recruiter dials up the IntelliView computer and then leaves the room. The candidate punches in answers to roughly 100 questions about work attitudes and other issues. In a few minutes, the recruiter can call Pinkerton (the company offering the service) and find out the results. On the basis of what the IntelliView interview reveals, the recruiter can delve more deeply into certain areas and, ultimately, have more information on which to base the hiring decision.

YOUR TASK As assistant recruiter for Canadian Tire, you think that IntelliView might help your firm. Plan a brief memo to Paula Wolski, director of human resources, in which you will suggest a test of the IntelliView system. Your memo should tell your boss why you believe your firm should test the system before making a long-term commitment.[6]

11. DAY AND NIGHT: PROBLEM-SOLVING REPORT ON STOCKING A 24-HOUR CONVENIENCE STORE

When a store is open all day, every day, when's the best time to restock the shelves? That's the challenge at Store 24, a retail chain that never closes. As the assistant manager of a Store 24 branch that just opened near your campus, you want to set up a restocking schedule that won't conflict with prime shopping hours. Think about the number of customers you're likely to serve in the morning, afternoon, evening, and overnight hours. Consider, too, how many employees might be working during these four periods.

YOUR TASK Plan a problem-solving report to be delivered in letter form. You'll be sending your report to the store manager (Isabel Chu) and the regional manager (Eric Angstrom), who must agree on a solution to this problem. Plan on discussing the pros and cons of each of the four periods, and include your recommendations for restocking the shelves.

12. PRACTISE DOCUMENTING RESEARCH USING APA STYLE

YOUR TASK Use Research Navigator in MyBusCommLab to find two articles about employee incentive programs. Write one paragraph summarizing the articles, and in the paragraph include a citation for a passage you have paraphrased and a citation for a direct quotation you have included. Use APA style to make the citations and to then write up the entries for the list of references. To review APA style, you can use Research Navigator or consult Appendix B, or look online at one of the following sites:

Diana Hacker's APA style guide: www.dianahacker.com/resdoc//p04_c09_o.html
Online! APA style guide: www.bedfordstmartins.com/online/cite6.html
American Psychological Association's APA style guide: http://apastyle.apa.org/

Come to class ready to discuss your experience of one of these resources. After the class discussion, decide which resource you would recommend to a company that wanted to provide a resource for employees.

13. PRACTISE SUMMARIZING: A BOOK REVIEW

Business associates are expected to be socially confident. In every office, those who are comfortable interacting with others and who know how to act in social situations gain more opportunities for advancement.

YOUR TASK Build your knowledge of polite interaction by exploring a book on the art of conversation—for example, *How to Win Friends and Influence People*, by Dale Carnegie. Practise your summarizing skills by selecting key points from two to three chapters of the book and putting the advice you find into your own words. Based on your reading of two or three chapters, would you recommend the book to classmates?[7]

Write your summary in three short paragraphs. Then write a shorter summary (140 characters or less) that you could post on Twitter.

Give your recommendation in a short oral report to your class.

The internet helps businesses make closer connections with other organizations and customers all over the planet. They use the internet to

- Share text, photos, slides, videos, and other data within the organization
- Permit employees to *telecommute,* or work away from a conventional office, whether at home, on the road, or across the country
- Participate in meetings through webcasting and virtual world technology
- Recruit employees cost-effectively
- Locate information from external sources
- Find new business partners and attract new customers
- Locate and buy parts and materials from domestic and international suppliers
- Promote and sell goods and services to customers in any location
- Provide customers with service, technical support, and product information
- Collaborate with local, national, and international business partners
- Inform investors, industry analysts, and government regulators about business developments

In addition, companies can set up special employee-only websites using an *intranet,* a private internal corporate network. Intranets use the same technology as the internet but restrict the information and access to members of the organization (regardless of a member's actual location). Once a company has an intranet, it can add an *extranet* that allows people to communicate and exchange data within a secure network of qualified people outside the organization—such as suppliers, contractors, and customers who use a password to access the system.

ONLINE REPORTING

Thanks to the internet, more and more companies are using online reports to keep employees, managers, investors, and other stakeholders informed. For example, companies with many branches and operations can have staff enter data into the computer system by following report formats on the screen. These reports are sent electronically to headquarters where corporate managers can track sales, adjust resources, and resolve potential problems much more quickly than if they had to wait for printed reports.

Well-known package-shipper FedEx lets customers access electronic reports to monitor the status of their shipments at any time. This reporting system not only helps FedEx serve its customers better but also puts valuable information in the hands of customers. And like many companies, FedEx posts its annual report and other corporate informational reports on its website for interested customers and investors.

Applications for Success

Answer the following questions:

1. **Ethical Choice** Do you think companies should monitor their employees' use of the internet and email? Explain your answer.
2. What kinds of electronic reports might a company want to post on its website?
3. What advantages and disadvantages do you see in asking managers to go beyond their informational operations reports and start filing electronic problem-solving reports on the company's intranet?

Writing and Completing Business Reports and Proposals

LEARNING OBJECTIVES

After studying this chapter, you will be able to

1. Discuss what decisions you must make when organizing a business report or proposal
2. Describe the structure of informational reports
3. Describe the structure of analytical reports and proposals
4. List several popular types of graphics and discuss when to use them
5. Name five characteristics of effective report content
6. Explain three tools that writers can use in long reports to help readers stay on track
7. Identify the prefatory parts of a formal report
8. Explain the purpose of an executive summary
9. Name the three supplemental parts of a formal report

TIPS FOR SUCCESS

"A good proposal reflects whether the writer has a clear idea of the project being proposed: why it is needed, why it is important, and how it will benefit the community."

—Sidney Sawyer
Manager,
Community Programs
VanCity Community Foundation

The VanCity Community Foundation in Vancouver provides grants and lending advice to non-profit organizations proposing initiatives to improve communities through community economic development. Sidney Sawyer is part of a team that assesses these proposals, evaluating many of them each year. "Proposal writers," says Sawyer, "create positive impressions by providing clear answers, using plain language, and providing facts to support the proposal." Proposals should be concise but contain enough detail to convince the audience that the idea is valuable, practical, and desirable. Proposals must contain a compelling argument—the key to a successful report.[1]

Step 2: Writing Business Reports and Proposals

Once you've planned out your document (see Chapters 3 and 10), you're ready to begin Step 2, writing business reports and proposals. Since so much of Step 2 is discussed in Chapter 4, the following sections cover only those aspects of writing that differ for reports and proposals. Think carefully about all the relevant tasks as you organize and compose your reports and proposals.

Organizing Reports and Proposals

Before you can compose a business report or proposal, you must organize the material you've collected, arranging it in a logical order that meets your audience's needs. You must carefully choose the format, length, order, and structure for your document.

DECIDING ON FORMAT AND LENGTH When you select the format for your report, you have four options:

- **Preprinted form.** Used for fill-in-the-blank reports. Most are relatively short (five or fewer pages) and deal with routine information, often mainly numerical.
- **Letter.** Commonly used for reports of five or fewer pages that are directed to outsiders. These reports include all the normal parts of a letter, and they may also have headings, footnotes, tables, and figures.

You may present a report in one of four formats: preprinted form, letter, memo, or manuscript.

- **Memo.** Commonly used for short (fewer than 10 pages), informal reports distributed within an organization. Like longer reports, they often have internal headings and sometimes include visual aids.
- **Manuscript.** Commonly used for reports that require a semi-formal or formal approach, whether a few pages or several hundred. A short, semi-formal manuscript report (five pages or fewer) may include only a few formal elements such as a title at the top of the first page and a brief covering email or memo to transmit the document to its receiver. It includes headings and uses graphics but does not include the many parts of a longer and more formal manuscript report such as a table of contents, list of illustrations, and so on. As length increases, formal reports require more elements both before the body text (prefatory parts) and after it (supplementary parts). The second half of this chapter explains these elements in more detail.

> Length depends on
> - Your subject
> - Your purpose
> - Your relationship with your audience

 Activities

> The direct approach saves time and makes the report easier to understand by giving readers the main idea first.

> The indirect approach is not effective for long reports.

> Business people often combine the direct and the indirect approach.

> The nature of the subject dictates the best way to structure the report.

The length of your report often depends on your subject, your purpose, and your relationship with your audience. When your readers are relative strangers, sceptical, or hostile, or if your material is nonroutine or controversial, you usually have to explain your points in greater detail, which results in a longer document. However, you can afford to be brief if you're on familiar terms with your readers, if they are likely to agree with you, and if the information is routine or uncomplicated.

CHOOSING THE DIRECT OR INDIRECT APPROACH The direct approach is by far the most popular and convenient order for business reports, saving time and making the report easier to follow. It also produces a more forceful report, because stating your conclusions confidently in the beginning makes you sound sure of yourself. However, if your readers have reservations about either you or your material, making strong statements at the beginning may intensify reader resistance. Also, confidence may sometimes be misconstrued as arrogance. So choose the direct approach for reports only when your credibility is high—when your readers trust you and are willing to accept your conclusions.

If your audience is sceptical or hostile, you may want to use the indirect approach, introducing your complete findings and discussing all supporting details before presenting your conclusions and recommendations. The indirect approach gives you a chance to prove your points and gradually overcome your audience's reservations. Even so, some readers will immediately flip back to the recommendations, thus defeating your purpose. The longer the message, the less effective an indirect approach is likely to be. Also, an indirect argument is harder to follow than a direct one.

Both direct and indirect approaches have merit, so business people often combine them, revealing their conclusions and recommendations as they go along, rather than treating them first or last. Figure 11.1 presents the introductions from two reports with the same general outline. In the direct version, a series of statements summarize the conclusion reached about each main topic on the outline. In the indirect version, the same topics are introduced in the same order but without any conclusions about them. Instead, the conclusions appear after evidence given in the report body.

Regardless of the format, length, or order you use, you must still decide how your ideas will be developed. Choose a logical structure that suits your topic and goals and makes the most sense to your audience.

STRUCTURING INFORMATIONAL REPORTS Informational reports provide nothing more than facts. Most readers will respond unemotionally, so you can use the direct approach. However, you need to present the facts logically and accurately so that readers will understand exactly what you mean and be able to use your information easily. For example, when describing a machine, make report headings correspond to each component. Or when describing an event, discuss it chronologically. Let the nature of your subject

FIGURE 11.1 Direct Approach Versus Indirect Approach in an Introduction

THE DIRECT APPROACH

Since the company's founding 25 years ago, we have provided regular repair service for all our electric appliances. This service has been an important selling point as well as a source of pride for our employees. However, we are paying a high price for our image. Last year, we lost $500 000 on our repair business.

Because of your concern over these losses, you have asked me to study the pros and cons of discontinuing our repair service. With the help of John Hudson and Susan Lefkowitz, I have studied the issue for the past two weeks and have come to the conclusion that we have been embracing an expensive, impractical tradition.

By withdrawing from the electric appliance repair business, we can substantially improve our financial performance without damaging our reputation with customers. This conclusion is based on three basic points that are covered in the following pages:

- It is highly unlikely that we will ever be able to make a profit in the repair business.
- Service is no longer an important selling point with customers.
- Closing down the service operation will create few internal problems.

THE INDIRECT APPROACH

Since the company's founding 25 years ago, we have provided repair service for all our electric appliances. This service has been an important selling point as well as a source of pride for our employees. However, the repair business itself has consistently lost money.

Because of your concern over these losses, you have asked me to study the pros and cons of discontinuing our repair service. With the help of John Hudson and Susan Lefkowitz, I have studied the issue for the past two weeks. The following pages present my findings for your review. Three basic questions are addressed:

- What is the extent of our losses, and what can we do to turn the business around?
- Would withdrawal hurt our sales of electric appliances?
- What would be the internal repercussions of closing down the repair business?

---

dictate the structure of your informational reports. Use a topical organization, arranging material according to one of the following:

- **Importance.** If you're reviewing five product lines, you might organize your report according to product sales, from highest to lowest.
- **Sequence.** If you're studying a process, discuss it step by step—1, 2, 3, and so on.
- **Chronology.** When investigating a chain of events, organize the study according to what happened in January, what happened in February, and so on.
- **Spatial orientation.** If you're explaining how a physical object works, describe it left to right (or right to left in some cultures), top to bottom, outside to inside.
- **Geography.** If location is important, organize your study according to geography, perhaps by region of Canada or by area of a city.
- **Category.** If you're asked to review several distinct aspects of a subject, discuss one category at a time, such as cost, profit, sales, or investment.

Some informational reports (especially compliance reports and internal reports) are prepared on preprinted forms, so they are organized according to the instructions supplied by the person requesting the information.

STRUCTURING ANALYTICAL REPORTS For analytical reports, your choice of structure depends on the reaction you anticipate. When you expect your audience to agree with you, choose a structure that focuses attention on conclusions and recommendations. When you expect your audience to disagree with you or to be hostile, choose a structure that focuses attention on the reasons behind your conclusions and

> Topical organization is arranging material in order of importance, sequence, chronology, spatial relationships, location, or categories.

> The structure of analytical reports depends on audience reaction and whether you focus on
> - Conclusions and recommendations
> - Logical arguments

 Document Makeovers

recommendations. Thus, the two most common approaches to structuring analytical reports are as follows:

- **Direct: Focusing on conclusions and recommendations.** When people are likely to accept your findings, structure your report around conclusions, using a direct approach. Readers interested mainly in your conclusions can grasp them quickly, and those wanting more detail can examine your analysis and data. When asked to solve a problem, structure your report around recommendations, using a direct approach:
  1. Establish a need for action in the introduction (briefly describing the problem or opportunity).
  2. Describe your solution to the problem (your conclusion) in general terms, and then list the actions required using action verbs for emphasis (your recommendations).
  3. Introduce the benefits that can result (using action verbs for emphasis).
  4. Explain each step more fully (giving details of procedures, costs, and benefits).
  5. Summarize your recommendations.

- **Indirect: Focusing on logical arguments.** When encouraging readers to weigh all the facts before presenting your conclusions or recommendations, use the indirect approach and arrange your ideas around the reasoning behind your report's conclusions and recommendations. Organize your material to reflect the thinking process that will lead readers to your conclusions.

Solicited proposals are best organized by using the client's criteria as the main points.

STRUCTURING BUSINESS PROPOSALS Just as with reports, choosing a structural approach for proposals depends on whether you expect your audience to be receptive. In general, your audience may be more receptive to solicited proposals, since the problem and the solution have already been identified. The writer structures the proposal as specified in the RFP (request for proposal), using a direct approach and focusing on recommendations.

The indirect approach may be a better choice for unsolicited proposals depending on how much you must convince your audience that a problem exists, and how much you must establish your credibility if you are unknown to the reader. Unfold your solution to the problem by focusing on logical argument, trying to persuade readers to accept your idea and award you a contract, and spelling out the terms of your proposal.

Document **Design**

Organizing Visual Aids

Use visuals to simplify, clarify, and emphasize important information.

When preparing reports, you'll often include visuals or graphics, to convey and emphasize important points. Carefully prepared visuals can help your audience understand your message and make your report more interesting. Even so, don't overdo the number of graphics. Use visuals selectively to support your primary message—to supplement your words, not to replace them.

Some information is clearest in words; other information is clearest as a graphic. For instance, detailed facts and figures may be confusing and tedious in paragraph form, but tables and charts organize and display such detail concisely and conveniently. Information that requires detailed description of physical relationships or procedures is clearest in a flow chart. Or you can simply draw attention to or emphasize a particular fact or detail by reinforcing that information visually.

Be sure to maintain a balance between your visuals and your words. The ideal blend depends on the nature of your subject. But illustrating every point dilutes the effectiveness of visuals. Plus, readers usually assume that the amount of space allocated to a topic indicates its relative importance. So by using visuals to illustrate a minor point, you may be sending a misleading message about its significance.

CHOOSING THE RIGHT VISUAL FOR THE JOB Once you decide which points to illustrate visually, select the type of graphic that will present your data most clearly and effectively

TABLE 11.1	Choosing the Right Illustration for the Job

WHEN YOUR PURPOSE IS TO	CHOOSE A
Present a large amount of data so that the reader can analyze the data in detail	Table
Compare up to five variables	Bar graph
Show trends/changes over time	Line graph
Show percentages of a whole	Pie chart
Show relationships	Organization charts or flow charts
Show parts, interrelationships, and features	Illustrations and diagrams

to your audience. Some types of visuals depict certain kinds of data better than others. Your choice depends on the nature of the message and on the type of data you are presenting. Use Table 11.1 to select the right illustration.

Tables To present detailed, specific information, choose a **table**, a systematic arrangement of data in columns and rows, with useful headings along the top and side. When preparing tables, be sure to

- Use common, understandable units, and clearly identify them: dollars, percentages, price per tonne, and so on
- Express all items in a column in the same unit, and round off for simplicity
- Label column headings clearly, and use a subhead if necessary
- Separate columns or rows with lines or extra space to make the table easy to follow
- Document the source of data using the same format as an endnote (see Appendix B)

> Use tables to help your audience understand detailed information.

Bar Charts A **bar chart** portrays numbers by the height or length of its rectangular bars, making a series of numbers easy to read or understand. Bar charts are particularly valuable when you want to

- Compare the size of several items at one time
- Show changes in one item over time
- Indicate the composition of several items over time
- Show the relative size of components of a whole

> Bar charts, in which numbers are visually portrayed by rectangular bars, can take a variety of forms.

As Figure 11.2 (on page 242) shows, bar charts allow readers to compare data. Bar charts work best when you want to dramatize a major point with only a few variables. For example, Figure 11.2 shows the change in Canadian immigration patterns.

You can be creative with bar charts in many ways. For instance, you can align the bars either vertically or horizontally (see Figures 11.2 and 11.3 on page 242).

Line Graphs Line graphs can show more complex relationships than bar graphs. A **line graph** illustrates trends over time or plots the relationship of two variables. In line graphs showing trends, the vertical, or y, axis shows the amount, and the horizontal, or x, axis shows the time or the quantity being measured. Plot lines on the same graph for comparative purposes, as shown in Figure 11.4 (on page 243). Try to use no more than three lines on any given graph, particularly if the lines cross. Ordinarily, both scales begin at zero and proceed in equal increments; however, the vertical axis can be broken to show that some of the increments have been left out. A broken axis is appropriate when the data are plotted far above zero, but be sure to clearly indicate the omission of data points.

> Use line charts
> - To indicate changes over time
> - To plot the relationship of two variables

Pie Charts Pie charts show how parts of a whole are distributed and are restricted to showing relationships at one point in time. Each segment represents a slice of a complete

> Use pie charts to show the relative sizes of the parts of a whole.

| FIGURE 11.2 | Bar Chart: Growth of Visible Minorities in Major Canadian Cities, 1981–2001 |

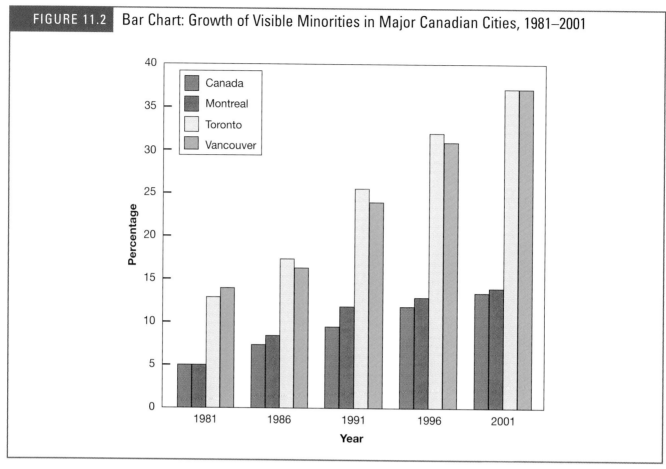

Source: Adapted from Statistics Canada, "Canadian Internet Use Survey," *The Daily*, Catalogue no. 11-001, June 12, 2008. http://dissemination.statcan.ca/Dailly/English/080612/d080812b.htm

| FIGURE 11.3 | Bar Chart: How Much Online North American Consumers Trust Sources of Information About Products or Services |

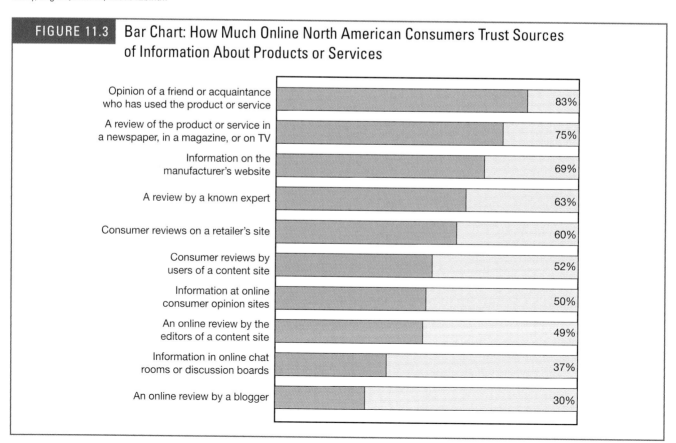

Source: Charlene Li and Josh Bernoff, *Groundswell* (Boston: Harvard Business Press, 2008), 22. Used with permission of Harvard Business Publishing.

| FIGURE 11.4 | Line Graph: Trends in Canadian Immigration from Europe and Asia |

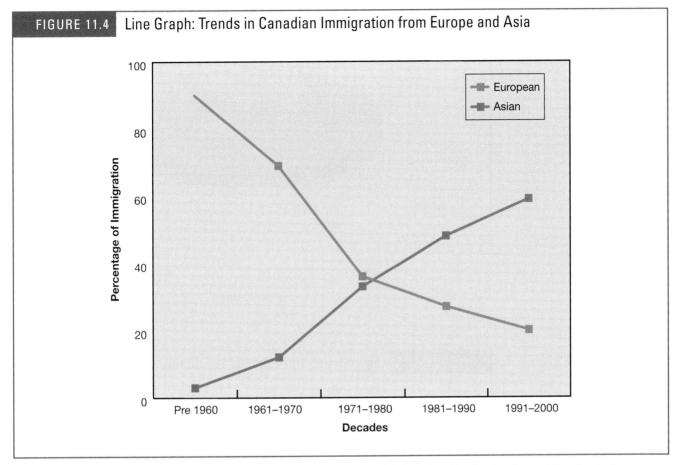

Source: Adapted from Statistics Canada, "Proportion of immigrants born in Europe and Asia by period of immigration, Canada," *Canada e-Book*, Catalogue no. 11-404, May 2003. http://www43.statcan.ca/02/02a/02a_graph/02a_graph-005_1e.htm

circle, or *pie*. As you can see in Figure 11.5 (on page 244), pie charts are an effective way to show percentages or to compare one segment with another. You can combine pie charts with tables to expand the usefulness of such visuals.

When composing pie charts, restrict the number of slices in the pie. Otherwise, the chart looks cluttered and is difficult to label. If necessary, lump the smallest pieces together in a "miscellaneous" category. Ideally, the largest or most important slice of the pie is placed at the twelve o'clock position; the rest are arranged clockwise either in order of size or in some other logical progression. Use different colours or patterns to distinguish the various pieces. To emphasize one piece, you can explode it or pull it away from the rest of the pie. Label all segments, and indicate their value either in percentages or in units of measure. Remember, the segments must add up to 100 percent if percentages are used or to the total number if numbers are used.

Flow Charts If you need to show physical or conceptual relationships rather than numerical ones, you might want to use a flow chart, illustrating a sequence of events from start to finish. Flow charts are indispensable when illustrating processes, procedures, and sequential relationships such as the workflow in a major project. The various elements in the process you want to portray may be represented by pictorial symbols or geometric shapes, as shown in Figure 11.6 (on page 244).

Organization Charts As the name implies, an organization chart illustrates the positions, units, or functions of an organization and the way they interrelate. An organization's normal communication channels are almost impossible to describe without the benefit of a chart like the one in Figure 11.7 (on page 245).

Use flow charts
- To show a series of steps from beginning to end
- To show sequential relationships

Use organization charts to depict the interrelationships among the parts of an organization.

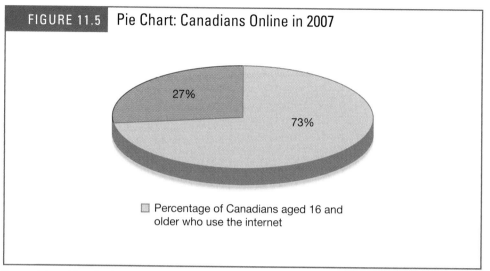

FIGURE 11.5 | Pie Chart: Canadians Online in 2007

27%

73%

☐ Percentage of Canadians aged 16 and
older who use the internet

Source: Adapted from Statistics Canada, "Canadian Internet Use Survey," *The Daily*, Catalogue no. 11-001, June 12, 2008. http://dissemination.statcan.ca/Daily/English/080612/d080812b.htm

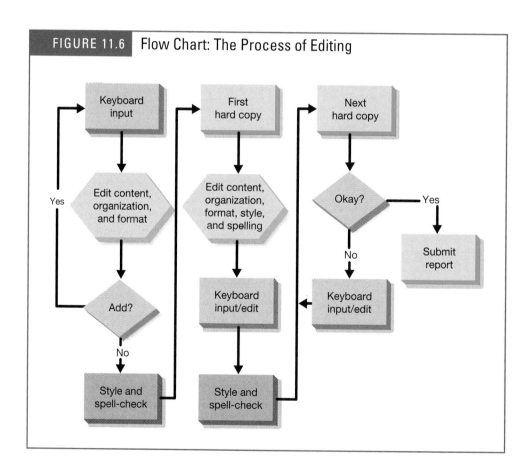

FIGURE 11.6 | Flow Chart: The Process of Editing

Computer-graphics systems cut the time and cost involved in producing visuals.

CREATING VISUALS WITH COMPUTERS Professional-looking graphics used to be extremely expensive and time-consuming to produce, but computer technology now allows business people to turn out professional-looking visuals. Using computer graphics gives you several advantages, including speed, accuracy, and ease of use. You can create freehand drawings, manipulate existing images, and display numbers in graphic form using software programs such as CorelDraw!, PowerPoint, Photoshop, Painter, Excel, and Visio—to name just a few.

FIGURE 11.7   Organization Chart: Administration and Faculty of Atlantic College

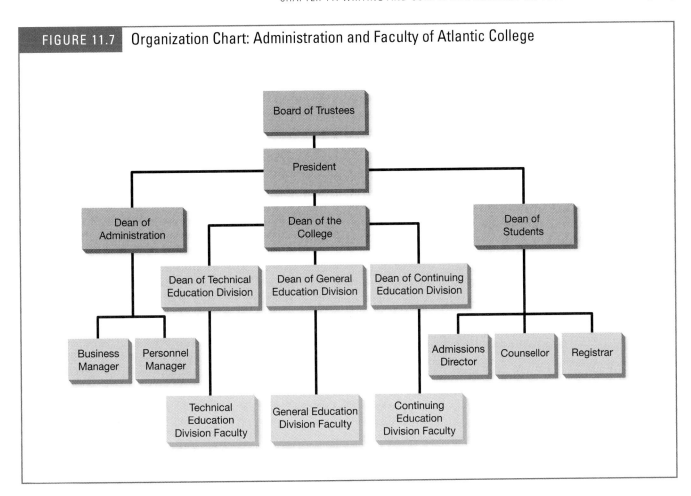

The style of your visuals communicates a subtle message about your relationship with your audience. The image you want to project should determine the visual you use.

INTEGRATING GRAPHICS WITH REPORT TEXT Graphics do not replace written explanations. Instead, they enhance and emphasize important aspects of the text of a report. Decisions about what to illustrate and which type of graphic to use should be based on your purpose and audience analysis. What needs to be emphasized? What concepts would be best shown in charts, photographs, or tables? Visual material complements the verbal content and to be effective, the visual material needs to be integrated.

When you insert a graphic into a report, be sure to properly integrate it by following three guidelines:

Guideline 1: Refer to the Graphic and Give It a Number, Title, and Labels Refer to the graphic in the text *before* it appears. Say what the graphic shows. For example, "Figure 12.2 compares the average number of power failures . . ." Another way to refer to the graphic is to include the reference in parentheses: "Since power failures have been frequent (Figure 12.2), we recommend an automatic data storage system to handle the surges discussed above (Table 12.4)."

Give each graphic a number and use separate numbering for tables and figures. In long documents divided into sections, identify the graphics by section numbers. For example, Figure 5.3 is the third figure in section 5.

Include a specific title for each graphic and consider having the title indicate what the reader should be noticing. The title sums up the key point of what is being shown.

How descriptive should your titles be? For example, will "Downturn in December Sales" suffice, or should you use the more specific "33 Percent Reduction in December Sales"? Base your decision about how descriptive your titles should be on whether your audience is receptive enough for you to be direct. Lastly, always use phrases instead of sentences so that your titles are easy to scan.

Also use clear, horizontal labelling to make the parts of the graphic easy to understand. Avoid a cluttered appearance, and use a legend if too many labels are needed. Be careful not to make the interpretation of the graphic too much work for the reader. Simplify the number of elements to make the material easy to understand.

Guideline 2: Place the Graphic Where It Is Needed Place the graphic as close as possible to where it is discussed. Allow a separate page for graphics larger than one half of a page. Graphics one half a page or smaller can be incorporated in the same page as the text. Place the graphic as close after the reference as possible.

Guideline 3: Explain the Graphic Sometimes a graphic is self-explanatory, but often your reader will benefit from a quick walk-through of its significant parts.

Some readers approach report content through a quick scan of the visual material, so making the graphics self-explanatory is helpful for these visual processors.

Composing Reports and Proposals

> A final outline is a work in progress.

Effective writers begin composing their first draft by preparing a final outline. In addition to guiding your writing effort, a final outline forces you to re-evaluate the information and visuals you've selected and the order in which you present them. Preparing a final outline also gives you a chance to rephrase your outline points to set the tone of your report.

Once you have a final outline, you are ready to write the report. Additional tasks include drafting the content, using a proper degree of formality, maintaining a consistent time perspective, and providing clues to help readers navigate your document.

> The most successful reports have certain characteristics.

DEVELOPING THE CONTENT As with other written business communications, the text of a report or proposal has three major sections: an introduction, a body, and a close. The content and length of each section varies with the type and purpose of the document, the document's organizational structure, the length and depth of the material, the degree of document formality, and the writer's relationship with the audience.

Successful report content is

- **Accurate.** In addition to checking for typos, double-check your facts and references.
- **Complete.** Include all the necessary information—no more, no less.
- **Balanced.** Present all sides of the issue fairly and equitably.
- **Structured clearly and logically.** Write uncluttered sentences and paragraphs that organize your ideas and proceed logically with clear, helpful transitions.[2]
- **Documented properly.** Give proper credit to your sources, as explained in Appendix B.

> For the most successful proposals, use the AIDA plan and follow some important guidelines.

Guidelines for Proposals Proposals persuade readers to do something (purchase goods or services, fund a project, implement a program). Thus, writing a proposal is similar to writing persuasive sales messages (see Chapter 9). Use the AIDA plan to gain attention, build interest, create desire, and motivate action. In your proposal[3]

- **Demonstrate your knowledge.** Show readers that you have the knowledge and experience to solve the problem. Provide enough information to win the job without giving away all your ideas so that your services aren't needed.

- **Provide concrete examples.** Avoid vague, unsupported generalizations such as "we are losing money on this program." Instead, include the math. Provide quantifiable details such as the amount of money being lost, how, why, and so on. Explain *how much* money your proposed solution will save. Spell out your plan, and give details on how the job will be done.
- **Research the competition.** Use trade publications and the internet to become familiar with your competitors' product lines, services, and prices. This strategy is especially important if you are competing against others for a job.
- **Prove that your proposal is workable.** Your proposal must be feasible for the audience. For instance, it would be foolish to recommend a solution that doubles the budget or requires three times the number of current employees.
- **Adopt a "you" attitude.** Relate your product, service, or personnel to the reader's exact needs, either as stated in the RFP for a solicited proposal or as discovered through your own investigation for an unsolicited proposal.
- **Package your proposal attractively.** Make sure your proposal is letter-perfect, inviting, and readable. Readers will judge the type of work you perform by your submitted proposal. If it contains errors, omissions, or inconsistencies, they will likely withhold approval.

Drafting the Introduction In the *introduction,* prepare your readers for the information that follows. Invite them to continue reading by telling them what the report is about, why the audience should be concerned, and how the report is organized. Your introduction should accomplish four tasks:

> Your introduction must prepare your audience for information that follows.

- Say why the report or proposal was written and what it proposes to solve.
- Introduce the report's subject (purpose) and indicate why that subject is important.
- Preview the main ideas and the order in which they'll be covered.
- Establish the tone of the document and your relationship with the audience.

In proposals, use the introduction to present the problem you want to solve and to summarize your solution. Orient readers to the remainder of the text. In a solicited proposal, refer to the RFP in your introduction; in an unsolicited one, use the introduction to mention any factors that led you to submit your proposal.

Drafting the Body In the *body* of your reports and proposals, include the major divisions or chapters that present, analyze, and interpret the information you gathered during your investigation. Give complete details of your proposed solution and specify what results you anticipate. The body contains the "proof," the detailed information necessary to support your conclusions and recommendations.

> The body contains the substance of your report or proposal.

Drafting the Close The *close* is the final section of the text in your report or proposal. Leave a strong and lasting impression. This is your last chance to make sure that your report says what you intended.[4] In proposals, the close is your last opportunity to persuade readers to accept your suggestions. In both formal and informal proposals, be brief, assertive, and confident. Your close should accomplish four goals:

> The close re-emphasizes your main ideas.

- Emphasize the main points of the message.
- Summarize reader benefits (if some change or other course of action is suggested).
- Refer back to all the pieces of the document and remind readers how those pieces fit together.
- Bring all the action items together in one place and give details about who should do what, when, where, and how.

For examples of some of the topics you might include in the introduction, body, and close of reports and proposals, see Table 11.2 (on page 248).

TABLE 11.2	Report and Proposal Contents

REPORT CONTENTS

Introduction
- **Authorization.** Review who authorized the report (when, how), who wrote it, and when it was submitted.
- **Problem/purpose.** Explain the reason for the report's existence and what the report will achieve.
- **Scope.** Describe what will and won't be covered in the report—indicating size and complexity.
- **Background.** Review historical conditions or factors that led up to the report.
- **Sources and methods.** Discuss the primary and secondary sources consulted and methods used.
- **Definitions.** List terms and their definitions—including any terms that might be misinterpreted. Terms may also be defined in the body, explanatory notes, or glossary.
- **Limitations.** Discuss factors beyond your control that affect report quality—not an excuse for a poor study or bad report.
- **Report organization.** Tell what topics are covered in what order.

Body—Main Sections
- **Explanations.** Give complete details of the problem, project, or idea.
- **Facts, statistical evidence, and trends.** Lay out the results of studies or investigations.
- **Analysis of action.** Discuss potential courses of action.
- **Pros and cons.** Explain advantages, disadvantages, costs, and benefits of a particular course of action.
- **Procedures.** Outline steps for a process.
- **Methods and approaches.** Discuss how you've studied a problem (or gathered evidence) and arrived at your solution (or collected your data).
- **Criteria.** Describe the benchmarks for evaluating options and alternatives.
- **Conclusions and recommendations.** Discuss what you believe the evidence reveals and what you propose should be done about it.
- **Support.** Give the reasons behind your conclusions or recommendations.

Close
- **For direct order.** Summarize key points (except in short memos), listing them in the order they appear in the body. Briefly restate your conclusions or recommendations, if appropriate.
- **For indirect order.** You may use the close to present your conclusions or recommendations for the first time—just be sure not to present any new facts.
- **For motivating action.** Spell out exactly what should happen next and provide a schedule with specific task assignments.

PROPOSAL CONTENTS

Introduction
- **Background or statement of the problem.** Briefly review the reader's situation, establish a need for action, and explain how things could be better. In unsolicited proposals, convince readers that a problem or opportunity exists.
- **Summary of proposed solution.** Briefly describe the change you propose, highlighting your key selling points and their benefits to show how your proposal will solve the reader's problem.
- **Scope.** State the boundaries of the proposal—what you will and will not do.
- **Report organization.** Orient the reader to the remainder of the proposal and call attention to the major divisions of thought.

Body—Main Sections
- **Proposed approach.** Describe your concept, product, or service.
- **Facts and evidence to support your conclusions.** Give complete details of the proposed solution and the anticipated results.
- **Benefits.** Stress reader benefits and emphasize any advantages you have over your competitors.
- **Work plan.** Describe how you'll accomplish what must be done (unless you're providing a standard, off-the-shelf item). Explain the steps you'll take, their timing, the methods or resources you'll use, and the person(s) responsible. State when work will begin, how it will be divided into stages, when you'll finish, and whether follow-up will be needed.
- **Statement of qualifications.** Describe your organization's experience, personnel, and facilities—relating it all to the reader's needs. Include a list of client references.
- **Costs.** Prove that your costs are realistic—break them down so that readers can see the cost of labour, materials, transportation, travel, training, and other categories.

Close
- **Review of argument.** Briefly summarize the key points.
- **Review of reader benefits.** Briefly summarize how your proposal will help the reader.
- **Review of the merits of your approach.** Briefly summarize why your approach will be more effective than that of competitors.
- **Restatement of qualifications.** Briefly re-emphasize why you and your firm should do the work.
- **Request.** Ask for a decision from the reader. Ask for authorization to proceed with your solution.

CHOOSING THE PROPER DEGREE OF FORMALITY If you know your readers reasonably well and if your report is likely to meet with their approval, you can generally adopt a fairly informal tone. You can speak to readers in the first person, referring to yourself as *I* and to your readers as *you*. This personal approach is often used in brief memo or letter reports, although there are many exceptions.

Use a more formal tone for longer reports, especially those dealing with controversial or complex information, and for reports that will be sent to other parts of the organization or to customers or suppliers. Also, communicating with people in other cultures often calls for more formality. Use an impersonal style, and avoid references to *you* and *I* (including *we, us,* and *our*). However, make sure that avoiding personal pronouns doesn't lead to overuse of phrases such as *there is* and *it is,* which are both dull and wordy. Also, be careful not to slip into passive voice more than necessary.

ESTABLISHING A CONSISTENT TIME PERSPECTIVE By switching from tense to tense throughout your report, you confuse readers. Use tense consistently.

Also be careful to observe the chronological sequence of events in your report. If you're describing the history or development of something, start at the beginning and cover each event in the order of its occurrence. If you're explaining the steps in a process, take each step in proper sequence.

HELPING READERS FIND THEIR WAY Readers have no concept of how the various pieces of your report relate to one another. Although you can see how each page fits into the overall structure, readers see your report one page at a time. So give them a preview or road map of your report's structure, and clarify how the various parts are related. Give them a sense of the overall structure of your document by using three tools:

- **Headings.** These brief titles cue readers about the content of a section. They improve readability (see Chapter 6) and clarify a report's framework. *Subheadings* (lower-level headings) help show which ideas are more important. Many companies specify a format for headings; if yours does, use it. Otherwise, use the scheme shown in Figure 11.8 (on page 250) or any other scheme that clearly shows the hierarchy.
- **Transitions.** These words or phrases tie ideas together and show how one thought is related to another. Whether words, sentences, or complete paragraphs, use transitions to help readers move from one section of a report to the next. When writing transitions, be sure to list coming topics in the order they are discussed.
- **Previews and reviews.** *Preview sections* introduce an important topic, helping readers get ready for new information. *Review sections* come after a body of material and summarize the information for readers, helping them absorb details while keeping track of the big picture.

> For informal reports, adopt a personal style, using the pronouns *I* and *you*.

> Being formal means putting your readers at a distance and establishing an objective, businesslike relationship.

> Be consistent in the verb tense you use, and follow a chronological sequence.

> Readers can lose their way unless you give them signposts telling them where they are and where they're going.

Step 3: Completing Business Reports and Proposals

 Activities

The process of writing a report or proposal doesn't end with a first draft. As Chapter 5 points out, once you have finished your first draft, you perform three tasks to complete your document: revise, produce, and proofread. Make sure you've scheduled enough time for production. Corrupted disk files, printing problems, and other glitches can consume hours. If you're preparing a long, formal report, you'll need extra time to prepare and assemble all the various components.

> Producing documents requires some special considerations when working with reports.

Components of a Formal Report

The parts included in a report depend on the type of report you are writing, the requirements of your audience, the organization you're working for, and the length of your

FIGURE 11.8   Heading Format for Reports

TITLE

The title is centred at the top of the page in all-capital letters, usually bold-faced, often in a large font (for example, 14 point), and often using a sans serif typeface. When the title runs to more than one line, the lines are usually arranged as an inverted pyramid (longer line on the top).

FIRST-LEVEL HEADING

A first-level heading indicates what the following section is about, perhaps by describing the subdivisions. All first-level headings are grammatically parallel, with the possible exception of such headings as "Introduction," "Conclusions," and "Recommendations." Some text appears between every two headings, regardless of their levels. Still boldfaced and sans serif, the font may be smaller than that used in the title but larger than the typeface used in the text (for example, 12 point) and still in all-capital letters.

Second-Level Heading

Like first-level headings, second-level headings indicate what the following material is about. All second-level headings within a section are grammatically parallel. Still boldfaced and sans serif, the font may either remain the same or shrink to the size used in the text, and the style is now initial capitals with lower case. Never use only one second-level heading under a first-level heading. (The same is true for every other level of heading.)

Headings and subheadings show the content at a glance.

Third-Level Heading

A third-level heading is worded to reflect the content of the material that follows. All third-level headings beneath a second-level heading should be grammatically parallel.

Fourth-Level Heading. Like all the other levels of headings, fourth-level headings reflect the subject that will be developed. All fourth-level headings within a subsection are parallel.

Fifth-level headings are generally the lowest level of heading used. However, you can indicate further breakdowns in your ideas by using a list:

Headings allow readers to scan a report and choose which sections to read.

1. *The first item in a list.* You may indent the entire item in block format to set it off visually. Numbers are optional.
2. *The second item in a list.* All lists have at least two items. An introductory phrase or sentence may be italicized for emphasis, as shown here.

The three basic divisions of a formal report:
- Prefatory parts
- Text
- Supplementary parts

report. The components listed in Figure 11.9 fall into three categories, according to their location in a report: prefatory parts, text, and supplementary parts.

Most prefatory parts (such as the table of contents) should be placed on their own pages. However, the various parts in the report text are often run together and seldom stand alone. If your introduction is only a paragraph long, don't bother with a page break before moving into the body of your report. If the introduction runs longer than a page, however, a page break can signal the reader that a major shift is about to occur in the flow of the report.

For an illustration of how the various parts fit together in an actual report, see Figure 11.10 (on page 253). This 14-page report was prepared by Linda Moreno, manager of the cost accounting department at Electrovision, a high-tech company. Electrovision's main product is optical character recognition equipment, which is used for sorting mail. Moreno's job is to help analyze the company's travel and entertainment costs. Moreno used direct order and organized her report based on conclusions and recommendations.

FIGURE 11.9 Parts of a Formal Report

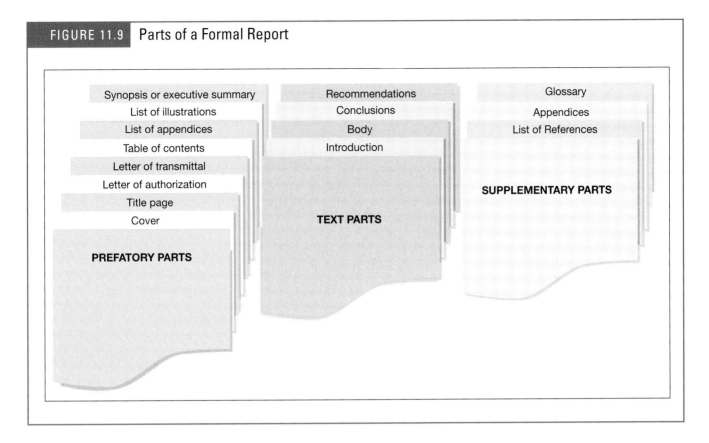

PREFATORY PARTS Prefatory parts are front-end materials that provide preliminary information so that readers can decide whether to and how to read the report.[5] Many of these parts—such as the table of contents, list of illustrations, and executive summary—are easier to prepare after the text has been completed, because they directly reflect the contents. Other parts can be prepared at almost any time.

> Prefatory parts come before the text but may be written after the text has been completed.

- **Cover.** Many companies have standard covers for reports. If your company doesn't provide them, you can find something suitable in a good stationery store. Report titles are often printed on these covers. Think carefully about the title you put on the cover. Give readers all the specific information they need (the who, what, when, where, why, and how of the subject), but be concise.
- **Title page.** The title page includes four blocks of information (see Moreno's Electrovision report): (1) the title of the report; (2) the name, title, and address of the person, group, or organization that authorized the report (usually the intended audience); (3) the name, title, and address of the person, group, or organization that prepared the report; and (4) the date on which the report was submitted.
- **Letter of authorization.** If you received written authorization to prepare the report, you may want to include that letter or memo in your report.
- **Letter of transmittal.** The letter of transmittal is often paper-clipped to the cover of the report or appears just after the title page. This routine document (which can also be a memo) begins with the main idea ("Here is the report you asked me to prepare on . . . "). The opening discusses scope, methods, and limitations. The middle can highlight important sections of the report, suggest follow-up studies, offer details to help readers use the report, and acknowledge help from others. The close can include a note of thanks for the assignment, an expression of willingness to discuss the report, and an offer to assist with future projects (see Figure 11.10 on page 254).
- **Table of contents.** The contents page lists report parts and text headings to indicate the location and relative importance of the information in the report. You may show only the top two or three levels of headings or only first-level headings. Word headings exactly as they are in the report text. List prefatory parts that come after the contents page and all supplementary parts (see Figure 11.10 on page 255).

- **List of illustrations.** The list of illustrations gives the titles and page numbers of visual aids. If you have enough space on a single page, include the list of illustrations under its heading directly beneath the table of contents. Otherwise, put the list on the page after the contents page. Tables and figures are numbered separately, so they should also be listed separately. The two lists can appear on the same page if they fit; otherwise, start each list on a separate page.
- **List of appendices.** Supplementary material or oversized documents may be appended to the main report. The list of appendices tells the contents of each appendix you have attached to the report. These items need a title and must be actually mentioned in the text of the report to appear in the appendices. At the back of the report, the appendices are put in the order of mention. For example, if you based your report on surveys or interviews, you might append the list of questions you used to show the scope of your inquiry. Appendices are usually given a letter (A, B, C) and the list would show the title of each and the page number where the items can be found. In very long reports with many appendices, each appendix may have separate page numbering.
- **Executive summary.** An executive summary is a fully developed "mini" version of the report, which may contain headings, transitions, and even visual aids. Executive summaries are for readers who lack the time or motivation to study the complete text. Keep the length of an executive summary to approximately 10 percent of the length of the report. Linda Moreno's Electrovision report provides one example of an executive summary.

Document Makeovers

Include a brief summary of any report you write to satisfy readers who may not have time to read the whole report.

Three main text parts of a report are
- Introduction
- Body
- Close

TEXT OF THE REPORT Although reports may contain a variety of components, the heart of a report is always the text, with its introduction, body, and conclusion. Moreno's executive summary contains key points from each section of the main report.

Linda Moreno's Electrovision report gives you a good idea of the types of supporting detail commonly included in the text body. Pay close attention to her effective use of visuals. Most inexperienced writers have a tendency to include too much data in their reports or to place too much data in paragraph format instead of using tables and charts. Include only the essential supporting data in the body, use relevant graphics and visuals, and place any additional information in an appendix.

In a long report, the closing section may be labelled "Conclusions and Recommendations." Since Moreno organized her report in a direct pattern, her closing is relatively brief. When using the indirect approach, you may use the close to present your conclusions and recommendations, which could make this section relatively extensive.

Supplementary parts present additional details and come after the text.

SUPPLEMENTARY PARTS Supplementary parts follow the text of the report and provide information for readers who seek more detailed discussion. Supplements are more common in long reports than in short ones. They typically include appendices, a bibliography, and an index.

- **Appendices.** An appendix contains additional information for those readers who want it—information related to the report but not included in the text because it is too lengthy, is too bulky, or lacks direct relevance. Appendices contain sample questionnaires and cover letters, sample forms, computer printouts, spreadsheets, and so on. Include each type of material in a separate appendix, mention all appendices in the text, and list them in the table of contents. Arrange them in the order of mention.
- **List of References or Bibliography.** The bibliography lists the secondary sources you consulted. In Moreno's report, she labelled her bibliography "References" because she listed only the works that were mentioned in the report, according to APA format. Moreno's Electrovision report uses the author-date system. An alternative is to use numbered endnotes (put at the end of the report). For more on citing sources, see Appendix B, "Documentation of Report Sources."

FIGURE 11.10 Linda Moreno's Formal Report

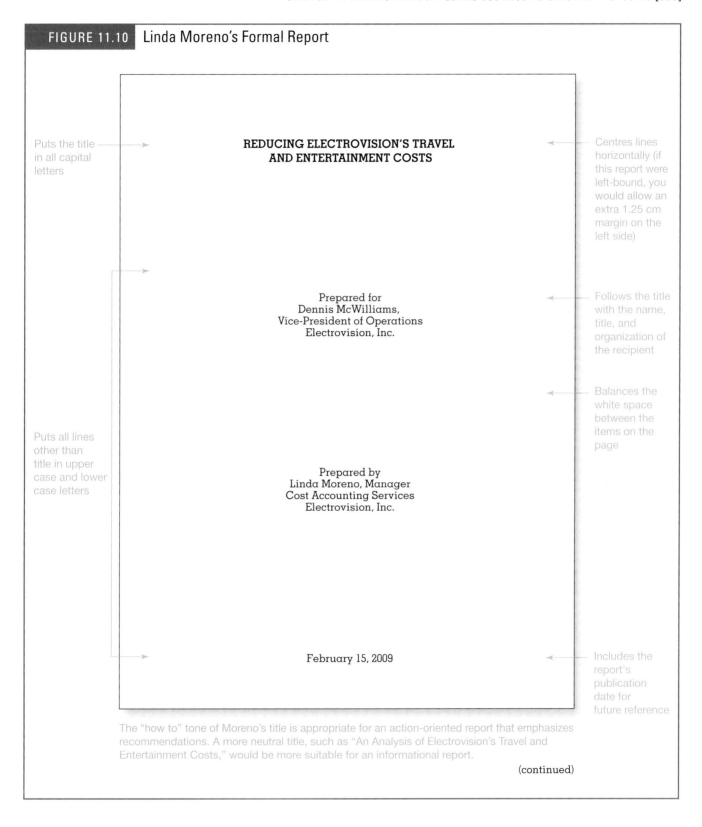

Puts the title in all capital letters

Puts all lines other than title in upper case and lower case letters

Centres lines horizontally (if this report were left-bound, you would allow an extra 1.25 cm margin on the left side)

Follows the title with the name, title, and organization of the recipient

Balances the white space between the items on the page

Includes the report's publication date for future reference

REDUCING ELECTROVISION'S TRAVEL AND ENTERTAINMENT COSTS

Prepared for
Dennis McWilliams,
Vice-President of Operations
Electrovision, Inc.

Prepared by
Linda Moreno, Manager
Cost Accounting Services
Electrovision, Inc.

February 15, 2009

The "how to" tone of Moreno's title is appropriate for an action-oriented report that emphasizes recommendations. A more neutral title, such as "An Analysis of Electrovision's Travel and Entertainment Costs," would be more suitable for an informational report.

(continued)

FIGURE 11.10 (Continued)

Uses memo format for transmitting this internal report; otherwise, letter format would be used for transmitting external reports

Presents the main conclusion right away (because Moreno expects a positive response)

Uses an informal, conversational style

Acknowledges help that has been received

Closes with thanks and an offer to discuss results (when appropriate, you could also include an offer to help with future projects)

MEMORANDUM

TO: Dennis McWilliams, Vice-President of Operations

FROM: Linda Moreno, Manager of Cost Accounting Services

DATE: February 15, 2009

SUBJECT: REDUCING ELECTROVISION'S TRAVEL AND ENTERTAINMENT COSTS

Here is the report you requested January 30, on Electrovision's travel and entertainment costs.

Your suspicion was right. We are spending far too much on business travel. Our unwritten policy has been "anything goes," leaving us with no real control over T&E expenses. Although this hands-off approach may have been understandable when Electrovision's profits were high, we can no longer afford the luxury.

To solve the problem we need to have someone with centralized responsibility for travel and entertainment costs, a clear statement of policy, an effective control system, and a business-oriented travel service that can optimize our travel arrangements. We should also investigate alternatives to travel, such as videoconferencing. Perhaps more important, we need to change our attitude.

Getting people to economize is not going to be easy. In the course of researching this issue, I've found that our employees are deeply attached to their first-class travel privileges. We'll need a lot of top-management involvement to sell people on the need for moderation. One thing is clear: People will be very bitter if we create a two-class system in which top executives get special privileges while the rest of the employees make the sacrifices.

I'm grateful to Mary Lehman and Connie McIlvain for their help in collecting and sorting five years' worth of expense reports.

Thanks for giving me the opportunity to work on this assignment. It's been informative. If you have any questions about the report, please give me a call at local 6877.

In this report, Moreno decided to write a brief memo of transmittal and include a separate executive summary. Short reports (fewer than 10 pages) often combine the synopsis or executive summary with the memo or letter of transmittal.

(continued)

FIGURE 11.10 (Continued)

Includes no element that appears before the "Contents" page

Words the headings exactly as they appear in the text

Numbers figures consecutively throughout the report

Numbers the contents pages with lower case roman numerals centred at the bottom margin

Includes only the page numbers where sections begin

LIST OF ILLUSTRATIONS

iii

Moreno included only first- and second-level headings in her table of contents, even though the report contains third-level headings. She prefers a shorter table of contents that focuses attention on the main divisions of thought. She used informative titles, which are appropriate for a report to a receptive audience.

(continued)

FIGURE 11.10 (Continued)

Begins by stating the purpose of the report

Presents the points in the executive summary in the same order as they appear in the report

Continues numbering the executive summary pages with lower case roman numerals centred about 2.5 cm from the bottom of the page

Uses subheadings that summarize the content of the main sections of the report without repeating what appears in the text

Targets a receptive audience with a hard-hitting tone in the executive summary (a more neutral approach would be better for hostile or sceptical readers)

Appears in the same typeface and type style as the text of the report. Uses single spacing because the report is single spaced, and follows the text's format for margins, paragraph indentions, and headings.

EXECUTIVE SUMMARY

This report analyzes Electrovision's travel and entertainment (T&E) costs and presents recommendations for reducing those costs.

Travel and Entertainment Costs Are Too High

T&E is a large and growing expense category for Electrovision. The company spends more than $16 million per year on business travel, a cost that is increasing by 12 percent annually. Employees make some 3500 trips a year, each trip averaging $4720. Airfares are the largest expense, followed by hotels and meals.

The nature of Electrovision's business requires extensive travel, but the company's costs seem excessive. Electrovision employees spend more than double what the average business traveller spends. Although the location of company facilities may partly explain this discrepancy, the firm's philosophy and managerial style invite employees to go first class and pay relatively little attention to travel costs.

Cuts Are Essential

Electrovision management now recognizes the need to gain more control over this element of costs. The company is entering a period of declining profits, prompting management to look for every opportunity to reduce spending. Also, rising airfares and hotel rates are making T&E expenses more important to the bottom line.

Electrovision Can Save $6 Million per Year

Electrovision should be able to save up to $6 million per year, based on the experience of other companies. A sensible travel-management program can save firms up to 35 percent a year (Gilligan 2006). Since we purchase more first-class tickets than the average, we should be able to achieve even greater savings.

The first priority should be hiring a director for T&E spending. This director should develop a written T&E policy, establish a cost-control system, retain a national travel agency, and investigate electronic alternatives to travel. Electrovision should make employees aware of the need to reduce T&E spending by forgoing unnecessary travel and by economizing on tickets, hotels, meals, and rental cars.

We should also negotiate preferential rates with travel providers. These changes are likely to hurt short-term morale. Management will need to explain the rationale for reduced spending and set an example by economizing on their own travel arrangements. On the plus side, cutting travel will reduce the burden on employees and help them balance their business and personal lives.

iv

Moreno included an executive summary, which provides a short form of the whole report, because her audience was mixed—some readers would be interested in the details of her report and some would prefer to focus on the big picture.

Moreno's impersonal style adds to the formality of her report. She chose an impersonal style for several reasons: (1) several members of her audience were considerably higher up in the organization and she did not want to sound too familiar, (2) she wanted the executive summary to be compatible with the text, and (3) her company prefers the impersonal style for formal reports.

Some writers prefer a more personal approach. Generally, you should gear your choice of style to your relationship with the readers.

(continued)

FIGURE 11.10 (Continued)

Centres the title of the report on the first page of the text, 5 cm from the top of the page (6.25 cm if top-bound)

REDUCING ELECTROVISION'S TRAVEL AND ENTERTAINMENT COSTS

INTRODUCTION

Electrovision has always encouraged a significant amount of business travel. To compensate employees for the inconvenience and stress of frequent trips, management has authorized generous travel and entertainment (T&E) allowances. This philosophy has been good for morale, but last year Electrovision spent $16 million on T&E—$7 million more than it spent on research and development.

This year's T&E costs will affect profits even more, due to changes in airfares and hotel rates. Also, the company anticipates that profits will be relatively weak for a variety of other reasons. Therefore, Dennis McWilliams, Vice-President of Operations, asked the accounting department to look into the T&E budget.

The purpose of this report is to analyze the T&E budget, evaluate the effect of changes in airfares and hotel costs, and suggest ways to tighten management's control over T&E expenses. The report outlines several steps to reduce our expenses, but the precise financial impact of these measures is difficult to project. Estimates are a "best guess" view of what Electrovision can expect to save.

For this report, the accounting department analyzed internal expense reports for the past five years to determine how much Electrovision spends on T&E. These figures were compared with average statistics compiled by RBC Dominion Securities as reported in the *Report on Business*'s Travel Index. We also analyzed trends and suggestions published in a variety of business journal articles to see how other companies are coping with the high cost of business travel.

This report reviews the size and composition of Electrovision's T&E expenses, analyzes trends in travel costs, and recommends ways to reduce the T&E budget.

THE HIGH COST OF TRAVEL AND ENTERTAINMENT

Many companies view T&E as an "incidental" cost of business, but the dollars add up. Electrovision's bill for airfares, hotels, rental cars, meals, and entertainment totalled to more than $16 million last year and has increased by 12 percent per year for the past five years. Compared to the average Canadian business, Electrovision's expenditures are high, largely because of management's generous policy on travel benefits.

1

Begins the introduction by establishing the need for action

Mentions sources and methods to increase credibility and to give readers a complete picture of the study's background

Uses the standard numeral 1 for the first page, centring the number about 2.5 cm from the bottom of the page

In her brief introduction, Moreno omitted the subheadings within the introduction and relied on topic sentences and on transitional words and phrases to indicate that she is discussing the purpose, scope, and limitations of the study. Moreno used single spacing and 2.5 cm side margins, common in business reports.

(continued)

FIGURE 11.10 (Continued)

2

Uses standard numerals to number the second and succeeding pages of the text in the upper right-hand corner where the top and right-hand margins meet

THE HIGH COST OF TRAVEL AND ENTERTAINMENT
$16 Million per Year Is Spent on Travel and Entertainment

Electrovision's annual T&E budget is 8 percent of sales. Because this is a relatively small expense category, compared with salaries and commissions, it is tempting to dismiss T&E costs as insignificant. But T&E is Electrovision's third-largest controllable expense, directly behind salaries and information systems.

Last year Electrovision personnel made 3390 trips. The average trip cost $4720 and involved a round-trip flight of 4800 km, meals, two to three days of hotel accommodations, and a rental car. About 80 percent of trips were made by 20 percent of the staff—top managers and sales personnel averaged 18 trips per year.

Figure 1 shows how the T&E budget is spent. Airfares and lodging account for $7 out of every $10 employees spend on T&E. This breakdown has been steady for the past five years and is consistent with other companies' distribution.

Introduces visual aids before they appear and indicates what readers should notice about the data

Places the visual aid as close as possible to the point it illustrates

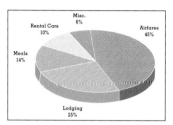

Figure 1
Airfares and Lodging Exceed Two-Thirds of Travel and Entertainment Budget

Makes placement of visual aid titles consistent throughout a report (options for placement include above, below, or beside the visual)

Although the composition of the T&E budget has been consistent, its size has not. With T&E costs increasing 12 percent per year for five years, roughly twice the rate of the company's sales growth (see Figure 2), T&E is Electrovision's fastest-growing expense item.

Numbers the visual aids consecutively and refers to them in the text by their numbers (if your report is a book-length document, you may number the visual aids by chapter; for example, Figure 4.2 would be the second figure in the fourth chapter)

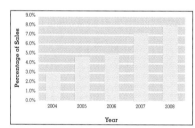

Figure 2
Travel and Entertainment Expenses Have Increased as a Percentage of Sales

Gives each visual aid a title that clearly indicates what it's about

Moreno opened the first main section of the body with a topic sentence that introduces an important fact about the subject of the section. Then she oriented the reader to the three major points developed in the section.

Moreno decided to use a bar chart in Figure 2 to express the main idea in terms of percentage and make the main idea easy to grasp.

(continued)

FIGURE 11.10 (Continued)

3

THE HIGH COST OF TRAVEL AND ENTERTAINMENT
Electrovision's Travel Expenses Exceed National Averages

Much of our travel budget is justified. Two major contributing factors are

- Our headquarters are on the west coast and our major customer is on the east coast, so we naturally spend a lot on cross-country flights.

- Corporate managers and division personnel make frequent trips between our headquarters on the west coast and the manufacturing operations in Windsor, Montreal, and Don Mills to coordinate these disparate operations.

However, even with such justifiable expenses, Electrovision spends considerably more on T&E than the average business traveller spends (see Figure 3).

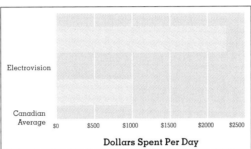

Electrovision

Canadian Average

$0 $500 $1000 $1500 $2000 $2500

Dollars Spent Per Day

Figure 3
Electrovision Employees Spend More Than Double the Canadian Average

Source: The Globe and Mail's Report on Business *and company records*

RBC Dominion's Travel Index calculates the average cost per day of business travel in Canada, based on average rates for airfare, hotel, and rental car. This average fluctuates weekly as travel companies change their rates, but it has been running about $1000 per day for the last year or so. In contrast, Electrovision's average daily expense over the past year has been $2250—125 percent higher than average. This figure is based on the average trip cost of $4720 and an average trip length of 2.1 days.

Spending Has Been Encouraged

Although a variety of factors may contribute to this differential, Electrovision's relatively high T&E costs are at least partially due to the company's philosophy and management style. Since many employees do not enjoy business travel, management has tried to make the trips more pleasant by authorizing first-class airfare, luxury hotel accommodations, and full-size rental cars. The sales staff is encouraged to entertain clients at top restaurants and to invite them to cultural and sporting events.

Leaves a bit more white space above a heading than below to help readers associate that heading with the text it describes

The chart in Figure 3 is simple, but it creates an effective visual comparison. Moreno included just enough data to make her point. She was as careful about the appearance of her report as she was about its content.

(continued)

FIGURE 11.10 (Continued)

4

THE HIGH COST OF TRAVEL AND ENTERTAINMENT

The cost of these privileges is easy to overlook, given the weakness of Electrovision's system for keeping track of T&E expenses:

- Monthly financial reports have no separate T&E category; this information is buried in Cost of Goods Sold and in Selling and General Expenses.

- Department heads can approve expense reports, no matter how large.

- Receipts are not required for expenditures of less than $100.

- Individuals are allowed to make their own travel arrangements.

- No one has responsibility for controlling the company's total T&E spending.

GROWING IMPACT ON PROFITS

During the past three years, the company's healthy profits have disguised the need for tighter controls over all aspects of the business. However, as we all know, the projection is for flat to declining profits over the next two years, which has prompted all of us to search for ways to cut costs. Also, rising airfares and hotel rates have increased the impact of T&E expenses on the company's finances.

Lower Profits Underscore the Need for Change

The next two years promise to be difficult for Electrovision. After several years of steady spending increases, Canada Post is tightening procurement policies for automated mail-handling equipment. Funding for our A-12 optical character reader has been cancelled. As a result, our marketing people expect sales to drop 15 percent. Even though Electrovision is negotiating several R&D contracts with nongovernment clients, the marketing department foresees no major procurements for two to three years.

At the same time, Electrovision is facing cost increases on several fronts. As we have known for several months, the new production facility now under construction in Montreal is behind schedule and over budget. Labour contracts in Windsor and Don Mills will expire within the next six months, and plant managers there anticipate that significant salary and benefits concessions may be necessary to avoid strikes.

Moreover, marketing and advertising costs are expected to increase as we attempt to strengthen these activities to better cope with competitive pressures. Given the expected decline in revenues and increase in costs, the executive committee's prediction that profits will fall by 12 percent in the coming fiscal year does not seem overly pessimistic.

Uses bulleted list to make it easy for readers to identify and distinguish related points

Uses informative headings to focus reader attention on the main points (such headings are appropriate when a report is in direct order and intended for a receptive audience; however, descriptive headings are more effective when a report is in indirect order and readers are less receptive)

Moreno designed her report to include plenty of white space so that pages having no graphics would appear inviting and easy to read.

(continued)

| FIGURE 11.10 | (Continued) |

5

GROWING IMPACT ON PROFITS
Airfares and Hotel Rates Are Rising

Business travellers got used to frequent fare wars and discounting in the travel industry. Excess capacity and aggressive price competition made travel a relative bargain. However, that situation has changed as many competitors have been forced out and the remaining players are keeping rates high. Last year we saw some of the steepest rate hikes in years. Business airfares jumped 40 percent in many markets. The trend is expected to continue, with rates increasing another 5 percent to 10 percent overall (Phillips 2007; Dahl 2008).

Since air and hotel costs account for 70 percent of Electrovision's T&E budget, the trend toward higher prices in these two categories will have serious effects on the company's expenses, unless management takes action to control these costs.

METHODS FOR REDUCING TRAVEL AND ENTERTAINMENT COSTS

By implementing a number of reforms, management can expect to reduce Electrovision's T&E budget by as much as 40 percent. This estimate is based on the general assessment made by Global Travel Inc. (Gilligan 2006) and our chance to reduce or eliminate first-class travel. However, these measures are likely to be unpopular with employees. To gain acceptance for such changes, management will need to sell employees on the need for moderation in T&E allowances.

Four Ways to Trim Expenses

By researching what other companies are doing to curb T&E expenses, the accounting department has identified four prominent opportunities that should enable Electrovision to save about $6 million annually in travel-related costs.

1. Institute Tighter Spending Controls

One person should be appointed director of travel and entertainment to lead the T&E budget-control effort. More than a third of all large companies now employ travel managers to keep costs in line ("Businesses Use Savvy Managers" 2008). Reporting to the vice-president of operations, the director should be familiar with the travel industry and well versed in both accounting and information technology. The director should establish a written T&E policy and implement a system for controlling T&E costs. Electrovision currently has no written policy on travel and entertainment, a step widely recommended by air travel experts (Smith 2008). Creating a policy would clarify management's position and serve as a vehicle for

Documents the facts to add weight to Moreno's argument

Gives recommendations an objective flavour by pointing out both the benefits and the risks of taking action

Because airfares represent Electrovision's biggest T&E expense, Moreno included a subsection that deals with the possible impact of trends in the airline industry. Airfares are rising, so it is especially important to gain more control over employees' air travel arrangements.

Moreno created a forceful tone by using action verbs in the third-level subheadings of this section. This approach is appropriate to the nature of the study and the attitude of the audience. However, in a status-conscious organization, the imperative verbs might sound a bit too presumptuous coming from a junior member of the staff.

Moreno carries over major headings to the next page so that readers can orient themselves to the report's organizational structure.

(continued)

FIGURE 11.10 (Continued)

6

METHODS FOR REDUCING TRAVEL AND ENTERTAINMENT COSTS

communicating the need for moderation. At a minimum, the policy should include provisions such as the following:

- Limiting all T&E to business purposes and getting approval in advance

- Ensuring that all employees travel by coach and stay in mid-range business hotels (with rare exceptions to be approved on a case-by-case basis)

- Applying policy equally to employees at all levels

To implement the new policy, Electrovision must create a system for controlling T&E expenses. Each department should prepare an annual T&E budget. These budgets should be presented in detail so that management can evaluate how T&E dollars will be spent and can recommend appropriate cuts. To help management monitor performance relative to these budgets, the T&E director should prepare monthly financial statements showing actual T&E expenditures by department.

The director of travel should also be responsible for retaining a business-oriented travel service that will schedule all employee business trips and look for the best travel deals, especially in airfares. In addition to centralizing Electrovision's reservation and ticketing activities, the agency will negotiate reduced group rates with hotels and rental car agencies. The agency should have offices nationwide so that all Electrovision facilities can channel their reservations through the same company. This step is particularly important in light of the differing airfares available from city to city. It's common to find dozens of fares along commonly travelled routes (Rowe 2007). Plus, the director can help coordinate travel across the company to secure group discounts when possible (Barker 2008; Miller 2008).

2. Reduce Unnecessary Travel and Entertainment

One of the easiest ways to reduce expenses is to reduce the amount of travelling and entertaining that occurs. An analysis of last year's expenditures suggests that as much as 30 percent of Electrovision's T&E is discretionary. The professional staff spent $2.8 million attending seminars and conferences last year. Some of these gatherings are undoubtedly beneficial, but the company could save money by sending fewer people and eliminating the less valuable functions.

Electrovision could also economize on trips between headquarters and divisions by reducing these visits and sending fewer people each time. Although face-to-face meetings are often necessary, management could try to resolve more internal issues through telephone, electronic, and written communication.

Electrovision can urge employees to economize by flying coach instead of first class or by taking advantage of discount fares. Instead of taking clients to dinner, Electrovision personnel can hold breakfast meetings, which tend to be less costly.

Breaks up text with bulleted lists, which not only call attention to important points but also add visual interest (you can also use visual aids, headings, and direct quotations to break up large, solid blocks of print)

Specifies the steps required to implement recommendations

Moreno uses references to research to support her claims.

(continued)

FIGURE 11.10 (Continued)

7

METHODS FOR REDUCING TRAVEL AND ENTERTAINMENT COSTS

Rather than ordering a $50 bottle of wine, employees can select a less expensive bottle or dispense with alcohol entirely. People can book rooms at moderately priced hotels and drive smaller rental cars.

3. Obtain Lowest Rates from Travel Providers

Apart from urging individual employees to economize, Electrovision can also save money by searching for the lowest available rates for airfares, hotels, and rental cars. Few Electrovision employees have the time or specialized knowledge to seek out travel bargains, making the most convenient and comfortable arrangements. However, by contracting with a professional travel service, the company will have access to professionals who can more efficiently obtain lower rates.

Judging by the experience of other companies, Electrovision may be able to trim 30 percent to 40 percent from the travel budget by looking for bargains in airfares and negotiating group rates with hotels and rental car companies. The company should be able to achieve these economies by analyzing travel patterns, identifying frequently visited locations, and selecting a few hotels that are willing to reduce rates in exchange for guaranteed business. Also, the company should be able to save up to 40 percent on rental car charges by negotiating a corporate rate.

The possibilities for economizing are promising; however, making the best arrangements is a complicated undertaking, requiring trade-offs such as the following:

- The best fares may not always be the lowest (e.g., indirect flights often cost less than direct ones, but they take longer, costing more in lost work time).

- The cheapest tickets may need to be booked far in advance, often impossible.

- Nonrefundable discount tickets are a drawback if the trip must be cancelled.

4. Replace Travel with Technological Alternatives

We might be able to replace a major portion of our interdivisional travel with electronic meetings, such as videoconferencing or real-time on-screen document sharing. Many companies use these tools to cut costs and reduce employee stress.

Rather than make specific recommendations in this report, I suggest that the new T&E director conduct an in-depth study of the company's travel patterns. An analysis of why employees travel and what they accomplish will highlight any opportunities for replacing face-to-face meetings. Part of this study should include limited testing of various electronic systems as a way of measuring their effect on both workplace effectiveness and overall costs.

Points out possible difficulties to show that all angles have been considered and to build reader confidence in the writer's judgment

Note how Moreno makes the transition from section to section. The first sentence under the first heading on this page refers to the subject of the previous paragraph and signals a shift in thought.

(continued)

FIGURE 11.10 (Continued)

Uses informative title for the table, which is consistent with the way headings are handled and is appropriate for a report to a receptive audience

8

METHODS FOR REDUCING TRAVEL AND ENTERTAINMENT COSTS
The Impact of Reforms

By implementing tighter controls, reducing unnecessary expenses, negotiating more favourable rates, and exploring "electronic travel," Electrovision should be able to reduce its travel and entertainment budget significantly. As Table 1 illustrates, the combined savings should be in the neighbourhood of $6 million, although precise figures are somewhat difficult to project.

Table 1

Electrovision Can Trim Travel and Entertainment Costs by an Estimated $6 Million per Year

Source of Savings	Amount Saved
Switching from first-class to coach airfare	$2 300 000
Negotiating preferred hotel rates	940 000
Negotiating preferred rental car rates	460 000
Systematically searching for lower airfares	375 000
Reducing interdivisional travel	675 000
Reducing seminar and conference attendance	1 250 000
TOTAL POTENTIAL SAVINGS	**$6 000 000**

To achieve the economies outlined in the table, Electrovision will incur expenses for hiring a director of travel and for implementing a T&E cost-control system. These costs are projected at $95 000: $85 000 per year in salary and benefits for the new employee and a one-time expense of $10 000 for the cost-control system. The cost of retaining a full-service travel agency is negligible because agencies receive a commission from travel providers rather than a fee from clients.

The measures required to achieve these savings are likely to be unpopular with employees. Electrovision personnel are accustomed to generous travel and entertainment allowances, and they are likely to resent having these privileges curtailed. To alleviate their disappointment

- Management should make a determined effort to explain why the changes are necessary.

- The director of corporate communication should develop a multi-faceted campaign to communicate the importance of curtailing T&E costs.

- Management should set an example by adhering strictly to the new policies.

- The limitations should apply equally to employees at all levels in the organization.

Table title is worded to help readers focus immediately on the point of the table

Includes dollar figures to help management envision the impact of the suggestions, even though estimated savings are difficult to project

Note how Moreno calls attention in the first paragraph to items in the following table, without repeating the information in the table.

The table puts Moreno's recommendations in perspective. She calls attention to the most important sources of savings and also spells out the costs required to achieve those results.

(continued)

FIGURE 11.10 (Continued)

9

Uses a descriptive heading for the last section of the text (in informational reports, this section is often called "Summary"; in analytical reports, it is called "Conclusions" or "Conclusions and Recommendations")

CONCLUSIONS

Electrovision is currently spending $16 million per year on travel and entertainment. Although much of this spending is justified, the company's costs are high relative to competitors', mainly because Electrovision has been generous with its travel benefits.

Electrovision's liberal approach to T&E expenses made sense during years of high profitability; however, the company is facing the prospect of declining profits for the next several years. Thus, management is motivated to cut costs in all areas of the business. Reducing T&E spending is particularly important because the impact of these costs will increase as airfares and hotel accommodations increase.

Summarizes conclusions in the first two paragraphs —a good approach because Moreno organized her report around conclusions and recommendations, so readers have already been introduced to them

Electrovision should be able to reduce T&E costs by as much as 40 percent by taking four important steps:

RECOMMENDATIONS

1. *Institute tighter spending controls.* Management should hire a T&E director to assume overall responsibility for relevant activities. Within the next six months, this director should develop a written travel policy, institute a T&E budget and a cost-control system, and retain a professional, business-oriented travel agency.

2. *Reduce unnecessary travel and entertainment.* Electrovision should encourage employees to economize on T&E spending. Management can authorize fewer trips and urge employees to be more conservative in their spending.

Uses a verb-first structure to emphasize actions.

Emphasizes the recommendations by presenting them in list format

3. *Obtain lowest rates from travel providers.* Electrovision should focus on obtaining the best rates on airline tickets, hotel rooms, and rental cars. By channelling all arrangements through a professional travel agency, the company can optimize its choices and gain clout in negotiating preferred rates.

4. *Replace travel with technological alternatives.* With the number of computers already installed in our facilities, it seems likely that we could take advantage of desktop videoconferencing and other distance-meeting tools. This won't be quite as feasible with customer sites, since these systems require compatible equipment at both ends of a connection, but it is certainly a possibility for communication with Electrovision's own sites.

Because these measures may be unpopular with employees, management should make a concerted effort to explain the importance of reducing travel costs. The director of corporate communication should be given responsibility for developing a plan to communicate the need for employee cooperation.

Moreno introduces no new facts in this entire section.

(continued)

FIGURE 11.10 (Continued)

10

REFERENCES

Barker, Julie. (2008, February). How to Rein in Group Travel Costs. *Successful Meetings*, p. 31.

Businesses Use Savvy Managers to Keep Travel Costs Down. (2008, July 17). *Christian Science Monitor*, p. 4.

Dahl, Jonathan. (2008, December 29). 2008: The Year Travel Costs Took Off. *The Globe and Mail*, section B6, p. 10.

Gilligan, Edward P. (2006, November). Trimming Your T&E Is Easier Than You Think. *Managing Office Technology*, pp. 39–41.

Miller, Lisa. (2008, July 7). Attention, Airline Ticket Shoppers. *National Post*, section B, p. 12.

Phillips, Edward H. (2007, January 8). Airlines Post Record Traffic. *Aviation Week & Space Technology*, p. 331.

Rowe, Irene Vilitos. (2007, October 12). Global Solution for Cutting Travel Costs. *European*, p. 30.

Smith, Carol. (2008, November 2). Rising Erratic Airfares Make Company Policy Vital. *Los Angeles Times*, section D4, p. 9.

Travel Costs Under Pressure. (2007, Februrary 15). *Purchasing*, p. 30.

Lists references alphabetically by the author's last name, and when the author is unknown, by the title of the reference (see Appendix B for additional details on preparing reference lists)

Moreno's list of references follows APA style.

• **Glossary.** A glossary is a list of definitions of terms used in the report. It is useful when some readers need definitions and some do not. Putting the definitions in a glossary at the back of the report gives readers a choice about reading them.

Components of a Formal Proposal

Formal proposals contain many of the same components as other formal reports (see Figure 11.11 on page 267). The difference lies mostly in the text, although a few of the prefatory parts are also different. With the exception of an occasional appendix, most proposals have few supplementary parts.

Formal proposals contain most of the same prefatory parts as other formal reports.

PREFATORY PARTS The cover, title page, table of contents, and list of illustrations, and executive summary are handled the same as in other formal reports. However, other prefatory parts are handled quite differently, such as the copy of the RFP and the letter of transmittal:

• **Copy of the RFP.** Instead of having a letter of authorization, a formal proposal may have a copy of the request for proposal (RFP), which is a letter or memo soliciting a proposal or a bid for a particular project. If the RFP includes detailed specifications, it may be too long to bind into the proposal; in that case, you may want to include only the introductory portion of the RFP. Another option is to omit the RFP or append it and simply refer to it in your letter of transmittal.

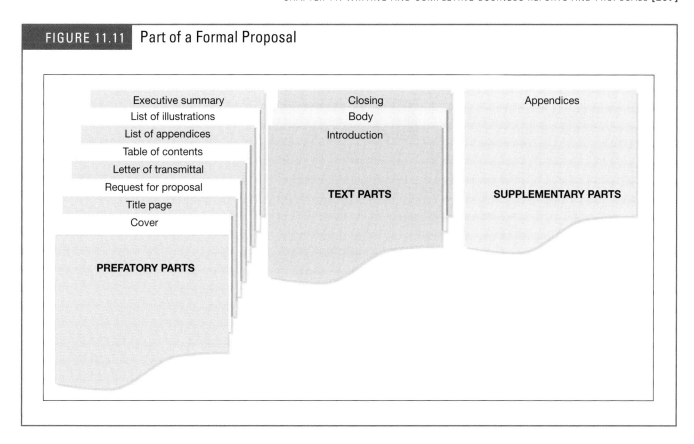

FIGURE 11.11 Part of a Formal Proposal

- **Letter of transmittal.** If the proposal is solicited, the transmittal letter follows the pattern for good-news messages, highlighting those aspects of your proposal that may give you a competitive advantage. If the proposal is unsolicited, the transmittal letter follows the pattern for persuasive messages (see Chapter 9). The letter must persuade the reader that you have something worthwhile to offer that justifies reading the entire proposal. Because the transmittal letter may be all that the client reads, it must be especially convincing.

CONTENTS OF THE PROPOSAL Just as with reports, the text of a proposal comprises an introduction, body, and a closing section. The introduction presents and summarizes the problem you intend to solve and your solution. The body includes any benefits the reader will receive from the solution and explains the complete details of the solution:

> Just like other business reports, proposals have three divisions of text: introduction, body, and close.

- How the job will be done
- How it will be broken into tasks
- What method will be used to do it (including the required equipment, material, and personnel)
- When the work will begin and end
- How much the entire job will cost (including a detailed breakdown)
- Why your company is qualified

The close emphasizes the benefits readers will realize from your solution, and it urges readers to act.

Figure 11.12 (on page 268) is an informal proposal submitted by Dixon O'Donnell, vice-president of O'Donnell & Associates, a geotechnical engineering firm that conducts a variety of environmental testing services. The company is bidding on the mass grading and utility work specified by AGI Builders. As you review this document, pay close attention to the specific items addressed in the proposal's introduction, body, and closing.

FIGURE 11.12 Dixon O'Donnell's Informal Solicited Proposal

O'Donnell
&
Associates, Inc.

1793 East Westerfield Road, Montreal, QC J4P 2X1
(819) 441-1148 Fax: (819) 441-1149 Email: dod@inter.net

July 28, 2009

Ms. Joyce Colton, P.E.
AGI Builders, Inc.
1280 Spring Lake Drive
Montreal, QC J7R 8T2

Dear Ms. Colton:

PROPOSAL NO. F-0087 FOR AGI BUILDERS, SAINT-BRUNO MANUFACTURING PLANT

Uses opening paragraph in place of an introduction

Grabs reader's attention by highlighting company qualifications

O'Donnell & Associates is pleased to submit the following proposal to provide construction testing services for the mass grading operations and utility work at the Saint-Bruno Manufacturing Plant, 1230 Parent Street, Saint-Bruno, Quebec. Our company has been providing construction-testing services in the Montreal area since 1972 and has performed more than 100 geotechnical investigations at airports within Ontario and Quebec—including Pearson International Airport, Dorval, and Mirabel.

Background

Uses headings to divide proposal into logical segments for easy reading

Acknowledges the two projects and their required time lines

It is our understanding that the work consists of two projects: (1) the mass grading operations will require approximately six months, and (2) the utility work will require approximately three months. The two operations are scheduled as follows:

Mass Grading Operations	September 2008–February 2009
Utility Work	March 2009–May 2009

Proposed Approach and Work Plan

Describes scope of project and outlines specific tests the company will perform

O'Donnell & Associates will perform observation and testing services during both the mass grading operations and the excavation and backfilling of the underground utilities. Specifically, we will
- perform field density tests on the compacted material as required by the job specifications using a nuclear moisture/density gauge
- conduct appropriate laboratory tests such as ASTM D-1557 Modified Proctors
- prepare detailed reports summarizing the results of our field and laboratory testing

Fill materials to be placed at the site may consist of natural granular materials (sand), processed materials (crushed stone, crushed concrete, slag), or clay soils.

(continued)

FIGURE 11.12 (Continued)

O'Donnell & Associates, Inc.   July 28, 2009   Page 2

Staffing

Explains who will be responsible for the various tasks

O'Donnell & Associates will provide qualified personnel to perform the necessary testing. Mr. Kevin Patel will be the lead field technician responsible for the project. A copy of Mr. Patel's resumé is included with this proposal for your review. Kevin will coordinate field activities with your job site superintendent and make sure that appropriate personnel are assigned to the job site. Overall project management will be the responsibility of Mr. Joseph Proesel. Project engineering services will be performed under the direction of Mr. Dixon O'Donnell, P.E. All field personnel assigned to the site will be familiar with and abide by the Project Site Health and Safety Plan prepared by Carlson Environmental, Inc., dated April 2009.

Encloses resumé rather than listing qualifications in the document

Qualifications

O'Donnell & Associates has been providing quality professional services since 1972 in

- Geotechnical engineering
- Materials testing and inspection
- Pavement evaluation
- Environmental services
- Engineering and technical support (CADD) services

Grabs attention by mentioning distinguishing qualifications

The company provides Phase I and Phase II environmental site assessments, preparation of LUST site closure reports, installation of groundwater monitoring wells, and testing of soil/groundwater samples for environmental contaminants. Geotechnical services include all phases of soil mechanics and foundation engineering, including foundation and lateral load analysis, slope stability analysis, site preparation recommendations, seepage analysis, pavement design, and settlement analysis.

O'Donnell & Associates' materials testing laboratory is certified by AASHTO Accreditation Program for the testing of Soils, Aggregate, Hot Mix Asphalt, and Portland Cement Concrete. A copy of our laboratory certification is included with this proposal. In addition to in-house training, field and laboratory technicians participate in a variety of certification programs, including those sponsored by the American Concrete Institute (ACI), Quebec Chapter.

Gains credibility by describing certifications

(continued)

FIGURE 11.12 (Continued)

O'Donnell & Associates, Inc.   July 28, 2009   Page 3

Costs
On the basis of our understanding of the scope of the work, we estimate the total cost of the two projects to be $100 260.00, as shown in the table.

Table of Cost Estimates

Cost Estimate: Mass Grading	Units	Rate ($)	Total Cost ($)
Field Inspection			
Labour	1320 hours	$38.50	$ 50 820.00
Nuclear Moisture Density Meter	132 days	35.00	4 620.00
Vehicle Expense	132 days	45.00	5 940.00
Laboratory Testing			
Proctor Density Tests	4 tests	130.00	520.00
(ASTM D-1557)			
Engineering/Project Management			
Principal Engineer	16 hours	110.00	1 760.00
Project Manager	20 hours	80.00	1 600.00
Administrative Assistant	12 hours	50.00	600.00
Subtotal			***$ 65 860.00***

Cost Estimate: Utility Work	Units	Rate ($)	Total Cost ($)
Field Inopcction			
Labour	660 hours	$ 38.50	$ 25 410.00
Nuclear Moisture Density Meter	66 days	35.00	2 310.00
Vehicle Expense	66 days	45.00	2 970.00
Laboratory Testing			
Proctor Density Tests	2 tests	130.00	260.00
(ASTM D-1557)			
Engineering/Project Management			
Principal Engineer	10 hours	110.00	1 100.00
Project Manager	20 hours	80.00	1 600.00
Administrative Assistant	15 hours	50.00	750.00
Subtotal			***$ 34 400.00***

Total Project Costs			**$100 260.00**

This estimate assumes full-time inspection services. However, our services may also be performed on an as-requested basis, and actual charges will reflect time associated with the project. We have attached our standard fee schedule for your review. Overtime rates are for hours in excess of 8.0 hours per day, before 7:00 a.m., after 5:00 p.m., and on holidays and weekends.

Builds interest by describing all services provided by the company

Itemizes costs by project and gives supporting detail

Provides alternative option in case full-time service costs exceed client's budget

(continued)

FIGURE 11.12 (Continued)

Uses brief closing to emphasize qualifications and ask for client decision

O'Donnell & Associates, Inc.   July 28, 2009   Page 4

Authorization

With a staff of more than 30 personnel, including registered professional engineers, resident engineers, geologists, construction inspectors, laboratory technicians, and drillers, we are convinced that O'Donnell & Associates is capable of providing the services required for a project of this magnitude.

If you would like our firm to provide the services as outlined in this proposal, please sign this letter and return it to us along with a certified cheque for $10 000 (our retainer) by August 15, 2009. Please call me if you have any questions regarding the terms of this proposal or our approach.

Provides deadline and makes response easy

Sincerely,

Dixon O'Donnell
Dixon O'Donnell
Vice-President

Enclosures

Accepted for AGI BUILDERS, INC.

By_____   Date _____

Makes letter a binding contract, if signed

ON THE JOB

Being able to write reports and proposals well will help you advance in your career. Reports are used by managers to make decisions. If you become known as someone whose reports are accurate, complete, concise, and articulate, your value to the company is increased. As well, writing proposals for improving company operations is a way to get your ideas in front of your manager and see them implemented.

Reviewing Key Points

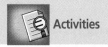
Activities

In this chapter you learned about writing business reports and proposals. When writing a report

- Use a direct pattern when resistance is low. Place conclusions and recommendations near the beginning for reader convenience.
- Use an indirect pattern when resistance is high. Place arguments and evidence before the conclusion and recommendations to help gain reader acceptance of the rationale behind the ideas.
- Include special format requirements when writing long, formal reports, such as
  - An executive summary
  - A table of contents
  - A list of illustrations
  - A list of appendices
  - A title page
- Use an executive summary to provide a condensed version of the whole report to allow the busy reader access to key points and to grasp your conclusions quickly.
- Choose the right graphics according to your purpose; use
  - Tables to summarize numerical data
  - Bar charts for comparisons
  - Line graphs to show trends
  - Charts to show relationships
- Control the style and tone by using the appropriate voice, personal pronouns, and consistent verb tenses. Use active voice when possible. Strive for a style that reflects the image of your organization and the formality of the situation.

mybuscommlab   Go to MyBusCommLab at www.pearson.ca/mybuscommlab for online exercises.

Practise Your Grammar

Exercises

Effective business communication starts with strong grammar skills. To improve your grammar skills, go to MyBusCommLab or Grammar-on-the-Go, where you'll find exercises and diagnostic tests to help you produce clear, effective communication.

Test Your Knowledge

Exercises

1. Name four options for report format.
2. What are some ways of organizing informational reports?
3. How would you determine whether to use a direct or indirect approach for structuring an analytical report?
4. What tools can you use to help readers follow the structure and flow of information in a long report?
5. What graphic would you use to compare one part with a whole?
6. What graphic type would you use to show trends?
7. What is an executive summary, and how does it differ from an introduction?
8. What information is included on the title page of a report?
9. What is a letter of transmittal, and where is it included in a formal report submission?
10. How are appendices ordered?

Apply Your Knowledge

1. Should a report always explain the writer's method of gathering evidence or solving a problem? Why or why not?
2. Would you use the direct or indirect approach to document inventory shortages at your manufacturing plant? To propose an employee stock-option plan? Why?

3. What similarities do you see between visuals and nonverbal communication? Explain your answer.

4. You're writing a report to the director of human resources on implementing teams throughout your company. You want to emphasize that since the new approach was implemented six months ago, absenteeism and turnovers have been sharply reduced in all but two departments. How do you visually present your data in the most favourable light? Explain.

5. **Ethical Choices** How would you report on a confidential survey in which employees rated their managers' capabilities? Both employees and managers expect to see the results. Would you give the same report to employees and managers? What components would you include or exclude for each audience? Explain your choices.

Running Cases

Video

CASE 1: Noreen

Noreen's boss likes the idea Noreen proposed to merge the Go Points department with the Petro-Go credit card sales/service department. The boss would like Noreen to write an analysis and justification report to support the idea and plan to merge the two departments into one.

As mentioned previously, the Go Points department is currently on the fourth floor and staffed by 20 sales/service reps. They (1) make sales calls to existing Petro-Go credit card holders to offer the points program, (2) receive calls from existing points program customers who have enquiries, and (3) call existing points customers to announce, for example, promotions and offers.

The Petro-Go credit card department is on the third floor and staffed by 30 sales/service reps. They (1) make sales calls to recruit new credit card customers, (2) receive calls from existing credit card holders who have enquiries, and (3) call existing credit card customers to announce, for example, promotions and offers.

Noreen thinks that by joining the credit card sales/service department with the Go Points department, customers will be better served by one-stop shopping.

She also feels that the credit card sales/service staff could easily modify their call routines to include information about the Go Points program, and the Go Points staff could easily be trained on the credit card policies and procedures.

QUESTIONS

a. What information must Noreen gather?
b. What logical arguments can Noreen use?
c. What are the five steps Noreen should follow to focus her report around recommendations?
d. What type of visuals might Noreen include in the report?
e. How will Noreen leave a strong and lasting impression on the reader at the end of her report?

YOUR TASK

With a partner, use your imagination to write an analytical memo report from Noreen to her managers (use your names) that gives an analysis of the situation and justifies the merger.

When structuring a report around recommendations, follow the five steps listed on page 240. Include at least one visual in your report.

CASE 2: Kwong

Kwong is working with the annual report project team to gather, summarize, and compile the annual report for ET Canada. The annual report will be posted on the internet and distributed to all shareholders. The report will include several charts and tables. Revenue will be reported, and Kwong will use a table to show product lines offered by ET and the revenue from each product over the past few years.

QUESTIONS

a. Why will placing the information in a table help the reader?
b. Would this annual report best be organized in chronological, geographical, or category order?
c. Should the company's annual report use the direct approach or the indirect approach?
d. List three factors Kwong should consider when he is deciding how many and what type of visuals to include in the annual report.

YOUR TASK

Create a letter to Kwong showing ET Canada's product line analysis for this year and last year. The letter is from the company's CIO (chief information officer). The letter contains a table showing revenues for each product line for this year and last year. Product lines are Local and Access, Long Distance, Wireless, Data, Video, Terminal Sales, and Other. The table also includes a column for percentage of change in revenue between this year and last year as well as column totals. The letter also contains a bar/column chart that displays the revenues for each product line for the two years. Kwong plans to add this information to ET Canada's annual report.

Practise Your Knowledge

ACTIVITIES

1. **Organizing Reports: Deciding on Format** Go to the library or visit the SEDAR website at site **www.sedar.com** to find annual reports from hundreds of Canadian companies. Review the annual report most recently released by Westport Innovations. Be prepared to discuss the following questions in class:
   a. How does Westport Innovations discuss its annual performance? Are the data presented clearly so that shareholders can draw conclusions about how well the company performed?
   b. What goals, challenges, and plans does the CEO emphasize in his discussion of results?
   c. How do the format and organization of the report enhance or detract from the information being presented?
2. **Organizing Reports: Choosing the Direct or Indirect Approach** Of the organizational approaches introduced in the chapter, which is best suited for writing a report that answers the following questions? Briefly explain why. (Note, you will write one report for each question item.)
   a. In which market segment—root beer, cola, or lemon-lime—should Fizz Drinks, Inc., introduce a new soft drink to take advantage of its enlarged research and development budget?
   b. Should Major Manufacturing, Inc. close down operations of its antiquated Bathurst, Nova Scotia, plant despite the adverse economic impact on the town that has grown up around the plant?
   c. Should you and your partner adopt a new accounting method to make your financial statements look better to potential investors?
   d. Should North Battleford Chemicals buy disposable test tubes to reduce labour costs associated with cleaning and sterilizing reusable test tubes?
   e. What are some reasons for the recent data loss at your school's computer centre, and how can we avoid similar problems in the future?
3. **Teamwork: Report Structure** You and a classmate are helping Linda Moreno prepare her report on Electrovision's travel and entertainment costs (see Figure 11.10). This time, however, the report is to be informational rather than analytical, so it will not include recommendations. Review the existing report and determine what changes would be needed to make it an informational report. Be as specific as possible. For example, if your team decides the report needs a new title, what title would you use? Now draft a transmittal memo for Moreno to use in conveying this informational report to Dennis McWilliams, Electrovision's vice-president of operations.
4. **Organizing Reports: Structuring Informational Reports** Assume that your school's president has received many student complaints about campus parking problems. You are appointed to chair a student committee organized to investigate the problems and recommend solutions. The president gives you the file labelled "Parking: Complaints from Students," and you jot down the essence of the complaints as you inspect the contents. Your notes look like this:
   - Inadequate student spaces at critical hours
   - Poor night lighting near the computer centre
   - Inadequate attempts to keep resident neighbours from occupying spaces
   - Dim marking lines
   - Motorcycles taking up full spaces
   - Discourteous security officers
   - Spaces (usually empty) reserved for school officials

- Relatively high parking fees
- Full fees charged to night students even though they use the lots only during low-demand periods
- Vandalism to cars and a sense of personal danger
- Inadequate total space
- Resident harassment of students parking on the street in front of neighbouring houses

Now prepare an outline for an informational report to be submitted to committee members. Use a topical organization for your report that categorizes this information.

5. **Choosing the Right Visual** You're preparing the annual report for FretCo Guitar Corporation. For each of the following types of information, select the right chart or visual to illustrate the text. Explain your choices.
   a. Data on annual sales for the past 20 years
   b. Comparison of FretCo sales, product by product (electric guitars, bass guitars, amplifiers, acoustic guitars), for this year and last year
   c. Explanation of how a FretCo acoustic guitar is manufactured
   d. Explanation of how the FretCo Guitar Corporation markets its guitars
   e. Data on sales of FretCo products in each of 12 countries
   f. Comparison of FretCo sales figures with sales figures for three competing guitar makers over the past 10 years

6. **Internet** One of the best places to see how data can be presented visually is in government statistical publications, which are often available on the internet. For example, Industry Canada publishes updates on Canadian trade with other countries. Visit the Industry Canada website at **www.ic.gc.ca** and click on "Resources for Business" to find the links to "Trade and Investment" and in "Trade" click on "Countries and Region Information" to find a report about a country that interests you. For example, you could read about what's new in trade with the People's Republic of China or Russia. Using what you learned in this chapter, evaluate the charts in the report. Do they present the data clearly? Are they missing any elements? What would you do to improve the charts? Print out a copy of the report to turn in with your answers, and indicate which charts you are evaluating.

7. **Composing Reports: Navigational Clues** Use Research Navigator in MyBusCommLab to locate and review a long business article in a journal or newspaper. Highlight examples of how the article uses headings, transitions, and previews and reviews to help the readers find their way.

8. **Ethical Choices** Your boss has asked you to prepare a feasibility report to determine whether the company should advertise its custom-crafted cabinetry in the weekly neighbourhood newspaper. Based on your primary research, you think they should. As you draft the introduction to your report, however, you discover that the survey administered to the neighbourhood newspaper subscribers was flawed. Several of the questions were poorly written and misleading. You used the survey results, among other findings, to justify your recommendation. The report is due in three days. What actions might you want to take, if any, before you complete your report?

9. **Producing Reports: Letter of Transmittal** You are president of the Friends of the Library, a non-profit group that raises funds and provides volunteers to support your local library. Every February, you send a report of the previous year's activities and accomplishments to the Municipal Arts Council, which provides an annual grant of $1000 toward your group's summer reading festival. Now it's February 6, and you've completed your formal report. Here are the highlights:
   - The back-to-school book sale raised $2000.
   - The holiday craft fair raised $1100.
   - Promotion and prizes for the summer reading festival cost $1450.
   - Materials for the children's program featuring a local author cost $125.
   - New reference databases for the library's career centre cost $850.
   - Bookmarks promoting the library's website cost $200.

   Write a letter of transmittal to Erica Maki, the council's director. Because she is expecting this report, you can use the direct approach. Be sure to express gratitude for the council's ongoing financial support.

10. **Internet** Visit WestJet's website (**www.westjet.com**) and select "Financial Reports" under "About Us" to find the company's most recent annual report. Read through the report and look at its visuals. What is the purpose of this document? Does the title communicate this purpose? What type of report is this, and what is the report's structure? Which prefatory and supplementary parts are included? Now analyze the visuals. What types are included in this report? Are they all necessary? Are the titles and legends sufficiently informative?

Expand Your Knowledge

Best of the Web

Preview Before You Produce A good way to get ideas for the best style, organization, and format of a report is by looking at copies of professional business reports. To find samples of different types of reports, you can use a metasearch engine, such as Ixquick Metasearch. Ixquick searches many engines simultaneously; in addition to searching in English, you can conduct your search in five other languages. See what Ixquick produces when you enter the phrase "business reports." Choose from various titles or descriptions to compare different kinds of reports. This research could result in your preparing better reports and proposals.

www.ixquick.com

EXERCISES

1. What is the purpose of the report you read? Who is its target audience? Explain why the structure and style of the report make it easy or difficult to follow the main idea.
2. What type of report did you read? Briefly describe the main message. Is the information well organized? If you answer "yes," explain how you can use the report as a guide for a report you might write. If you answer "no," explain why the report is not helpful.
3. Drawing on what you know about the qualities of a good business report, review a report and describe what features contribute to its readability.

Exploring the Web on Your Own

Review these chapter-related websites to learn more about writing reports and proposals.

1. Need some help using graphics software? Get started at the About.com graphics software website. Take the tutorials, view the illustrated demonstrations, and read the instructional articles at **www.graphicssoft.about.com/cs/howtos/index.htm**.
2. Looking for the perfect transitional word? Cues and Transitions for the Reader, at **www.managementhelp.org/writing/cuestran.htm**, has some recommendations to help you.
3. Develop a better business plan by following the advice at Canadian Business Service Centres at **www.cbsc.org**, or at Services for Canadian Business at **www.businessgateway.ca**, or at the Small Business Association website, **www.sba.gov/starting/indexbusplans.html**.

Cases

The "Cases" section of Chapter 10 asked you to complete planning tasks for 12 informal cases (both informational and analytical). Your instructor may ask you to go back and choose some of those cases to prepare and write as fully developed reports. Following are some formal reports your instructor may assign.

Short Formal Reports

1. CLIMBING THE LADDER: SHORT REPORT SUMMARIZING DATA ABOUT CORPORATE OPPORTUNITIES FOR WOMEN (NO ADDITIONAL RESEARCH REQUIRED)

As assistant to the director of human resources for a large advertising firm, you hear the concerns of many employees. Lately, increasing numbers of women have been complaining about being passed up for promotions and management positions. They feel that men receive preferential treatment, even though many women are more highly qualified.

Your team has already conducted some research into the problem. Table 11.3 shows several key statistics about the men and women working for your company.

Table 11.4 depicts how executives in Fortune 1000 companies see the barriers to the advancement of women, and Table 11.5 (on page 278) shows why female executives believe that women should have more opportunities in the corporate world. These data may help shed light on the possibility of sex discrimination at your company. Because your company believes in fair and equal treatment for all employees, regardless of gender, you know your boss will be interested in this information.[6] Although the source of the information is from the United States, you know it has relevance for your company.

YOUR TASK Write a short report to the director of human resources, interpreting and summarizing the information in these tables. Suggest a possible course of action to remedy the situation at your company.

WEB SKILLS 2. PICKING THE BETTER PATH: SHORT RESEARCH REPORT ASSISTING A CLIENT IN A CAREER CHOICE (ADDITIONAL RESEARCH REQUIRED)

You are employed by Open Options, a career-counselling firm, where your main function is to help clients make career choices. Today a client with the same name as

---

TABLE 11.3   Statistics for Male and Female Managers

EMPLOYEE STATISTICS	FEMALE MANAGERS	MALE MANAGERS
Average number of years with the company	12.3	9.5
Average number of years of management experience	7.2	6.9
Percentage who have an MBA or other advanced degree	74%	63%
Average annual salary	$76 000	$84 000
Average number of times promoted	4.2	4.4

TABLE 11.4   Why Female Executives Don't Advance into Corporate Leadership Positions

REASON CITED	ACCORDING TO FEMALE EXECUTIVES (%)	ACCORDING TO MALE CEOS (%)
Male stereotyping preconceptions	52	25
Exclusion from informal networks	49	15
Lack of general management/line experience	47	82
Inhospitable corporate culture	35	18
Women not in pipeline long enough	29	64

TABLE 11.5	Why Female Executives Think Companies Should Increase the Number of Female Senior Managers	

REASON	STRONGLY AGREE (%)	AGREE (%)
Women are large part of management talent pool	29	69
Women contribute unique perspective	32	61
Women are large part of consumer base	45	36
Companies have social responsibility	41	10
Shareholders want more executive women	41	7
Customers want more executive women	34	7
Lawsuits are increasing	40	5

yours (what a coincidence!) came to your office and asked for help deciding between two careers—careers that you yourself had been interested in (an even greater coincidence!).

YOUR TASK Research the two careers, and prepare a short report that your client can study. Your report should compare at least five major areas, such as salary, working conditions, and educational requirements. Interview the client to understand her or his personal preferences regarding each of the five areas. For example, what is the minimum salary the client will accept? By comparing the client's preferences with the research material you collect, you will have a basis for concluding which of the two careers is best. The report should end with a career recommendation. Note: Two good places for career-related information are two publications of Human Resources and Social Development Canada, both available in print (in libraries) and online at the sites noted:

* *National Occupational Classification 2006*, online at www5.hrsdc.gc.ca/NOC-CNP
* *Job Futures*, online at http://jobfutures.ca

Another good source for detailed information about career opportunities, trends, and qualifications is the *Occupational Outlook Handbook*, published by the U.S. Bureau of Labor Statistics, available in print at the library and online at http://stats.bls.gov/oco/ocoiab.htm.

Long Formal Reports Requiring Additional Research

3. IS THERE ANY JUSTICE? REPORT CRITIQUING LEGISLATION

Plenty of people complain about their MPs and MLAs, but few are specific about their complaints. Here's your chance.

YOUR TASK Write a formal report about a law that you believe should have been, or should not have been, enacted. Be objective. Write the report using specific facts to support your beliefs. Reach conclusions and offer your recommendation at the end of the report. As a final step, you might send a copy of your report to an appropriate provincial or federal official or member of the Legislative Assembly in your province or to your member of Parliament.

4. TRAVEL OPPORTUNITIES: REPORT COMPARING TWO DESTINATIONS FOR AN EMPLOYEE INCENTIVE PROGRAM

You work for a subsidiary of the world's largest publishing company in Toronto as a human resources manager. Your company sends the top Canadian sales representative and his or her family on an all-expenses paid trip to a luxury resort to join top sellers from throughout the company. You have been working with the New York office that has arranged past trips and have been given the responsibility for recommending this year's resort. You have three in mind that you need to research: the Grand Wailea in Maui, Hawaii; the Phoenician in Phoenix, Arizona; and the Chateau Whistler in Whistler, B.C.

YOUR TASK Prepare a report comparing the three resorts. Establish some criteria that you can use to decide which resort to recommend, such as that the price for each attendee's trip (including meals, airfare, car rental, and accommodation) has to be within a budget of CAN $25 000. The trip takes place each February. What other criteria would be useful in assessing these resorts for your purpose? Using resources in your library, on the internet, and perhaps from travel agencies, analyze the destinations to see which one meets your criteria. At the end of the report, recommend the resort for this year's travel incentive.

5. SECONDARY SOURCES: REPORT BASED ON LIBRARY RESEARCH

Perhaps one of the following questions has been on your mind:

a. Which is the best university or college at which to pursue an undergraduate degree in business?

b. How can you organize a student group to make your campus safer at night?

c. Which of three companies that you would like to work for has the most responsible environmental policies?

d. What market factors led to the development of a product that you use frequently, and how are those factors different today?

e. Which three Canadian companies have had the best stock price performance over the past 30 years and why?

f. What are the best small-business opportunities available today?

YOUR TASK Answer one of those questions, using secondary sources for information. Be sure to document your sources in APA style (see Appendix B). Give conclusions and recommendations in your report.

6. DOING BUSINESS ABROAD: REPORT SUMMARIZING THE SOCIAL AND BUSINESS CUSTOMS OF A FOREIGN COUNTRY

Your company would like to sell its products overseas. But first, management must have a clear understanding of the social and business customs of the foreign countries where they intend to do business.

YOUR TASK Choose a non-English-speaking country, and write a long formal report summarizing the country's social and business customs. Review appropriate sections of Chapter 1 as a guide for the types of information you could include in your report.

7. BREWING UP SALES: FORMAL PROPOSAL TO SUPPLY COFFEE TO PETER'S DOUGHNUTS

You are assistant to the president of Lighthouse Roasters, a small but growing coffee-roasting company. Lighthouse has made a name for itself by offering fresh, dark-roasted gourmet coffees; however, Lighthouse Roasters does not operate its own stores (unlike Starbucks and other competitors). Instead, Lighthouse sells roasted gourmet coffee beans to retailers such as restaurants, bakeries, and latte carts. These retailers use the Lighthouse beans to make the coffee beverages they sell.

Lighthouse's total cost to produce a kilogram of roasted gourmet beans is $2.75. The company wholesales a kilogram of roasted gourmet beans for an average price of $4.50. Competitors who sell regular coffee beans typically charge about $3.00 per kilogram. However, the average price of a gourmet coffee beverage is $1.50, about $0.50 more than beverages made with regular coffee (including both brewed coffee and espresso drinks). Each kilogram of coffee yields about 40 beverages.

With 76 doughnut shops across five provinces, Peter's Doughnuts has seen its sales decline in recent months, after Starbucks began opening stores close by Peter's shops. Starbucks not only sells gourmet coffee but also carries a selection of pastries that compete with doughnuts. Peter's management figures that by offering gourmet coffee, it will win back customers who like doughnuts but who also want darker-roasted gourmet coffees. Therefore, Peter's has invited you to submit a proposal to be its exclusive supplier of coffee. Peter's anticipates that it will need 400 kg of coffee a month during the colder months (October–March) and 300 kg during the warmer months (April–September). The company has said it wants to pay no more than $6.95 per kilogram for Lighthouse coffee.

YOUR TASK Using your imagination to supply the details, write a proposal describing your plan to supply coffee to Peter's Doughnuts. Considering your costs, will you meet Peter's pricing demands, or will you attempt to gain a higher price?

8. HELPING THE COMMUNITY: FORMAL PROPOSAL TO SOLVE A LOCAL PROBLEM USING PRIMARY RESEARCH

Look around your campus or local community for a problem you are interested in. Maybe it is related to campus parking, food services, or a neighbourhood playground that is run down. Maybe the lack of training given to workers at your part-time job may be causing poor sales.

What types of solutions may be possible? What information and facts would you need to have to present a solution to this problem? What types of primary research could you do to gather information for your proposal? Is it practical to survey a representative sample of people who use the service or whose opinion would be helpful to include in the proposal? Would interviews with a representative sample of those affected by the proposal be useful? Work with your professor to define the scope of your proposal and to identify suitable kinds of primary research you will do for the assignment. Identify a "real" audience for your proposal and design your research methods. Here are a few sample proposal scenarios: You could write a proposal to

- A community association to fund a playground renovation

- A college board of governors to light the student parking area

- A college board of governors and student association to provide an evening "safe walk" program
- The City to fund an arts or cultural event
- The City or a private foundation to fund restoration of a stream in your area
- Your part-time employer to request funding for staff training on avoiding harassment or fostering multicultural communication

The best topic would be a problem that you would like to solve in real life.

YOUR TASKS

1. Define your topic, audience, and purpose and get your topic approved by your professor.
2. Identify what sources of information you will need to research.
3. Find articles or technical material about your subject. What were the experiences of other companies or agencies that implemented a similar idea? Keep a list of references to include with the proposal.
4. Research the cost of implementing your idea.
5. What support exists for your proposal? Prepare questions for interviews and a survey and bring them to class for feedback. Are you asking the right questions to get appropriate evidence for your proposal? Are your questions unbiased? What is a representative sample of people to interview or survey?
6. Conduct your surveys/interviews and summarize the results.
7. Write your proposal draft and bring it to class for feedback.
8. Submit the final copy of the proposal with a list of references. Include an envelope containing all copies of your completed surveys/interview summaries.

9. HELPING YOUNG WORKERS BE SAFE ON THE JOB: PROPOSAL FOR A SAFETY ORIENTATION FOR NEW HIRES

Assume you work as an office manager (a position that includes hiring responsibilities) for Undergo, a small but growing construction company that specializes in the installation of underground services, including water, sewer, and electrical piping. In the past year the staff has grown from 20 to 80; the company has multiple worksites and projects and 45 new male employees between the ages of 17 and 25.

Since no one else on staff is assigned responsibility for safety, you have handled some of the safety duties in the office, such as checking the vocational certifications of all new staff, filing accident investigation and inspection reports, and keeping training records. You also get notices from the provincial workers' compensation

board, and recently they sent a bulletin stating that the injury rate for young (especially male) workers is much higher than for other workers. You learned that every day 30 young workers are injured, and every week 5 are permanently disabled in workplace injuries.[7] Since you are in the "young worker" age bracket yourself, these statistics troubled you and motivated you to take some action at Undergo.

You know your company's supervisors do a great job in giving new hires training on-the-job and in covering hazard avoidance; but nothing is written down about what is covered, and without records, if a serious accident occurred, the company would be in a very bad legal position. As well, without some sort of checklist or guide, the topics covered are not necessarily the same for each new hire. Now that the company has grown, you believe the company needs to have a formal safety orientation program. Further, you think written records about this training should be kept. You decide to research what material might be available for developing a safety orientation program for young workers. You also think that some of the training material your company has is outdated—it mostly consists of print materials in dusty binders in the site trailers. You intend to see if any web-based materials are available on some general safety topics (such as ladder safety, using fall-arrest equipment, housekeeping on construction sites, wearing personal protective clothing, and so on). Each of your company's worksites has a trailer and a laptop, so you might be able to get some material on YouTube that could help motivate young workers to work safely.

YOUR TASK Write a proposal to the company's owner to establish an orientation program for all new hires. You decide the orientation would take about two hours and be run in a site office by each supervisor gaining the new employee(s).

If your proposal is approved, you will put together the program and train the supervisors on how to give a safety orientation. Begin your research by going online to look into your province's workers' compensation board resources. Your proposal should describe the topics to be covered in the orientation, the costs (including your time to put together the session, train the supervisors in how to run it, and design some forms to guide and record the training), the reasons why the company should have such a program (benefits), and some of the resources you would like to have for the program.

10. PROPOSAL: PODCASTING ABOUT PRODUCTS

You work for Tim Hortons in the human resources department in the Halifax regional office. Your job is to co-ordinate training material for the more than 30 store managers and their 400 employees in the region. You update the company's training manuals and send out product updates that are put into product knowledge binders for the employees to read. Recently one of the managers, Mark Harding, commented to you that it was difficult to get the employees to read the product update manual. "Even when the traffic slows down, and employees have time to read, they just don't seem to want to and the environment isn't really set up for reading either. It's a real hassle nagging them, but when they don't know about the products we lose sales" he complained. "This week alone five employees didn't know the new process for making a new popular drink and had to have a supervisor spend 30 minutes with each of the five on different shifts. That's how poor employee knowledge costs us money. And it is not just the starting wage employee time, it's also the supervisory time that is wasted. So, I keep nagging them."

You replied, "I've heard this complaint from other store managers and maybe it is time to try something that may be more appealing to the age group of your employees. What do you think of using podcasts for this kind of employee training? Starbucks has used podcasts to tell staff about new products. They play the podcasts when staff members are in the store without customers, like at opening and closing."

"Sounds like it would be more interesting than a manual, but what about if you forget something and want to look it up?" asked Mark.

"The podcasts would be in addition to the print training materials—the podcasts just provide a different way to get the information," you say.

Mark added, "But surely we don't want our employees to be plugged into MP3 players while they are in the store—that would not improve employee communication."

"True enough, what we would do is play the audio files on the in-store system, and if employees want to download files to review after work hours, they could," you reply.

You decide to persuade your boss, the manager of human resources (Martin Law), to experiment with podcasting for employee communication. He may be a tough sell. He is 55, has been with the company for the last 10 years, and is not that oriented to social technologies. While not a bean counter, he is very interested in the business's bottom line. He'll need to know the costs and benefits. He'd want to know that other businesses are using this technology to some advantage. A little research would be helpful on that.

You are not too worried about the cost of producing the podcasts. You would write the scripts and hire a local freelance broadcaster ($200/hour) to record 10-minute programs that can be played in the stores during opening and closing. You figure there would be enough material to make a weekly podcast, but to get it going, you decide starting small is best, so you want to propose making five podcasts that would be released every two weeks during the fall promotion period. As well, you'll start off with just one voice making the recordings, and if it is popular, work into using sound effects, music, and more than one voice recording. Who knows, if the idea works in this region, maybe it could be used nationally. How will you evaluate its success?

You find out the department could buy some recording and editing software called Recordforall for approximately $70, but you also want to purchase a high-quality recorder such as an R-09HR Edirol MP3 Recorder ($600) to produce the podcasts. It would take you four hours to learn how to use the editing software, two to three hours to write the script for each podcast, and two to three hours to edit each program. The finished programs would be available as MP3 files to be used in the store or downloaded by employees and listened to on non-work time. You figure the number of employees who would be reached would make the effort worthwhile.

YOUR TASK Write a proposal to Martin Law. Include a description of your idea, how it would work, what it would cost, and of course, what benefits would be gained. Tip: Use your math skills to estimate savings so that you can be persuasive with your audience.

11. FINDING A SOCIAL NETWORKING TECHNOLOGY FOR A BUSINESS APPLICATION

Using the Purdy's scenario in Chapter 9, Case 14, research a social networking strategy you are interested in to determine its advantages and disadvantages for the marketing department of Purdy's Chocolates. Purdy's goal would be to create opportunities for relationship building and interactivity with customers online. What social technology would you recommend?

What would be involved in getting the strategy implemented and what success has it had in other businesses? How costly is the strategy to implement? What types of resources do you need and what is the ongoing cost of monitoring or maintaining the online presence? For example, you might propose that the marketing department produce product knowledge podcasts to use in each of its 50 branches. Or, you may investigate and propose the use of a Facebook event to promote the product. Or, perhaps you'd like to investigate the best uses of wikis—maybe the department could use a wiki to develop marketing literature for a new product. How can the company build relationships either with customers or employees online?

YOUR TASK Write a proposal to implement the strategy at Purdy's (or at another company with which you are familiar).

12. REPORTING ON COMPANY USE OF FACEBOOK

You work as an administrator for Westport Innovations, a high-tech firm that makes bus engines that run on hydrogen and compressed natural gas. Your high-tech environment is exciting to work in and the field has been expanding rapidly, with sales in South America, China, and India. Many of the employees working at Westport are engineers and designers. Your company needs to attract the brightest talent and is looking for ways to expand recruitment and move away from traditional campus recruitment. You have been asked to research how companies are using Facebook and other social technologies to recruit employees.

YOUR TASK Summarize your findings in a report to the human resources department manager. Consult at least ten sources, including three business journal articles. Provide a list of references in APA format.

Top Tips for Writing Reports That Tell the Truth

Put nothing in writing that you're unwilling to say in public, and write nothing that may embarrass or jeopardize your employer. Does this mean you should cover up problems? Of course not. However, when you're dealing with sensitive information, be discreet. Present the information in such a way that it will help readers solve a problem. Avoid personal gripes, criticisms, alibis, attempts to blame other people, sugarcoated data, and unsolicited opinions.

To be useful, the information must be accurate, complete, and honest. But remember, being honest is not always a simple matter. Everyone sees reality a little differently, and individuals describe what they see in their own way. To restrict the distortions introduced by differences in perception, follow these guidelines:

- **Describe facts or events in concrete terms.** Indicate quantities whenever you can. Say that "Sales have increased 17 percent," or that "Sales have increased from $40 000 to $43 000 in the past two months." Don't say, "Sales have skyrocketed."
- **Report all relevant facts.** Regardless of whether these facts support your theories or please your readers, they must be included. Omitting the details that undermine your position may be convenient, but it is misleading and inaccurate.
- **Put the facts in perspective.** Taken out of context, the most concrete facts are misleading. If you say "Stock values have doubled in three weeks," you offer an incomplete picture. Instead, say "Stock values have doubled in three weeks, rising from $2 to $4 per share."
- **Give plenty of evidence for your conclusions.** Statements such as "We have to reorganize the sales force or we'll lose market share" may or may not be

true. Readers have no way of knowing unless you provide enough data to support your claim.

- **Present only verifiable conclusions.** Check facts, and use reliable sources. Don't draw conclusions too quickly (one rep may say that customers are unhappy, but that doesn't mean they all are). And don't assume that one event caused another (sales may have dipped right after you switched ad agencies, but that doesn't mean the new agency is at fault—the general state of the economy may be responsible).
- **Keep your personal biases in check.** Even if you feel strongly about your topic, keep those feelings from influencing your choice of words. Don't say, "Locating a plant in Kingston is a terrible idea because the people there are mostly students who would rather play than work and who don't have the ability to operate our machines." Such language not only offends but also obscures the facts and provokes emotional responses.

Applications for Success

1. When would you use vague language instead of concrete detail? Would this action be unethical or merely one form of emphasizing the positive?
2. Recent budget cuts have endangered the daycare program at your local branch of a national company. You're writing a report for headquarters about the grave impact on employees. Describe the situation in a single sentence that reveals nothing about your personal feelings but that clearly shows your position.
3. When writing an unsolicited proposal to a potential client, you need to persuade your audience to consider hiring your firm or purchasing your product. How can you be persuasive and completely truthful at the same time?

Planning, Writing, and Delivering Oral Presentations

After studying this chapter, you will be able to

1. Explain how planning an oral presentation differs from planning a written document
2. Describe the five tasks that go into organizing oral presentations
3. List three challenges you must keep in mind while composing your presentation
4. Discuss four elements involved in creating effective slides
5. List 10 ways to overcome your anxiety and feel more confident
6. Discuss two factors in presenting visuals effectively
7. Discuss six guidelines for handling questions effectively

Leanne Anderson helps business people become better public speakers by training them to focus on their audience's needs. She believes that knowing your audience is the most important element of a successful speech. She also advocates being a ruthless editor, because a good way to make your presentation stand out from others is to write a well-organized speech that is clear, concise, and focused. "Economy of language is the real key to good communication," she says. "That means choosing the best way of saying something to get the desired result."[1]

The Three-Step Oral Presentation Process

Like Leanne Anderson, chances are you'll have an opportunity to deliver a number of oral presentations throughout your career. You may not speak before large audiences of employees or the media, but you'll certainly be expected to present ideas to your colleagues, make sales presentations to potential customers, or engage in other kinds of spoken communication. For instance, if you're in the human resources department, you may give orientation briefings to new employees or explain company policies, procedures, and benefits at assemblies. If you're familiar with your department's procedures, you may conduct training programs. Regardless of your job or the purpose of your presentation, you will be more effective if you adopt an oral presentation process that follows three familiar steps (see Figure 12.1):

1. Plan your presentation.
2. Write your presentation.
3. Revise and rehearse your presentation.

> The process for preparing oral presentations has three familiar steps.

Step 1: Planning Speeches and Presentations

Planning oral presentations is similar to planning any other business message: It requires analyzing your purpose and your audience, investigating and researching necessary information, and adapting your message to the occasion and your audience so that you can establish a good relationship. However, because presentations are delivered orally under

> Preparing oral presentations requires some special communication techniques to ensure your audience hears what you say.

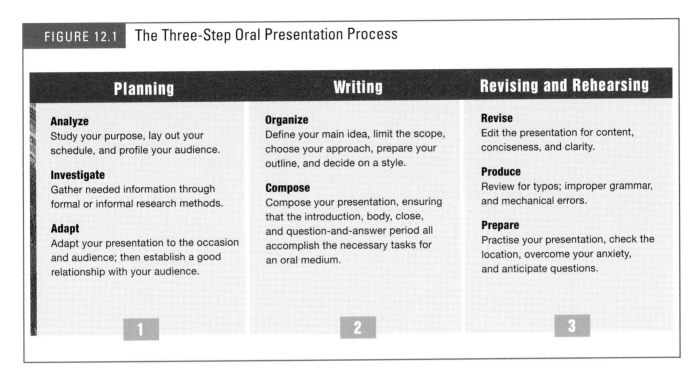

FIGURE 12.1 The Three-Step Oral Presentation Process

Planning	Writing	Revising and Rehearsing
Analyze Study your purpose, lay out your schedule, and profile your audience.	**Organize** Define your main idea, limit the scope, choose your approach, prepare your outline, and decide on a style.	**Revise** Edit the presentation for content, conciseness, and clarity.
Investigate Gather needed information through formal or informal research methods.	**Compose** Compose your presentation, ensuring that the introduction, body, close, and question-and-answer period all accomplish the necessary tasks for an oral medium.	**Produce** Review for typos; improper grammar, and mechanical errors.
Adapt Adapt your presentation to the occasion and audience; then establish a good relationship with your audience.		**Prepare** Practise your presentation, check the location, overcome your anxiety, and anticipate questions.
1	2	3

relatively public circumstances, they require a few special communication techniques. For one thing, a presentation is a one-time event; your audience cannot leaf back through printed pages to review something you said earlier. So you must make sure that audience members will hear what you say and remember it. You must capture their attention immediately and keep them interested. Therefore, begin by defining your purpose clearly while thinking of ways to engage your audience.

Clarify Your Purpose

The four basic reasons for giving a presentation are to inform, to persuade, to motivate, and to entertain. The purpose of your oral presentation will govern the content you include and the style in which you present the content. Most of your presentations or speeches will be informative, requiring a straightforward statement of the facts. If you're involved in marketing or sales, however, you'll probably be writing and delivering persuasive presentations and speeches using the organizational and writing techniques discussed in Chapter 9. Motivational speeches tend to be more specialized, so many companies bring in outside professional speakers to handle this type of presentation. Entertainment speeches are perhaps the rarest in the business world; they are usually limited to after-dinner speeches and to speeches at conventions or retreats.

> The content and style of speeches and presentations vary, depending on your purpose.

Analyze Your Audience

Whatever your purpose, your speech will be more effective if you keep your audience interested in your message. To do so, you must understand who your audience members are and what they need. If you're involved in selecting the audience or if you're speaking to a group of peers at work, you'll certainly have information about listener characteristics. But in many cases, you'll be speaking to a group of people you know very little about. You'll want to investigate their needs and characteristics before showing up to speak. Identify audience interests related to your topic. Research to find relevant facts and examples. You can also ask your host or some other contact person for help with audience analysis, and you can supplement that information with some educated estimates of your own. For a reminder of how to analyze an audience, review Chapter 3's "Develop

> What you know about your audience affects your main idea, scope, approach, outline, and style.

FIGURE 12.2	Audience Analysis Checklist

AUDIENCE ANALYSIS CHECKLIST

Determine Audience Size and Composition
✓ Estimate how many people will attend.
✓ Consider whether they have some political, religious, professional, or other affiliation in common.
✓ Analyze the mix of men and women, ages, socio-economic and ethnic groups, occupations, and geographic regions represented.

Predict the Audience's Probable Reaction
✓ Analyze why audience members are attending the presentation.
✓ Determine the audience's general attitude toward the topic: interested, moderately interested, open-minded, unconcerned, or hostile.
✓ Analyze the mood that people will be in when you speak to them.
✓ Find out what kind of backup information will most impress the audience: technical data, historical information, financial data, demonstrations, samples, and so on.
✓ Consider whether the audience has any biases that might work against you.
✓ Anticipate possible objections or questions.

Gauge the Audience's Level of Understanding
✓ Analyze whether everybody has the same background and experience.
✓ Determine what the audience already knows about the subject.
✓ Decide what background information the audience will need to better understand the subject.
✓ Consider whether the audience is familiar with your vocabulary.
✓ Analyze what the audience expects from you.
✓ Think about the mix of general concepts and specific details you will need to present.

an Audience Profile" and see Figure 12.2. For even more insight into audience evaluation (including emotional and cultural issues), consult a good public-speaking textbook.

 Document Makeovers

Step 2: Writing Speeches and Presentations

You may never actually write out a presentation word for word. But that doesn't mean that developing its content will be any easier or quicker than preparing a written document. Speaking intelligently about a topic may actually involve more work and more time than preparing a written document about the same topic.

Organize Your Speech or Presentation

> The tasks you perform when organizing oral messages are similar to those you perform for written messages.

Organize an oral message just as you would organize a written message, by focusing on your audience as you define your main idea, limit your scope, choose your approach, prepare your outline, and decide on the most effective style for your presentation.

- **Define the main idea.** What is the one message you want audience members to walk away with? The "you" attitude helps keep your audience's attention and convinces people that your points are relevant.
- **Limit your scope.** Tailor the material to the time allowed, which is often strictly regulated. Speakers can deliver about one paragraph (125 to 150 words) a minute (or between 20 and 25 double-spaced, typed pages per hour). To make three basic points in a 10-minute presentation, allow about 2 minutes (about two paragraphs) to explain each point, devote a minute each to the introduction and the conclusion, and leave 2 minutes for questions.
- **Choose your approach.** If you have 10 minutes or less to deliver your message, organize your presentation like a letter or a brief memo. Organize longer presentations like reports. Regardless of length, use direct order if the audience is receptive and indirect if you expect resistance. Simplicity of organization is especially valuable in oral presentations, since listeners can't review a paragraph or flip pages back and

forth, as they can when reading. One approach that is worth experimenting with is "Pecha Kucha," a technique that began in Japan's art and design community in 2003 and has now spread around the world. Pecha Kucha, whose name is the Japanese word for "chit-chat," is a format that limits speakers to the use of 20 slides, each shown for a maximum of 20 seconds, to form a strict 6 minute and 40 second presentation "timebox." First used in nightclubs with a series of presentations on varied art and design topics, the "20 × 20" method has spread into the business world, where the limitations on time and number of slides are appreciated. If you want to use Pecha Kucha, organize your presentation with these constraints in mind and rehearse your oral delivery to stay within the 6:40 time limit.

- **Prepare your outline.** Your outline helps you keep your presentation both audience centred and within the allotted time. Figure 12.3 is the outline for a 30-minute

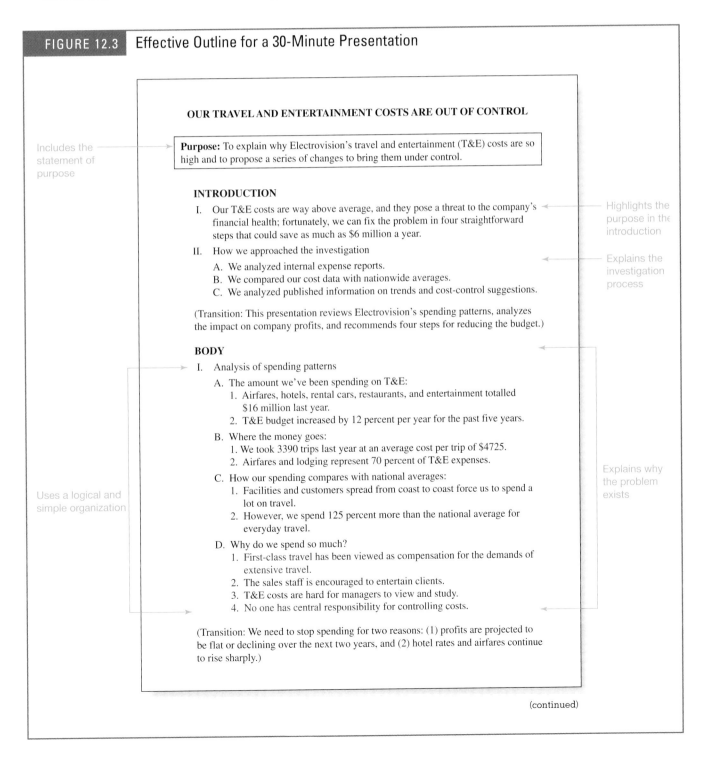

FIGURE 12.3 Effective Outline for a 30-Minute Presentation

Includes the statement of purpose

OUR TRAVEL AND ENTERTAINMENT COSTS ARE OUT OF CONTROL

Purpose: To explain why Electrovision's travel and entertainment (T&E) costs are so high and to propose a series of changes to bring them under control.

INTRODUCTION

I. Our T&E costs are way above average, and they pose a threat to the company's financial health; fortunately, we can fix the problem in four straightforward steps that could save as much as $6 million a year.

II. How we approached the investigation
   A. We analyzed internal expense reports.
   B. We compared our cost data with nationwide averages.
   C. We analyzed published information on trends and cost-control suggestions.

(Transition: This presentation reviews Electrovision's spending patterns, analyzes the impact on company profits, and recommends four steps for reducing the budget.)

BODY

I. Analysis of spending patterns
   A. The amount we've been spending on T&E:
      1. Airfares, hotels, rental cars, restaurants, and entertainment totalled $16 million last year.
      2. T&E budget increased by 12 percent per year for the past five years.
   B. Where the money goes:
      1. We took 3390 trips last year at an average cost per trip of $4725.
      2. Airfares and lodging represent 70 percent of T&E expenses.
   C. How our spending compares with national averages:
      1. Facilities and customers spread from coast to coast force us to spend a lot on travel.
      2. However, we spend 125 percent more than the national average for everyday travel.
   D. Why do we spend so much?
      1. First-class travel has been viewed as compensation for the demands of extensive travel.
      2. The sales staff is encouraged to entertain clients.
      3. T&E costs are hard for managers to view and study.
      4. No one has central responsibility for controlling costs.

(Transition: We need to stop spending for two reasons: (1) profits are projected to be flat or declining over the next two years, and (2) hotel rates and airfares continue to rise sharply.)

Highlights the purpose in the introduction

Explains the investigation process

Explains why the problem exists

Uses a logical and simple organization

(continued)

FIGURE 12.3 (Continued)

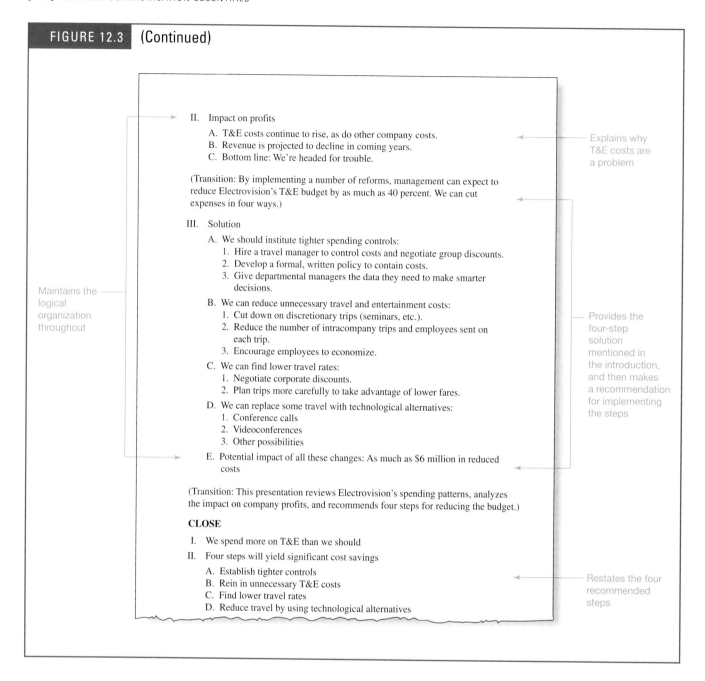

II. Impact on profits
   A. T&E costs continue to rise, as do other company costs.
   B. Revenue is projected to decline in coming years.
   C. Bottom line: We're headed for trouble.

Explains why T&E costs are a problem

(Transition: By implementing a number of reforms, management can expect to reduce Electrovision's T&E budget by as much as 40 percent. We can cut expenses in four ways.)

III. Solution
   A. We should institute tighter spending controls:
      1. Hire a travel manager to control costs and negotiate group discounts.
      2. Develop a formal, written policy to contain costs.
      3. Give departmental managers the data they need to make smarter decisions.
   B. We can reduce unnecessary travel and entertainment costs:
      1. Cut down on discretionary trips (seminars, etc.).
      2. Reduce the number of intracompany trips and employees sent on each trip.
      3. Encourage employees to economize.
   C. We can find lower travel rates:
      1. Negotiate corporate discounts.
      2. Plan trips more carefully to take advantage of lower fares.
   D. We can replace some travel with technological alternatives:
      1. Conference calls
      2. Videoconferences
      3. Other possibilities
   E. Potential impact of all these changes: As much as $6 million in reduced costs

Maintains the logical organization throughout

Provides the four-step solution mentioned in the introduction, and then makes a recommendation for implementing the steps

(Transition: This presentation reviews Electrovision's spending patterns, analyzes the impact on company profits, and recommends four steps for reducing the budget.)

CLOSE

I. We spend more on T&E than we should
II. Four steps will yield significant cost savings
   A. Establish tighter controls
   B. Rein in unnecessary T&E costs
   C. Find lower travel rates
   D. Reduce travel by using technological alternatives

Restates the four recommended steps

analytical presentation based on Linda Moreno's Electrovision report (see Chapter 11). It is organized around conclusions and presented in direct order. If you plan to give your presentation from notes rather than from written text, your outline can also become your final "script."

- **Decide on an appropriate style.** Choose your style to fit the occasion, audience size, subject, purpose, budget, location, and preparation time. When speaking to a small group in a conference room, encourage participation with a casual style. For a large audience at an important event, establish a more formal atmosphere: perhaps speaking from a stage or platform, standing behind a lectern, and using a microphone.

Compose Your Speech or Presentation

Developing a major presentation is much like writing a formal report, except that you need to adjust your technique to an oral channel. Speaking before a group offers certain opportunities:

- **Immediate audience feedback.** You can transmit information, but you can also receive audience feedback without delay.
- **Immediate modification to suit audience needs.** You can adjust both the content and the delivery of your message as you go along, in order to clarify or to be more compelling. Instead of simply expressing your ideas, you can draw ideas from your audience and then reach a mutually acceptable conclusion.
- **Nonverbal reinforcement.** You also have the opportunity to use nonverbal cues to express your meaning and emphasize what's important.

Using an oral communication channel presents you with challenges you need not face in written reports. As you compose each part of your presentation, think about how you will face each challenge:

- **Maintaining control.** The more you expect to interact with your audience, the less control you'll have of the situation.
- **Helping your audience follow what you're saying.** Since listeners cannot refer back and forth to what has been or will be said, you must work harder to clarify where you're going and help them stay on track.
- **Shifting topics smoothly.** Halfway through your presentation, a comment from someone in the audience might force you to shift topics. If you anticipate such shifts, you can prepare for them as you compose your presentation.

As you develop your speech, think carefully about how to handle each part: introduction, body, and close.

INTRODUCTION A good introduction arouses the audience's interest in your topic, establishes your credibility, and prepares the audience for what will follow. That's a lot to pack into the first few minutes of your presentation. So, of the total time you allocate to writing your oral presentation, plan on spending a disproportionate amount on developing your introduction. In the introduction, you want to

- **Arouse audience interest.** Get a good start by capturing the audience's attention (several methods are listed in Table 12.1 on page 290). If you are presenting to a small group, you can involve the audience by encouraging comments from listeners. However, when speaking to a large group, responding to comments can interrupt the flow of information, weaken your argument, and reduce your control of the situation. In that case, it's often best to ask people to hold questions until you're finished—be sure to allow ample time after your remarks.
- **Build your credibility.** Establish your credentials quickly—people will decide about you within a few minutes.[2] Building credibility is easy with a familiar, open-minded audience. For strangers (especially skeptical ones), try letting someone else introduce you. If introducing yourself, keep your comments simple, and don't be afraid to mention your accomplishments:

  I'm Karen Whitney. I've worked in the telemarketing department for the past five years, specializing in small-business markets. Vice-President John Barre asked me to talk to you about our telemarketing methods so that you'll have a better idea of how to get started.

- **Preview your presentation.** Help your audience understand the structure and content of your message. Give them cues to help them figure out how the main points of the

TABLE 12.1	Five Ways to Get Attention and Keep It
Use humour	Even though the subject of most business presentations is serious, including a light comment now and then can perk up the audience. Just be sure the humour is relevant to the presentation and not offensive to the audience.
Tell a story	Slice-of-life stories are naturally interesting and can be compelling. Be sure your story illustrates an important point.
Pass around a sample	Psychologists say that you can get people to remember your points by appealing to their senses. The best way to do so is to pass around a sample. If your company is in the textile business, let the audience handle some of your fabrics. If you sell chocolates, give everybody a taste.
Ask a question	Asking questions will get the audience actively involved in your presentation and, at the same time, will give you information about them and their needs.
State a startling statistic	People love details. If you can interject an interesting statistic, you can often wake up your audience.

Get attention with specific examples, anecdotes, and audience involvement.

message fit together. Summarize the main idea, identify the supporting points, and indicate the order in which you'll develop them. Establish the framework so that your audience will understand how the facts and figures are related to your main idea as you move into the body of your presentation.

Simplify the body by covering no more than three or four main points.

BODY The bulk of your speech or presentation is devoted to a discussion of the three or four main points in your outline. Use the same organizational patterns you would use in a letter, memo, or report, but keep things simple—limit the body to three or four main points. Make sure that your organization is clear and that your presentation holds the audience's attention.

Help your audience follow your presentation by using clear transitions between sentences and paragraphs, as well as between major sections.

Connecting Your Ideas To show how ideas are related, a written report uses typographical and formatting clues: headings, paragraph indentions, white space, and lists. However, an oral presentation must rely on words to link various parts and ideas.

For the small links between sentences and paragraphs, use one or two transitional words: *therefore, because, in addition, in contrast, moreover, for example, consequently, nevertheless,* or *finally.* To link major sections of a presentation, use complete sentences or paragraphs, such as "Now that we've reviewed the problem, let's take a look at some solutions." Every time you shift topics, be sure to stress the connection between ideas. Summarize what's been said, then preview what's to come.

Emphasize your transitions by repeating key ideas, using gestures, changing your tone of voice, or introducing a visual aid.

The longer your presentation, the more important your transitions become. If you will be presenting many ideas, audience members may have trouble absorbing them and seeing the relationships among them. Your listeners need clear transitions to guide them to the most important points. Furthermore, they need transitions to pick up any ideas they may have missed. So by repeating key ideas in your transitions, you can compensate for lapses in your audience's attention. When you actually give your presentation, you might also want to call attention to the transitions by using gestures, moving to a new position, changing your tone of voice, or introducing a visual aid (discussed later in this chapter).

Holding Your Audience's Attention To communicate your points effectively, you must do more than connect your ideas with clear transitions. You also have to hold your audience's attention. Here are a few helpful tips for engaging an audience:

- **Relate your subject to your audience's needs.** People are interested in things that affect them personally. Present every point in light of your audience's needs and values.
- **Anticipate your audience's questions.** Try to anticipate as many questions as you can, and address these questions in the body of your presentation. You'll also want to prepare and reserve additional material to use during the question-and-answer period should the audience ask for greater detail.
- **Use clear, vivid language.** People become bored when they don't understand the speaker. If your presentation will involve abstract ideas, plan to show how those abstractions connect with everyday life. Use familiar words, short sentences, and concrete examples.
- **Explain the relationship between your subject and familiar ideas.** Show how your subject is related to ideas that audience members already understand, so that you give people a way to categorize and remember your points.[3]
- **Ask opinions or pause occasionally for questions or comments.** Getting audience feedback helps you determine whether your listeners have understood a key point. Feedback also gives your audience a change from listening to participating. Plan your pauses, even noting them in your outline so that you won't forget to pause once you're on stage.

> Make a special effort to capture wandering attention.

CLOSE The close of a speech or presentation is almost as important as the beginning because audience attention peaks at this point. Plan to devote writing time to the ending. When developing your conclusion, begin by telling listeners that you're about to finish, so that they'll make one final effort to listen intently. Don't be afraid to sound obvious. Consider saying something such as "in conclusion" or "to sum it all up." You want people to know that this is the home stretch.

- **Restating your main points.** Repeat your main idea in the close. Emphasize what you want your audience to do or think, state the key motivating factor, and restate the three or four main supporting points. A few sentences are enough to refresh people's memories. One speaker ended a presentation by repeating his four specific recommendations and concluding with a memorable statement to motivate his audience:

> Make the close should leave a strong and lasting impression.

  We can all be proud of the way our company has grown. If we want to continue that growth, however, we will have to adjust our managers' compensation program to reflect competitive practices. If we don't, our best people will look for opportunities elsewhere.

  In summary, our survey has shown that we need to do four things to improve executive compensation:

  - Increase the overall level of compensation
  - Install a cash bonus program
  - Offer a variety of stock-based incentives
  - Improve our health insurance and pension benefits

  By making these improvements, we can help our company grow to compete on a global scale.

- **Describing the next steps.** If you expect listeners to take action, explain who is responsible for doing what. (You might present a slide listing each item with a completion date and the name of persons responsible.) Alert people to potential difficulties or pitfalls.

- **Ending on a strong note.** Make your final remarks encouraging and memorable. Conclude with a quote, a call to action, or some encouraging words. You might stress the benefits of action, express confidence in the listeners' ability to accomplish the work ahead, or end with a question or statement that leaves people thinking. Your final words give the audience a satisfied feeling of completeness. Don't introduce new ideas or alter the mood of the speech.

 Document Makeovers

Step 3: Revising and Rehearsing Speeches and Presentations

To complete your oral presentation, evaluate the content of your message and edit your remarks for clarity and conciseness—as you would for any business message. Develop any visual aids for your presentation, and coordinate them with your delivery. Finally, master the art of delivery through practice and preparation, by building your confidence, and by polishing the way you present visuals and handle questions.

Using Visual Aids in Your Speech or Presentation

> Visual aids help the audience remember important points.

Visual aids can improve the quality and impact of your oral presentation by creating interest, illustrating points that are difficult to explain in words alone, adding variety, and increasing the audience's ability to absorb and remember information. Visual aids help your audience; they are estimated to improve learning because humans can process visuals much faster than text.[4] Visual aids also help you as speaker; they help you remember the details of your message (no small feat in a lengthy presentation), and they improve your professional image (speakers who use visuals generally appear better prepared and more knowledgeable than other speakers).

 **Model** Document

> When preparing visual aids for oral presentations, you have a variety of media to choose from.

SELECTING THE RIGHT TYPE OF VISUAL To enhance oral presentations, you can choose from a variety of visual aids. Among the most popular types are:

- **Electronic presentation.** This slide show is a series of electronic slides created and stored on computer. Using software such as Microsoft PowerPoint, Lotus Freelance Graphics, or CorelDRAW, you can incorporate text, photos, sound, video, graphics, and animation into your slides. You show these slides using a liquid crystal display (LCD) projector.[5]
- **Overhead transparency.** This piece of clear plastic contains text or a graphic. You show a transparency by placing it on the lit window of an overhead projector, which casts the image onto a large screen. You can create transparencies by hand, but you're more likely to use word-processing, page-layout, or presentation software. We sometimes refer to transparencies as slides because their content and design elements are so similar to electronic slides.
- **Chalkboard or whiteboard.** These writing surfaces are effective tools for recording points made during small-group brainstorming sessions. Because these visual aids are produced on the spot, they offer flexibility; however, they're too informal for some situations.
- **Flip chart.** These large sheets of paper are attached at the top like a tablet and can be propped on an easel so that you can flip the pages as you speak. With felt-tip markers, you can also record ideas generated during a discussion.
- **Other visual aids.** Product or material samples help your audience experience your subject directly. Scale models represent objects conveniently. Slide presentations,

TABLE 12.2	Advantages and Disadvantages of Overhead and Electronic Slides

ADVANTAGES OF OVERHEAD TRANSPARENCIES

- Inexpensive and easy to create. You can prepare high-quality overheads using a computer and a high-resolution colour inkjet or laser printer.
- Simple to use. They require little extra equipment to show: Most conference rooms or classrooms have overhead projectors.
- Can be projected in full daylight. Speakers can maintain eye contact with their listeners.
- Can be altered during presentation. Speakers can use special markers to write on transparencies as they present information.

DISADVANTAGES

- Must be replaced if content changes.
- Fragile. They easily chip, flake, scratch, and tear.
- Protective frames of cardboard or plastic and transparent sleeves are costly and bulky to store and transport.
- Must be aligned carefully (one at a time) on the overhead projector, limiting the speaker's ability to move freely about the room.

ADVANTAGES OF ELECTRONIC SLIDES

- Easy to change in real time. You can change a graphic, add a bulleted phrase, even alter slide sequence with a simple click of the mouse.
- Make dazzling professional presentations. You can add animation, video clips, sound, hypertext, and other multimedia effects, as well as preprogram and automate the release of text and graphic elements.
- Easy to store, transport, and customize for different audiences.
- Allow you to feature one text point at a time.

DISADVANTAGES

- Display equipment is expensive, can be complicated to use, and may not be available in all situations.
- Most people spend too much time focusing on the technical components of a presentation, paying more attention to the animation and special effects than to the audience.
- Inexperienced presenters tend to use too many special effects, creating a visual overload of pictures and graphics that dazzle or hypnotize the audience but blur the key message.

television, and videotapes show demonstrations, interviews, and other events. Also, slides, movies, TV, and videos can stand alone (without a speaker) to communicate with dispersed audiences at various times.

The two most popular visual aids are overhead transparencies and electronic presentations. Even though these two visual aids differ in some features and delivery, both are a collection of slides that must be well written and well designed to be effective. Once the slides are created, they are either printed on clear plastic sheets (for overhead transparencies) or stored electronically and further embellished with multimedia effects (for electronic presentations). Both overhead transparencies and electronic slides have advantages and disadvantages, as Table 12.2 points out.

> Overhead transparencies and electronic presentations both consist of a series of slides.

LIMITING THE NUMBER OF VISUALS Even if you produce an outstanding set of slides, they'll do you no good if you can't complete your presentation in the allotted time. Having too many visuals can detract from your message. It forces you either to rush through a presentation or to skip visuals—some of which may be critical to your message.

> Limit the number of slides to a few good ones.

Covering less information in a relaxed style is much better than covering too much information in a hurried and disorganized manner. Build enough time into your presentation for a smile, an anecdote, or further illustration of a point. Remember that most audiences won't be angry if you let them out early, but they might be upset if you keep them late.

Gauging the correct number of visuals depends on the length of your presentation and the complexity of the subject matter. If you are using electronic slides, try to average one slide for every 90 seconds you speak. For a 30-minute presentation, you would create about 20 slides.[6] Of course, you may spend more time discussing some slides than others, so the best way to find the "right" number is to time your presentation as you practise.

TABLE 12.3	Colour and Emotion	
COLOUR	EMOTIONAL ASSOCIATIONS	BEST USE
■	Peaceful, soothing, tranquil, cool, trusting, relaxing	Background for electronic business presentations (usually dark blue); safe and conservative
□	Neutral, innocent, pure, wise	Font colour of choice for most electronic business presentations with a dark background
□	Warm, bright, cheerful, enthusiastic	Text bullets and subheadings with a dark background
■	Losses in business, passion, danger, action, pain	Promote action or stimulate audience; seldom used as a background
▭	Money, growth, assertiveness, prosperity, envy	Highlight and accent colour

 **Model** Document

> Slides are most effective when they are simple and are used sparingly.

> Colour can increase the appeal and impact of your slides.

CREATING EFFECTIVE SLIDES Once you've planned out what a slide is going to say, organize the content as you would for any written message. Then compose and polish the written content before focusing on the slide's design elements.

Simplicity is the key to effective design. Since people cannot read and listen effectively at the same time, your slides must be simple enough for the audience to understand in a moment or two. Use phrases only. Sentences and paragraphs require prolonged reading. Keep content and graphics simple and readable, select design elements that enhance your message without overshadowing it, be consistent in your design selections, and use special effects selectively.

Choosing Colour Colour is a critical design element. It grabs the viewer's attention, emphasizes important ideas, creates contrast, and isolates slide elements. Colour can make your slides more attractive, lively, and professional (see Table 12.3). Indeed, colour visuals can account for 60 percent of an audience's acceptance or rejection of an idea.[7] When choosing colour, remember these important guidelines:

- **Use colour to stimulate the right emotions.** If you wish to excite your audience, add some warm colours such as red and orange to your slides. If you wish to achieve a more relaxed and receptive environment, stick to blue.[8]
- **Be sensitive to cultural differences.** When creating slides for international audiences, remember that colour may have a different meaning from culture to culture.
- **Limit colour selections to a few complementary ones.** Avoid using too many colours in your slides. Also, remember that some colours work together better than others.
- **Use contrasting colours to increase readability.** For backgrounds, titles, and text, avoid choosing colours that are close in hue: yellow text on a white background, brown on green, blue on black, blue on purple, and so on.[9]
- **Adjust colour choices to room light.** Since most electronic presentations are shown in a dark room, use dark colours such as blue for the background, a midrange of brightness for illustrations, and light colours for text. If you are showing overhead transparencies in well-lit rooms, reverse the colours: Use light colours for the background and dark colours for text.[10]

Choosing Background Designs A slide's background can silently persuade viewers to pay attention or encourage them to look the other way. Many companies hire professional graphic artists to develop a custom background design to be used in all company slides. These custom designs generally include a company logo and company colours.

If you're not using a company design, you have several options. Popular software programs such as Microsoft's PowerPoint come with a collection of professionally developed

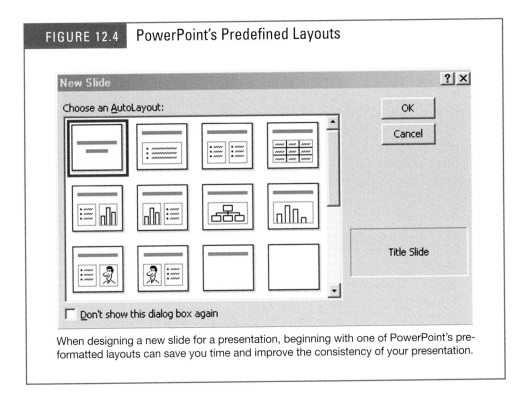

FIGURE 12.4   PowerPoint's Predefined Layouts

When designing a new slide for a presentation, beginning with one of PowerPoint's pre-formatted layouts can save you time and improve the consistency of your presentation.

background designs. Some designs are effective for business presentations; others are too busy or too colourful to be used in business settings. You can also purchase collections of slide backgrounds over the internet, obtain them from other software packages, or create your own.

Regardless of your source, be careful when choosing slide backgrounds. Avoid backgrounds whose heavy colour, busy patterns, or strong graphics compete with your text. Choose a design that is simple, is appropriate for the presentation subject, and will appeal to the audience. Make sure that graphic elements such as borders and company logos repeat on every visual. Such consistency not only makes your slides easier to read but also gives your presentation a clean, professional look. Another way to achieve design consistency is to use the layout templates that are included with most presentation software packages. As Figure 12.4 shows, each layout contains placeholders for specific slide elements such as a title, graphic art, or bulleted text.

> Select a background design that fits with your message and your audience.

> Layout templates are easy to use.

Choosing Fonts and Type Styles   Most software programs offer an immense selection of fonts. However, even though decorative fonts appear attractive, few of them project well on screen.

> Use a strong, simple font.

When selecting fonts and type styles for slides, follow these guidelines:
- Avoid script or decorative fonts.
- Limit your fonts to one or two per slide (if two fonts are used, reserve one for headings and the other for bulleted items).
- Use boldface type for electronic slides so that letters won't look washed out.
- Avoid italicized type because it is difficult to read when projected.
- Use both upper case and lower case letters, with extra white space between lines of text.

Bigger is not always better when it comes to type size. Large type can force text from one line to two and diminish the slide's white space. Use between 24- and 36-point type for electronic presentations, reserving the larger size for titles and the smaller size for bullet items. Headings of the same level of importance should use the same font, type size, and colour. Once you've selected your fonts and type styles, test them for readability by viewing sample slides from a distance.

> Test your font and type style selections by viewing slides from the back of the room.

Don't overdo special effects.

Slide sorter view makes it easier to check your slides for consistency and logical organization.

Good handouts keep the audience informed without overwhelming them with information.

Use handouts to provide detail. If you use magazine articles, seek permission to avoid copyright infringement.

Manage handouts carefully to avoid distractions.

Adding Animation and Special Effects Unlike transparencies, electronic slide shows can include a number of special effects, such as sound, animation, and video. You can even automate your program to move from one slide to the next without the speaker's intervention. The biggest challenge to overcome is the tendency to use too many of these features, which can include

- **Transitions.** The way that one electronic slide replaces another on screen is called a *transition*. Effective transitions can make your presentation flow smoothly from slide to slide so that you keep your audience's attention. Most electronic software packages include a number of effective transition effects, such as blind, box, checkerboard, dissolve, wipe, fade, paintbrush, and split. Use the same transitions throughout your presentation.

- **Builds.** The way that text and graphics are released for viewing is called a *build*. You can make your bullet points appear one at a time, line by line, to draw audience attention to the point being discussed. The most basic build effects are flys (making an element appear to fly in) and dissolves (altering the intensity of an element's colour as you discuss it while fading the other colours into the background). Use the same builds throughout your presentation.

- **Hyperlinks.** By coding text, graphics, or pictures with hypertext markup language, you can build interactivity into electronic slides. When you click on a slide's hyperlink with a mouse, you are taken to a different slide in your presentation, to other files on your computer, or even to a webpage on the internet. Hyperlinks are a great tool for illustrating fine details without having to incorporate each detail into a slide.

Electronic presentation software can help you plan, write, and revise your slides. As Figure 12.5 shows, the *slide sorter view* lets you see a file's entire batch of slides at once, making it relatively easy to add and delete slides, reposition slides, and check slides for design consistency. You can also use this view to preview animation and transition effects and experiment with design elements.

CREATING EFFECTIVE HANDOUTS Handouts are a terrific way to offer your audience additional material without overloading your slides with information. Candidates for good handout material include the following.[11]

- **Complex charts and diagrams.** Charts and tables that are too unwieldy for the screen or that demand thorough analysis are better as handouts. One common approach is to create a stripped-down version of a chart or graphic for the presentation slide and include a more detailed version in your handout.

- **Report parts.** In most cases lengthy research reports promise information overload and are inappropriate for handouts. But photocopies of specific pages that highlight or underline relevant text are welcome material.

- **Websites.** Lists of websites related to your topic are useful. In addition to providing the URL address, annotate each item with a one- or two-sentence summary of each site's content.

- **Copies of presentation slides.** In many cases, audiences like to have small print versions of the slides used by the speaker (about three to a page) along with accompanying comments and blank lines for note-taking.

Other good handout materials include brochures, pictures, outlines, and a copy of the presentation agenda.

Timing the distribution of handouts is a difficult decision. You must base that decision on the content of your handouts, the nature of your presentation, and whether you plan to use the material during the talk. Some speakers distribute handout materials before the presentation; other speakers advise the audience of the types of handouts but delay distributing anything until they have finished speaking.

| FIGURE 12.5 | Slide Sorter View |

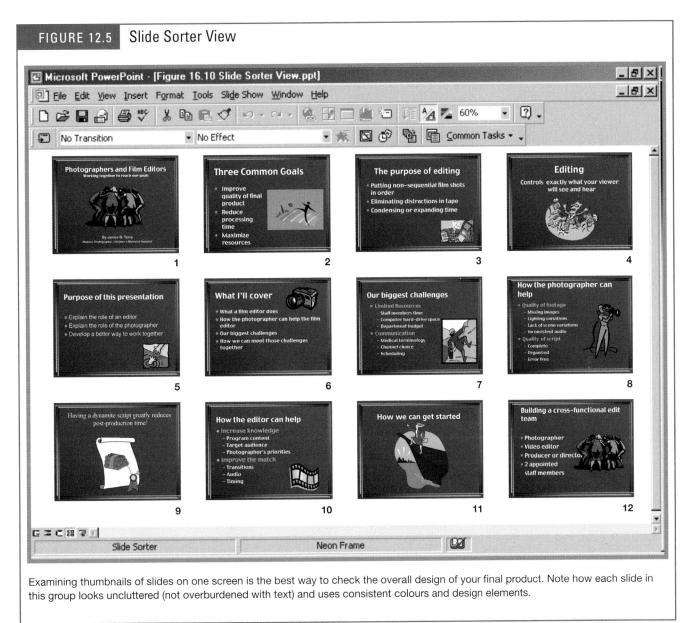

Examining thumbnails of slides on one screen is the best way to check the overall design of your final product. Note how each slide in this group looks uncluttered (not overburdened with text) and uses consistent colours and design elements.

To help you decide when to distribute handouts, how many visuals to include, or how to coordinate your slides with what you have to say, you'll need to practise delivering your speech.

Mastering the Art of Delivery

Giving a speech is quite different from preparing one. Once you've planned and written your presentation and developed your visuals, you're ready to begin practising your delivery. You have a variety of delivery methods to choose from, some of which are easier to handle than others:

- **Speaking from notes.** Making a presentation with the help of an outline, note cards, or visual aids is probably the most effective and easiest delivery mode. This approach gives you something to refer to and still allows for eye contact and interaction with the audience. If your listeners look puzzled, you can expand on a point or rephrase it. (Generally, note cards are preferable to sheets of paper, because nervousness is easier to see in shaking sheets of paper.)
- **Memorizing.** Unless you're a trained actor, avoid memorizing your speech, especially a long one. You're likely to forget your lines, and your speech will sound stilted.

> Speaking from notes is generally the best way to handle delivery.

> Avoid both memorized and recited delivery and avoid reading.

Besides, you'll often need to address audience questions during your speech, so you must be flexible enough to adjust your speech as you go. However, memorizing a quotation, an opening paragraph, or a few concluding remarks can bolster your confidence and strengthen your delivery.

- **Reading.** If you're delivering a technical or complex presentation, you may need to read parts of it. Policy statements by government officials are sometimes read because the wording may be critical. If you choose to read your speech, practise enough so that you can still maintain eye contact with your audience. Triple-spaced copy, wide margins, and large type will help. You might even want to include stage cues, such as *pause, raise hands, lower voice.* However, in most business presentations you will be more effective if you do not read. You'll want to connect with the audience.

- **Impromptu speaking.** You might have to give an impromptu, or unrehearsed, speech if you're called on to speak unexpectedly or if you've agreed to speak but neglected to prepare your remarks. Avoid speaking unprepared unless you've spoken countless times on the same topic or are an extremely good public speaker. When you're asked to speak "off the cuff," take a moment to think through what you'll say. Then avoid the temptation to ramble.

> **Before you speak**
> - Practise
> - Prepare the location
> - Consider cultural differences

PREPARE TO SPEAK Regardless of which delivery mode you use, be sure that you're thoroughly familiar with your subject. Knowing what you're talking about is the best way to build your self-confidence. Also, practising helps keep you on track, helps you maintain a conversational tone with your audience, and boosts your confidence and composure. Practise in front of a mirror. If possible, rehearse on videotape to see yourself as your audience will. Practise in front of people.

In addition to knowing your material and practising your delivery, check the room and seating arrangements to ensure that they're appropriate for your needs. Check the outlets, projection equipment, pointer, extension cords, and any other small but crucial items you might need.

Also, make sure you're prepared to address audiences from other cultures. You may need to adapt the content of your presentation or the way you deliver it.

OVERCOME ANXIETY AND STAGE FRIGHT If you're nervous about facing an audience and experience stage fright, you're not alone. Even speakers with years of experience feel some anxiety about getting up in front of an audience. Although you might not be able to make your nervous feelings disappear, you can learn to cope with your anxiety.

> Several techniques can help you become a more confident speaker.

Feeling More Confident Nervousness shows that you care about your audience, your topic, and the occasion. If your palms get wet or your mouth goes dry, don't think of nerves, think of excitement. Such stimulation can give you the extra energy you need to make your presentation sparkle. Here are some ways to become a more confident speaker:[12]

- **Prepare more material than necessary.** Combined with a genuine interest in your topic, extra knowledge will reduce your anxiety.
- **Rehearse.** The more familiar you are with your material, the less panic you'll feel.
- **Think positively.** See yourself as polished and professional, and your audience will too.
- **Visualize your success.** Use the few minutes before you actually begin speaking to tell yourself you're on and you're ready.
- **Take a few deep breaths.** Before you begin to speak, remember that your audience is silently wishing you success.
- **Be ready.** Have your first sentence memorized and on the tip of your tongue.
- **Be comfortable.** If your throat is dry, drink some water.
- **Don't panic.** If you feel that you're losing your audience during your speech, try to pull them back by involving them in the action; ask for their opinions or pause for questions.

- **Keep going.** Things usually get better as you go.
- **Focus on your message and audience.** Perhaps the best way to feel more confident is to focus outside yourself. If you're busy thinking about your subject and observing your audience's response, you'll tend to forget your fears.

Appearing More Confident As you practise delivering your presentation, try to be aware of the nonverbal signals you're transmitting. Regardless of how you feel inside, your effectiveness greatly depends on how you look and sound.

Well-delivered presentations start with your first minute at the podium, so don't rush. As you approach the speaker's lectern, walk slowly, breathe deeply, and stand up straight. Face your audience, adjust the microphone, count to three slowly, and then survey the room. When you find a friendly face, make eye contact and smile. Count to three again and begin your presentation.[13] If you are nervous, this slow, controlled beginning will help you establish rapport and appear more confident.

Be particularly careful to practise maintaining eye contact with your audience. Pick out several people positioned around the room, and shift your gaze from one to another. Looking directly at your listeners will make you appear sincere, confident, and trustworthy. It also helps you get an idea of the impression you're creating.

Your posture is also important in projecting more confidence. Stand tall, with your weight on both feet and your shoulders back. Avoid gripping the lectern. In fact, practise stepping out from behind the lectern to help your audience feel more comfortable with you and to express your own comfort and confidence in what you're saying. Use your hands to emphasize your remarks with appropriate gestures. Meanwhile, vary your facial expressions to make the message more dynamic.

Finally, think about the sound of your voice. Studies indicate that people who speak with lower vocal tones at a slightly faster than average rate are perceived as being more credible.[14] Practise speaking in a normal, conversational tone but with enough volume for everyone to hear you. Try to sound poised and confident, varying your pitch and speaking rate to add emphasis. Don't ramble. Use silence instead of meaningless filler words such as *um, you know, okay,* and *like.* Silence adds dramatic punch and gives the audience time to think about the message. Remember, speak clearly and crisply, articulating all the syllables, and sound enthusiastic about what you're saying.

PRESENT VISUALS EFFECTIVELY When practising your presentation, run through it about five times using your visuals. Your credibility is dramatically enhanced when you move seamlessly through your presentation.

Speaking Without Reading The most common mistake people make when delivering a presentation is reading their slides. When using PowerPoint, touch the "B" key to black out the screen so you can connect directly with your listeners. When you read to audience members, you lose contact with them. As your voice loses its inflection, listeners lose interest and eventually stop paying attention. Plus, listeners expect you to add valuable information not included on the slides. You must know enough about the subject of your presentation to elaborate on your visuals, so do your research.

As you practise, try not to be dependent on your slides. Some people can deliver a perfect presentation without notes. But for those who require notes, electronic software gives you an added advantage. Speaker's notes (as shown in Figure 12.6 on page 300) are a helpful tool included with most popular electronic presentation software packages. You can display these notes along with a scaled-down version of your slide on a computer screen so that only you can see the notes. As with visuals, don't read your speaker's notes aloud word for word. Instead, use them to list important facts or to remind yourself of comments you should make as you present the slide. For instance, you might include a note such as "Explain the impact of last year's bad weather on sales."

Don't rush the opening.

Use eye contact, posture, gestures, and voice to convey an aura of mastery and to keep your audience's attention.

Don't read your slides to the audience.

Use speaker's notes to jog your memory.

FIGURE 12.6 Speaker's Notes

Speaker Notes [?] [X]

Slide: 1

Lighting variations: Mention colour combinations to avoid because they do not photograph well together.

Lack of scene variations: Remind photographers that editing department is a good resource for hospital scene footage.

Inconsistent Audio: Emphasize the importance of matching appropriate music tracks to the subject matter.

Close

How the photographer can help

- **Quality of footage**
  - Missing images
  - Lighting variations
  - Lack of scene variations
  - Inconsistent audio
- **Quality of script**
  - Complete
  - Organized
  - Error-free

Figure 12.6a Speaker's notes

Figure 12.6b Corresponding slide

Speaker's notes, such as the ones displayed in Figure 12.6a, are an added benefit of using electronic presentations. The notes are displayed only on the presenter's screen while the corresponding slide, Figure 12.6b, is presented to the audience.

Introduce your slides before you show them.

With electronic slides, you are not tied to the projector or front of the room.

Practise placing overhead transparencies on a projector so it becomes second nature.

Introducing Visuals All visual aids must be properly introduced. Too many speakers show a visual first and then introduce it. Introduce the next visual aid *before* you show it. State your transition out loud:

"We can get started with this new program by introducing these policies . . . "

"The next segment of my presentation discusses . . . "

"The three most significant issues facing our company are . . . "

Also avoid referring to a slide in your transitional comments. For instance, don't say "The next slide illustrates . . . " Instead, match your words to the slide and let the audience make the proper connection.

If you're using overhead transparencies, introduce the next overhead as you remove the old one and position the new one on the projector. Immediately cover all but the first bulleted phrase with a sheet of paper to prevent the audience from reading ahead. Then step aside to give the audience about five seconds to look it over before you start discussing it. As you advance through your discussion, you can move the paper down the transparency to uncover the next bullet, or use a pointer. When you are finished using the transparency, cover it until you're ready to introduce a new slide. Keep in mind that placing overhead transparencies on a projector takes a bit more time than clicking a mouse. The audience will probably have little interest in reading the old transparency once your comments move forward.[15]

If you are using electronic slides, introduce the slide before you show it and then give the audience a few seconds to view the title and design elements. With electronic slides, you have more control over the release of information. For instance, you can release bulleted points or sections of a graph as you discuss them. This control gives you more flexibility to move about the room. Take advantage of this benefit. Moving around can increase audience involvement and enhance your impact. You may even want to invest in a mouse with an extended cord or a battery-operated remote mouse to maximize your freedom to walk around.

Use a pointer to guide the audience to a specific part of a visual. It is not a riding crop, conductor's baton, leg scratcher, or walking stick. Use the pointer only at the time you need it, then fold it and remove it from sight. If you are using a laser pointer that puts a focused dot of light on the desired part of your visual, don't overdo it. A laser pointer is an excellent tool if used judiciously, but in the hands of the overzealous presenter, it can become a distraction.[16]

HANDLE QUESTIONS RESPONSIVELY The question-and-answer period is one of the most important parts of an oral presentation. At the beginning of your presentation explain when the audience can ask questions and be sure to leave time for them. Questions give you a chance to obtain important information and feedback, to emphasize points you made earlier, to work in material that didn't fit into the formal presentation, and to overcome audience resistance by building enthusiasm for your point of view. Without questions, you might just as well write a report.

Many speakers do well delivering their oral presentation, only to falter during the question-and-answer period. But if you spend time anticipating these questions, you'll be ready with answers. Some experts recommend that you hold back some dramatic statistics as ammunition for the question-and-answer session.[17] If your message is unpopular, you should also be prepared for hostile questions. Treat them as legitimate requests for information. Maintaining your professionalism will improve your credibility. Follow these guidelines to ensure an effective question-and-answer period:

- **Respond appropriately.** Answer the question you're asked. Don't sidestep it, ignore it, or laugh it off. If an adequate answer would take too long, say, "I'm sorry, we don't have time to explore that issue right now, but if you'll see me after the presentation, I'll be happy to discuss it with you." If you don't know the answer, don't pretend to. Say, "I don't have those figures. I'll get them for you as quickly as possible."
- **Focus on the questioner.** Pay attention to body language and facial expression to determine what the question really means. Nod your head in acknowledgement, and repeat the question aloud to confirm your understanding and ensure that everyone has heard it. If a question is vague, ask for clarification before giving a simple, direct answer. If asked to choose between two alternatives, don't feel you must. Offer your own choice if it makes more sense.[18]
- **Maintain control of the situation.** Prevent anyone from monopolizing this period. State a time or question limit per person. Asking people to identify themselves before they speak helps them behave themselves.[19] Avoid lengthy debate. You might respond with a brief answer before moving on to the next questioner. Or you might admit that you and the questioner have different opinions and offer to get back to the questioner once you've done more research.[20]
- **Maintain self-control.** If a question flusters or angers you, answer honestly but stay cool. Maintain eye contact, answer the question as well as you can, and try not to show your feelings. Don't get into an argument. Defuse hostility by paraphrasing the question and asking the questioner to confirm that you've understood it correctly. Break long, complicated questions into parts. Respond accurately and unemotionally; then move on.
- **Motivate questions.** If listeners are too timid or hostile to ask questions, consider planting your own. If a friend or the event organizer starts off, others will join in. When all else fails, say something like "I know from experience that most questions are asked after the question period. So I'll be around afterwards to talk."[21]
- **Signal the end of your speech.** When your allotted time is up, halt the question-and-answer session, even if people still want to talk. Say, "Our time is almost up. Let's have one last question." After you reply, summarize the main idea of the presentation and thank people for their attention. Conclude the way you began, by looking around the room and making eye contact. Then gather your notes and leave the podium, shoulders straight, head up.

> Anticipate questions and be ready with answers so that you can
> - Emphasize your most important points
> - Refer to material that didn't fit in the formal presentation
> - Overcome audience resistance

> Answer questions effectively by
> - Using body language to show you're listening
> - Keeping answers short and to the point
> - Stating some ground rules to maintain control
> - Responding unemotionally
> - Helping listeners ask you questions

ON THE JOB

If you are invited to participate in a group presentation, you have a chance to show-case your leadership skills. "Teamwork is crucial, even at the lectern," says media and presentation coach Jim Gray.[22] Jim's tips for giving team presentations are to

- Pick a leader and decide on content and roles
- Have the leader introduce the topic and speakers and sum up at the end
- Keep it simple—have a maximum of four presenters
- Allocate time according to speaker strengths
- Look and act like a team, including gazing at the speaker when it is not your turn to talk
- Rehearse transitions and learn each others' parts in case you have to step in

Reviewing Key Points

In this chapter, you learned to plan your speeches and presentations by studying your purpose and profiling your audience. You learned how to organize and compose your presentation, and how to develop the introduction, body, and close. To make your introduction effective, capture attention, establish credibility, and preview the content. Develop the body by anticipating audience interests, providing specific examples and anecdotes relevant to the audience, and emphasizing the most important points with visual aids. Use analogies, audience-oriented examples, and vivid language to keep the audience's attention. Add transitional phrases, gestures, and visuals to ensure that the audience follows as you move between sections in your talk. In the closing, restate key points, tell what's next, and end with a quote, a provocative question, or a memorable remark.

The chapter suggested following these guidelines for preparing visuals:

- Select the appropriate type of visual (electronic slides, transparencies, flip charts, white boards, or handouts) depending on the formality, size of the venue, and subject matter.
- Limit the number of visuals so that they will have maximum effect.
- Make slides easy to scan by keeping them simple, limiting points to phrases only, ensuring a minimum amount of information is on each one, and choosing a simple, boldface font and using upper and lower case letters.

To build confidence and create effective delivery, you should

- Rehearse to practise timing and word choice
- Avoid memorizing, reciting, and reading
- Maintain eye contact with the audience
- Use posture and eye contact to convey a nonverbal message of confidence
- Use movement and gestures to provide emphasis and variety
- Vary your voice in volume, rhythm, and pace
- Avoid reading visuals from the screen
- Invite questions and exercise self-control when answering them

Practise Your Grammar

Effective business communication starts with strong grammar skills. To improve your grammar skills, go to MyBusCommLab or Grammar-on-the-Go, where you'll find exercises and diagnostic tests to help you produce clear, effective communication.

Test Your Knowledge

1. How does the purpose for giving an oral presentation influence how the speaker delivers it?
2. Why is simplicity of organization important in oral communication?
3. What three goals should you accomplish during the introduction of an oral presentation?
4. How can a speaker get and keep the audience's attention?
5. What three tasks should you accomplish in the close of your presentation?
6. When creating slides for oral presentations, which should you do first: select the background design for your slides or write your bulleted phrases? Explain your answer.
7. What is the advantage of practising an oral presentation with visual aids before a live audience?
8. As a speaker, what nonverbal signals can you send to appear more confident?
9. What should speakers do to create effective delivery?
10. What can speakers do to maintain control during the question-and-answer period of a presentation?

Apply Your Knowledge

1. Why is it important to limit the scope of oral presentations?
2. How might the audience's attitude affect the amount of audience interaction during or after a presentation? Explain your answer.
3. If you were giving an oral presentation on the performance of a company product, what three attention-getters might you use to enliven your talk?
4. From the speaker's perspective, what are the advantages and disadvantages of responding to questions from the audience throughout an oral presentation, rather than just afterward? From the listener's perspective, which approach would you prefer? Why?
5. **Ethical Choices** How can you use design elements and special effects to persuade an audience? Is it ethical to do so?

Running Cases

CASE 1: Noreen

The Petro-Go senior management team has decided to move forward with the merger of the Go Points department and the credit card sales/service department. They approved Noreen's proposal and report and decided to implement this plan across all national and international centres. Noreen is about to deliver a business presentation to the staff in both departments. She needs to introduce herself, explain how the departments have merged, and discuss how job roles will change. She plans to show the new organizational chart during her presentation and mention that all centres will merge the two departments, so all credit card sales/service staff will also market the points program and all Go Points staff will now conduct credit card sales and offer service to existing credit card customers. Staff will be provided with product, systems, and service training as well as new phone scripts and procedures manuals.

QUESTIONS

a. What features will the members of Noreen's audience have in common? What resistance might she face and what could she do to overcome it?
b. When creating visual slides, what principles must Noreen remember?
c. Is the direct or indirect approach best?
d. How can Noreen arouse the audience's interest in this topic?

YOUR TASK

Prepare this presentation. Assume you are Noreen. Create a speech outline and an electronic slide show. Deliver the presentation to a group.

CASE 2: Kwong

Kwong has to prepare a presentation for his final course in his CGA program and seeks his manager's permission to use ET Canada as his case study. Kwong will have to gather some company information and get approval to use it for his course project. Kwong's manager would like to see his project before Kwong presents it to his class. Kwong plans to discuss the software systems used at ET Canada and the policies and procedures the company follows to gather information electronically from the national branches into the head office. System screen shots (pictures of data screens) will be used and charts, graphs, or other reported information may be included in Kwong's presentation.

QUESTIONS

a. What must Kwong consider when sharing company data with the public?
b. How can Kwong arouse the audience's interest in this topic?

c. Should Kwong prepare handouts for the audience? For what kinds of information? If so, when should he hand them out?
d. How will Kwong ensure that the audience can clearly see the screen shots and other visuals in the slide show?
e. What should Kwong include in the introductory part of the speech?

YOUR TASK

Prepare two slides Kwong could use in the introduction of his presentation.

Practise Your Knowledge

ACTIVITIES

1. **Analyze This Document** Pick a speech from *Vital Speeches of the Day,* a publication containing recent speeches on timely and topical subjects. As an alternative, select a speech from an online source such as the speech archives of a large company's website. For example, go to **www.bombardier.com** and follow the links from "What's New" to the "Media Centre" and then click on "Speeches." Select a speech that interests you. Examine both the introduction and the close; then analyze how these two sections work together to emphasize the main idea. What action does the speaker want the audience to take? Next, identify the transitional sentences or phrases that clarify the speech's structure for the listener, especially those that help the speaker shift between supporting points. Using these transitions as clues, list the main message and supporting points; then indicate how each transitional phrase links the current supporting point to the succeeding one. Now, prepare a brief (two- to three-minute) oral presentation summarizing your analysis for your class.

2. **Internet** For many years, Toastmasters has been dedicated to helping its members give speeches. Instruction, good speakers as models, and practice sessions aim to teach members to convey information in lively and informative ways. Visit the Toastmasters website at **www.toastmasters.org** and carefully review the linked pages

about listening, speaking, voice, and body. Evaluate the information and outline a three-minute presentation to your class telling why Toastmasters and its website would or would not help you and your classmates write and deliver an effective speech.

3. **Mastering Delivery: Analysis** Attend a presentation at your school or in your town, or watch a speech on television. Categorize the speech as one that motivates or entertains, one that informs or analyzes, or one that persuades or urges collaboration. Then compare the speaker's delivery with the concepts presented in this chapter. Write a two-page report analyzing the speaker's performance and suggesting improvements.

4. **Mastering Delivery: Nonverbal Signals** Observe and analyze the delivery of a speaker in a school, work, or other setting. What type of delivery did the speaker use? Was this delivery appropriate for the occasion? What nonverbal signals did the speaker use to emphasize key points? Were these signals effective? Which nonverbal signals would you suggest to further enhance the delivery of this oral presentation—and why?

5. **Ethical Choices** Think again about the oral presentation you observed and analyzed in Activity 4. How could the speaker have used nonverbal signals to unethically manipulate the audience's attitudes or actions?

6. **Teamwork** You've been asked to give an informative 10-minute talk on vacation opportunities in your home province. Draft your introduction, which should last no more than two minutes. Then pair off with a classmate and analyze each other's introductions. How well do these two introductions arouse the audience's interest, build credibility, and preview the presentation? Suggest how these introductions might be improved.

7. **Completing Oral Presentations: Self-Assessment** How good are you at planning, writing, and delivering oral presentations? Rate yourself on each of the following elements of the oral presentation process. Then examine your ratings to identify where you are strongest and where you can improve, using the tips in this chapter.

Element of Presentation Process	Always	Frequently	Occasionally	Never
1. I start by defining my purpose.	_____	_____	_____	_____
2. I analyze my audience before writing an oral presentation.	_____	_____	_____	_____
3. I match my presentation length to the allotted time.	_____	_____	_____	_____
4. I begin my oral presentation with an attention-getting introduction.	_____	_____	_____	_____
5. I look for ways to build credibility as a speaker.	_____	_____	_____	_____
6. I cover only a few main points in the body of my presentation.	_____	_____	_____	_____
7. I use transitions to help listeners follow my ideas.	_____	_____	_____	_____
8. I review main points and describe next steps in the close.	_____	_____	_____	_____
9. I practise my presentation beforehand.	_____	_____	_____	_____
10. I prepare in advance for questions and objections.	_____	_____	_____	_____
11. I conclude oral presentations by summarizing my main idea.	_____	_____	_____	_____

8. **Delivering Oral Presentations: Tips for Success Topic Suggestions** (some research needed)
Choose one of the informative or persuasive presentation topics below.

Inform classmates or management trainees about
a. How to dress for success
b. How to work with the other gender in the workplace
c. Nonverbal communication and your persona at work
d. The etiquette for a business lunch
e. Business culture—choose a country

Japan	Germany
India	England
Korea	Australia
Iran	Canada
Saudi Arabia	United States
France	

f. Interview dos and don'ts
g. Employee incentive programs
h. Building an effective exhibit for a trade show
i. Environmental best practices for the office

Persuade management that
- j. The company should purchase and display Canadian art in the workplace
- k. The company should start a recycling program
- l. The company should sponsor a young worker safety program
- m. The long-term care facility should sponsor an exercise program for the elderly residents
- n. The city council should build more sports and recreation facilities
- o. The company should hold a Dress-up Thursday (or Casual Friday).

Your Task Choose a topic and purpose, research the material using MyBusCommLab's Research Navigator or library materials, and prepare a 5–10 minute presentation to be given to your class as specified by your instructor.

9. **Practising Presentation Skills: Introduce a Classmate** (no research needed)
Work in groups of two. Interview each other to find out enough information to introduce each other to the group.

What did the person do before this course?

Do they have any work or educational experiences?

What activities does the person enjoy in his or her spare time?

What are the person's strengths? What is the person's career goal?

Your Task Prepare a 1-minute introduction of your classmate. Your instructor will invite you to present to the class or to a small group of five.

10. **Practising Presentations: Present a Personal View** (no research needed)
Take a few minutes to develop three to five points about one of the following topics to prepare for a practice oral presentation. Most of the topics can be developed by thinking of the 5Ws: What is it? Why is it enjoyable or worthwhile? When/where can you do it? You can also think about how you can find it. Add a brief introduction and a summary and you have a short presentation!
- a. A sport you enjoy
- b. A book you'd recommend
- c. A movie you think everyone should see
- d. A website you'd recommend
- e. Software you'd recommend
- f. An online retail site you like
- g. A television program worth watching
- h. A hobby you enjoy
- i. A course you would recommend
- j. A life skill it's important to have
- k. Tips for getting along with others
- l. Tips for studying
- m. Tips for getting good marks on assignments
- n. Tips for having a balanced life as a student
- o. Tips for how to stay healthy at school

Your Task Prepare a 1–2 minute oral presentation on one of the topics. Your instructor will invite you to present to the class or to a small group of five students.

Expand Your Knowledge

Best of the Web

Speak with Flair The Virtual Presentation Assistant (VPA) offers abundant resources with related links to other websites that contain useful articles, reviews, or supplemental materials for planning presentations. You can also connect to popular media and library pages with worldwide research information. You'll find examples of presentation types, suggestions for selecting and focusing your topic, tips on audience analysis, delivery, using visual aids,

and various other guidelines to help you prepare and deliver an effective oral presentation. If you need inspiration, check out this site.
www.public-speaking.org

EXERCISES

1. Suppose you have been asked to prepare an oral presentation on a business issue currently in the news. How could you use what you've discovered at the VPA site to help you select a topic? How could you use this site to find additional information or supplementary materials related to your topic?
2. According to this website, what factors should you consider when analyzing your audience?
3. What topics or information will entice you to return to this site or its links? (If you don't find the Virtual Presentation Assistant useful, explain why.)

Exploring the Web on Your Own

Review these chapter-related websites on your own to enhance your oral presentation skills and knowledge.

1. Visit TED (Technology, Entertainment, Design) at www.ted.com to watch videos of excellent speakers talking about a wide variety of topics on technology, science, art, culture, and more. Each week, more speeches and presentations by leading authors, researchers, and business people are posted. For example, you can hear Daniel Goleman talk about emotional intelligence, or Nicholas Negroponte talk about his "One Laptop per Child" project.
2. Learn to prepare, write, and polish your oral presentations at www.speechsuccess.com and www.successtips.com.

Nerves: The Secret Weapon of Polished Presenters

What do Barbra Streisand, Liza Minnelli, and Donny Osmond have in common? These professional performers and many others admit to being nervous about public speaking. If the pros can feel fear, it's no wonder beginners are sometimes scared speechless. Survey after survey has confirmed that public speaking is the number one fear in Canada and the United States—so if you're anxious about stepping in front of an audience, you're not alone.

Nervousness might make your hands tremble, your knees knock, your mouth feel dry, or your stomach churn. As bad as these symptoms can be, remember that nerves are a good indicator of your concern for the occasion, your subject, and your audience. If you didn't care, you wouldn't be anxious. A speaker who cares is more likely to seek out every method of communicating with the audience.

Remember also that you'll feel a little less nervous with every oral presentation. Once you see how the audience responds to your first attempt, you'll realize that you did better than you feared you would. People in the audience want you to succeed; they're interested in learning from you or being inspired by your words, not in straining to hear the sound of your knees knocking together.

You can harness your nerves by focusing on what you want to accomplish. In the words of actress Carol Channing, "I don't call it nervousness—I prefer to call it concentration." Like Channing, you can concentrate your efforts on making that all-important connection with your audience. But don't make the mistake of expecting perfection. Put that nervous energy into planning, preparing, and practising. Turn your negative fears into positive energy, and you'll be better equipped to face your audience the first time and every time.

You might start by listing statements that describe each of your fears: (1) the behaviour that will show your fear, (2) the effect this behaviour will have, and (3) the action you can take to change the behaviour and get rid of the fear. For example, if you're afraid that you won't be as good as you would like to be, you might say, "I'll leave out parts of my speech or act nervous (behaviour), so I won't impress the audience or get my message across (effect)." The solution is to make the speech your own before addressing your audience (action). Practise, practise, practise. Tape-record your speech or videotape yourself and look for strengths and weaknesses. Practise out loud until you've mastered the speech and it's yours. If you like your speech, your audience will like it, and you'll get your message across.

Or perhaps you're saying something like "I'll look scared (behaviour), and the audience will sense my nervousness and will snicker and make fun of me (effect)." The solution is to act confident—even if you don't feel it (action). Listeners want you to succeed, and they can't see what's happening inside you. Don't apologize for anything. If you make a mistake, don't start over; just keep going. Then enjoy the applause—your moment in the spotlight.

Applications for Success

Learn how to overcome your fear of public speaking by visiting www.pe2000.com/pho-speaking.htm.
Answer the following questions:

1. Think of any lectures or presentations you've recently attended. Have you ever noticed a speaker's level of anxiety? Did any speakers succeed in overcoming this fear? Describe the ways a particular speaker visibly conquered his or her nervousness. If that speaker failed, what techniques might have helped?

2. As a member of the audience, what can you do to help a speaker overcome his or her nervousness? Briefly explain.

3. Using the "behaviour-effect-action" structure, list one of your fears and show how you plan to counter it in your next speech.

Searching for Employment and Preparing Employment Messages

LEARNING OBJECTIVES

After studying this chapter, you will be able to

1. Discuss three results of how today's constantly changing workplace is affecting the employment-search process
2. Explain three things you can do to help you adapt to the changing workplace
3. Summarize six tasks you can do before and during your job search
4. Discuss how to choose the appropriate resumé organization, and list the advantages or disadvantages of the three options
5. List the major elements to include in a traditional resumé
6. Describe what you can do to adapt your resumé to a scannable format
7. Define the purpose of application letters, and explain how to apply the AIDA organizational approach to them

Stephanie Sykes' department at BCE Corporate Services provides recruitment and human resource planning to help Bell Canada attract and retain talented employees. Bell Canada receives more than 60 000 applications each year. "What stands out in an application," says Sykes, "is clarity and simplicity. Tell me why you want to work for Bell and what you will bring to our company. Technical skills show through easily but remember that most companies are also looking for people with leadership skills or potential."

Building Toward a Career

As Stephanie Sykes will tell you, getting the job that's right for you takes more than sending out a few resumés and application letters. Before entering the workplace, you need to learn as much as you can about your capabilities and the job marketplace.

Understanding Today's Changing Workplace

The workplace today is changing constantly.[1] The attitudes and expectations of both employers and employees are being affected not only by globalization, technology, diversity, and teams but also by deregulation, shareholder activism, corporate downsizing, mergers and acquisitions, outsourcing, and entrepreneurialism (people starting their own business or buying a franchise).[2] The results of constant change are threefold.

Numerous forces are changing today's workplace.

- **How often people look for work.** Rather than looking for lifelong employees, many employers now hire temporary workers and consultants on a project-by-project basis. Likewise, rather than staying with one employer for their entire career, growing numbers of employees are moving from company to company.
- **Where people find work.** Fewer jobs are being created by large companies. One expert predicts that soon 80 percent of the labour force will be working for firms employing fewer than 200 people. Moreover, self-employment seems to be an increasingly attractive option for many former employees.[3]

- **The type of people who find work.** Employers today are looking for people who are able and willing to adapt to diverse situations and who continue to learn throughout their careers. Companies want team players with strong work records, leaders who are versatile, and employees with diversified skills and varied job experience.[4] Plus, most employers expect employees to be sensitive to intercultural differences.[5]

Adapting to the Changing Workplace

Before you limit your employment search to a particular industry or job, do some advance preparation. Analyze what you have to offer, what you hope to get from your work, and how you can make yourself more valuable to potential employers. This preliminary analysis will help you identify employers who are likely to want you and vice versa.

LEARN WHAT YOU HAVE TO OFFER When seeking employment, you must tell people about yourself, about who you are. So you need to know what talents and skills you have. You'll need to explain how these skills will benefit potential employers. Follow these guidelines:

> To determine what you have to offer, carefully examine your functional skills, your education and experience, and your personality traits.

- **Jot down 10 achievements you're proud of.** Did you learn to ski, take a prize-winning photo, tutor a child, edit your school paper? Think about what skills these achievements demanded (leadership skills, speaking ability, and artistic talent may have helped you coordinate a winning presentation to your school's administration). You'll begin to recognize a pattern of skills, many of which might be valuable to potential employers.
- **Look at your educational preparation, work experience, and extracurricular activities.** What do your knowledge and experience qualify you to do? What have you learned from volunteer work or class projects that could benefit you on the job? Have you held any offices, won any awards or scholarships, mastered a second language?
- **Take stock of your personal characteristics.** Are you aggressive, a born leader? Or would you rather follow? Are you outgoing, articulate, great with people? Or do you prefer working alone? Make a list of what you believe are your four or five most important qualities. Ask a relative or friend to rate your traits as well.

DECIDE WHAT YOU WANT TO DO Knowing what you *can* do is one thing. Knowing what you *want* to do is another. Don't lose sight of your own values. Discover the things that will bring you satisfaction and happiness on the job.

> When deciding what you want to do, envision your ideal day at work: your activities, independence, salary, career goals, environment, location, position, and relationships.

- **What would you like to do every day?** Talk to people in various occupations about their typical workday. You might consult relatives, local businesses, or former graduates (through your school's alumni relations office). Read about various occupations. Start with your college or university library or placement office.
- **How would you like to work?** Consider how much independence you want on the job, how much variety you like, and whether you prefer to work with products, machines, people, ideas, figures, or some combination thereof. Do you like physical work, mental work, or a mix? Constant change or a predictable role?

> Set goals; assess your needs and preferences.

- **What specific compensation do you expect?** What do you hope to earn in your first year? What kind of pay increase do you expect each year? What's your ultimate earnings goal? Would you be comfortable getting paid on commission, or do you prefer a steady paycheque? Are you willing to settle for less money in order to do something you really love?
- **Can you establish some general career goals?** Consider where you'd like to start, where you'd like to go from there, and the ultimate position you'd like to attain. How soon after joining the company would you like to receive your first promotion?

Your next one? What additional training or preparation will you need to achieve them?

- **What size of company would you prefer?** Do you like the idea of working for a small, entrepreneurial operation? Or would you prefer a large corporation?
- **What type of operation is appealing to you?** Do you prefer to work for a profit-making company or a non-profit organization? Are you attracted to service businesses or manufacturing operations? Do you want regular, predictable hours, or do you thrive on flexible, varied hours? Would you enjoy a seasonally varied job such as education (which may give you summers off) or retailing (with its selling cycles)?
- **What location would you like?** Would you like to work in a city, a suburb, a small town, an industrial area, or an uptown setting? Do you favour a particular part of the country? A country abroad? Do you like working indoors or outdoors?
- **What facilities do you envision?** Is it important to you to work in an attractive place, or will simple, functional quarters suffice? Do you need a quiet office to work effectively, or can you concentrate in a noisy, open setting? Is access to public transportation or freeways important?
- **What sort of corporate culture are you most comfortable with?** Would you be happy in a formal hierarchy with clear reporting relationships? Or do you prefer less structure? Are you looking for a paternalistic firm or one that fosters individualism? Do you like a competitive environment? One that rewards teamwork? What qualities do you want in a boss?

MAKE YOURSELF MORE VALUABLE TO EMPLOYERS Take positive steps toward building your career. Before you graduate from university or college or while you're seeking employment, you can do a lot. The following suggestions will help potential employers recognize the value of hiring you:

- **Keep an employment portfolio.** Keep samples that show your ability to perform (classroom or work evaluations, certificates, awards, papers you've written). Your portfolio is a great resource for writing your resumé, and it gives employers tangible evidence of your professionalism.
- **Take interim assignments.** As you search for a permanent job, consider temporary, volunteer, or freelance work. Also gain a competitive edge by participating in an internship program. These temporary assignments not only help you gain valuable experience and relevant contacts but also provide you with important references and with items for your portfolio.[6]
- **Work on polishing and updating your skills.** Whenever possible, join networks of professional colleagues and friends who can help you keep up with your occupation and industry. While waiting for responses to your resumé, take a computer course, or seek out other educational or life experiences that would be hard to get while working full-time.

> Make yourself more valuable to potential employers by tracking what you've done, broadening your experience, and constantly improving your skills.

Even after you've been hired, continue improving your skills. Distinguish yourself from your peers and continue increasing your value to current and potential employers. Becoming a lifelong learner will help you reach your personal goals in the workplace:[7]

- Obtain as much technical knowledge as you can.
- Learn to accept and adapt to change.
- Regularly read publications such as *The Globe and Mail, Canadian Business, Maclean's,* and *Report on Business.*
- View each job as a chance to expand your knowledge, experience, and social skills.
- Take on as much responsibility as you can (listen to and learn from others while actively pursuing new or better skills).
- Stay abreast of what's going on in your organization and industry to understand the big picture.

> Your career-building efforts don't stop after you are hired.

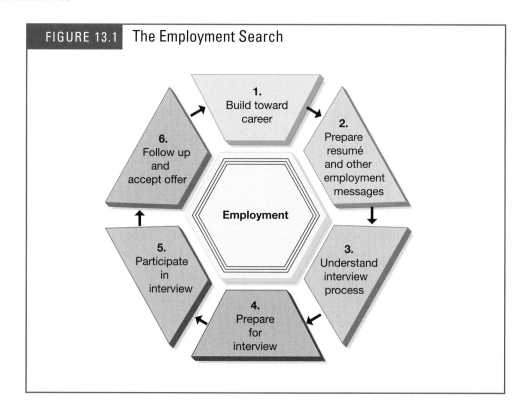

FIGURE 13.1 The Employment Search

Seeking Employment in the Changing Workplace

The search for employment is a process.

Look at Figure 13.1 for an idea of what an employment search entails. The first two tasks are discussed in this chapter; the rest are discussed in Chapter 14. Gather as much information as you can, narrowing it as you go until you know precisely the companies you want to approach.

To learn all you can about the job opportunities available, consistently pursue six tasks.

Begin by finding out where the job opportunities are, which industries are strong, which parts of the country are booming, and which specific job categories offer the best prospects for the future. From there you can investigate individual organizations, doing your best to learn as much about them as possible. To prepare for and successfully complete your search for employment, do the following:

* **Stay abreast of business and financial news.** Subscribe to a major newspaper (print or online) and scan the business pages every day. Watch some television programs that focus on business. Consult the *National Occupational Classification* (Human Resources Development Canada, in print and online at **www5.hrsdc.gc.ca/NOC-CNP**) and Job Futures (Human Resources and Social Development Canada, in print and online at **www.jobfutures.ca**). View forecasts about various job titles to develop ideas for a career. In addition to the national edition of Job Futures, you can also check provincial editions. B.C. Work Futures (**www.workfutures.bc.ca**) provides forecasts about occupational profiles and includes links to other provinces' Work Futures sites. Alberta's Work Futures site gives you links that list the biggest companies in Alberta. Another source of detailed information about occupations and trends is the *U.S. Occupational Outlook Handbook,* published in print and online at **www.bls.gov/oco/print/ocos021.htm**. Often the online versions of these materials are most up to date.
* **Research specific companies.** Compile a list of specific organizations that appeal to you (by consulting directories of employers at the library, at your career centre, or on the web). Consult company profiles, press releases, financial information, and information on employment opportunities. Find out about a company's mission, products, annual reports, and employee benefits. Send an email request for annual reports, brochures, or newsletters.

- **Look for job openings.** Check company websites for job openings, or find sites that list openings from multiple companies—many of which allow you to search by region, industry, job title, company, skills, or requirements (see Figure 13.2). And don't forget to look in newspapers, sign up for campus interviews, network, and find career counselling.
- **Respond to job openings.** You can respond directly to job listings by posting tailor-made resumés (that match required qualifications) and by sending email resumés and focused cover letters directly to the people doing the hiring. Since companies receive thousands of electronic resumés a day, also consider a printed letter or a phone call.[8]
- **Network.** Find people in your field by participating in business organizations (such as the Canadian Marketing Association or the Canadian Institute of Management Association). Visit organizations, contact their personnel departments, and talk with key employees. On the web, locate and communicate with potential employers using discussion groups, social networking sites such as LinkedIn (**www.linkedin.com**), Usenet newsgroups (that post messages on electronic bulletin boards), and Listservs (that email messages to every member). Once you locate a potential contact, send an email requesting information about the company or about job openings.
- **Find career counselling.** College placement offices offer counselling, credential services, job fairs, on-campus interviews, and job listings. They provide workshops in job-search techniques, resumé preparation, interview techniques, and more.[9] College- and university-run online career centres are excellent.

FIGURE 13.2 **A Sample Site for Searching Multiple Companies**

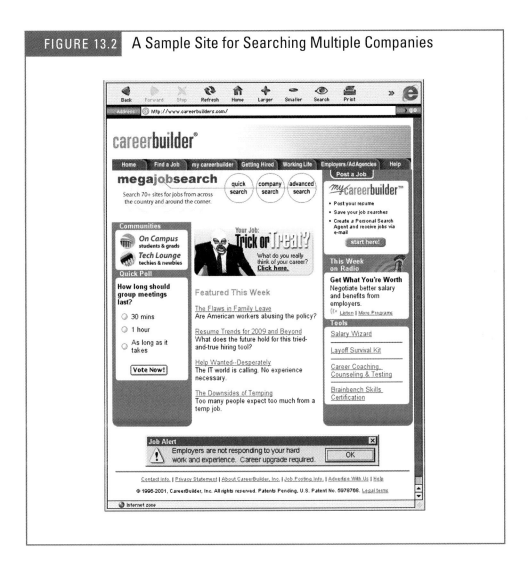

Preparing Resumés

While looking for employment, you'll need to send out messages such as resumés and application letters. Whenever you send out such employment messages, you have an opportunity to showcase your communication skills—skills valued highly by the majority of employers. So write these messages carefully by following the three-step writing process (see Figure 13.3).

Planning Your Resumé

A resumé is a structured, written summary of a person's education, employment background, and job qualifications. Many people have misconceptions about the value and function of resumés—see Table 13.1. As with other business messages, planning a resumé means analyzing your purpose and audience, gathering information, and adapting the document to your purpose and audience.

- **Analyze your purpose and audience.** Your resumé must be more than a simple list of jobs you've held. It is a form of advertising intended to stimulate an employer's interest in you—in meeting you and learning more about you. With this purpose in mind, put yourself in your audience's position and tailor your resumé to satisfy audience needs.
- **Investigate pertinent information.** Gather every scrap of pertinent personal history you can and have it at your fingertips: all details of previous jobs (dates, duties, accomplishments), all relevant educational experience (formal degrees, skill certificates, academic or civic awards), all relevant information about personal endeavours (dates of membership in an association, offices you held in a club or organization, presentations you made to a community group).
- **Adapt your resumé to your audience.** Your resumé must make an impression quickly. Focus on your audience. Ask yourself what key qualifications this employer will be looking for. Decide which qualifications are your greatest strengths. Choose three or four of your most relevant accomplishments and what resulted from these accomplishments. A good resumé is flexible and can be customized for various situations and employers.

Don't exaggerate, and don't alter the past or claim skills you don't have. However, don't dwell on negatives, either. By knowing yourself and your audience, you'll focus successfully on the strengths needed by potential employers.

> As with other business messages, the three-step writing process can help you plan, write, and complete your resumé and other employment messages.

 Document Makeovers

> Your resumé concisely summarizes your educational and employment background and shows your qualifications for a job.

> To get an interview, analyze your audience's needs, have all the facts at your fingertips, and tailor your resumé to various audiences and situations.

FIGURE 13.3 Three-Step Writing Process for Employment Messages

Planning	Writing	Completing
Analyze Study your purpose and your audience to tailor your message for maximum effect. **Investigate** Gather relevant information about you and about the employer you're targeting. **Adapt** Establish a good relationship by highlighting those skills and qualifications that match each employer.	**Organize** Use the AIDA approach in letters and choose the most appropriate resumé format to highlight your strongest points. **Compose** Make your letters friendly, businesslike, and slightly more formal than usual. For resumés, use action verbs and make your style direct, brief, and crisp.	**Revise** Evaluate content, revising for both clarity and conciseness. **Produce** Ensure a clean, sharp look whether your message is in print, email, or online. **Proofread** Look carefully for errors in spelling and mechanics that can detract from your professionalism.
1	2	3

TABLE 13.1	Fallacies and Facts About Resumés

FALLACY	FACT
⊗ The purpose of a resumé is to list all your skills and abilities.	☑ The purpose of a resumé is to kindle employer interest and generate an interview.
⊗ A good resumé will get you the job you want.	☑ All a resumé can do is get you in the door.
⊗ Your resumé will be read carefully and thoroughly by an interested employer.	☑ Your resumé probably has less than 45 seconds to make an impression.
⊗ The more good information you present about yourself in your resumé, the better.	☑ Too much information on a resumé may actually kill the reader's appetite to know more.
⊗ If you want a really good resumé, have it prepared by a resumé service.	☑ Prepare your own resumé—unless the position is especially high-level or specialized. Even then, you should check out services carefully before using one.
⊗ Using a Word template will make a professional impression.	☑ Design your own resumé to be distinct and show your communication skills.

Writing Your Resumé

 **Activities**

To write a successful resumé, you need to convey seven qualities that employers seek. You want to show that you
- Think in terms of results
- Know how to get things done
- Are well rounded
- Show signs of progress
- Have personal standards of excellence
- Are flexible and willing to try new things
- Possess strong communication skills

As you organize and compose your resumé, think about how you can convey those seven qualities.

ORGANIZE YOUR RESUMÉ AROUND YOUR STRENGTHS Although you may want to include a little information in all categories, emphasize the information that has a bearing on your career objective, and minimize or exclude any that is irrelevant or counterproductive. Call attention to your best features and downplay your weaknesses—but be sure you do so without distorting or misrepresenting the facts.[10] To focus attention on your strongest points, adopt the appropriate organizational approach—make your resumé chronological, functional, or a combination of the two. The "right" choice depends on your background and your goals.

> Select an organizational pattern that focuses attention on your strengths.

 **Model** Document

The Chronological Resumé In a **chronological resumé**, the "Work Experience" section dominates and is placed immediately after the name and address and the objective. You list your jobs sequentially in reverse order, beginning with the most recent position and working backwards toward earlier jobs. Under each job listing, describe your responsibilities and accomplishments, giving the most space to the most recent positions. If you're just starting your career, you can vary this chronological approach by putting your educational qualifications before your experience, thereby focusing attention on your training and academic credentials.

> Most recruiters prefer the chronological plan: a historical summary of your education and work experience.

The chronological approach is the most common way to organize a resumé, and many employers prefer it. This approach has three key advantages: (1) employers are familiar with it and can easily find information, (2) it highlights growth and career progression, and (3) it highlights employment continuity and stability.[11] The chronological approach is especially appropriate if you have a strong employment history and are aiming for a job that builds on your current career path. This is the case for Lareine Chan. Compare the ineffective and effective versions of Chan's resumé in Figure 13.4 and 13.5.

The Functional Resumé A **functional resumé** emphasizes a list of skills and accomplishments, identifying employers and academic experience in subordinate sections. This pattern stresses individual areas of competence, so it's useful for people who are just entering the job market, who want to redirect their careers, or who have little continuous career-related experience. The functional approach also has three advantages: (1) without having to read through job descriptions, employers can see what you can do for them, (2) you can emphasize earlier job experience, and (3) you can de-emphasize any lack of career progress or lengthy unemployment.

Figure 13.6 (on page 318) illustrates how Glenda Johns uses the functional approach to showcase her qualifications for a career in retail. Although she has not held any paid, full-time positions in retail sales, Johns has participated in work-experience programs, and she knows a good deal about the profession from research and from talking with people in the industry. She organized her resumé in a way that demonstrates her ability to handle such a position. Bear in mind, however, that many employment professionals assume that candidates who use this organization are trying to hide something.[12]

A functional resumé focuses attention on your areas of competence.

FIGURE 13.4 Ineffective Chronological Resumé

Lareine Chan

5687 Crosswoods Drive, Richmond, BC V59 2T1
Home: (604) 273-0086   Office: (604) 273-6624

I have been staff accountant/financial analyst at Inter-Asian Imports in Vancouver, B.C., from March 2004 to present.

- I have negotiated with major suppliers.
- I speak both Cantonese and Mandarin fluently, and I was recently encouraged to implement an electronic funds transfer for vendor disbursements.
- In my current position, I am responsible for preparing accounting reports.
- I have audited financial transactions.
- I have also been involved in the design of a computerized model to adjust accounts for fluctuations in currency exchange rates.
- I am skilled in the use of Excel, Access, HTML, and Visual Basic.

Was staff accountant with Monsanto Agricultural Chemicals in Shanghai, China (October 2000 to March 2004).

- While with Monsanto in Shanghai, I was responsible for budgeting and billing.
- I was responsible for credit-processing functions.
- I was also responsible for auditing the travel and entertainment expenses for the sales department.
- I launched an online computer system to automate all accounting functions.
- Also during this time, I was able to travel extensively in Asia.

I have my Master's of Business Administration with emphasis on international business, which I earned while attending University of British Columbia in Vancouver, B.C., from 1998 to 2000.

Bachelor of Business Administration (1995–1998), earned while attending Memorial University in St. John's, Newfoundland and Labrador.

Annotations: Fails to combine accounting expertise with international experience in the minds of employers by stating it in an overall objective. Uses bulleted lists ineffectively: Lacks parallelism; Lacks logical organization; Often highlights wrong information; Uses the word "I" too often; Uses too many unnecessary words (such as "I was responsible for"); Fails to highlight important skills by breaking them out into a separate list. Includes too many words in educational information and lacks parallelism. Organizes information chronologically but hides that fact with awkward format. Fails to draw reader's attention to important points: Fails to provide the sort of specific information on duties and accomplishments that catches an employer's eye; Fails to use concise, active language consistently to describe duties. Lacks informative headings throughout, making it difficult for potential employers to find work-related, educational, or skills information easily.

FIGURE 13.5 Effective Chronological Resumé

Combines accounting expertise with international experience in the minds of employers by stating it in a summary of qualifications

Organizes information chronologically and emphasizes that organization with format

Makes each description concise, easy to read, and informative:

• Avoids the word "I" throughout

• Uses no unnecessary words

Highlights important skills by breaking them out into a list in a separate section

---

LAREINE R. CHAN
5687 Crosswoods Drive
Richmond, BC V59 2T1
lchan@telus.net

Home: (604) 273-0086   Office: (604) 273-6624

SUMMARY OF QUALIFICATIONS

• Master of Business Administration, International Business
• Seven years of experience in accounting for international trade
• Fluent in Mandarin, Cantonese, and skilled in use of accounting software

EXPERIENCE

Financial Analyst, INTER-ASIAN IMPORTS (Vancouver, B.C.)
   March 2004–present

• Preparing accounting reports for wholesale giftware importer ($15 million annual sales)
• Auditing financial transactions with suppliers in 12 Asian countries
• Creating a computerized model to adjust accounts for fluctuations in currency exchange rates
• Negotiating joint-venture agreements with major suppliers in China and Japan
• Implementing electronic funds transfer for vendor disbursements, improving cash flow, and eliminating payables clerk position

Staff Accountant, Monsanto Agricultural Chemicals (Shanghai, China)
   October 2000–March 2004

• Handled budgeting, billing, and credit-processing functions for the Shanghai branch of an agricultural chemicals manufacturer
• Audited travel and entertainment expenses for the sales department
• Assisted in launching an online system to automate all accounting functions

EDUCATION

Master's of Business Administration, International Business, University of British Columbia, Vancouver, British Columbia, 1998–2000

Bachelor of Business Administration, Accounting, Memorial University, St. John's Newfoundland and Labrador, 1995–1998

INTERCULTURAL AND TECHNICAL SKILLS AND INTERESTS

Fluent in Cantonese and Mandarin   CPR, Industrial First Aid, Level C
Travelled extensively in Asia and Canada   Reading, Tennis, Skiing
Excel, Access, HTML, Visual Basic   Volunteer, Big Sisters of Canada

REFERENCES

Meghan McCandless   Dr. Anna Wilson
Manager   Professor
Accounting Division   International Business
Inter-Asian Imports   University of British Columbia
4312 Pender Street   1200 Westbrook Mall
Vancouver, BC V5J 2T4   Vancouver, BC V62 1B4
604 669 1276   604 222 8943
mmccandless@interasian.com   awilson@interchange.ubc.ca

Draws reader's attention to important points:

• Provides the sort of specific information on duties and accomplishments that catches an employer's eye

• Highlights duties and work achievements in bulleted lists

• Uses active language to describe duties

Includes informative headings throughout, making it easy for potential employers to find work-related, educational, or skills information

| FIGURE 13.6 | Functional Resumé |

Glenda S. Johns

Home: 457 Mountain View Road
Clear Lake, Manitoba R2H 0J9
(204) 733-5971

College: 1254 Main Street
Brandon, Manitoba R5Y 2P5
(204) 438-5254

OBJECTIVE: Retailing position

RELEVANT SKILLS

- **Personal Selling/Retailing**
  - Led housewares department in employee sales for spring 2008
  - Created end-cap and shelf displays for special promotions
  - Sold the most benefit tickets during college fundraising drive for local community centre
- **Public Interaction**
  - Commended by housewares manager for resolving customer complaints amicably
  - Performed in summer theatre productions in Clear Lake, MB
- **Managing**
  - Trained part-time employees in cash register operation and customer service
  - Reworked employee schedules as assistant manager
  - Organized summer activities for children 6–12 years old for town of Clear Lake, Manitoba—including reading programs, sports activities, and field trips

(Margin note: Describes relevant skills first because Johns is a recent graduate)

(Margin note: Uses action verbs to enhance resumé effectiveness)

EDUCATION

- Diploma in Business Administration (E-Business) (3.81 GPA /4.0 scale), Red River Community College, June 2008
- Courses included marketing, accounting, retail management, website design, e-marketing, and consumer behaviour

WORK EXPERIENCE

- **Assistant Manager**, housewares, at Jefferson's Department Store during off-campus work experience program, Brandon, Manitoba (fall 2007–spring 2008)
- **Sales Clerk**, housewares, at Jefferson's Department Store during off-campus work experience program, Brandon, Manitoba (fall 2006–spring 2007)
- **Assistant Director**, Summer Recreation Program, Clear Lake, Manitoba (summer 2006)
- **Actor**, Cobblestone Players, Clear Lake, Manitoba (summer 2005)

(Margin note: Describes but does not emphasize Johns' sketchy work history)

LEADERSHIP EXPERIENCE

- Student Co-Chair for Clear Lake Women's Club Fashion Show, 2008 (raised $45 000)
- President of Student Housing Society, 2007
- Student representative (high school) to Clear Lake Chamber of Commerce (2 years)

(Margin note: Calls attention to leadership abilities and experience by listing her leadership positions in a separate section)

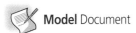

Model Document

A combination resumé is a hybrid of the chronological and functional resumés.

The Combination Resumé A **combination resumé** includes the best features of the chronological and functional approaches. Nevertheless, it is not commonly used, and it has two major disadvantages: (1) it tends to be longer, and (2) it can be repetitious if you have to list your accomplishments and skills in both the functional section and the chronological job descriptions.[13] When Erica Vorkamp developed her resumé, she chose not to use a chronological pattern, which would focus attention on her lack of recent work experience. As Figure 13.7 shows, she used a combination approach to emphasize her abilities, skills, and accomplishments while also including a complete job history.

FIGURE 13.7 Combination Resumé

Erica Vorkamp
993 Church Street, Mission, BC V5R 1P8
(604) 885-2153

evor@shaw.ca

OBJECTIVE To obtain a position as a special events coordinator

SKILLS AND CAPABILITIES

- Plan and coordinate large-scale public events
- Develop community support for concerts, festivals, and the arts
- Manage publicity for major events
- Coordinate activities of diverse community groups
- Establish and maintain financial controls for public events
- Negotiate contracts with performers, carpenters, electricians, and suppliers
- Use computer software for project management, desktop publishing, and database management

SPECIAL EVENT EXPERIENCE

- Arranged 2007's week-long Arts and Entertainment Festival for the Public Library, involving performances by 25 musicians, dancers, actors, magicians, and artists

- Coordinated a 2006 Parent Association Carnival, an all-day festival with game booths, live bands, contests, and food service that raised $7600 for a local school

- Organized the 2005 Western Convention for 800 members of the Canadian Figure Skating Officials, which extended over a three-day period and required arrangements for hotels, meals, speakers, and special tours

- Served as chairperson for the 2004 to 2007 Children's Helpline Show, a luncheon for 450 that raised $5000–$6700 for children at risk

EDUCATION

- Diploma, Marketing Management, British Columbia Institute of Technology (Burnaby, B.C.), 2005

EMPLOYMENT HISTORY

- ScotiaBank (Langley, B.C.), 2005–2007, Operations Processor; tracked cheques with a lost/stolen status, contacted customers by phone, registered payment amounts, verified receipt reports, researched cheque authenticity, managed orientation program for entry-level trainees

- BCIT Marketing Department (Burnaby, B.C.), 2003–2005, part-time Administrative Assistant

ACTIVITIES & INTERESTS

- Volunteer, Mission Public Library (two years)—Read stories to children
  Prepare podcast readings for CNIB

- Slow pitch softball—player on community team (three years)

- Fitness and yoga enthusiast

- Figure skater—competed at high performance level from 1998–2002, now skate for fun

AWARDS & ACHIEVEMENTS

- BCIT Marketing Department Award for Best Proposal (2005)

- Second in B.C. Provincial Figure Skating Championships (2002)

- Employee of the Month, ScotiaBank (May 2006 to February 2007)

REFERENCES

Sarah Burns	Peter Voljic	Mary Fraser
Dean, School of Business	Head Librarian	Program Chair
BC Institute of Technology	Mission Public Library	Children's Helpline Foundation
3700 Willingdon Avenue	316 Front Street	626 Royal Avenue
Burnaby, BC V5G 3H2	Mission, BC V5R 3J9	New Westminster, BC V6P 1T4
604 434 5734	604 882 1964	604 524 1856
s.burns@bcit.ca	pvoljic@telus.net	mfraser@helpline.org

Relates all capabilities and experience to the specific job objective, giving a selective picture of the candidate's abilities

Includes event attendance statistics and fundraising results to quantify accomplishments

Includes work history (even though it has little bearing on job target) because Vorkamp believes recruiters want to see evidence that she's held a paying position

TABLE 13.2	Action Verbs to Use in Resumés			
accomplished	coordinated	initiated	participated	set up
achieved	created	installed	performed	simplified
administered	demonstrated	introduced	planned	sparked
approved	developed	investigated	presented	streamlined
arranged	directed	joined	proposed	strengthened
assisted	established	launched	raised	succeeded
assumed	explored	maintained	recommended	supervised
budgeted	forecasted	managed	reduced	systematized
chaired	generated	motivated	reorganized	targeted
changed	identified	operated	resolved	trained
compiled	implemented	organized	saved	transformed
completed	improved	oversaw	served	upgraded

To capture attention quickly, leave out the word I, and begin your phrases with strong, action verbs.

COMPOSE YOUR RESUMÉ TO IMPRESS To save your readers time and to state your information as forcefully as possible, write your resumé using a simple and direct style. Use short, crisp phrases instead of whole sentences, and focus on what your reader needs to know. Avoid using the word *I*. Instead, start your phrases with impressive action verbs such as the ones listed in Table 13.2. For instance, you might say, "Coached a Little League team to the regional playoffs" or "Managed a fast-food restaurant and four employees." Here are some additional examples of how to phrase your accomplishments using active statements that show results:

Avoid Weak Statements	**Use Active Statements That Show Results**
Responsible for developing a new filing system	Developed a new filing system that reduced paperwork by 50 percent
I was in charge of customer complaints and all ordering problems	Handled all customer complaints and resolved all product order discrepancies
Won a trip to Europe for opening the most new customer accounts in my department	Generated the highest number of new customer accounts in my department
Member of special campus task force to resolve student problems with existing cafeteria assignments	Assisted in implementing new campus dining program allowing students to eat at any college dorm

Elements to include in your resumé are your name and address, academic credentials, employment history, activities and achievements, and relevant personal data.

The opening section shows at a glance
• Who you are
• How to reach you

Name and Address The first thing an employer needs to know is who you are and where you can be reached: your name, address, phone number, and email address (or URL, if you have one). If you have contact information at school and at home, you can include both. Similarly, if you have a work phone and a home phone, list both and indicate which is which. Many resumé headings are nothing more than the name and address centred at the top of the page. You don't really need to include the word *resumé*. Just make sure the reader can tell in an instant who you are and how to communicate with you.

Include your email address.

Stating your objective helps the recruiter categorize you.

Career Objective Experts disagree about the need to state a career objective on your resumé. Some argue that your objective is obvious from your qualifications. Some also maintain that such a statement only limits you as a candidate (especially if you want to be considered for a variety of openings) because it labels you as being interested in only one thing. Other experts argue that employers will try to categorize you anyway, so you might as well make sure they attach the right label. Remember, your goal is to generate interest immediately. If you decide to state your objective, make it effective by being as specific as possible about what you want:

A software sales position in a growing company requiring international experience

Advertising assistance with print media emphasis requiring strong customer-contact skills

If you have different types of qualifications (such as a certificate in secretarial science and two years' experience in retail sales), prepare separate resumés, each with a different objective. If your immediate objective differs from your ultimate one, combine the two in a single statement:

A marketing position with an opportunity for eventual managerial status

Proposal writer, with the ultimate goal of becoming a contracts administrator

Summary of Qualifications Instead of stating your objective, you might summarize your qualifications in a brief statement that highlights your strongest points, particularly if you have had a good deal of varied experience. Use a short, simple phrase:

Summary of qualifications: Ten years of experience in commission selling with track record of generating new customer leads through creative advertising and community leadership positions

> Use a summary of qualifications instead of an objective if you have several key qualifications to highlight.

Or, you could put a heading at the beginning of your resumé, "Summary of Qualifications," and under it list three or four points summarizing the main reasons that the company should hire you. You may want to add together the months of experience you have had in short, part-time jobs to get a total and express how that experience is transferable to the professional environment you are entering. For example, if you had a number of part-time jobs in restaurants and retail each lasting several months, you might say "three years of experience in the hospitality industry" and highlight it in the summary as follows:

Summary of Qualifications
- Bachelor of Commerce, University of British Columbia
- Three years of experience in customer service
- Bilingual (French/English)
- Skilled in office and accounting software

The career objective or summary may be the only section read fully by the employer, so if you include either one, make it strong, concise, and convincing.

In Figure 13.8 (on page 322) Charlene Tang has used a "Highlights of Qualifications" section in her resumé to emphasize the combination of her education and experience. Since she is an applicant with both post-secondary education and several years of job experience, she combines these key qualifications in the opening segment. In addition, since Charlene immigrated to Canada recently, she wants to show she has improved her English through English language training and through studying business once in Canada. These qualifications are less significant than her professional designation, but they show she has made the transition to work culture in Canada. She also chose an English language instructor for her reference to show that her language skills are strong.

Education If you're still in school, education is probably your strongest selling point, so present your educational background in depth, choosing facts that match the position you are seeking. Give this section a heading such as "Education" or "Professional Training." Then, starting with the school you most recently attended, list the name and location of each one, the term of your enrolment (in months and years), your major and minor fields of study, significant skills and abilities you've developed in your course work, and the degrees, diplomas, or certificates you've earned. If you're working on an uncompleted degree or diploma, include in parentheses the expected date of completion. Showcase your qualifications by listing skills courses that have directly equipped you for

> If education is your strongest selling point, discuss it thoroughly and highlight it visually.

FIGURE 13.8 Resumé of Charlene Tang

Charlene Tang

#412, 692 High Street
Sherbrooke, Quebec J1H 5N1
819-561-6740
chartang@gmail.com

HIGHLIGHTS OF QUALIFICATIONS

- Ten years' experience in office administration, including one year in leasing
- Diploma in Business Administration plus Master's in Economics
- Computer skills in MS Office and Simply Accounting
- Languages include Mandarin and basic French

WORK EXPERIENCE

Lease Administrator/Sales Coordinator   **2008–2009**
Atticus Financial Group, Sherbrooke, QC

- Prepare quotes and contracts
- Process and submit credit applications
- Follow up with customers and vendors via phone, fax, and email
- Report to management on application/funding status

Office Administrator   **1994–2004**
Tianjin Tax Bureau, Tianjin, China

- Managed and coordinated a high volume of financial documents
- Assigned work schedules and maintained department records
- Liaised with budgeting, accounting, and collections departments

EDUCATION

Diploma of Technology (Business Administration)   **2007–2008**
British Columbia Institute of Technology, Burnaby, B.C.
Graduated with Honours

- Accounting   • Microsoft Applications
- Business Law   • Business Communication

English Language College Preparation Program   **2005–2006**
Vancouver Community College, Vancouver, B.C.

Masters of Economics   **1996–1998**
Bachelor of Economics   **1990–1994**
Tianjin Finance & Economics University, Tianjin, China

ACTIVITIES

Volunteering

- French Cultural Centre, Vancouver   2006–2008
- Tutor in Economics, Burnaby   2007–2008
- *Run for the Cure* Vancouver & Sherbrooke   2008 & 2009
- Jogging, reading, and watching movies with friends

REFERENCES

Gretchen Quiving
Communication Instructor
B.C. Institute of Technology
3700 Willingdon Avenue
Burnaby, BC V5G 5H2
G.Quiving@bcit.co
(604) 434-5734

Rob Svetic
Accounts Manager
Atticus Financial
823 Main Street
Sherbrooke, QC
Rob.Svetic@atticus.com
(819) 689-4319

the job you are seeking, and indicate any scholarships, awards, or academic honours you've received.

The education section also includes off-campus training sponsored by business or government. Include any relevant seminars or workshops you've attended, as well as the certificates or other documents you've received. Whether you list your grades depends on the job you want and the quality of your grades. If you choose to show a grade-point average, be sure to mention the scale, especially if a five-point scale is used instead of a four-point scale.

Education is usually given less emphasis in a resumé after you've worked in your chosen field for a year or more. If work experience is your strongest qualification, save the section on education for later in the resumé and provide less detail.

In Figure 13.9 (on page 324), Alex Warren's resumé devotes most of the space to education and related activities since Alex is just entering the workforce and does not have a lot of work experience. If you must rely mostly on your education at this stage in your job-hunting career, don't worry. Young workers have other advantages for employers, often bringing enthusiasm and energy into the workplace. Notice that Alex conveys skills from his past jobs that are transferable into an accounting job. He also keeps his resumé to one page, suitable for a young applicant.

Work Experience, Skills, and Accomplishments Like the education section, the work-experience section focuses on your overall theme. Tailor your description to highlight the relationship between your previous responsibilities and your target field. Call attention to skills you've developed and your progression from jobs of lesser to greater responsibility.

When describing your work experience, list your jobs in reverse chronological order, with the current or last one first. Include any part-time, summer, or intern positions, even if unrelated to your current career objective. Employers will see that you have the ability to get and hold a job—an important qualification in itself. If you have worked your way through school, say so. Employers interpret this behaviour as a sign of character.

Each listing includes the name and location of the employer. If readers are unlikely to recognize the organization, briefly describe what it does. When you want to keep the name of your current employer confidential, identify the firm by industry only ("a large film-processing laboratory") or use the name but request confidentiality in the application letter or in an underlined note ("Resumé submitted in confidence") at the top or bottom of the resumé. If an organization's name or location has since changed, state the current name and location and then "formerly . . . "

Before each job listing, state your functional title, such as "salesperson." If you were a dishwasher, say so. Don't try to make your role seem more important by glamorizing your job title, functions, or achievements. Employers are checking on candidates' backgrounds more than they used to, so inaccuracies are likely to be exposed sooner or later. Also state how long you worked on each job, from month/year to month/year. Use the phrase "to present" to denote current employment. If a job was part-time, say so.

Devote the most space to the jobs that are related to your target position. If you were personally responsible for something significant, be sure to mention it ("Devised a new collection system that accelerated payment of overdue receivables"). Facts about your skills and accomplishments are the most important information you can give a prospective employer, so quantify them whenever possible:

Designed a new ad that increased sales by 9 percent

Raised $2500 in 15 days for cancer research

You may also include a section describing other aspects of your background that pertain to your career objective. If you were applying for a position with a multinational organization, you would mention your command of another language or your travel experience. Other skills you might mention include the ability to operate a computer, word processor, or other specialized equipment. You might title a special section

The work experience section lists all the related jobs you've had:
- Name and location of employer
- What the organization does (if not clear from its name)
- Your function title
- How long you worked there
- Your duties and responsibilities

Quantify your accomplishments whenever possible.

Include facts that are related to your career objective:
- Command of other languages
- Computer expertise
- Date you can start working

FIGURE 13.9 Resumé of a Young Applicant

Alex Warren

952 Oxford Street
Winnipeg, MB R3H 059

(204) 737-2954
alex_warren@gmail.com

EDUCATION

Completed first year of **Accounting Diploma, Red River College,**
Winnipeg, Manitoba, September 2008–present. Skills include
- Journalizing accounting entries, accounts receivable and payable
- Preparing financial statements and bank reconciliations
- Producing end-of-period reports and statements
- Using Word, Excel, Simply Accounting, Quick Books, and PowerPoint

Graduated, Kelvin Secondary School, Winnipeg, Manitoba, June 2008

WORK EXPERIENCE

Server, Salisbury House Restaurant, Winnipeg, Weekends
June 2006–present
- Serve up to 500 customers per shift accurately and efficiently and support others on work team
- Handle cash of approximately $5000 per shift

Cleaner, Manitoba Historical Society, Winnipeg, Summers 2006–2007
- Cleaned museum five evenings per week
- Took care with valuable exhibits and worked with no supervision

SKILLS AND ACTIVITIES

- Organized, disciplined, hardworking
- Skilled in accounting software, and spreadsheets
- Active in hockey and cross country running

ACCOMPLISHMENTS

- Kelvin School Physical Education Award 2007
- Most Valuable Player—Western Canada High School Hockey Championships 2007
- Canadian Hockey Referee Certification Level 3, 2006

VOLUNTEER EXPERIENCE

- Hockey Coach for Grade 5 & 6 team at Grosvenor Elementary, 2006–2007
- Hockey Referee, River Heights Hockey Club, 2007–2008
- *River Run* Water Booth Volunteer 2004–2007

REFERENCES

Johanna Vik, Manager
Salisbury House
Winnipeg, MB
(204) 488-1630
jvik@gmail.com

Mr. Paul Black, Counsellor
Kelvin Secondary School
Winnipeg, MB
(204) 488-7815
pblack@sympatico.ca

"Computer Skills" or "Language Skills" and place it near your "Education" or "Work Experience" section. If samples of your work might increase your chances of getting the job, insert a line at the end of your resumé offering to supply a portfolio of them on request.

References Experts debate the value of putting references in a resumé. Some say that putting them in is unnecessary and takes up valuable space since they are not used until after the interview. In this case, bring reference information from past employment and education to the interview. Ensure that you have the reference's name, job title, company name and address, telephone number, and email address. Also have the person's permission. Talk to references about what they will say about you.

Others say that having references in the resumé shows you are organized and it may make it easy for the recruiter to call references without any further communication with you. Also, it may be possible to create a positive impression of the applicant if the reference named is impressive. If you do decide to put references in, since you are limited in space, consider putting in two: one from work and one from education. Personal references are not as persuasive.

Activities and Achievements Your resumé should also describe any volunteer activities that demonstrate your abilities. Include the category "Volunteer Experience." List projects that require leadership, organization, teamwork, and cooperation. Emphasize career-related activities, such as "member of the Student Marketing Association." List skills you learned in these activities, and explain how these skills are related to the job you're applying for. Include speaking, writing, or tutoring experience; participation in athletics or creative projects; fundraising or community-service activities; and offices held in academic or professional organizations. (However, mention of political or religious organizations may be a red flag to someone with differing views, so use your judgment.)

Note any awards you've received. Again, quantify your achievements whenever possible. Instead of saying that you addressed various student groups, state how many and the approximate audience sizes. If your activities have been extensive, you may want to group them into divisions such as "College Activities," "Community Service," "Professional Associations," "Seminars and Workshops," and "Speaking Activities." An alternative is to divide them into two categories: "Service Activities" and "Achievements, Awards, and Honours."

Interests Including interests can enhance the employer's understanding of how you would fit in the company.[14] For instance, candidates applying for a bodyguard position with Pinkerton's security division may want to list martial arts achievements among their personal interests. Someone applying to Mountain Equipment Co-op may want to list outdoor activities. Such information helps show how a candidate will fit in with the organization's culture.

Some information is best excluded from your resumé. Federal human rights laws prohibit employers from discriminating on the basis of gender, marital or family status, age, race, religion, national origin, and physical or mental disability. So be sure to exclude any items that could encourage discrimination. Experts also recommend excluding from resumés salary information, reasons for leaving jobs, names of previous supervisors, your social insurance number, and other identification codes. Save these items for the interview, and offer them only if the employer specifically requests them.

AVOID RESUMÉ DECEPTION In an effort to put your best foot forward, you may be tempted to avoid a few points that could raise questions about your resumé. Although statistics on the prevalence of resumé inflation are difficult to gather, the majority of recruiters agree that distortion is common. Avoid the most frequent forms of deception:

- **Do not claim educational credits you don't have.** Candidates may state (or imply) that they earned a degree when, in fact, they never attended the school or attended

---

Draw attention to key qualifications by making them section titles, for example, "Language Skills."

Model Document

Nonpaid activities may provide evidence of work-related skills.

Provide only the personal data that will help you get the job.

Do not misrepresent your background or qualifications.

but did not complete the regular program. A typical claim might read, "Majored in commerce at Queen's University."

- **Do not inflate your grade-point average.** Students who feel pressured to impress employers with their academic performance may claim a higher GPA than they actually achieved.
- **Do not stretch dates of employment to cover gaps.** Many candidates try to camouflage gaps in their work history by giving vague dates of employment. For example, a candidate who left a company in January 1994 and joined another in December 1995 might cover up by showing that the first job ended in 1994 and the next began in 1995.
- **Do not claim to be self-employed if you were not.** Another common way people cover a period of unemployment is by saying that they were "self-employed" or a "consultant." Only include this experience if you were operating an independent business.
- **Do not claim to have worked for companies that are out of business.** Candidates who need to fill a gap in their work record sometimes say they worked for a firm that has gone out of business. Checking such claims is difficult because the people who were involved in the disbanded business are hard to track down.
- **Do not omit jobs that might cause embarrassment.** Being laid off from one or two jobs is understandable when corporate mergers and downsizing are commonplace. However, a candidate who has lost several jobs in quick succession may seem a poor employee to recruiters.
- **Do not exaggerate expertise or experience.** Candidates often inflate their accomplishments by using verbs somewhat loosely. Words such as *supervised, managed, increased, improved,* and *created* imply that the candidate was personally responsible for results that, in reality, were the outcome of a group effort.

If you misrepresent your background and your resumé raises suspicion, you will probably get caught, and your reputation will be damaged. A deceptive resumé can seriously affect your ability to get hired and pursue your career (see Table 13.3).

TABLE 13.3	How Far Can You Go to Make Your Resumé Strong and Positive?

DO	DON'T
☑ **Tell the truth.** If you lie, you will almost certainly get caught, and the damage to your career could be significant.	⊗ **Fabricate.** Academic degrees and jobs are checked first. Fabrications will cost you the job, before or after you're hired.
☑ **Make your story positive.** Most blemishes on your record can be framed in a positive way.	⊗ **Make blatant omissions.** Failing to disclose a job that didn't work out is almost as bad as making one up.
☑ **Sanitize your record.** Clear up unresolved issues such as tax liens and lawsuits.	⊗ **Exaggerate successes.** Be ready to prove any claim about your accomplishments.
☑ **Think small.** Candidates with criminal histories or other career impediments should focus on smaller companies, which are less likely to conduct background checks.	⊗ **Go overboard.** There's usually no need to disclose career or personal history that's more than 15 years old. If asked directly, answer truthfully—but with a minimum of elaboration.

Completing Your Resumé

The last step in the three-step writing process for resumés is no less important than the other two. As with any other business message, you need to revise your resumé, produce it in an appropriate form, and proofread it for any errors.

REVISE YOUR RESUMÉ The key to writing a successful resumé is to adopt the "you" attitude and focus on your audience. Think about what the prospective employer needs, and then tailor your resumé accordingly. Employers read thousands of resumés every year, and they complain about common problems.

Do not submit a resumé that is

- **Too long.** One or two pages is a good length. The resumé should be concise, relevant, and to the point.
- **Too short or sketchy.** The resumé should give enough information for a proper evaluation of the applicant.
- **Hard to read.** A lack of "white space" and of devices such as indentions and bold-facing makes the reader's job more difficult.
- **Wordy.** Descriptions are verbose, with numerous words used for what could be said more simply.
- **Too slick.** The resumé will appear to have been written by someone other than the applicant, which raises the question of whether the qualifications have been exaggerated.
- **Misspelled and ungrammatical throughout.** Recruiters conclude that candidates who make spelling and grammar mistakes lack good verbal skills, which are important on the job.
- **Boastful.** The overconfident tone makes the reader wonder whether the applicant's self-evaluation is realistic.
- **Dishonest.** The applicant claims to have expertise or work experience that he or she does not possess.

> Avoid common resumé problems.

MAKE YOUR RESUMÉ EASY TO SCAN With less than a minute to make a good impression, your resumé needs to look sharp and grab a recruiter's interest in the first few lines. A typical recruiter devotes 45 seconds to each resumé before tossing it into either the "maybe" or the "reject" pile.[15] Most recruiters scan through a resumé rather than read it from top to bottom. If the content in your resumé doesn't stand out, chances are the recruiter won't look at it long enough to judge your qualifications at a glance.

To give your printed resumé the best appearance possible, use a simple typeface on high-grade, letter-sized bond paper (in white or some light earth tone). Your stationery and envelope should match. Leave ample margins all around, and make sure that any corrections are unnoticeable. Avoid italic typefaces, which are difficult to read, and use a quality printer.

Keep your resumé to one or two pages. If you have a great deal of experience and are applying for a higher-level position, you may need to prepare a somewhat longer resumé.

Lay out your resumé to make important information easy to spot at a glance.[16] Break up the text with headings that call attention to various aspects of your background, such as work experience and education. Underline or capitalize key points, or set them off in the left margin. Use lists to itemize your most important qualifications, and leave plenty of white space, even if doing so forces you to use two pages rather than one. Use bold-face or visual elements to draw the eye to important qualifications.

> Check what stands out. Have you highlighted key selling points?

> The key characteristics of a good resumé are
> - Neatness
> - Simplicity
> - Accuracy
> - Honesty
> - Scannability

BE PREPARED TO SUBMIT YOUR RESUMÉ ELECTRONICALLY Many large organizations encourage applicants to submit resumés electronically. Most large companies use scanning systems to handle large volumes of applications. By scanning these resumés into their electronic database, companies can quickly narrow the field of applicants. But companies with fewer than 100 employees seldom use such systems.[17] If you're unsure whether an employer accepts Word files for your resumé and letter, call and ask, or visit the company's website.

> Reformatting your traditional resumé is helpful if it will be scanned or if you will be posting it on the internet or submitting it via email.

You may wish to prepare a second copy of your resumé in PDF format to be sent when you know the company uses electronic scanning or to be uploaded to a website or posted online.

Using Keywords Since many companies do use electronic scanning of resumés, you can emphasize certain keywords to help employers select your resumé from the thousands they scan. Both mechananized and human scanners generally search for nouns (since verbs tend to be generic rather than specific to a particular position or skill). To maximize the number of matches (or "hits") include keywords and phrases that define your skills, experience, and professional affiliations. Integrate these keywords throughout the "Education" and "Experience" sections of your resumé or in the list of skills or highlights you put near the beginning. Here are some sample keywords you might include if you were in accounting:

> Accountant, Corporate Controller, Receivables, Payables, Inventory, Cash Flow, Financial Analysis, Payroll Experience, Reconciliations, Corporate Taxes, Activity-Based Budgeting, Problem-Solving, Computer Skills, Excel, Access, Quick Books, Bachelors Degree in Accounting, CPA, Articulate, Team Player, Flexible, Willing to Travel, Fluent in French, Computer Skills, Networks, HTML, HMML, Simply Accounting

One way to identify which keywords to include in your resumé is to underline all the skills listed in ads for the types of jobs you're interested in. Make sure these ads match your qualifications and experience. Include *interpersonal keywords* that tell what kind of person you are (see Table 13.4).

Balancing Common Language with Current Jargon Another way to maximize hits on your resumé is to use words that potential employers will understand (for example, say *keyboard*, not *input device*). Also, use abbreviations sparingly (except for common ones such as BA or MBA). At the same time, learn and use the important buzzwords in your field. Look for current jargon in the want ads of major newspapers such as *The Globe and Mail* and in other resumés in your field that are posted online. Be careful to check and recheck the spelling, capitalization, and punctuation of any jargon you include, and use only those words you see most often.

Submitting Your Scannable Resumé If an employer gives you an option of submitting a scannable resumé by mail, by fax, or by email, choose email. Email puts your resumé directly into the employer's database, bypassing the scanning process. If you send your resumé in a paper format by regular mail or by fax, you run the risk that an OCR scanning program will create an error when reading it.

Keywords help potential employers sort through an entire database of resumés.

Use words your employer will understand by including some jargon specific to your field.

Email is the best way to transmit your resumé.

TABLE 13.4 Interpersonal Keywords

ability to delegate	communication skills	follow instructions	open minded	self-accountable
ability to implement	competitive	follow through	oral communication	self-managing
ability to plan	conceptual ability	follow up	organizational skills	sensitive
ability to train	creative	high energy	persuasive	setting priorities
accurate	customer oriented	industrious	problem solving	supportive
adaptable	detail minded	innovative	public speaking	takes initiative
aggressive work	empowering others	leadership	results oriented	team player
analytical ability	ethic	multi-tasking	risk taking	tenacious
assertive	flexible	open communication	safety conscious	willing to travel

When submitting your resumé by email, attach it as a Word or PDF document and paste your resumé into the body of your email message. Whenever you know a reference number or a job ad number, include it in your email subject line.

CONSIDER YOUR ONLINE PROFILE If you wish to post your resumé on your webpage, provide employers with your URL. As you design your website resumé, think of important keywords to use as hyperlinks—words that will grab an employer's attention and make the recruiter want to click on that hyperlink to learn more about you. You can make links to papers you've written, recommendations, and sound or video clips. Don't distract potential employers from your credentials by using hyperlinks to organizations or other websites.

Do not use photos, and avoid providing information that reveals your age, gender, race, marital status, or religion. Because a website is a public access area, you should also leave out the names of references and previous employers. Either mention that references are available on request, or say nothing. Also, instead of naming companies, simply refer to "a large accounting firm" or "a wholesale giftware importer." Finally, include a PDF version of your resumé on your webpage so that prospective employers can download it into their company's database.

Some applicants create an "e-portfolio" which includes a resumé, application letter, and sample documents or examples of work. This approach makes a lot of sense for those in creative fields or where samples of your work may help the employer decide to hire you. However, keep in mind that most recruiters won't take the time to use search engines to find your site.[18] Avoid asking employers to put effort into finding your resumé. Submitting a Word or PDF file via email makes the action easy for the employer.

Another way to reach employers is to build a profile in a social networking site such as LinkedIn (www.linkedin.org). But be careful about what material you have on a social networking site or personal website before bringing prospective employers to it. Many employers consider checking online sources a part of screening and a high percentage of employers have used Facebook and other social networking sites to look into the character of applicants. Images from Facebook can also help applicants, however. Consider the example of a recruiter looking for a financial officer for a music industry position. Concerned about how the financial applicant would fit with a company in the creative business, the recruiter found pictures of the applicant playing his electric guitar on Facebook and saw that the applicant had a genuine interest in music.

PROOFREAD YOUR RESUMÉ Your resumé is a concrete example of how you will prepare material on the job. So in every format, remember to pay close attention to mechanics and details. Check all headings and lists for parallelism, and be sure that your grammar, spelling, and punctuation are correct.

Once your resumé is complete, update it continually. As already mentioned, employment is becoming much more flexible these days, so it's likely you'll want to change employers. Besides, you'll also need your resumé to apply for membership in professional organizations and to work toward a promotion. Keeping your resumé updated is a good idea.

Preparing Other Types of Employment Messages

Although your resumé will take the greatest amount of time and effort, you'll also need to prepare other employment messages, including application letters, application forms, and follow-up notes.

Application Letters

Whenever you submit your resumé, accompany it with a cover, or application letter to let readers know what you're sending, why you're sending it, and how they can benefit from reading it. Because your application letter is in your own style (rather than the choppy, shorthand style of your resumé), it gives you a chance to show your communication skills and some personality.

> If submitting your resumé by email, attach it as a Word or PDF document and also paste it into the body of your email.

> One advantage of posting your resumé on your website is the opportunity to use hyperlinks.

> Many employers check Facebook to find out about the character of applicants.

> Keep your resumé up to date.

 Document Makeovers

 Model Document

 Activities

Always send your resumé and application letter together, because each has a unique job to perform. The purpose of your resumé is to get employers interested enough to contact you for an interview. The purpose of your application letter is to get employers interested enough to read your resumé.

SHOW YOU KNOW THE COMPANY Before drafting a letter, learn something about the organization you're applying to; then focus on your audience so that you can show you've done your homework. Imagine yourself in the recruiter's situation, and show how your background and talents will solve a particular problem or fill a specific need the company has. The more you can learn about the organization, the better you'll be able to capture the reader's attention and convey your interest in the company.[19] During your research, find out the name, title, and department of the person to whom you are writing. Reaching and addressing the right person is the most effective way to gain attention. Avoid phrases such as "To Whom It May Concern" and "Dear Sir or Madam."

KEEP IT SHORT When putting yourself in your reader's shoes, remember that this person's in-box is probably overflowing with resumés and cover letters. So respect your reader's time. A good application letter should be no longer than one page. It should maintain a friendly, conversational tone. Highlight the specific points the company is looking for. Show that you know the job.

If you're sending a **solicited application letter**—in response to an announced job opening—you'll usually know what qualifications the organization is seeking. You'll also have more competition because hundreds of other job seekers will have seen the listing and may be sending applications too. The letter in Figure 13.10 was written in response

> Application letters are intended to interest readers enough to read your resumé.

> Research the company so you can show specifically how you "fit" into their workplace.

> You write a solicited application letter in response to an announced job opening.

FIGURE 13.10 Sample Solicited Application Letter

2893 Jack Pine Road
Hamilton, ON L2H 8Y7

February 3, 2009

Ms. Angela Clair
Director of Administration
Cummings and Welbane, Inc.
770 Campus Point Drive
Hamilton, ON L8N 3T2

Dear Ms. Clair:

JOINING YOUR FIRM AS AN OFFICE ASSISTANT

Please consider me for the office assistant position you advertised in the January 31 issue of the *Toronto Star*. In addition to experience in a variety of office settings, I am trained in the software used in your office.

I recently completed a three-course sequence at Hamilton College on Microsoft Office. I learned how to use Word and Excel to speed up report-writing tasks and manage databases. A workshop on "Writing and Editing with the Unix Processor" gave me experience with other valuable applications such as composing and formatting sales letters, financial reports, and presentation slides.

These skills have been invaluable to me as assistant to the chief nutritionist at Cara Food Services (please refer to my resumé). The order-confirmation system I designed has sharply reduced late shipments and improved inventory levels.

I would appreciate an interview with you. Please telephone me any afternoon between 3 and 5 p.m. at (905) 220-6139 to let me know the day and time most convenient for you.

Sincerely,

Nick Caruso

Nick Caruso

Enclosure: Resumé

States the reason for writing and links the writer's experience to stated qualifications

Explains an achievement mentioned in the resumé and refers the reader to the enclosure

Discusses how specific skills apply to the job sought, showing that Caruso understands the job's responsibilities

Asks for an interview and facilitates action

FIGURE 13.11	Sample Unsolicited Application Letter

Gains attention in the first paragraph

Interests reader with knowledge of the company's policy toward promotion

Points out qualities that aren't specifically stated in her resume

Focuses on the audience and displays the "you" attitude, even though the last paragraph uses the word "I"

1254 Main Street
Summerside, PE C1N 3C4

June 16, 2009

Ms. Patricia Downings
Store Manager
The Bay
840 South Oak
Charlottetown, PE C2R 5H6

Dear Ms. Downings:

APPLICATION FOR MANAGERIAL POSITION

Please accept this application for your next management trainee position. The opportunity to develop a career at The Bay, with its industry-leading inventory practices, fits my career goals, and I would deliver on your expectations for a hardworking, enthusiastic, and competent employee.

As a clerk at *Zellers*, I stocked shelves, answered customer enquiries, and built displays. I gained experience in nine different departments and often worked extra shifts and evenings. Patience with customer questions helped me develop good listening skills and identify opportunities for new products. Recognizing that many customers can go online instead of coming into the store, I built relationships whenever I could to help encourage return visits. While completing team projects at Ryerson, I learned how to lead, listen, encourage others' ideas, and speak up tactfully when needed. The interpersonal skills gained in these projects will be useful in serving your customers and in becoming the kind of manager that others will trust.

In addition to customer service skills, I bring strong administrative skills. During my diploma in retailing, I gained knowledge of marketing and experience in solving problems by analyzing spreadsheets. I have used databases at *Zellers* for stock-taking, ordering, and producing month-end merchandising reports. I also studied international sourcing during my special projects course and learned about many of The Bay's best practices. The reach of The Bay's purchasing is exciting. Please look over my resumé, to see other skills I can bring to the job.

I understand that The Bay prefers to promote its managers from within the company, so I am seeking an entry-level position. I will telephone you early next Wednesday to arrange a meeting to discuss my qualifications, or please call me at (204) 733-5981.

Sincerely,

Glenda Johns

Glenda Johns

Enclosure: Resumé

to a help-wanted ad. Nick Caruso highlights his chief qualifications and mirrors the requirements specified in the ad.

In some respects, an **unsolicited letter**—sent to an organization that has not announced an opening—stands a better chance of being read and receiving individualized attention. In her unsolicited application letter in Figure 13.11, Glenda Johns manages to give a snapshot of her qualifications and skills. She gains attention by focusing on the needs of the employer.

Both solicited and unsolicited letters present your qualifications similarly. The main difference is in the opening paragraph. In a solicited letter, you need no special attention-getter because you have been invited to apply. In an unsolicited letter, you need to start by capturing the reader's attention and interest.

Like your resumé, your application letter is a form of advertising, so organize it as you would a sales letter: Use the AIDA approach, focus on your audience, and emphasize reader benefits (as discussed in Chapter 9). Make sure your style projects confidence. To

You write an unsolicited application letter to an organization that has not announced a job opening.

Getting Attention

Follow the AIDA approach when writing your application letter: attention, interest, desire, action.

sell a potential employer on your merits, you must believe in them and sound as though you do.

> The opening of an application letter captures attention, gives the reason you're writing, and states which job you're applying for.

The opening paragraph of your application letter must also state your reason for writing and the position you are applying for. Table 13.5 highlights some important ways to spark interest and grab attention in your opening paragraph. All these openings demonstrate the "you" attitude, and many indicate how the applicant can serve the employer. You can give your reason for writing by saying something like the following examples:

> Please consider my application for an entry-level position in technical writing.

> Your firm advertised a fleet sales position (on September 23, 2009, in the *Edmonton Sun*).

Another way to state your reason for writing is to use a subject line in the opening of your letter:

> Subject: Application for Bookkeeper Position

TABLE 13.5	Tips for Getting Attention in Application Letters

TIP	EXAMPLE
Unsolicited Application Letters	
• Show how your strongest skills will benefit the organization. A 20-year-old in her third year of college might begin like this:	When your export division needs an administrative assistant who can word-process 95 words per minute and who is bilingual in English and French, please call me.
• Describe your understanding of the job's requirements and then show how well your qualifications fit them.	Your annual report states that Petro-Canada runs employee-training programs about workforce diversity. The difficulties involved in running such programs can be significant, as I learned while tutoring inner-city high-school students last summer. My 12 pupils were enrolled in vocational training programs and came from diverse backgrounds. The one thing they had in common was a lack of familiarity with the typical employer's expectations. To help them learn the "rules of the game," I developed exercises that cast them in various roles: boss, customer, new recruit, and co-worker. Of the 12 students, 10 subsequently found full-time jobs and have called or written to tell me how much they gained from the workshop.
• Mention the name of a person known to and highly regarded by the reader.	When Janice McHugh of your franchise sales division spoke to our business communication class last week, she said you often need new marketing graduates at this time of year.
• Refer to publicized company activities, achievements, changes, or new procedures.	Today's issue of the *Globe* reports that you may need the expertise of computer programmers versed in robotics when your London bottling plant automates this spring.
• Use an opening that addresses a current issue faced by the company.	Social networking technologies enable people to connect, share their stories, and build friendships. My skills in using these technologies could help build strong relationships with customers and employees that can result in your company benefiting from the stories customers have to tell about your products.
Solicited Application Letters	
• Identify the publication in which the ad ran; then describe what you have to offer.	Your ad in the April issue of *Travel & Leisure* for a cruise-line social director sounds like an exciting opportunity. My eight years of experience as an event planner has given me skills to do this job well.

BUILDING INTEREST AND INCREASING DESIRE The middle section of your application letter presents your strongest selling points in terms of their potential benefit to the organization, thereby building interest in you and creating a desire to interview you. If you already mentioned your selling points in the opening, don't repeat them. Simply give supporting evidence. Be careful not to repeat the facts presented in your resumé; instead, interpret those facts for the reader. Spell out a few of your key qualifications, and back up your assertions with some convincing evidence of your ability to perform:

> The middle section of an application letter
> • Summarizes your relevant qualifications
> • Emphasizes your accomplishments
> • Suggests desirable personal qualities
> • Justifies salary requirements
> • Refers to your resumé

Poor: I completed three college courses in business communication, earning an A in each course, and have worked for the past year at Imperial Construction.

Improved: Using the skills gained from three semesters of training in business communication, I developed a collection system for Imperial Construction that reduced its 2008 bad-debt losses by 3.7 percent, or $9902, over those of 2007. Instead of using timeworn terminology, the new system's collection letters offered discount incentives for speedy payment.

Improved: Experience in customer relations and courses in public relations have taught me how to handle the problem-solving tasks that arise in a leading retail clothing firm like yours. Such important tasks include identifying and resolving customer complaints, writing letters and emails that build good customer relations, and above all, promoting the organization's positive image.

When writing a solicited letter responding to an advertisement, be sure to discuss each requirement specified in the ad.

The middle of your application letter also demonstrates a few significant job-related qualities, such as your diligence or your ability to work hard, learn quickly, handle responsibility, or get along with people:

> While attending university full-time, I trained three hours a day with the track team. In addition, I worked part-time during the school year and up to 60 hours a week each summer in order to be totally self-supporting while in university. I can offer your organization the same level of effort and perseverance.

Toward the end of this section, refer the reader to your resumé by citing a specific fact or general point covered there:

> As you can see in the attached resumé, I've been working part-time with a local publisher since my second year of college, and during that time, I have successfully resolved more than a few "client crises."

MOTIVATING ACTION The final paragraph of your application letter has two important functions: to ask the reader for a specific action and to make a reply easy. In almost all cases, the action you request is an interview. Don't demand it, however; try to sound natural and appreciative. Offer to come to the employer's office at a convenient time or, if the firm is some distance away, to meet with its nearest representative. Make the request easy to fulfil by stating your phone number and the best time to reach you—or, if you wish to be in control, by mentioning that you will follow up with a phone call in a few days.

> Close by asking for an interview and making the interview easy to arrange.

> After you have reviewed my qualifications, could we discuss the possibility of putting my marketing skills to work for your company? Because I will be on spring break the week of March 8, I would like to arrange a time to talk then. I will call in late February to schedule a convenient time when we could discuss employment opportunities at your company.

Once you have edited and proofread your application letter, mail it and your resumé promptly, especially if they have been solicited.

You may need to vary your approach according to your reader's culture.

ADAPTING STYLE AND APPROACH TO CULTURE The AIDA approach isn't appropriate for job seekers in every culture. If you're applying for a job abroad or want to work with a subsidiary of an organization that is based in another country, you may need to adjust your tone. Blatant self-promotion is considered bad form in some cultures. Other cultures stress group performance over individual contributions. As for format, recruiters in some countries (including France) prefer handwritten letters to printed or typed ones—another good reason to research a company carefully before drafting your application letter. For Canadian and U.S. companies, let your letter reflect your personal style. Be yourself, but be businesslike too; avoid sounding cute. Don't use slang or a gimmicky layout.

Application Forms

An application form is a standardized data sheet that simplifies comparison of applicants' credentials.

Before considering you for a position, some organizations require you to fill out and submit an application form, a standardized data sheet that simplifies the comparison of applicants' qualifications. Organizations will use your application form as a convenient one-page source of information about your qualifications, so try to be thorough and accurate when filling it out. Have your resumé with you to remind you of important information, and if you can't remember something and have no record of it, provide the closest estimate possible.

Model Document

Activities

Application Follow-Ups

Use a follow-up letter to let the employer know you're still interested in the job.

If your application letter and resumé do not bring a response within a month or so, follow up with a second letter to keep your file active. This follow-up letter also gives you a chance to update your original application with any recent job-related information:

> Since applying to you on May 3 for an executive assistant position, I have completed a course in office management at Red River Community College. I achieved a first-class standing in the course. I am now a proficient user of MS Office, including competency in Excel spreadsheets.

> Please keep my application in your active file, and let me know when you need a skilled executive assistant.

Even if you've received a letter acknowledging your application and saying that it will be kept on file, send a follow-up letter three months later to show that you are still interested:

> Three months ago I applied for an underwriting position, and I want to let you know that I am still very interested in joining your company.

> I recently completed a four-week temporary work assignment at a large local insurance agency. I learned several new verification techniques and gained experience in delivering online service. This experience could increase my value to your underwriting department.

> Please keep my application in your active file, and let me know when a position opens for a capable underwriter.

A follow-up letter can demonstrate that you're sincerely interested in working for the organization, that you're persistent in pursuing your goals, and that you're upgrading your skills to make yourself a better employee. And it might just get you an interview.

ON THE JOB

Just as you put a lot of effort into a professional appearance for your resumé, do the same when presenting yourself for an interview. Before the interview, check what supervisors in that company wear to work and dress to fit in. Avoid revealing, flashy, or evening clothing. Your grooming and clothing contribute to the impression that new acquaintances form of you.

Reviewing Key Points

In this chapter you learned about searching for employment and preparing resumés and letters of application. You learned how to research career and job prospects by checking forecasts in occupational handbooks and how to organize resumés. You can choose to show your work history in reverse chronological order or by categorizing your skills in a functional resumé. Whichever way you decide to organize your resumé, you should

- Keep the length to one or two pages
- Summarize and select key information according to job requirements
- Use headings and lists to highlight important information
- Include education, work and volunteer experience, market-related skills, and interests
- Be accurate, concise, clear, and use parallel structure
- Use verbs to create a dynamic style
- Make the resumé easy to skim by using layout, white space, indentation, headings, boldface, and visual features for emphasis

If the company of interest uses computer software to scan applicants' resumés, you will need to use keywords in your document and check with the company for submission requirements.

In letters of application

- Write the letter as you would a "sales" letter and use the AIDA approach
- Open with the job request
- Use research to show how you "fit" the company
- Emphasize the skills you can contribute
- Ask for an interview in the last paragraph and "make the action easy"
- Keep it to one page
- Follow up if the company has not responded

mybuscommlab   Go to MyBusCommLab at www.pearson.ca/mybuscommlab for online exercises.

Practise Your Grammar

Exercises

Effective business communication starts with strong grammar skills. To improve your grammar skills, go to MyBusCommLab or Grammar-on-the-Go, where you'll find exercises and diagnostic tests to help you produce clear, correct communication.

Test Your Knowledge

Exercises

1. In what three ways is the employment search affected by the results of today's changing workplace?
2. What three things can you do to make yourself more valuable to an employer?
3. What is a resumé, and why is it important to adopt a "you" attitude when preparing one?
4. How does a chronological resumé differ from a functional resumé, and when is each appropriate?
5. What elements are commonly included in a resumé?
6. What are some of the most common problems with resumés?
7. Why is it important to provide keywords in a resumé?
8. What advantages do resumés sent by email have over resumés sent by fax or by mail?
9. How does a solicited application letter differ from an unsolicited letter?
10. How does the AIDA approach apply to an application letter?

Apply Your Knowledge

1. According to experts in the job-placement field, the average job seeker relies too heavily on the resumé and not enough on other elements of the job search. Which elements do you think are most important? Please explain.
2. One of the disadvantages of resumé scanning is that some qualified applicants will be missed because the technology isn't perfect. However, more companies are using this approach. Do you think that resumé scanning is a good idea? Please explain.
3. Stating your career objective on a resumé or application might limit your opportunities by labelling you too narrowly. Not stating your objective, however, might lead an employer to categorize you incorrectly. Which outcome is riskier? Do summaries of qualifications overcome such drawbacks? If so, how? Explain briefly.
4. When writing a solicited application letter and describing the skills requested in the employer's ad, how can you avoid using "I" too often? Explain and give examples.
5. **Ethical Choices** Between your second and third year, you quit school for a year to earn the money to finish university. You worked as a clerk in a finance company, checking references on loan applications, typing, and filing. Your manager made a lot of the fact that he had never attended university. He seemed to resent you for pursuing your education, but he never criticized your work, so you thought you were doing okay. After you'd been working there for six months, he fired you, saying that you failed to be thorough enough in your credit checks. You were actually glad to leave, and you found another job right away at a bank doing similar duties. Now that you've graduated from university, you're writing your resumé. Will you include the finance company job in your work history? Please explain. What other ethical issue could you be concerned about?

Running Cases

Video

CASE 1: Noreen

The Go Points department and the credit card sales/service department have merged, and Petro-Go plans to combine these two departments in all their international centres. The senior management team is hiring for a new position of Merger Project Manager and Noreen wants to apply. The project is expected to last two years and the chosen candidate will travel to 12 countries and 40 call centres to implement the merger.

QUESTIONS

a. What is the purpose of the cover letter and resumé?
b. What skills should Noreen emphasize?
c. How many pages long should her resumé be?
d. What is the best organizational style for Noreen's resumé? Why?
e. What common mistakes with resumé fonts must Noreen ensure she doesn't make?

YOUR TASK

Create a cover letter and resumé for Noreen. Refer to the cases about Noreen at the end of each chapter in this book to read about her skills and background. You may use your imagination to add skills and experience to Noreen's resumé as you see fit.

CASE 2: Kwong

Kwong has obtained his CGA credentials and opened an accounting firm. His firm, CG Accounting, has been operating for three months and has 20 corporate account customers and 167 personal account customers. His sister is working in his office as the office administrator, and he has one other tax preparer working on the accounts with him. His sister is leaving, and he needs to hire a new administrator who will answer phones, advise customers, prepare forms for signature, take care of emails and filing, and so on. He has placed a job advertisement in the newspaper and is now reviewing resumés.

QUESTIONS

a. List three main skills Kwong will look for.
b. Is past experience necessary?
c. What skills should the cover letter emphasize?
d. List two questions Kwong might ask an over-qualified candidate.
e. List two questions Kwong might ask an under-qualified candidate.

YOUR TASK

Create a cover letter to apply for this position. Use your resumé and fit it to this position. Work in pairs and exchange your cover letter and resumé with another student. Each of you will give feedback and suggestions for improvement to the other.

⊘ Practise Your Knowledge

ACTIVITIES

1. **Analyze This Document** Read the following resumé; then (1) analyze its strengths and weaknesses and (2) revise the document so that it follows the guidelines presented in this chapter.

Sylvia Manchester

765 Belle Fleur Blvd.

St-Laurent, QC H4L 3X9

(514) 312-9504

smanchester@bce.net

PERSONAL: Single, excellent health, 5980, 116 lb.; hobbies include cooking, dancing, and reading.

JOB OBJECTIVE: To obtain a responsible position in marketing or sales with a good company.

Education: BSc degree in biology, Dalhousie University. Graduated with a 3.0 average. Member of the varsity volleyball team. President of Dalhousie Chess Club.

WORK EXPERIENCE

Fisher Scientific Instruments, 2006 to present, field sales representative. Responsible for calling on customers and explaining the features of Fisher's line of laboratory instruments. Also responsible for writing sales letters, attending trade shows, and preparing weekly sales reports.

Fisher Scientific Instruments, 2002–2004, customer service representative. Was responsible for handling incoming phone calls from customers who had questions about delivery, quality, or operation of Fisher's line of laboratory instruments. Also handled miscellaneous correspondence with customers.

Medical Electronics, Inc. 2000–2001, administrative assistant to the vice-president of marketing. In addition to handling typical secretarial chores for the vice-president of marketing, I was in charge of compiling the monthly sales reports, using figures provided by members of the field sales force. I also was given responsibility for doing various market research activities.

Ottawa Convention and Visitors Bureau. 1998–1999, summers, tour guide. During the summers of my university years, I led tours of Ottawa for tourists visiting the city. My duties included greeting conventioneers and their spouses at hotels, explaining the history and features of the city during an all-day sightseeing tour, and answering questions about Ottawa and its attractions. During my fourth summer with the bureau, I was asked to help train the new tour guides. I prepared a handbook that provided interesting facts about the various tourist attractions, as well as answers to the most commonly asked tourist questions. The bureau was so impressed with the handbook they had it printed up so that it could be given as a gift to visitors.

Dalhousie University. 1998–1999, part-time clerk in admissions office. While I was a student in university, I worked 15 hours a week in the admissions office. My duties included filing, processing applications, and handling correspondence from high-school students and administrators.

2. **Analyze This Document** Read the following letter; then (1) analyze its strengths and weaknesses and (2) revise the letter so that it follows the guidelines presented in this chapter.

I'm writing to let you know about my availability for the brand manager job you advertised. As you can see from my enclosed resumé, my background is perfect for the position. Even though I don't have any real job experience, my grades have been outstanding considering that I went to a top-ranked business school.

I did many things during my undergraduate years to prepare me for this job:

* Earned a 3.4 out of a 4.0 with a 3.8 in my business courses
* Elected representative to the student governing association
* Selected to receive the Terry Fox Award
* Worked to earn a portion of my tuition

I am sending my resumé to all the top firms, but I like yours better than any of the rest. Your reputation is tops in the industry, and I want to be associated with a business that can pridefully say it's the best.

If you wish for me to come in for an interview, I can come on a Friday afternoon or anytime on weekends when I don't have classes. Again, thanks for considering me for your brand manager position.

3. **Analyze This Document** Read the following letter; then (1) analyze its strengths and weaknesses and (2) revise the letter so that it follows the guidelines presented in this chapter.

Did you receive my resumé? I sent it to you at least two months ago and haven't heard anything. I know you keep resumés on file, but I just want to be sure that you keep me in mind. I heard you are hiring health-care managers and certainly would like to be considered for one of those positions.

Since I last wrote you, I've worked in a variety of positions that have helped prepare me for management. To wit, I've become lunch manager at the restaurant where I work, which involved a raise in pay. I now manage a wait staff of 12 girls and take the lunch receipts to the bank every day.

Of course, I'd much rather be working at a real job, and that's why I'm writing again. Is there anything else you would like to know about me or my background? I would really like to know more about your company. Is there any literature you could send me? If so, I would really appreciate it.

I think one reason I haven't been hired yet is that I don't want to leave Winnipeg. So I hope when you think of me, it's for a position that wouldn't require moving. Thanks again for considering my application.

4. **Work-Related Preferences: Self-Assessment** What work-related activities and situations do you prefer? Evaluate your preferences in each of the following areas. Use the results as a good start for guiding your job search.

Activity or Situation	Strongly Agree	Agree	Disagree	No Preference
1. I want to work independently.	_____	_____	_____	_____
2. I want variety in my work.	_____	_____	_____	_____
3. I want to work with people.	_____	_____	_____	_____
4. I want to work with products or machines.	_____	_____	_____	_____
5. I want physical work.	_____	_____	_____	_____
6. I want mental work.	_____	_____	_____	_____
7. I want to work for a large organization.	_____	_____	_____	_____
8. I want to work for a non-profit organization.	_____	_____	_____	_____
9. I want to work for a small family business.	_____	_____	_____	_____
10. I want to work for a service business.	_____	_____	_____	_____
11. I want regular, predictable work hours.	_____	_____	_____	_____
12. I want to work in a city location.	_____	_____	_____	_____
13. I want to work in a small town or suburb.	_____	_____	_____	_____
14. I want to work in another country.	_____	_____	_____	_____
15. I want to work outdoors.	_____	_____	_____	_____
16. I want to work in a structured environment.	_____	_____	_____	_____

5. **Teamwork** Working with another student, change the following statements to make them more effective for a traditional resumé by using action verbs.
   a. Have some experience with database design
   b. Assigned to a project to analyze the cost accounting methods for a large manufacturer
   c. Was part of a team that developed a new inventory control system
   d. Am responsible for preparing the quarterly department budget
   e. Was a manager of a department with seven employees working for me
   f. Was responsible for developing a spreadsheet to analyze monthly sales by department
   g. Put in place a new program for ordering supplies

6. **Resumé Preparation: Work Accomplishments** Using your team's answers to Activity 5, make the statements stronger by quantifying them (make up any numbers you need).

7. **Ethical Choices** Assume that you achieved all the tasks shown in Activity 5 not as an individual employee but as part of a work team. In your resumé, must you mention other team members? Explain your answer.

8. **Resumé Preparation: Using Keywords** Using your revised version of the resumé in Activity 1, prepare a fully formatted print resumé. Identify and use keywords and make all the changes needed to complete this resumé.

9. **Ethical Choices: Use of Facebook to Check the Character of Applicants** Many recruiters and managers are using Facebook, LinkedIn, and other online spaces to find out more about applicants. Do you think this is an ethical practice? Discuss in groups of four and be ready to share your views with the class. What should applicants do in response to this practice? How can applicants manage their "online personas"? In your group, prepare a list of suggestions.

   After your class discussion, write a short reflection on your online persona. What can employers learn about you online? How can you manage your presence? Do you have a professional profile online?

10. **Online Presence** Develop a LinkedIn profile for yourself at www.linkedin.com.

Expand Your Knowledge

Best of the Web

Post an Online Resumé At Careerbuilder, you'll find sample resumés, tips on preparing different types of resumés (including scannable ones), links to additional articles, and expert advice on creating resumés that bring positive results. After you've polished your resumé-writing skills, you can search for jobs online using the site's numerous links to national and international industry-specific websites. You can access the information at Monster.ca to develop your resumé and then post it with prospective employers—all free. Take advantage of what this site offers, and get ideas for writing or improving a new resumé.

www.careerbuilder.ca
www.monster.ca

EXERCISES

1. Before writing a new resumé, make a list of action verbs that describe your skills and experience.
2. Describe the advantages and disadvantages of chronological and functional resumé formats. Do you think a combination resumé would be an appropriate format for your new resumé? Explain why or why not.
3. List some of the tips you learned for preparing an electronic resumé.

Exploring the Web on Your Own

Review these chapter-related websites on your own to learn more about writing resumés and cover letters.

1. Learn how to produce cover letters with brilliance, flair, and speed at So You Wanna Write a Cover Letter? **www.soyouwanna.com/site/syws/coverletter/coverletter.html**.
2. For expert advice on writing resumés and cover letters, go to WetFeet, **www.wetfeet.com**.

Cases

Apply each step in Figure 13.3 to the following cases, as assigned by your instructor.

Building Toward a Career

1. TAKING STOCK AND TAKING AIM: APPLICATION PACKAGE FOR THE RIGHT JOB

Think about yourself. What are some things that come easily to you? What do you enjoy doing? In what part of the country would you like to live? Do you like to work indoors? Outdoors? A combination of the two? How much do you like to travel? Would you like to spend considerable time on the road? Do you like to work closely with others or more independently? What conditions make a job unpleasant? Do you delegate responsibility easily, or do you like to do things yourself? Are you better with words or numbers? Better at speaking or writing? Do you like to work under fixed deadlines? How important is job security to you? Do you want your supervisor to state clearly what is expected of you, or do you like the freedom to make many of your own decisions? What industries interest you? What are your core values? For example, are you community-oriented or keen on working in the "green economy"? Use a site such as WetFeet to help you form your career goals (**www.wetfeet.com**).

YOUR TASK After answering these questions, gather information about possible jobs that suit your profile by consulting reference materials (from your university or college library or placement centre) and by searching the internet (using some of the search strategies discussed in Chapter 10). Next, choose a location, a company, and a job that interests you. With guidance from your instructor, decide whether to apply for a job you're qualified for now or one you'll be qualified for with additional education. Research specific information to include in your letter. Then, as directed by your instructor, write one or more of the following: (a) a resumé, (b) a letter of application, (c) a follow-up letter to your application letter.

WEB SKILLS 2. SCANNING THE POSSIBILITIES: RESUMÉ FOR THE INTERNET

In your search for a position, you discover CareerMag, a website that lists hundreds of companies advertising on the internet. Your chances of getting an interview with a leading company will be enhanced if you submit your resumé and cover letter electronically. On the web, explore **www.careermag.com**.

YOUR TASK Prepare a resumé that could be submitted to one of the companies advertising at the CareerMag website. Print out the resumé for your instructor.

3. ANALYZING THE AUDIENCE: CUSTOMIZING YOUR APPLICATION

Motley Fool (**www.fool.com**) is an online investment magazine accessed via the web. Its founders and writers are extremely creative and motivated. The many benefits and eccentric atmosphere of the organization are intriguing. If you were to apply to this company, what kinds of skills and personality traits would you emphasize? Why? What messages about the corporate culture come across on its website? How would these messages influence your approach to a job application? What types of recruitment strategies are emphasized on the website?

YOUR TASK Discuss with a classmate and, together, write an opening paragraph of an email job application. What type of creative "hook" could you use?

Writing a Resumé and an Application Letter

4. "HELP WANTED": APPLICATION FOR A JOB LISTED IN THE CLASSIFIEDS SECTION

Among the jobs listed in today's *Vancouver Sun* are the following:

ACCOUNTING ASSISTANT

Established leader in the vacation ownership industry has immediate opening in its Richmond corp. accounting dept. for an accounting assistant. Responsibilities include bank reconciliation, preparation of deposits, AP, and cash receipt posting. Join our fast-growing company and enjoy our great benefits package. Flex work hours, medical, dental insurance. Fax resumé to Lisa: 604-564-3876.

ADMINISTRATIVE ASSISTANT

Fast-paced Yaletown office seeks professional with strong computer skills. Proficient in MS Word & Excel, PowerPoint a plus. Must be detail oriented, able to handle multiple tasks, and possess strong communication skills. Excellent benefits, salary, and work environment. Fax resumé to 604-350-8649.

CUSTOMER SERVICE

A nationally known computer software developer has an exciting opportunity in customer service and inside sales support in its fast-paced Burnaby office. You'll help resolve customer problems over the phone, provide information, assist in account management, and administer orders. If you're friendly, self-motivated, energetic, and have two years of experience, excellent problem-solving skills, organizational, communication, and PC skills, and communicate well over the phone, send resumé to J. Haber, 233 North Lake Shore Drive, Burnaby, BC V1H 5N1.

SALES-ACCOUNT MANAGER

Aqua Springs Water Company is seeking an Account Manager to sell and coordinate our programs to major accounts in the Alberta market. The candidate should possess strong analytical and selling skills and demonstrate computer proficiency. Previous sales experience with major account level assignment desired. A degree in business or equivalent experience preferred. For confidential consideration please mail resumé to Steven Crane, Director of Sales, Aqua Springs Water Company, 133 N. Railroad Avenue, Langley, BC V5J 4S2

YOUR TASK Send a resumé and an application letter to one of these potential employers.

Writing Other Types of Employment Messages

5. CRASHING THE LAST FRONTIER: LETTER OF INQUIRY ABOUT JOBS IN INUVIK

Your friend can't understand why you would want to move to the Arctic. So you explain: "What really decided it for me was that I'd never seen the northern lights."

"But what about the bears? The 60-degree-below winters? The permafrost?" asks your friend.

"No problem. Anyhow, I want to live in the North. Inuvik has lots of small businesses, like a frontier town in the West about 150 years ago. I think it still has homesteading tracts for people who want to do their own building and are willing to stay for a certain number of years."

"Your plans seem a little hasty," your friend warns. "Maybe you should write for information before you just take off. How do you know you could get a job?"

YOUR TASK Take your friend's advice and write to the Chamber of Commerce, Inuvik, NT X0E 2YR. Ask what types of employment are available to someone with your education and experience, and ask who specifically is hiring year-round employees.

Netting a Job on the Web

Can the web provide the answer to all your employment dreams? Perhaps . . . or perhaps not. As the web grows, the employment information it provides is constantly expanding. And you're fortunate because you don't have to start from scratch like some intrepid adventurer. For helpful hints and useful web addresses, you can turn to books such as *What Color Is Your Parachute?* by Richard Nelson Bolles. Other places to check out online include the following:*

- **National Job Bank** (jb-ge.hrsdc-drhc.gc.ca). Human Resources and Social Development Canada hosts the Service Canada site, which posts thousands of jobs and offers helpful resumé and application tips. It includes links to provincial job opportunities, labour market information, and other job-hunting services.
- **WORKink** (www.workink.com). The Canadian Council on Rehabilitation and Work hosts a "virtual employment resource centre" with support from HRSDC. It is administered with provincial and territorial partners. Although WORKink's mission is to facilitate and enhance resources available for employment of people with disabilities, its service is useful for any job seeker.
- **The Monster Board** (www.monster.ca). Posts openings and resumés. Heavily marketed, it brings a flood of employers (many with fewer than 500 employees).
- **Yahoo!HotJobs** (www.hotjobs.yahoo.com). A member-based site that charges companies a hefty fee to post openings or search through resumés. Job seekers can create a personal page to manage their search and collect statistics on how many companies have retrieved their resumé. The site has a "Yahoo!HotJobs Canada" link (ca.hotjobs.yahoo.com/).

- **Net-Temps** (www.net-temps.com). Maintained by career consultants; offers several thousand updated listings and real-time seminars. Network forums help you develop new contacts and job leads. Includes chat room for online interviews. Check the link to "Canada" under "Search Jobs by Career Channel."
- **Careerbuilder** (www.careerbuilder.ca). Offers a network of career services, job-search information, and tips on how to succeed once you're hired. Includes a database of 20 000 openings.
- **MonsterTrak** (www.monstertrak.com). Has formed partnerships with campuses and serves as a virtual career centre for students and alumni. Many entry-level postings.

Applications for Success

1. Surfing the web can chew up a disproportionate amount of your job-seeking time. Explain how you can limit the amount of time you spend on the web and still make it work for you.
2. When posting your resumé on the web, you're revealing a lot of information about yourself that could be used by people other than employers (salespeople, people competing for similar positions, con artists). What sort of information might you leave off your web resumé that would certainly appear on a traditional resumé?
3. Visit at least two of these online indexes, and check out features such as job searches, career centres, and tips for finding employment. Compare the features of the indexes and choose the one you find the most convenient and helpful. Explain your choice in a one-page email to your instructor.

*Direct links to these websites can be accessed at the Riley Guide (www.rileyguide.com).

Interviewing for Employment and Following Up

LEARNING OBJECTIVES

After studying this chapter, you will be able to

1. Define *employment interview* and explain its dual purpose
2. Discuss the three stages in a typical sequence of interviews
3. Identify and briefly describe six types of employment interviews
4. List six tasks you need to complete to prepare for a successful job interview
5. Explain the three stages of a successful employment interview
6. Describe four ways you can respond to unethical or illegal questions during an interview
7. Name three common employment messages that follow an interview and state briefly when you would use each one

In her job at Ray & Berndtson, Tanton Mitchell, an international executive search firm, Caroline Jellinck interviews more than 100 people each year. When evaluating candidates, she looks for people who are confident without being arrogant and who can be specific, yet succinct in their replies. "The only way to judge if someone is going to be successful in the future," says Jellinck, "is to know where they have been successful in the past. Realistic, honest stories about past achievements can give interviewers a picture of future potential."

Understanding the Interviewing Process

Interviewers are not trying to intimidate or scare people; employers want to find out as much as they can. Employment interviews have a dual purpose:

- **Organization's main objective.** To find the best person available for the job
- **Applicant's main objective.** To find the job best suited to his or her goals and capabilities

While recruiters are trying to decide whether you are right for them, you must decide whether the company is right for you.

An **employment interview** is a formal meeting during which both employer and applicant ask questions and exchange information to see whether the applicant and the organization are a good match. Because interviewing takes time, you'll want to begin seeking jobs well in advance of the date you want to start work. Some students begin their job search as much as nine months before graduation. It takes an average of 10 interviews to get one job offer, so if you hope to have several offers to choose from, expect to go through 20 or 30 interviews during your job search.[1] Also, in one company you may face a series of interviews, each with a different purpose.

> An interview helps both the interviewer and the applicant achieve their goals.

> In a typical job search, you can expect to have many interviews before you accept a job offer.

The Typical Sequence of Interviews

Not all organizations interview potential candidates the same way. However, many employers interview an applicant two or three times before deciding to make a job offer.

THE SCREENING STAGE The preliminary *screening stage* can be held on campus to help employers screen out unqualified applicants. These interviews are fairly structured: Applicants are often asked roughly the same questions so that all the candidates will be measured against the same criteria. In some cases, technology has transformed the initial, get-to-know-you interview, allowing employers to screen candidates by phone, video, or computer.[2]

Your best approach to the screening stage is to follow the interviewer's lead. Keep your responses short and to the point. Time is limited, so talking too much can be a big mistake. However, try to differentiate yourself from other candidates. Without resorting to gimmicks, call attention to one key aspect of your background. Then the recruiter can say, "Oh yes, I remember Scott—the one who sold used Toyotas in Edmonton." Just be sure the trait you accentuate is relevant to the job in question. Also be ready to demonstrate a particular skill (perhaps problem solving) if asked to do so. Candidates who meet the company's requirements are invited to visit company offices for further evaluation.

> During the screening stage of interviews, try to differentiate yourself from other candidates.

THE SELECTION STAGE The next stage of interviews helps the organization narrow the field a little further. Typically, if you're invited to visit a company, you'll talk with several people: a member of the human resources department, one or two potential colleagues, and your potential supervisor. You might face a panel of several interviewers who ask you questions during a single session. By noting how you listen, think, and express yourself, they can decide how likely you are to get along with colleagues.

Show interest in the job. Relate your skills and experience to the organization's needs. Touch briefly on all your strengths, but explain three or four of your best qualifications in depth. At the same time, probe for information that will help you evaluate the position objectively. As important as it is to get an offer, it's also important to learn whether the job is right for you. Also, be sure to listen attentively, ask insightful questions, and display enthusiasm. If the interviewers agree that you're a good candidate, you may receive a job offer, either on the spot or a few days later by phone or mail.

> During the selection stage of interviews, cover all your strengths and relate them to the organization's needs.

THE FINAL STAGE You may be invited back for a final evaluation by a higher-ranking executive with the authority to make an offer and negotiate terms. This person may already have concluded that your background is right and may be more concerned with sizing up your personality. You both need to see whether there is a good psychological fit, so be honest about your motivations and values. An underlying objective of the *final stage* is often to sell you on the advantages of joining the organization.

> During the final stage, emphasize your personality, describing your motivations and values honestly.

Types of Interviews

Organizations use various types of interviews to discover as much as possible about applicants.

- **Structured interviews.** Generally used in the screening stage, structured interviews are controlled by the employer, who asks a series of prepared questions in a set order. All answers are noted. Although useful in gathering facts, the structured interview is generally a poor measure of an applicant's personal qualities. Nevertheless, some companies use structured interviews to create uniformity in their hiring process.[3]
- **Open-ended interviews.** Less formal and unstructured, these interviews often have a relaxed format. The interviewer asks broad, open-ended questions, encouraging applicants to talk freely. Such interviews bring out an applicant's personality and test professional judgment. However, some candidates reveal too much, rambling on

> Interviews vary from employer to employer.

about personal or family problems, so strike a balance between being friendly and remembering that you're in a business situation.

- **Group interviews.** To judge interpersonal skills, some employers meet with several candidates simultaneously to see how they interact. For example, the Walt Disney Company uses group interviews when hiring people for its theme parks. During a 45-minute session, the Disney recruiter watches how three candidates relate to one another. Do they smile? Are they supportive of one another's comments? Do they try to score points at each other's expense?[4]
- **Stress interviews.** Perhaps the most unnerving, stress interviews are set up to see how well a candidate handles stressful situations (an important qualification for certain jobs). You might be asked pointed questions designed to irk or unsettle you. You might be subjected to long periods of silence, criticisms of your appearance, deliberate interruptions, and abrupt or even hostile reactions by the interviewer.
- **Video interviews.** To cut travel costs, many large companies use videoconferencing systems. You need to prepare a bit differently for a video interview by (1) requesting a preliminary phone conversation to establish rapport with the interviewer, (2) arriving early enough to get used to the equipment and setting, (3) speaking clearly but no more slowly than normal, (4) sitting straight and looking up but not down, and (5) showing some animation (but not too much since it will appear blurry to the interviewer).[5]
- **Situational interviews.** Many companies claim that interviewing is about the job, not about a candidate's five-year goals, weaknesses or strengths, challenging experiences, or greatest accomplishments. An interviewer describes a situation and asks, "How would you handle this?" So the situational interview is a hands-on, at-work meeting between an employer who needs a job done and a worker who must be fully prepared to do the work.[6]

Regardless of the type of interview you may face, a personal interview is vital because your resumé can't show whether you're lively and outgoing or subdued and low-key, able to take direction or able to take charge. Each job requires a different mix of personality traits. The interviewer's task is to find out whether you will be effective on the job.

Preparing for a Job Interview

Just as written messages need planning, employment interviews need preparation.

It's perfectly normal to feel a little anxious before an interview. But good preparation will help you perform well. Be sure to consider any cultural differences when preparing for interviews, and base your approach on what your audience expects. The advice in this chapter is most appropriate for companies and employers in Canada and the United States. Before the interview, do some more research, think ahead about questions, bolster your confidence, polish your interview style, plan to look good, and be ready when you arrive.

Do Some Additional Research

Be prepared to relate your qualifications to the organization's needs.

You will already have researched the companies you sent your resumé to. But now that you've been invited for an interview, you'll want to fine-tune your research and brush up on the facts you've collected (see Table 14.1). Learning about the organization and the job enables you to show the interviewer just how you will meet the organization's particular needs.

Think Ahead About Questions

Planning ahead for the interviewer's questions will help you handle them more confidently and intelligently. Moreover, you will want to prepare intelligent questions of your own.

TABLE 14.1	Finding Out About the Organization and the Job

WHERE TO LOOK FOR INFORMATION

• *Company website*	Provides corporate profile, news, scope of operations, locations, can give a sense of the company's values, involvement in charities or in environmental issues, and may have link to blogs or webcasts
• *Annual report*	Summarizes operations; describes products, lists events, names key personnel
• *In-house magazine or newspaper*	Reveals information about company operations, events, personnel
• *Product brochure or publicity release*	Gives insight into firm's operations and values (obtain from public relations office)
• *Stock research report*	Helps assess stability and growth prospects (obtain online or from stockbroker)
• *Newspaper's business or financial pages*	Contain news items about organizations, current performance figures
• *Periodicals indexes*	Contain descriptive listings of magazine/newspaper articles about firms (obtain from library)
• *Better Business Bureau and Chamber of Commerce*	Distribute information about some local organizations
• *Former and current employees*	Have insight into job and work environment
• *College placement office*	Collects information on organizations that recruit and on job qualifications and salaries

WHAT TO FIND OUT ABOUT THE ORGANIZATION

• *Full name*	How the firm is officially known (e.g., CIBC is Canadian Imperial Bank of Commerce)
• *Location*	Where the organization's headquarters, branch offices, and plants are
• *Age*	How long the organization has been in business
• *Products*	What goods and services the organization produces and sells
• *Industry position*	What the organization's current market share, financial position, and profit picture are
• *Earnings*	What the trends in the firm's stock prices and dividends are (if firm is publicly held)
• *Growth*	How the firm's earnings/holdings have changed in recent years and prospects for expansion
• *Organization*	What subsidiaries, divisions, and departments make up the whole

WHAT TO FIND OUT ABOUT THE JOB

• *Job title*	What you will be called (e.g., sales representative)
• *Job functions*	What the main tasks of the job are
• *Job qualifications*	What knowledge and skills the job requires
• *Career path*	What chances for ready advancement exist
• *Salary range*	What the firm typically offers and what is reasonable in this industry and geographic area
• *Travel opportunities*	How often, long, and far you'll be allowed (or required) to travel
• *Relocation opportunities*	Where you might be allowed (or required) to move and how often

PLANNING FOR THE EMPLOYER'S QUESTIONS Employers usually gear their interview questions to specific organizational needs. You can expect to be asked about your skills, achievements, and goals, as well as about your attitude toward work and school, your relationships with others (work supervisors, colleagues, and fellow students), and occasionally your hobbies and interests. For a look at the types of questions often asked, see Table 14.2 (on page 348). Jot down a brief answer to each one. Then read over the answers until you feel comfortable with each of them.

> Practise answering interview questions.

Although practising your answers will help you feel prepared and confident, you don't want to memorize responses or sound over-rehearsed. Try giving a list of interview questions to a friend or relative and have that person ask you various questions at random. Such practice helps you learn to articulate answers and to look at the person as you answer.

TABLE 14.2	Twenty-Five Common Interview Questions

QUESTIONS ABOUT COLLEGE OR UNIVERSITY

1. What courses did you like most? Least? Why?
2. Do you think your extracurricular activities were worth the time you spent on them? Why or why not?
3. When did you choose your major? Did you ever change your major? If so, why?
4. Do you feel you did the best academic work you are capable of?
5. Which of your college or university years was the toughest? Why?

QUESTIONS ABOUT EMPLOYERS AND JOBS

6. Why do you want to work for this company?
7. What jobs have you held? Why did you leave?
8. What percentage of your post-secondary expenses did you earn? How?
9. Why did you choose your particular field of work?
10. What is your management style?
11. What important trends do you see in our industry?
12. Why do you think you would like this particular type of job?

QUESTIONS ABOUT PERSONAL ATTITUDES AND PREFERENCES

13. Do you prefer to work in any specific geographic location? If so, why?
14. How much money do you hope to be earning in 5 years? In 10 years?
15. What do you think determines a person's progress in a good organization?
16. What personal characteristics do you feel are necessary for success in your chosen field?
17. Tell me about yourself or tell me a story.
18. Do you like to travel?
19. Do you think grades should be considered by employers? Why or why not?

QUESTIONS ABOUT WORK HABITS

20. Do you prefer working with others or by yourself?
21. What type of boss do you prefer?
22. Have you ever had any difficulty getting along with colleagues or supervisors? With instructors? With other students?
23. Would you prefer to work in a large or a small organization? Why?
24. How do you feel about overtime work?
25. What have you done that shows initiative and willingness to work?

PLANNING FOR BEHAVIOURAL QUESTIONS It has become quite popular for employers to choose behaviour-based questions to solicit how you would act in certain situations related to the position. These questions give you a situation and ask how you would respond or they ask you to give examples from your experience that relate to challenging situations you might face on the job. For example, for a customer service position, an interviewer may ask "tell me about a time when you had to deal with a difficult person. What did you do?" The purpose of the question is to identify whether you know how to handle conflict. Table 14.3 lists other samples of behavioural questions. In management interviews, expect a majority of the questions to be behavioural.

In your answers to these kinds of questions, follow a four-part approach:

1. Describe a specific situation.
2. Tell what your role was.
3. Tell what action you took.
4. Describe the positive result of your actions.

Find specific examples from your past (work, education, extracurricular activities, or volunteer experiences) for each question you anticipate.

TABLE 14.3	Sample Behavioural Questions

1. Describe a situation where you had to persuade someone to do things your way.
2. Give an example of when you communicated well with someone even though that person may not have liked you or you didn't like the person.
3. In your work experience have you had to handle a problem when your manager was not available?
4. Give an example of a difficult situation you have faced and how you handled it.
5. If you were in the store by yourself and a customer began to act in a loud and threatening manner, how would you react?
6. If you observed a fellow employee acting in an unsafe manner, what would you do?
7. If you were in training, and the supervisor training you criticized you in front of a customer, how would you react?
8. Think of a past supervisor or instructor who you have worked with closely and who you respect. What would that supervisor say are your strengths?
9. What would your supervisor say that you could improve?

PLANNING QUESTIONS OF YOUR OWN The questions you ask in an interview are just as important as the answers you provide. By asking intelligent questions, you demonstrate your understanding of the organization, and you can steer the discussion into those areas that allow you to present your qualifications to best advantage. Before the interview, prepare a list of questions you need answered in order to evaluate the organization and the job. Here's a list of some things you might want to find out:

- **Are these my kind of people?** Observe the interviewer, and if you can, arrange to talk with other employees.
- **Can I do this work?** Compare your qualifications with the requirements described by the interviewer.
- **Will I enjoy the work?** Know yourself and what's important to you. Will you find the work challenging? Will it give you feelings of accomplishment, of satisfaction, and of making a real contribution?
- **Is the job what I want?** You may never find a job that fulfils all your wants, but the position you accept should satisfy at least your primary ones. Will it make use of your best capabilities? Does it offer a career path to the long-term goals you've set?
- **Does the job pay what I'm worth?** By comparing jobs and salaries before you're interviewed, you'll know what's reasonable for someone with your skills in your industry.
- **What kind of person would I be working for?** If the interviewer is your prospective boss, watch how others interact with that person, tactfully query other employees, or pose a careful question or two during the interview. If your prospective boss is someone else, ask for that person's name, job title, and responsibilities. Try to learn all you can.
- **What sort of future can I expect with this organization?** How healthy is the organization? Can you look forward to advancement? Does the organization offer insurance, pension, vacation, or other benefits?

Rather than bombarding the interviewer with these questions the minute you walk in the room, use a mix of formats to elicit this information. Start with a warm-up question to help break the ice. You might ask, "What departments usually hire new graduates?" After that, you might build rapport by asking an open-ended question that draws out the interviewer's opinion ("How do you think internet sales will affect the company's continued growth?"). Indirect questions can elicit useful information and show that you've prepared for the interview ("I'd really like to know more about the company's plans for expanding its corporate presence on the web" or "That recent *Toronto Star* article about the company was very interesting"). Any questions you ask should be uniquely yours so that you don't sound like every other candidate. Do not ask questions that you could

> You are responsible for deciding whether the work and the organization are compatible with your goals and values.

> Assess whether the job satisfies your needs.

> Types of questions to ask during an interview:
> - Warm-up
> - Open-ended
> - Indirect

TABLE 14.4	Sample Questions to Ask the Interviewer

QUESTIONS ABOUT THE JOB	QUESTIONS ABOUT THE ORGANIZATION
What are the job's major responsibilities (if not published)?	What are the organization's major strengths? Weaknesses?
What qualities do you want in the person who fills this position?	What makes your organization different from others in the industry?
Do you want to know more about my related training?	Does the organization have any plans for new products? Acquisitions?
What is the first problem that needs the attention of the person you hire?	How would you define your organization's managerial philosophy?
Would relocation be required now or in the future?	What additional training does your organization provide?
Why is this job now vacant?	Do employees have an opportunity to continue their education with help from the organization?
What can you tell me about the person I would report to?	

research and answer before the interview. For a list of other good questions you might use as a starting point, see Table 14.4.

Take your list of typed questions to the interview. If you need to, jot down brief notes during the meeting, and be sure to record answers in more detail afterwards. Having a short list of typed questions should impress the interviewer with your organization and thoroughness. The questions should also reflect that you have already done some research on the company and know a lot about it. For example, only ask "What are your organization's major markets?" if that information is not readily available in sources. If you ask "What are your organization's major competitors?" when this information can be researched easily, you will miss an opportunity to show you are interested enough in the company to have done the research. Having a list of questions will show that you're there to evaluate the organization and the job as well as to sell yourself; but watch for cues and avoid overdoing it.

Bolster Your Confidence

If you feel shy or self-conscious, remember that recruiters are human too.

Building your confidence helps you make a better impression. The best way to counteract any apprehension is to remove its source. You may feel shy or self-conscious because you think you have some flaw that will prompt others to reject you. But you're much more conscious of your limitations than other people are.

If some aspect of your appearance or background makes you uneasy, correct it or offset it by exercising positive traits such as warmth, wit, intelligence, or charm. Instead of dwelling on your weaknesses, focus on your strengths so that you can emphasize them to an interviewer. Make a list of your good points and compare them with what you see as your shortcomings. Remember that you're not alone. All the other candidates for the job are just as nervous as you are. Even the interviewer may be nervous.

Polish Your Interview Style

Staging mock interviews with a friend is a good way to hone your style.

Confidence helps you walk into an interview, but once you're there, you want to give the interviewer an impression of poise, good manners, and good judgment. You can develop an adept style by staging mock interviews with a friend. After each practice session, try to identify opportunities for improvement. Have your friend critique your performance, using the list of interview faults shown in Figure 14.1. You can tape-record or videotape these mock interviews and then evaluate them yourself.

Nonverbal behaviour has a significant effect on the interviewer's opinion of you.

As you stage your mock interviews, pay particular attention to your nonverbal behaviour. In Canada, you are more likely to have a successful interview if you maintain eye contact, smile frequently, sit in an attentive position, and use frequent hand gestures. These nonverbal signals convince the interviewer that you're alert, assertive, dependable,

| FIGURE 14.1 | Marks Against Applicants (in General Order of Importance) |

WHAT EMPLOYERS DON'T LIKE TO SEE IN CANDIDATES

- ☒ Poor personal appearance
- ☒ Overbearing, overaggressive, conceited demeanour; a "superiority complex"; a know-it-all attitude
- ☒ Inability to express ideas clearly; poor voice, diction, grammar
- ☒ Lack of knowledge or experience
- ☒ Poor preparation for the interview
- ☒ Lack of interest in the job
- ☒ Lack of planning for career; lack of purpose, goals
- ☒ Lack of enthusiasm; passive and indifferent demeanour; lack of vitality
- ☒ Lack of confidence and poise; appearance of being nervous and ill at ease
- ☒ Insufficient evidence of achievement
- ☒ Failure to participate in extracurricular activities
- ☒ Overemphasis on money; interest only in the best dollar offer
- ☒ Poor scholastic record; just got by
- ☒ Unwillingness to start at the bottom; expecting too much too soon
- ☒ Tendency to make excuses
- ☒ Evasive answers; hedges on unfavourable factors in record
- ☒ Lack of tact, maturity, courtesy
- ☒ Poor listening skills
- ☒ Condemnation of past employers
- ☒ Lack of social skills
- ☒ Marked dislike for schoolwork
- ☒ Failure to look interviewer in the eye

confident, responsible, and energetic.[7] Some companies based in Canada are owned and managed by people from other cultures, so during your research, find out about the company's cultural background and preferences regarding nonverbal behaviour.

The sound of your voice can also have a major impact on your success in a job interview.[8] You can work with a tape recorder to overcome voice problems. If you tend to speak too rapidly, practise speaking more slowly. If your voice sounds too loud or too soft, practise adjusting it. Work on eliminating speech mannerisms such as *you know, like,* and *um,* which might make you sound inarticulate.

Plan to Look Good

"Looks count," says Jellinck, "not in your physical features, but in the way you present yourself. Candidates need to be well turned out and professional." When it comes to clothing, the best policy is to dress conservatively. Wear the best-quality businesslike clothing you can, preferably in a dark, solid colour. Avoid flamboyant styles, colours, and prints. Even in companies where interviewers may dress casually, it's important to show good judgment by dressing (and acting) in a professional manner. Good grooming makes any style of clothing look better. Make sure your clothes are clean and unwrinkled, your shoes unscuffed and well shined, your hair neatly styled and combed, your fingernails clean, and your breath fresh.

> To look like a winner,
> - Dress conservatively
> - Be well groomed
> - Smile when appropriate

Be Ready When You Arrive

Plan to take a small notebook, a pen, a list of the questions you want to ask, two copies of your resumé (protected in a folder), a list of references, an outline of what you have learned about the organization, and any past correspondence about the position. You may also want to take a small calendar, a transcript of your grades, and a portfolio containing samples of your work, performance reviews, and certificates of achievement. In an era when many people exaggerate their qualifications, visible proof of your abilities carries a lot of weight.[9]

Be sure you know when and where the interview will be held. The worst way to start any interview is to be late. Allow a little extra time in case you run into a problem on the way.

Once you arrive, relax. Be polite to the interviewer's assistant. If the opportunity presents itself, ask a few questions about the organization or express enthusiasm for the job. Refrain from smoking before the interview, and avoid chewing gum in the waiting room.

> Be prepared for the interview by
> - Taking proof of your accomplishments
> - Arriving on time
> - Waiting graciously

Interviewing for Success

As discussed earlier, how you handle a particular interview depends on where you stand in the sequence of interviews. Is this your first interview in the screening process? Have you made it to the selection interview or even the final interview? Regardless of where you are in the process, every interview will proceed through three stages: the warm-up, the question-and-answer session, and the close.

The Warm-Up

> The first minute of the interview is crucial.

Of the three stages, the warm-up is the most important, even though it may account for only a small fraction of the time you spend in the interview. Psychologists say that 50 percent of an interviewer's decision is made within the first 30 to 60 seconds, and another 25 percent is made within 15 minutes. If you get off to a bad start, it's extremely difficult to turn the interview around.[10]

Body language is important at this point. Because you won't have time to say much in the first minute or two, you must sell yourself nonverbally. Make eye contact and maintain it during the interview. Begin by using the interviewer's name if you're sure you can pronounce it correctly. If the interviewer extends a hand, respond with a firm but gentle handshake, and wait until you're asked to be seated. Let the interviewer start the discussion, and listen for cues that tell you what he or she is interested in knowing about you as a potential employee.

The Question-and-Answer Stage

Questions and answers will consume the greatest part of the interview. The interviewer will ask you about your qualifications and discuss many of the points mentioned in your resume. You'll also be asking questions of your own.

> Tailor your answers to emphasize your strengths.

HANDLING QUESTIONS Let the interviewer lead the conversation, and never answer a question before he or she has finished asking it. Surprisingly, the last few words of the question might alter how you respond. As questions are asked, tailor your answers to make a favourable impression. Don't limit yourself to yes-or-no answers. If you're asked a difficult question, be sure you pause to think before responding.

If you periodically ask a question or two from the list you've prepared, you'll not only learn something but also demonstrate your interest. Probe for what the company is looking for in its new employees so that you can show how you meet the firm's needs. Also try to zero in on any reservations the interviewer might have about you so that you can dispel them.

> Paying attention to both verbal and nonverbal messages can help you turn the question-and-answer stage to your advantage.

LISTENING TO THE INTERVIEWER Paying attention when the interviewer speaks can be as important as giving good answers or asking good questions. Listening should make up about half the time you spend in an interview. For tips on becoming a better listener, see Chapter 2.

The interviewer's facial expressions, eye movements, gestures, and posture may tell you the real meaning of what is being said. Be especially aware of how your comments are received. Does the interviewer nod in agreement or smile to show approval? If so, you're making progress. If not, you might want to introduce another topic or modify your approach.

FIELDING DISCRIMINATORY QUESTIONS In North America, employers cannot legally discriminate against a job candidate on the basis of race, colour, gender, age (from 40 to 70), marital status, religion, national origin, or disability. In general, the following topics should not be directly or indirectly introduced by an interviewer:[11]

- Your religious affiliation or organizations and lodges you belong to
- Your national origin, age, marital status, or former name
- Your spouse, spouse's employment or salary, dependants, children, or child-care arrangements
- Your height, weight, gender, pregnancy, or any health conditions or disabilities that are not reasonably related to job performance
- Arrests or criminal convictions that are not related to job performance

| Some questions should not be asked by interviewers. |

Table 14.5 compares specific questions that may and may not be asked during an employment interview.

How to Respond If your interviewer asks these personal questions, how you respond depends on how badly you want the job, how you feel about revealing the information asked for, what you think the interviewer will do with the information, and whether you want to work for a company that asks such questions. If you don't want the job, you can tell the interviewer that you think a particular question is unethical or simply refuse to answer—responses that will leave an unfavourable impression.[12] If you do want the job, you might (1) ask how the question is related to your qualifications, (2) explain that the information is personal, (3) respond to what you think is the interviewer's real concern, or (4) answer both the question and the concern. If you answer an unethical or unlawful question, you run the risk that your answer may hurt your chances, so think carefully before answering.[13]

| Think in advance about how you might respond to unlawful interview questions. |

The Close

Like the opening, the end of the interview is more important than its duration would indicate. In the last few minutes, you need to evaluate how well you've done. You also need to correct any misconceptions the interviewer might have.

| Conclude the interview with courtesy and enthusiasm. |

TABLE 14.5 Interview Questions That May and May Not Be Asked

YOU MAY ASK THIS	BUT NOT THIS
What is your name?	What is your maiden name?
Are you over 18?	When were you born?
Did you graduate from high school?	When did you graduate from high school?
[No questions about race are allowed.]	What is your race?
Can you perform [specific tasks]?	Do you have physical or mental disabilities?
	Do you use drugs or alcohol?
	Are you taking any prescription drugs?
Would you be able to meet the job's requirement to frequently work weekends?	Would working on weekends conflict with your religion?
Do you have the legal right to work in Canada?	What country are you a citizen of?
Have you ever been convicted of a crime?	Have you ever been arrested?
This job requires that you speak French. Do you?	What language did you speak in your home when you were growing up?

CONCLUDING GRACEFULLY You can generally tell when the interviewer is trying to conclude the session. He or she may ask whether you have any more questions, sum up the discussion, change position, or indicate with a gesture that the interview is over. When you get the signal, respond promptly, but don't rush. Be sure to thank the interviewer for the opportunity and express an interest in the organization. If you can do so comfortably, try to pin down what will happen next, but don't press for an immediate decision.

If this is your second or third visit to the organization, the interview may culminate with an offer of employment. You have two options: Accept it or request time to think it over. The best course is usually to wait. If no job offer is made, the interviewer may not have reached a decision yet, but you may tactfully ask when you can expect to know the decision.

> Be realistic in your salary expectations and diplomatic in your negotiations.

DISCUSSING SALARY If you do receive an offer during the interview, you'll naturally want to discuss salary. However, let the interviewer raise the subject. If asked your salary requirements, say that you would expect to receive the standard salary for the job in question. If you have added qualifications, point them out: "With my 18 months of experience in the field, I would expect to start in the middle of the normal salary range." Some applicants find the internet a terrific resource for salary information.

When to Negotiate If you don't like the offer, you might try to negotiate, provided you're in a good bargaining position and the organization has the flexibility to accommodate you. You'll be in a fairly strong position if your skills are in short supply and you have several other offers. It also helps if you're the favourite candidate and the organization is booming. Even though many organizations are relatively rigid in their salary practices, particularly at the entry level, in Canada and the United States and in some European countries, it is perfectly acceptable to ask, "Is there any room for negotiation?"

What to Negotiate Even if you can't bargain for more money, you may be able to win some concessions on benefits and perquisites. The value of negotiating can be significant because benefits often cost the employer 25 percent to 45 percent of your salary. Don't inquire about benefits, however, until you know you have a job offer.

Interview Notes

> Keep a written record of your job interviews.

If yours is a typical job search, you'll have many interviews before you accept an offer. For that reason, keep a notebook. As soon as the interview ends, jot down the names and titles of the people you met. Briefly summarize the interviewer's answers to your questions. Then quickly evaluate your performance during the interview.[14] In addition to improving your performance during interviews, interview notes will help you keep track of any follow-up messages you'll need to send.

Following up After the Interview

> Two types of follow-up messages:
> - Thank-you message
> - Inquiry

Touching base with the prospective employer after the interview, either by phone or in writing, shows that you really want the job and are determined to get it. Following up brings your name to the interviewer's attention once again and reminds him or her that you're waiting for the decision.

The two most common forms of follow-up are the thank-you message and the inquiry. These messages are often handled by letter, but an email or a phone call can be just as effective, particularly if the employer seems to favour a casual, personal style.

Thank-You Message

> A note or phone call thanking the interviewer
> - Is organized like a routine message
> - Closes with a request for a decision or future consideration

Express your thanks within two days after the interview, even if you feel you have little chance for the job. Acknowledge the interviewer's time and courtesy, and be sure to restate the specific job you're applying for. Convey your continued interest, then ask politely for a decision.

Keep your thank-you message brief (less than five minutes for a phone call or only one page for an email or letter), and organize it like a routine message. Demonstrate the "you" attitude, and sound positive without sounding overconfident. The following sample thank-you letter shows how to achieve all this in three brief paragraphs:

Reminds the interviewer of the reasons for meeting and graciously acknowledges the consideration shown to the applicant

After talking with you yesterday, touring your sets, and watching the television commercials being filmed, I remain very enthusiastic about the possibility of joining your staff as a television/film production assistant. Thanks for taking so much time to show me around.

During our meeting, I said that I would prefer not to relocate, but I've reconsidered. I would be pleased to relocate wherever you need my skills in set decoration and prop design.

Indicates the writer's flexibility and commitment to the job if hired

Reminds the recruiter of special qualifications

Ends with a request for a decision

Now that you've explained the details of your operation, I feel quite strongly that I can contribute to the sorts of productions you're lining up. You can also count on me to be an energetic and positive addition to your crew. Please let me know your decision as soon as possible.

Closes on a confident, "you"-oriented note

Even if the interviewer has said that you're unqualified for the job, a thank-you message may keep the door open. Riley Mullins followed up a recent job interview with a thank-you message sent by email the same day (see Figure 14.2).

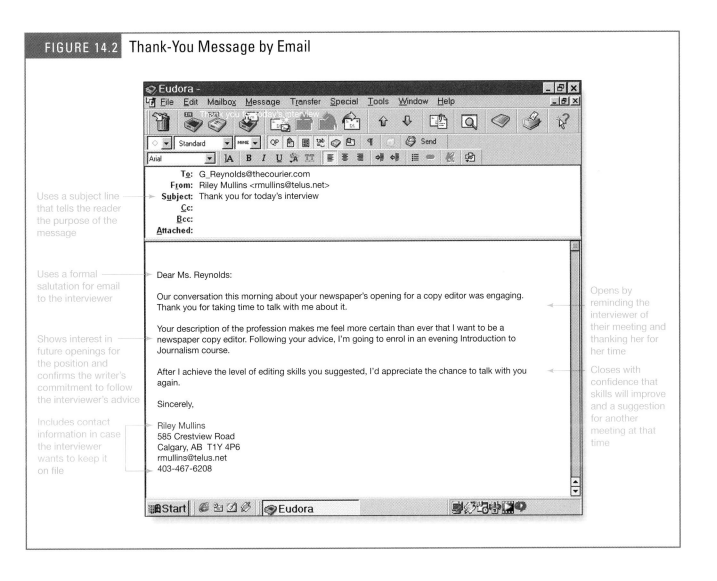

FIGURE 14.2 Thank-You Message by Email

Uses a subject line that tells the reader the purpose of the message

Uses a formal salutation for email to the interviewer

Shows interest in future openings for the position and confirms the writer's commitment to follow the interviewer's advice

Includes contact information in case the interviewer wants to keep it on file

To: G_Reynolds@thecourier.com
From: Riley Mullins <rmullins@telus.net>
Subject: Thank you for today's interview
Cc:
Bcc:
Attached:

Dear Ms. Reynolds:

Our conversation this morning about your newspaper's opening for a copy editor was engaging. Thank you for taking time to talk with me about it.

Your description of the profession makes me feel more certain than ever that I want to be a newspaper copy editor. Following your advice, I'm going to enrol in an evening Introduction to Journalism course.

After I achieve the level of editing skills you suggested, I'd appreciate the chance to talk with you again.

Sincerely,

Riley Mullins
585 Crestview Road
Calgary, AB T1Y 4P6
rmullins@telus.net
403-467-6208

Opens by reminding the interviewer of their meeting and thanking her for her time

Closes with confidence that skills will improve and a suggestion for another meeting at that time

 **Model** Document

An inquiry about a hiring decision follows the plan for a direct request.

Letter of Inquiry

If you're not advised of the interviewer's decision by the promised date or within two weeks, you might make an inquiry. A letter of inquiry is particularly appropriate if you've received a job offer from a second firm and don't want to accept it before you have an answer from the first. The following email illustrates the general plan for a direct request; the writer assumes that a simple oversight, and not outright rejection, is the reason for the delay:

Identifies the position and introduces the main idea →

Places the reason for the request second →

When we talked on April 7 about the fashion coordinator position in your North York showroom, you said you would be making your decision before May 1. I would still like the position very much, so I'm eager to know what conclusion you've reached.

To complicate matters, another firm has now offered me a position and has asked that I reply within the next two weeks.

Because your company seems to offer a greater challenge, I would appreciate knowing about your decision by Thursday, May 12. If you need more information before then, please let me know.

← Makes a courteous request for specific action last, while clearly stating a preference for this organization

ON THE JOB

Three Ways to Impress the Interviewer
1. Know specifics about the company and position
2. Ensure your grooming is impeccable
3. Arrive early

Reviewing Key Points

This chapter discussed interviewing for employment and following up. Companies often conduct three interviews to screen, select, and approve a candidate. Each interview type has stages. In the warm-up stage you hope to make a positive impression through nonverbal communication and through a warm, friendly, and professional approach. In the question-and-answer stage you give specific examples, showing you know the company and what you can contribute. In the closing stage, you recap your main strengths. When you get an interview, you should

- Research the company so that you can ask good questions, show how you would fit and contribute, and determine how to dress appropriately
- Be early and well groomed
- Anticipate questions and prepare your answers
- Listen carefully, answer succinctly, and do not interrupt
- Give examples of skills and traits needed for the job
- Follow up after the interview with a specific thank-you note or call

If you haven't heard back from the company in a reasonable period, follow up with a letter expressing your continued interest.

Practise Your Grammar

 Exercises

Effective business communication starts with strong grammar skills. To improve your grammar skills, go to MyBusCommLab or Grammar-on-the-Go, where you'll find exercises and diagnostic tests to help you produce clear, correct communication.

Test Your Knowledge

 Exercises

1. What should your objective be during a selection interview?
2. How does a structured interview differ from an open-ended interview and a situational interview?
3. What typically occurs during a stress interview?
4. Why are the questions you ask during an interview as important as the answers you give to the interviewer's questions?
5. What is the best way to polish your interview style?
6. What are the three stages of every interview, and which is the most important?
7. How should you respond if an interviewer at a company where you want to work asks you a question that seems too personal or unethical?
8. What are some behavioural questions you might expect in an interview in your field?
9. What makes a thank-you message effective after an interview?
10. What is the purpose of sending a letter of inquiry after an interview?

Apply Your Knowledge

1. How can you distinguish yourself from other candidates in a screening interview and still keep your responses short and to the point? Explain.
2. What can you do to make a favourable impression when you discover that an open-ended interview has turned into a stress interview? Briefly explain your answer.
3. If you want to switch jobs because you can't work with your supervisor, how can you explain this situation to a prospective employer? Give an example.
4. During a group interview you notice that one of the other candidates is trying to monopolize the conversation. He's always the first to answer, his answer is the longest, and he even interrupts the other candidates while they are talking. The interviewer doesn't seem to be concerned about his behaviour, but you are. You would like to have more time to speak so that the interviewer could get to know you better. What should you do?
5. **Ethical Choices** Why is it important to distinguish unethical or illegal interview questions from acceptable questions? Explain.

Running Cases

 Video

CASE 1: Noreen

After submitting her cover letter and resumé for the position of merger project manager, Noreen is selected for an interview. Noreen arrives 10 minutes early. She remains in the waiting area until she is asked to enter the meeting room. She walks in and sees six senior management staff sitting around a large table. She is asked to sit down. The managers introduce themselves to Noreen. Noreen knows two of them already.

QUESTIONS

a. What should Noreen wear to the interview?
b. What questions might she be asked?
c. What questions might she have?

d. Since this is an internal interview (she already works for the company), should she assume this will be an informal or casual interview?

e. List three things that Noreen should not discuss during the interview.

YOUR TASK

Role-play this interview. In a group, have one person be Noreen. Noreen needs to prepare answers and questions for the interview. The group needs to prepare questions and answers for Noreen. Conduct the interview, then assume Noreen gets a call after the interview and is offered the position. In a second role play Noreen needs to negotiate more money than offered as well as obtain a written guarantee that she may return to her previous position or equivalent upon project completion (end of job).

CASE 2: Kwong

Kwong is interviewing potential candidates for the office administrator position in his firm, CG Accounting. Some are overqualified and some have no work experience at all, which in his opinion makes them underqualified. One job applicant is very impressive and answers Kwong's questions confidently and accurately during the interview. Kwong feels this person has the right college education, but the applicant has no work experience. He decides to hire this applicant anyway.

QUESTIONS

a. Will the job applicant do well in the job without work experience?

b. What would the "right college education" be in this case?

c. Should Kwong discuss salary during the interview?

d. Is Kwong legally allowed to ask the applicant if he or she is able to work overtime?

e. List three ways the applicant can demonstrate his or her interest in the position during the interview.

YOUR TASK

Role-play this interview in a group of three students. One student can play Kwong, one can play his administrator, and the other can play the job applicant. The job applicant needs to prepare answers for the interviewers, and Kwong and his administrator need to prepare questions to ask the job applicant.

In this play, ask the job applicant if he or she feels over- or underqualified for this position and have the applicant explain his or her answer. Have Kwong ask the applicant why he or she is applying for this position and how long he or she plans to stay in this position. Have Kwong's administrator ask if the applicant is married and what religion the applicant practices. Kwong's administrator should explain that he or she is asking because there is overtime work during tax season and the company wants to ensure the availability of employees. These are illegal questions to ask during a job interview in Canada, so have the actors in the role-play deal with them.

⊜ Practise Your Knowledge

ACTIVITIES

1. **Analyze This Document** Read the following document; then (1) analyze its strengths and weaknesses and (2) revise the document so that it follows this chapter's guidelines.

Thank you for the really marvellous opportunity to meet you and your colleagues at Epcor Utilities. I really enjoyed touring your facilities and talking with all the people there. You have quite a crew! Some of the other companies I have visited have been so rigid and uptight that I can't imagine how I would fit in. It's a relief to run into a group of people who seem to enjoy their work as much as all of you do.

I know that you must be looking at many other candidates for this job, and I know that some of them will probably be more experienced than I am. But I do want to emphasize that my two-year hitch in the Navy involved a good deal of engineering work. I don't think I mentioned all my shipboard responsibilities during the interview.

Please give me a call within the next week to let me know your decision. You can usually find me at my residence in the evening after dinner (phone: 877-9080).

2. **Analyze This Document** Read the following document; then (1) analyze its strengths and weaknesses and (2) revise the document so that it follows this chapter's guidelines.

> I have recently received a very attractive job offer from the Warrington Company. But before I let them know one way or another, I would like to consider any offer that your firm may extend. I was quite impressed with your company during my recent interview, and I am still very interested in a career there.
>
> I don't mean to pressure you, but Warrington has asked for my decision within 10 days. Could you let me know by Tuesday whether you plan to offer me a position? That would give me enough time to compare the two offers.

3. **Analyze This Document** Read the following document; then (1) analyze its strengths and weaknesses and (2) revise the document so that it follows this chapter's guidelines.

> I'm writing to say that I must decline your job offer. Another company has made me a more generous offer, and I have decided to accept. However, if things don't work out for me there, I will let you know. I sincerely appreciate your interest in me.

4. **Teamwork** Divide the class into two groups. Half the class will be recruiters for a large chain of national department stores looking to fill manager trainee positions (there are 15 openings). The other half of the class will be candidates for the job. The company is specifically looking for candidates who demonstrate these three qualities: initiative, dependability, and willingness to assume responsibility.
   a. Have each recruiter select and interview an applicant for 10 minutes.
   b. Have all the recruiters discuss how they assessed the applicant against each of the three desired qualities. What questions did they ask or what did they use as an indicator to determine whether the candidate possessed the quality?
   c. Have all the applicants discuss what they said to convince the recruiters that they possessed each of these qualities.

5. **Internet** Select a large company (one that you can easily find information about) where you might like to work. Use internet sources to gather some preliminary research on the company.
   a. What did you learn about this organization that would help you during an interview there?
   b. What internet sources did you use to obtain this information?
   c. Armed with this information, what aspects of your background do you think might appeal to this company's recruiters?
   d. If you choose to apply for a job with this company, what keywords would you include on your resumé, and why?

6. **Interviews: Being Prepared** Prepare written answers to 10 of the questions listed in Table 14.2, "Twenty-Five Common Interview Questions."

7. **Interviews: Understanding Qualifications** Write a short memo to your instructor discussing what you believe are your greatest employment strengths and weaknesses. Next, explain how these strengths and weaknesses would be viewed by interviewers evaluating your qualifications.

8. **Classroom Practice in Answering Behavioural Interview Questions** In the following activity, use the four-step method to develop your answer:
   1. Describe a specific situation (from work, education, volunteering, or extracurricular activities).
   2. Tell what your role was.
   3. Tell what action you took.
   4. Describe the positive result.

Part A

Below are five behavioural interview questions. Write a response to one of them.
   1. Describe a situation in which you were able to use persuasion to successfully convince someone to see things your way.
   2. Describe an instance when you had to think on your feet to extricate yourself from a difficult situation.
   3. Give a specific example of a time when you used good judgment and logic in solving a problem.
   4. Describe a time when you were faced with problems or stresses that tested your coping skills.
   5. Give an example of a time in which you had to be relatively quick in coming to a decision.

Part B

Pick a partner and take turns answering the question you selected in Part A. Give the presenter feedback on

- The content of the answer
- Use of the four-part response
- The delivery manner
- The nonverbal message sent by the speaker

Part C

Revise your answer based on your partner's feedback and submit it to your instructor. Find more practice sample answers at www.quintcareers.com/sample_behavioral.html

9. **Writing Case Questions Designed to Find Out How You Would Behave in Difficult Situations** With a partner, describe a difficult situation you might face in a particular job that you would like to have. For example, what difficulties might arise in your position as an accountant for a film production company or as an administrator on a construction site?

   After you have your scenario written, apply the four-step process to develop a suitable answer. Be prepared to share your scenario and your ideas on how to answer the question with the class.

10. **Preparing for Behavioural Interview Questions** Visit www.quintcareers.com and search "Interview Questions" to find a link to "Job Interview Questions Database." Select 10 questions, prepare your answers, and compare them to the sample answers provided on the website. Write a short summary explaining how your answers compared to the samples given. What should you add or leave out of your answers?

Expand Your Knowledge

Best of the Web

Planning for a Successful Job Interview How can you practise for a job interview? What are some questions that you might be asked, and how should you respond? What questions are you not obligated to answer? Job-interview.net provides mock interviews based on actual job openings. It provides job descriptions, questions and answers for specific careers and jobs, and links to company guides and annual reports. You'll find a step-by-step plan that outlines key job requirements, lists practice interview questions, and helps you put together practice interviews. The site offers tips on the keywords to look for in a job description that will help you narrow your search and anticipate the questions you might be asked on your first or next job interview. www.job-interview.net

EXERCISES

1. What are some problem questions you might be asked during a job interview? How would you handle these questions?
2. Choose a job title from the list, and read more about it. What did you learn that could help during an actual interview for the job you selected?
3. Developing an "interview game plan" ahead of time helps you make a strong, positive impression during an interview. What are some of the things you can practise to help make everything you do during an interview seem to come naturally?

Exploring the Web on Your Own

Review these chapter-related websites on your own to learn more about interviewing for jobs.

1. Get more than 2000 pages of career advice at Monster.ca, www.monster.ca, and talk to career experts in your choice of industry or profession.
2. Learn how to prepare for and handle yourself with care during a job interview at SoYouWannaAceAJobInterview, www.soyouwanna.com/site/syws/aceinterview/aceinterview.html.
3. Follow the steps at Job-interview.net, www.job-interview.net, and be prepared for your next job interview.

Cases

Interviewing with Potential Employers

1. INTERVIEWERS AND INTERVIEWEES: CLASSROOM EXERCISE IN INTERVIEWING

Interviewing is clearly an interactive process involving at least two people. The best way to practise for interviews is to work with others.

YOUR TASK You and all other members of your class are to write letters of application for an entry-level or management-trainee position requiring a pleasant personality and intelligence but a minimum of specialized education or experience. Sign your letter with a fictitious name that conceals your identity. Next polish (or prepare) a resumé that accurately identifies you and your educational and professional accomplishments.

Now, three members of the class who volunteer as interviewers divide among themselves all the anonymously written application letters. Then each interviewer selects a candidate who seems the most pleasant and convincing in his or her letter. At this time the selected candidates identify themselves and give the interviewers their resumés.

Each interviewer then interviews his or her chosen candidate in front of the class, seeking to understand how the items on the resumé qualify the candidate for the job. At the end of the interviews, the class may decide who gets the job and discuss why this candidate was successful. Afterwards, retrieve your letter, sign it with the right name, and submit it to the instructor for credit.

WEB SKILLS 2. INTERNET INTERVIEW: EXERCISE IN INTERVIEWING

Using the Work Futures site for your province, locate the home page of a company you would like to work for (use the links to other provinces on www.workfutures.bc.ca to find your province's site). Then identify a position within the company for which you would like to apply. Study the company using any online business resources you choose, and prepare for an interview with that company.

YOUR TASK Working with a classmate, take turns interviewing each other for your chosen positions. Inter-viewers should take notes during the interview. Once the interview is complete, critique each other's performance (interviewers should critique how well candidates prepared for the interview and answered the questions; interviewees should critique the quality of the questions asked). Write a follow-up letter thanking your interviewer, and submit the letter to your instructor.

Following up After the Interview

3. A SLIGHT ERROR IN TIMING: LETTER ASKING FOR DELAY OF AN EMPLOYMENT DECISION

You botched your timing and applied for your third-choice job before going after what you really wanted. What you want to do is work in retail at Holt Renfrew in Toronto; what you have been offered is a retail job with Longhorn Leather and Lumber, 40 km away in Etobicoke.

You review your notes. Your Longhorn interview was three weeks ago with the human resources manager, R. P. Bronson, a congenial person who has just written to offer you the position. The store's address is 27 Flanigan Drive, Etobicoke, ON M6H 2L1. Mr. Bronson notes that he can hold the position open for 10 days. You have an interview scheduled with Holt's next week, but it is unlikely that you will know the store's decision within this 10-day period.

YOUR TASK Write to R. P. Bronson, requesting a reasonable delay in your consideration of his job offer.

4. JOB HUNT: SET OF EMPLOYMENT-RELATED LETTERS TO A SINGLE COMPANY

Where would you like to work? Pick a real or an imagined company, and assume that a month ago you sent your resumé and application letter. Not long afterwards, you were invited to come for an interview, which seemed to go very well.

YOUR TASK Use your imagination to write the following: (a) a thank-you letter for the interview, and (b) a note of inquiry.

Workplace Skills

Interview Strategies: Answering the 16 Toughest Questions

The answers to challenging interview questions can reveal a lot about a candidate. You can expect to face several such questions during every interview. If you're prepared with thoughtful answers that are related to your specific situation, you're bound to make a good impression. Here are 16 tough questions and guidelines for planning answers that put your qualities in the best light.

1. **What was the toughest decision you ever had to make?** Be prepared with a good example, explaining why the decision was difficult and how you decided.

2. **Why do you want to work for this organization?** Show that you've done your homework, and cite some things going on in the company that appeal to you.

3. **Why should we employ you?** Emphasize your academic strengths, job skills, and enthusiasm for the firm. Tie specific skills to the employer's needs, and give examples of how you can learn and become productive quickly. Cite past activities to prove you can work with others as part of a team.

4. **If we hire you, what changes would you make?** No one can know what to change in a position before settling in and learning about the job and company operations. State that you would take a good hard look at everything the company is doing before making recommendations.

5. **Can we offer you a career path?** Reply that you believe so, but you need to know more about the normal progression within the organization.

6. **What are your greatest strengths?** Answer sincerely by summarizing your strong points: "I can see what must be done and then do it," or "I'm willing to make decisions," or "I work well with others."

7. **What are your greatest weaknesses?** Describe a weakness so that it sounds like a virtue—honestly revealing something about yourself while showing how it works to an employer's advantage. If you sometimes drive yourself too hard, explain that it has helped when you've had to meet deadlines.

8. **What didn't you like about previous jobs you've held?** State what you didn't like and discuss what the experience taught you. Avoid making slighting references to former employers.

9. **How do you spend your leisure time?** Rather than focusing on just one, mention a cross-section of interests—active and quiet, social and solitary.

10. **Are there any weaknesses in your education or experience?** Take stock of your weaknesses before the interview, and practise discussing them in a positive light. You'll see they're minor when discussed along with the positive qualities you have to offer.

11. **Where do you want to be five years from now?** This question tests (1) whether you're merely using this job as a stopover until something better comes along and (2) whether you've given thought to your long-term goals. Saying that you'd like to be company president is unrealistic, and yet few employers want people who are content to sit still. Your answer should reflect your long-term goals and the organization's advancement opportunities.

12. **What are your salary expectations?** If you're asked this at the outset, say, "Why don't we discuss salary after you decide whether I'm right for the job?" If the interviewer asks this after showing real interest in you, speak up. Do your homework, but if you need a clue about salary levels, say, "Can you discuss the salary range with me?"

13. **What would you do if . . . ?** This question tests your resourcefulness. For example: "What would you do if your computer broke down during an audit?" Your answer is less important than your approach to the problem—and a calm approach is best.

14. **What type of position are you interested in?** Job titles and responsibilities vary from firm to firm. So state your skills ("I'm good with numbers") and the positions that require those skills ("accounts payable").

15. **Tell me something about yourself.** Answer that you'll be happy to talk about yourself, and ask what the interviewer wants to know. If this point is clarified, respond. If it isn't, explain how your skills can contribute to the job and the organization. This is a great chance to sell yourself.

16. **Do you have any questions about the organization or the job?** Employers like candidates who are interested in the organization. Convey your interest and enthusiasm. Be sure that your answers are sincere, truthful, and positive. Take a moment to compose your thoughts before responding, so that your answers are to the point.

Applications for Success

Improve your interviewing skills by visiting the "Interviewing" section at Yahoo!HotJobs (http://ca.hotjobs.yahoo.com/interview).

Answer the following questions:

1. When an interviewer asks you a question, what makes one answer more effective than another? Consider some of the ways answers can vary: specific versus general, assertive versus passive, informal versus formal.

2. Think of four additional questions that pertain specifically to your resumé. Practise your answers.

3. Which of the 16 questions seems the toughest to you? In no more than two paragraphs, write out your answer to the question that you think is the toughest of all. Then submit your work to your instructor.

Format and Layout of Business Documents

The format and layout of business documents vary from country to country; they even vary within Canada. In addition, many organizations develop their own variations of standard styles, adapting documents to the types of messages they send and the kinds of audiences they communicate with. The formats described here are more common than others.

First Impressions

Your documents tell readers a lot about you and about your company's professionalism. So all your documents must look neat, present a professional image, and be easy to read. Your audience's first impression of a document comes from the quality of its paper, the way it is customized, and its general appearance.

Paper

To give a quality impression, business people consider carefully the paper they use. Several aspects of paper contribute to the overall impression:

- **Weight.** Paper quality is judged by weight. The weight most commonly used by Canadian businesses is 20-pound paper, but 16- and 24-pound versions are also used.
- **Cotton content.** Paper quality is also judged by the percentage of cotton in the paper. Cotton doesn't yellow over time the way wood pulp does, plus it's both strong and soft. For letters and outside reports, use paper with a 25 percent cotton content. For memos and other internal documents, you can use a lighter-weight paper with lower cotton content.
- **Size.** In Canada, the standard paper size for business documents is 8½ by 11 inches. Standard legal documents are 8½ by 14 inches.
- **Colour.** White is the standard colour for business purposes, although neutral colours such as grey and ivory are sometimes used.

Many companies also design and print standardized forms for memos and frequently written reports that always require the same sort of information (such as sales reports and expense reports). They use computers to generate their standardized forms, which can save them both money and time.[1]

Appearance

Produce your business documents using a printer. Certain documents, however, should be handwritten (such as a note of condolence). Be sure to handwrite, print, or type the envelope to match the document. However, even a letter on the best-quality paper with the best-designed letterhead may look unprofessional if it's poorly produced. So pay close attention to all the factors affecting appearance, including the following:

- **Margins.** Companies in Canada make sure that documents (especially external ones) are centred on the page, with margins of at least 2.5 cm all around.
- **Line length.** Lines are rarely right-hand justified, because the resulting text looks too much like a form letter and can be hard to read (even with proportional spacing). Varying line length makes the document look more personal and interesting.
- **Line spacing.** You can adjust the number of blank lines between elements (such as between the date and the inside address) to ensure that a short document fills the page vertically or that a longer document extends at least two lines of the body onto the last page.
- **Character spacing.** Use proper spacing between characters and after punctuation. For example, Canadian conventions include leaving one space after commas, semicolons, colons, and sentence-ending periods. Each letter in a person's initials is followed by a period and a single space. However, abbreviations such as U.S.A. or MBA may or may not have periods, but they never have internal spaces.
- **Special symbols.** When using a computer, use appropriate symbols to give your document a professional look (see Table A.1 for examples).
- **Corrections.** Messy corrections are obvious and unacceptable in business documents. Reprint any letter, report, or memo requiring a lot of corrections.

TABLE A.1	Special Symbols on Computer	
	COMPUTER SYMBOL	TYPED SYMBOL
Case fractions	½	1/2
Copyright	©	(c)
Registered trademark	®	(R)
Cents	¢	None
British pound	£	None
Paragraph	¶	None
Bullets	●, ◆, ■, ❑, ✓, ☑, ⊗	*, #, 0
Em dash	—	-- (two hyphens)
En dash	–	- (one hyphen)

Reports

Enhance your report's effectiveness by paying careful attention to its appearance and layout. Follow whatever guidelines your organization prefers, always being neat and consistent throughout. If it's up to you to decide formatting questions, the following conventions may help you decide how to handle margins, headings, spacing and indention, and page numbers.

Margins

All margins on a report page are at least 2.5 cm wide. For double-spaced pages, use 2.5-cm margins; for single-spaced pages, set margins between 3 cm and 3.75 cm. The top, left, and right margins are usually the same, but the bottom margins can be one and a half times deeper. Some special pages also have deeper top margins. Set top margins as deep as 5 cm for pages that contain major titles: prefatory parts (such as the table of contents or the executive summary), supplementary parts (such as the endnotes or bibliography), and textual parts (such as the first page of the text or the first page of each chapter).

If you're going to bind your report at the left or at the top, add 1.25 cm to the margin on the bound edge (see Figure A.1). The space taken by the binding on left-bound reports makes the centre point of the text 0.5 cm to the right of the centre of the paper. Be sure to centre headings between the margins, not between the edges of the paper. Computers can do this for you automatically.

Other guidelines for report formats are found in Figure 11.10.

Headings

Headings of various levels provide visual clues to a report's organization. Chapter 11's Figure 11.9 illustrates one good system for showing these levels, but many variations exist. No matter which system you use, be sure to be consistent.

Spacing and Indentions

If your report is double-spaced (perhaps to ease comprehension of technical material), indent all paragraphs five character spaces (or about 1.25 cm). In single-spaced reports, block the paragraphs (no indentions) and leave one blank line between them.

Make sure the material on the title page is centred and well balanced, as on the title page of the sample report in Chapter 11 (Figure 11.10).

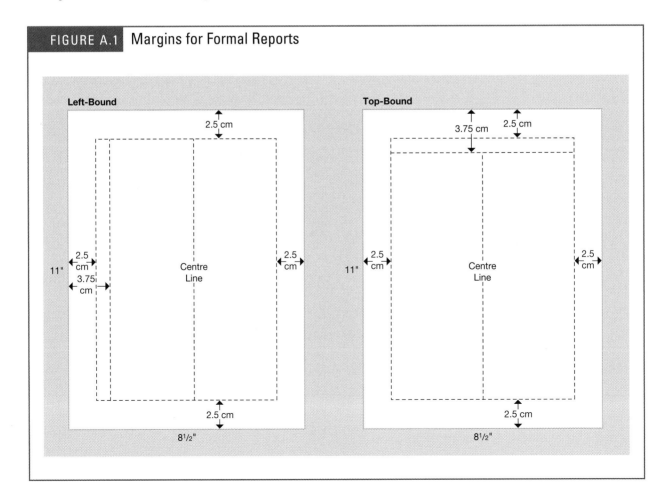

FIGURE A.1 Margins for Formal Reports

Page Numbers

Remember that every page in the report is counted; however, not all pages show numbers. The first page of the report, the title page, is unnumbered. All other pages in the prefatory section are numbered with a lower case roman numeral, beginning with *ii* and continuing with *iii, iv, v,* and so on. The unadorned (no dashes, no period) page number is centred at the bottom margin.

Number the first page of the text of the report with the unadorned standard numeral 1, centred at the bottom margin (double- or triple-spaced below the text). In left-bound reports, number the following pages (including the supplementary parts) consecutively with unadorned standard numerals (2, 3, and so on), placed at the top right-hand margin (double- or triple-spaced above the text). For top-bound reports and for special pages having 5-cm top margins, centre the page numbers at the bottom margin.

A sample report page showing headings and layout is shown in Figure A.2.

FIGURE A.2	Sample Report Page—Excerpt from an Internal Report on Recruiting

Paragraphs are single spaced with double spaces between

Specific headings tell what is in each section

INTRODUCTION

On Feb. 12, you asked our department to look into a way to reduce our company's costs for hiring. Our company currently spends $1340 per new hire for recruiting and interviewing. Three human resource officers work full time to source applicants and arrange interviews. Recent research shows that recruiting over the internet, called "e-cruiting," could not only save us time and money, but also extend the reach of our recruitment.

USE OF INTERNET FOR RECRUITING

Currently 30 000 to 100 000 internet sites are devoted to recruiting and more than 150 million people are using the internet in North America. Last year, 74 percent of those people over the age of 18 used the internet to look for a job. That number represents a huge pool of potential talent that we might tap. Craigslist is an example of the type of network we could use for advertising and recruitment.

POTENTIAL FOR COST-SAVING

Using the internet for recruitment has the potential for saving money. The Bank of Montreal is reported to have saved $1 million by relying on e-cruiting this year. Currently only 2 percent of our building-industry competitors are using this new technique to find good employees. We could be among the first in our industry to use the technique.

TWO WAYS E-CRUITING CAN HELP

E-cruiting can improve our current methods of recruitment in two ways.

Subheadings are distinguished by a different type style

Faster Access to Available Candidates
We can use software to scan and screen potential candidates from huge online data banks of resumés. We list the qualifications we need, and the job sites send us the resumés of candidates who have those qualifications. This approach will save our company approximately 6 hours of work per hiring. The pre-screening process will already be done—and this service is free.

Reduced Costs to Advertise
We can list our job openings on the major career websites such as monster.ca, hotjobs.com, or careermosaic.com for only $100–$300 per month—a lot less than the $1000 we pay for local newspaper advertisements. Plus, the online listing reaches a potentially unlimited audience, and it has no word limit. You can describe the openings in as much detail as you like. This way, we may attract some candidates who don't post their resumés online but who do check the web for job openings.

TIME SAVINGS
Bank of Montreal and The Bay, who use e-cruiting, report they have cut hiring times from six weeks to one hour.

Number the pages—but leave the page number off the first page

Email

Because email messages can act both as memos (carrying information within your company) and as letters (carrying information outside your company and around the world), their format depends on your audience and purpose. You may choose to have your email resemble a letter or you may decide to keep things as simple as an interoffice memo. A modified memo format is appropriate for most email messages.[2] All email programs include two major elements: the header and the body (see Figure A.3).

Header

The email header depends on the particular program you use. Some programs even allow you to choose between a shorter and a longer version. However, most headers contain similar information.

- **To:** Contains the name of the receiver and/or audience's email address. Most email programs also allow you to send mail to an entire group of people all at once. First, you create a distribution list. Then you type the name of the list in the *To:* line instead of typing the addresses of every person in the group.[3]
- **From:** Contains your email address.
- **Date:** Contains the day of the week, date (day, month, year), time, and time zone.
- **Subject:** Describes the content of the message and presents an opportunity for you to build interest in your message.
- **Cc:** Allows you to send copies of a message to more than one person at a time. It also allows everyone on the list to see who else received the same message.

- **Bcc:** Lets you send copies to people without the other recipients knowing—a practice considered unethical by some.[4]
- **Attachments:** Contains the name(s) of the file(s) you attach to your email message. The file can be a document, a digital image, an audio or video message, a spreadsheet, or a software program.[5]

Body

The rest of the space below the header is for the body of your message. In the *To:* and *From:* lines, some headers actually print out the names of the sender and receiver (in addition to their email addresses). Other headers do not.

Include a greeting such as "Hello" in your email. As pointed out in Chapter 6, greetings personalize your message. Do not use casual greetings such as "Hey." Leave one line space above and below your greeting to set it off from the rest of your message. You may end your greeting with a colon (formal), a comma (conversational), or even two hyphens (informal)—depending on the level of formality you want.

Your message begins one blank line space below your greeting. Just as in memos and letters, skip one line space between paragraphs and include headings, numbered lists, bulleted lists, and embedded lists when appropriate. Limit your line lengths to a maximum of 80 characters by inserting a hard return at the end of each line.

One blank line space below your message, include a simple closing, often just one word. A blank line space below that, include your signature. Whether you type your name or use a signature file, including your signature personalizes your message.

FIGURE A.3 | A Typical Email Message

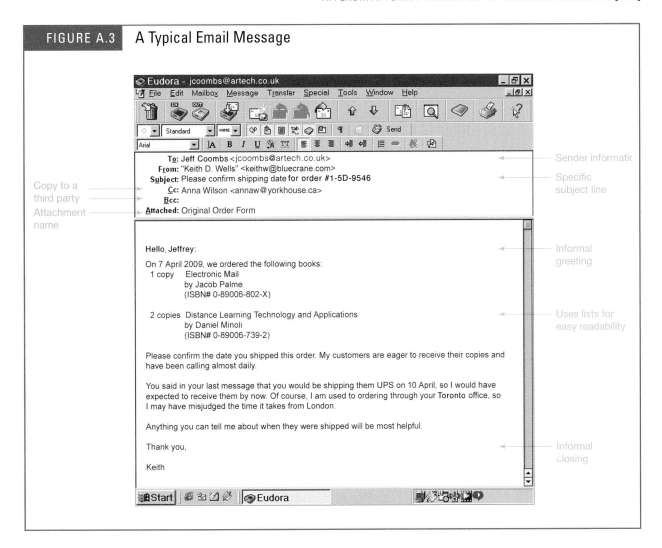

Memos

Many organizations have memo forms preprinted, with labelled spaces for the recipient's name (or sometimes a checklist of all departments in an organization or all persons in a department), the sender's name, the date, and the subject (see Figure A.4). If such forms don't exist, you can use a memo template (which comes with word-processing software and provides margin settings, headings, and special formats), or you can use plain paper.

On your document, include a title such as *MEMO* or *INTEROFFICE CORRESPONDENCE* (all in capitals) centred at the top of the page or aligned with the left margin. Also at the top, include the words *To, From, Date,* and *Subject*—followed by the appropriate information—with a blank line between, as shown here:

```
                    MEMO
    TO:
    FROM:
    DATE:
    SUBJECT:
```

Sometimes the heading is organized like this:

```
                    MEMO
    TO:              DATE:
    FROM:            SUBJECT:
```

You can arrange these four pieces of information in almost any order. The date sometimes appears without the heading *Date*. The subject may be presented with the letters *Re:* (in place of *SUBJECT:*) or without any heading (but in capital letters so that it stands out clearly). You may want to include a file or reference number, introduced by the word *File*.

The following guidelines will help you effectively format specific memo elements:

- **Addressees.** When sending a memo to a long list of people, include the notation *See distribution list* or *See below* in the *To* position at the top; then list the names at the end of the memo. Arrange this list alphabetically, except when high-ranking officials deserve more prominent placement. You can also address memos to groups of people—*All Sales Representatives, Production Group, New Product Team.*
- **Subject line.** The subject line of a memo helps busy co-workers quickly find out what your memo is about. Although the subject "line" may overflow onto a second line, it's most helpful when it's short (but still informative).
- **Body.** Start the body of the memo on the second or third line below the heading. Like the body of a letter, it's usually single-spaced with blank lines between paragraphs. Indenting paragraphs is optional. Handle lists, important passages, and subheadings as you do in letters.
- **Second page.** If the memo carries over to a second page, head the second page just as you head the second page of a letter.
- **Writer's initials.** Unlike a letter, a memo doesn't require a complimentary close or a signature, because your name is already prominent at the top. However, you may initial the memo—either beside the name appearing at the top of the memo or at the bottom of the memo—or you may even sign your name at the bottom, particularly if the memo deals with money or confidential matters.
- **Other elements.** Treat elements such as reference initials, enclosure notations, and copy notations just as you would in a letter.

Informal, routine, or brief reports for distribution within a company are often presented in memo form (see Chapter 10). Don't include report parts such as a table of contents and appendices.

MEMORANDUM

To: Jodie Whitehead, Director of Public Relations

From: Jessie Long, Associate Director of Human Resources

Date: May 19, 2009

Re: **IMPROVING COMPANY RECRUITMENT**

Employee turnover in our company is at 20 percent, and filling these vacancies can take us up to one year. High turnover is costing our company time and money. Giving employees a small amount of company stock could help us reduce our costs by improving retention.

How the Stock Program Would Work

Employees would be given $200 worth of stock after the first three months with the company and $500 of stock after they have been with the company for two years. At this point they would also have an option of purchasing additional stock at a 10 percent discount.

Human Resources would track when the stock option should be offered to each employee. The offer would be renewed every five years. The cost of offering this benefit to all our staff is $43 000 for the first seven-year period. The cost of recruitment and hiring is already $35 000 for the previous three years.

Advantages of Offering Applicants a Stock Bonus

- We can still honour our internal pay scale
- Employees expecting stock will feel they have more invested in the company.
- When employees realize stock gains, they will be more likely to stay employed.
- We are able to offer a benefit to counter the competitive forces outside our company without hiring additional staff or losing productivity.

ACTION

Is it possible to meet with you on Wednesday, May 15th, to further discuss ways to decrease employee turnover? Please let me know your thoughts.

Letters

Canadian businesses commonly use letterhead stationery, which may be either professionally printed, or designed in-house using word-processing templates and graphics. The letterhead includes the company's name and address, usually at the top of the page but sometimes along the left side or even at the bottom. Other information may be included in the letterhead as well: the company's telephone number, email address, fax number, website address, product lines, date of establishment, slogan, and symbol (logo). Well-designed letterhead gives readers[6]

- Pertinent reference data
- A favourable image of the company
- A good idea of what the company does

For as much as it's meant to accomplish, the letterhead should be as simple as possible.

In Canada, businesses always use letterhead for the first page of a letter. Successive pages are usually plain sheets of paper that match the letterhead in colour and quality. Some companies use a specially printed second-page letterhead that bears only the company's name. All business letters have certain elements in common. Several of these elements appear in every letter; others appear only when desirable or appropriate.

Standard Letter Parts

The letter in Figure A.5 shows the placement of standard letter parts. The writer of this business letter had no letterhead available but correctly included a heading. All business letters typically include the following eight elements.

HEADING Letterhead (the usual heading) shows the organization's name, full address, telephone number (almost always), and email address (often). If letterhead stationery is not available, the heading includes a return address (but no name) and starts 13 lines from the top of the page, which leaves a 5-cm top margin.

DATE If you're using letterhead, place the date at least one blank line beneath the lowest part of the letterhead. Without letterhead, place the date immediately below the return address. The usual method of writing the date in Canada uses the full name of the month (no abbreviations), followed by the day (in numerals, without *st, nd, rd,* or *th*), a comma, and then the year: July 14, 2009 (7/14/09). Some organizations follow other conventions (see Table A.2). To maintain the utmost clarity in international correspondence, always spell out the name of the month in dates.[7]

When communicating internationally, you may also experience some confusion over time. Some companies in Canada refer to morning (A.M.) and afternoon (P.M.), dividing a 24-hour day into 12-hour blocks so that they refer to four o'clock in the morning (4:00 A.M.) or four o'clock in the afternoon (4:00 P.M.). European companies refer to one 24-hour period so that 0400 hours (4:00 A.M.) is always in the morning and 1600 hours (4:00 P.M.) is always in the afternoon.[8] Make sure your references to time are as clear as possible, and be sure you clearly understand your audience's time references.

INSIDE ADDRESS The inside address identifies the recipient of the letter. For Canadian correspondence, begin the inside address at least one line below the date. Precede the addressee's name with a courtesy title, such as *Dr., Mr.,* or *Ms.* The accepted courtesy title for women in business is *Ms.,* although a woman known to prefer the title *Miss* or *Mrs.* is always accommodated. If you don't know whether a person is a man or a woman (and you have no way of finding out), omit the courtesy title. For example, *Terry Smith* could be either a man or a woman. The first line of the inside address would be just *Terry Smith,* and the salutation would be *Dear Terry Smith.* The same is true if you know only a person's initials, as in *S. J. Adams.*

Spell out and capitalize titles that precede a person's name, such as *Professor* or *General* (see Table A.3 on page 374 for the proper forms of address). The person's organizational title, such as *Director,* may be included on this first line (if it is short) or on the line below; the name of a department may follow. In addresses and signature lines, don't forget to capitalize any professional title that follows a person's name:

Mr. Ray Johnson, Dean

Ms. Patricia T. Higgins
Assistant Vice-President

However, professional titles not appearing in an address or signature line are capitalized only when they directly precede the name.

President Kenneth Johanson will deliver the speech.

Maria La Mothe, president of ABC Enterprises, will deliver the speech.

The Honourable Helen Masters, member of Parliament from Nepean, will deliver the speech.

If the name of a specific person is unavailable, you may address the letter to the department or to a specific position within the department. Also, be sure to spell out company names in full, unless the company itself uses abbreviations in its official name.

FIGURE A.5 — Standard Letter Parts

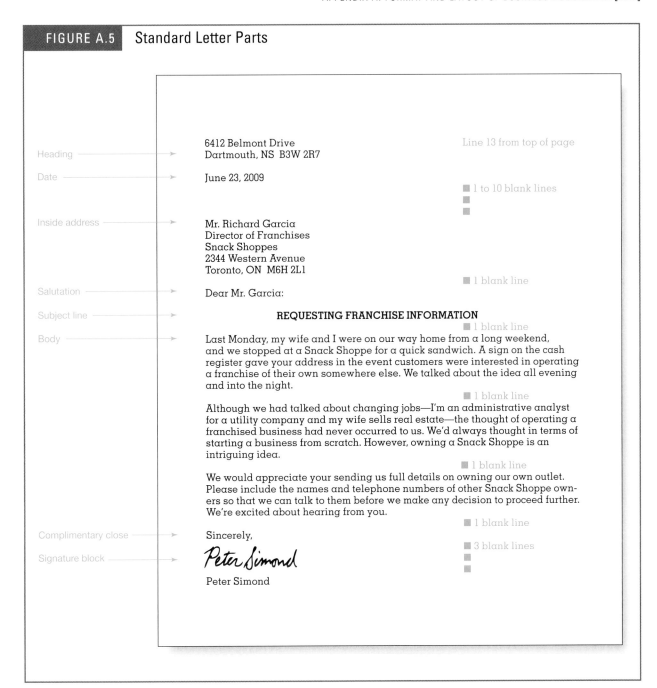

Heading → 6412 Belmont Drive
Dartmouth, NS B3W 2R7

Date → June 23, 2009

Inside address → Mr. Richard Garcia
Director of Franchises
Snack Shoppes
2344 Western Avenue
Toronto, ON M6H 2L1

Salutation → Dear Mr. Garcia:

Subject line → REQUESTING FRANCHISE INFORMATION

Body → Last Monday, my wife and I were on our way home from a long weekend, and we stopped at a Snack Shoppe for a quick sandwich. A sign on the cash register gave your address in the event customers were interested in operating a franchise of their own somewhere else. We talked about the idea all evening and into the night.

Although we had talked about changing jobs—I'm an administrative analyst for a utility company and my wife sells real estate—the thought of operating a franchised business had never occurred to us. We'd always thought in terms of starting a business from scratch. However, owning a Snack Shoppe is an intriguing idea.

We would appreciate your sending us full details on owning our own outlet. Please include the names and telephone numbers of other Snack Shoppe owners so that we can talk to them before we make any decision to proceed further. We're excited about hearing from you.

Complimentary close → Sincerely,

Signature block → *Peter Simond*
Peter Simond

Line 13 from top of page

■ 1 to 10 blank lines
■
■

■ 1 blank line

■ 1 blank line

■ 1 blank line

■ 1 blank line

■ 1 blank line

■ 3 blank lines
■
■

TABLE A.2 — Common Date Forms

CONVENTION	DESCRIPTION	DATE—MIXED	DATE—ALL NUMERALS
Canadian and U.S. standard	Month (spelled out) day, year	July 14, 2009	7/14/09
Alternative	Day (in numerals) month (spelled out) year	14 July 2009	14/7/09
European	Replace diagonal line with periods	14 July 2009	14.7.2009
International standard	Year month day	2009 July 14	2009,7,14

TABLE A.3	Forms of Address	

PERSON	IN ADDRESS	IN SALUTATION
Personal Titles		
Man	Mr. [first & last name]	Dear Mr. [last name]:
Woman (marital status unknown)	Ms. [first & last name]	Dear Ms. [last name]:
Woman (single)	Ms. or Miss [first & last name]	Dear Ms. *or* Miss [last name]:
Woman (married)	Ms. or Mrs. [wife's first & last name] *or* Mrs. [husband's first & last name]	Dear Ms. *or* Mrs. [last name]:
Woman (widowed)	Ms. or Mrs. [wife's first name & last name]	Dear Ms. *or* Mrs. [last name]:
Woman (separated or divorced)	Ms. or Mrs. [first & last name]	Dear Ms. *or* Mrs. [last name]:
Two men (or more)	Mr. [first & last name] and Mr. [first & last name]	Dear Mr. [last name] and Mr. [last name]: *or* Messrs. [last name] and [last name]:
Two women (or more)	Ms. [first & last name] and Ms. [first & last name] *or* Mrs. [first & last name] and Mrs. [first & last name]	Dear Ms. [last name] and Ms. [last name]: *or* Mses. [last name] and [last name]: Dear Mrs. [last name] and Mrs. [last name]: *or* Dear Mesdames [last name] and [last name]: *or* Mesdames:
	Miss [first & last name] Mrs. [first & last name]	Dear Miss [last name] and Mrs. [last name]:
One woman and one man	Ms. [first & last name] and Mr. [first & last name]	Dear Ms. [last name] and Mr. [last name]:
Couple (married)	Mr. and Mrs. [husband's first & last name]	Dear Mr. and Mrs. [last name]:
Couple (married with different last names)	[title] [first & last name of husband] [title] [first & last name of wife]	Dear [title] [husband's last name] and [title] [wife's first & last name]:
Couple (married professionals with same title and same last name)	[title in plural form] [husband's first name] and [wife's first & last name]	Dear [title in plural form] [last name]:
Couple (married professionals with different titles and same last name)	[title] [first & last name of husband] and [title] [first & last name of wife]	Dear [title] and [title] [last name]:
Professional Titles		
President of a college or university (doctor)	Dr. [first & last name], President	Dear Dr. [last name]:
Dean of a school of college or university	Dean [first & last name] *or* [title] Miss [first & last name] Dean of [school]	Dear Dean [last name]: *or* Dear [title] [last name] Miss [last name]:
Professor	Professor [first & last name]	Dear Professor [last name]:
Physician	[first & last name], M.D.	Dear Dr. [last name]:

(continued)

TABLE A.3 (Continued)

PERSON	IN ADDRESS	IN SALUTATION
Governmental Titles		
Prime Minister of Canada	The Prime Minister	Dear Mr. *or* Madam Prime Minister:
Member of Parliament	Honourable [first & last name]	Dear Honourable Member of Parliament [last name]:
Mayor	Honourable [first & last name] Mayor of [name of city]	Dear Mayor [last name]:
Judge	The Honourable [name]	Dear Judge [last name]:
Religious Titles		
Priest	The Reverend [first & last name], [initials of order, if any]	Reverend Sir: (formal) *or* Dear Father [last name]: (informal)
Rabbi	Rabbi [first & last name]	Dear Rabbi [last name]:
Minister	The Reverend [first & last name], [title, if any]	Dear Reverend [last name]:

Other address information includes the treatment of buildings, house numbers, and compass directions (see Table A.4 on page 376). The following example shows all the information that may be included in the inside address and its proper order for Canadian correspondence:

Dr. H. C. Armstrong
Research and Development
Commonwealth Mining Consortium
The Chelton Building, Suite 301
585 Second Street SW
Calgary, Alberta T2P 2P5

The order and layout of address information vary from country to country. So when addressing correspondence for other countries, carefully follow the format and information that appear in the company's letterhead. However, when you're sending mail from Canada, be sure that the name of the destination country appears on the last line of the address in capital letters. Use the English version of the country name so that your mail is routed to the right country. Then, to be sure your mail is routed correctly within the destination country, use the foreign spelling of the city name (using the characters and diacritical marks that would be commonly used in the region).

For example, the following address uses *Köln* instead of *Cologne*:

H.R. Veith, Director	Addressee
Eisfieren Glaswerk	Company name
Blaubachstrabe 13	Street address
Postfach 10 80 07	Post office box
D-5000 Köln I	District, city
GERMANY	Country

Be sure to use organizational titles correctly when addressing international correspondence. Job designations vary around the world. In England, for example, a managing director is often what a Canadian company would call its chief executive officer or president, and a British deputy is the equivalent of a vice-president. In France, responsibilities are assigned to individuals without regard to title or organizational structure, and in China the title *project manager* has meaning, but the title *sales manager* may not.

To make matters worse, business people in some countries sign correspondence without their names typed below. In Germany, for example, the belief is that employees represent the company, so it's inappropriate to emphasize personal names.[9]

SALUTATION In the salutation of your letter, follow the style of the first line of the inside address. If the first line is a person's name, the salutation is *Dear Mr.* or *Ms. Name.* The formality of the salutation depends on your relationship with the addressee. If in conversation you would say "Mary," your letter's salutation should be *Dear Mary,* followed by a colon. Otherwise, include the courtesy title and last name, followed by a colon. Presuming to write *Dear Lewis* instead of *Dear Professor Chang* demonstrates a disrespectful familiarity that the recipient will probably resent.

If the first line of the inside address is a position title such as *Director of Personnel,* then use *Dear Director.* If the addressee is unknown, use a polite description, such as *Dear Alumnus, Dear SPCA Supporter,* or *Dear Voter.* If the first line is plural (a department or company), then use *Ladies and Gentlemen* (look again at Table A.3).

TABLE A.4	Inside Address Information

DESCRIPTION	EXAMPLE
Capitalize building names.	Welland Building
Capitalize locations within buildings (apartments, suites, rooms).	Suite 1073
Use numerals for all house or building numbers, except the number *one*.	One Trinity Lane
	637 Adams Avenue, Apt. 7
Spell out compass directions that fall within a street address	1074 West Connover Street
Abbreviate compass directions that follow the street address	783 Main Street, N.E., Apt. 27

SUBJECT LINE The subject line tells recipients at a glance what the document is about (and indicates where to file the letter for future reference). It usually appears below the salutation, either against the left margin, indented (as a paragraph in the body), or centred. It can be placed above the salutation or at the very top of the page, and it can be underscored. Some businesses omit the word *Subject*. The subject line may take a variety of forms, including the following:

> Subject: RainMaster Sprinklers
>
> FALL 2008 SALES MEETING
>
> Reference Order No. 27920

BODY The body of the letter is your message. Almost all letters are single-spaced, with one blank line before and after the salutation or opening, between paragraphs, and before the complimentary close. The body may include indented lists, entire paragraphs indented for emphasis, and even subheadings. If it does, all similar elements should be treated in the same way. Your department or company may select a format to use for all letters.

COMPLIMENTARY CLOSE The complimentary close begins on the second line below the body of the letter. Alternatives for wording are available, but currently the trend seems to be toward using one-word closes, such as *Sincerely*. In any case, the complimentary close reflects the relationship between you and the person you're writing to. Avoid cute closes, such as *Yours for bigger profits*. If your audience doesn't know you well, your sense of humour may be misunderstood.

SIGNATURE BLOCK Leave three blank lines for a written signature below the complimentary close, and then include the sender's name (unless it appears in the letterhead). The person's title may appear on the same line as the name or on the line below:

> Yours truly,
>
> Raymond Dunnigan
>
> Director of Human Resources

Your letterhead indicates that you're representing your company. However, if your letter is on plain paper or runs to a second page, you may want to emphasize that you're speaking legally for the company. The accepted way of doing that is to place the company's name in capital letters a double space below the complimentary close and then include the sender's name and title four lines below that:

> Sincerely,
>
> WENTWORTH INDUSTRIES
>
> (Mrs.) Helen B. Taylor
>
> President

If your name could be taken for either a man's or a woman's, a courtesy title indicating gender should be included, with or without parentheses. Also, women who prefer a particular courtesy title should include it:

> Mrs. Nancy Winters
>
> (Miss) Celine Dufour
>
> Ms. Pat Li
>
> (Mr.) Jamie Saunders

Additional Letter Parts

Letters vary greatly in subject matter and thus in the identifying information they need and the format they adopt. The letter in Figure A.6 shows how these additional parts should be arranged. The following elements may be used in any combination, depending on the requirements of the particular letter:

- **Addressee notation.** Letters that have a restricted readership or that must be handled in a special way

| FIGURE A.6 | Additional Letter Parts |

WORLDWIDE TALENT AGENCY
2314 BLOOR STREET W.
TORONTO, ON M3B 5TG
(416) 695-2864

Date → November 18, 2009

Line 13 or 1 blank line below letterhead
■ 1 to 10 blank lines
■
■
■

Addressee notation → CONFIDENTIAL

■ 1 blank line

Attention: Scheduling Coordinator
Peachtree Lecture Bureau
2920 S. Bennett Parkway
Brantford, ON N3T 5V2

■ 1 blank line

Ladies and Gentlemen:

■ 1 blank line

Subject: Contract No. 27-83176

■ 1 blank line

Here is some additional information for you to consider. Please note that the
five speakers you would like to have attend the special event are all available.

■ 5 blank lines
■
■
■
■

Second-page heading → Peachtree Lecture Bureau
November 18, 2009
Page 2

■ 1 blank line

This information should clarify our commitment to you. I look forward to good
news from you in the near future.

■ 1 blank line

Sincerely,

■ 1 blank line

Company name → WORLDWIDE TALENT AGENCY

■ 3 blank lines
■
■

Elizabeth Spencer

J. Elizabeth Spencer
President

■ 1 blank line

Reference initials → nt

■ 1 blank line

Enclosure notation → Enclosures: Talent Roster
Commission Schedule

■ 1 blank line

Copy notation → Copy to Everett Cunningham, Chairperson of the Board, InterHosts, Inc.

■ 1 blank line

Mailing notation → Special Delivery

■ 1 blank line

Postscript → PS: The lunch you treated me to the other day was a fine display of hospitality.
Thanks again.

should include such addressee notations as *Personal, Confidential,* or *Please Forward.* This sort of notation appears a double space above the inside address, in all-capital letters.

- **Attention line.** Although not commonly used today, an attention line can be used if you know only the last name of the person you're writing to. It can also direct a letter to a position title or department. Place the attention line on the first line of the inside address and put the company name on the second.[10] An attention line may take any of the following forms or variants of them:

  Attention Dr. McHenry

  Attention Director of Marketing

  Attention Marketing Department

- **Second-page heading.** Use a second-page heading whenever an additional page is required. Some companies have second-page letterhead (with the company name and address on one line and in a smaller typeface). The heading bears the name (person or organization) from the first line of the inside address, the page number, the date, and perhaps a reference number. Leave two blank lines before the body. Make sure that at least two lines of a continued paragraph appear on the first and second pages. Never allow the closing lines to appear alone on a continued page. Precede the complimentary close or signature lines with at least two lines of the body. Also, don't hyphenate the last word on a page. All the following are acceptable forms for second-page headings:

  Ms. Melissa Baker

  May 10, 2009

  Page 2

  Ms. Melissa Baker, May 10, 2009, Page 2

  Ms. Melissa Bake   -2-   May 10, 2009

- **Company name.** If you include the company's name in the signature block, put it all in capital letters a double space below the complimentary close. You usually include the company's name in the signature block only when the writer is serving as the company's official spokesperson or when letterhead has not been used.

- **Reference initials.** When business people keyboard their own letters, reference initials are unnecessary, so they are becoming rare. When one person dictates a letter and another person produces it, reference initials show who helped prepare it. Place initials at the left margin, a double space below the signature block:

- **Enclosure notation.** Enclosure notations appear at the bottom of a letter, one or two lines below the reference initials. Some common forms include the following:

  Enclosure

  Enclosures (2)

  Enclosures: Resumé

         Photograph

- **Copy notation.** Copy notations may follow reference initials or enclosure notations. They indicate who's receiving a *courtesy copy* (*cc*) or they simply use *copy* (*c*). Recipients are listed in order of rank or (rank being equal) in alphabetical order. Among the forms used are the following:

  cc: David Wentworth, Vice-President

  c: Dr. Martha Littlefield

  Copy to Hans Vogel

         748 Chesterton Road

         Kitimat, BC V8C 5V1

  When sending copies to readers other than the person receiving the original letter, place *bc, bcc,* or *bpc* ("blind copy," "blind courtesy copy," or "blind photocopy") along with the name and any other information **only on the copy, not on the original.**

- **Mailing notation.** You may place a mailing notation (such as *Special Delivery* or *Registered Mail*) at the bottom of the letter, after reference initials or enclosure notations (whichever one is last) and before copy notations. Or you may place it at the top of the letter, either above the inside address on the left-hand side or just below the date on the right-hand side. For greater visibility, mailing notations may appear in capital letters.

- **Postscript.** A postscript is an afterthought to the letter, a message that requires emphasis, or a personal note. It is usually the last thing on any letter and may be preceded by *P.S., PS., PS:,* or nothing at all. Since postscripts usually indicate poor planning, generally avoid them. However, they're common in sales letters as a punch line to remind readers of a benefit for taking advantage of the offer.

Letter Formats

A letter format is the way of arranging all the basic letter parts. Sometimes a company adopts a certain format as its policy; sometimes the individual letter writer or preparer is allowed to choose the most appropriate format. In Canada, three major letter formats are commonly used:

- **Block format.** Each letter part begins at the left margin. The main advantage is quick and efficient preparation (see Figure A.7).
- **Modified block format.** Same as block format, except that the date, complimentary close, and signature block start near the centre of the page (see Figure A.8 on page 380). The modified block format does permit indentions as an option. This format mixes preparation speed with traditional placement of some letter parts. It also looks more balanced on the page than the block format does.

- **Simplified format.** Instead of using a salutation, this format often weaves the reader's name into the first line or two of the body and often includes a subject line in capital letters (see Figure A.9 on page 381). With no complimentary close, your signature appears after the body, followed by your printed (or typewritten) name (usually in all capital letters). This format is convenient when you don't know the reader's name; however, some people object to it as mechanical and impersonal (a drawback you can overcome with a warm writing style). Because certain letter parts are eliminated, some line spacing is changed.

FIGURE A.7 **Block Letter Format**

NATIONAL
GEOGRAPHIC
SOCIETY

September 5, 2009 — Line 13 or 1 line below letterhead / 1 to 10 blank lines

Mr. Stanley Comiskey, General Manager
The Map Store
475 Kenwood Dr.
Calgary, AB T5W 2X6

— 1 blank line

Dear Mr. Comiskey:

— 1 blank line

DELIVERY OF MAPS

— 1 blank line

You should receive your shipment of wall maps and topographical maps within two weeks, just in time for the holiday shopping season. The merchandise is being shipped by UPS. As the enclosed invoice indicates, the amount due is $352.32.

— 1 blank line

When preparing to ship your order, I noticed that this is your fifteenth year as a National Geographic Society customer. During that period, you have sold more than 3750 maps! Thanks for your hard work marketing our maps to the public.

— 1 blank line

Your customers should be particularly excited about the new CD-ROM Topo maps with GPS upgrade. The Topo GPS is the ultimate planning software for outdoor recreation. GPS enthusiasts will love using this CD-ROM to plan treks, interact with maps, and live track with a GPS receiver.

— 1 blank line

Next month, you'll receive our spring catalogue. Notice the new series of wall maps that offer a mural-sized panorama. They come in three sections that hang like wallpaper. As a special introductory incentive, you'll receive 15 percent off on all items in this line until the end of January. Please order soon.

— 1 blank line

Sincerely,

— 3 blank lines

Zeneesia Johnson

Ms. Zeneesia Johnson
Commerical Service Representative

kjc — 1 blank line

Enclosure — 1 blank line

1145 17th Street N.W., Washington, D.C. 20036-4688

FIGURE A.8	Modified Block Letter Format

Greyhound Canada

P.O. Box 850 • Calgary, AB T2E 4S7

■ line 13 from top of page   November 3, 2009
■ 1 to 10 blank lines
■

Mrs. Eugenia Preston, President
Drayton Valley High School PAC
P.O. Box 335
Drayton Valley, AB T7A 1T9
    ■ 1 blank line
Dear Mrs. Preston:
    ■ 1 blank line

TRAVELLING TO EDMONTON
    ■ 1 blank line

Thank you for inviting us to participate in your "Government Experience" program. So that your honours students can experience government firsthand, we will be delighted to provide one of our motor coaches next May at a 15 percent discount to transport up to 40 students and 7 teachers from Drayton Valley to Edmonton and back.
    ■ 1 blank line

Our buses seat 47 passengers, are fully equipped with restrooms and reclining seats, and are climate controlled for year-round comfort. You can rely on us for your charter transportation needs:
    ■ 1 blank line

- Our intensive, ongoing driver-training program ensures your safety and satisfaction.
- Our competitive pricing allows us to compete both locally and nationwide.
- Our state-of-the-art maintenance facilities are located in all major Canadian cities to ensure quality, reliability, and excellent service.
    ■ 1 blank line

Please give me a call at (403) 997-4646 to discuss the specific date of your event, departure times, and the discounted price for your trip. Together, we'll make sure your students have a day that's not only fun and educational but safe and secure. I look forward to hearing from you.
    ■ 1 blank line

                            Yours truly,
    ■ 3 blank lines
    ■
    ■

                            Ronald Struthers
                            Vice-President, Public Relations
    ■ 1 blank line

pf
    ■ 1 blank line

Enclosure

The most common formats for intercultural business letters are the block style and the modified block style. *Standard punctuation* uses a colon after the salutation (a comma if the letter is social or personal) and a comma after the complimentary close. *Open punctuation* uses no colon or comma after the salutation or the complimentary close.

| FIGURE A.9 | Simplified Block Letter Format |

KELLY
SERVICES

May 5, 2009

Line 13 from top of page
■ 1 to 10 blank lines
■
■
■

Ms. Gillian Savard, President
Scientific and Technical Contracts, Inc.
6348 Ste-Croix Avenue
Montreal, QC H3P 1T4

■ 2 blank lines
■

NEW SERVICES

■ 2 blank lines
■

Thank you, Ms. Savard, for your recent inquiry about our services. Our complete line of staffing services offers high-level professionals with the skills you require. From the office to the factory, from the tech site to the trade show, from the law firm to the lab—we can provide you with the people and the expertise you need.

■ 1 blank line

I have enclosed a package of information for your review, including specific information on our engineers, designers/drafters, and engineering support personnel. The package also contains reprints of customer reviews and a comparison sheet showing how our services measure up against those of competing companies. We identify qualified candidates and recruit through a network of professional channels to reach candidates whose skills match the specific engineering disciplines you require.

■ 1 blank line

Please call me with any questions you may have. Whether you need a temporary employee for a day or an entire department staffed indefinitely, our staffing solutions give you the freedom you need to focus and the support you need to succeed. I will be glad to help you fill your staffing needs with Kelly professionals.

■ 3 blank lines
■
■

Rudy Cohen

RUDY COHEN
CUSTOMER SERVICE SPECIALIST

■ 1 blank line

jn

■ 1 blank line

Enclosures

999 WEST AVE • MONTREAL, QUEBEC H3Z 1A4
TELEPHONE (514) 362-444

Envelopes

For a first impression, the quality of the envelope is just as important as the quality of the stationery. Letterhead and envelopes should be of the same paper stock, have the same colour ink, and be imprinted with the same address and logo. Most envelopes used by Canadian businesses are No. 10 envelopes (9½ inches long), which are sized for an 8½-by-11-inch piece of paper folded in thirds. Figure A.10 (on page 382) shows the most common size.

Addressing the Envelope

The address is always single-spaced with all lines aligned on the left. The address on the envelope is in the

---

FIGURE A.10 Prescribed Envelope Format

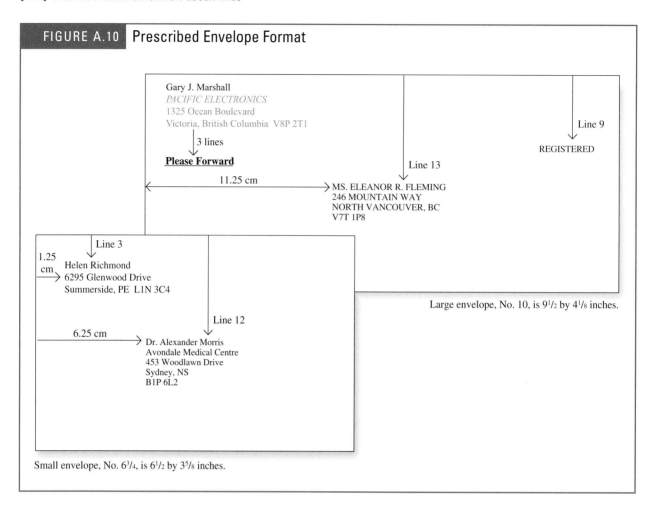

same style as the inside address and presents the same information. The order to follow is from the smallest division to the largest:

1. Name and title of recipient
2. Name of department or subgroup
3. Name of organization
4. Name of building
5. Street address and suite number, or post office box number
6. City, province, and postal code
7. Name of country (if the letter is being sent abroad)

Because Canada Post uses optical scanners to sort mail, envelopes for quantity mailings, in particular, should be addressed in the prescribed format. No punctuation is included, and all mailing instructions of interest to the post office are placed above the address area (see Figure A.10). Canada Post requires that the city is all in capitals, and the postal code is placed on the line below the name of the city. The post office scanners read addresses from the bottom up, so if a letter is to be sent to a post office box rather than to a street address, the street address should appear on the line above the box number. Figure A.10 also shows the proper spacing for addresses and return addresses.

Canada Post Corporation and the U.S. Postal Service have published lists of two-letter mailing abbreviations for provinces, territories, and states (see Table A.5). Postal authorities prefer no punctuation with these abbreviations. Canadian postal codes are alphanumeric, with a three-character "area code" and a three-character "local code" separated by a single space (K2P 5A5). Canadian postal codes may be separated from the province by two spaces or put in the bottom line of the address all by itself.

International Mail

Postal service differs from country to country. For example, street addresses are uncommon in India, and the mail there is unreliable.[11] It's usually a good idea to send international correspondence by airmail and to ask that responses be sent that way as well.

TABLE A.5 — Two-Letter Mailing Abbreviations for Canada and the United States

PROVINCE/ TERRITORY OR STATE	ABBREVIATION	PROVINCE/ TERRITORY OR STATE	ABBREVIATION	PROVINCE/ TERRITORY OR STATE	ABBREVIATION
Canada		Delaware	DE	New Jersey	NJ
Alberta	AB	District of Columbia	DC	New Mexico	NM
British Columbia	BC	Florida	FL	New York	NY
Manitoba	MB	Georgia	GA	North Carolina	NC
New Brunswick	NB	Guam	GU	North Dakota	ND
Newfoundland and Labrador	NL	Hawaii	HI	Ohio	OH
Northwest Territories	NT	Idaho	ID	Oklahoma	OK
Nova Scotia	NS	Illinois	IL	Oregon	OR
Nunavut	NU	Indiana	IN	Pennsylvania	PA
Ontario	ON	Iowa	IA	Puerto Rico	PR
Prince Edward Island	PE	Kansas	KS	Rhode Island	RI
Quebec	QC	Kentucky	KY	South Carolina	SC
Saskatchewan	SK	Louisiana	LA	South Dakota	SD
Yukon Territory	YT	Maine	ME	Tennessee	TN
		Maryland	MD	Texas	TX
United States		Massachusetts	MA	Utah	UT
Alabama	AL	Michigan	MI	Vermont	VT
Alaska	AK	Minnesota	MN	Virginia	VA
American Samoa	AS	Mississippi	MS	Virgin Islands	VI
Arizona	AZ	Missouri	MO	Washington	WA
Arkansas	AR	Montana	MT	West Virginia	WV
California	CA	Nebraska	NE	Wisconsin	WI
Colorado	CO	Nevada	NV	Wyoming	WY
Connecticut	CT	New Hampshire	NH		

parentheses). Finally, include the page range of the article: *Journal of Business Communication, 36*(4), 72. (In this example, the volume is 36, the number is 4, and the page number is 72.)

- Include personal communications (such as letters, memos, email, and conversations) only in text, not in reference lists.
- Electronic references include author, date of publication, title of article, name of publication (if one), volume, date of retrieval (month, day, year), and the source.
- For electronic references, indicate the actual year of publication, and the exact date of retrieval.
- For electronic references, specify the URL, leave periods off the ends of URLs.

Chicago Humanities Style

The Chicago Manual of Style recommends two types of documentation systems. The *documentary-note,* or *humanities,* style gives bibliographic citations in notes—either footnotes (when printed at the bottom of a page) or endnotes (when printed at the end of the report). The humanities system is often used in literature, history, and the arts. The other system strongly recommended by *Chicago* is the *author-date* system, which cites the author's last name and the date of publication in the text, usually in parentheses, reserving full documentation for the reference list (or bibliography). For the purpose of comparing styles, we will concentrate on the humanities system, which is described in detail in *Chicago*.

In-Text Citation—Chicago Humanities Style

To document report sources in text, the humanities system relies on superscripts—standard numerals placed just above the line of type at the end of the reference:

> Toward the end of his speech, Myers sounded a note of caution, saying that even though the economy is expected to grow, it could easily slow a bit.[10]

The superscript lets the reader know how to look for source information in either a footnote or an endnote (see Figure B.2). Some readers prefer footnotes so that they can simply glance at the bottom of the page for information. Others prefer endnotes so that they can read the text without a clutter of notes on the page. Also, endnotes relieve the writer from worrying about how long each note will be and how much space it will take away from the page. Both footnotes and endnotes are handled automatically by today's word-processing software.

For the reader's convenience, you can use footnotes for **content notes** (which may supplement your main text with asides about a particular issue or event, provide a cross-reference to another section of your report, or direct the reader to a related source). Then you can use endnotes for **source notes** (which document direct quotations, paraphrased passages, and visual aids). Consider which type of note is most common in your report, and then choose whether to present these notes all as endnotes or all as footnotes. Regardless of the method you choose for referencing textual information in your report, notes for visual aids (both content notes and source notes) are placed on the same page as the visual.

Bibliography—Chicago Humanities Style

The humanities system may or may not be accompanied by a bibliography (because the notes give all the necessary bibliographic information). However, endnotes are arranged in order of appearance in the text, so an alphabetical bibliography can be valuable to your readers. The bibliography may be titled *Bibliography, Reference List, Sources, Works Cited* (if you include only those sources you actually cited in your report), or *Works Consulted* (if you include uncited sources as well). This list of sources may also serve as a reading list for those who want to pursue the subject of your report further, so you may want to annotate each entry—that is, comment on the subject matter and viewpoint of the source, as well as on its usefulness to readers. Annotations may be written in either complete or incomplete sentences. (See the annotated list of style manuals on page 384.) A bibliography may also be more manageable if you subdivide it into categories (a classified bibliography), either by type of reference (such as books, articles, and unpublished material) or by subject matter (such as government regulation, market forces, and so on). Following are the major conventions for developing a bibliography according to *Chicago* style (see Figure B.3):

- Exclude any page numbers that may be cited in source notes, except for journals, periodicals, and newspapers.
- Alphabetize entries by the last name of the lead author (listing last name first). The names of second and succeeding authors are listed in normal order. Entries without an author name (or issuing organization) are alphabetized by the first important word in the title.
- Format entries as hanging indents (indent second and succeeding lines three to five spaces).
- Arrange entries in the following general order: (1) author name, (2) title information, (3) publication information, (4) date, (5) periodical page range.

| FIGURE B.2 | Sample Endnotes—Chicago Humanities Style |

NOTES

Journal article with volume and issue numbers

1. James Assira, "Are They Speaking English in Japan?" *Journal of Business Communication* 36, no. 4 (Fall 2007): 72.

Brochure

2. BestTemp Staffing Services, *An Employer's Guide to Staffing Services,* 2d ed. (Denver: BestTemp Information Center, 2006), 31.

Newspaper article, no author

3. "Buying Asian Supplies on the Net," *The Globe and Mail,* 12 February 2007, sec. D, p. 3.

Annual report

4. Eurotec, *2008 Annual Report* (New York: Eurotec, Inc., 2008), 48.

Magazine article

5. Holly Graves, "Prospecting Online," *Report on Business,* 17 November 2006, 43–5.

Television broadcast

6. Daniel Han, "Trade Wars Heating Up Around the Globe," *CNN Headline News* (Atlanta: CNN, 5 March 2006).

Internet, World Wide Web

7. "Intel—Company Capsule," Hoover's Online [accessed 8 March 2007], 3 screens; available from www.hoovers.com/capsules/13787.html.

Book, component parts

8. Sonja Kuntz, "Moving Beyond Benefits," in *Our Changing Workforce,* ed. Randolf Jacobson (New York: Citadel Press, 2008), 213–27.

Unpublished dissertation or thesis

9. George H. Morales, "The Economic Pressures on Industrialized Nations in a Global Economy" (Ph.D. diss., University of San Diego, 2007), 32–47.

Paper presented at a meeting

10. Charles Myers, "HMOs in Today's Environment" (paper presented at the Conference on Medical Insurance Solutions, Chicago, Ill., August 2008), 16–17.

Online magazine article

11. Preston Norwalk, "Training Managers to Help Employees Accept Change," in Business Line [online] (San Francisco, 2005 [updated 17 September 2007; accessed 3 October 2007]); available from www.busline.com/news.

CD-ROM encyclopedia article, one author

12. Robert Parkings, "George Eastman," *The Concise Columbia Encyclopedia* (New York: Columbia University Press, 2008) [CD-ROM].

Interview

13. Georgia Stainer, general manager, Day Cable and Communications, interview by author, Topeka, Kan., 2 March 2007.

Newspaper article, one author

14. Evelyn Standish, "Global Market Crushes OPEC's Delicate Balance of Interests," *Wall Street Journal,* 19 January 2006, sec. A, p. 1.

Book, two authors

15. Miriam Toller and Jay Fielding, *Global Business for Smaller Companies* (Rocklin, Calif.: Prima Publishing, 2008), 102–3.

Government publication

16. U.S. Department of Defense, *Stretching Research Dollars: Survival Advice for Universities and Government Labs* (Washington, D.C.: GPO, 2008), 126.

- Use quotation marks around the titles of articles from magazines, newspapers, and journals—capitalizing the first and last words, as well as all other important words (except prepositions, articles, and coordinating conjunctions).
- Use italics to set off the names of books, newspapers, journals, and other complete publications—capitalizing the first and last words, as well as all other important words.
- For journal articles, include the volume number and the issue number (if necessary). Include the year of publication inside parentheses and follow with a colon and the page range of the article: *Journal of Business Communication* 36, no. 4 (2008): 72. (In this source, the volume is 36, the number is 4, and the page is 72.)
- Use brackets to identify all electronic references: [Online database] or [CD-ROM].
- Explain how electronic references can be reached: Available from www.spaceless.com/WWWVL.
- Give the citation date for online references: Cited 23 August 2008.

FIGURE B.3 Sample Bibliography—Chicago Humanities Style

BIBLIOGRAPHY

Assira, James. "Are They Speaking English in Japan?" *Journal of Business Communication* 36, no. 4 (Fall 2007): 72.

BestTemp Staffing Services. *An Employer's Guide to Staffing Services.* 2d ed. Denver: BestTemp Information Center, 2006.

"Buying Asian Supplies on the Net." *The Globe and Mail,* 12 February 2007, sec. D.

Eurotec. *2008 Annual Report.* New York: Eurotec, Inc., 2008.

Graves, Holly. "Prospecting Online." *Report on Business,* 17 November 2006, 43–5.

Han, Daniel. "Trade Wars Heating Up Around the Globe." *CNN Headline News.* Atlanta: CNN, 5 March 2006.

"Intel—Company Capsule." *Hoover's Online* [accessed 8 March 2007]. 3 screens; Available from www.hoovers.com/capsules/13787.html.

Kuntz, Sonja. "Moving Beyond Benefits." In Our Changing Workforce, edited by Randolf Jacobson. New York: Citadel Press, 2008.

Morales, George H. "The Economic Pressures on Industrialized Nations in a Global Economy." Ph.D. diss., University of San Diego, 2007.

Myers, Charles. "HMOs in Today's Environment." Paper presented at the Conference on Medical Insurance Solutions, Chicago, Ill., August 2008.

Norwalk, Preston. "Training Managers to Help Employees Accept Change." In *Business Line* [online]. San Francisco, 2005 [updated 17 September 2007; accessed 3 October 2007]. Available from www.busline.com/news.

Parkings, Robert. "George Eastman." *The Concise Columbia Encyclopedia.* New York: Columbia University Press, 2008. [CD-ROM].

Stainer, Georgia, general manager, Day Cable and Communications. Interview by author. Topeka, Kan., 2 March 2007.

Standish, Evelyn. "Global Market Crushes OPEC's Delicate Balance of Interests." *Wall Street Journal,* 19 January 2006, sec. A.

Toller, Miriam, and Jay Fielding. *Global Business for Smaller Companies.* Rocklin, Calif.: Prima Publishing, 2008.

U.S. Department of Defense. *Stretching Research Dollars: Survival Advice for Universities and Government Labs.* Washington, D.C.: GPO, 2008.

Labels: Journal article with volume and issue numbers; Brochure; Newspaper article, no author; Annual report; Magazine article; Television broadcast; Internet, World Wide Web; Book, component parts; Unpublished dissertation or thesis; Paper presented at a meeting; Online magazine article; CD-ROM encyclopedia article, one author; Interview; Newspaper article, one author; Book, two authors; Government publication

MLA Style

The style recommended by the Modern Language Association of America is used widely in the humanities, especially in the study of language and literature. Like APA style, MLA style uses brief parenthetical citations in the text. However, instead of including author name and year, MLA citations include author name and page reference.

In-Text Citation—MLA Style

To document report sources in text using MLA style, insert the author's last name and a page reference inside parentheses following the cited material: (Matthews 63). If the author's name is mentioned in the text reference, the name can be omitted from the parenthetical citation: (63). The citation indicates that the reference came from page 63 of a work by Matthews. With the author's name, readers can find complete publication information in the alphabetically arranged list of works cited that comes at the end of the report.

> Some experts recommend both translation and back-translation when dealing with any non-English-speaking culture (Assira 72).

> Toller and Fielding make a strong case for small companies succeeding in global business (102–03).

List of Works Cited—MLA Style

The *MLA Style Manual* recommends preparing the list of works cited first so that you will know what information to give in the parenthetical citation (for example, whether to add a short title if you're citing more than one work by the same author, or whether to give an initial or first name if you're citing two authors who have the same last name). The list of works cited appears at the end of your report, contains all the works that you cite in your text, and lists them in alphabetical order. Following are the major conventions for developing a reference list according to MLA style (see Figure B.4):

- Format entries as hanging indents.
- Double space inside and between entries

- Arrange entries in the following general order: (1) author name, (2) title information, (3) publication information, (4) date, (5) periodical page range, (6) medium of publication (print, web, CD-ROM, etc).
- List the lead author's name in reverse order (last name first), using either full first names or initials. List second and succeeding author names in normal order.
- Use quotation marks around the titles of articles from magazines, newspapers, and journals—capitalize all important words.
- Italicize the names of books, newspapers, journals and other complete publications, capitalizing all main words in the title.
- For journal articles, include the volume number and the issue number (if necessary). Include the year of publication inside parentheses and follow with a colon, the page range of the article, and the publication medium: *Journal of Business Communication* 36.4 (2004): 72. Print. (In this source, the volume is 36, the number is 4, and the page is 72, and the researcher read the source in print form.)
- Electronic sources are less fixed than print sources, and they may not be readily accessible to readers. The newly revised MLA guidelines (2008) point out that many researchers now look for material online, using titles or authors to find material because URLs are often not that helpful. They change frequently, can be long and cumbersome to type and are prone to transcription errors. Include URLs only if no other path to the information is available.
- The date for electronic sources should contain both the date assigned in the source and the date accessed by the researcher.
- If you do include the URL for electronic sources, it must be as accurate and complete as possible, from access-mode identifier (http, ftp, gopher, telnet) to all relevant directory and file names. Be sure to enclose this path inside angle brackets: <http://www.hoovers.com/capsules/13787.html>
- MLA guidelines now encourage writers to include the name of the database used to find the material where appropriate. Put the title of the database in italic: Dhillon, Surjit. *Tips for Doing Business in India.* Vancouver: Raincoast Press, 2008. *Google Book Search.* Web. 9 July 2008.

FIGURE B.4 Sample Works Cited—MLA Style

WORKS CITED

Journal article with volume and issue numbers

Assira, James. "Are They Speaking English in Japan?" *Journal of Business Communication* 36.4 (2007): 72–76. Print.

Brochure

BestTemp Staffing Services. *An Employer's Guide to Staffing Services.* 2d ed. Denver: BestTemp Information Center, 2006. Print.

Newspaper article, no author

"Buying Asian Supplies on the Net." *The Globe and Mail* 12 Feb. 2007: D3. Print.

Annual report

Eurotec. *2008 Annual Report.* New York: Eurotec, Inc., 2008. Print.

Magazine article

Graves, Holly. "Prospecting Online." *Report on Business* 17 Nov. 2006: 43–45. Print.

Television broadcast

Han, Daniel. "Trade Wars Heating Up Around the Globe." *CNN Headline News.* CNN, Atlanta. 5 Mar. 2006. Television.

Internet, World Wide Web

"Intel—Company Capsule." *Hoover's Online.* 2007. Hoover's Company Information. 8 Mar. 2007. Web. 20 October 2008.

Book, component parts

Kuntz, Sonja. "Moving Beyond Benefits." *Our Changing Workforce.* Ed. Randolf Jacobson. New York: Citadel Press, 2008. 213–27. Print.

Image from the internet

"Scarborough, Ontario." Map. Google Maps. *Google,* 20 Oct. 2008. Web. 20 Oct. 2008.

Paper presented at a meeting

Myers, Charles. "HMOs in Today's Environment." Conference on Medical Insurance Solutions. Chicago. 13 Aug. 2004.

Online magazine article

Norwalk, Preston. "Training Managers to Help Employees Accept Change." *Business Line* 17 July 2005. Web. 8 Mar. 2007.

CD-ROM encyclopedia article, one author

Parkings, Robert. "George Eastman." *The Concise Columbia Encyclopedia.* New York: Columbia UP, 2008. CD-ROM.

Interview

Stainer, Georgia, general manager, Day Cable and Communications. Telephone interview. 2 Mar. 2008.

Newspaper article, one author

Standish, Evelyn. "Global Market Crushes OPEC's Delicate Balance of Interests." *Wall Street Journal* 19 Jan. 2006: A1. Print.

Book, two authors

Toller, Miriam, and Jay Fielding. *Global Business for Smaller Companies.* Rocklin, CA: Prima Publishing, 2008. Print.

Government publication

United States. Department of Defense. *Stretching Research Dollars: Survival Advice for Universities and Government Labs.* Washington: GPO, 2008. Print.

Correction Symbols

Instructors often use these short, easy-to-remember correction symbols and abbreviations when evaluating students' writing. You can use them too, to understand your instructor's suggestions and to revise and proofread your own letters, memos, and reports.

Content and Style

Acc	Accuracy. Check to be sure information is correct.
ACE	Avoid copying examples.
ACP	Avoid copying problems.
Adp	Adapt. Tailor message to reader.
App	Approach. Follow proper organizational approach. (Refer to Chapter 4.)
Assign	Assignment. Review instructions for assignment.
AV	Active verb. Substitute active for passive.
Awk	Awkward phrasing. Rewrite.
BC	Be consistent.
BMS	Be more sincere.
Chop	Choppy sentences. Use longer sentences and more transitional phrases.
Con	Condense. Use fewer words.
CT	Conversational tone. Avoid using overly formal language.
Depers	Depersonalize. Avoid attributing credit or blame to any individual or group.
Dev	Develop. Provide greater detail.
Dir	Direct. Use direct approach; get to the point.
Emph	Emphasize. Develop this point more fully.
EW	Explanation weak. Check logic; provide more proof.
Fl	Flattery. Avoid compliments that are insincere.
FS	Figure of speech. Find a more accurate expression.
GNF	Good news first. Use direct order.
GRF	Give reasons first. Use indirect order.
GW	Goodwill. Put more emphasis on expressions of goodwill.
H/E	Honesty/ethics. Revise statement to reflect good business practices.
Imp	Imply. Avoid being direct.
Inc	Incomplete. Develop further.
Jar	Jargon. Use less specialized language.
Log	Logic. Check development of argument.
Neg	Negative. Use more positive approach or expression.

Obv	Obvious. Do not state point in such detail.
OC	Overconfident. Adopt humbler language.
OM	Omission.
Org	Organization. Strengthen outline.
OS	Off the subject. Close with point on main subject.
Par	Parallel. Use same structure.
Pom	Pompous. Rephrase in down-to-earth terms.
PV	Point of view. Make statement from reader's perspective rather than your own.
RB	Reader benefit. Explain what reader stands to gain.
Red	Redundant. Reduce number of times this point is made.
Ref	Reference. Cite source of information.
Rep	Repetitive. Provide different expression.
RS	Resale. Reassure reader that he or she has made a good choice.
SA	Service attitude. Put more emphasis on helping reader.
Sin	Sincerity. Avoid sounding glib or uncaring.
SL	Stereotyped language. Focus on individual's characteristics instead of on false generalizations.
Spec	Specific. Provide more specific statement.
SPM	Sales promotion material. Tell reader about related goods or services.
Stet	Let stand in original form.
Sub	Subordinate. Make this point less important.
SX	Sexist. Avoid language that contributes to gender stereotypes.
Tone	Tone needs improvement.
Trans	Transition. Show connection between points.
UAE	Use action ending. Close by stating what reader should do next.
UAS	Use appropriate salutation.
UAV	Use active voice.
Unc	Unclear. Rewrite to clarify meaning.
UPV	Use passive voice.
USS	Use shorter sentences.
V	Variety. Use different expression or sentence pattern.
W	Wordy. Eliminate unnecessary words.
WC	Word choice. Find a more appropriate word.
YA	"You" attitude. Rewrite to emphasize reader's needs.

Grammar, Mechanics, and Usage

Ab	Abbreviation. Avoid abbreviations in most cases; use correct abbreviation.
Adj	Adjective. Use adjective instead.
Adv	Adverb. Use adverb instead.
Agr	Agreement. Make subject and verb or noun and pronoun agree.
Ap	Appearance. Improve appearance.
Apos	Apostrophe. Check use of apostrophe.
Art	Article. Use correct article.
BC	Be consistent.
Cap	Capitalize.
Case	Use cases correctly.
CoAdj	Coordinate adjective. Insert comma between coordinate adjectives; delete comma between adjective and compound noun.
CS	Comma splice. Use period or semicolon to separate clauses.
DM	Dangling modifier. Rewrite so that modifier clearly relates to subject of sentence.
Exp	Expletive. Avoid expletive beginnings, such as *it is, there are, there is, this is,* and *these are.*
F	Format. Improve layout of document.
Frag	Fragment. Rewrite as complete sentence.
Gram	Grammar. Correct grammatical error.
HCA	Hyphenate compound adjective.
lc	Lower case. Do not use capital letter.
M	Margins. Improve frame around document.
MM	Misplaced modifier. Place modifier close to word it modifies.
NRC	Nonrestrictive clause (or phrase). Separate from rest of sentence with commas.
P	Punctuation. Use correct punctuation.
Par	Parallel. Use same structure.
PH	Place higher. Move document up on page.
PL	Place lower. Move document down on page.
Prep	Preposition. Use correct preposition.
RC	Restrictive clause (or phrase). Remove commas that separate clause from rest of sentence.
RO	Run-on sentence. Separate two sentences with comma and coordinating conjunction or with semicolon.
SC	Series comma. Add comma before *and* or *or.*
SI	Split infinitive. Do not separate *to* from rest of verb.
Sp	Spelling error. Consult dictionary.
S-V	Subject-verb pair. Do not separate with comma.
Syl	Syllabification. Divide word between syllables.
WD	Word division. Check dictionary for proper end-of-line hyphenation.
WW	Wrong word. Replace with another word.

Proofreading Marks

SYMBOL	MEANING	SYMBOL USED IN CONTEXT	CORRECTED COPY
═══ ‖	Align horizontally	meaningful result	meaningful result
‖	Align vertically	1. Power cable 2. Keyboard	1. Power cable 2. Keyboard
≡≡≡	Capitalize	Pepsico, Inc.	PepsiCo, Inc.
⌐⌐ ⌐	Centre	Awards Banquet	Awards Banquet
◡	Close up space	self- confidence	self-confidence
ℓ	Delete	harrassment and abuse	harassment
(ds)	Double-space	text in first line text in second line (ds)	text in first line text in second line
∧	Insert	turquoise shirts	turquoise and white shirts
∨	Insert apostrophe	our teams goals	our team's goals
∧	Insert comma	a, b and c	a, b, and c
=	Insert hyphen	third quarter sales	third-quarter sales
⊙	Insert period	Harrigan et al	Harrigan et al.
∨ ∨	Insert quotation marks	This team isn't cooperating.	This "team" isn't cooperating.
#	Insert space	real estate testcase	real estate test case
/	Lower case	TULSA, South of here	Tulsa, south of here
⌐⌐	Move down	Sincerely,	Sincerely,
⌐	Move left	Attention: Security	Attention: Security
⌐	Move right	February 2, 2004	February 2, 2004
⌐⌐	Move up	THIRD-QUARTER SALES	THIRD-QUARTER SALES
(STET)	Restore	staff talked openly and frankly (STET)	staff talked openly
∫	Run lines together	Manager, Distribution	Manager, Distribution
(ss)	Single space	text in first line text in second line (ss)	text in first line text in second line
⬭	Spell out	(COD)	cash on delivery
(sp)	Spell out	(sp) Assn. of Biochem. Engrs.	Association of Biochemical Engineers
⌐	Start new line	Marla Fenton, Manager, Distribution	Marla Fenton, Manager, Distribution
¶	Start new paragraph	¶The solution is easy to determine but difficult to implement in a competitive environment like the one we now face.	The solution is easy to determine but difficult to implement in a competitive environment like the one we now face.
∼	Transpose	airy, light, casual tone	light, airy, casual tone
(bf)	Use boldface	Recommendations (bf)	**Recommendations**
(ital)	Use italics	Quarterly Report (ital)	*Quarterly Report*

Endnotes

CHAPTER 1

1. Judi Hess, Vice-President, Eastman Kodak, General Manager, Enterprise Solutions—Graphic Communications Group, personal communication, 24 April 2007.

2. Adapted from Essie Calhoun and Antonio Perez quoted on Kodak.com website [accessed on 29 May 2007]. www.kodak.com/global/en/corp/diversity/index.jhtml?pq-path=2879/3649.

3. Conference Board of Canada, *Employability Skills 2000+* [accessed 13 June 2003], www.conferenceboard.ca/nbec.

4. "Interpersonal Skills Are Key in Office of the Future," *TMA Journal,* July–August 1999, 53.

5. Charlene Li and Josh Bernoff, *Groundswell* (Boston: Harvard Business Press, 2008), 22.

6. Lillian H. Chaney and Jeanette S. Martin, *Intercultural Business Communications* (Upper Saddle River, N.J.: Prentice Hall, 2000), 1–2.

7. James M. Citrin and Thomas J. Neff, "Digital Leadership," *Strategy and Business,* First Quarter 2000, 42–50; Gary L. Neilson, Bruce A. Pasternack, and Albert J. Viscio, "Up the E-Organization," *Strategy and Business,* First Quarter 2000, 52–61; Statistics Canada. (April 2003). *Plant Turnover and Productivity Growth in Canadian Manufacturing* [accessed 18 June 2003], www.statcan.ca/Daily/english/030402/d030402d.htm.

8. Some material adapted from Courtland L. Bovée, John V. Thill, Marian Burk Wood, and George P. Dovel, *Management* (New York: McGraw-Hill, 1993), 537–538.

9. Former U.S. Supreme Court Justice Potter Stewart, cited in A. Thomas Young, "Ethics in Business: Business of Ethics," *Vital Speeches,* 15 September 1992, 725–730.

10. Philip C. Kolin, *Successful Writing at Work,* 6th ed. (Boston: Houghton Mifflin, 2001), 24–30.

11. David Grier, "Confronting Ethical Dilemmas: The View from Inside—A Practitioner's Perspective," *Vital Speeches,* 1 December 1989, 100–104.

12. Joseph L. Badaracco Jr., "Business Ethics: Four Spheres of Executive Responsibility," *California Management Review,* Spring 1992, 64–79; Kenneth Blanchard and Norman Vincent Peale, *The Power of Ethical Management* (1989; reprint, New York: Fawcett Crest, 1991), 7–17.

13. Blanchard and Peale, *The Power of Ethical Management,* 7–17; Badaracco, "Business Ethics: Four Spheres of Executive Responsibility," 64–79.

14. Larry A. Samovar and Richard E. Porter, "Basic Principles of Intercultural Communication," in *Intercultural Communication: A Reader,* 6th ed., edited by Larry A. Samovar and Richard E. Porter (Belmont, Calif.: Wadsworth, 1991), 12.

15. Gus Tyler, "Tokyo Signs the Paychecks," *New York Times Book Review,* 12 August 1990, 7.

16. Otto Kreisher, "Annapolis Has a New Attitude Toward Sexual Harassment," *San Diego Union,* 30 July 1990, A-6.

17. Linda Beamer, "Teaching English Business Writing to Chinese-Speaking Business Students," *Bulletin of the Association for Business Communication* 57, no. 1 (1994): 12–18.

18. Edward T. Hall, "Context and Meaning," in *Intercultural Communication,* edited by Samovar and Porter, 46–55.

19. Beamer, "Teaching English Business Writing to Chinese-Speaking Business Students."

20. Charley H. Dodd, *Dynamics of Intercultural Communication,* 3d ed. (Dubuque, Iowa: Brown, 1991), 69–70.

21. Larry A. Samovar and Richard E. Porter, *Communication Between Cultures.* 2nd ed. (Belmont, Calif.: Wadsworth, 1995), 104.

22. James Wilfong and Toni Seger, *Taking Your Business Global* (Franklin Lakes, N.J.: Career Press, 1997), 277–278.

23. Philip R. Harris and Robert T. Moran, *Managing Cultural Differences,* 3d ed. (Houston: Gulf, 1991), 260.

24. Sharon Ruhly, *Intercultural Communication,* 2d ed., MODCOM (Modules in Speech Communication) (Chicago: Science Research Associates, 1982), 14.

25. Samovar and Richard Porter, *Communication Between Cultures,* 2nd ed., 90.

26. Guo-Ming Chen and William J. Starosta, *Foundations of Intercultural Communication* (Boston: Allyn & Bacon, 1998), 288–289.

27. Richard W. Brislin, "Prejudice in Intercultural Communication," in *Intercultural Communication,* edited by Samovar and Porter, 366–370.

28. Mona Casady and Lynn Wasson, "Written Communication Skills of International Business Persons," *Bulletin of the Association for Business Communication* 57, no. 4 (1994): 36–40.

29. Statistics Canada. (2001). "The Labour Force." The Canada E-book, *The People* [accessed 3 July 2003], http://142.206.72.67/02/02e/02e_009_e.htm.

30. Anne Howland. Mix of Age Groups Can Cause Friction. *Vancouver Sun,* 26 May 2007.

31. Amy Glass, "Understanding Generational Differences for Competitive Success," *Industrial & Commercial Training,* 39, no. 2, 2007, 98–103.

32. Brian Morton, "In a Technical World, Soft Skills Set You Apart." *Financial Post.* 30 May 2007.

33. The Cost of Conflict. Webpage for the Centre for Conflict Resolution International [accessed 4 July 2007] www.conflictatwork.com/conflict/cost_e.cfm. Derrick Penner. "The Cost of Workplace Conflict." *National Post.* 31 March 2003, p. BE4.

34. Karen Fritscher-Porter, "Taming Workplace Incivility." *OfficePro* magazine. June/July 2003 [accessed 15 June 2007] www.iaap-hq.org/ResearchTrends/taming_workplace_incivility.htm; Denise Balkiissoon. Omar El Akkad. Craig Silverman, The 30-Minute EMBA. *Report on Business* 29 September 2006, p. 103, retrieved from http://0-proquest.umi.com.innopac.lib.bcit.ca/pdqdweb?index=7&did=1137251451&SrchM. [accessed 15 June 2007]; Carole Kanchier, "Good Etiquette Makes for Good Business", *Vancouver Sun.* 15 February 2003.

35. "The Rude Age" *Maclean's* magazine, February 2007.

36. Jensen J. Zhao and Calvin Parks, "Self-Assessment of Communication Behavior: An Experiential Learning Exercise for Intercultural Business Success," *Business Communication Quarterly* 58, no. 1 (1995): 20–26; Dodd, *Dynamics of Intercultural Communication,* 142–143, 297–299; Stephen P. Robbins, *Essentials of Organizational Behavior,* 6th ed. (Paramus, N.J.: Prentice Hall, 1999), 345.

37. "When Rumors Disrupt Your Staff," *Working Woman,* October 1992, 36.

CHAPTER 2

1. Michael H. Mescon, Courtland L. Bovée, and John V. Thill, *Business Today* (Upper Saddle River, N.J.: Prentice Hall, 1999), 203.

2. Robbins, *Essentials of Organizational Behavior,* 98.

3. Larry Cole and Michael Cole, "Why Is the Teamwork Buzz Word Not Working?" *Communication World,* February/ March 1999, 29; Patricia Buhler, "Managing in the 90s: Creating Flexibility in Today's Workplace," *Supervision,* January 1997, 241; Allison W. Amason, Allen C. Hochwarter, Wayne A. Thompson, and Kenneth R. Harrison, "Conflict: An Important Dimension in Successful Management Teams," *Organizational Dynamics,* Autumn 1995, 201.

4. "Better Meetings Benefit Everyone: How to Make Yours More Productive," *Working Communicator Bonus Report,* July 1998.

5. Anders Gronstedt, "Training in Virtual Worlds," Infoline, Issue 0803, March 2008.

6. William C. Waddell and Thomas A. Rosko, "Conducting an Effective Off-Site Meeting," *Management Review,* February 1993, 40–44.

7. "Better Meetings Benefit Everyone."

8. Bob Lamons, "Good Listeners Are Better Communicators," *Marketing News,* 11 September 1995, 131; Phillip Morgan and H. Kent Baker, "Building a Professional Image: Improving Listening Behavior," *Supervisory Management,* November 1985, 35–36.

9. Robyn D. Clarke, "Do You Hear What I Hear?" *Black Enterprise,* May 1998, 129; Dot Yandle, "Listening to Understand," *Pryor Report Management Newsletter Supplement* 15, no. 8 (August 1998): 13.

10. Sherwyn P. Morreale and Courtland L. Bovée, *Excellence in Public Speaking* (Orlando, Fla.: Harcourt Brace, 1998), 72–76; Lyman K. Steil, Larry L. Barker, and Kittie W. Watson, *Effective Listening: Key to Your Success* (Reading, Mass.: Addison-Wesley, 1983), 21–22.

11. Patrick J. Collins, *Say It with Power and Confidence* (Upper Saddle River, N.J.: Prentice Hall, 1997), 40–45.

12. Collins, *Say It with Power and Confidence,* 40–45.

13. Augusta M. Simon, "Effective Listening: Barriers to Listening in a Diverse Business Environment," *Bulletin of the Association for Business Communication* 54, no. 3 (September 1991): 73–74.

14. Jo Ind, "Hanging on the Telephone," *Birmingham Post,* 28 July 1999, PS10.

15. Lin Walker, *Telephone Techniques* (New York: Amacom, 1998), 46–47.

16. Ind, "Hanging on the Telephone"; Dorothy Neal, *Telephone Techniques,* 2nd ed. (New York: Glencoe McGraw-Hill, 1998), 31; Walker, *Telephone Techniques,* 46–47.

17. Ind, "Hanging on the Telephone"; Neal, *Telephone Techniques;* Walker, *Telephone Techniques;* Jeannie Davis, *Beyond "Hello"* (Aurora, Colo.: Now Hear This, Inc., 2000), 2–3.

18. Susan Ford, "Voice Messaging Systems," *Toledo Business Journal,* 1 November 2001, 26.

19. Mike Bransby, "Voice Mail Makes a Difference," *Journal of Business Strategy,* January–February 1990, 7–10.

20. Bransby, "Voice Mail Makes a Difference."

21. "Ten Steps to Caller-Friendly Voice Mail," *Managing Office Technology,* January 1995, 25; Rhonda Finniss, "Voice Mail: Tips for a Positive Impression," *Administrative Assistant's Update,* August 2001, 5; "How to Get the Most out of Voice Mail," *CPA Journal,* February 2000, 11.

22. Ruth Davidhizar and Ruth Shearer, "The Effective Voice Mail Message," *Hospital Material Management Quarterly,* 45–49; "How to Get the Most out of Voice Mail."

23. Davidhizar and Shearer, "The Effective Voice Mail Message."

24. Graham, Unrue, and Jennings, "The Impact of Nonverbal Communication in Organizations."

25. Dale G. Leathers, *Successful Nonverbal Communication: Principles and Applications* (New York: Macmillan, 1986), 19.

26. Gerald H. Graham, Jeanne Unrue, and Paul Jennings, "The Impact of Nonverbal Communication in Organizations: A Survey of Perceptions," *Journal of Business Communication* 28, no. 1 (Winter 1991): 45–62.

CHAPTER 3

1. Adapted from RBC Royal Bank's website [accessed 23 June 2003], www.rbcroyalbank.com.

2. Sanford Kaye, "Writing Under Pressure," *Soundview Executive Book Summaries* 10, no. 12, part 2 (December 1988): 1–8.

3. Peter Bracher, "Process, Pedagogy, and Business Writing," *Journal of Business Communication* 24, no. 1 (Winter 1987): 43–50.

4. Mahalingam Subbiah, "Adding a New Dimension to the Teaching of Audience Analysis: Cultural Awareness," *IEEE Transactions on Professional Communication* 35, no. 1 (March 1992): 14–19; Ronald E. Dulek, John S. Fielden, and John S. Hill, "International Communication: An Executive Primer," *Business Horizons,* January–February 1991, 20–25; Dwight W. Stevenson, "Audience Analysis Across Cultures," *Journal of Technical Writing and Communication* 13, no. 4 (1983): 319–330.

5. Laurey Berk and Phillip G. Clampitt, "Finding the Right Path in the Communication Maze," *IABC Communication World,* October 1991, 28–32.

6. Berk and Clampitt, "Finding the Right Path in the Communication Maze."

7. Raymond M. Olderman, *10 Minute Guide to Business Communication* (New York: Alpha Books, 1997), 19–20.

8. Mohan R. Limaye and David A. Victor, "Cross-Cultural Business Communication Research: State of the Art and Hypotheses for the 1990s," *Journal of Business Communication* 28, no. 3 (Summer 1991): 277–299.

9. "Doing Business with Americans? Use E-mail or Voicemail," *Canadian Press Newswire*, 4 August 2000; "Netiquette," *Financial Post (National Post)* 29 September 1999, C8.

10. Elizabeth Blackburn and Kelly Belanger, "You-Attitude and Positive Emphasis: Testing Received Wisdom in Business Communication," *Bulletin of the Association for Business Communication* 56, no. 2 (June 1993): 1–9.

11. Annette N. Shelby and N. Lamar Reinsch Jr., "Positive Emphasis and You Attitude: An Empirical Study," *Journal of Business Communication* 32, no. 4 (1995): 303–322.

12. Lisa Taylor, "Communicating About People with Disabilities: Does the Language We Use Make a Difference?" *Bulletin of the Association for Business Communication* 53, no. 3 (September 1990): 65–67.

13. Charlene Li and Josh Bernoff, *Groundswell* (Boston: Harvard Business Press, 2008).

14. Adapted from Jeff Buckstein, "Hurt It Through the Grapevine," *The Globe & Mail,* 25 May 2007, C1.

15. Seth Godin, *Meatball Sundae* (New York: Penguin, 2007), 75.

CHAPTER 4

1. Julie Galle, writer/producer, weather.com, personal communication, 27 June 2001; Chuck Salter, "Weathering the Storm," *Fast Company,* December 2000, 186–200; Keith Flamer, "Eye of the Storm," *Broadcasting & Cable,* 25 September 2000, 84–86.

2. Susan Hall and Theresa Tiggeman, "Getting the Big Picture: Writing to Learn in a Finance Class," *Business Communication Quarterly* 58, no. 1 (1995): 12–15.

3. Carol S. Mull, "Orchestrate Your Ideas," *Toastmaster,* February 1987, 19.

4. Ernest Thompson, "Some Effects of Message Structure on Listener's Comprehension," *Speech Monographs* 34 (March 1967): 51–57.

5. Mary A. DeVries, *Internationally Yours* (Boston: Houghton Mifflin, 1994), 61.

6. Randolph H. Hudson, Gertrude M. McGuire, and Bernard J. Selzler, *Business Writing: Concepts and Applications* (Los Angeles: Roxbury, 1983), 79–82.

7. Peter Crow, "Plain English: What Counts Besides Readability?" *Journal of Business Communication* 25, no. 1 (Winter 1988): 87–95.

8. Portions of this section are adapted from Courtland L. Bovée, *Techniques of Writing Business Letters, Memos, and Reports* (Sherman Oaks, Calif.: Banner Books International, 1978), 13–90.

9. Alinda Drury, "Evaluating Readability," *IEEE Transactions on Professional Communication* PC-28 (December 1985): 12.

10. Denise Faguy, "Subtle Differences: Inside Canada's Aftermarket," *Aftermarket Insider* 15 (2002): 1 [accessed 2 June 2003], www.aftermarket.org/Information/Aftermarket_Insider/canada.asp; Lori Doss, "Tim Hortons makes plans to roll out hundreds of new branches," *Nation's Restaurant News,* 10 June 2002, 95–96; Hollie Shaw, "Tim Hortons in Push to Overtake McDonald's: Plans More Outlets." *National Post*, 24 May 2002, FP1; Tim Hortons website [accessed 2 June 2003], www.timhortons.com.

CHAPTER 5

1. Jamie Baillie, Chief of Staff, Office of the Premier, Province of Nova Scotia, personal comunication, 26 June 2003.

2. William Zinsser, *On Writing Well,* 5th ed. (New York: HarperCollins,1994), 126.

3. Zinsser, *On Writing Well,* 9.

4. "Message Lost in Some Memos," *USA Today,* 25 March 1987, 1A.

5. Zinsser, *On Writing Well,* 7, 17.

6. Mary A. DeVries, *Internationally Yours* (Boston: Houghton Mifflin, 1994), 160.

7. Patsy Nichols, "Desktop Packaging," *Bulletin of the Association for Business Communication* 54, no. 1 (March 1991): 43–45; Raymond W. Beswick, "Designing Documents for Legibility," *Bulletin of the Association for Business Communication* 50, no. 4 (December 1987): 34–35.

8. "The Process Model of Document Design," *IEEE Transactions on Professional Communication* PC-24, no. 4 (December 1981): 176–178.

9. William Wresch, Donald Pattow, and James Gifford, *Writing for the Twenty-First Century: Computers and Research Writing* (New York: McGraw-Hill, 1988), 192–211; Melissa E. Barth, *Strategies for Writing with the Computer* (New York: McGraw-Hill, 1988), 108–109, 140, 172–177.

CHAPTER 6

1. Courtland L. Bovée and John V. Thill, *Business Communication Today,* 6th ed. (Upper Saddle River, N.J.: Prentice Hall, 2003), 90–91.

2. Mary A. DeVries, *Internationally Yours* (Boston: Houghton Mifflin, 1994), 168; Susan Benjamin, *Words at Work,* (Reading, Mass.: Addison-Wesley, 1997), 61, 140–141.

3. Jill H. Ellsworth and Matthew V. Ellsworth, *The Internet Business Book* (New York: Wiley, 1994), 91.

4. Lance Cohen, "How to Improve Your E-Mail Messages," http://galaxy.einet/galaxy/Business-and-Commerce/Management/Communications/How_to_Improve_YourEmail.html.

5. Renee B. Horowitz and Marion G. Barchilon, "Stylistic Guidelines for E-Mail," *IEEE Transactions on Professional Communication* 37, no. 4 (December 1994): 207–212; Cohen, "How to Improve Your E-Mail Messages."

6. David Angell and Brent Heslop, *The Elements of E-Mail Style* (Reading, Mass.: Addison-Wesley, 1994), 20.

7. Horowitz and Barchilon, "Stylistic Guidelines for E-Mail," Angell and Heslop, *The Elements of E-Mail Style,* 22.

8. Benjamin, *Words at Work,* 61, 140–141.

9. Adapted from "How Microsoft Reviews Suppliers," *Fast Company,* Issue 17 [accessed 3 September 1998], http://fastcompany.com/online/17/msoftreviews.html.

10. Adapted from Carl Quintanilla, "Work Week: Pizza, Pizza," *Wall Street Journal,* 18 August 1998, A1.

11. Adapted from Davide Dukcevich, "Instant Business: Retailer Lands' End Profits from Online Chat," Forbes.com, Special to ABCNEWS.com, 29 July 2002 [accessed 21 July 2003] www.abcnews.go.com/sections/business/DailyNews/forbes_landsend.com; Lands' End website [accessed 5 December 2003] www.landsend.com; Forbes.com

staff, "Instant Messaging at Work," Forbes.com, 26 July 2002 [accessed 21 July 2003] www.forbes.com/2002/07/23/0723im/html; Tischelle George and Sandra Swanson with Christopher T. Heun, "Not Just Kid Stuff," *Information Week*, 3 September 2001 [accessed 21 July 2003] www.informationweek.com/story/IWK20010830S0030.

CHAPTER 7

1. Courtland L. Bovée, John V. Thill, and Barbara E. Schatzman, *Business Communication Today,* 7th ed. (Upper Saddle River, N.J.: Prentice Hall, 2003), 184.

2. Daniel P. Finkelman and Anthony R. Goland, "Customers Once Can Be Customers for Life," *Information Strategy: The Executive's Journal,* Summer 1990, 5–9.

3. Donna Larcen, "Authors Share the Words of Condolence," *Los Angeles Times,* 20 December 1991, E11.

4. Adapted from Bruce Frankel and Alex Tresniowski, "Stormy Skies," *People Weekly,* 31 July 2000, 112–115.

5. Adapted from Keith H. Hammonds, "Difference Is Power," *Fast Company,* 36, 258 [accessed 11 July 2000], www.fastcompany.com/online/36/power.html; Terri Morrison, Wayne A. Conaway, and George A. Borden, *Kiss, Bow, or Shake Hands* (Avon, Mass.: Adams Media Corp., 1994), 1–5.

6. Adapted from Floorgraphics website [accessed 18 June 2001], www.floorgraphics.com; John Grossman, "It's an Ad, Ad, Ad, Ad World," *Inc.,* March 2000, 23–26; David Wellman, "Floor'Toons," *Supermarket Business,* 15 November 1999, 47; "Floorshow," *Dallas Morning News,* 4 September 1998, 11D.

7. Adapted from Jamba Juice website [accessed 19 July 2001], www.jambacareers.com/benefits.html; Brenda Paik Sunoo, "Blending a Successful Workforce," *Workforce,* March 2000, 44–48; Michael Adams, "Kirk Perron: Jamba Juice," *Restaurant Business,* 15 March 1999, 38; "Live in a Blender," *Restaurant Business,* 1 December 2000, 48–50; David Goll, "Jamba Juices Up 24-Hour Fitness Clubs," *East Bay Business Times,* 30 June 2000, 6.

8. Adapted from Dylan Tweney, "The Defogger: Slim Down That Homepage," *Business 2.0,* 13 July 2001 [accessed 1 August 2001], www.business2.com/articles/web/0,1653,16483,FF.html.

9. Adapted from Barbara Carton, "Farmers Begin Harvesting Satellite Data to Boost Yields," *Wall Street Journal,* 11 July 1996, B4.

10. Adapted from Bernard Weinraub, "New Harry Potter Book Becoming a Publishing Phenomenon," *New York Times,* 3 July 2000 [accessed 12 July 2000], www.nytimes.com/library/books/070300potter-parties.html; Laura Miller, "Pottermania at Midnight," *Salon.com,* 8 July 2000 [accessed 12 July 2000], www.salon.com/books/features/2000/07/08/potter/; David D. Kirkpatrick, "Harry Potter Magic Halts Bedtime for Youngsters," *New York Times,* 9 July 2000 [accessed 12 July 2000], www.nytimes.com/library/books/070900potter-goblet.html; David D. Kirkpatrick, "Vanishing Off the Shelves," *New York Times,* 10 July 2000 [accessed 10 July 2000], www.nytimes.com/library/books/071000rowling-goblet.html.

11. Adapted from "Entrepreneurs Across America," *Entrepreneur Magazine Online* [accessed 12 June 1997], www.entrepreneurmag.com/entmag/50states5.hts#top.

CHAPTER 8

1. Jeffrey R. Caponigro, President & CEO, Caponigro Public Relations, Inc., personal communication, 17 July 2001; Jeffrey R. Caponigro, *The Crisis Counselor* (Southfield, Mich.: Barker Business Books, 1998), 151–221.

2. Mark H. McCormack, *On Communicating* (Los Angeles: Dove Books, 1998), 87.

3. Curtis Sittenfeld, "Good Ways to Deliver Bad News," *Fast Company,* April 1999, 58–60.

4. Ram Subramanian, Robert G. Insley, and Rodney D. Blackwell, "Performance and Readability: A Comparison of Annual Reports of Profitable and Unprofitable Corporations," *Journal of Business Communication* 30, no. 2 (1993): 49–61.

5. *Techniques for Communicators* (Chicago: Lawrence Ragan Communication, 1995), 18.

6. Adapted from the Disclosure Project website [accessed 20 August 2001], www.disclosureproject.org; Katelynn Raymer and David Ruppe, "UFOs, Aliens and Secrets," ABCNews.com, 10 May 2001 [accessed 20 August 2001], http://more.abcnews.go.com/sections/scitech/DailyNews/ufo010509.html; Rachael Myer, "UFO Probe Sought," *Las Vegas Review-Journal,* 11 May 2001 [accessed 20 August 2001], www.lvrj.com/cgi-bin/printable.cgi?/lvrj_home/2001/May-11-Fri-2001/news/16064080.html.

7. Adapted from Wolf Blitzer, "More Employers Taking Advantages of New Cyber-Surveillance Software," *CNN.com,* 10 July 2000 [accessed 11 July 2000], www.cnn.com/2000/US/07/10/workplace.eprivacy/index.html.

8. Adapted from Union Bank of California teleservices, personal communication, 16 August 2001.

9. Adapted from Associated Press, "Children's Painkiller Recalled," CNN.com/Health, 16 August 2001 [accessed on 22 August 2001], www.cnn.com/2001/HEALTH/parenting/08/16/kids.drug.recalled.ap/index.html; Perrigo Company website [accessed 29 August 2001], www.perrigo.com.

10. Adapted from Julie Vallese, "Motorized Scooter Injuries on the Rise," CNN.com/U.S., 22 August 2001 [accessed 22 August 2001], www.cnn.com/2001/US/08/22/scooter.advisory/index.html; The Sports Authority website [accessed 28 August 2001], www.thesportsauthority.com.

11. Pascal Zachary, "Sun Microsystems Apologizes in Letter for Late Payments," *Wall Street Journal,* 11 October 1989, B4.

12. Adapted from Associated Press, "Employers Restricting Use of Cell Phones in Cars," CNN.com/Sci-Tech, 27 August 2001 [accessed 27 August 2001], www.cnn.com/2001/TECH/08/27/cellphones.cars.ap/index.html; Julie Vallese, "Study: All Cell Phones Distract Drivers," CNN.com/U.S., 16 August 2001 [accessed 7 September 2001], www.cnn.com/2001/US/08/16/cell.phone.driving/index.html.

13. Adapted from Simon Fraser University website [accessed 6 March 2008] "Mass Alert Notification System Goes Online," press release, 6 March 2008, www.sfu.ca/pamr/media_releases/media_releases_archive/media_release03060801.html.

14. Adapted from Courtland Bovée and John Thill, *Business Communication Essentials,* 2nd US edition (New Jersey: Pearson Education, 2006), p. 23; Adapted from Sean Doherty, "Dynamic Communications," *Network Computing,* 3 April 2003, 14, no. 6: 26 [accessed 24 July 2003] http://search.epnet.com/direct.asp?an-9463336&db=tg=AN; R.P. Srikanth,

"IM Tools Are the Latest Tech Toys for Corporate Users," *Express Computer*, 2 July 2002 [accessed 21 July 2003] www.expresscomputeronline.com/20020701/indtrend1.shtml.

CHAPTER 9

1. Courtland L. Bovée, John V. Thill, and Barbara E. Schatzman, *Business Communication Today*, 7th ed. (Upper Saddle River, N.J., Prentice Hall, 2003), 264.

2. Jay A. Conger, "The Necessary Art of Persuasion," *Harvard Business Review*, May–June 1998, 84–95; Jeanette W. Gilsdorf, "Write Me Your Best Case for . . ." *Bulletin of the Association for Business Communication* 54, no. 1 (March 1991): 7–12.

3. "Vital Skill for Today's Managers: Persuading, Not Ordering Others," *Soundview Executive Book Summaries*, September 1998, 1.

4. Mary Cross, "Aristotle and Business Writing: Why We Need to Teach Persuasion," *Bulletin of the Association for Business Communication* 54, no. 1 (March 1991): 3–6.

5. Robert T. Moran, "Tips on Making Speeches to International Audiences," *International Management*, April 1980, 58–59.

6. Gilsdorf, "Write Me Your Best Case for . . ."

7. Raymond M. Olderman, *10-Minute Guide to Business Communication* (New York: Macmillian Spectrum/Alpha Books, 1997), 57–61.

8. Gilsdorf, "Write Me Your Best Case for . . ."

9. William North Jayme, quoted in Albert Haas Jr., "How to Sell Almost Anything by Direct Mail," *Across the Board*, November 1986, 50.

10. Robert L. Hemmings, "Think Before You Write," *Fund Raising Management*, February 1990, 23–24.

11. Conrad Squires, "How to Write a Strong Letter, Part Two: Choosing a Theme," *Fund Raising Management*, November 1991, 65–66.

12. Adapted from Michael H. Mescon, Courtland L. Bovée, and John V. Thill, *Business Today*, 10th ed. (Upper Saddle River, New Jersey: Prentice Hall, 2002), 272–274; Jason Roberson, "Rush-hour Rebellion," *Dallas Business Journal*, 22 June 2001, 31; Carole Hawkins, "Ready, Set, Go Home," *Black Enterprise*, August 2001, 118–124; Wayne Tompkins, "Telecommuting in Transition," *Louisville (KY.) Courier-Journal*, 9 July 2001, 01C.

13. Adapted from Mescon, Bovée, and Thill, *Business Today*, 269; Peter Baker, "Work: Have Fun. And That's an Order," *The Observer* (London), 3 January 1999, 011; "The Power of Laughter," Oprah.com [accessed 29 September 2001], www.oprah.com/living/lifemake/experts/tracy/expert_tracy_laughter.html.

14. Kevin M. Savetz, "Preventive Medicine for the Computer User," *Multimedia Online* 2, no. 2 (June 1996): 58–60.

15. Adapted from the American Red Cross website [accessed 3 October 2001], www.redcross.org; American Red Cross San Diego Chapter website [accessed 3 October 2001], www.sdarc.org/blood.htm.

16. Adapted from Annelena Lobb, "Identity Theft Survival Guide," CNN.com [accessed 4 April 2002], www.money.cnn.com/2002/04/03/pf/q_identity/index.htm; Inspector John Sliter, cited in Julia Chua, "Identity Theft—Robbery in the New Millennium," CBC Special Report [accessed 20 May 2003], www.cbc.ca/consumers/indepth/identity/index.html.

17. Adapted from Julian E. Barnes, "Fast-Food Giveaway Toys Face Rising Recalls," *New York Times*, 16 August 2001, A1; Product Safety Program Healthy Environments and Consumer Safety [accessed 20 May 2001], www.hc-sc.gc.cc/hecs-sesc/cps/mechanical.htm; Shirley Leung, "Burger King Recalls 2.6 Million Kids Meal Toys," *Wall Street Journal*, 1 August 2001, B2.

18. Adapted from Hotel del Coronado website [accessed 7 September 2001], www.hoteldel.comda; Museum of Natural History website [accessed 2 September 2001], www.flmnh.ufl.edu/fish/Sharks/Statistics/statsus.htm; "Sharks Attack Three Off Florida's East Coast," CNN.com, 20 August 2001 [accessed 21 August 2001], www.cnn.com/2001/US/08/19/shark.attack/index.html; "Year of Shark 'Hype,' Says Expert," CNN.com, 4 September 2001 [accessed 4 September 2001], www.cnn.com/2001/US/09/03/shark.perspective/; "Boy Dies After Shark Attack," CNN.com, 2 September 2001 [accessed 2 September 2001], www.cnn.com/2001/US/09/02/shark.attack/index.html; "Labor Day Shark Attack Survivor Hanging On," CNN.com, 5 September 2001 [accessed 5 September 2001], www.cnn.com/2001/US/09/04/shark.attacks/index.html; Thurston Hatcher, "Florida Panel Embraces Ban on Shark Feeding," CNN.com, 7 September 2001 [accessed 7 September 2001], www.cnn.com/2001/US/09/06/shark.feeding/ index.html.

19. Adapted from Michael S. James, "No Expiration on Recall Risk," ABCNews.com, 31 August 2001 [accessed on 31 August 2001], http://abcnews.go.com/sections/living/DailyNews/meat_recall010830.html; James F. Balch, M.D., and Phyllis A. Balch, C.N.C, *Prescription for Nutritional Healing*, 2nd ed. (Garden City Park, N.Y.: Avery Publishing Group, 1997), 277–282.

20. Adapted from CNET Shopper.com [accessed 1 October 2001], http://shopper.cnet.com/shopping/0-1257.html?tag=sh.

21. Adapted from Gateway website [accessed 2 October 2001], www.gateway.com; Gateway customer service sales representative, 1-800-GATEWAY, personal interview, 10 October 2001.

22. Adapted from Bruce Haring, "Trouble Getting up to Speed," *USA Today*, 27 December 1999, D3, D2; Mike Rogoway, "AT&T Seeks to Improve Internet Connections," *Vancouver (Wash.) Columbian*, 9 March 2001, E1.

23. Adapted from Margo Kelly, "The Emerging Green Economy," *CBC News*, 10 March 2008 [accessed 15 March 2008] www.cbc.ca/news/goinggreen/greenrush.html.

24. Adapted from Sarah Plaskitt, "Case Study: Hilton Uses SMS with Success," *B&T Marketing & Media*, 27 June 2002 [accessed 22 July 2003] www.bandt.com.au/articles/ce/0c00eace.asp; "Wireless Messaging Briefs," *Instant Messaging Planet*, 4 October 2002 [accessed 22 July 2003] www.instantmessagingplanet.com/wireless/print.php/10766_1476111; Hilton Hotels Corporation, *Hoover's Company Capsules*, 1 July 2003 [accessed 24 July 2003] www.proquest.com; Matthew G. Nelson, "Hilton Takes Reservations Wireless," *Information Week*, 25 June 2001, 99 [accessed 24 July 2003] www.web22.epnet.com; Hilton Hotels websites [accessed 15 January 2004] www.hilton.com.

25. Charlene Li and Josh Bernoff, *Groundswell* (Boston: Harvard Business Press, 2008), 104–106.

26. Adapted from WestJet website [accessed 9 July 2008] http://c5dsp.westjet.com/guest/contacts/donationRequest.jsp; jsessionid=R91LLzNGyqY7Z6RkM1KvQx3bnHQqVQgGgfp021dVvKGP Tn7ZqH2Q!-1595351148.

CHAPTER 10

1. Tom Sant, *Persuasive Business Proposals* (New York: American Management Association, 1992), summarized in *Soundview Executive Book Summaries* 14, no. 10, pt. 2 (October 1992): 3.

2. Information for this section was obtained from BCIT Library Electronic Resources, "Business" [accessed 2 June 2003] www.lib.bcit.ca/eResources/databases/subject.php?subject= Business; "Finding Industry Information" [accessed 3 November 1998], www.pitt.edu/~buslibry/industries.htm; Thomas P. Bergman, Stephen M. Garrison, and Gregory M. Scott, *The Business Student Writer's Manual and Guide to the Internet* (Upper Saddle River, N.J.: Prentice Hall, 1998), 67–80; Ernest L. Maier, Anthony J. Faria, Peter Kaatrude, and Elizabeth Wood, *The Business Library and How to Use It* (Detroit: Omnigraphics, 1996), 53–76; Sherwyn P. Morreale and Courtland L. Bovée, *Excellence in Public Speaking* (Fort Worth, Tex.: Harcourt Brace College Publishers, 1998), 166–171.

3. Jason Zien, "Measuring the Internet," About.com, 13 July 1999 [accessed 17 July 1999], internet.about.com/library/ weekly/1999/aa071399a.htm; "FAST Aims for Largest Index," *Search Engine Watch,* 4 May 1999 [accessed 17 July 1999], searchenginewatch.internet.com/sereport/99/05-fast.htm.

4. Adapted from BCIT Library Electronic Resources Data bases & Indexes, "Business" [accessed 2 June 2003], www.lib.bcit.ca/ eResources/databases/subject.php?sybhect=Business; interview with Linda Matsuba, Business Librarian, B.C. Institute of Technology, 2 June 2003.

5. Maier, Faria, Kaatrude, and Wood, *The Business Library and How to Use It,* 84–97; Matt Lake, "Desperately Seeking Susan OR Suzie NOT Sushi," *New York Times,* 3 September 1998, D1, D7.

6. Adapted from Bob Smith, "The Evolution of Pinkerton," *Management Review,* September 1993, 54–58.

7. Adapted from Kate Sangha, conversation, 9 May 2008.

CHAPTER 11

1. Courtland L. Bovée, John V. Thill, and Barbara E. Schatzman, *Business Communication Today,* 7th ed. (Upper Saddle River, N.J., Prentice Hall, 2003), 442.

2. David A. Hayes, "Helping Students GRASP the Knack of Writing Summaries," *Journal of Reading* (November 1989): 96–101.

3. Philip C. Kolin, *Successful Writing at Work,* 6th ed. (Boston: Houghton Mifflin, 2001), 552–555.

4. A. S. C. Ehrenberg, "Report Writing—Six Simple Rules for Better Business Documents," *Admap,* June 1992, 39–42.

5. Michael Netzley and Craig Snow, *Guide to Report Writing* (Upper Saddle River, N.J.: Prentice Hall, 2001), 57.

6. Bickley Townsend, "Room at the Top," *American Demographics,* July 1996, 28–37.

7. WorkSafeBC, *Backgrounder: Training and Orientation for Young and New Workers,* WorkSafeBC Publications (pamphlet),

2007; WorksafeBC, *Three Steps to Effective Worker Education and Training 2007 Edition,* WorksafeBC Publications, 2007.

CHAPTER 12

1. Courtland L. Bovée, John V. Thill, and Barbara E. Schatzman, *Business Communication Today,* 7th ed. (Upper Saddle River, N.J., Prentice Hall, 2003), 494.

2. Walter Kiechel III, "How to Give a Speech," *Fortune,* 8 June 1987, 180.

3. *Communication and Leadership Program* (Santa Ana, Calif.: Toastmasters International, 1980), 44, 45.

4. "Polishing Your Presentation," 3M Meeting Network [accessed 8 June 2001], www.mmm.com/meetingnetwork/ readingroom/meetingguide_pres.html.

5. Kathleen K. Weigner, "Visual Persuasion," *Forbes,* 16 September 1991, 176; Kathleen K. Weigner, "Showtime!" *Forbes,* 13 May 1991, 118.

6. Kevan Allbee, David L. Green, and Kari Woolf, "Pre-Show Business," *Presentations,* May 2001, 50–54.

7. Margo Halverson, "Choosing the Right Colors for Your Next Presentation," 3M Meeting Network [accessed 8 June 2001], www.mmm.com/meetingnetwork/readingroom/ meetingguide_right_color.html.

8. Carol Klinger and Joel G. Siegel, "Computer Multimedia Presentations," *CPA Journal,* June 1996, 46.

9. Jon Hanke, "Five Tips for Better Visuals," 3M Meeting Network [accessed 8 June 2001], www.mmm.com/ meetingnetwork/presentations/pmag_better_visuals.html.

10. Hanke, "Five Tips for Better Visuals."

11. Ted Simons, "Handouts That Won't Get Trashed," *Presentations,* February 1999, 47–50.

12. Sherwyn P. Morreale and Courtland L. Bovée, *Excellence in Public Speaking,* 24–25.

13. Judy Linscott, "Getting On and Off the Podium," *Savvy,* October 1985, 44.

14. Iris R. Johnson, "Before You Approach the Podium," *MW,* January–February 1989, 7.

15. Edward P. Bailey, *Writing and Speaking at Work* (Upper Saddle River, N.J.: Prentice Hall, 1999), 138–145.

16. Patrick J. Collins, *Say It with Power and Confidence* (Upper Saddle River, N.J.: Prentice Hall, 1997), 122–124.

17. Sandra Moyer, "Braving No Woman's Land," *The Toastmaster,* August 1986, 13.

18. "Control the Question-and-Answer Session," *Soundview Executive Book Summaries* 20, no. 6, pt. 2 (June 1998): 4.

19. "Control the Question-and-Answer Session."

20. Teresa Brady, "Fielding Abrasive Questions During Presentations," *Supervisory Management,* February 1993, 6.

21. Adapted from Ronald L. Applebaum and Karl W. E. Anatol, *Effective Oral Communication: For Business and the Professions* (Chicago: Science Research Associates, 1982), 240–244.

22. Jim Gray, "Teamwork Crucial—Even at the Lectern," *The Globe & Mail,* 1 June 2007, C1.

CHAPTER 13

1. Camille DeBell, "Ninety Years in the World of Work in America," *Career Development Quarterly* 50, no. 1 (September 2001): 77–88.

2. John A. Challenger, "The Changing Workforce: Workplace Rules in the New Millenium," *Vital Speeches of the Day* 67, no. 23 (15 September 2001): 721–728.

3. Marvin J. Cetron and Owen Davies, "Trends Now Changing the World: Technology, the Workplace, Management, and Institutions," *Futurist* 35, no. 1 (March/April 2001): 27–42.

4. Amanda Bennett, "GE Redesigns Rungs of Career Ladder," *Wall Street Journal*, 15 March 1993, B1, B3.

5. Robin White Goode, "International and Foreign Language Skills Have an Edge," *Black Enterprise*, May 1995, 53.

6. Nancy M. Somerick, "Managing a Communication Internship Program," *Bulletin of the Association for Business Communication* 56, no. 3 (1993): 10–20.

7. Joan Lloyd, "Changing Workplace Requires You to Alter Your Career Outlook," *Milwaukee Journal Sentinel*, 4 July 1999, 1; DeBell, "Ninety Years in the World of Work in America."

8. Stephanie Armour, "Employers: Enough Already with the E-Résumés," *USA Today*, 15 July 1999, 1B.

9. Cheryl L. Noll, "Collaborating with the Career Planning and Placement Center in the Job-Search Project," *Business Communication Quarterly* 58, no. 3 (1995): 53–55.

10. Pam Stanley-Weigand, "Organizing the Writing of Your Resume," *Bulletin of the Association for Business Communication* 54, no. 3 (September 1991): 11–12.

11. Richard H. Beatty and Nicholas C. Burkholder, *The Executive Career Guide for MBAs* (New York: Wiley, 1996), 133.

12. Beatty and Burkholder, *The Executive Career Guide for MBAs*, 151.

13. Rockport Institute, "How to Write a Masterpiece of a Résumé" [accessed 16 October 1998], **www.rockportinstitute. com/ résumés.html.**

14. Rockport Institute, "How to Write a Masterpiece of a Résumé."

15. Beverly Culwell-Block and Jean Anna Sellers, "Résumé Content and Format—Do the Authorities Agree?" *Bulletin of the Association for Business Communication* 57, no. 4 (1994): 27–30.

16. Janice Tovey, "Using Visual Theory in the Creation of Résumés: A Bibliography," *Bulletin of the Association for Business Communication* 54, no. 3 (September 1991): 97–99.

17. Regina Pontow, "Electronic Résumé Writing Tips" [accessed 18 October 1998], **www.provenresumes.com/ reswkshps/electronic/scnres.html.**

18. Pontow, "Electronic Résumé Writing Tips."

19. William J. Banis, "The Art of Writing Job-Search Letters," *CPC Annual*, 36th ed. (1992): 42–50.

CHAPTER 14

1. Sylvia Porter, "Your Money: How to Prepare for Job Interviews," *San Francisco Chronicle*, 3 November 1981, 54.

2. Stephanie Armour, "The New Interview Etiquette," *USA Today*, 23 November 1999, B1, B2.

3. Samuel Greengard, "Are You Well Armed to Screen Applicants?" *Personnel Journal*, December 1995, 84–95.

4. Charlene Marmer Solomon, "How Does Disney Do It?" *Personnel Journal*, December 1989, 53.

5. Marcia Vickers, "Don't Touch That Dial: Why Should I Hire You?" *New York Times*, 13 April 1997, F11.

6. Nancy K. Austin, "Goodbye Gimmicks," *Incentive*, May 1996, 241.

7. Robert Gifford, Cheuk Fan Ng, and Margaret Wilkinson, "Nonverbal Cues in the Employment Interview: Links Between Applicant Qualities and Interviewer Judgments," *Journal of Applied Psychology* 70, no. 4 (1985): 729.

8. Dale G. Leathers, *Successful Nonverbal Communication* (New York: Macmillan, 1986), 225.

9. Shirley J. Shepherd, "How to Get That Job in 60 Minutes or Less," *Working Woman*, March 1986, 119.

10. Shepherd, "How to Get That Job in 60 Minutes or Less," 118.

11. H. Anthony Medley, *Sweaty Palms: The Neglected Art of Being Interviewed* (Berkeley, Calif.: Ten Speed Press, 1993), 179.

12. Gerald L. Wilson, "Preparing Students for Responding to Illegal Selection Interview Questions," *Bulletin of the Association for Business Communication* 54, no. 2 (1991): 44–49.

13. Jeff Springston and Joann Keyton, "Interview Response Training," *Bulletin of the Association for Business Communication* 54, no. 3 (1991): 28–30; Gerald L. Wilson, "An Analysis of Instructional Strategies for Responding to Illegal Selection Interview Questions," *Bulletin of the Association for Business Communication* 54, no. 3 (1991): 31–35.

14. Harold H. Hellwig, "Job Interviewing: Process and Practice," *Bulletin of the Association for Business Communication* 55, no. 2 (1992): 8–14.

APPENDIX A

1. Mel Mandell, "Electronic Forms Are Cheap and Speedy," *D&B Reports*, July–August 1993, 44–45.

2. U.S. Postal Service, *Postal Addressing Standards* (Washington, D.C.: GPO, 1992), 3.

3. Lennie Copeland and Lewis Griggs, *Going International: How to Make Friends and Deal Effectively in the Global Marketplace*, 2nd ed. (New York: Random House, 1985), 24–27.

4. Renée B. Horowitz and Marian G. Barchilon, "Stylistic Guidelines for E-Mail," *IEEE Transactions on Professional Communications*, 37, no. 4 (1994): 207–212.

5. William Eager, *Using the Internet* (Indianapolis: Que Corporation, 1994), 10.

6. "When Image Counts, Letterhead Says It All," *Stamford (Conn.) Advocate and Greenwich Times*, 10 January 1993, F4.

7. Linda Driskill, *Business and Managerial Communication: New Perspectives* (Orlando, Fla.: Harcourt Brace Jovanovich, 1992), 470.

8. Driskill, *Business and Managerial Communication*, 470.

9. Copeland and Griggs, *Going International*, 24–27.

10. Mary A. De Vries, *Internationally Yours* (Boston: Houghton Mifflin, 1994), 8.

11. Copeland and Griggs, *Going International*, 24–27.

Credits

TEXT

19 Business Communication Notebook, adapted from "Culture Quiz," *Workforce,* January 1998, 25; Valerie Frazee, "Establishing Relations in Germany," *Global Workforce,* April 1997, 16–17; James Wilfong and Toni Seger, *Taking Your Business Global* (Franklin Lakes, N.J.: Career Press, 1997), 282; Valerie Frazee, "Keeping Up on Chinese Culture," *Global Workforce,* October 1996, 16–17; David A. Ricks, "International Business Blunders: An Update," *Business & Economic Review,* January–March 1988, 11–14. **38** Business Communication Notebook adapted from "Air Travel Fears to Drive Videoconferencing Market," *Electronic Commerce News,* 15 October 2001, 11; "Amid Terrorism Fears, More Businesses Are Conducting Virtual Meetings," *Palm Beach Post,* 14 October 2001, 4F; Charles E. Ramirez, "Videoconference Demand Up: More Companies Seek Services After Attacks," *Detroit News,* 10 October 2001, 1; Fred O. Williams, "Reluctant Travelers: Videoconferencing Gets Boost from Businesses," *Buffalo News,* 7 October 2001, B11; Wayne Tompkins, "Face-to-Face Meetings Are Less Likely for Now," *Courier-Journal,* 1 October 2001, 05C; Benny Evangelista, "Meetings via Video: More Businesses Skipping Travel, Tuning Into Video-conferencing, *San Francisco Chronicle,* 1 October 2001, E1; James R. Healey, "Business Travelers Keep Their Feet on the Ground: Videoconferencing, Telecommuting Replace Good Old Face-to-Face," *USA Today,* 26 September 2001, B.01; Thomas E. Weber, "E-World: After Terrorist Attacks, Companies Rethink In-Person Meetings," *Wall Street Journal,* 24 September 2001, B1. **56** Business Communication Notebook adapted from Mary Beth Currie and Daniel Black, "E-merging Issues in the Electronic Workplace," *Ivey Business Journal,* January–February 2001, 18–29; John J. DiGilio, "Electronic Mail: From Computer to Courtroom," *Information Management Journal,* April 2000, 32–44; Mike Elgan, "The Trouble with E-Mail," *Windows Magazine,* November 1998, 31; Jerry Adler, "When E-Mail Bites Back," *Newsweek,* 23 November 1998, 45–46; Amy Harmon, "Corporate Delete Keys Busy as E-Mail Turns Up in Court," *New York Times,* 12 November 1998, A1, C2. **95** Business Communication Notebook adapted from Reid Goldsborough, "Words for the Wise," *Link-Up,* September–October 1999, 25–26; John Morkes and Jakob Nielsen, *How to Write for the Web* [accessed 23 April 2000], www.useit.com/papers/webwriting/writing.html; Jakob Nielsen, *Reading on the Web* [accessed 23 April 2000], www.useit.com/alertbox/9710a.html; Jakob Nielsen, *Failure of Corporate Websites* [accessed online 23 April 2000], www.useit.com/alertbox/982028.html; Shel Holtz, "Writing for the Wired World," *International Association of Business Communicators,* 1999, 6–9; "Web Writing: How to Avoid Pitfalls," *Investor Relations Business,* 1 November 1999, 15; Michael Lerner, "Building Worldwide Websites," IBM [accessed 23 April 2000], www.4.ibm.com/software/developer/library/web-localization.html; Steve Outing, "Some Advice on Writing, Web-Style," *E&P Online* [accessed 23 April 2000], www.mediainfo.com/ephome/news/newshtm/stop/st061899.htm; *Good Documents Website* [accessed 15 July 2001], www.gooddocuments.com/techniques/techniqueshome.htm; Jakob Nielsen, *Microcontent: How to Write Headlines, Page Titles, and Subject Lines* [accessed online 23 April 2000], www.useit.com/alertbox/980906.html; Jakob Nielsen, P.J. Schemenaur, and Jonathan Fox, "Writing for the Web," Sun Microsystems website [accessed 23 April 2000], www.sun.com/980713/webwriting; Amy Gahran, "Writing for the Web and Creating Effective Online Content," *Webword.com* [accessed 31 May 2000], www.webword.com/interviews/gahran.html. **121** Business Communication Notebook adapted from William Lutz, "Life Under the Chief Doublespeak Officer," *USA Today,* 17 October 1996, 15A; Toddi Gutner, "At Last, the Readable Prospectus," *Business Week,* 13 April 1998, 11; Philip Maher, "One for the Writers," *Investment Dealers' Digest,* 17 November 1997, 41; Ronald G. Shafer, "Government Bureaucrats to Learn a New Language: Simple English," *Wall Street Journal,* 2 June 1998, B1; Peder Zane, "For Investors, an Initial Public Offering of English," *New York Times,* 25 August 1996, 7; Dan Seligman, "The Gobbledygood Profession," *Forbes,* 7 September 1998, 174–175; Michael Weiss and James Hildebrandt, "Art of Clear Writing Lost in Sea of Legalese," *San Antonio Business Journal,* 28 October 1996 [accessed September 1998], www.amcity.com/sanantonio/stories/102896/editorial2.htm. **139** Procedure adapted from "Basic Steps to Lockout" WorkSafeBC Pamphlet, 2008. **152** Business Communication Notebook adapted from Mary A. DeVries, *Internationally Yours* (Boston: Houghton Mifflin, 1994), 195; Myron W. Lustig and Jolene Koester, *Intercultural Competence* (New York: HarperCollins, 1993), 66–72; Mary Munter, "Cross-Cultural Communication for Managers," *Business Horizons,* May–June 1993, 69–78; David A. Victor, *International Business Communication* (New York: Harper Collins, 1992), 137–168; Larry A. Samovar and Richard E. Porter, *Intercultural Communication: A Reader,* 6th ed. (Belmont, Calif.: Wadsworth, 1991), 109–110; Larry A. Samovar and Richard E. Porter, *Communication Between Cultures* (Belmont, Calif.: Wadsworth, 1991), 235–244; Carley H. Dodd, *Dynamics of Intercultural Communication,* 3d ed. (Dubuque, Iowa: Wm. C. Brown, 1989), 69–73. **178** Business Communication Notebook adapted from Stephanie Armour, "E-Mail Lets Companies Deliver Bad News from Afar," *USA Today,* 20 February 2001, B1; Cheryl Maday, "How to Break Bad News," *Psychology Today,* November–December 1999, 18; Nancy Flynn and Tom Flynn, *Writing Effective E-Mail* (Menlo Park, Calif: Crisp Learning, 1998), 4. **207** Business Communication Notebook adapted from Ronald A. Anderson, Ivan Fox, David P. Twomey, and Marianne M. Jennings, *Business Law and the Legal Environment* (Cincinnati: West Educational Publishing, 1999), 229–230, 237–240, 247, 524–526, 567; *Sales Letter Tips* [accessed 26 June 2000], www.smartbiz.com/sbs/arts/sbs47.htm; *Instant Sales Letters* [acessed 26 June 2000], instantsalesletters.com. **236** Business Communication Notebook adapted from Paul Franson, *High*

Tech, High Hope (New York: Wiley, 1998), 252; John R. L. Rizza, "Extranets: The Internet Gets Down to Business," *Entrepreneurial Edge* 3 (1998): 76–78; Samuel Greengard, "Extranets Linking Employees with Your Vendors," *Workforce,* November 1997, 28–34. **283** Business Communication Notebook adapted from Joan Minninger, *The Perfect Memo* (New York: Doubleday, 1990), 169–170. **308** Business Communication Notebook adapted from Sherwyn P. Morreale and Courtland L. Bovée, *Excellence in Public Speaking* (Fort Worth, Tex: Harcourt Brace, 1998), 7; Leon Fletcher, "A Remedy for Stage Fright," *The Toastmaster,* June 1994, 8–10; Greg Dahl, "Fear of Fear," *The Toastmaster,* June 1994, 10–11; "A Survival Guide to Public Speaking," *Training & Development Journal,* September 1990, 15–16, 18–25; Arden K. Watson, "Ask an Expert," in Morreale and Bovée, *Excellence in Public Speaking,* 42. **343** Business Communication Notebook adapted from Richard N. Bolles, "Career Strategizing or, What Color Is Your Web Parachute?" *Yahoo! Internet Life,* May 1998, 116, 121; Tara Weingarten, "The All-Day, All-Night, Global, No-Trouble Job Search," *Newsweek,* 6 April 1998, 17; Michele Himmelberg, "Internet an Important Tool in Employment Search," *San Diego Union-Tribune,* 7 September 1998, D2; Gina Imperato, "35 Ways to Land a Job Online," *Fast Company,* August 1998, 192–197; Roberta Maynard, "Casting the Net for Job Seekers," *Nation's Business,* March 1997, 28–29; Human Resources Development Canada's National Job Bank, http://jb-ge.hrdc-drhc.gc.ca [accessed 15 July 2003]; Canadian Council on Rehabilitation and Work's virtual employment resource centre, WORKink, www.workink.com [accessed 10 July 2003]. **362** Business Communication Notebook adapted from "Career Strategies," *Black Enterprise,* February 1986, 122. Copyright © 1986, Black Enterprise Magazine, The Earl Graves Publishing Company, Inc., New York, NY. All rights reserved.

FIGURES AND TABLES

26 (Table 2.1) Copyright, Dr. Lyman K. Steil, president, Communication Development, Inc., St. Paul, Minn. Prepared for the Sperry Corporation. Reprinted with permission of Dr. Steil and Unisys Corporation. **132** (Figure 7.5) Courtesy Herman Miller. **242** (Figure 11.2) Adapted from Statistics Canada, "Proportion of Visible Minorities." http://142.206.72.67/02/02a/02a/02a_graph/02a_graph_006_le.htm [accessed 2 July 2003].

242 (Figure 11.3) "How Much Online North American Consumers Trust Sources of Information About Products or Services." Adapted from Charlene Li and Josh Bernhoff, *Groundswell,* Forester Research, 2008. Reprinted with permission from Harvard Business Press. **243** (Figure 11.4) Statistics Canada, "Trends in Canadian Immigration from Europe and Asia 2001." http://142.206.72.67/02/02a/02a_graph/02a_graph005_le.htm [accessed 2 July 2003]. **244** (Figure 11.5) Brad Reagan, "Sounding Off," *Wall Street Journal,* 29 October 2001, R4; (Figure 11.6) Iris I. Varner, *Contemporary Business Report Writing,* 2d ed. (Chicago: Dryden Press, 1991), 75. **277** (Table 11.3) Catalyst, New York, cited in Bickley Townsend, "Room at the Top," *American Demographics,* July 1996, 31; (Table 11.4) Catalyst, New York, cited in Bickley Townsend, "Room at the Top," *American Demographics,* July 1996, 31. **278** (Table 11.5) Catalyst, New York, cited in Bickley Townsend, "Room at the Top," *American Demographics,* July 1996, 33. **290** (Table 12.1) Adapted from Eric J. Adams, "Management Focus: User-Friendly Presentation Software," *World Trade,* March 1995, 92. **320** (Table 13.2) Rockport Institute, "How to Write a Masterpiece of a Résumé" [accessed 16 October 1998], www.rockportinstitute.com/résumés.html. **326** (Table 13.3) Adapted from Anne Field, "Coach, Help Me Out with This Interview," *Business Week,* 22 October 2001, 134E4, 134E6; Joan E. Rigdon, "Deceptive Résumés Can Be Door-Openers but Can Become an Employee's Undoing," *Wall Street Journal,* 17 June 1992, B1; Diane Cole, "Ethics: Companies Crack Down on Dishonesty," *Managing Your Career,* Spring 1991, 8–11; Nancy Marx Better, "Résumé Liars," *Savvy,* December 1990–January 1991, 26–29. **328** (Table 13.4) Joyce Lain Kennedy and Thomas J. Morrow, *Electronic Resume Revolution* (New York: John Wilcy & Sons, 1994). **348** (Table 14.2) Adapted from *The Northwestern Endicott Report* (Evanston, Ill.: Northwestern University Placement Center). **349** (Table 14.3) Adapted from Charlene Li and Josh Bernhoff, *Groundswell,* Forester Research, 2008. Reprinted with permission from Harvard Business Press. **350** (Table 14.4) Adapted from H. Lee Rust, *Job Search: The Completion Manual for Jobseekers* (New York: American Management Association, 1979), 56. **351** (Figure 14.1) Adapted from *The Northwestern Endicott Report* (Evanston, Ill.: Northwestern University Placement Center. **353** (Table 14.5) "Dangerous Questions," *Nation's Business,* May 1999, 22.

Index